LAW FOR LEGAL EXECUTIVES

PART I, YEAR II

LAW FOR LEGAL EXECUTIVES

PART I, YEAR II

Contract and Consumer Law
Employment Law
Family Law
Wills, Probate and Succession

Sixth Edition

GRAHAM ROWLEY, BA (Hons), LCGI, MIOSH, MCGI

JANET E. STEVENSON, Solicitor

BRENDAN GREENE, LLB, MA

TIMOTHY BLAKEMORE, LLB, LLM, Cert Ed, Solicitor

OXFORD
UNIVERSITY PRESS

OXFORD
UNIVERSITY PRESS

Great Clarendon Street, Oxford OX2 6DP

Oxford University Press is a department of the University of Oxford.
It furthers the University's objective of excellence in research, scholarship,
and education by publishing worldwide in

Oxford New York

Auckland Bangkok Buenos Aires Cape Town Chennai
Dar es Salaam Delhi Hong Kong Istanbul Karachi Kolkata
Kuala Lumpur Madrid Melbourne Mexico City Mumbai Nairobi
São Paulo Shanghai Singapore Taipei Tokyo Toronto

Oxford is a registered trade mark of Oxford University Press
in the UK and in certain other countries

Published in the United States
by Oxford University Press Inc., New York

First published 1992
Reprined 1993
Second edition 1994
Third edition 1996
Fourth edition 1998
Reprinted 1999
Fifth edition 2000
Sixth edition 2002

The moral rights of the authors have been asserted
Database right Oxford University Press (maker)

British Library Cataloguing in Publication Data

Data available

Library of Congress Cataloging in Publication Data

Data available

ISBN 0–19–925527–X

1 3 5 7 9 10 8 6 4 2

Typeset in Adobe Minion and ITC Stone Sans
by RefineCatch Limited, Bungay, Suffolk
Printed in Great Britain by
T.J. International Ltd, Padstow, Cornwall

Contents

Preface   xiii

Table of Cases   xv

1   Contract and Consumer Law

LAW OF CONTRACT

Introduction   1

Nature of contract   2

    1   Introduction   2

    2   Business bias   3

    3   Distinctions between contract and tort 4

    4   Observations   5

Formation of a contract   5

    1   Introduction   5

    2   Agreement   6

    3   Intention to create legal relations   22

    4   Consideration   27

    5   Requirements as to form   35

    6   Privity   39

Contents of a contract   45

    1   Introduction   45

    2   Representations and terms   45

    3   The parol evidence rule   48

    4   Express and implied terms   49

    5   Warranties, conditions and innominate terms 52

    6   Terms dealing with secondary obligations 56

Exclusion clauses   58

    1   Introduction   58

    2   Common law rules   59

    3   Statutory rules dealing with exclusion clauses 65

    4   The Unfair Contract Terms Act 1977   66

    5   The Unfair Terms in Consumer Contracts Regulations 1999 74

Vitiating elements   77

    1   Introduction   77

2   Illegality   77
3   Mistake   86
4   Misrepresentation   91
5   Duress and undue influence   98
6   Capacity   106

Discharge of the contract   108

1   Introduction   108
2   Discharge by performance   108
3   Discharge by agreement   111
4   Discharge by frustration   113
5   Discharge by breach   118

Remedies for breach of contract   120

1   Introduction   120
2   Damages   120
3   *Quantum meruit*   128
4   Specific performance   128
5   Injunctions   132
6   Limitation of actions   133

CONSUMER LAW

Introduction   134

Sale of Goods Act 1979   136

1   Introduction   136
2   Contracts of sale and other contracts   136
3   The implied terms   137
4   Title   138
5   Description   139
6   Satisfactory quality   141
7   Fitness for purpose   146
8   Relationship between section 14(2) and (3)   148
9   Sale by sample   149
10   Excluding the implied terms under sections 12 to 15   150
11   Remedies   150
12   Transfer of property   152
13   Transfer of property in specific goods   153
14   Transfer of property in unascertained goods   156
15   Reserving a right of disposal   159
16   Transfer of risk   160

17	Transfer of property in goods by a non-owner	162
18	Estoppel	162
19	Mercantile agents	163
20	Common law and statutory powers	164
21	Sale under a voidable title	164
22	Sale by a seller in possession	164
23	Sale by a buyer in possession	165
24	Sale of cars on hire-purchase under Part III of the Hire-Purchase Act 1964	165
25	Reform of rules on passing of property by a non-owner	166
26	Duties in performing the contract	167
27	Remedies under the Sale of Goods Act 1979	167

Supply of Goods and Services Act 1982 — 168

1	Introduction	168
2	Contracts involving the transfer of ownership of goods	169
3	Hire of goods	170
4	Services	171

Supply of Goods (Implied Terms) Act 1973 — 172

1	Introduction	172
2	Right to sell	173
3	Description	173
4	Satisfactory quality and fitness for purpose	173
5	Sample	173
6	Conditions	173
7	Exclusion of implied terms	174
8	Minor breaches of condition	174

Consumer Credit Act 1974 — 174

1	Introduction	174
2	Types of credit	175
3	Terminology of the Act	177
4	Agreements covered by the Act	179
5	The licensing system	181
6	Seeking business	182
7	Formation of the credit agreement	183
8	Cancellation	186
9	Rights to end the contract	188
10	Remedies	191

Consumer Protection Act 1987   193

  1   Introduction   193

  2   Contract   193

  3   Negligence   194

  4   Breach of statutory duty   194

  5   Consumer Protection Act 1987   195

Questions   202

2 Employment Law

Introduction   205

Employment   206

  1   The contract and its formation   206

  2   Express terms   207

  3   Implied terms   211

  4   Unfair or wrongful dismissal   215

  5   Unfair dismissal—a detailed consideration   219

  6   Discrimination: sex discrimination, equal pay and race
discrimination   243

  7   The Disability Discrimination Act 1995   257

Health and safety at work   261

  1   Introduction   261

  2   The rules of negligence   261

  3   The regulations   267

  4   Manslaughter   291

  5   Health and Safety at Work etc. Act 1974   292

  6   Sample health and safety policy document   305

Questions   309

3 Family Law

Introduction   311

Requirements for a valid marriage   312

  1   The nature of marriage   312

  2   The prohibited degrees   315

  3   Age   317

  4   Single status   317

  5   Gender   318

  6   Polygamous marriages   320

  7   Void and voidable marriages   320

Invalidity and failure of marriage   321

  1   Methods of terminating a marriage   321

  2   Nullity   322

  3   Divorce   328

  4   Judicial separation   340

  5   Methods of terminating a marriage compared   341

Financial provision after a final decree   341

  1   Introduction   341

  2   Orders available to the court   343

  3   Statutory guidelines   348

  4   The interrelationship of orders   355

Financial provision in the family proceedings court   356

  1   The domestic jurisdiction of the magistrates   356

  2   Grounds for an order   359

  3   Consent orders   361

  4   Child orders   361

  5   Orders in the High Court or county court   362

Children   363

  1   Introduction   363

  2   The orders available under the Children Act 1989   373

  3   Local authorities   379

  4   Financial provision   390

Questions   397

4   Wills, Probate and Succession

Introduction   399

Introductory principles—formalities and validity   400

  1   Wills and codicils   400

  2   Capacity   401

  3   *Animus testandi* (intention of making a will)   401

  4   Preparing the will   402

  5   Statutory requirements for a valid will   403

  6   Privileged wills (wills of soldiers on actual military service and sailors at sea)   406

Main clauses in a will   409

  1   Introduction   409

  2   The revocation of former wills   409

3	Appointment of executors	409
4	Funeral arrangements and special wishes concerning a body	410
5	Appointment of guardians	410
6	Dispositions in the will	411
7	Extension of trustee powers	411
8	Attestation clause	415

Gifts contained in wills — 415

1	Introduction	415
2	Inheritance tax considerations	416
3	Categories of gift	417
4	Gifts of land	417
5	Legacies or bequests—gifts of personalty	421
6	Residuary gifts	423
7	The survivorship period	424
8	Circumstances in which a beneficiary may lose a beneficial interest	424

Revocation of wills — 426

1	Voluntary revocation—s. 20 of the Wills Act 1837	426
2	Revocation by marriage or remarriage	428
3	Revocation by dissolution or annulment of marriage	428

Intestacy — 429

1	Total or partial intestacy?	429
2	The statutory trust for sale	429
3	Who is entitled to the estate?	430
4	Other powers and duties under s. 33, Administration of Estates Act 1925	434
5	The matrimonial home	434
6	Possible hardship caused by present intestacy rules	435
7	Commorientes and intestacy	436
8	Donationes mortis causa—'death bed gifts'	436

Personal representatives — 437

1	Appointment of personal representatives	437
2	Appointment of executors	438
3	Appointment of administrators	441
4	Grant of letters of administration *de bonis non administratis*	443
5	Powers and duties of personal representatives	444
6	Applying for the grant	447
7	Other affidavit evidence	455

Inheritance (Provision for Family and Dependants) Act 1975   457

   1   Introduction   457

   2   Against whom may a claim be made?   457

   3   When must the claim be made?   457

   4   Who may claim under the Inheritance (Provision for Family and
       Dependants) Act 1975?   458

   5   What must the applicant prove?   459

   6   Matters which the court must consider when making orders for
       provision (s. 3, Inheritance (Provision for Family and Dependants)
       Act 1975)   460

   7   Orders which may be made   462

   8   Conclusion   463

Inheritance tax   463

   1   What is inheritance tax?   463

   2   Introduction of inheritance tax   464

   3   When is inheritance tax chargeable?   464

   4   Transfer of value   465

   5   Rate of tax   466

   6   Reliefs from tax   466

Questions   468

Index   471

Preface

This edition has been prepared after 18 months or so of the Human Rights Act 1998 being in force, but with surprisingly little need for dramatic changes as a result. It has, however, been a confusing period in respect of legislation in family law, and this has meant some difficult decisions concerning the scope of the family law chapter. The Lord Chancellor has now announced that the divorce provisions in the Family Law Act 1996 will be repealed, and so these are now covered rather more briefly than in the previous edition, but still with sufficient detail to show how a new law of divorce could be drafted in the future. The child support provisions in the Child Support Pensions and Social Security Act 2000 were to come into force in April 2002, but were postponed at the last moment. These are covered in detail, rather than the 'old' (but still operating) formulae, in the expectation that they will be implemented sooner rather than later. The Adoption and Children Bill 2002 will make several important changes in the law over a range of topics, but was still wending its way through Parliament at the time of writing and is therefore still vulnerable to last-minute changes of policy. Its provisions have been noted when relevant, but as possibilities rather than certainties. The courts have been relatively quiet, although the House of Lords has caused some considerable re-thinking of ancillary relief principles on divorce by their decision in *White* v *White* (2000), and in care proceedings by their decision in *Re W and B (Children) (Care Plan)* (2001). In contract and consumer law, on the other hand, the courts have been unusually busy. The House of Lords has made important rulings on undue influence in *Royal Bank of Scotland* v *Etridge (No. 2)* (2001); damages based on the profits made in *Attorney General* v *Blake* (2000); and damages for disappointment in *Farley* v *Skinner* (2001). The Court of Appeal has given guidance on auctions held 'without reserve' in *Barry* v *Heathcote Ball* (2001); mistaken identity in *Shogun Finance* v *Hudson* (2001); and breach of Article 6 of the European Convention on Human Rights in *Wilson* v *First County Trust* (2001). The employment law chapter has also been updated to include: the Part-Time Workers (Prevention of Less Favourable Treatment) Regulations 2000 and Draft Regulations regarding fixed-term contract employees, updated rights relating to maternity, the decisions of the House of Lords in *Johnson* v *Unisys Ltd* (2001), *Halfpenny* v *IGC Medical Systems Ltd* (2000), *Preston and Others* v *Wolverhampton Health Care NHS Trust and Others* (2001), *Lubbe* v *Cape plc* (2000), *Lister and Others* v *Hesley Hall Ltd* (2001), which extends the principle of vicarious liability; the Court of Appeal decision in *Attorney-General's Reference* (No. 2 of 1999) (CA) 2000—regarding Great Western Trains' liability for manslaughter; and many other new cases and statutory updates relating to employment and safety in the workplace. In family law, the implementation of the divorce provisions of the Family Law Act 1996 has been postponed indefinitely but the pension-sharing provisions are being brought into force in December 2000. Some important new legislation was still progressing through Parliament at the time that this edition went to print (the Child Support, Pensions and Social Security Bill and Children (Leaving Care) Bill). The House of Lords have reviewed the guidelines for financial provision (*Piglowska* v *Piglowska* (1999)) and the threshold criteria for care orders (*Lancashire County Council* v *A* (2000)). The Chapter on wills, probate and succession refers to the latest Inheritance Tax Threshold, figures for excepted estates, when a reduced Inland Revenue Account may be delivered, and some of the provisions of the Trustee Act 2000.

We have endeavoured to state the law as it stood at 30 April 2002.

Graham Rowley
Janet E. Stevenson
Brendan Greene
Timothy Blakemore

Table of Cases

A v National Blood Authority [2001] 3 All ER 289 . . . 201, 266

A (Permission to Remove Child from Jurisdiction: Human Rights), re [2000] 2 FLR 225 . . . 374

Abouzaid v Mothercare (2001) *The Times*, 20 February . . . 200

Adams, re (2001) LTL 12/12/2001 . . . 461

Adams v Lindsell (1818) 1 B & Ald 681, 106 ER 250 . . . 18

Addis v Gramophone Co. Ltd (1909) AC 488 . . . 126, 236

Adler v Dickson [1954] 3 All ER 397 . . . 64

AEG Ltd v Logic Resource Ltd (1995) Sol Jop 1161 . . . 61

Affréteurs Réunis SA, Les v Leopold Walford (London) Ltd [1919] AC 801 . . . 42

Ailsa Craig Fishing Co. Ltd v Malvern Fishing Co. Ltd [1983] 1 All ER 101 . . . 70

Alaskan Trader, The, (No. 2) [1984] 1 All ER 129 . . . 119

Alexander v Rolls Royce Motor Cars Ltd [1996] RTR 95 . . . 122

Allen v Amalgamated Construction Co. Ltd (ECJ) (Case C234/98) *The Times*, 10 December 1999 . . . 216

Allen v Avon Rubber Co. Ltd (CA) [1986] ICR 695 . . . 276

Alliance Bank Ltd v Broom (1864) 2 Dr & Sm 289, 62 ER 631 . . . 31

Allonby v Accrington and Rossendale College and Others [2001] ICR 1189 . . . 244

Aluminium Industrie Vaassen BV v Romalpa Aluminium Ltd [1976] 2 All ER 552 . . . 159

Amalgamated Investment and Property Co. Ltd v John Walker & Sons Ltd [1976] 3 All ER 509 . . . 115

Andrews v Hopkinson [1956] 3 All ER 422 . . . 64

Anglia Television Ltd v Reed [1971] 3 All ER 690 . . . 123

Anyanwu and Another v South Bank Student Union and Another [2001] 2 All ER 353 . . . 244

Aparau v Iceland Frozen Foods plc (CA) [2000] 1 All ER 228 . . . 218

Application by Badeck and Others (ECJ) (2000) case C–158/97 . . . 246

Argyll v Argyll [1965] 1 All ER 611 . . . 314

Armhouse Lee Ltd v Chappell (1996) *The Times*, 7 August . . . 80

Armour v Thyssen Edelstahlwerke AG [1991] 2 AC 339 . . . 160

Ashmore v Corporation of Lloyd's (No. 2) [1992] 2 Lloyd's Rep 620 . . . 51

Associated Newspapers Ltd v Wilson [1995] 2 All ER 100 . . . 232

Aswan Engineering Establishment Co. v Lupdine Ltd [1987] 1 All ER 135 . . . 143

Atari Corp. Ltd v Electronics Boutique [1998] 1 All ER 1010 . . . 156

Atlantic Baron, The [1978] 3 All ER 1170 . . . 99

Atlas Express Ltd v Kafco (Importers and Distributors) Ltd [1989] 1 All ER 641 . . . 99

Attorney-General v Blake [2000] 4 All ER 385 . . . 121

Attorney-General's Reference (No. 2 of 1999) (CA) [2000] 3 WLR 195 . . . xiii, 291

Attwood v Lamont [1920] 3 KB 571 . . . 85

Attwood v Small (1838) 6 Cl & Fin 232, 7 ER 684 . . . 93

Auguste Noel Ltd v Curtis (EAT) [1990] ICR 604 . . . 226

Austin Rover Group Ltd v H M Inspector of Factories (HL) [1989] 2 All ER 1087 . . . 298

Avery v Bowden (1855) 5 E & B 714, 119 ER 647 . . . 119

B (A Minor) (Residence Order: ex parte), re [1992] 2 FLR 1 . . . 369, 370, 377

B (Adoption: Natural Parent), re (2001) *The Times*, 17 December . . . 367

B (Minors) (Care: Contact: Local Authority's Plans), re [1993] 1 FLR 543 . . . 371, 385, 389

B v B (Consent Order: Variation) [1995] 1 FLR 9 . . . 350

B v UK [2000] 1 FLR 1 327 . . . 366

B v France [1992] 2 FLR 249 . . . 319

Baker v Jones [1954] 2 All ER 553 . . . 82

Baker Refractories v Bishop [2002] 2 All ER 1 . . . 212

Baldry v Marshall [1925] 1 KB 260 . . . 146

Balfour v Balfour [1919] 2 KB 571 . . . 23

Balfour v Foreign and Commonwealth Office (CA) [1994] ICR 277 . . . 226

Banco Exterior Internacional v Thomas [1997] 1 All ER 46 . . . 103

Banik *v* Banik [1973] 3 All ER 45 . . . 336

Bank of Credit and Commerce International SA (in liquidation) *v* Ali (ChD) (1999) *The Times*, 25 January . . . 214

Bannerman *v* White (1861) 10 CBNS 844, 142 ER 685 . . . 46

Barber *v* Guardian Royal Exchange Assurance Co. (ECJ) [1990] ICR 616 . . . 249

Barber *v* RJB Mining UK Ltd (QBD) [1999] IRLR 308; ICR 679 . . . 210

Barclays Bank plc *v* Coleman [2000] 1 All ER 385 . . . 101

Barclays Bank plc *v* O'Brien [1993] 4 All ER 417 . . . 99, 101, 102, 202

Barder *v* Barder [1987] 2 All ER 440 . . . 354

Barking and Dagenham LBC *v* Camara (EAT) [1988] ICR 865 . . . 256

Barry *v* Heathcote Ball & Co Ltd [2001] 1 All ER 944 . . . 7, 65

Bartlett *v* Marcus (Sidney) Ltd [1965] 2 All ER 753 . . . 145

Barton (Alexander) *v* Armstrong [1975] 2 All ER 465 . . . 98

Beale *v* Taylor [1967] 3 All ER 253 . . . 140

Bellinger *v* Bellinger [2002] 1 All ER 311; [2001] 2 FLR 1048 . . . 319

Bence Graphics *v* Fasson UK Ltd [1997] 1 All ER 979 . . . 125

Bergin *v* Bergin [1983] 1 All ER 905 . . . 359

Bernstein *v* Pamson Motors (Golders Green) Ltd [1987] 2 All ER 220 . . . 151

Beswick *v* Beswick [1967] 2 All ER 1197 . . . 40, 44

Bettini *v* Gye (1876) 1 QBD 183 . . . 53

Birkett *v* Acorn Business Machines Ltd [1999] 2 All ER (Comm) 429 . . . 79

Birmingham City Council *v* H [1994] 1 FLR 224 . . . 389

Bishopsgate Motor Finance Corp Ltd *v* Transport Brakes Ltd [1949] 1 All ER 37 . . . 162

Bisset *v* Wilkinson [1927] AC 177 . . . 92

Blackpool and Fylde Aero Club Ltd *v* Blackpool Borough Council [1990] 3 All ER 25 . . . 10

Board of Governors of St Matthias Church of England School *v* Crizzle (EAT) [1993] ICR 401 . . . 257

Bolton *v* Mahadeva [1972] 2 All ER 1322 . . . 110

Bonnesen *v* Bonnesen [1989] Fam Law 230 . . . 329

Bouette *v* Rose [2000] 1 All ER 665 . . . 458

Bowerman *v* ABTA (1996) CLC 451 . . . 17

Boyle *v* Equal Opportunities Commission (ECJ) (1998) (Case C-411/96) . . . 242

Bradbury *v* Morgan (1862) 1 H & C 249, 158 ER 877 . . . 22

Bridgewater, in the estate of [1965] 1 All ER 717 . . . 427

Brinkibon *v* Stahag Stahl [1982] 1 All ER 293 . . . 15

British Coal Corporation *v* Smith and Others (HL) [1996] 3 All ER 97 . . . 252

British Crane Hire Corprn Ltd *v* Ipswich Plant Hire Ltd [1974] 1 All ER 1059 . . . 62

British Gas plc *v* Sharma (EAT) [1991] ICR 19 . . . 257

British Reinforced Concrete Engineering Co. Ltd *v* Schelff [1921] 2 Ch 292 . . . 84

British Road Services Ltd *v* Arthur V. Crutchley & Co. Ltd [1968] 1 All ER 811 . . . 65

British Steel Corpn *v* Cleveland Bridge and Engineering Co. Ltd [1984] 1 All ER 504 . . . 128

British United Shoe Machinery Co. Ltd *v* Clarke (EAT) [1978] ICR 70 . . . 228

Brodie *v* Brodie [1917] P 271 . . . 313

Brogden *v* Metropolitan Rlwy Co. (1877) 2 App Cas 666 . . . 11

Brookes *v* J & P Coates (UK) Ltd (QBD) [1984] ICR 158 . . . 273

Brown *v* Rentokil Ltd (C-394/36) (CA) (1998) *The Times*, 2 July . . . 246

Bullock *v* Alice Ottley School (CA) [1993] ICR 138 . . . 245

Burridge *v* Burridge [1982] 3 All ER 80 . . . 358

Butler Machine Tool Co. Ltd *v* Ex-Cell-O Corporation (England) Ltd [1979] 1 All ER 965 . . . 65

Buxton *v* Buxton [1965] 3 All ER 150 . . . 360

Buxton *v* Equinox Design Ltd (EAT) [1999] IRLR 158; ICR 269 . . . 259

Byrne & Co. *v* Leon van Tienhoven & Co. (1880) 5 CPD 344 . . . 20

C (Interim Care Order: Residential Assessment), Re [1997] 1 FLR 1 . . . 385

C *v* C (A Minor) (Custody: Appeal) [1991] 1 FLR 223 . . . 370

C *v* C (Custody of Child) (No. 2) [1992] 1 FCR 206 . . . 370

C *v* C (Financial Relief: Short Marriage) [1997] 2 FLR 26 . . . 350

Cain *v* Leeds Western Health Authority (EAT) [1990] ICR 54 . . . 226

Cammell Laird & Co. Ltd v Manganese Bronze and Brass Co. Ltd [1934] AC 402 . . . 148

Canterbury City Council v Howletts and Port Lympne Estates Ltd (QBD) [1997] ICR 925 . . . 293

Cantor Fitzgerald Intentional v Callaghan (CA) [1999] 2 All ER 411 . . . 208

Capper Pass Ltd v Lawton (EAT) [1977] ICR 83 . . . 252

Car and Universal Finance Co. Ltd v Caldwell [1964] 1 All ER 290 . . . 95, 164

Care First Partnership Ltd v Roffey and Others [2001] IRLR 85 . . . 223

Carlill v Carbolic Smoke Ball Co. [1892] 2 QB 484, [1893] 1 QB 256 . . . 8, 17

Carmichael v National Power plc [1999] 1 WLR 2042 . . . 207–8

Carlos Federspiel & Co. SA v Charles Twigg & Co. Ltd [1957] Lloyd's Rep 240 . . . 157

Carter-Fea v Carter-Fea [1987] Fam Law 131 . . . 331, 397

Casey v Morane Ltd [2001] IR LR 166; ICR 316 . . . 263

Casey's Patents, Re, Stewart v Casey [1892] 1 Ch 104 . . . 29

Cehave NV v Bremer Handelsgesellschaft GmbH [1975] 3 All ER 739 . . . 55

Cellulose Acetate Silk Co. Ltd v Widnes Foundry (1925) Ltd [1933] AC 20 . . . 56

Central London Property Trust Ltd v High Trees House Ltd [1947] KB 130 . . . 34

Cerberus Software Ltd v Rowley [2001] IRLR 160; ICR 1241 . . . 218

Chapelton v Barry UDC [1940] 1 All ER 356 . . . 60

Chaplin v Hicks [1911] 2 KB 786 . . . 126

Chappell & Co. Ltd v Nestlé Co. Ltd [1959] 2 All ER 701 . . . 30

Charter v Sullivan [1957] 1 All ER 809 . . . 125

Cheese v Thomas [1994] 1 All ER 35 . . . 106

Chief Constable of West Yorkshire Police v Khan [2001] 4 All ER 834 . . . 255

CIBC Mortgages plc v Pitt [1993] 4 All ER 433 . . . 100, 102, 202

Citibank NA v Brown Shipley & Co. Ltd [1991] 2 All ER 690 . . . 89

City and Westminster Properties (1934) Ltd v Mudd [1958] 2 All ER 733 . . . 48

Clark and Tokeley Ltd (t/a Spellbrook Ltd) v Oakes (CA) (1998) IRLR 577 . . . 215, 229

Cleary v Cleary [1974] 1 WLR 73 . . . 330

Codd v Thomson Tour Operations Ltd (2000) The Times 20 October . . . 263–4

Cohen v Roche [1927] 1 KB 169 . . . 129

Collins v Godefroy (1831) 1 B & Ad 950, 109 ER 1040 . . . 31

Coloroll Pension Trustees Ltd v Russell and others (1994) The Times, 30 November . . . 250

Commission for New Towns v Cooper Ltd [1995] 2 All ER 929 . . . 37

Conway v Rimmer (1968) 1 All ER 874 . . . 226

Cook's Goods, re [1902] P 114 . . . 440

Co-operative Insurance Society Ltd v Argyll Stores Ltd [1997] 3 All ER 297 . . . 131

Corbett v Corbett [1970] 2 All ER 33 . . . 318

Cossey v UK [1991] 2 FLR 492 . . . 319

Court v Szuba (QBD) [1982] ICR 380 . . . 296

Couturier v Hastie (1856) 5 HLC 673, 10 ER 1065 . . . 86

Coventry, re, Coventry v Coventry [1979] 3 All ER 815 . . . 460

Cowan v Cowan [2001] 3 WLR 684; 2 FLR 192 . . . 352

Cowley v South African Airways (ET) (1999) The Times, 3 August . . . 247

Cox v H.C.B. Angus Ltd (QBD) [1981] ICR 683 . . . 275

Craven-Ellis v Canons Ltd [1936] 2 KB 403 . . . 128

Crédit Lyonnaise v Burch [1997] 1 All ER 144 . . . 103, 202

Crosville Wales Ltd v Tracey (CA) (1995) Independent, 29 August . . . 231

Crown Suppliers (Property Services Agency) v Dawkins (CA) [1993] ICR 517 . . . 254

Crowther v Shannon Motor Co. [1975] 1 All ER 139 . . . 148

Croydon London Borough Council v A [1992] 3 All ER 788 . . . 376

Cundy v Lindsay (1878) 3 App Cas 459 . . . 89

Curtis v Chemical Cleaning and Dyeing Co. [1951] 1 All ER 631 . . . 64

Cutter v Powell (1795) 6 Term Rep 320, 101 ER 573 . . . 109

D (A Child), re [2001] 1 FLR 972 . . . 366

D (A Minor) (Care or Supervision), re [1993] 2 FLR 423 . . . 368, 383, 385, 388

D (Care: Natural Parent Presumption), re (1999) FLR 134 . . . 369

D & C Builders v Rees [1965] 3 All ER 837 . . . 33

Darby v GKN Screws and Fasteners Ltd (QBD) [1986] ICR 1 . . . 275

Davies, in the estate of [1951] 1 All ER 920 ... 427

Davis and Others v MJ Wyatt (Decorators) Ltd (EAT) (2000) *The Times*, 24 October ... 210–11

Davis Contractors Ltd v Fareham UDC [1956] 2 All ER 145 ... 115

De Lassalle v Guildford [1901] 2 KB 215 ... 48

Dedman v British Building and Engineering Appliances Ltd (CA) [1974] 1 All ER 420 ... 220

Defrenne v Sabina [1979] ECR 1365, [1978] 3 CMLR 312 ... 250, 251

Delaney v Staples (HL) [1992] 1 All ER 944 ... 208

Denny, Mott and Dickson Ltd v James B Fraser & Co. Ltd [1944] 1 All ER 678 ... 114

Devis (W) and Sons Ltd v Atkins (HL) [1977] ICR 662 ... 226

Dick Bentley Productions Ltd v Harold Smith Motors Ltd [1965] 2 All ER 65 ... 47

Dickinson v Dodds (1876) 2 ChD 463 ... 20

Dietmann v Brent London BC (CA) [1988] ICR 842 ... 217, 225

Digital Equipment Co. Ltd v Clements (CA) [1998] ICR 258 ... 236

Dimond v Lovell [1999] 3 All ER 1 ... xiii, 185

Director General of Fair Trading v First National Bank [2001] 2 All ER (Comm) 1000; 3 WLR 1297 ... 76

Dixon v London Fire and Civil Defence Authority (CA) (1993) *The Times*, 22 March ... 275

Dodds v Yorkshire Bank Finance [1992] CCLR 92 ... 166

Donoghue v Stevenson (HL) [1932] AC 562, [1932] All ER Rep 1 ... 265

Dorman Long (Steel) Ltd v Bell (HL) [1964] 1 All ER 617 ... 275

Doughty v Turner Manufacturing Co. Ltd (CA) [1964] 1 All ER 98 ... 262

Dudley MBC v Colorvision plc [1997] CCLR 19 ... 182

Dunlop Pneumatic Tyre Co. Ltd v New Garage and Motor Co. Ltd [1915] AC 79 ... 57

Dunlop Pneumatic Tyre Co. Ltd v Selfridge & Co. Ltd [1915] AC 847 ... 39

E (Residence: Imposition of Conditions) re [1997] 2 FLR 638 ... 374

Eagland v British Telecommunications plc (EAT) [1990] ICR 248 ... 207

East v Maurer [1991] 2 All ER 733 ... 97

East Lindsey DC v Daubney (EAT) [1977] ICR 566 ... 224

Eastbourne Borough Council v Foster (CA) [2002] ICR 234; [2001] LGR 529 ... 209

EC Commission v UK (C-300/95) [1997] All ER (EC) 481 ... 200

Ecay v Godfrey (1947) 80 Ll L Rep 286 ... 46

Edgar v Met. Office [2002] ICR 149 ... 237

Edgington v Fitzmaurice (1885) 29 ChD 459 ... 92

Edmonds v Lawson (QBD) (1999) [2000] 2 WLR 1091 ... 209

Edwards v Skyways Ltd [1964] 1 All ER 494 ... 26

Elmi v Harrods Ltd (CA) [1998] 1 All ER 52 ... 256

Ely v YKK Fasteners (UK) Ltd (CA) [1994] ICR 164 ... 234

Enderby v Frenchay Health Authority (no 2)(CA) [2000] IRLR 257; ICR 612 ... 253

Entores Ltd v Miles Far East Corpn [1955] 2 All ER 493 ... 15

Errington v Errington and Woods [1952] 1 All ER 149 ... 21

Esso Petroleum Co. Ltd v Harper's Garage (Stourport) Ltd [1967] 1 All ER 699 ... 85

Evans (J) & Son (Portsmouth) Ltd v Andrea Merzario Ltd [1976] 2 All ER 930 ... 64

Everet v Williams (1724) 220 LT 117 ... 79

F & H Entertainments Ltd v Leisure Enterprises Ltd (1976) 120 SJ 331 ... 94

Farley v Skinner [2001] 4 All ER 801 ... 122

Felthouse v Bindley (1862) 11 CBNS 869, 142 ER 1037 ... 16

Ferodo Ltd v Barnes (EAT) [1976] ICR 439 ... 225

Fibrosa Spolka Akcyjna v Fairbairn Lawson Combe Barbour Ltd [1942] 2 All ER 122 ... 117

Financings Ltd v Stimson [1962] 3 All ER 386 ... 21

First National Bank plc v Syed [1991] 2 All ER 250 ... 192

Firstpost Homes v Johnson [1995] 4 All ER 355 ... 36

Fisher v Bell [1960] 3 All ER 731 ... 7

Fitch v Dewes (HL) [1921] 2 AC 158, [1921] All ER Rep 15 ... 83, 214

Foakes v Beer [1884] 9 App Cas 605 ... 33

Folkes v King [1923] 1 KB 282 ... 163

Ford v Ford [1987] Fam Law 232 ... 323, 324

Ford v GKR Construction (CA) [2000] 1 All ER 802 . . . 267

Ford v Warwickshire County Council (HL) [1983] ICR 273 . . . 222

Ford Motor Co. Ltd v Amalgamated Union of Engineering and Foundry Workers [1969] 2 All ER 481 . . . 26

Ford Motor Co. (England) Ltd v Armstrong (1915) 31 TLR 267 . . . 57

Forster & Sons Ltd v Suggett (1918) 35 TLR 87 . . . 83

Forthright Finance Ltd v Ingate [1997] 4 All ER 99 . . . 189

Foster v Biosol (2001) 59 BMLR 178 . . . 197

Foster v Driscoll [1929] 1 KB 470 . . . 80

Fraser v State Hospitals Board for Scotland (2000) The Times 12 September . . . 212

Fraser v Winchester Health Authority (CA) (1999), (2000) 55 BMLR 122 . . . 272

Frost v Aylesbury Dairy Co. [1905] 1 KB 608 . . . 148

Frost v Chief Constable of South Yorkshire (HL) (1998) 3 WLR 1509 . . . 263, 309

Fuller v Fuller [1973] 2 All ER 650 . . . 332

G (Child Case: Avoiding Delay), re [1991] FCR 562 . . . 371

Gamerco v ICM/Fair Warning Agency Ltd [1995] 1 WLR 1226 . . . 117

Garcia v Garcia [1992] 1 FLR 256 . . . 337

Geddling v Marsh [1920] 1 KB 668 . . . 145

General Medical Council v Goba (EAT) [1988] ICR 885 . . . 255

George Mitchell (Chesterhall) Ltd v Finney Lock Seeds Ltd [1983] 2 All ER 737 . . . 69

GF1 Group Inc. v Eaglestone (QBD) [1994] IRLR 119 . . . 214

Gibson v East Riding of Yorkshire District Council CA [2000] IRLR 598; ICR 890 . . . 210

Gibson v Manchester City Council (CA) [1978] 2 All ER 583, (HL) [1979] 1 All ER 972 . . . 9, 11

Gillick v West Norfolk and Wisbech Area Health Authority [1986] AC 112 . . . 363

Glasbrook Bros Ltd v Glamorgan County Council [1925] AC 270 . . . 31

Glasgow City Council and Others v Marshall and Others [2000] 1 All ER 641 . . . 252

Gloucester County Council v P [1999] 2 FLR 61 . . . 373

Glynn v Margetson & Co. [1893] AC 351 . . . 63

Godley v Perry [1960] 1 All ER 36 . . . 149

Gojkovic v Gojkovic [1992] 1 All ER 267 . . . 350

Goldcorp Exchange Ltd (in receivership), re [1994] 2 All ER 806 . . . 157

Goldsoll v Goldman [1915] 1 Ch 292 . . . 85

Goodwin v The Patent Office (EAT) (1999) ICR 302 . . . 258

Governing Body of Clifton Middle School and Others v Askew (CA) [1999] IRLR 708; ICR 286 . . . 229

Graham and others v Secretary of State for Social Security and another (1995) The Times, 25 September . . . 251, 260

Grant v Australian Knitting Mills Ltd [1936] AC 85 . . . 139

Great Northern Rlwy Co. v Witham (1873) LR 9 CP 16 . . . 13

Grenfell v Grenfell [1978] 1 All ER 561 . . . 329, 334, 353

Griffin v London Pensions Fund Authority (EAT) [1993] ICR 564 . . . 249

Griffiths v Peter Conway Ltd [1939] 1 All ER 685 . . . 147

Grist v Bailey [1966] 2 All ER 875 . . . 87

Gunion v Roche Products Ltd (Outer House, Court of Session) (1994) The Times, 4 November . . . 276

H (A Minor) (Parental Responsibility), re [1993] 1 FLR 484 . . . 366, 386

H (A Minor) (Shared Residence), re [1994] 1 FLR 717 . . . 374

H (Minors) (Access), re [1992] 1 FLR 148 . . . 375

H (Minors) (Sexual Abuse: Standard of Proof), re [1996] 1 All ER 1 . . . 381

H (Parental Responsibility: Contact), re [1998] 1 FLR 855 . . . 366

H v H (Financial Provision: Capital Assets) [1993] 2 FLR 335 . . . 349

Haberman-Belterman (C-421/92) [1994] IRLR 364 . . . 245

Hadley v Baxendale (1854) 9 Exch 341, 156 ER 145 . . . 124

Haley v London Electricity Board (HL) [1964] 3 All ER 185 . . . 268

Halfpenny v IGE Medical Systems Ltd (HL) 2000 . . . xiii, 241, 263

Hall v Woolston Hall Leisure Ltd [2000] 4 All ER 787 . . . 244

Hardwick Game Farm v Suffolk Agricultural and Poultry Producers' Association [1969] 1 All ER 309 . . . 62

Hare v Murphy Bros Ltd [1974] 3 All ER 940 . . . 114

Harlingdon and Leinster Enterprises Ltd v Christopher Hull Fine Art Ltd [1990] 1 All ER 737 . . . 140

Harlow v National Westminster Bank (1994) *The Times*, 3 January . . . 460

Harris v Nickerson (1873) LR 8 QB 286 . . . 7

Harris v Sheffield United FC Ltd [1987] 2 All ER 838 . . . 31

Harris v TSB (CA) [2000] IRLR 157 . . . 213

Harris v Wyre Forest DC [1989] 2 All ER 514 . . . 59

Harrods Ltd v Remick [1998] 1 All ER 52 . . . 256

Harrods Ltd v Seeley [1998] 1 All ER 52 . . . 256

Hartley v Ponsonby (1857) 7 E & B 872 . . . 32

Hartog v Colin and Shields [1939] 3 All ER 566 . . . 88

Harvela Investments Ltd v Royal Trust Co. of Canada (CI) Ltd [1985] 2 All ER 966 . . . 10

Harvest Town Circle Ltd v Rutherford [2001] IRLR 599 . . . 249

Harvey v Facey [1893] AC 552 . . . 9

Hayes and Others v Security Facilities Division (CA) [2001] IRLR 81 . . . 206

Health and Safety Executive v Spindle Select Ltd (QBD) (1996) *The Times*, 9 December . . . 294

Healy v Howlett & Sons [1917] 1 KB 337 . . . 158

Hedley Byrne & Co. Ltd v Heller & Partners Ltd [1963] 2 All ER 575 . . . 4, 94

Heil v Rankin and Another (2000) *The Times* 20 June . . . 262

Helby v Matthews [1895] AC 471 . . . 175

Hendy Lennox (Industrial Engines) Ltd v Grahame Puttick Ltd [1984] 2 All ER 152 . . . 160

Heppie and Others v Adjudication Officer (2000) case C–196/98, *The Times*, 30 May . . . 251

Herne Bay Steam Boat Co. v Hutton [1903] 2 KB 683 . . . 115

Hertford Foods Ltd v Lidl UK GmbH (2001) LTL 20/6/2001

Hicking v Basford Group Ltd [1999] All ER (EC) 1 . . . 254

Hill v James Crowe (Cases) Ltd (QBD), [1978] 1 All ER 812 . . . 265

Hilton International Hotels (UK) Ltd v Kaissi (EAT) [1994] ICR 578 . . . 206

Hirachand Punamchand v Temple [1911] 2 KB 330 . . . 33

Hirani v Hirani (1982) 4 FLR 232 . . . 325, 397

Hochster v De La Tour (1853) 2 E & B 678, 118 ER 922 . . . 119

Hoenig v Isaacs [1952] 2 All ER 176 . . . 110

Hollier v Rambler Motors (AMC) Ltd [1972] 1 All ER 399 . . . 62

Holwell Securities Ltd v Hughes [1974] 1 All ER 161 . . . 18

Home Counties Dairies Ltd v Skilton [1970] 1 All ER 1227 . . . 84

Hong Kong Fir Shipping Co. Ltd v Kwasaki Kisen Kaisha Ltd [1962] 1 All ER 474 . . . 54

Hopkins v Norcros plc (CA) [1994] ICR 11 . . . 218

Hough and others v Leyland DAF Ltd (EAT) [1991] ICR 696 . . . 228

Houghton v Trafalgar Insurance Co. Ltd [1953] 2 All ER 1409 . . . 62

Hounslow London Borough Council v A [1993] 1 WLR 291 . . . 371, 383

Hughes v Asset Managers plc [1995] 3 All ER 669 . . . 78

Hughes v Metropolitan Rlwy Co. (1877) 2 App Cas 439 . . . 34

Humphreys v Oxford University [2000] 1 All ER 996 . . . 229

Hussain and others v J. H. Walker Ltd (EAT) [1996] ICR 291 . . . 247

Hutton v Warren (1836) 1 M & W 466 . . . 50

Hyde v Wrench (1840) 3 Beav 334, 49 ER 132 . . . 12

Hyde v Hyde and Woodmansee (1866) LR 1 P & D 130 . . . 314, 318

IRC v Fry (2001) *The Times* 10 December; STC 1715 . . . 19

J (A Minor) (Property Transfer), re [1993] 2 FLR 56 . . . 390

J v C [1969] 1 All ER 788 . . . 367

Jackson v Horizon Holidays Ltd [1975] 3 All ER 92 . . . 43

Jackson v Union Marine Co. Ltd (1874) LR 10 CP 125 . . . 116

Jameson v Central Electricity Generating Board (HL) [1999] 1 All ER 193 . . . 265

Jarvis v Swan Tours Ltd [1973] 1 All ER 71 . . . 122

Jebson v Ministry of Defence [2000] 1 WLR 2055 . . . 263

Jelley v Iliffe [1981] 2 All ER 29 . . . 459

Johansen v Norway (1997) 23 EHRR 33 . . . 386

John Lewis plc v Coyne [2001] IRLR 139 . . . 234

Johnson v Unisys Ltd [2001] 2 All ER 801 . . . xiii, 236

Johnston v Caddies Wainwright Ltd (CA) [1983] ICR 407 . . . 275

Jolly v Sutton London Borough Council [2000] 3 All ER 409 . . . 265

Jones v Padavatton [1969] 2 All ER 616 . . . 24

Jones v Tower Boot Co. Ltd (CA) [1997] 2 All ER 406 . . . 254

Jones v Vernons Pools Ltd [1938] 2 All ER 626 . . . 24

Jones (Deceased), re [1981] 1 All ER 1 . . . 407

Jones, re, Jones v Midland Bank Trust Co. Ltd (1997) The Times, 29 April . . . 425

Joshua Wilson and Bros Ltd v Union of Shop Distributive and Allied Workers (EAT) [1978] ICR 614 . . . 227

Junior Books Ltd v Veitchi Co. Ltd [1983] 3 All ER 201 . . . 4

K (Contact: Mother's Anxiety), re (1999) 2 FLR 703 . . . 375

K (Deceased), re [1985] 2 All ER 833 . . . 425

K v H (Child Maintenance) [1993] 2 FLR 61 . . . 371

K v K (Minors: Property Transfer) [1992] 2 FLR 220 . . . 377, 390

Kalake v Freie Hansestadt Bremen (1995) The Times, 26 October . . . 246

Kassim v Kassim [1962] 3 All ER 426 . . . 326

Kaur v Singh [1972] 1 All ER 292 . . . 324

Kenny v Hampshire Constabulary (EAT) [1999] IRLR 76; ICR 27 . . . 259

Kenyon-Brown v Desmond Banks & Co. (2000) Lloyd's Rep Bank 80 . . . 103

Ketley (A.) Ltd v Scott [1981] ICR 241 . . . 192

Khan v General Medical Council (EAT) [1993] ICR 627 . . . 255

Kinder v Camberwell BC (KBD) [1944] 2 All ER 315 . . . 280

King's Norton Metal Co. Ltd v Edridge, Merrett & Co. Ltd (1897) 14 TLR 98 . . . 88

Kleinwort Benson Ltd v Malaysia Mining Corpn Bhd [1989] 1 All ER 785 . . . 25

Knott v Bolton (1995) EGCS 59 . . . 122, 123

Knowles v Liverpool City Council (HL) [1993] 4 All ER 321 . . . 300

Koonjul v Thameslink Healthcare Services NHS Trust (2000) The Times 18 May; P1QR 123 . . . 285

Krell v Henry [1903] 2 KB 740 . . . 115, 117

Kyte v Kyte [1988] 1 FLR 469 . . . 351

L (A Child) (Contract: Domestic Violence), re [2000] 4 All EU 609; 2 FLR 334 . . . 375

Lampleigh v Brathwait (1615) Hob 105, 80 ER 255 . . . 29

Lamplough v Lotus Cars (1977) The Times, 26 October . . . xiv, 129

Lancashire County Council v A [2000] 2 All ER 97 . . . 382

Larner v British Steel plc (CA) [1993] ICR 551 . . . 276

Le Brocq v Le Brocq [1964] 3 All ER 464 . . . 332

Le Marechal v WSS (Western) Ltd (CA) (1992) The Times, 9 December . . . 218

Leach v Lindeman [1985] 2 All ER 754 . . . 462

Leaf v International Galleries [1950] 1 All ER 693 . . . 96

Leverton v Clwyd CC (HL) [1989] ICR 33 . . . 253

Levez v TM Jennings (Harlow Pools) Ltd; Hicking v Basford Group Ltd (EAT) (1999) All ER (EC) 1, (1998) (ECJ) (Case C-326/96) . . . 254

L'Estrange v F Graucob Ltd [1934] 2 KB 394 . . . 60

Linford Cash and Carry Ltd v Thomson and Others (EAT) [1989] ICR 518 . . . 225

Link v Secretary of State for Trade and Industry [2001] ICR 1096 . . . 230

Lister v Romford Ice and Cold Storage Co. Ltd (HL) [1957] 1 All ER 125 . . . 213, 266

Lister and Others v Hesley Hall Ltd [2001] 2 All ER 769 . . . xiii, 266

Liverpool City Council v Hatton (2002) BBC News (Health) Website, 5 February . . . 212

Liverpool City Council v Irwin [1976] 2 All ER 39 . . . 51

Livingstone-Stallard v Livingstone-Stallard [1974] 2 All ER 776 . . . 331

Lloyds Bank plc v Waterhouse (1990) 10 Tr LR 161 . . . 91

Lumley v Wagner (1852) 1 De GM & C 604, 42 ER 687 . . . 132

Lubbe v Cape plc (HL) 2000 . . . xiii, 263

M (A Minor) (Care Order: Threshold Conditions), re [1994] 3 All ER 298 . . . 380

M v M (Minors) (Removal from Jurisdiction) [1992] 2 FLR 303 . . . 374

McMichael v UK [1995] 2 FCR 718 . . . 386

Macmillan Inc. v Bishopsgate Investment Trust plc (No. 2) [1993] ICR 385 . . . 211

Mahmud v Mahmud [1994] SLT 599 . . . 326

Makepeace v Evans Brothers (Reading) (a firm) and Another (2000) The Times 13 June; BLR 737 . . . 264

Malik v Bank of Credit and Commerce International SA (In Liquidation) (CA) [1997] IRLR 462 . . . 127, 213, 236

Maritime National Fish Ltd v Ocean Trawlers Ltd [1935] AC 524 . . . 116

Marley (UK) Ltd v Anderson (EAT) [1994] ICR 295 . . . 221

Marshall v Southampton and South-West Hampshire Area Health Authority (Teaching) (No. 2) (ECJ) [1993] ICR 893 . . . 253–4

Martin v Boulton and Paul (Steel Construction) Ltd (QBD) [1982] ICR 366 . . . 294

Martin v Lancashire County Council [2000] 3 All ER 544 . . . 262

Martin v Martin [1978] Fam 12 . . . 346, 355

Mason v Provident Clothing and Supply Co. Ltd [1913] AC 724 . . . 84

McArdle, re [1951] 1 All ER 905 . . . 28

McCausland v Duncan Lawrie Ltd [1996] 4 All ER 995 . . . 37

McKenzie v Crosville Motor Services Ltd (EAT) [1990] ICR 172 . . . 230

Mecca Leisure Group plc v Chatprachong (EAT) [1993] ICR 688 . . . 257

Mehta v Mehta [1945] 2 All ER 690 . . . 326

Mennell v Newell and Wright (Transport Contractors) Ltd (EAT) [1997] ICR 1039. . . 234

Merritt v Merritt [1970] 2 All ER 760 . . . 23

Mesher v Mesher [1980] 1 All ER 126 . . . 346

Messina v Smith [1971] 2 All ER 1046 . . . 327

MHC Consulting Services Ltd v Tansell [2000] IRLR 387; ICR 789 . . . 258

Microbeads AG v Vinhurst Road Markings Ltd [1975] 1 All ER 529 . . . 138

Mihalis Angelos, The [1970] 3 All ER 125 . . . 55

Militante v Ogunwomoju [1994] Fam Law 17 . . . 326

Ministry of Defence v Cannock and others (EAT) (1994), [1995] 2 All ER 449 . . . 243

Ministry of Defence v Wheeler (CA) [1998] 1 All ER 790 . . . 236, 243

Mitchell v Arkswood Plastics (Engineering) Ltd (EAT) (1993) The Times, 12 September . . . 224

Monie v Coral Racing Ltd (CA) [1981] ICR 109 . . . 225, 263

Montgomery v Johnson Underwood Ltd (2001) The Times 16 March; [2001] ICR 819 . . . 219

Moody (Deceased), re, Moody v Stevenson [1992] 2 All ER 524 . . . 461

Moorcock, The (1889) 14 PD 64 . . . 51

Moore & Co. and Landauer & Co., re [1921] 2 KB 519 . . . 140, 141, 152

Moran v University College Salford (No. 2) (1993) The Times, 23 November . . . 25

Morgan v Manser [1947] 2 All ER 666 . . . 114

Morris v Breaveglen Ltd (CA) [1993] ICR 766 . . . 264

Moualem v Carlisle City Council (QBD) (1994) 158 JP 1110 . . . 298

Munt v Munt [1983] Fam Law 81 . . . 358

Murray v Foyle Meats Ltd (HL) [1999] 3 All ER 769 . . . 227

Museprime Properties Ltd v Adhill Properties Ltd (1990) 61 P & CR 111 . . . 93

Nagarajan v London Regional Transport (HL) [1999] 3 WLR 425 . . . 256

Nash v Inman [1908] 2 KB 1 . . . 107

National Federation of Self-Employed and Small Businesses Ltd v Philpott (EAT)[1997] ICR 518 . . . 245

National Westminster Bank plc v Morgan [1985] 1 All ER 821 . . . 100

Neath v Hugh Steeper Ltd (ECJ) [1994] IRLR 91 . . . 249

Nelhams v Sandells Maintenance Ltd and another (CA) (1995) The Times, 15 June; [1996] 46 Con LR 40 . . . 264

New Zealand Shipping Co. Ltd v A. M. Satterthwaite & Co. Ltd [1975] AC 154 . . . 6

Newham London Borough Council v National and Local Government Officers Association (CA) [1993] ICR 189 . . . 231

Newtons of Wembley Ltd v Williams [1964] 3 All ER 532 . . . 165

Niblett v Confectioners' Materials Co. [1921] 3 KB 387 . . . 138

Nicolene Ltd v Simmonds [1953] 1 All ER 822 . . . 14

Noel v London Underground Ltd (CA) [1999] IRLR 621; ICR 109 . . . 221

Nordenfelt v Maxim Nordenfelt Guns and Ammunition Co. Ltd [1894] AC 535 . . . 84

Norris v Southampton City Council [1982] ICR 177 . . . 114

North West Thames Regional Health Authority v Noone (CA) [1988] ICR 813 . . . 256

Northern General Hospital National Health Service Trust v Gale (EAT) [1993] ICR 638 . . . 215

Norweb plc v Dixon [1995] 3 All ER 952 . . . 5

Nottingham County Council v P [1993] 3 All ER 815 . . . 370, 379

Nottingham Patent Brick and Tile Co. v Butler (1885) 15 QBD 261 . . . 92

Nottingham University v Fishel [2000] IRLR 471; ICR 1462 . . . 213

Octavius Atkinson and Sons Ltd v Morris (EAT) [1988] ICR 880 . . . 228

O'Laoire v Jackel International Ltd (No. 2) (CA) [1991] ICR 718 . . . 206, 218

Olley v Marlborough Court Ltd [1949] 1 All ER 127 . . . 61

O'Neill v Governors of St Thomas More Roman Catholic Voluntary Aid Upper School (EAT) [1997] ICR 33 . . . 246

Oscar Chess Ltd v Williams [1957] 1 All ER 325 . . . 47

Overland Shoes Ltd v Schenkers Ltd (1998) The Times, 26 February . . . 72

Overseas Medical Supplies Ltd v Orient Transport Services Ltd [1999] All ER (Comm) 981 . . . 70

P (A Minor) (Education), re [1992] 1 FLR 316 . . . 368

PB Leasing v Patel and Patel (1995) CCLR 82 . . . 185

Page v Freight Hire Tank Haulage Ltd (EAT) [1981] ICR 299 . . . 251

Page v Smith (HL) (1995) 2 All ER 736 . . . 263, 309

Page One Records Ltd v Britton [1967] 3 All ER 822 . . . 133

Parker v Clark [1960] 1 All ER 93 . . . 23

Parkinson v College of Ambulance Ltd and Harrison [1925] 2 KB 1 . . . 79, 80

Parkinson v March Consulting (CA) (1997) The Times, 9 November . . . 223

Parr v Whitbread & Co. plc (EAT) [1990] ICR 427 . . . 225

Parsons (H) (Livestock) Ltd v Uttley Ingham & Co. Ltd [1978] 1 All ER 525 . . . 125

Partridge v Crittenden [1968] 2 All ER 421 . . . 8

Patel v Ali [1984] 1 All ER 978 . . . 130

Peachdart Ltd, re [1983] 3 All ER 204 . . . 159

Peake v Automotive Products Ltd (CA) [1977] ICR 968 . . . 245, 261

Pearce v Brooks (1866) LR 1 Ex 213 . . . 79

Pearce v Governing Body of Mayfield School (2001) The Times 9 October . . . 244

Pearson v Franklin [1994] 1 FLR 246 . . . 377

Pename v Paterson (EAT) [1989] ICR 12 . . . 208

Percy (G.) Trentham Ltd v Archital Luxfer Ltd [1993] 1 Lloyd's Rep 25 . . . 11

Petch v Commissioners of Customs and Excise (CA) [1993] ICR 789 . . . 1, 213

Pharmaceutical Society of Great Britain v Boots Cash Chemists (Southern) Ltd [1953] 1 All ER 482 . . . 8

Pheasant v Pheasant [1972] 1 All ER 587 . . . 332, 397

Phelps v Hillingdon London Borough Council [2000] 4 All ER 504 . . . 266

Phillips v Brooks Ltd [1919] 2 KB 243 . . . 89

Photo Production Ltd v Securicor Transport Ltd [1980] 1 All ER 556 . . . 3, 63

Pickard v Sears (1837) 6 Ad & El 469, 112 ER 179 . . . 163

Piglowska v Piglowska (1999) 1 WLR 1360 . . . xiii–xiv, 352

Pignataro v Gilroy [1919] 1 KB 459 . . . 158

Pilkington v Wood [1953] 2 All ER 810 . . . 127

Pinnell's Case (1602) 5 CoRep 117a, 77 ER 237 . . . 32, 33

Pitt v PHH Asset Management Ltd [1993] 4 All ER 961 . . . 14

Planche v Colburn (1831) 8 Bing 14, 131 ER 305 . . . 110, 128

Plant Construction plc v Clive Adams Associates and Another (1998) 58 Con LR 1 . . . 265

Polkey v A E Dayton Services Ltd (HL) [1988] ICR 142 . . . 227, 228

Port of London Authority v Payne (CA) [1994] IRLR 9 . . . 237

Posner v Scott-Lewis [1986] 3 All ER 513 . . . 131

Post Office v Adekeye (CA) [1997] ICR 110 . . . 256

Post Office v Jones [2001] ICR 805 . . . 260

Poussard v Spiers and Pond (1876) 1 QBD 410 . . . 53

Powell v Lee (1908) 99 LT 284 . . . 16

Preist v Last [1903] 2 KB 148 . . . 146

Preston and Others v Wolverhampton Health Care NHS and Others (HL) 2001 . . . xiii, 251

Price v Easton (1833) 4 B & Ad 433, 110 ER 518 . . . 30

Provident Financial Group plc v Hayward (CA) [1989] ICR 160 . . . 214

Quadrant Visual Communications Ltd v Hutchison Telephone (UK) Ltd [1993] BCLC 442 . . . 130

R (A Minor) (Blood Transfusion), re [1993] 2 FLR 757 . . . 377

R v Associated Octel Co. Ltd (HL) [1996] 4 All ER 846 . . . 291, 297

R v Board of Trustees of the Science Museum (CA) [1993] ICR 876 . . . 297

R v British Coal Corporation ex parte Vardy (QBD) [1993] ICR 720 . . . 228

R v Chief Constable of Merseyside Police ex parte Bennion [2001] IRLR 442; ICR 136 . . . 235

R v Clarke (1927) 40 CLR 227 . . . 19

R v Cornwall County Council ex parte LH (1999) 1, [2000] 1 FLR 236 . . . 386

R v Croydon Justices ex parte W. H. Smith Ltd (2000) *The Times* 22 November . . . 293

R v F Howe and Son (Engineers) Ltd (CA) (1999) 2 All ER 249 . . . 290

R v Gateway Foodmarkets Ltd (CA) [1997] 3 All ER 78 . . . 291, 293

R v General Medical Council ex parte Virik (CA) (1995) . . . 255

R v Jackson [1891] 1 QB 671 . . . 313

R v Mara (CA) [1987] ICR 165 . . . 297

R v Nelson Group Services (Maintenance) Ltd (CA) [1998] 4 All ER 331 . . . 297

R v R [1991] 4 All ER 481 . . . 314

R v Rhone-Poulenc Rover Ltd (CA) (1995) *The Times*, 1 December . . . 298

R v Secretary of State for Education and Employment and Another ex parte McNally [2002] ICR 15 . . . 235

R v Secretary of State for Employment ex parte Equal Opportunities Commission (HL) [1994] 2 WLR 409 . . . 216

R v Secretary of State for Employment ex parte Seymouth-Smith and Another (HL) (1997) *The Times*, 14 March . . . 216

R v Secretary of State for Trade and Industry ex parte Broadcasting, Entertainment, Cinematographic and Theatre Union 2001 case C-173/99 . . . 210

R v Tan [1983] 2 All ER 12 . . . 319

R & B Customs Brokers Co. Ltd v United Dominions Trust Ltd [1988] 1 All ER 847 . . . 67

Railtrack plc v Smallwood [2001] ICR 714 . . . 292

Ramsgate Victoria Hotel Co. Ltd v Montefiore (1866) LR 1 Ex 109 . . . 21

Rapley, re [1983] 3 All ER 248 . . . 407

Ratcliffe and others v North Yorkshire County Council (HL) [1995] 3 All ER 597. . . 247

Redgrave v Hurd (1881) 20 ChD 1 . . . 93

Rees v UK [1987] 2 FLR 111 . . . 319

Reid v Camphill Engravers (EAT) [1990] ICR 435 . . . 223

Richards v Richards [1984] AC 174 . . . 330

Richardson v LRC Products (2001) 59 BMLR 185 . . . 197

Richardson v Richardson [1993] 4 All ER 673 . . . 354

Roberts v Birds Eye Walls Ltd (ECJ) [1994] ICR 338 . . . 249

Robinson v Post Office (CA) [1974] 2 All ER 737 . . . 262

Rogers v Parish (Scarborough) Ltd [1987] 2 All ER 232 . . . 144

Rose and Frank Co. v J R Crompton & Bros Ltd [1925] AC 445 . . . 25

Routledge v McKay [1954] 1 All ER 855 . . . 47

Rowland v Divall [1923] 2 KB 500 . . . 138

Royal Bank of Scotland v Etridge (No. 2) [2001] 4 All ER 449 . . . 99, 101, 103, 104–5, 202

Royscot Trust Ltd v Rogerson [1991] 3 All ER 294 . . . 97

Rubicon Computer Systems Ltd v United Paints Ltd (1999) LTL 12/11/99 . . . 139

Rushton v Turner Bros Asbestos Co. Ltd [1959] 3 All ER 517 . . . 280, 296

Ruxley Electronics and Construction Ltd v Forsyth [1995] 3 All ER 268 . . . 126

Ryan v Mutual Tontine Westminster Chambers Association [1893] 1 Ch 116 . . . 131

Saeed v Royal Wolverhampton Hospitals NHS Trust [2001] ICR 903 . . . 235

St Albans City and District Council v ICL [1996] 4 All ER 481 . . . 71

St John Shipping Corpn v Joseph Rank Ltd [1956] 3 All ER 683 . . . 78

Samuels v Davis [1943] KB 526 . . . 168–9

Sanders v F M Lloyd and Co. Ltd [1982] ICR 360 . . . 274

Sandwell DC v Jones [2002] 2 All ER 1 . . . 212

Santos v Santos [1972] 2 All ER 246 . . . 333, 335

Sarker v South Tees Acute Hospitals NHS Trust (EAT) [1997] ICR 673 . . . 218

Saunders v Anglia Building Society [1971] 1 All ER 243 . . . 90

Sayers v Harlow UDC [1958] 2 All ER 342 . . . 128

Scammell (G.) and Nephew Ltd v Ouston [1941] 1 All ER 14 . . . 13

Scanfuture UK Ltd v Secretary of State for Trade and Industry [2001] ICR 1096 . . . 230

Schawel v Reade [1913] 2 IR 64 . . . 46

Schuller v Schuller [1990] 2 FLR 193 . . . 349

Scotson v Pegg (1861) 6 H & N 295, 158 ER 121 . . . 32

Seaton v Seaton [1986] 2 FLR 398 . . . 355

Secretary of State for Employment *v* Clark (CA) [1997] ICR 64 . . . 246

Selectmove Ltd, re [1995] 2 All ER 531 . . . 16, 33, 35

Sen *v* Headley [1991] 2 All ER 637 . . . 437

Sewell *v* Electrolux Ltd (CA) (1997) *The Times*, 7 November . . . 262

Shanklin Pier Ltd *v* Detel Products Ltd [1951] 2 All ER 471 . . . 42, 48

Shaw *v* Groom [1970] 1 All ER 702 . . . 80

Sheffield and Horsham *v* UK (1998) 3 FCR 141 . . . 319

Sheriff *v* Klyne Tugs (Lowestoft) Ltd (CA) (1999) IRLR 481 . . . 256

Shogun Finance Ltd *v* Hudson [2002] IWLR 867 . . . 90, 166

Siboen & The Sibotre, The [1976] 1 Lloyd's Rep 293 . . . 98

Sidhu *v* Aerospace Composite Technology Ltd [2000] IRLR 602; [2001] ICR 167 . . . 255

Simpkins *v* Pays [1955] 3 All ER 10 . . . 24

Sindicato de Médicos de Asistencia Pública *v* Conselleria de Sanidad y Consumo de la Generalidad Valenciana case C-303/98 . . . 210

Singh *v* Singh [1971] 2 All ER 828 . . . 323, 324, 325, 397

Sita (GB) Ltd *v* Burton and others (EAT) (1996) *The Times*, 5 December . . . 223

Skilton *v* T & K Home Improvements Ltd (CA) [2000] IRLR 595; ICR 1162 . . . 209

Slater *v* Finning [1996] 3 All ER 398 . . . 147

Slaughter *v* C Brewer and Sons Ltd (EAT) [1990] ICR 730 . . . 224

Smith *v* Eric S Bush [1989] 2 All ER 514 . . . 69, 93

Smith *v* Secretary of State for Trade and Industry (EAT) (1999) *The Times*, 15 October . . . 230

Smith *v* Smith [1991] 2 All ER 306 . . . 350, 351, 354

Smith New Court Securities Ltd *v* Scrimgeour Vickers Ltd [1996] 4 All ER 398 . . . 97

Snapes *v* Adam (CA) (1998) *The Times*, 8 May 1998 . . . 462

Somerset CC *v* Barber [2002] 2 All ER 1 . . . 212

Sorbie *v* Trust House Forte Hotels Ltd (EAT) [1977] ICR 55 . . . 252

Spice Girls *v* Aprilia World Service BV [2002] IPD 2 5024 . . . 95

Spring *v* Guardian Assurance plc (HL) [1994] 3 All ER 129 . . . 213

Spring *v* National Amalgamated Stevedores and Dockers Society [1956] 1 WLR 585 . . . 52

Stapylton Fletcher Ltd, re and re Ellis Son & Vidler [1995] 1 All ER 192 . . . 157

Stark *v* The Post Office [2000] ICR 1013 . . . 278

Startup *v* Macdonald (1843) 6 Man & C 593, 134 ER 1029 . . . 111

Stephens (GW) and Son *v* Fish (EAT) [1989] ICR 324 . . . 220

Sterns Ltd *v* Vickers Ltd [1923] 1 KB 78 . . . 161

Stevenson *v* Rogers (1998) [1999] 1 All ER 613. . . xiii, 67, 142

Stevenson, Jaques & Co. *v* McLean (1880) 5 QBD 346 . . . 9, 12

Stickney *v* Keeble [1915] AC 386 . . . 129

Stilk *v* Myrick (1809) 2 Camp 317, 170 ER 1168 . . . 31, 32

Stocznia *v* Latvian Shipping Co. [1998] 1 All ER 883 . . . 27

Sudbrook Trading Estate Ltd *v* Eggleton [1982] 3 All ER 1 . . . 13

Suisse Atlantique Société d'Armement Maritime SA *v* Rotterdamsche Kolen Centrale NV [1966] 2 All ER 61 . . . 63

Sumpter *v* Hedges [1898] 1 QB 673 . . . 110

Surrey County Council *v* Bredero Homes Ltd [1992] 3 All ER 302 . . . 121

Sutcliffe and Eaton Ltd *v* R Pinney (EAT) [1977] IRLR 349 . . . 232

Suter *v* Suter [1987] 2 All ER 336 . . . 348, 350, 354

Swain *v* Denso Marston Ltd [2000] ICR 1079 . . . 285

T (Paternity: Ordering Blood Tests), re [2001] 2 FLR 1190 . . . 367

T *v* S (Financial Provision for Children) [1994] 2 FLR 883 . . . 391

Tarling *v* Baxter (1827) 6 B & C 360, 108 ER 484 . . . 154

Tasci *v* Pekalp of London Ltd [2001] ICR 633 . . . 295

Taylor *v* Caldwell (1863) 8 B & S 826, 122 ER 309 . . . 113, 116

Taylor *v* Secretary of State of Scotland [2000] 3 All ER 90 . . . 245

Thake *v* Maurice [1984] 2 All ER 513 . . . 50

Thomas *v* Chief Adjudication Officer (ECJ) [1993] ICR 673 . . . 251, 260

Thompson *v* London, Midland and Scottish Rlwy Co. [1930] 1 KB 41 . . . 61

Thompson (W L) Ltd v Robinson (Gunmakers) Ltd [1955] 1 All ER 154 . . . 125

Thornton v Shoe Lane Parking Ltd [1971] 1 All ER 686 . . . 60

Thurlow v Thurlow [1975] 2 All ER 979 . . . 331, 351, 397

Tinn v Hoffmann & Co. (1873) 29 LT 271 . . . 20

Tinsley v Milligan [1993] 3 All ER 65 . . . 81

TNT Express Worldwide (UK) Ltd v Brown [2001] ICR 182 . . . 255

Tribe v Tribe [1995] 4 All ER 236 . . . 81

Trotman v North Yorkshire County Council (1998) *The Times*, 10 October; 1999 LGR 584 . . . 266

Tsakiroglou & Co. Ltd v Noblee Thorl GmbH [1961] 2 All ER 179 . . . 115

Tulk v Moxhay (1848) 2 Ph 774, 41 ER 1143 . . . 41

Underwood Ltd v Burgh Castle Brick and Cement Syndicate [1922] 1 KB 343 . . . 154

Union Eagle Ltd v Golden Achievement Ltd [1997] 2 All ER 215 . . . 54

University of Manchester v Jones (CA) [1993] ICR 474 . . . 247

Veedfald v Athus Amtskommune (2001) Case C 203/99 ECJ . . . 200

Vokes v Bear (NIRC) [1974] ICR 1 . . . 228

Victoria Laundry (Windsor) Ltd v Newman Industries Ltd [1949] 1 All ER 997 . . . 124

Vitol SA v Norelf Ltd (1996) AC 800 . . . 119

Vroege v NCIV Instituut voor Volkshuisvesting BV and another [1995] ICR 635 . . . 250

W (A Minor) (Residence Order), re [1992] 2 FLR 332 . . . 369

Wand B (Children) (Care Plan), re [2001] 2 FLR 582 . . . 384, 389

W v UK (1987) 10 EHRR 29 . . . 367

Wachtel v Wachtel [1973] Fam 72 . . . 351

Walford v Miles [1992] 1 All ER 453 . . . 14

Walker v Northumberland CC (QBD) (1994) *The Times*, 24 November . . . 211, 309

Walls Meat Co. Ltd v Selby (CA) [1989] ICR 601 . . . 228

Wandsworth London Borough Council v National Association of Schoolmasters/Union of Women Teachers (CA) [1994] ICR 81 . . . 209

Warlow v Harrison (1859) 1 E & E 309, 120 ER 925 . . . 7

Warner Bros Pictures Inc v Nelson [1936] 3 All ER 160 . . . 132

Watford Electronics Ltd v Sanderson CFL Ltd [2001] 1 All ER (Comm) 696 . . . 72

Wearing v Pirelli Ltd (HL) [1977] ICR 90 . . . 280

Webb v EMO Air Cargo (UK) Ltd (HL) [1994] IRLR 27; (ECJ) (Case C32/93) [1995] 4 All ER 577 . . . 239, 245

Webster v Cecil (1861) 30 Beav 62, 54 ER 812 . . . 130

West Bromwich Building Society Ltd v Townsend (QBD) [1983] ICR 257 . . . 294

Westwood v Post Office (HL) [1973] 3 All ER 184 . . . 274, 279, 295

Wetherall (Bond Street WI) Ltd v Lynn (EAT) [1978] 1 WLR 200 . . . 223

Whiffen v Milham Ford Girls' School and Another [2001] IRLR 468; LGR 309 . . . 244, 247

Whirlpool (UK) Ltd and Magnet Ltd v Gloucester County Council (1993) (LEXIS) . . . 199

White v White [2000] 1 All ER 1; 3 WLR 1571 . . . 350, 352, 461

White and Carter (Councils) Ltd v McGregor [1961] 3 All ER 1178 . . . 119, 127

Whiting v Whiting [1988] 2 All ER 275 . . . 354

Wickman Machine Tool Sales Ltd v Schuler (L) AG [1973] 2 All ER 39 . . . 55

William Sindall v Cambridgeshire County Council [1994] 3 All ER 932 . . . 96

Williams v Bayley (1866) LR I HL 200 . . . 100, 202

Williams v Carwardine (1833) 4 B & Ad 621, 110 ER 590 . . . 19

Williams v Roffey Bros & Nicholls (Contractors) Ltd [1990] 1 All ER 512 . . . 32, 33, 99, 112

Wilson v Best Travel Ltd [1993] 1 All ER 353 . . . 52, 171

Wilson v First Country Trust [2001] 3 All ER 229 . . . 185

Wilson v Rickett, Cockerell & Co. Ltd [1954] 1 All ER 868 . . . 145

Wiluszynski v Tower Hamlets LBC (CA) [1989] ICR 493 . . . 208

With v O'Flanagan [1936] Ch 575 . . . 92

Wolverhampton Corpn v Emmons [1901] 1 KB 515 . . . 132

Wong Mee Wan v Kwan Kin Travel Services Ltd [1995] 4 All ER 745 . . . 52

Wood v Scarth (1855) 2 K & J 33, 69 ER 682 . . . 87

Wood *v* Smith [1991] 2 All ER 939, [1992] 3 All ER 556 . . . 404

Wormell *v* RHM Agriculture (East) Ltd [1987] 3 All ER 75 . . . 147

Wright *v* Rugby Borough Council (ET), (1984) *The Times*, 29 October . . . 246

Yates Building Co. Ltd *v* R J Pulleyn & Sons (York) Ltd (1975) 119 SJ 370 . . . 19

Young *v* National Power plc (2000) *The Times*, 23 November . . . 254

Z and others *v* UK [2001] 2 FLR 612 . . . 379

1

Contract and Consumer Law

LAW OF CONTRACT

Introduction

A contract is a legally binding agreement between two or more parties. Not all agreements are legally binding and it is this feature which distinguishes a contract. The law of contract sets out the rules which apply to such agreements; when they are made, when they are broken and the remedies available on breach. The ultimate sanction for breaking a contract is to take legal action in the courts, but even if legal proceedings are taken, 98 per cent of civil cases are settled out of court.

Many people see the law of contract as being remote from their lives and more to do with business and large organisations. While it is true that individual claims are few in the High Court, they number one third of small claims in the county courts. Whether the contract is to build a Channel Tunnel or to buy a kilo of apples, it will be governed by the same basic rules of contract law. It is a popular misconception that a contract has to be in writing, when it could equally be made orally or by conduct. In everyday life people constantly make contracts, for example, buying a newspaper, going to the hairdressers, getting on a bus, doing the weekly shopping. Written agreements would be a hindrance to both parties in all such cases.

Contract law is essentially a case law subject and familiarity with leading decisions is vital in appreciating how the principles are developed and applied. It will also be seen that there are some thin distinctions between cases, some conflicting decisions and some gaps, where questions remain to be answered, like the simple matter of getting on a bus—is this an offer or an acceptance? Sometimes even well-established doctrines of contract law are questioned, for example, in *G. Percy Trentham Ltd* v *Architual Luxfer Ltd* (1993) the Court of Appeal said there was no need for an offer and matching acceptance in all cases. The Human Rights Act 1998 will have to be followed in respect of contracts made with public authorities, in particular Article 6 of the European Convention on Human Rights provides a right to a fair trial in the event of a dispute and its wider impact on contract law will have to be monitored.

This treatment of contract law is fairly traditional, as the main aim is to set out the basic rules clearly. The nature of a contract is examined as are the rules regarding the formation of a contract, such as offer and acceptance. The next section looks at the contents of the agreement, including the thorny problems of exemption clauses and unfair contract terms. Even though there is a binding agreement, there are many factors which may undermine it such as illegality, mistake, misrepresentation, duress, undue influence and incapacity, which are looked at in turn. This is followed by how a contract is brought to an end and finally the variety of remedies available when a contract is broken.

It is important to recognise that putting the rules into neat compartments, as above, is simplistic, in the sense that it isolates matters which are frequently connected. A real life problem is unlikely to fit neatly into one of these defined categories, but will need knowledge from a number of them and an understanding of how they relate. This awareness of the relationships is vital in advising clients. Of equal importance is the awareness of the distinction between having legal rights and being able to enforce them. The problems of cost, delay and risk in going to trial have been examined in *Law for Legal Executives, Part One, Year One*. Even in the light of the reforms to the civil justice system following Lord Woolf's report, *Access to Justice, (1996)*, sound legal advice may involve suggesting alternatives such as arbitration or not to sue in any circumstances!

Nature of contract

1 Introduction

A contract is a binding agreement. It is also an agreement which has been made voluntarily by the parties. The law of contract is therefore a branch of private law as opposed to public law, the latter being rules imposed by the state. This is not to say that the state does not impose some rules in contracts—for example, terms implied by Acts of Parliament. Contract deals with those agreements which the law will enforce, the obligations such agreements create and the remedies available for breach of such agreements. Adams and Brownsword make the point that 'there were no English textbooks on contract before 1790' (Adams and Brownsword, *Understanding Contract Law*, (1994)). Prior to this books were written by and for practising lawyers and were based on precedents. It was not until Victorian times that writers began to identify underlying principles and to develop theories. There was a parallel development in the study of law as an academic discipline in universities, rather than as a practical subject. This conflict between theory and practice can be seen in contemporary decisions of the courts, which often do not fit easily into the categories created by academic textbook writers!

The law of contract sets out general rules, which can apply to a broad range of situations. However, the law has also developed particular rules for specific types of contract and examples of these include shipping, building, the sale of goods, banking and insurance.

Contract law, like any other branch of law does not exist in a vacuum. Atiyah in *An Introduction to the Law of Contract* (5th ed. (1995)), identifies the connection between the rules of contract and prevailing political philosophies. The idea of *'laissez faire'* became increasingly important in the nineteenth century, and this could be seen in the emergence of the principle of 'freedom of contract'. This meant that people were free to make whatever contracts they wanted, on whatever terms they wanted. The twentieth century witnessed the emergence of the welfare state, and this could be seen in more state regulation of the rules of contract. Atiyah argues that this latter trend was reversed in the 1980s. Further regulation is likely via European law, which will have an increasing effect on contract law, for example, Directive 93/13 on unfair terms in consumer contracts which has been implemented by the Unfair Terms in Consumer Contracts Regulations 1999 and the Distance Selling Directive 1999/7 implemented by the Consumer Protection (Distance Selling) Regulations 2000.

2 Business bias

One important feature of a contract which has been identified, is its binding nature. This is of vital importance for people and businesses, in making agreements for the sale of goods and services, that they know such agreements can be enforced by the law. Without the structure provided by the law of contract, people in a democratic society would have great difficulty in making such agreements. The alternative of state control has not been too successful, as events in Eastern Bloc countries have shown.

The law of contract fulfils two functions here, for both individuals and businesses:

(a) it provides a framework to solve disputes by setting out the detailed rules to govern the relationship between the parties; and

(b) it enables people to plan for the future knowing that agreements they have made can ultimately be enforced by the courts.

A typical breach of contract case will involve two large companies, as in the following example.

Photo Production Ltd v Securicor Transport Ltd (1980)
The defendant's security guard was on night patrol at the claimant's factory and deliberately started a fire which burned down the factory causing £615,000 worth of damage. When the claimants claimed this as damages, the defendants successfully relied on an exclusion clause in the contract.

The number of cases actually reaching court is very small compared with the number of actions started but many businesses may not even resort to the law. Sometimes the law is used as a bargaining weapon but it is often the case that business relationships are based on goodwill, and taking legal action is not likely to improve this! Nevertheless the vast majority of cases reaching the courts involve businesses and it is no surprise that this has influenced the development of the law. For example the practice of businesses using 'standard form' contracts which severely restricted the rights of consumers, led to the courts developing rules against such use and eventually to statutory measures.

3 Distinctions between contract and tort

A contract is an agreement under which a party voluntarily takes on obligations.

> EXAMPLE
>
> Michele goes into a restaurant and orders a meal. This is a contract entered into voluntarily, under which Michele impliedly agrees to pay for the meal.

A tort on the other hand is an obligation imposed by the law.

> EXAMPLE
>
> Michele accidentally drives her car on to the pavement and knocks someone down. This is the tort of negligence and her liability to pay damages arises by operation of law and not by agreement.

A party is strictly liable for carrying out their obligations in contract. Strict liability means that the defendant is liable irrespective of whether they are at fault or not.

> EXAMPLE
>
> Food sold by a shop must be of satisfactory quality. If it is not, then the shop is liable for breach of contract, irrespective of whether the shop is at fault.

By contrast in tort, as a general rule, it has to be shown that the other party is at *fault* in some way, as in the tort of negligence.

> EXAMPLE
>
> Michele drives on to the pavement and injures someone. For negligence to be proved, it would have to be shown she was not paying attention or had not checked the car properly.

In contract a party can claim compensation for economic loss, i.e. financial loss rather than injury or damage to property. In tort, however, a party cannot claim for economic loss, unless they establish liability for a negligent statement (*Hedley Byrne & Co. Ltd* v *Heller & Partners Ltd* (1963)) or a close relationship of proximity can be established (*Junior Books Ltd* v *Veitchi Co. Ltd* (1983)).

The aim of damages in contract is normally to put the parties in the position they would have been in if the contract had been fulfilled. In tort, the aim is to put the parties in the position they were in originally, before the tort was committed. However, it is now possible to claim damages in contract on the same basis as tort; this is known as *reliance* loss (see *Remedies for Breach*, 2.2).

The period within which a claim must be brought is six years in both contract and tort. If damages for personal injuries are claimed, the period is reduced to three years.

However, the time the period begins to run is the time of the breach of contract, but in tort it is when the damage occurs which may be later than the time the tort was committed.

It is important to remember that there can be concurrent liability in contract and tort, but a party who sues for both cannot recover twice in respect of the same damage.

EXAMPLE

If Daniel hails a taxi to take him to the station and it crashes because it is going too fast, then he may sue in contract or tort.

4 Observations

It is not easy to set out the exact nature of a contract. Saying it is an agreement which is freely made by each side does not tell the whole truth. Even when the doctrine of 'freedom of contract' was in its prime few contracts made by individuals were entered entirely freely. How many individuals today are free to dictate the terms of their contracts of employment to their employers? Many agreements are not contractual in nature, for example treatment provided for a patient under the National Health Service or agreements for the supply of electricity (*Norweb plc* v *Dixon* (1995)), as in both such cases there is a statutory duty to provide the service. The scope of contract law is also difficult to define. Although there is a body of 'general rules of contract' many of these rules have permeated the development of special branches of law such as employment law (see Chapter 2). Contract law is also influenced by political philosophies and has been increasingly affected by statutes, for example the Unfair Contract Terms Act 1977. Many academics now see contract as part of the wider law of obligations, which encompasses principles of contract, tort and restitution. The law of contract must continue to be receptive to changes in the way that society and business operate and it must be able to deal with new problems and challenges as they arise, if it is not to be seen as an anachronism of nineteenth-century rules, with little relevance to modern commercial life.

Formation of a contract

1 Introduction

A distinction is made between *simple* contracts and contracts made by *deed* (sometimes called specialty contracts). The rules of contract law deal with simple contracts, which are the vast majority of contracts. This section examines the 'ingredients' needed for a legally binding, simple contract. There must be an agreement between the parties; each party must provide consideration; and each party must have an intention to create legal relations. Sometimes the law requires a contract to take a particular form; it may require a deed, or writing or written evidence. Another relevant rule is the principle of *privity*, that the contract is only binding on the parties to it, but there are numerous exceptions to this.

There are three basic ingredients needed to make a legally binding contract:

(a) agreement (generally consisting of an offer and an acceptance);

(b) intention to create legal relations;

(c) consideration.

If any one of these is missing, there cannot be a binding contract.

2 Agreement

A contract is an agreement between two or more parties, giving rise to obligations which are enforced by the law. The courts take an *objective* view of whether or not the parties have made an agreement. If the parties appear to have agreed, the courts will say there is a binding contract, irrespective of what the parties believed. In some cases a party cannot be regarded as agreeing, for example a gift made by deed does not require the agreement of the recipient and contracts made on someone's standard terms hardly involve the agreement of the other party.

2.1 Offer

The traditional approach is for the courts to apply an objective test to the dealings between the parties and to look for:

(a) a firm offer; and

(b) an acceptance of that offer.

The courts may hold that a contract exists, even though the events do not fit nicely into the above categories. In *New Zealand Shipping Co. Ltd v A.M. Satterthwaite & Co. Ltd* (1975) Lord Wilberforce said: 'English law having committed itself to a rather technical and schematic doctrine of contract, in application takes a practical approach, often at the cost of forcing the facts to fit uneasily into the marked slots of offer, acceptance and consideration'. See 2.2.2 below.

An offer is a proposition put by one person to another. The person making the offer is called the *offeror*. The person to whom the offer is made is called the *offeree*. The offeror must intend that a binding contract is made if the offer is accepted.

An offer may be made orally, in writing or by conduct. It is not essential for the word 'offer' to be used. The offer may be made to an individual *or* a group of people *or* to the whole world.

2.1.1 Offers distinguished from invitations to treat

An invitation to treat is something less than an offer. It is important to make this distinction, because an invitation to treat cannot be 'accepted' and turned into a contract. However, it is not always easy to make the distinction, particularly if the preliminary negotiations are complicated or drawn out. It can be illustrated by looking at the following situations: auctions, the display of goods, advertisements, the mere statement of price, requests for information and tenders.

2.1.1.1 Auctions   The normal rule is that the bidder makes the offer, for example by nodding their head. This offer may then be accepted by the auctioneer striking the table with his gavel. Before this happens, either party may withdraw.

Is the advertising of an auction an offer to hold it?

Harris v *Nickerson* (1873)

The claimant saw an advert for an auction which was to include office furniture. The claimant travelled to the auction, but found the furniture was not put up for sale and then claimed damages for breach of contract. It was held that the advert was not an offer but an invitation to treat, otherwise everyone who attended would claim expenses.

Is the advertising of an auction 'without reserve' an offer to sell to the highest bidder? In *Warlow* v *Harrison* (1859) it was stated *obiter* that it was an offer, provided that the auction was actually held, but there was no obligation to hold the auction. The approach in *Warlow* v *Harrison* (1859) was followed in the next case.

Barry v *Heathcote Ball & Co. Ltd* (2001)

The defendant auctioneers put two new machines up for sale 'without reserve'. The cost of the machines new was £14,000 each. The claimant made bids of £200 for each machine but the defendant withdrew them from sale because the bids were too low. The defendant later sold the machines for £750 each. The claimant sued for breach of contract. The Court of Appeal held that by stating the sale was without reserve the defendant auctioneer created a second contract (or collateral contract) between the defendant auctioneer and the claimant. The defendant was offering to sell to the highest bidder and the consideration by the bidder was to make a bid, which is a detriment to the bidder because it could be accepted and it is also a benefit to the defendant because a sale 'without reserve' attracts more bidders. By withdrawing the machines the defendant was breaking the contract. The judge at the trial had awarded the claimant damages of £27,600, the difference between the contract price (£400) and the market price (£28,000). The defendant argued that the damages should be the amount the machines were actually sold for, but the Court of Appeal said that amount would not put the claimant in a position to buy two new machines and it confirmed that the trial judge was correct in awarding £27,600.

2.1.1.2 Display of goods for sale   If goods are put in a shop window or on the shelf in a supermarket, with a price on, does this amount to an offer? Note that the same rules apply even if there is no price on the goods.

Fisher v *Bell* (1960)

A shopkeeper had a box of flick knives in his window priced at 4s 0d each (20 pence). Under the Restriction of Offensive Weapons Act 1959 it was an offence to 'offer for sale' such a weapon. Had the shopkeeper made an offer for sale? The court decided that the display was not an 'offer' but an invitation to treat, otherwise customers could accept such offers and the shop might not have enough stock.

The problem of whether goods on supermarket shelves amount to an offer was dealt with in the following case.

Pharmaceutical Society of Great Britain v *Boots Cash Chemists Ltd* (1953)

Under the Pharmacy and Poisons Act 1933 certain listed drugs had to be sold under the supervision of a pharmacist. Boots opened a supermarket with a pharmacist at the cash desk to supervise sales. The question arose at what point did the sale take place? Were goods on the shelf an offer or an invitation to treat? It was held by the Court of Appeal that the customer made the offer at the cash desk, so the sale was supervised. Goods on the shelf represented merely an invitation to treat.

2.1.1.3 Advertisements   Normally an advertisement will not be regarded as an offer. This was seen in the following criminal case.

Partridge v *Crittenden* (1968)

Partridge put an advert in the paper stating: 'Bramblefinch cocks and hens 25s (£1.25) each'. A Mr Thompson ordered one and this was sent by post. Partridge was then charged with unlawfully 'offering for sale' a live bird, contrary to the Protection of Birds Act 1954. It was held by the Divisional Court that the advert was an invitation to treat. It was not specific enough to be an offer and it was unlikely that Partridge intended every 'acceptance' to be binding, so no offence was committed under the Act.

However, in some cases an advertisement may be an offer and an example is the following famous case.

Carlill v *Carbolic Smoke Ball Co.* (1893)

The defendants made 'smokeballs'. They advertised these in the press offering to pay £100 to anyone who caught influenza: 'after having used the ball three times daily for two weeks according to the printed directions supplied with each ball. £1,000 is deposited with Alliance Bank, Regent Street, showing our sincerity in the matter'. The claimant bought a smokeball and used it according to the instructions, but still caught influenza. The defendants argued that:

(a) the advert was not intended to be binding;

(b) no offer was made to any particular person;

(c) if there was an offer it was too vague;

(d) if there was an offer, there was no acceptance.

It was held by the Court of Appeal that:

(a) the deposit of money showed an intention to be bound, therefore the advert was an offer;

(b) it was possible to make an offer to the world at large, which is accepted by anyone who buys a smokeball;

(c) the offer of protection would cover the period of use;

(d) the buying and using of the smokeball amounted to acceptance. Therefore the claimant was entitled to £100.

2.1.1.4 Mere statement of price A distinction is drawn between a definite offer which is intended to be binding and a simple statement of a price, which is not meant to be binding.

Harvey v *Facey* (1893)

The claimants sent a telegram to the defendants: 'Will you sell Bumper Hall Pen? Telegraph lowest cash price'. The defendants replied by telegraph: 'Lowest price £900'. The claimants then telegraphed: 'We agree to buy . . . for £900 asked by you'. The Privy Council held that the defendants' telegram was not an offer but simply an indication of the minimum price the defendants would want, if they decided to sell. The claimants' second telegram could not be an acceptance.

More recently the matter has been considered by the House of Lords in the following case.

Gibson v *Manchester City Council* (1979)

The claimant told the council that he wished to buy his council house. He received a letter from the council stating that it ' . . . may be prepared to sell the house to you at the purchase price of £2,725 less 20 per cent %£2,180'. It also stated: 'This letter should not be regarded as a firm offer of a mortgage' and asked him to make a formal application to buy the house. The claimant did this. Before the sale could be completed, local elections resulted in a change of council and the new council decided not to sell council houses. The claimant now claimed that he had a binding contract. It was held at first instance, and in the Court of Appeal, that there was a binding contract. The House of Lords, reversing the lower courts, held that the words 'may be prepared to sell' did not mean 'I will sell'; and in conjunction with the request to make a formal application to buy, the council's letter could not be regarded as an offer. The claimant's application could not then be treated as an acceptance.

2.1.1.5 Request for information A distinction is also drawn between a definite offer and a request for information which cannot be turned into a contract. See *Stevenson, Jaques & Co.* v *McLean* (1880) at 2.2.2.2 below.

2.1.1.6 Tenders A statement that goods are to be sold by tender is not normally regarded as an offer to sell them. A statement inviting tenders for the supply of goods is not normally an offer, unless it states that the lowest tender will be accepted. In both of these situations the 'offer' is from the person who submits the tender, and no contract is made unless the person inviting tenders accepts an offer.

EXAMPLE

A council invites tenders for the supply of packed lunches to schools for the 2004 education year. Boris submits a tender to supply them for £250,000. This is an offer and will only become a contract if the council accepts it.

A problem arose over 'referential' bids, i.e., when one party makes a bid by reference to someone else's bid.

Harvela Investments Ltd v *Royal Trust Co. of Canada (CI) Ltd* (1985)

The first defendants were selling land and invited sealed bids from the claimants and the second defendants, stating: 'We confirm that if the offer made by you is the highest offer received by us we bind ourselves to accept that offer'. The claimants made a bid of $2,175,000. The second defendants made a bid '$2,100,000 or $101,000 in excess of any other offer which you may receive expressed as a fixed monetary amount whichever is higher'. The first defendants accepted the second defendants' offer. The House of Lords decided that the first defendants' statement was an offer to accept the highest bid, but the aim of such tenders was to make those bidding make fixed bids. The referential bid made by the second defendants was therefore invalid. If both parties bidding had made referential bids, it would not have been possible to decide on the highest bid. Therefore the claimants' bid had to be accepted.

A related problem emerged in the following case.

Blackpool and Fylde Aero Club Ltd v *Blackpool Borough Council* (1990)

The council airport was run by the claimants under licence. When this came up for renewal, the council invited tenders to operate the airport to be submitted by noon on a fixed date. The claimants' tender was put in the council's letter box well before noon but the box was not emptied and their tender was not considered. The claimants claimed the council was in breach of contract in not considering all tenders received before noon. The Court of Appeal held that although the council was not under an obligation to accept any tender or the highest tender, that did not mean it was under no obligation. There was a contract about the tender process and it was an implied term of that contract that all bids received before noon would be considered. The defendants therefore had to consider the claimants' tender.

2.2 Acceptance

2.2.1 Introduction

When an offer has been 'accepted' a binding contract is made. Two things must be established, firstly that the offeree has accepted as a fact and secondly that this has been communicated to the offeror.

2.2.2 The fact of acceptance

In simple agreements like buying goods from a corner shop, it is usually quite clear when the acceptance has occurred. If the negotiations are complicated or protracted, however, it may be difficult or even impossible to tell the exact point at which an offer has been accepted. If it is impossible, the question then arises whether a binding contract can be made in the absence of a matching offer and acceptance.

Brogden v *Metropolitan Railway Company* (1877)

B supplied coal to MRCfor years, without an agreement. MRCsent a draft agreement to B and B filled in the name of an arbitrator in a blank space, signed it and sent it back to MRC. A clerk put the agreement in his desk. B continued to supply coal but two years later a dispute arose and B said that there was no binding agreement. It was held that B's returning of the document was not an acceptance, as inserting a new term was a counter offer. But B's returning of the document could be an offer which could be regarded as accepted, either when MRC ordered coal or when B actually supplied it. Therefore a binding contract was made by conduct.

Lord Denning has suggested on a number of occasions that there can be a binding agreement even without a matching offer and acceptance:

. . . but, as I understand the law, there is no need to look for a strict offer and acceptance. You should look at the correspondence as a whole and at the conduct of the parties and see therefrom whether the parties have come to an agreement on everything that was material. (*Gibson* v *Manchester City Council* (1979) in the Court of Appeal.)

On further appeal, the House of Lords rejected Lord Denning's approach and followed the traditional analysis, while accepting that in certain cases it was possible to have a binding contract without an offer and acceptance. A further attempt to move away from the traditional approach has been made recently.

G. Percy Trentham Ltd v *Archital Luxfer Ltd* (1993)

T were the main contractors to build industrial units and they subcontracted the windows to L. The work was done and paid for. T then claimed damages from L because of defects in the windows. L argued that even though there had been letters, phone calls and meetings between the two parties, there was no matching offer and acceptance and so no contract. In the Court of Appeal Steyn LJ made a number of points:

(a) The courts take an objective approach to deciding if a contract has been made.

(b) In the vast majority of cases a matching offer and acceptance will be the mechanism to create a contract, but this is not necessary for a contract based on performance.

(c) The fact that the contract has been carried out (executed) by both parties makes it unrealistic to argue that there was no intention to create legal relations or that it is void for uncertainty.

(d) If a contract is made by performance, it is possible to say that the contract covers pre-contract performance.

Applying these points to the case, there was a binding contract by performance, even though it was impossible to say precisely when, in terms of offer and acceptance. Both parties had provided executed consideration.

The effect of this decision does not mean that offer and acceptance are no longer needed but it shows that the courts are willing to step outside the confines of the doctrine of offer and acceptance if the above requirements are met. A number of cases cannot be explained on the basis of the traditional approach but can be on this approach. One problem, however, is it does not decide the exact point at which a contract is made, which might be important in some circumstances.

There are a number of rules the courts have developed dealing with acceptance.

2.2.2.1 Acceptance must fit the offer   To make a binding contract the acceptance must exactly match the offer. This is called the *mirror image rule.* If the offeree qualifies the offer in some way or changes the terms of the offer, this will *not* be a valid acceptance.

2.2.2.2 Counter offers   If the offeree changes the terms of the offer this is known as a counter offer and the effect of this is to *cancel* the original offer. The following case provides the classic example of this.

Hyde v Wrench (1840)

On 6 June W wrote offering to sell his estate to H for £1,000. On 8 June H replied by letter offering £950. W wrote rejecting H's offer on 27 June. Finally on 29 June H offered £1,000. W refused to sell and H sued for breach of contract. It was held that H's letter of 8 June was a counter offer, which cancelled W's offer of 6 June. H could not accept it later.

The courts have distinguished between such counter offers and what is merely a request for information.

Stevenson, Jaques & Co. v McLean (1880)

On Saturday the defendant offered to sell iron to the claimant at '40 shillings (£2) a ton—open until Monday'. On Monday the claimant sent a telegram: 'Please wire whether you would accept 40 shillings for delivery over two months or if not longest limit you would give' and this arrived at 10 a.m. As the claimant had had no reply to this, at 1.34 p.m. he sent another telegram: 'We accept 40 shillings a ton cash'. At 1.25 p.m. the defendant had sent a telgram to the claimant: 'Sold iron to third party' and this arrived at 1.46 p.m. The claimant sued the defendant for breach of contract and the defendant argued that the claimant's first telegram was a counter offer, so the claimant's second telegram could not be an acceptance. It was held that the claimant's first telegram was not a counter offer but only an enquiry, so a binding contract was made by the claimant's second telegram.

2.2.2.3 Conditional acceptance   If the offeree puts a *condition* in the acceptance, then it will not be binding.

EXAMPLE

Basil offers to sell his Ford Focus to Alice for £5,000. Alice agrees to buy it, if it passes an inspection by the Automobile Association. This is not a binding agreement.

The offeree should use clear and simple language to ensure that a contract is binding.

2.2.2.4 Tenders A person may invite others to 'tender' for the supply of goods and services. A typical example of this is a local authority asking for tenders to provide transport to take pupils to school. This invitation is not an offer. If the other person then submits a tender, this may be regarded as an offer. Two possible situations arise.

EXAMPLES

(1) The council asks for one bus to be available for 200 days a year. If Bob submits a tender, this is an offer, which the council may accept. If it does, a binding contract is made.
(2) The council asks for one bus to be available for up to 200 days. If Bob submits a tender which the council accepts, then Bob's tender is regarded as a 'standing offer' and each request by the council for a bus can be treated as an acceptance of that standing offer.

Great Northern Railway Co. v Witham (1873)
GNR advertised for tenders for the supply of stores and W replied: 'I undertake to supply the company for 12 months with such quantities as the company may order from time to time'. GNR accepted this tender and later placed orders which W supplied. Later W refused to supply an order. It was held that W's tender was a standing offer, which GNR could accept by placing an order. The refusal to supply by W was a breach of contract, but it could also be regarded as revoking W's standing offer for the future, so W did not have to meet any further orders.

2.2.2.5 Certainty Even if the fact of acceptance has been established, the agreement may not be binding because it is too vague or some important term has not been agreed. The courts are in favour of bringing certainty to agreements but they will not make up a contract for the parties.

G. Scammell and Nephew Ltd v Ouston (1941)
O offered to 'buy' a van from S 'on hire purchase terms' over two years. S accepted this offer but terms were never agreed and S did not provide a van. O sued for non-delivery. It was held by the House of Lords that there were so many different hire purchase terms it could not be certain which ones the parties meant. It was not up to the court to 'invent' a contract for the parties.

It is possible to make a binding contract even though some main points have been left to be decided in the future as long as a way has been provided to determine these points.

Sudbrooke Trading Estate Ltd v Eggleton (1982)
The lessee of premises was granted an option to buy the freehold. The price was to be fixed by two valuers, one of whom was to be appointed by the lessee and one by the lessor or, if the valuers could not agree, by an umpire appointed by the valuers. The lessor refused to appoint a valuer and claimed the option was void for uncertainty.

The House of Lords held that as the lessee had exercised his option, each party was under a duty to appoint a valuer and this was ordered by the court.

The courts try to maintain contracts if at all possible.

Nicolene Ltd v Simmonds (1953)

The claimant and defendant agreed on the quantity and price of steel to be sold to the defendant, who added, 'the usual conditions of acceptance apply'. The defendant did not deliver and, when sued, argued that there was no agreement on the conditions of acceptance. It was held by the Court of Appeal that there were no 'usual conditions' so these words were meaningless and could be severed from the contract, which was binding.

The next case is a recent example of an uncertain agreement.

Walford v Miles (1992)

M was negotiating the sale of a business to W. M agreed not to negotiate with anyone else if W provided a letter from his bank saying the purchase money was available. W provided this letter but M sold to a third party. W claimed that there was a binding 'lockout' agreement. The House of Lords held that the agreement not to negotiate with anyone else was too uncertain, as it was for an unspecified time. It was accepted that a lockout for a specified period could be enforceable.

This precedent was later applied by the Court of Appeal.

Pitt v PHH Asset Management Ltd (1993)

The defendant was selling property for which two people had made offers. The defendant agreed to accept the claimant's offer, and not to consider any other offers, on the basis that the claimant would exchange within two weeks of receiving a contract. The defendant sold to the other interested party for a higher amount. The Court of Appeal held that this was a binding lockout agreement. The defendant's consideration was a promise not to consider other offers and the claimant's consideration was a promise to exchange within two weeks of receiving a contract. Note that this was not a contract for the sale of an interest in land.

Sometimes agreements are not binding because of the words used by the parties.

EXAMPLE

Building contractors who employ sub-contractors often appoint the sub-contractor by using a 'letter of intent'. This means that they will only engage the sub-contractor if the main contractor gets the contract. Such a letter is not therefore binding.

2.2.3 Communication of acceptance

The fact someone has decided to accept an offer does not amount to an 'acceptance' in law.

2.2.3.1 The general rule   The general rule is that the offeror *must be told of the acceptance.* The acceptance is communicated to the offeror when it is brought to his notice. Even if the parties deal face to face, the onus is on the offeree to make sure that the offeror knows of the acceptance.

'Suppose, for instance, that I shout an offer to a man across a river . . . but I do not hear his reply because it is drowned by an aircraft flying overhead. There is no contract at that moment. If he wishes to make a contract, he must wait till the aircraft is gone and then shout back his acceptance so that I can hear what he says.' (Denning LJ in *Entores Ltd* v *Miles Far East Corporation* (1955), see below.)

The same rule applies to all instantaneous methods of communication.

Entores Ltd v *Miles Far East Corporation* (1955)

The claimants were a London company and the defendants were based in Amsterdam. The claimants made an offer by telex to buy goods from the defendants. This offer was accepted by a telex received in London. The claimants then claimed breach of contract by the defendants and the question arose as to where the contract was made. It was held by the Court of Appeal that where communication was instantaneous, as here, there was no binding agreement until the acceptance was received by the offeror. The acceptance was received in London and so the contract was made in London.

However, the question remains, in the absence of case law, how this general rule should be applied to modern methods of communication like faxes and electronic mail (e-mail). Is the acceptance valid:

(a) when received on the machine?

(b) when received in office hours?

(c) when it is read?

(d) when it is read by the person it was sent to?

If the general rule is strictly applied, the acceptance will not be valid until read by the person it is sent to. There are also difficulties applying the rules if an acceptance is sent out of office hours or is left on a telephone answering machine. This is clearly not 'instantaneous' and cannot be regarded as valid on receipt. An *obiter* statement in *Brinkibon* v *Stahag Stahl* (1983) in the House of Lords has said that as regards communications outside business hours, they can be decided only by looking at the intention of the parties and business practice, but as a general rule they cannot be valid until the start of business. The development of electronic commerce has raised questions about the application of the rules to contracts made via the Internet. In applying the general rules goods advertised on a website could be seen as an invitation to treat. Using the rule that acceptance is valid when received, if an offer has been made on a website it could be argued that someone who visits that site and clicks with their 'mouse' is accepting the offer.

2.2.3.2 Communication must be by an authorised person Communication of acceptance must be made by the offeree *or* someone authorised by the offeree. If someone 'accepts' on behalf of the offeree, without having authority to do so, this will not be a valid acceptance.

Powell v Lee (1908)

The claimant applied for a job as a headmaster and the school managers decided to appoint him. One of the managers, acting without authority, told the claimant he had been appointed. Later the managers decided to appoint someone else. The claimant sued for breach of contract. It was held that the claimant's offer had not been officially accepted and so there was no contract.

2.2.3.3 Silence cannot be acceptance   If the offeree keeps silent in response to an offer, this is not acceptance. This rule applies even if the offeror states that if he hears nothing he will treat silence as acceptance.

Felthouse v Bindley (1862)

The claimant had discussed buying a horse from his nephew and eventually wrote to him saying: 'If I hear no more about him, I consider the horse mine at £30 15s (i.e. £30.75)'. The nephew did not reply but wanted to sell the horse to his uncle and some time later when he was having a sale, he told the auctioneer(the defendant) not to sell the horse. By mistake the horse was sold. The uncle sued the auctioneer in the tort of conversion. He could only succeed in this if he could show that the horse was his. It was held that even though the nephew had intended to accept his uncle's offer, he had not communicated his acceptance and therefore there was no contract. The uncle's claim failed.

The above rule has been applied by statute, to goods and services which have not been requested. The Unsolicited Goods and Services Act 1971 (and the amending Act of 1975) provided that a consumer who received unsolicited goods did not accept them by keeping quiet, but became owner if the sender did not collect them within six months. These rules have now been replaced by the Consumer Protection (Distance Selling) Regulations 2000 as regards consumer contracts but not business contracts. Under reg. 24 (inertia selling), unsolicited goods now become an unconditional gift immediately. Under reg. 24(1) this applies if:

(a) the unsolicited goods are sent to a person with a view to his acquiring them;

(b) the recipient has no reasonable cause to believe they were sent with a view to being acquired for business; and

(c) the recipient has not agreed to acquire the goods or return them.

Under reg. 24(2) the recipient may treat the goods as an 'unconditional gift'. Regulation 24(4) provides that if unsolicited goods are sent to someone other than for the purpose of business, it is a criminal offence to demand payment.

In *Felthouse* v *Bindley* (1862) above, it was the offeror (the uncle) who was trying to impose on the offeree that silence to an offer was an acceptance. In *Re Selectmove, Re* (1995), Peter Gibson LJ considered the position if it was the offeree (the nephew in *Felthouse* v *Bindley*) who wished to say that silence would be acceptance, and in an *obiter* statement he said 'I can see no reason in principle why that should not be an exceptional circumstance such that the offer can be accepted by silence'.

2.2.3.4 Exceptions to the rule that acceptance must be communicated

(A) UNILATERAL CONTRACTS

In a unilateral contract one party (the *promisor*) promises to do something for another (the *promisee*), if that other does a particular task. But only one person is bound, the promisor, if the promisee carries out the task. The promisee does not have to do the task. Unilateral contracts are sometimes called 'if' contracts, as the offer can be put in the form, 'If you use our smokeball and catch a cold, we will pay you £100'.

> EXAMPLE
>
> In the *Carbolic Smoke Ball* case the company promised to give £100 to anyone who used a smokeball and still caught influenza. No one was obliged to use a smokeball.

This is in contrast to the more usual *bilateral* contract, under which both parties are bound to carry out their part of the contract.

> EXAMPLE
>
> Alice promises to sell her bike to Bob and Bob promises to pay her £50 for it.

In unilateral contracts the normal rule for communication of acceptance to the offeror does not apply. Carrying out the stipulated task is enough to constitute acceptance of the offer.

> EXAMPLE
>
> In the *Carbolic Smoke Ball* case the fact of Miss Carlill buying and using the smokeball was an acceptance of the company's offer; there was no need to tell them she was accepting their offer.

A recent example of a unilateral contract occurred in the next case.

Bowerman v *ABTA* (1995)

The claimants, a teacher and a pupil, booked a school skiing holiday with a tour operator who was a member of ABTA. In the tour operator's office, an ABTA notice stated 'ABTA . . . ensures that if you are abroad you will be able to return to the United Kingdom'. The operator became insolvent, and although ABTA provided another holiday they refused to refund the claimants' holiday insurance premiums. It was held that the notice was a unilateral offer which was accepted by booking with an ABTA member. The claimants were entitled to their premiums.

(B) DISPENSING WITH COMMUNICATION OF ACCEPTANCE

The offeror may waive the need for the offeree to communicate acceptance. This waiver may be express or implied.

> EXAMPLE
>
> Alice orders goods by telephone from Bob. Bob can accept this offer by sending the goods; there is no need for Bob to communicate his acceptance.

(c) THE POSTAL RULE

If the post is a reasonable means of acceptance and the letter is properly addressed and stamped and it is posted in the proper manner, then the *postal rule* applies. This states that the letter of acceptance is effective from the moment it is posted. This rule applies even if the letter is delayed or lost. It was first set out in the following case.

Adams v *Lindsell* (1818)

On 2 September the defendants, who were wool dealers, wrote to the claimants, who were manufacturers, offering to sell wool and asking for a reply 'in the course of post'. The defendants' letter was wrongly addressed and did not arrive until 5 September. The claimants sent a letter of acceptance on 5 September, which the defendants received on 9 September. However, the defendants had sold the wool to a third party on 8 September. It was held that a binding contract was made when the claimants posted their letter of acceptance on 5 September, so the defendants were in breach of contract.

The effect of this rule is that it puts the risk of delay or loss on the offeror. The post will be regarded as a reasonable means of acceptance if the offer has been made by post or if the post is at least as quick as the way the offer was made. If the offeree wrongly addresses or stamps the letter the rule does not apply. Further, the letter must be posted in the correct manner by putting it in a letter box. Handing a letter to a postman is not sufficient. If the offeror states that he must actually be told of acceptance or that a particular method of acceptance must be used, apart from the post, the rule will be excluded.

How the postal rule might be applied to modern methods of communication remains to be seen. A telemessage, a message dictated over the telephone and then delivered, could be treated as acceptance when dictated but there is no direct authority. Similarly with private courier services, the acceptance could be treated as valid on delivery of the message to the courier. Much will depend on the intention of the parties.

2.2.3.5 Method of acceptance   The offeror may provide that acceptance *must* only be communicated in a particular way. If the offeree uses a different method, the acceptance will not be valid and no contract will be made.

Holwell Securities Ltd v *Hughes* (1974)

The defendant gave the claimants an option to buy property, which could be exercised 'by notice in writing to the defendant' up to 19 April 1972. On 14 April the claimants posted a letter exercising this option but the letter was lost in the post and the claimants claimed specific performance. It was held by the Court of Appeal that the provision for notice to the defendant meant *actual notice* and the postal rule did not apply. No contract was made.

The offeror may set out a particular method of acceptance without making it clear that this is the only way. In such circumstances the offeree may use an equally efficacious method of acceptance.

Yates Building Co. Ltd v *R.J. Pulleyn & Sons (York) Ltd* (1975)

The defendants granted the claimants an option to buy land, exercisable by notice in writing to be sent by 'registered or recorded delivery post'. The claimants sent a letter accepting this offer by ordinary post, which was received by the defendants who refused to accept it as valid. It was held by the Court of Appeal that this method of acceptance was valid and was no disadvantage to the offeror, as the method stipulated was only to ensure delivery and that had happened.

Following the prescribed method of acceptance will not be an acceptance if the offeree does not know about the offer.

IRC v *Fry* (2001)

The defendant owed income tax. He sent a cheque for a smaller amount plus a letter stating that the Inland Revenue could accept his offer by presenting the cheque. The Inland Revenue told the defendant that his offer was not accepted but that his cheque would be presented for payment in accordance with normal procedures. The Inland Revenue later claimed the balance. It was held that an offer would normally be accepted by following the prescribed manner of acceptance. But presenting the cheque only led to a presumption of acceptance of the letter. This presumption was rebutted by the evidence that presenting the cheque was simply following normal office procedures and the defendant had to pay the balance.

2.2.3.6 Does the offeree have to know about the offer?   As a general principle, a person can only accept an offer if they know about it. A problem arises with unilateral contracts if someone accepts the offer, without knowing about it. This can be viewed as two separate and unrelated acts.

EXAMPLE

Alice offers £100 reward for the return of Pavlov her lost dog. If Bob returns the dog without knowing about the reward, can Bob claim it?

R v *Clarke* (1927) (Australia)

Following the murder of two policemen, a reward of £1,000 was offered for information and a free pardon was offered to any accomplices. Clarke had seen the offer but gave information to save himself as he was a suspect. Later he claimed the reward. It was held that the reward money was not present in his mind when he gave the information. The court said that there cannot be consent without knowledge and ignorance of the offer is the same, whether it is due to not hearing or to forgetting. Therefore Clarke was not entitled to the money.

Motive was considered in an earlier case.

Williams v *Carwardine* (1833)

The defendant offered a £20 reward for information leading to the conviction of a murderer. The claimant knew of this offer and gave information that it was her husband after he had beaten her. It was held that the claimant was entitled to the reward, she knew about it and her motive (spite) in giving the information was irrelevant.

A similar problem arises in relation to two identical offers which cross in the post. Does this create a binding contract?

EXAMPLE

Alice sends a letter offering to sell her dog to Bob for £100 and Bob sends a letter offering to buy Alice's dog for £100. The letters cross in the post.

In such circumstances there is no *offer* and a related *acceptance* of that offer, so there is no binding contract (*Tinn* v *Hoffmann & Co.* (1873)).

2.2.4 Termination of the offer

An offer may end in a number of ways. It may be accepted, rejected, revoked, or end through a counter offer, lapse of time, failure of a condition or the death of one of the parties. The following section will examine these situations.

2.2.4.1 *Acceptance*   Once an offer has been accepted, a binding contract is made and the offer ends. The detailed rules for acceptance have been set out above.

2.2.4.2 *Rejection*   If the offeree rejects the offer that is the end of it. The offeror must be told. It is of course open to the offeror to make a fresh offer, but the original offer is now dead.

2.2.4.3 *Revocation*   The general rule is that the offeror may revoke or withdraw his offer any time up to acceptance. Even if the offeror promises to keep the offer open, he may revoke it. However, if the offeree provides *consideration* for such a promise, then this can be treated as a contract in itself and the offeror must then keep the offer open for the agreed time.

If the offeror wants to revoke the offer, he must tell the offeree. This rule applies even if the post is used, so that a posted revocation will only take effect when it is received by the offeree.

Byrne & Co. v Leon Van Tienhoven & Co. (1880)

On 1 October the defendants posted a letter to the claimants offering to sell them tinplate. On 8 October the defendants posted a letter revoking their earlier offer because of a sudden rise in the price of tinplate. On 11 October the claimants received the offer and accepted immediately by telegram. On 15 October the claimants posted a letter confirming their acceptance. On 20 October the defendants' letter of revocation arrived. It was held that the revocation was not effective until it was received by the offeree on 20 October. This was too late as a contract was made on 11 October when the claimants sent a telegram.

The revocation need not be communicated by the offeror personally, it is sufficient if it is done through a reliable third party.

Dickinson v Dodds (1876)

Dodds made a written offer to sell a house to Dickinson, the offer to remain open until Friday at 9 a.m. On Thursday Dodds sold the house to someone else and

Dickinson was told of the sale by Berry, a reliable third party. Dickinson then delivered an 'acceptance' to Dodds before 9 a.m. on Friday. It was held by the Court of Appeal that the offer had been effectively withdrawn when Dickinson heard of the sale, it was not necessary for the revocation to be made by Dodds. It was clear that Dodds no longer wished to sell to Dickinson who could not therefore accept the offer.

In *unilateral* contracts a problem arises with revocation, if the offeror attempts to revoke the offer after the offeree has started to carry out the acceptance. Applying the general rule, the offeror can revoke at any time until the acceptance is completed.

Errington v Errington (1952)
A father bought a house on mortgage for his son and daughter in law and promised them that if they paid off the mortgage, they could have the house. They began to do this but before they had finished paying the father died. His executors now claimed the house. It was held by the Court of Appeal that the father's offer could not be revoked while the couple were paying the mortgage.

On the basis of this case once the offeree has started to perform the contract, the offeror cannot withdraw without giving them a reasonable chance to complete the acceptance.

2.2.4.4 Counter offer   If the offeree changes the terms of the offer, this is a counter offer and its effect is to cancel the original offer. It is open to the offeror to make a new offer and this is what often happens in practice (see 2.2.2.2 above).

2.2.4.5 Lapse of time   If an offer is stated to be open until a particular time, any acceptance after that is invalid. If there is no time limit, the offer is only open for a 'reasonable' time.

Ramsgate Victoria Hotel Co. Ltd v Montefiore (1866)
The defendant offered to buy shares in the claimant company on 8 June. The company sent a letter of allotment accepting this offer on 23 November, but the defendant refused to pay for the shares. It was held that the long period of time that had elapsed meant that the defendant's offer had ended and it could not therefore be accepted.

What amounts to a *reasonable time* will depend on the facts of each case. Obviously offers to sell fresh fruit or to buy shares in companies must be accepted quickly.

2.2.4.6 Failure of a condition   An offer may be made subject to a *condition* and if this condition is not satisfied, the offer will end. Such a condition may be express or implied.

Financings Ltd v Stimson (1962)
The defendant saw a car at a garage and agreed to take it on hire purchase through the claimants. The defendant signed the agreement and paid a deposit. Two days later he returned the car saying that he was not satisfied with it. The car was then damaged by another party. The day after this the claimants signed the hire-purchase agreement, thus accepting the defendant's offer. The Court of Appeal decided that the defendant's offer was subject to an *implied condition* that the car was in the same state when the

offer was accepted as when the offer was made. But as the offer was accepted by the claimants after the car had been damaged, the defendant's offer had lapsed and there was no contract.

2.2.4.7 Death

(A) DEATH OF OFFEROR

The offeree cannot accept an offer after notice of the offeror's death. However, if the offeree does not know of the offeror's death, and there is no personal element involved, then he may accept the offer.

Bradbury v Morgan (1862)

L guaranteed his brother's account with the claimants. L died but the claimants did not know this and continued to supply goods. The defendants (L's executors) refused to pay for goods supplied after L's death. It was held that L's offer continued until the claimants knew about his death and they were therefore entitled to be paid.

If there was a personal element involved, for example an offer to give piano lessons, then this offer would lapse on the death of the offeror, irrespective of the offeree's knowledge of the death.

(B) DEATH OF OFFEREE

If the offeree dies, then the offer cannot be accepted by someone else on the offeree's behalf.

3 Intention to create legal relations

3.1 Introduction

The parties must intend the agreement to be legally binding. But how can the court find out what is in the parties' minds? As was said in one case 'the devil himself knows not the intent of man'. The nearest the courts can get to discovering this intention is to apply an *objective* test and judge the situation by what was said and done. The law divides agreements into two groups, *social (or domestic)* agreements and *business* agreements. This section will also briefly look at collective agreements made between trade unions and employers.

3.2 Social agreements

The first question to deal with is, what is a social agreement? This probably covers agreements between family members, couples living together, friends and workmates. The law does not want to become involved in such cases for policy reasons, that if such contracts were binding, the courts would be full of families suing one another! Consequently the law presumes that social agreements are not intended to be legally binding. A *presumption* is really only a rule of evidence rather than an unchangeable rule of law. This means a presumption may be changed by strong evidence to show the opposite intention. It is up to the party wishing to change (or rebut) the presumption to give evidence of this. The cases show it is a difficult task to rebut such a presumption.

Greene promises to take his friend Blakemore to the pub at lunch time and buy him a pint of lager if Blakemore buys the sandwiches. When they get to the pub, although Blakemore buys the sandwiches, Greene refuses to buy the drinks. This is only a social agreement and Blakemore cannot enforce it.

Balfour v *Balfour* (1919)

The Balfours lived in Ceylon but came to England on holiday. Mrs Balfour was advised to stay in England for health reasons. Before he returned to Ceylon, Mr Balfour promised to give her £30 per month maintenance. He made a number of payments but then the marriage broke up and he stopped paying. Mrs Balfour sued for breach of contract. It was held by the Court of Appeal that agreements between husbands and wives are not contracts because the parties do not intend them to be binding. The agreement was made when they were living together and was intended to be a temporary domestic arrangement.

The following case is in contrast to this.

Merritt v *Merritt* (1970)

The husband left his wife. Later they met in the husband's car to make arrangements for the future. The husband agreed to pay £40 per month maintenance, out of which the wife was to pay the mortgage. The husband also agreed that when the mortgage was paid off he would transfer the house from joint names to the wife's name. He wrote this down on a piece of paper and signed it. When the mortgage was paid off he refused to transfer the house. The Court of Appeal held that, *when the agreement was made*, the husband and wife were no longer living together, therefore they must have intended the agreement to be binding, as they would base their future actions on it. This was the most important point. The writing helped to show this intention. The husband had to transfer the house to the wife.

In what other circumstances will the presumption be rebutted? If a social agreement will have serious consequences for the parties, this may rebut the presumption.

Parker v *Clark* (1960)

The Parkers were in their 40s and the Clarks were in their 70s. Mrs Parker was a niece of Mrs Clark. The Parkers visited the Clarks (who lived in a big, old house) and an agreement was made that the Parkers would sell their own house and come to live with the Clarks. Both families would share the bills and the Clarks would then leave the house to the Parkers. Later Mrs Clark wrote to the Parkers setting out the details of expenses and confirming the arrangements. The Parkers then sold their house and moved in with the Clarks. Mr Clark changed his will leaving the house to the Parkers. Later the two couples fell out and the Parkers were asked to leave. The Parkers now claimed damages for breach of contract. It was held that the exchange of letters showed the two couples were serious, but when the Parkers took the drastic step of selling their own home it showed that they intended the agreement to be binding. Also when Mr Clark changed his will it showed that he intended the agreement to be binding. Therefore the Parkers were entitled to damages.

What if the agreement is not precise?

Jones v Padavatton (1969)

Mrs Jones lived in Trinidad and her daughter had a good job in Washington. Mrs Jones offered to give her daughter an allowance of £42 per month if she would come to England and study to become a barrister. The daughter accepted this offer in 1962. In 1964 because of accommodation problems the mother bought a house in London in which the daughter lived. Part of the house was let out and the rent covered the daughter's allowance. In 1967 they fell out and the mother claimed the house. By this time the daughter had not even passed half of the exams. It was held that there were two agreements: (a) the agreement to study was a family arrangement and not intended to be binding. Even if it was intended to be binding, because the terms were definite, it was subject to an implied term that it was for a reasonable time. Five years was such a time; (b) the agreement for the house was too vague. Could the daughter have the house indefinitely? There was no intention on the part of the mother to give up the house. Therefore the mother was not liable on the maintenance agreement and could also claim the house.

Apart from husbands and wives and parents and children, agreements may be made by other family members.

Simpkins v Pays (1955)

The defendant (grandmother), her daughter and a paying lodger (claimant) shared a house. They all contributed one third of the stake in entering a competition in a Sunday newspaper. It was sent in under the grandmother's name. One week she won £750 but refused to share the money. It was held that contributing a share of the stake was not the most important factor. The most important factor was the presence of the outsider which rebutted the presumption that it was a family agreement and not intended to be binding. The parties *did* intend the agreement to be binding and all were entitled to an equal share of the winnings.

3.3 Business agreements

In business agreements the presumption is that the parties intended to create legal relations and make a contract. After all, one of the aims of the law of contract is to help people to make agreements. This presumption can be changed by strong evidence to the contrary.

Jones v Vernons Pools Ltd (1938)

The claimant sent in his pools coupon, which contained a winning combination. The defendants said that they had not received it. Further they argued that the agreement was not binding, because the coupon contained a clause which stated that the transaction was 'binding in honour only'. The court held that although this appeared to be a business agreement, i.e., giving money to a company for a service, the clause in the agreement meant that it was based on the honour of the parties. In other words, it was not legally binding and there was no liability to pay the claimant.

Honour clauses, such as the following, are still used by pools companies: 'I have read the rules which govern this entry and agree that this transaction is binding in honour only . . . I also acknowledge that any collector through whom my coupon is submitted is my agent and any arrangement between me and them is likewise binding in honour only'.

EXAMPLE

Could you sue in contract if the collector pocketed your stakemoney and you would have won £1,000,000?

Recently the courts have considered the legal status of the offer of a university place.

Moran v University College Salford (No. 2) (1993)

A student applied to a university, received an unconditional offer and accepted the offer, so that under the admissions scheme he could not apply for other places. The student then left his job and accommodation. Later the university said the offer was made in error and was not intended to be binding. The student now claimed a mandatory injunction to make the university admit him. The Court of Appeal held that the unconditional offer was intended to create a legal relationship and when the student accepted there was a strong case for saying there was an agreement. But the order would be refused pending trial of the action for damages.

A complicated situation occurred in the following case.

Rose & Frank Co. v J.R. Crompton and Brothers Ltd (1925)

The defendants made carbon paper in England. In July 1913 they made an agreement giving the claimants the sole right to sell the defendants' carbon paper in the USA for three years with an option to extend that time. The agreement contained the following clause: 'This is not a formal legal agreement and shall not be subject to the legal jurisdiction of the courts in the United States or England'. Later the agreement was extended to last until 1920. In 1919 the defendants ended the agreement, without giving notice in accordance with its terms. They also refused to carry out orders received before they ended the agreement. The claimants sued for breach of contract. The House of Lords held that in effect there were two contracts: (a) the agreement to give the claimants selling rights. This did not create any legal obligations because of the clause which clearly showed the parties' intentions. The defendants did not have to give notice; (b) specific orders which had been accepted by the defendants before they had ended the agreement could be treated as separate and binding contracts. The defendants had to complete these.

Another type of agreement sometimes used is the 'letter of comfort'.

Kleinwort Benson Ltd v Malaysia Mining Corporation Bhd (1989)

The claimant bank lent £10m to a subsidiary of the defendants, who gave the claimants a letter of comfort. This stated: 'It is the company's policy to ensure that the business of its subsidiary is at all times in a position to meet its liabilities . . . '. The subsidiary went into liquidation and the claimants claimed payment from the defendants. The Court of Appeal, reversing the High Court decision, said that this letter was merely a moral promise and was not intended to be legally binding. A statement of the defendants' policy could be changed and the claimants took this risk.

If a clause is put in an agreement and the clause is ambiguous then the courts will intervene.

Edwards v Skyways Ltd (1964)

The claimant was employed as a pilot by the defendants. In 1962 he was made redundant. Under his contract of employment he had a choice between (a) withdrawing his pension contributions or (b) leaving them and claiming a pension at 50 years old. The claimant was a member of the British Air Line Pilots Association (BALPA) which had made an agreement with the defendants that anyone taking option (a) would be given an ex gratia payment (i.e., a gift). The claimant was told about this in a BALPA newsletter. He then chose option (a) but did not get his ex gratia payment. He sued for breach of contract. The defendants argued that the use of the words 'ex gratia' showed that there was no intention to create a legal relationship. It was held that this agreement related to business matters, therefore it was presumed to be binding. It was up to the defendants to prove that it was not and they had failed to do this. The use of the words 'ex gratia' as meaning 'without liability' applied to existing liability and not the liability to make the actual payment. Therefore they had to pay the pilot.

3.4 Collective agreements

A collective agreement is usually made between trade unions and employers concerning such matters as working conditions, pay, hours etc. Are such agreements binding?

Ford Motor Co. Ltd v AUEW (1969)

The claimants made an agreement in 1955 with 19 trade unions including the defendants. This agreement, in writing, was made after a good deal of thought on both sides and contained the following clause: 'At each stage of the procedure set out in the agreement every attempt will be made to resolve issues raised and until such procedure has been carried through there will be no stoppage of work or other industrial action'. In 1969 some of the unions which had signed the agreement declared a strike. The claimants claimed this was a breach of contract and asked for an injunction to stop the strike. It was held that this was clearly a commercial matter and presumed initially to be binding. It was therefore up to the union to prove otherwise. Because of the nature of such agreements, i.e., that they consist largely of optimistic aspirations, and because of the circumstances in which they are made, the court said they are binding in honour only.

Such agreements are now governed by the Trade Union and Labour Relations (Consolidation) Act 1992, s. 179, which reverses the normal presumption for business agreements (i.e., collective agreements are not binding unless made in writing and stated to be legally enforceable).

4 Consideration

4.1 Introduction

One of the essential ingredients of a simple contract is consideration. Both parties to the contract must provide consideration if they wish to sue on the contract. The law of contract will not enforce a bare promise.

> EXAMPLE
>
> Alice promises to give £100 to Basil. If Alice changes her mind and will not pay, Basil cannot sue.

The test of whether there has been a total failure of consideration is whether the promisor has performed part of the contract and not whether the promisee has received anything.

Stocznia v *Latvian Shipping Co.* (1998)

The claimant shipbuilders agreed to design and build ships for the defendants. The contract provided that property in the ships did not pass until delivery and that the price was to be paid in instalments as the ships were being built. The defendants failed to pay the first instalment and the claimants rescinded the contract under a clause allowing rescission on default by the defendants. The claimants claimed the unpaid instalment. The defendants argued that a clause in the contract covered the situation which had arisen and excluded the claimants' right to sue for the instalment, and that the claimants were not entitled to any money because they had failed to provide any consideration. It was held by the House of Lords that clear words were needed to rebut the presumption that a party did not intend to give up its remedies for breach of contract. By exercising their right of rescission under the contract the claimants did not intend to give up their right to claim money owed. Even though the claimants had not transferred property in the ships to the defendants, it was part of the contract to design and build the ships, so the claimants had provided consideration.

If a contract is made by deed, then consideration is not needed. Note that a deed no longer needs to be sealed but must be witnessed. In the above example, if Alice's promise was made by deed, then Basil could sue to enforce it.

This section will examine the rules developed by the courts about acceptable types of consideration, what is valid as consideration, who must provide consideration and related matters about part payment of debts and the equitable doctrine of promissory estoppel.

These 'rules' of consideration should be seen in the context of the overall purpose of consideration, which is to act as a *filter* to decide which agreements can be enforced and which cannot be. This is much the same as the purpose behind deciding if there is an intention to create a legal relationship.

4.2 Definition

The courts have provided a number of definitions of consideration. In the nineteenth century the emphasis was on a benefit given or a detriment suffered. The modern view of consideration derives from a definition given by Sir Frederick Pollock (*Principles of Contract*):

An act or forbearance of one party or the promise thereof, is the price for which the promise of the other is bought and the promise thus given for value is enforceable.

This involves an exchange between the parties under which the act or promise of one is given for the promise of the other. It can be seen from this definition that a *promise* to do something is consideration.

4.3 Types of consideration

4.3.1 *Executory consideration*

An executory act is one which is yet to be done. Executory consideration is a promise to do something. If one party makes a promise in exchange for a promise from the other, then both parties provide executory consideration. Such consideration is perfectly valid, even though neither party has actually done anything.

EXAMPLE

Alice orders one dozen bottles of Guinness from Bob's off-licence and agrees to pay for them on delivery in one week's time. If Bob does not deliver them, this is a breach of contract and Alice can sue.

4.3.2 *Executed consideration*

If one party makes a promise in exchange for an act by the other party, when that act is completed, it is executed consideration. A good example of this is a unilateral contract, which only comes into existence when the act has been performed and is thus executed consideration.

EXAMPLE

Alice offers £50 reward for the return of her lost handbag. If Basil finds the bag and returns it, Basil's consideration is executed.

4.3.3 *Past consideration*

Past consideration is something which has been done before the promise is made. The rule is that *past consideration is no consideration*, so it is not valid and cannot be used to sue on a contract.

EXAMPLE

Alice gives Bertie a lift from Northampton to London in her car. When they arrive in London, Bertie promises to give Alice £5 towards the petrol. Alice cannot enforce this promise as her consideration, giving Bertie a lift, is past.

Re McArdle (1951)

A father left his house to his wife and then to his three children, A, B and C. During the wife's lifetime the three children lived in the house. A's wife did some decorating and sometime after this A, B and C promised to pay her £488 and they signed a document to this effect. It was held by the Court of Appeal that the decorating was done before the promise was made and was therefore past. A's wife was not entitled to the money.

4.3.3.1 Exceptions to this rule

(A) PREVIOUS REQUEST
If the promisor has previously asked the other party to provide goods or services, then a promise made after they are provided will be treated as binding.

Lampleigh v Brathwait (1615)
B killed someone and then asked L to get him a pardon from the King. L eventually found the King, got the pardon and gave it to B who promised to pay L £100 for his trouble. It was held that although L's consideration was past (he had got the pardon), B's earlier request could be linked with B's later promise to pay, and treated as one agreement, so it could be implied at the time of the request that L would be paid.

(B) BUSINESS SITUATIONS
If something is done in a business context and it is clearly understood by both sides that it will be paid for, then past consideration will be valid.

Re Casey's Patents (1892)
A and B owned a patent and C was the manager who had worked on it for two years. A and B then promised C a one-third share in the invention for his help in developing it. It was held by the Court of Appeal that even though C's consideration was in the past, it had been done in a business situation, at the request of A and B and it was understood by both sides that C would be paid.

(C) THE BILLS OF EXCHANGE ACT 1882
Under s. 27(1) it is provided that any antecedent debt or liability is valid consideration for a bill of exchange.

> EXAMPLE
>
> Alice mows Bob's lawn and a week later Bob gives Alice a cheque for £10. Alice's work is valid consideration in exchange for the cheque.

4.4 Rules of consideration

4.4.1 Consideration need not be adequate
Both parties to the contract must get something and it must have some value. As long as it has some value it will be treated as valid consideration, as the courts will not investigate contracts to see if the parties have got equal value. Cases have decided that 'love and affection' is not valid consideration.

4.4.2 Consideration must move from the promisee

The person who wishes to enforce the contract must show that they provided consideration, it is not enough to show that someone provided consideration. Normally there will only be two parties and the claimant will be the promisee (the person to whom the promise is made). It is up to the promisee to show that consideration 'moved from' (i.e., was provided by) them. The consideration does not have to move to the promisor. If there are three parties involved, problems may arise.

> **EXAMPLE**
>
> Alice, Basil and Chris agree that Alice will mow Basil's lawn if Chris gives Alice £20. Basil cannot enforce this promise as he has not provided consideration.

Price v Easton (1833)

The defendant made a contract with X that in return for X doing work for him, the defendant would pay the claimant £19. X did the work but the defendant did not pay, so the claimant sued. It was held that the claimant's claim must fail, as he had not provided consideration.

This rule that the promisee cannot sue if he does not provide consideration, is closely related to another rule of contract, that only the parties to the contract may sue on it. This is known as the rule of *privity*. (See the effect of the Contracts (Rights of Third Parties) Act 1999 at 6.3 below.)

4.4.3 Consideration must be sufficient

Sufficient consideration means something the law recognises as valid. There are many cases deciding what is and what is not regarded as sufficient.

4.4.3.1 Trivial items   The courts have accepted things of little value as being sufficient consideration.

Chappell & Co. Ltd v Nestlé Co. Ltd (1959)

The defendants sold a record 'Rockin' Shoes' to the public in exchange for 1s 6d (7½p) plus three chocolate wrappers, the latter were thrown away on receipt. The defendants were obliged to pay the owners (claimants) a percentage of the selling price and they offered this percentage based on 1s 6d. The question was whether this amount was the selling price or did the value of the wrappers add to it? It was held by the House of Lords that the wrappers were part of the consideration, it was irrelevant that they were thrown away.

4.4.3.2 Forbearance to sue   If one person has a claim against another but agrees not to pursue the claim, that is a forbearance. Such a claim may be in contract or tort. A promise not to sue is good consideration, if made in return for a promise by the other to settle the claim. But what if the claim is not a valid one, can giving it up be good consideration? The courts have determined that the consideration consists of not giving up a legal right but the claim to such a right. The person giving up the claim must show it is reasonable and that they honestly believe they will win.

Alliance Bank Ltd v *Broom* (1864)

The defendant owed an unsecured debt of £22,000 to the claimant. When the claimant asked for some security, the defendant promised to provide some goods but never produced them. When the claimant tried to enforce the agreement for the security, the defendant argued that the claimant had not provided any consideration. The court held that normally in such a case, the bank would promise not to enforce the debt, but this was not done here. By not suing, however, the bank had shown forbearance and this was valid consideration, so the agreement to provide security was binding.

4.4.3.3 Existing duties

(A) DUTIES IMPOSED BY LAW

If someone is under a public duty to do a particular task, then agreeing to do that task is not sufficient consideration for a contract.

Collins v *Godefroy* (1831)

The defendant promised to pay the claimant six guineas if the claimant would attend court and give evidence for the defendant. The claimant had been served with a subpoena (i.e., a court order telling someone they must attend). It was held that as the claimant was legally obliged to attend court, a promise to do this was not valid consideration.

If someone acts over and above their public duty, then this may be valid consideration.

Glasbrook Bros Ltd v *Glamorgan County Council* (1925)

During a miners' strike, a mine owner asked for police to be billeted on the premises. The police said this was not necessary, but the mine owner promised to pay £2,200 if they would do so, and the police complied with this request. When the police claimed the money, the mine owner refused to pay saying that the police had simply carried out their public duty. The House of Lords held that although the police were bound to provide protection, they had a discretion as to the form it should take. As they believed mobile police were sufficient, they had acted over their normal duties and were entitled to payment.

In the more recent case of *Harris* v *Sheffield United FC Ltd* (1987) it was held that the football club had to pay for police to control the crowds at football matches.

(B) DUTIES IMPOSED UNDER AN EXISTING CONTRACT

If someone promises to do something they are already bound to do under a contract, that is not valid consideration.

Stilk v *Myrick* (1809)

A ship sailed from London to the Baltic and whilst there two out of 11 crew deserted. The captain promised to pay the remaining crew extra money if they sailed the ship back, but later refused to pay. It was held that as the sailors were already bound by their contract to sail back, promising to sail back was not valid consideration and the captain did not have to pay.

This was distinguished in the following later case.

Hartley v Ponsonby (1857)

Out of 36 crew, 19 deserted. The captain promised the remaining crew extra money to sail back, but later refused to pay saying they were only doing their normal jobs. It was held that sailing the ship back in such dangerous conditions was over and above their normal duties and they were entitled to the money.

The principle set out in *Stilk* v *Myrick* has recently been amended by the following case.

Williams v Roffey Bros & Nicholls (Contractors) Ltd (1990)

The defendants were the main contractors to refurbish a block of flats and the claimants were sub-contractors for the carpentry. The claimants got into financial difficulties and were concerned that they might not be able to finish on time or at all. The defendants then agreed to pay them an extra £575 per flat. The claimants finished eight flats and claimed the extra money. In the Court of Appeal the defendants argued that the claimants were only doing what they were contractually bound to do and so had not provided consideration. The court held that there were benefits to the defendants including (a) making sure the claimants continued their work, (b) avoiding payment under a liquidated damages clause of the main contract payable if the claimants were late, (c) avoiding the expense and trouble of getting someone else. Therefore the claimants were entitled to payment.

The courts seem to have taken account of the reality of business life, that sometimes a party to a contract obtains a practical benefit or avoids a burden by getting the other party to carry out their part of the contract. Clearly if there is a practical benefit to the promisor, the promisee carrying out existing duties does now provide valid consideration.

(C) DUTIES UNDER AN EXISTING CONTRACT WITH A THIRD PARTY

If a party promises to do something for a second party, but is already bound by contract to do this for a third party, this is good consideration.

Scotson v Pegg (1861)

S contracted to deliver coal to X 'or his order'. X sold the coal to P and told S to deliver the coal to P. Then P promised S to unload at a fixed rate. S sued for breach of this promise and P argued that the promise was not binding, because S had not provided consideration as S was bound by his contract with X to deliver the coal. It was held that delivery of the coal was a benefit to P and was valid consideration. It could also be seen as a detriment to S, as they could have broken their contract with X and paid damages.

4.5 Part payment of a debt

4.5.1 The rule in Pinnel's case

If one person owes a sum of money to another and agrees to pay *part* of this sum in full settlement, this is not valid consideration, because he is already legally bound to pay the full amount. This is based on the same principle as *Stilk* v *Myrick*.

Pinnel's case (1602)
Cole owed Pinnel £8 10s 0d (£8.50) which was due on 11 November. At Pinnel's request, Cole paid £5 2s 2d (£5.11) on 1 October, which Pinnel accepted in full settlement of the debt. It was held that part payment in itself was not sufficient consideration, there had to be a new element, like a chattel, payment at a different place or an earlier date. As payment had been made on an earlier date this was valid consideration.

At one time part payment by cheque was regarded as valid consideration because cheques are easy to carry and can be transferred, but this rule was changed by *D&C Builders* v *Rees* (1965).

Recently it has been argued, on the basis of *Williams* v *Roffey Bros & Nicholls (Contractors) Ltd*, that a promise to pay an existing debt could be valid consideration.

Re Selectmove Ltd (1995)
S owed tax to the Inland Revenue and made an 'agreement' to pay by instalments. S began paying but the Inland Revenue demanded full payment immediately. S argued that the Inland Revenue obtained benefits from this agreement by getting the amount due and saving the trouble of going to court. The Court of Appeal distinguished *Williams* v *Roffey Bros & Nicholls (Contractors) Ltd* on the basis that it was to supply goods and services, while this was to pay a sum of money. The Court said the agreement to pay by instalments was not binding on the Inland Revenue, as S had not provided consideration. The Court also said that because the Inland Revenue collector had no authority to make the 'agreement', his silence was not acceptance of the company's proposal, and neither could an estoppel arise from the Inland Revenue's implied promise not to enforce the debt.

This distinction between providing goods and services and paying a debt is not wholly convincing, but the Court was bound by the precedent of *Foakes* v *Beer* (1884) which confirmed the rule in *Pinnel's case*.

4.5.2 Exceptions to the rule in Pinnel's case
Apart from the exceptions mentioned in Pinnel's case itself, there are others.

4.5.2.1 Part payment by a third party   If part payment by a third party is accepted in full settlement, this is valid.

Hirachand Punamchand v Temple (1911)
A father paid a smaller sum to a moneylender to pay his son's debts, which the moneylender accepted in full settlement. Later the moneylender sued for the balance. It was held that the part payment was valid consideration, as to allow the moneylender's claim would be fraud on the father.

4.5.2.2 Composition agreements   This is an agreement between a debtor and a group of creditors, under which the creditors agree to accept a percentage of their debts in

full settlement. The courts do not allow an individual creditor to sue the debtor for the balance, as effectively this would be fraud on the other creditors who had all agreed to the percentage.

4.6 Promissory estoppel

4.6.1 The principle of estoppel

If someone makes a promise that another acts on, at common law because that other did not provide consideration for the promise they cannot sue for breach of contract, if the promisor goes back on the promise. However, the courts of Equity developed the principle of equitable estoppel or as it is now generally known, promissory estoppel. The principle is that if someone (the promisor) makes a promise, which another person acts on, the promisor is stopped (or estopped) from going back on the promise, even though the other person did not provide consideration.

The important aspects of the principle are set out below.

4.6.2 Existing legal relationship

There must be an existing legal relationship, which will usually be a contract.

4.6.3 A promise

One party makes a promise which is intended to be binding.

This promise may be express or implied and an example of the latter is the next case.

Hughes v Metropolitan Railway Company (1877)

In October the landlord gave the tenant six months' notice to repair or forfeit the lease. In November the landlord and tenant began negotiations for the sale of the premises, but these ended in December without agreement. Meanwhile the tenant had not done the repairs and when the six months period was up, the landlord sought possession. It was held by the House of Lords that beginning negotiations implied that as long as they went on, the landlord would not enforce the notice. Therefore the notice did not run during the period of negotiations.

This case was an example of equitable estoppel as the implied statement was about existing fact. The principle was extended to statements about the future in the following case and became known as promissory estoppel.

Central London Property Trust Ltd v High Trees House Ltd (1947)

In 1939 the claimants let a block of flats to the defendants for £2,500 a year. Because of the war the defendants could not get enough tenants and in 1940 the claimants agreed in writing to accept half rent. After the war in 1945 all the flats were occupied and the claimants claimed the full rent for the period 1940–5 and the future. As a test claim they asked for the full rent for the second half of 1945. It was held that even though the defendants did not provide consideration for the claimants' promise to accept half rent, this promise was intended to be binding and was acted on by the defendants. Therefore the claimants were estopped from going back on their promise and could not claim the full rent for 1940–5. However, they could claim full rent for the second half of 1945 as the promise only lasted during war conditions.

In *Re Selectmove* (1995), it was argued on behalf of the company that there was an implied promise by the Inland Revenue that they would not enforce the debt and therefore they should be estopped from going back on this promise. The Court said that an estoppel did not arise because the Inland Revenue official did not have the authority to make the agreement.

4.6.4 *Reliance on the promise*

The party the promise is made to must have relied on it. If a party acts on the basis of the promise, this shows reliance on it. For example, in the *High Trees* case the tenant actually paid half rent. It has been said that the promisee must act to his detriment, although some judges have said it is sufficient merely to have acted on the promise.

EXAMPLE

Alice is expecting some overtime pay after working late for four weeks. She receives her pay slip from her employer Bertie, showing £1,000 extra on her usual monthly salary. Honestly believing this is her overtime, Alice spends it on a new moped. Bertie now claims £800 back saying it was paid due to a computer error. Under the principle of promissory estoppel Alice would not have to repay that money.

4.6.5 *Inequitable to let the promisor go back on the promise*

The principle of estoppel was developed by the courts of equity and it is up to the court to exercise its discretion whether the principle should apply in a particular case. For example, if the promisor withdrew his promise shortly after making it, the court may let the promisor go back on the promise. In *Re Selectmove, Re* (1995), it was said that even if there was an estoppel, because the company had not continued to pay the instalments it would not be inequitable to allow the Inland Revenue to go back on the promise.

4.6.6 *A shield not a sword*

A person cannot sue someone on the basis of the principle of estoppel, they need to establish a contract to sue. However, estoppel can be used as a defence to a claim.

4.6.7 *Suspends rights*

A question arises whether the principle of estoppel merely suspends rights or extinguishes them.

The prevalent authorities are in favour of it merely suspending rights, which can be revived by giving reasonable notice or by conditions changing. An example of this is the *High Trees* case, as after the war all the flats were let and the landlord could once again charge full rent.

5 Requirements as to form

5.1 Introduction

Although it is widely believed that contracts have to be in writing, the general rule is that no formalities are required to make a valid contract. It may be made orally, in writing or by conduct or any combination of these methods. However, some contracts have to be made in a particular form, either by deed, in writing or evidenced in writing. This is additional to the requirements of agreement, intention and consideration.

5.2 Contracts which must be made by deed

A deed is a formal written document and the traditional requirements for deeds were abolished by the Law of Property (Miscellaneous Provisions) Act 1989, s. 1(1). A deed may now be drawn up on any substance and does not need to be sealed. To be a deed, a document must now make it clear on its face or by its description or how it is signed, that it is intended to be a deed (s. 1(2)). As regards individuals, the deed must be signed by the individual in the presence of a witness, who must then sign. Alternatively, it may be signed on behalf of an individual at his direction and in his presence and the presence of two witnesses, who must also sign. The deed must then be delivered to the other party.

A contract to convey the legal estate in land, and an assignment of a lease for three years or more, must be by deed (Law of Property Act 1925).

5.3 Contracts which must be in writing

The law requires some contracts to be made in writing to draw the attention of the parties to the seriousness of the undertaking or to protect one of the parties. The most important examples are contracts for the sale of land and consumer credit agreements.

5.3.1 Contracts for the sale of land

Under the Law of Property (Miscellaneous Provisions) Act 1989, s. 2(1):

A contract for the sale or other disposition of an interest in land can only be made in writing and only by incorporating all the terms which the parties have expressly agreed in one document or, where contracts are exchanged, in each.

Under s. 2(3):

The document incorporating the terms or, where contracts are exchanged, one of the documents incorporating them (but not necessarily the same one) must be signed by or on behalf of each party to the contract . . .

This section repeals s. 40, Law of Property Act 1925, and applies to all contracts made after 27 September 1989. All contracts for the sale of land or an interest in land, like an easement or a mortgage, must now be in writing and be signed by the parties. If the requirements of s. 2 are not met, the contract is invalid.

Recent decisions of the Court of Appeal have involved interpretation of these requirements.

Firstpost Homes v *Johnson* (1995)

The buyer of land prepared a letter with his name typed on it, stating that the seller wished to sell the land on the enclosed plan. Only the seller signed the letter, but both parties signed the plan. The seller then died and her personal representatives argued that there was no written contract within s. 2 of the 1989 Act. The court held that the letter and plan were two separate documents. The fact that the buyer's name was on the letter was not sufficient, the requirement for a signature meant a handwritten signature. As the buyer had not signed there was no binding contract.

Commission for New Towns v *Cooper Ltd* (1995)
This involved the sale of land by the exchange of letters. It was argued this was enough to be within s. 2(3) 'where contracts are exchanged'. It was held by the Court of Appeal that the phrase 'contracts are exchanged' meant the process by which each party prepares and signs a contract and then exchanges it for an identical contract signed by the other party. Therefore there was no binding contract.

McCausland v *Duncan Lawrie Ltd* (1996)
The buyer and seller of land both signed a written contract of sale. Later the parties, realising that the completion date was a Sunday, agreed to change completion to the previous Friday and exchanged letters setting out this new date. But there was no single document incorporating the change which was signed by both of them. The buyers did not complete on the Friday. It was held that to comply with s. 2 of the 1989 Act any variation in a contract for the sale of land had to be in writing and signed by both parties, and this had not been done.

Some contracts are excluded from the above requirements and do not have to be in writing: contracts for leases for three years or less; contracts made under the Financial Services Act 1986; contracts for the sale of land made at public auctions.

5.3.2 *Consumer credit agreements*
Under the Consumer Credit Act 1974, s. 60, a regulated consumer credit agreement must be in writing and in the specific form required by regulations. If the agreement is not in writing, it cannot be enforced by the creditor without a court order.

5.3.3 *Assignments of choses in action*
A chose in action is an intangible right, for example a debt. Such a right may only be transferred by a process called assignment and this assignment must be in writing (Law of Property Act 1925, s. 136).

5.3.4 *Negotiable instruments*
A negotiable instrument is a document giving a right to a sum of money and under the Bills of Exchange Act 1882 it must be in writing. For example, cheques and bills of exchange must be in writing.

5.3.5 *Distance selling contracts*
Under the Consumer Protection (Distance Selling) Regulations 2000 certain requirements apply to a 'distance contract'. This is defined under reg. 3(1) as 'any contract concerning goods or services concluded between a supplier and a consumer under an organised distance sales or service provision scheme run by the supplier who, for the purposes of the contract, makes exclusive use of one or more means of distance

communication up to and including the moment at which the contract is concluded'. These regulations came into force on 31 October 2000.

The type of contracts which these regulations will apply to include contracts made via catalogues, telephone, e-mail, fax and the internet.

Certain formalities are required under contracts covered by the regulations. Regulation 7(1) provides that information must be given to the consumer before the contract is concluded. This information includes the identity of the supplier (and if payment in advance is required, the supplier's address); a description of the goods or services; the price; delivery charges; arrangements for payment; and the right of cancellation. Under reg. 7(2) the supplier must ensure that the information required is provided in a clear and comprehensible manner appropriate to the means of distance communication used. Under reg. 8 the supplier must provide the consumer 'in writing, or other durable medium which is available' the information required under reg. 7. The information could be given in writing or by an e-mail which could be printed by the consumer.

Under reg. 10 the consumer has the right to cancel the contract within seven days by notice in writing or other durable medium. If the notice is sent by post it takes effect on the day it is posted and if by fax or e-mail on the day it is sent.

Some contracts are excluded from the regulations under reg. 5: contracts for the sale of land; financial services; contracts made via automatic vending machines; and contracts made at auctions.

5.4 Contracts which must be evidenced in writing

5.4.1 Introduction
Here the law asks for some written evidence of the contract, which is less formal than requiring the contract to be in writing. Only contracts of guarantee must now be evidenced in writing.

5.4.2 Contracts of guarantee
A guarantee is an agreement to meet the debts or liabilities of someone else. It is different from a manufacturer's guarantee, which does not have to be in any particular form although normally will be in writing.

The requirements were first set out in the Statute of Frauds 1677, s. 4, which provided that no action could be brought on a ' . . . promise to answer for the debt, default or miscarriages of another person . . . unless the agreement . . . or some memorandum or note . . . shall be in writing and signed by the party to be charged'.

There must be three parties to a guarantee: the debtor; the creditor; the guarantor. The guarantor promises the creditor that if the debtor does not pay the creditor, then the guarantor will do so. The debtor still has *primary* liability and the guarantor will only be liable if the debtor does not pay (*secondary* liability).

A guarantee must be distinguished from an *indemnity*. Here there are only two parties, one agrees to pay in place of the debtor. The indemnifier takes on *primary* liability. An indemnity is not covered by s. 4 and does not have to be evidenced in writing.

EXAMPLE

Alice borrows £100 from Bertie's Bank and Chris promises to pay Bertie's Bank if Alice does not repay the money. This is a guarantee and must be evidenced in writing.

The word 'miscarriages' in the Statute of Frauds 1677 covers torts as well as contracts. The promise must be made to the creditor, if it is made to the debtor s. 4 does not apply.

If the requirements of s. 4 are not met, the guarantee cannot be enforced in a court. However, it does not mean that it is invalid and if the guarantor pays up there is no problem. In practice the creditor will invariably make the guarantor sign a written agreement. It is always risky for an individual to sign a guarantee, because they may not fully realise the implications and that they may be required to pay on it.

6 Privity

6.1 Introduction

The vast majority of contracts are made between *two parties* and only those parties are affected. In some situations however, it is possible for an outside party (i.e., a *third* party) to be involved in some way. The *principle of privity* (or *doctrine of privity*) states that only the parties to the contract can sue on the contract or be sued on the contract. The original rule meant that a third party could neither sue on such a contract nor be sued on it. The rule of privity has been amended by the Contracts (Rights of Third Parties) Act 1999 which gives rights to third parties in certain defined circumstances. This Act will be examined below after considering the original rule and the exceptions to the rule.

There are two aspects to the doctrine of privity, firstly that a contract cannot give *benefits* to third parties and secondly that a contract cannot impose *obligations* on a third party. It is easier to accept that a third party should be able to receive a benefit from a contract rather than have obligations imposed on them, but under the rule of privity, strictly, neither can happen. There are exceptions to both of these cases. The following case provides an example of the doctrine in practice.

Dunlop Pneumatic Tyre Co. Ltd v *Selfridge & Co. Ltd* (1915)
Dunlop sold tyres to Dew on terms that the buyers would not sell below list price and that, if they resold, Dew would put a similar term in the contracts. Dew sold to Selfridge, who agreed not to sell below list price and to pay £5 to Dunlop for every tyre sold in breach of this agreement. Selfridge sold below list price and Dunlop sued them. The House of Lords held that as Dunlop were not a party to the contract between Dew and Selfridge and had not provided any consideration, they had no rights under it.

Viscount Haldane LC said in the above case that two principles were fundamental to the law. First that only a party to a contract can sue on the contract and secondly that only someone who had given consideration could enforce a contract. These can be seen as two aspects of the same principle, so someone can only sue on a contract if they are a party to it and have provided consideration.

A number of exceptions have been made to the doctrine of privity and there have also been several attempts at extending these exceptions.

6.2 Exceptions to the doctrine of privity

6.2.1 Exceptions made by statute

6.2.1.1 Married Women's Property Act 1882, s. 11   This provides that if a husband or wife insures his or her life for the benefit of their spouse or children, this will create a trust in favour of the objects of the policy.

> EXAMPLE
>
> Alan takes out a policy of life insurance with Basil for Christine his wife. If Alan dies, Christine may sue Basil even though she was not a party to the contract.

6.2.1.2 Bills of Exchange Act 1882, s. 29   This provides that the holder in due course of a cheque who has given value for it, may sue any prior party who has signed it. The holder's rights are not limited to suing the person with whom they made the contract, i.e., who gave them the cheque.

6.2.1.3 Law of Property Act 1925, s. 56   This provides that a person may take an interest in 'land or other property' even though they may not be named as a party to the agreement. It was argued in the following case that 'other property' included a contract.

Beswick v Beswick (1966)
A husband sold his business to his nephew, on terms that the husband would receive a weekly payment for life and on his death his widow would receive £5 a week for life. The nephew only made one payment to the widow. The widow sued as (a) administratrix of her husband's estate and (b) as the widow. It was held by the House of Lords that her claim as widow failed, as she was not a party to the contract made between her husband and the defendant but her claim as administratrix was as representative of her husband, who was a party to the contract and she was awarded specific performance. The House stated that s. 56 only applied to land and could not be extended to other property, rejecting Lord Denning's claim in the Court of Appeal that she could sue personally under s. 56.

6.2.1.4 Law of Property Act 1925, s. 136   This provides that a chose in action may be assigned. The assignment must be in writing; be the assignment of the whole interest; and notice in writing must be given to the debtor. The assignee who was not a party to the original contract can sue on that contract.

Alice owes Basil £100. Basil can assign this debt to Christine. This enables Christine to sue Alice, even though Christine was not a party to the original loan.

6.2.2 Agency

Agency arises when one person (principal) appoints a representative (agent) to make contracts with someone else (third party). The principal can sue and be sued on contracts they have not made. This seems to conflict with the principle of privity. It is argued against this that the third party will usually know that the agent is only acting as an agent and will drop out, so the real contract is between the principal and the third party. The rules of agency, however, recognise situations which do not comply with this justification.

6.2.2.1 Apparent authority   An agent may have no actual authority but may appear to the third party to have authority. Contracts made will be binding on the principal, so he is liable on a contract he did not want to make.

EXAMPLE

Danny is manager of a public house owned by Eve. Danny has been told not to buy cigarettes from any representatives, as Eve can obtain them cheaper. Danny buys cigarettes on credit from Freddie, a travelling salesman. This contract will be binding on Eve.

6.2.2.2 Undisclosed principal   Here the agent does not tell the third party that he is acting as an agent. As long as the agent has authority to make the contract it is binding on the principal, who can sue and be sued on the contract. The principal is liable, even though the third party does not know the principal existed.

Despite these objections, agency is accepted to meet the realities of the business world.

6.2.3 Covenants on land

In land law on the sale of land or the assignment of a lease, the law has recognised that covenants in such agreements can 'run with the land', so that they will be binding on later purchasers and can impose obligations on them. This is an exception to the rule of privity that only the parties to the original agreement are bound by it. In *Tulk* v *Moxhay* (1848) it was held that a purchaser of land in Leicester Square was bound by a restrictive covenant not to build in the garden imposed by the original landowner.

Attempts have been made to extend the idea of covenants running with land to goods, but, with one exception which must be confined to its particular facts concerning a charterparty, these have not been successful.

6.2.4 Trusts

A trust arises when one person (settlor) gives property or money to another (trustee), to hold for the benefit of a third party (beneficiary). The beneficiary can enforce the trust, even though they are not a party to the agreement between the settlor and the trustee.

EXAMPLE

Alice makes an agreement with Basil, to give Basil money to hold on trust for the benefit of Christine. Christine can enforce this trust, even though she was not a party to the agreement between Alice and Basil.

Attempts have been made to extend the idea of a trust to a normal contract situation. For example, where Alice makes a contract with Basil for the benefit of Christine, it has been argued that Basil is holding his contractual rights against Alice, 'on trust' for Christine. If this is accepted, then Christine could sue Alice for breach of trust and get round the principle of privity.

Les Affréteurs Réunis SA v *Leopold Walford (London) Ltd* (1919)

Walford negotiated the hire of a ship between the ship owners (claimants) and the hirers. The contract between the owners and hirers provided that the owners would pay Walford 3 per cent commission. They did not pay and Walford sued them. The House of Lords held that the hirers could be regarded as trustees of the commission for Walford, who could join the hirers to the action as either co-claimants or co-defendants. Walford was therefore able to enforce this contract even though he was not a party to it.

No formalities are needed to create a trust as long as there is evidence of an intention to do so. However, the courts have been reluctant to use the trust device and have emphasised that there is a difference between a trust and a contract made between two people for the benefit of a third party. One influential factor has been that the terms of a contract may be varied by the parties, but not the terms of a trust. A finding that a trust had been created would mean that the contract could not be changed.

6.2.5 Collateral contracts

This is a device used to create a second contract which exists alongside the main contract and evades the rule of privity.

Shanklin Pier Ltd v *Detel Products Ltd* (1951)

The claimants employed X to paint their pier and specified that the defendants' paint should be used, as the defendants had told the claimants that the paint would last ten years. X bought the paint from the defendants and painted the pier, but the paint only lasted three months. The claimants could not sue the defendants on the contract for the sale of the paint, as the claimants were not parties to this contract. It was held that a collateral contract existed between the claimants and the defendants under which the consideration provided by the claimants was a promise that X would buy the paint from the defendant and the consideration by the defendant was a promise that the paint would last ten years. Therefore the claimants won the case.

6.3 Contracts (Rights of Third Parties) Act 1999

6.3.1 Avoiding the doctrine of privity

There have been many attempts to get round the doctrine of privity, but the courts seem to have restricted these within narrow confines. One avenue which is always open to a third party is to get one of the parties to the contract to sue on their behalf. One problem then faced by the third party is that the person suing will not have suffered loss and will only be entitled to nominal damages.

Jackson v Horizon Holidays Ltd (1975)

The claimant booked a holiday in Ceylon for his family, with the defendants. The hotel had few of the facilities promised, the room was damp and the food awful. The question arose whether the members of the family could recover compensation, as they were not parties to the contract. The Court of Appeal held that the claimant was entitled to damages for himself and his family. This judgment was later criticised by the House of Lords, which said that damages for the family could only be justified because the claimant saw his family suffering.

Another possible avenue is if a third party can establish a claim in the tort of negligence. However claims in tort for economic loss will not generally be successful.

The strict application of the doctrine of privity led to injustice in many cases and both the courts and Parliament created exceptions. The Law Commission examined the doctrine in *Privity of Contract: Contracts for the Benefit of Third Parties* Report No. 242 (1996) which resulted in the passing of the Contracts (Rights of Third Parties) Act 1999. The Act provides,

1.—(1) ... a person who is not a party to a contract (a 'third party') may in his own right enforce a term of the contract if—

  (a) the contract expressly provides that he may, or

  (b) subject to subsection (2), the term purports to confer a benefit on him.

(2) Subsection (1)(b) does not apply if on a proper construction of the contract it appears that the parties did not intend the term to be enforceable by the third party.

It is clear that under s. 1(1)(a) a contract which expressly gives a third party the right to sue can be enforced by that third party.

Under s. 1(1)(b) the third party will have the right to sue if the contract 'purports to confer a benefit on him' but even if this is proved, the parties to the contract may show that they did not intend the third party to be able to enforce this right.

It is provided under s. 1(3) that the third party must be identified by name or as a member of a class or as answering a particular description. Further, the third party does not have to be in existence at the time the contract is made.

EXAMPLE

Enforceable rights may be given to a person born after the contract was made or a company formed after the contract was made.

Section 1(4) provides that the third party's rights to enforce the contract are subject to the other terms of the contract. Under s. 1(5) the third party has all the remedies available in the case of a breach of contract. Under s. 1(6) the third party may rely on any exclusion clauses in the contract.

6.3.2 Changes to the contract

It is provided in s. 2 that if a third party has a right to enforce a contract the parties to that contract cannot end the contract or change it without the third party's consent if:

(a) the third party has told the promisor that he agrees to the term; or

(b) the promisor is aware that the third party has relied on the term; or

(c) the promisor should have foreseen that the third party would rely on the term and the third party has actually relied on it.

The aim of this section is to stop the parties ending the contract or altering it without the third party's consent, if the third party has agreed to the contract or acted in reliance on it.

This section is subject to any term of the contract which allows the parties to alter it without the third party's consent.

6.3.3 Defences

Under s. 3 if a third party sues the promisor on the contract, the promisor may rely on any defence or set-off which would have been available against the other party to the contract (the promisee). The promisor also has similar rights against the third party which would have been available if the third party had been a party to the contract. These rights are subject to any express term of the contract which may take them away.

EXAMPLE

If the third party has made a misrepresentation to the promisor, the promisor may rely on this when sued by the third party.

Under s. 10 the Act came into force on 11 November 1999 but it does not apply to contracts made within six months of that date unless the contract provided otherwise. The Act does apply to all contracts made on or after 11 May 2000.

6.3.4 Effect of the Act

Many contracting parties may simply exclude the provisions of the Act so that third parties cannot bring claims under the contract. However, the Act will bring benefits to third parties. A third party will be able to rely on an exclusion clause in the contract if this was intended to benefit them. For example, if a contract between the owner of goods and the shipper contains an exclusion clause in favour of the shipper, a third party, such as stevedores unloading the goods, would be able to rely on the clause if it was intended to benefit them. In a situation like _Beswick v Beswick_ (1966), Mrs Beswick would now be able to sue in her own right under the Act as the contract was made for her benefit and purports to confer a benefit on her. The Act will also give rights to members of a family where a holiday is booked for them by, for example, the mother. One problem area may be s. 1(1)(b) where a contract term 'purports to confer a benefit' on a third party. This would cover a situation where something done directly for the third party, for example, paying him a sum of money, but its exact scope remains to be seen.

Contents of a contract

1 Introduction

When it is clear that a valid contract has been made, it is still necessary to determine what the details of the contract are. These details set out the rights and obligations of the parties and are known as the *terms of the contract*. In very simple contracts the terms will be few and clear, for example Alice buying a newspaper from Basil. However, if a party is buying something expensive or complicated, for example Alice buys a helicopter from Bob, it is likely that the parties have been involved in negotiations and have then drawn up a detailed written contract. It is unlikely that everything which has been spoken or written is treated as a term of the contract, some matters may simply be *representations* which are not part of the contract. Further, the details of the contract may not only be what was *written* down, but may include things that were *said* or even things that are *implied* either by Act of Parliament or the courts. Even if it is agreed what is to be included, it is unlikely that all the terms are of equal importance and it will be necessary to classify them accordingly. Another important matter to decide is how far the parties can *exclude* or *limit* their liability. This section will examine the differences between representations and terms of the contract; the various categories of terms recognised by the law as being express or implied and the concurrent categories of conditions, warranties and innominate (or intermediate) terms; the effect of the parol evidence rule; the significance of terms being liquidated damages clauses or penalty clauses. Exclusion clauses and unfair contract terms are dealt with at the end of the following section.

2 Representations and terms

2.1 Introduction

It may be clearly established what the parties said and what was written down but this does not mean that all these are part of the contract. A distinction is made between:

(a) representations—statements which induce the contract but are not treated as part of it; and

(b) terms—statements which are actually part of the contract.

The importance of this distinction arises if a particular statement is untrue. If the statement is classed as a *representation,* a party will only have a claim to damages if the statement was fraudulent or negligent. If it was innocent then under the Misrepresentation Act 1967 it is up to the discretion of the court whether to award damages. If the untrue statement is classed as a *term* of the contract, then damages are available as of right, in all cases. It is usually better for the party affected to show that the statement is a term of the contract. In some circumstances a statement which is a representation is treated by the courts as a term of the contract.

2.2 Guidelines used by the courts in making the distinction

The test used by the courts to determine whether a statement is a representation or a term of the contract, is the intention of the parties. Did they *intend* the statement to be a term of the contract? The courts use an objective test and look at the facts from the viewpoint of the reasonable man.

2.2.1 *Manner in which statement is made*

If the person making the statement asks the other party to check its truth, the statement is unlikely to be treated as a term of the contract.

Ecay v *Godfrey* (1947)

The seller of a boat said the boat was sound but advised the buyer to have it checked. It was held that the seller did not intend this statement to be a term of the contract.

If the maker of the statement tries to stop the other party checking the truth, it is likely to be treated as a term.

Schawel v *Reade* (1913)

A buyer wanted a horse for stud purposes and was about to examine it, when the seller said 'You need not look for anything, the horse is perfectly sound'. The horse was, in fact, no good. The House of Lords held that this statement was important to the buyer, who was stopped from checking it and it could therefore be treated as a term of the contract.

2.2.2 *Importance of the statement*

A statement is likely to be a term if it was so important that the buyer would not have made the contract unless it was a term.

Bannerman v *White* (1861)

The defendant was buying hops and asked if sulphur had been used in growing them, adding that if it had, he would not even bother to ask the price. The seller said that sulphur had not been used but this was untrue. The court held that the seller must have realised how important this statement was to the buyer and therefore it could be treated as a term of the contract.

2.2.3 *Special knowledge or skill*

If one of the parties has special knowledge or skill compared with the other, which would enable them to discover the truth of a statement, that is an important factor in deciding if the statement is a term. The effect of special knowledge can be seen by contrasting the following two cases.

— They should know, and should it have said

Dick Bentley Productions Ltd v Harold Smith (Motors) Ltd (1965)

The second claimant told the defendant he wanted a 'well vetted Bentley car'. The defendant said he had one which had only done 20,000 miles on a new engine. The claimant bought the car but the contract did not mention the mileage. In fact, it had done 100,000 miles on the new engine. It was held by the Court of Appeal that the defendant was in a position to know about the truth of his statement or at least find out. The statement about mileage could be treated as a term of the contract.

Oscar Chess Ltd v Williams (1957)

Relying on his registration book, the defendant said his Morris was a 1948 model and was allowed £290 by the claimant garage on a part exchange. Eight months later the claimants found it was a 1939 model worth only £175. The Court of Appeal held that the defendant was not an expert, but the claimants were. The statement about age could not be treated as a term of the contract, only a representation.

2.2.4 *Time of the statement*

The time the statement was made is important in deciding if it is a term of the contract. If there is a large gap between making the statement and making the contract, this may show the parties did not intend it to be a term.

Routledge v McKay (1954)

This involved a private sale of a motorbike, which the defendant said was a 1942 model. A week later the claimant bought it but the written contract did not mention the year of manufacture. In fact it was a 1930 model. The Court of Appeal said that as the statement had been made well before the contract, it was not intended to be a term of the contract.

In the above case there was a clear time gap between the statement and the contract, during which no further negotiations took place, but the courts have treated contracts as being made over a period of time.

2.3 Collateral contracts

The problem of whether a statement is a representation or a term of the contract can be avoided by the use of a device developed by the courts called a *collateral* contract. The word 'collateral' means side by side or secondary. Using the doctrine of collateral contracts the courts can say that a statement which is not a term of the main contract is not simply a representation, but a term of another contract (a collateral contract), which exists alongside the main contract.

2.3.1 *Requirements for a collateral contract*

   (a) All the ingredients of a contract must be present, including intention, offer, acceptance and consideration.

   (b) There must be evidence that the parties intended the term to take effect as a collateral contract and not simply as a term of the main contract.

An example of how a collateral contract arises can be seen in the following case.

De Lassalle v Guildford (1901)

The claimant would not sign the lease of the defendant's house, until the defendant made an oral promise that the drains were in good order. The lease did not mention this promise and it turned out that the drains needed to be repaired. The Court of Appeal held that although the statement about the drains was not in the main contract (the lease), it could be regarded as part of a collateral contract. The consideration for the defendant's promise that the drains were in good order, was the claimant's promise to sign the lease. This was a breach of the collateral contract. The consideration for the main contract was the promise to pay the rent.

In theory a collateral contract cannot contradict the main contract, but the courts have not always followed this.

City and Westminster Properties (1934) Ltd v Mudd (1958)

The defendant leased a shop from the claimant and slept in a roomnext door. The defendant then signed a new lease which stated that the premises would be used for 'business purposes', but only after being given an oral promise that he could sleep on the premises. The court held that there was a collateral contract that the defendant could sleep on the premises. The claimant's consideration was a promise not to enforce the term in the main contract that the premises would only be used for business and the defendant's consideration was a promise to sign the new lease.

In most cases the main contract and the collateral contract will be between the same two parties, but sometimes a third party may be involved.

Shanklin Pier Ltd v Detel Products Ltd (1951)

The claimants employed X to paint their pier and told X to buy the paint from the defendants. The claimants had earlier been told by the defendants that their paint would last ten years. In fact it lasted three months. It was held that although the main contract for the paint was between the defendants and X, there was a collateral contract between the claimants and the defendants, under which the claimants promised X would buy the paint from the defendants and the defendants promised the paint would last ten years. This was a breach of the collateral contract and the defendants were liable to pay the cost of repainting.

3 The parol evidence rule

3.1 The rule

A contract may be made in any form, but if it is a mixture of written and oral terms this causes a problem as to which of the oral terms are part of the contract. The *parol evidence rule* says that parol evidence cannot be admitted to add to, vary or contradict a written document. 'Parol' means any extrinsic evidence outside the contract. In most cases this will mean oral evidence, but the rule also covers outside written evidence, for example a letter written by one of the parties. The main reason for this rule is that without it, a written contract could easily be contradicted and would then be worthless. Also if the parties put the agreement into writing, they should be bound by that writing.

Although the rule originally helped to make contracts certain, it also led to injustice in many cases. The courts have therefore developed a large number of *exceptions* to the rule. The Law Commission recommended that the rule should be abolished (Working Paper No. 154, Cmnd 970 (1976)) but by 1986 concluded that it did not stop the courts accepting parol evidence if this was consistent with the intention of the parties.

3.2 Exceptions to the parol evidence rule

3.2.1 Not whole contract
If the written agreement was not intended to be the whole contract, parol evidence is admissible.

3.2.2 Evidence of validity
It only stops evidence being given about the content of the contract, not evidence about the validity of the contract, for example that one party has not provided consideration or that there has been a misrepresentation.

3.2.3 Implied terms
It only applies to express terms. If the contract does not mention something normally implied by law, parol evidence may be given to show it should be included.

3.2.4 Non-operation
Parol evidence may be given to show that the contract has not yet started to operate, for example a condition has not been fulfilled.

3.2.5 Custom
Parol evidence is allowed to show a local or trade custom. – *e.g. Baker's Dozen is 13*

3.2.6 Rectification
Equity allows a written contract to be rectified by parol evidence if the written agreement does not represent the true agreement.

3.2.7 Collateral contract
Parol evidence of a collateral contract is allowed.

4 Express and implied terms

4.1 Introduction
The terms of a contract may be classified in two main ways:

   (a) express or implied terms; and

   (b) warranties, conditions or innominate terms.

Neither group (a) nor group (b) is exclusive, so any individual term will be in both groups, for example, an implied condition.

4.2 Express terms

The express terms of a contract are those details which the parties have agreed on. They may be written or oral. If the whole contract is in writing, then it will be clear what the express terms are. The parol evidence rule applies and outside evidence is not allowed, unless it comes within one of the exceptions. If the contract is unwritten, then all the evidence will be oral evidence. It is also possible to have a contract which is partly written and partly oral.

EXAMPLE

Alice agrees to buy a television from Basil for £800, and Basil promises it has a 30-inch screen, stereo speakers and can receive satellite signals. The express terms are: the price of £800; that the television has a 30-inch screen; that the television has stereo speakers; that the television can receive satellite signals. *Implied term would be that it works!*

Even if it is clear what the express terms are, it may still be necessary to interpret what the words used mean. In *Thake v Maurice* (1984) a vasectomy described as 'irreversible' by a surgeon had to be interpreted in the light of surgical operations, which meant that virtually nothing can be given a 100 per cent guarantee, so the Court of Appeal held that it did not mean irreversible.

4.3 Implied terms

4.3.1 Introduction

As well as the express terms of the contract, there may be other terms which are implied and automatically become part of the contract, without the parties having to mention them. Such terms are equally as valid as express terms. Terms may be implied by custom, Act of Parliament or the courts. Originally implied terms were based on the intention of the parties, as matters the parties intended to put in, but it is now accepted that in many cases terms are implied simply by the law imposing obligations on parties.

4.3.2 *Terms implied by custom*   — *prob. not v. imp. nowadays*

If there is a local or trade custom this will be implied in the contract, unless it is inconsistent with the terms of the contract.

Hutton v Warren (1836) *— date*

The claimant tenant was given notice to quit his farm and had to leave before the harvest. It was held that a local custom could be implied, which gave the tenant a fair allowance for seed and labour. *Tillage, sowing + cultivation*

4.3.3 *Terms implied by statute*

Many terms originally implied in contracts by the courts, later came to be incorporated in statutes. These terms will automatically become part of the contract without the parties having to mention them, if the particular requirements of that statute are met.

EXAMPLES

Under the Sale of Goods Act 1979 where the seller sells goods in the course of a business, the goods must be of *satisfactory quality* and *fit for their purpose*.

Under the Supply of Goods and Services Act 1982 where services are supplied in the course of a business, it is implied that the supplier will carry out the service with *reasonable care* and *skill*.

Under the Supply of Goods (Implied Terms) Act 1973 it is implied that goods taken on hire purchase correspond with their *description*.

4.3.4 Terms implied by the courts ✕ *imp. ones*

At common law the courts have power to imply terms in contracts. The courts will not imply a term because the term seems reasonable or because it will improve the contract. They have used two *tests* to help them decide whether or not to imply a term. Both tests are essentially ways of determining the intention of the parties. The first test is one of *business efficacy*, that the term is needed to make the contract viable. How this test works can be seen in the following case.

The Moorcock (1889) *the hidden rock in the dock*

The claimant made a contract to unload his boat at the defendant's tidal dock. When the tide went out the boat was damaged on a rock at the bottom of the dock, which neither party realised was there. The contract did not provide the dock would be safe. It was held by the Court of Appeal that both parties would have agreed to an implied term that the dock should be safe; the claimant would want his boat undamaged; the defendant as a businessman would want the dock to be safe, otherwise he would not get any custom. Therefore such a term could be implied to give the contract business efficacy.

does it make sense? Reason presumed intention

The second test is the *officious bystander test.* "You don't want to do that"

This says that if, at the time the parties made the contract, an officious bystander had suggested an express provision, both parties would have said to him: 'Oh, of course'. A term could then be implied. *so obvious it goes without saying*

Both tests were applied in the following case.

Ashmore v Corporation of Lloyd's (No. 2) (1992)

A group of Lloyd's investors (known as 'names') made huge losses on insurance claims. They argued that there was an implied term in their contract with Lloyd's that Lloyd's should tell them about any matters which could affect their interests. The court applied the test of business efficacy, but contracts with Lloyd's could work without such a term. The officious bystander test was then applied, but clearly Lloyd's would not have said 'Oh, of course' to such a term. Therefore the claimant's claim failed.

The following case is the leading case on implied terms.

Liverpool City Council v Irwin (1976)

The defendants lived on the ninth storey of the claimants' tower block. The defendants did not have a formal tenancy agreement but had signed a list of conditions

£.50

which set out obligations for the tenants but none for the landlord. Because of vandalism the lifts were broken, stairs unlit and rubbish chutes blocked. The defendants withheld rent claiming that the claimants were in breach of an implied term to keep the property in good repair. The House of Lords held that rights could be implied in favour of the defendants to use of the facilities and that the claimants should keep them in 'reasonable' repair. The council had done this, bearing in mind the common nature of those facilities.

The officious bystander test was used the following case.

Wilson v Best Travel Ltd (1993)

The claimant booked a holiday in Greece through the defendant tour operator. He fell through a glass door in the hotel and was injured and claimed that (a) there was an implied term that the hotel would be reasonably safe or (b) there was a breach of a duty to provide services with care and skill under the Supply of Goods and Services Act 1982, s. 13. In applying the officious bystander test, the court said the defendant would not have said 'Oh, of course' to such a term, as the defendant had no control over the hotel. As the brochure had stated that the hotels were inspected, this service would have to be carried out with reasonable care and skill. But as the doors met Greek standards (although not British ones) the defendants had acted with care and skill. It was held that the claimant's claim failed.

A further example of a term being implied occurred in a recent case.

Wong Mee Wan v Kwan Kin Travel Services Ltd (1995)

The claimant's daughter lived in Hong Kong and booked a package tour of China with the first defendant, a Hong Kong travel company. When the party reached China they were joined by a tour guide employed by the second defendant, a Chinese travel company. The main part of the tour involved visiting and crossing a lake. When the party arrived the ferry had gone and they had to make the crossing in a speedboat owned by the third defendant. The official driver refused to make a third trip, so another employee took over. The employee drove too fast, crashed into another boat and the claimant's daughter was drowned. The claimant claimed breach of contract on behalf of her daughter's estate. It was held by the Privy Council that the first defendant had agreed to provide and not merely arrange the services in the programme. There was an implied term that the services would be provided with reasonable skill and care, even if some services were to be carried out by others. As no steps were taken to see that the driver was competent, this was a breach of that duty.

A term will not be implied if one of the parties to the contract does not know about the matter: *Spring* v *National Amalgamated Stevedores and Dockers Society* (1956).

5 Warranties, conditions and innominate terms

5.1 Introduction

The terms in a contract are not all of equal importance. Whether they are express or implied, they can also be divided into warranties, conditions and innominate (or intermediate) terms depending on their importance in the contract.

5.2 Warranties

A warranty means a *minor* term of the contract. This meaning must be distiguished from 'manufacturer's warranty' where it means a guarantee of goods. If a warranty is broken, then it will cause some loss but will not affect the main purpose of the contract. The only remedy available to the party suffering the loss is to claim damages; they cannot end the contract.

> EXAMPLE
>
> Alice buys a car from Bertie, which Bertie has told her has a radio fitted. When the car is delivered, Alice finds it does not have a radio. Alice cannot end the contract but may claim damages amounting to the cost of the radio.

The following case provides an example of a breach of *warranty*.

Bettini v *Gye* (1876)

The claimant agreed to sing in opera for the defendant and also agreed to turn up for rehearsals six days before the start of the engagement. When the claimant turned up two days before the start, the defendant refused to have him. The court held that the main purpose was to sing in opera and missing some of the rehearsals was merely a breach of a warranty. The defendant could not treat the contract as ended but could only claim damages.

5.3 Conditions

A condition is a *major* term of the contract. A condition has been described as something which 'goes to the root of the contract'. If a condition is broken, the party who suffers has a choice. They may either (a) treat the contract as ended, or (b) they may carry on with the contract. In either case they can claim damages. But note the effect of the Sale and Supply of Goods Act 1994 on a non-consumer buyer (see below).   *Can repudiate the contract*

> EXAMPLE
>
> Alice buys a car from Bertie's Garage, who agree to deliver it. Later Alice tries to start it and discovers that the engine has been taken out. Alice has a choice to end the contract or continue with it.

The classic example is provided by the following case.

Poussard v *Spiers and Pond* (1876)

The claimant agreed to take the leading role in an opera starting on 28 November, put on by the defendant. The claimant was ill and did not turn up until 4 December, by which time the defendants had taken on someone else. The claimant sued for breach of contract. The court held that it was vitally important the opera started well and the claimant had broken a condition so the defendants were entitled to end the contract.

Breach of a condition resulted in harsh consequences in the next case.

Union Eagle Ltd v Golden Achievement Ltd (1997)

The claimant agreed to buy a flat in Hong Kong from the defendant and paid 10 per cent deposit. The contract provided that time was to be of the essence, and that if the buyer failed to comply with any of the terms it would lose its deposit. The time for completion of the transaction was 5.00 p.m. on 30 September 1991, but the buyer was 10 minutes late. The seller refused to complete the sale and kept the deposit. The buyer claimed specific performance of the contract. It was held by the Privy Council that the buyer had failed to comply with a condition of the contract and was not entitled to specific performance. The contract had made express provision for this event and it brought certainty to the law to know that the contract would be followed.

The original Sale of Goods Act 1893 defined the terms 'warranties' and 'conditions' and provided the remedies of damages and repudiation respectively. After this it was believed that all contract terms could be classed as either warranties or conditions but this was changed by *Hong Kong Fir Shipping Co. Ltd* v *Kawasaki Kisen Kaisha Ltd* (1962) (see 5.4 below).

5.4 Innominate terms or intermediate

Usually it will be clear which terms are important and which are not, however it may sometimes be difficult to put a term in one of the traditional two categories. Such a term is called an *innominate* (no name) or *intermediate* (neither a condition nor a warranty) term. In the case of a breach of an innominate term, the court will ask the question: 'has the innocent party been deprived of substantially what it was intended they should get under the contract?' If the answer is 'yes', then the contract can be treated as ended; if the answer is 'no', then only damages can be claimed.

Hong Kong Fir Shipping Co. Ltd v Kawasaki Kisen Kaisha Ltd (1962)

The claimants owned a ship which they chartered to the defendants for 24 months in February 1957. The contract provided that the ship would be 'in every way fitted for ordinary cargo service'. But the engines were old and the staff incompetent and the ship was delayed for 20 weeks and would not be ready until September, so in June the defendants repudiated the contract for breach of 'condition'. The claimants claimed damages for wrongful repudiation. The Court of Appeal held that the clause was neither a condition nor a warranty but an intermediate term. The effect of the breach by the claimants meant that the ship was still available for 19 out of 24 months, so the defendants could not treat the contract as discharged, they could only claim damages. Diplock LJ said:

> There are, however, many contractual undertakings ... which cannot be categorised as being 'conditions' or 'warranties' ... Of such undertakings, all that can be predicated is that some breaches will and others will not, give rise to an event which will deprive the party not in default of substantially the whole benefit which it was intended he should obtain from the contract.

The courts do not keep to the prior classification of the term as a condition or a warranty, but adopt a 'wait and see' approach to examine the consequences of the breach. If the consequences are serious the term is treated as a condition, if the consequences are minor, it is treated as a warranty.

Cehave NV v *Bremer Handelsgesellschaft GmbH* (1975)

Buyers paid £100,000 for citrus pulp pellets to be shipped 'in good condition'. About one third of the shipment was damaged and the buyers rejected the goods. The sellers sold to a second buyer, who in turn resold to the original buyer for £33,000, who used them for the original purpose of feeding cattle. It was held by the Court of Appeal that the term about shipment 'in good condition' was neither a condition nor a warranty, but an intermediate term. As the buyers had used the pellets for their original purpose, the effect of the breach was not serious and the buyers had no right to reject the goods but could only claim damages.

5.5 How the courts currently approach terms

5.5.1 The intention of the parties

The courts may try to determine the intention of the parties about a particular term at the time they made the contract. If the parties have described the term as a *condition*, that is not necessarily conclusive, if a breach will only cause minor loss. *[looking at the intention of the parties, "condition" here really just meant "term".]*

Wickman Machine Tool Sales Ltd v *L. Schuler AG* (1973)

The defendants appointed the claimant as agent to sell for them for a period of four years, and it was provided that it was a 'condition' that the claimant would visit six customers each week. The claimant missed a few visits and the defendants ended the contract for breach of the 'condition'. The House of Lords held that the parties could not have intended that failing to make e.g., one visit out of a possible 1,400 should have such drastic results. The parties must have used the word 'condition' to mean a term and this breach did not entitle the defendants to end the contract.

Consequently, if the parties wish a term to be a condition, it is not enough to call it a condition, they should also provide that breach of that condition gives a right to end the contract.

The intention of the parties may be gleaned not only from the language of the contract but the circumstances. *[Reintroduction of certainty]*

The Mihalis Angelos (1970)

This concerned the charter of a ship which was stated to be ready to load on 1 July. In fact it was not ready until 23 July. The Court of Appeal held that in the charter of ships, the time stated is traditionally very important and this clause was a condition, so the charterer could repudiate the contract.

5.5.2 The effects of the breach

The courts instead of looking to see the intention of the parties may examine the particular breach to see if the results are serious or not. An example of this approach is the *Hong Kong* case at 5.4 above.

[So spell out the remedy in the contract for the things you see as crucial to the contract]

The courts are faced with balancing the opposing claims of *certainty* by determining what the terms are in advance and *flexibility* by waiting to see what type of breach occurs. In particular trades, it is important for the parties to achieve certainty and the courts have recognised this.

6 Terms dealing with secondary obligations

6.1 Introduction

The obligations under a contract may be divided into *primary* and *secondary* obligations. The *primary* obligations set out what each party is to do. If a party fails to do what has been agreed, that is a breach of contract and will give rise to *secondary* obligations to pay damages. These secondary obligations may be implied by common law or statute. The common law provides that if a party breaks the primary obligations under a contract, they must pay compensation (damages), which will be fixed by the courts. The parties may provide in the contract for the payment of damages, in the event of a breach of primary obligations. These clauses are known as *agreed damages, liquidated damages* or *penalty* clauses. One reason for using them is to save going to court. The courts have drawn an important distinction between liquidated damages and penalties.

6.2 Liquidated damages clauses

This is a genuine attempt to estimate the loss suffered if one party breaks the contract. The courts treat such a clause as valid and the amount stated is followed, whether the actual loss is greater or smaller.

Cellulose Acetate Silk Co. Ltd v *Widnes Foundry (1925) Ltd* (1933)

The defendants agreed to build a factory for the claimants by a certain date and to pay £20 a week for every week they were late. The defendants were 30 weeks late and the claimants claimed their actual loss which was £5,850. The House of Lords held that the sum of £20 a week was a genuine estimate of loss, and so it was a liquidated damages clause and was binding. The defendants only had to pay £600.

6.3 Penalty clauses   *Objective Test*

A penalty clause is an amount payable by the party who breaks the contract. It can be seen as a threat hanging over them to make them perform their part of the contract. If a clause is a penalty clause, it can only be enforced up to the amount of actual loss.

6.4 Distinguishing between liquidated damages and penalties

In deciding whether a provision in the contract is a liquidated damages or a penalty clause, the courts will determine the intention of the parties by interpreting the contract, i.e., was the aim to ensure performance or a genuine attempt to assess damages for breach? The courts apply an objective test at the time the contract is made. Rules for guidance in making this assessment were laid down by Lord Dunedin

Guidelines / Presumptions

in *Dunlop Pneumatic Tyre Co. Ltd* v *New Garage and Motor Co. Ltd* (1915). These rules are only presumptions and may be changed by evidence to the contrary. Neither are they exhaustive and other factors may be taken into consideration.

(a) If parties use the words *penalty* or *liquidated damages* this is not conclusive.

(b) If a large amount is payable compared with the possible loss, it will be a penalty.

(c) If the breach consists of not paying an amount of money and the clause provides for payment of a larger amount, it is a penalty.

(d) If a single amount is payable for serious and minor losses, it is a penalty.

(e) If estimating the loss is very difficult, the sum stated may still be liquidated damages.

How these rules have been applied by the courts can be illustrated by contrasting the following two cases.

Dunlop Pneumatic Tyre Co. Ltd v *New Garage and Motor Co. Ltd* (1915)

The claimant supplied tyres to the defendant, who agreed not to tamper with the marks, not to sell below list price, not to export without consent and to pay £5 'liquidated damages' for each breach. The defendant sold a tyre below list price and the claimant claimed the amount of liquidated damages. The House of Lords set out the above guidelines and applied them to the case. It was held that although the clause might seem to be a penalty, because one sum was payable for several breaches, in these circumstances precise estimation of loss was difficult and as this was a genuine attempt, it was a liquidated damages clause.

Ford Motor Co. (England) Ltd v *Armstrong* (1915)

The defendant retailer was supplied by the claimant and agreed not to sell the claimant's cars or parts below list price, not to sell to other dealers, not to exhibit without consent and to pay £250 for every breach as being 'the agreed damage which the manufacturer will sustain'. The Court of Appeal held that the same sum was payable for different kinds of breach and it was a substantial amount, therefore it must be a penalty.

The Competition Act 1998 prohibits any agreements to fix selling prices.

6.5 Effect of the Unfair Terms in Consumer Contracts Regulations 1999

A clause which requires a consumer to pay compensation which is out of proportion, may be invalid under the above regulations.

UCTA 1977 *(handwritten)*

n clauses

:tion

Protecting one party against the other the other Eng. law doesn't like (handwritten)

1.1 Use of exclusion clauses

An exclusion clause is a term in a contract which *excludes* one of the parties from liability for breach of contract. Under the principle of freedom of contract, whereby parties were free to make whatever agreements they liked, these clauses flourished. But with the development of standard form contracts, especially in consumer trans-actions, the parties were not in equal bargaining positions and the courts devised ways of restricting the effect of exclusion clauses. A number of statutes were also passed to control the use of these clauses, the most important one being the Unfair Contract Terms Act 1977. More recently the Unfair Terms in Consumer Contracts Regulations 1999 have replaced the earlier 1994 Regulations which implemented the European Directive on unfair terms in consumer contracts. The regulations apply only to consumer contracts.

Exclusion clauses play a useful role in determining the obligations and risks which each party accepts in a contract and this remains true if the parties are in an equal bargaining position. But if they are not in an equal position, such clauses are usually used to exploit the weaker party. In spite of the stance taken by the courts in restricting the effect of exclusion clauses, and the statutory restrictions, the ingenuity of draftsmen in excluding or limiting liability continues to exercise the judges.

This section will firstly examine the rules developed by the courts at common law, which apply to all exclusion clauses. Secondly it will examine the effect of statutes on these clauses, particularly the Unfair Contract Terms Act 1977 which applies to only some types of contracts. Thirdly, the new regulations will be examined and their impact assessed.

1.2 Types of exclusion clause — 4 types *(handwritten)*

There are a wide variety of exclusion clauses, the main types being the following.

1.2.1 An *exclusion* (or *exemption*) clause

This exempts a party to a contract from liability for breaches of contract caused by them.

> EXAMPLE
>
> Red Rose Garden Centre sells a lawnmower to Violet who signs a contract containing the following clause: 'the seller is not liable for any defects in the goods supplied'.

1.2.2 A *limitation* clause

This limits the liability of a party to a fixed amount, if they commit a breach of contract.

EXAMPLE

As in the above example, if the clause said: 'Liability is limited to £100 for any losses arising from breach of contract by the seller'.

1.2.3 A disclaimer

This is a clause which provides that a particular obligation does not arise under a contract. In *Harris* v *Wyre Forest DC* (1989) it was argued that the disclaimer clause prevented a duty arising, but the House of Lords ruled that such clauses could not be given this effect, as they would get round the Unfair Contract Terms Act 1977. Disclaimers were within s. 13, Unfair Contract Terms Act 1977 and had to be reasonable.

EXAMPLE

As in the example in 1.2.1 above, if the contract of sale said: 'The seller disclaims all responsibility for the quality of the goods supplied'.

1.2.4 An indemnity clause

This provides that one party to the contract may reclaim any damages he has to pay arising out of the contract, from the other party. So although liability is initially accepted, the effect of such a clause is that the other party bears the loss.

[handwritten margin note: Indemnity]

EXAMPLE

As in the example in 1.2.1 above if the contract provided: 'Violet shall indemnify Red Rose Garden Centre for any losses arising for any reason whatsoever, from the use of the lawnmower'. If the lawnmower was faulty and exploded, damaging property of Nettle (Violet's neighbour) and Nettle sued Red Rose Garden Centre for negligence, any damages paid by Red Rose Garden Centre could be reclaimed from Violet.

Generally the rules which apply to the above type of clause are the same but there are some important differences, for example, limitation clauses are treated less strictly than exclusion clauses.

2 Common law rules

2.1 Introduction

The courts have three hurdles which have to be crossed before they recognise an exclusion clause as being valid. First, the clause must be incorporated as a term of the contract; secondly, it must cover the breach which occurs; thirdly, it may fail for a number of other reasons, like misrepresentation. These hurdles will be examined in turn.

2.2 Incorporation

A party who wishes to rely on an exclusion clause must show it is part of the contract and this can be done in any *one* of three ways:

(a) signature;

(b) notice;

(c) course of dealing.

2.2.1 Signature

If someone *signs* a contract, it is binding on them, even if they do not read it. Any exclusion clauses in the contract will also be binding. If someone reads a contract which they do not understand but still sign, it will be binding.

L'Estrange v F. Graucob Ltd (1934)

The claimant bought a cigarette machine for her café from the defendant and signed a sales agreement, in very small print, without reading it. The agreement provided that 'any express or implied condition, statement or warranty . . . is hereby excluded'. The machine did not work properly and the claimant sued for breach of contract. It was held that because the claimant had signed the agreement it was binding on her and her claim failed.

   Note that this case must now be read in the light of the Unfair Contract Terms Act 1977, but would the result be different?

2.2.2 Notice

If nothing is signed, an exclusion clause may still become part of the contract through *notice*. This may be contained in a document given to a party or a poster put up where the contract is made. Such a notice will only become part of the contract if the other party knows about it *or* they have been given 'reasonable' notice of it. The first situation is relatively clear but in the second case a number of factors are taken into account in deciding if 'reasonable' notice has been given.

2.2.2.1 The kind of document   The exclusion clause will only be effective if it is contained in a *contractual document*, that is, a document which a party would expect to contain the terms of a contract.

Chapelton v Barry UDC (1940)

The claimant hired a deckchair for 2d (1p) and was given a ticket, which he put in his pocket without reading. On the back of the ticket it stated that the council was not liable for any damage arising from use. When he sat on the chair it collapsed and he was injured. It was held that the claimant did not expect the ticket to contain terms, it was merely a receipt and not a contractual document, so the council was liable.

   This is in contrast to someone who deposits luggage at a left luggage office, who would expect the ticket which he received for his luggage to contain the terms on which items could be left.

2.2.2.2 The type of liability   The more *unusual* the liability imposed by the clause, the more the party relying on it has to do to bring it to the other's notice.

Thornton v Shoe Lane Parking Ltd (1971)

The claimant drove into the defendant's car park and was given a ticket by an automatic machine, which stated that it was issued subject to conditions displayed inside

[handwritten margin notes: "Must show exclusion clause", "how was V badly injured", "grevous exclusion clause", "shift in law."]

the car park. One of these conditions excluded liability for damage to vehicles or injury to customers, this latter being very unusual. The claimant was injured due partly to the defendant's negligence. The Court of Appeal held that because the clause was so unusual an explicit warning was needed. 'In order to give sufficient notice, it would need to be printed in red ink with a red hand pointing to it—or something equally startling' (Lord Denning).

AEG Ltd v *Logic Resource Ltd* (1995)

The buyer sent an order for cathode ray tubes to the seller and received a confirmation, which stated at the bottom, 'ORDERS ARE SUBJECT TO OUR CONDITIONS OF SALE—FOR EXTRACT SEE REVERSE'. On the back it set out five conditions and stated that the others were available on request. A term which was not on the back excluded all conditions and warranties, although it gave a warranty that the goods were free of defects caused by faulty materials or bad workmanship. It also required the buyer to pay for returning faulty goods. It was held by the Court of Appeal that because this term excluded the implied terms in the Sale of Goods Act and required the buyer to return defective goods, it was an onerous term. It had not been drawn to the buyer's attention and was not incorporated in the contract.

2.2.2.3 When the notice was given Notice of the exclusion clause must be given *before* or *at the time the contract is made.*

Olley v *Marlborough Court Ltd* (1949)

The claimant booked into the defendant's hotel. While staying there, her mink coat was stolen from her room. A notice on the back of the bedroom door excluded liability for loss of items not deposited in the safe. It was held by the Court of Appeal that the contract was made at the reception desk and new terms could not be brought in later, so the exclusion notice was ineffective.

Giving a person a ticket which refers to conditions can be treated as valid notice as long as those conditions are actually available.

If the court considers that *reasonable steps* have been taken to bring the exclusion notice to the attention of the other party, then the notice is effective, even if the other party does not know about it.

Thompson v *London, Midland and Scottish Railway Co.* (1930)

The claimant's niece bought her an excursion ticket, on the front of which it said 'See Back' and on the back it said 'Issued subject to the conditions set out in the timetable'. These conditions excluded liability for injury. The claimant stepped out of the train before it reached the platform and was injured. It was held that even though the claimant was illiterate, she had been given reasonable notice of the terms, as she should have asked her niece to read them to her. Therefore she was not entitled to compensation.

[handwritten margin note: "she can only ask her if she knew there was a condition there."]

2.2.3 Course of dealing

If nothing is signed and no notice is given, an exclusion clause may still become part of the contract if there has been a *consistent course of dealing* between the parties. As long as reasonable notice has been given during the course of dealing, it does not matter that the other party has not read the terms. It is important that the dealings are 'consistent' in the sense that notice is usually given, even though it may not have been given on a particular occasion. If notice is sometimes given, but sometimes not, this will not be consistent.

Hollier v Rambler Motors (AMC) Ltd (1972)

The claimant had used the defendant garage three or four times over five years and on some occasions had signed a contract, which excluded the defendants from liability for damage by fire. On this occasion nothing was signed and the claimant's car was badly damaged in a fire. It was held that there was not a regular course of dealing, therefore the defendants were liable. The court referred to *Hardwick Game Farm* v *Suffolk Agricultural Poultry Producers' Association* (1969) in which more than 100 notices had been given over a period of three years, which did amount to a course of dealing.

Even if there is no course of dealing, an exclusion clause may still become part of the contract through *trade usage* or *custom*.

British Crane Hire Corporation Ltd v Ipswich Plant Hire Ltd (1974)

The claimants supplied a crane to the defendants on the basis of a telephone contract made quickly, without mentioning conditions of hire. The claimants later sent a copy of their conditions but before the defendants could sign them, the crane sank in marshy ground. The conditions, which were similar to those used by all firms in the business, said that the hirer should indemnify the owner for all expenses in connection with use. It was held that as the defendants knew the conditions were in common use in the industry, the claimants could assume that if the defendants accepted the crane, they accepted the conditions and therefore the defendants were liable for the expense involved in recovering the crane.

2.3 Construction

If the first hurdle of incorporation is overcome, the courts will construe or interpret the words used to see if they cover the particular breach that has occurred. The main rules of construction are the contra proferentem rule, the main purpose rule and what is now the defunct rule of fundamental breach.

2.3.1 The contra proferentem rule

This states that if there is any doubt or ambiguity about an exemption clause, it will be construed *against* the party relying on it.

Houghton v Trafalgar Insurance Co. Ltd (1953)

The claimant's motor insurance policy provided that the defendant insurers would not be liable, if the claimant carried an 'excess load'. The claimant had an accident while carrying six people in a five seater car. The Court of Appeal held that the term 'excess load' could mean either too many people or too much weight. It was given the latter meaning, which meant that the defendants were liable on the policy.

2.3.2 The main purpose rule

The court looks at the whole contract to determine the *main purpose* and anything inconsistent with this, including exclusion clauses, is rejected.

Glynn v *Margetson & Co.* (1893)

Carriers agreed to take oranges from Malaga to Liverpool under a contract which allowed the ship to call at any port in Europe or Africa. The ship sailed 350 miles east from Malaga to pick up another cargo. When it arrived in Liverpool the oranges had gone bad. The House of Lords held that the main purpose was to deliver a perishable cargo of oranges to Liverpool and in the light of this the wide words of the clause could be ignored and the ship could only call at ports *en route*. Therefore the carriers were liable.

2.3.3 Fundamental breach

It should be made clear that the doctrine of fundamental breach no longer operates. It provided that if a party put a clause in a contract excluding their liability for a fundamental breach of contract (i.e. very serious breach), then the exclusion clause was invalid. This doctrine was followed for a number of years but doubt was cast on it in the *Suisse Atlantique* case (1966) when the House of Lords made an *obiter* statement that an exclusion clause is not automatically invalid if it covers a fundamental breach of contract. They said it was a matter of construction of the clause, i.e., did it cover the event which had happened? If so, then the exclusion clause should be valid. Even after this the courts continued to apply the doctrine of fundamental breach but the matter was finally decided in the following case.

Photo Production Ltd v *Securicor Transport Ltd* (1980)

The claimants employed the defendants to guard their factory. One night the defendants' employee deliberately started a fire which burned down the factory, causing £615,000 worth of damage. A clause in the contract provided that: 'Under no circumstances shall Securicor be responsible for any injurious act or default by any employee . . . unless such act or default could have been foreseen and avoided by the exercise of due diligence on the part of Securicor'. The claimants sued for breach of contract and the Court of Appeal decided that this was a fundamental breach of contract by the defendants and they could not rely on the clause. The House of Lords held that whether an exclusion clause could cover a fundamental breach was a matter of construction. Here the clause was clear and wide enough to cover what had happened, therefore it was valid and the defendants were not liable.

2.4 Other reasons for failure of an exclusion clause

2.4.1 Introduction

If an exclusion clause clears the two hurdles in 2.3.1 and 2.3.2 above, it may still fail for a number of reasons including misrepresentation, the fact that it is overridden by an oral promise, that a third party may be relying on it or that there is a collateral contract.

2.4.2 Misrepresentation

If someone signs a document containing an exclusion clause, it will not be binding if they were induced to sign by fraud or misrepresentation.

Curtis v Chemical Cleaning and Dyeing Co. (1951)

The claimant took a wedding dress with sequins on to the defendants for cleaning. She was asked to sign a form which excluded the defendants from liability for 'any damage howsoever arising'. She asked what it meant and was told it excluded the defendants from liability for damage to the sequins, so she signed it. The dress was returned stained. It was held by the Court of Appeal that the defendants could not rely on the clause as the claimant had only signed because of the misrepresentation and they were liable to pay damages.

2.4.3 Overriding oral promise

If an oral term of the contract contradicts the exclusion clause, then the exclusion clause will be ignored. Such a situation occurred in *J. Evans & Son (Portsmouth) Ltd* v *Andrea Merzario Ltd* (1976) where an oral assurance that goods would be carried inside a ship was part of the contract and was held to override the written exclusion clause.

2.4.4 Third parties

A third party is someone apart from the two parties to the contract. Under the rule of privity someone not a party to the contract could not benefit from it and consequently could not rely on an exclusion clause in the contract.

Adler v Dickson (1954)

The claimant was a passenger on a P & O ship under a contract which excluded the liability of employees for negligence. The claimant fell off the gangplank due to the negligence of employees and sued the captain. It was held by the Court of Appeal that the captain was a third party as regards the contract between the claimant and P & O and could not rely on the exclusion clause in that contract.

Following the passing of the Contracts (Rights of Third Parties) Act 1999, the third party in the above case would be able to take advantage of the exclusion clause if the requirements of the Act were met.

2.4.5 Collateral contracts

This is a separate contract alongside the main contract.

Andrews v Hopkinson (1956)

The claimant saw a car in the defendant's garage, which the defendant described as follows: 'It's a good little bus. I would stake my life on it'. The claimant agreed to take it on hire-purchase and the defendant sold it to a finance company who made a hire-purchase agreement with the claimant. When the car was delivered the claimant signed a note saying he was satisfied about its condition. Shortly afterwards, due to a defect in the steering, the car crashed. The claimant was stopped from suing the finance company because of the delivery note but he sued the defendant. It was held that there was a collateral contract with the defendant who promised the car was in good condition and in return the claimant promised to make the hire purchase agreement.

In *Barry* v *Heathcote Ball & Co. Ltd* (2001) the Court of Appeal explained that at an auction 'without reserve', the main contract was between the seller of the goods and the bidder. In addition there was a collateral contract between the auctioneer and the bidder under which the bidder promised to bid and the auctioneer promised to sell to the highest bidder.

2.5 The battle of the forms

A problem arises if *one* party sends a form saying that the contract is made on those terms but the *second* party accepts by sending a form with their own terms on and stating that the contract is on the second party's terms. The 'rule of thumb' here is that the contract will be made on the last set of terms sent.

British Road Services Ltd v *Arthur V. Crutchley & Co. Ltd* (1968)
BRS delivered whisky to AC's warehouse. BRS's driver gave AC a delivery note which contained BRS' conditions. AC stamped the note 'Received under AC's conditions'. The whisky was stolen. It was held that AC stamping the delivery note was a counter offer which was accepted by BRS handing over the whisky. The contract was made on AC's conditions.

Commercial reality is not always as simple as this analysis: see the case of *Butler Machine Tool Co. Ltd* v *Ex-Cell-O Corporation (England) Ltd* (1979).

In a recent case the court said that neither party's terms had been incorporated in the contract.

Hertford Foods Ltd v *Lidl UK GmbH* (2001)
HF made a contract to supply L with tins of corned beef. The contract was made informally over the phone. HF sent a letter to confirm the price and delivery dates but L sent its 'Fixed Quantity Contract' which HF said was not acceptable. L ordered certain quantities of corned beef and HF made some deliveries but because of problems in Brazil where HF obtained its supplies it could not fulfill the orders. L then said it would obtain further supplies and under its own terms, HF would have to pay for them. HF argued that under its standard terms it was not liable if failure was due to 'any cause beyond the seller's reasonable control'. It was held by the Court of Appeal that neither party had made it clear that its own terms applied. Although a contract existed, it was not made on the terms of either party. HF could not therefore rely on the *force majeure* clause in its standard terms and was in breach of contract for failure to deliver.

3 Statutory rules dealing with exclusion clauses

Although statutes have been used to control exclusion clauses since the Canals and Railways Act 1854, they have mainly dealt with particular uses and it was not until the

Unfair Contract Terms Act 1977 that general rules were laid down. Examples of particular statutes include the following.

3.1 Transport Act 1962, s. 43(7) (now dealt with by UCTA 1977)

British Rail shall not carry passengers on terms excluding or limiting their liability for death or bodily injury.

3.2 Public Passenger Vehicles Act 1981, s. 29

In contracts to carry passengers on public service vehicles any attempt to exclude liability for death or injury is invalid.

3.3 Road Traffic Act 1988, s. 149

Any agreement between the user of a vehicle and a passenger, restricting liability to the passenger, is invalid.

3.4 Fair Trading Act 1973, Part II

The Secretary of State for Trade has power to prohibit prejudicial trade practices and in exercising this power has made the use of exclusion clauses in contracts to supply goods or services to consumers a criminal offence (Consumer Transactions (Restrictions on Statements) Order 1976, amended 1978).

3.5 Consumer Protection Act 1987, s. 7

Liability for damage caused by defective products cannot be excluded or limited.

4 The Unfair Contract Terms Act 1977

4.1 To what does the Act apply?

The Act applies to both contract and tort. Generally, it only applies to *business liability* but there are some exceptions to this.
   The Act does *not* apply to:

(a) insurance contracts;

(b) the sale of land;

(c) intellectual property, e.g. copyright;

(d) contracts relating to companies;

(e) the sale of shares;

(f) the carriage of goods by sea.

4.2 Important definitions

There are some important definitions in the Act which need to be examined before looking at the main provisions.

4.2.1 Business liability

The Act applies mainly to 'business liability', which is defined as liability arising from things done in the course of a business or from the occupation of business premises (s. 1(3)). Business includes professions and the activities of Government departments, local and public authorities (s. 14). The exceptions are sale of goods, supply of goods and hire-purchase contracts where the Act also applies to private contracts.

4.2.2 Dealing as a consumer

It is provided by s. 12 that a party 'deals as consumer' if:

(a) he does not make the contract in the course of a business; and

(b) the other party does make the contract in the course of a business; and

(c) if goods are supplied, they are a type ordinarily supplied for private use.

EXAMPLES

Ali, a private individual, buys a word processor from Office Equipment Ltd—a consumer sale.

Chris, an accountant, buys a desk for his business from Office Equipment Ltd—not a consumer sale as both parties are acting in the course of a business.

Daniel, a private individual, buys some industrial shelving from Office Equipment Ltd—not a consumer sale as such goods are not normally bought for private use.

Eve, a private individual, buys a word processor through a private advertisement in the local newspaper—not a consumer sale, as neither party is acting in business.

A sale may be a consumer sale even if the buyer is a business. It will be outside s. 12 only if the purchase is an integral part of the business.

R & B Customs Brokers Co. Ltd v *United Dominions Trust Ltd* (1988)

The claimant company bought a car for a director to be used for business and private use. It had bought cars two or three times before. The contract excluded the implied conditions about merchantable quality. The car leaked badly. The Court of Appeal held that buying a car was not an 'integral' part of the claimant's business of shipbroking and to be integral the claimants would have to buy cars regularly. This was a consumer sale and the implied conditions could not be excluded, therefore the defendants were liable.

But note the decision in *Stevenson* v *Rogers* (1999) in respect of s. 14(2) of the Sale of Goods Act 1979; see *Sale of Goods Act 1979*, 6.1 below. A buyer at an *auction* can never deal as a consumer (Unfair Contract Terms Act 1977, s. 12(2)).

4.2.3 Types of exclusion clause

A party to a contract may try to disguise an exclusion clause, even though the effect of such a clause is to exclude liability. Section 13 tries to stop this and forbids the following.

(a) Restrictive or onerous conditions.

EXAMPLE

Goods must be returned post paid to the supplier.

(b) Excluding or restricting the remedies.

EXAMPLE

Damages shall not exceed the cost of the goods.

(c) Excluding or restricting evidence.

EXAMPLE

Only written evidence will be accepted.

4.2.4 Negligence
Under s. 1(1) this covers:

(a) failing to take reasonable care in carrying out a contract; or

(b) failing to meet a common law duty of care (i.e., tort); or

(c) failing to meet the duty of care under the Occupiers' Liability Act 1957.

4.2.5 The test of reasonableness
Some exclusion clauses are subject to a test of reasonableness under the Unfair Contract Terms Act 1977 and if they do not pass this test, they are void. Exclusion clauses in contracts must be fair and reasonable having regard to the circumstances which were or ought to have been in the minds of the parties when the contract was made (s. 11(1)).

In deciding whether an exclusion clause is *reasonable*, the matters set out in schedule 2 to the 1977 Act (see below) must be taken into account. These are only guidelines, however, and are not meant to be exclusive, so other factors may be relevant.

(a) *The relative bargaining strength of the parties*

EXAMPLE

If a contract between ICI plc and an individual contains an exclusion clause, that is evidence it is unreasonable.

(b) *Did the customer receive an inducement to agree to the exclusion or could the customer have made the contract somewhere else without the exclusion?*

EXAMPLE

If a buyer gets the price of goods reduced in return for agreeing to the exclusion.

If the customer could make a similar contract somewhere else, without the exclusion clause, this is evidence that the exclusion is reasonable because the customer had a choice.

(c) *Whether the customer knew or ought to have known of the exclusion*

EXAMPLE

If the other party has made the customer aware of the clause, that is evidence it is reasonable.

(*d*) *If the clause excludes liability unless some condition is fulfilled, whether meeting that condition is practicable.*

EXAMPLE

If the seller of a car provides that complaints must be made within 48 hours, this would not be practicable.

(*e*) *Whether the goods were made or adapted for the buyer.*

EXAMPLE

If goods have been made specially to the buyer's design then it is reasonable for the maker to exclude his liability for defects not arising from manufacture.

An example of how the test of reasonableness works can be seen in the following case. Although the events took place before the Unfair Contract Terms Act 1977 became law, it is based on a similar test under the Sale of Goods Act 1979.

George Mitchell (Chesterhall) Ltd v *Finney Lock Seeds Ltd* (1983)

The claimant, a farmer in a small way of business, bought cabbage seeds from the defendants, a national seed company. When the seeds grew, the plants consisted of just a few loose leaves and were unfit for human consumption. The claimant claimed £61,513 loss of profit. The defendants then pointed out a clause on the back of the invoice supplied with the seeds, which limited liability to the cost of the seeds at £192. The House of Lords held that the clause was part of the agreement because it had been used for many years in such contracts, also the wording was clear and it covered this event. The clause had, however, been imposed by a large company, without negotiation with the National Farmers' Union; the defendants could insure against the risk; the defendants could have tested the seeds but the farmers could not tell how the seeds would develop until the crop had grown; and most important was evidence that the defendants had paid compensation above the price of seed in cases where they thought a claim was genuine, which was an admission that the clause was unfair. On this evidence the clause was unreasonable and the claimant was entitled to compensation.

Further guidance on what is meant by reasonableness was given in the following cases.

Smith v *Eric S. Bush* (1989)

A house buyer applied to a building society, which engaged a valuer to value the property. The valuer negligently failed to check that a chimney breast which had been removed was properly supported. The buyer was told to get his own survey. The buyer was given a copy of the valuation report, which contained an exclusion clause, and in reliance on it bought the house. When the chimney collapsed he sued the valuer. The House of Lords held that a valuer who valued a house, knowing the valuation would be relied on by the purchaser, owed a duty to the purchaser to carry out the valuation with care and skill particularly as he knew the purchaser was paying for the report. In determining if the exclusion clause was reasonable the court took into account the fact the purchaser could not object to the clause; the purchaser was buying a modest house and could not afford a second survey; the task of the valuer was fairly simple and excluding liability was unreasonable; the valuer was better able to bear the loss. In all the circumstances the clause was unreasonable and invalid.

Overseas Medical Supplies Ltd v *Orient Transport Services Ltd* (1999)
OTS made a contract to transport goods for OMS. OMS had asked OTS to insure the goods but this was not done. A clause in the contract provided that if the transporter (OTS) arranged insurance they did so as agent of the customer and if they failed to arrange insurance, liability was limited to £600. The goods were lost and OMS sued. It was held by the Court of Appeal that OMS were not in a strong bargaining position as regards the insurance and it was unclear from the conditions whether they applied if OTS failed to insure, particularly as OMS had paid extra for insurance. The clause was unreasonable and OTS were liable for the cost of the goods.

4.2.6 Limitation clauses
The courts have drawn a distinction between *exclusion* clauses and *limitation* clauses.

Ailsa Craig Fishing Co. Ltd v *Malvern Fishing Co. Ltd* (1983)
ACF engaged Securicor to watch their ship in Aberdeen harbour. The contract provided that Securicor's liability was 'not to exceed £1,000 in respect of any one claim not related to fire or theft'. One night Securicor's guard did not bother patrolling and ACF's ship fouled MF's ship and both ships sank. The House of Lords held that a clause limiting rather than excluding liability should not be judged by the 'specially exacting standards' applied to exclusion clauses. Here the clause was clear and Securicor's liability was limited to the amount stated.

The Unfair Contract Terms Act 1977 provides in s. 11(4) that in determining whether a limitation clause is reasonable, apart from the matters in schedule 2, the following should also be taken into account:

(a) the resources available to a party; and

(b) whether insurance cover was available.

EXAMPLE

If one party is wealthy, this is evidence that such a clause is unreasonable. If insurance is not available, this is evidence the clause is reasonable.

4.3 The main provisions of the Unfair Contract Terms Act 1977

4.3.1 Death and injury
A person cannot exclude or restrict his business liability for death or injury resulting from negligence (s. 2(1)). The negligence may be in performing a contract or in tort.

EXAMPLE

As Alice is parking her car in the car park at Basil's public house the car goes into a pothole and Alice is injured. A notice at the entrance states: 'No liability for injury to persons using these premises'. This notice is invalid and of no effect.

4.3.2 Damage to property

A person cannot exclude his business liability for damage to property resulting from negligence, unless the term is reasonable (s. 2(2)). The negligence may be in performing a contract or in tort.

EXAMPLE

As in the above example, if the notice stated: 'No liability for damage to vehicles' and only Alice's car was damaged when it went into the pothole, then the exclusion notice must be reasonable.

4.3.3 Breach of contract

A clause excluding liability for breach of contract, or allowing substantially different performance from that expected, or no performance, must be reasonable when one party deals as a consumer (s. 3).

EXAMPLE

Alice buys a bicycle from Basil's shop and the contract allows Basil to substitute any model for the make chosen by the customer—this must be reasonable.

Such a clause must also be reasonable when the parties are dealing on written standard terms.

EXAMPLE

Two businessmen make an agreement using a standard form contract—any exclusion clause must be reasonable.

St Albans City and District Council v ICL (1996)

The claimants bought computer software from the defendants under a contract made on the defendants' standard terms, which limited liability to £100,000. The software was faulty and this resulted in overstating the number of people resident in the area for council tax purposes by nearly 3,000. As a result, in 1990–91 (i) the claimants set the community charge too low and lost £484,000, which they would otherwise have collected; and (ii) because of the higher number of payers Hertfordshire County Council charged the claimants more, in the precept issued against the district council (£685,000). The claimants sued the defendants for breach of contract and claimed damages of £1.3m. It was held in the High Court that as the parties were of unequal bargaining power, a small council and a large international company, and the defendants were insured for £50m, this clause was unreasonable. In the Court of Appeal the defendants argued, first, that the claimants did not deal on the defendants' written standard terms because the claimants had negotiated the terms before making the contract. The Court said that 'deals' means 'makes a deal' so that the standard terms did apply. Secondly, the defendants argued that the limitation clause was reasonable. The Court said that the clause was unreasonable for the reasons given by the trial judge. As regards the damages claim, the Court made a distinction between (a) the increased precept payment: the claimants could recover damages for the increased payment, as otherwise it would have to reclaim that amount from its charge payers, who would lose out; and (b) the community charge: the claimants could not recover damages for this because they had charged an extra amount in 1991–92 to cover the amount lost in 1990–91. The charge payers would have had to pay this in 1990–91 but for the defendants' breach of contract. Therefore the damages were reduced by £484,000.

Further guidance was given on the test of reasonableness in the following cases.

Overland Shoes Ltd v *Schenkers Ltd* (1998)

S made a contract to transport a cargo of shoes for O, from China to England. The standard form contract of the British International Freight Association was used, which contained a clause stating that the customer was to pay S all sums due without any deductions. S claimed freight charges and O wished to set off VAT owed to them by S. This clause was caught by s. 13 of the Unfair Contract Terms Act 1977 and had to satisfy the test of reasonableness. It was held at first instance that the clause was reasonable. In confirming this decision the Court of Appeal said that the clause was widely used throughout the world and had been negotiated by representatives of all parties.

Watford Electronics Ltd v *Sanderson CFL Ltd* (2001)

The claimants made a contract to buy computer software from the defendants. The contract was negotiated between the parties and contained some of the defendant's standard conditions, which were added to the contract. These excluded liability for any indirect or consequential losses; limited liability to the price of the contract (£104,596); and included a clause which stated that the contract was the 'entire agreement' and did not include any statements or representations. The software did not work properly and the claimants had to buy another system from another supplier. The claimants then sued for breach of contract and claimed £5.5m including replacement costs and loss of profits. At first instance the court said that the contract was within s. 3 of the Unfair Contract Terms Act 1977 and even though some changes had been made it could still be regarded as being made on 'standard terms'. In the circumstances the terms were unreasonable. On appeal the Court of Appeal stated that the contract had been negotiated between two experienced businessmen, the parties were of equal bargaining power, the limitation clause had been negotiated and in fact the claimants used a similar one in their own terms. In all the circumstances the clauses were reasonable and the claimants were not entitled to damages.

4.3.4 Sale of goods and hire-purchase

Section 12 of the Sale of Goods Act 1979 provides that the seller of goods has a right to sell them. A party to a contract cannot exclude his liability for breach of s. 12 (s. 6(1), Unfair Contract Terms Act 1977). This applies to all sales of goods, whether consumer sales or otherwise. *Description, satisfactory quality, fitness for purpose and sample (ss. 13, 14(2), (3), 15, Sale of Goods Act 1979):* here a distinction is made between consumer and non-consumer sales.

4.3.4.1 Consumer sales A party cannot exclude their liability for breach of these implied terms (s. 6(2), Unfair Contract Terms Act 1977).

4.3.4.2 Non-consumer sales A party may exclude their liability for breach of these implied terms, but only if this is *reasonable* (s. 6(3), Unfair Contract Terms Act 1977).

Note that s. 6 applies to *any* contract for the sale of goods or hire purchase, whereas the Unfair Contract Terms Act 1977 normally only applies to *business liability*. However, the effect of this is not as drastic as it seems as regards the implied terms, as ss. 14(2), 14(3) and 15, Sale of Goods Act 1979 do not apply to private sales.

It is also provided that these rules apply to hire purchase contracts which are covered by the Supply of Goods (Implied Terms) Act 1973.

Similar rules apply to contracts for the supply of goods, where goods are supplied in conjunction with a service, for example central heating is installed (s. 7, Unfair Contract Terms Act 1977).

4.3.5 Indemnity clauses

Someone who deals as a consumer cannot be made to indemnify another person, unless this term is *reasonable*. This indemnity could arise in contract or tort and could be in respect of acts of a third party.

> EXAMPLE
>
> Alice takes her car to France on the ferry and a term in the contract provides that Alice will indemnify the ferry company for any claims arising from transporting the car. If the car breaks loose and damages other cars, the company would claim against Alice, but such a clause would have to be reasonable and this is unlikely in consumer contracts.

4.3.6 Manufacturers' guarantees

If goods in consumer use cause damage as a result of negligence in manufacture or distribution, then liability *cannot* be excluded by a clause in a manufacturers' guarantee. This applies to goods of a type normally supplied for private use.

> EXAMPLE
>
> Alice buys a vacuum cleaner from Bertie's Electrical Stores which has been made by Clever Manufacturers. Alice signs a guarantee provided by Clever, which promises to guarantee the vacuum cleaner for 12 months in return for Alice giving up her rights under the Sale of Goods Act 1979. This clause is invalid.

The term 'in consumer use' has a special meaning here, which covers goods which are not solely used for a business.

> EXAMPLE
>
> Daniel, a businessman, buys a company car from Eve's Garage which Daniel also uses privately. This will be treated as *in consumer use*.

4.3.7 Misrepresentation

If a contract has a clause excluding or restricting liability for misrepresentation or the remedies available for misrepresentation, that clause is not valid unless it is *reasonable* (s. 8, Unfair Contract Terms Act 1977).

5 The Unfair Terms in Consumer Contracts Regulations 1999

5.1 Introduction

In April 1993 the Council of Ministers adopted Directive 93/13 on unfair terms in consumer contracts. It is recognised that suppliers are in a strong position compared to individual consumers. The United Kingdom's response was a statutory instrument, the Unfair Terms in Consumer Contracts Regulations 1994, which came into effect on 1 July 1995. These Regulations were replaced by the Unfair Terms in Consumer Contracts Regulations 1999 which came into force on 1 October 1999. The new Regulations are intended to be closer in wording to the Directive.

5.2 Outline of the regulations

Regulation 4 provides that they apply to unfair terms in contracts made between a seller or supplier and a consumer. This means that the Regulations only apply to consumer contracts.

Regulation 5 provides that any term which has not been individually negotiated will be regarded as unfair, if contrary to the requirement of good faith, it causes a significant imbalance against the rights of the consumer.

A term will always be regarded as not individually negotiated if it was drafted before the contract, so that the consumer cannot influence the term. Even if a particular term has been individually negotiated, the Regulations still apply to the remainder of the contract.

Regulation 6(1) says that in determining whether a term is 'unfair', the nature of the goods and services, all the circumstances at the time of the contract and all the terms of the contract shall be taken into account.

Regulation 6(2) provides that in deciding the fairness of a term, the definition of the subject-matter and the adequacy of the price shall not be taken into account. These are known as the 'core terms' of the contract and clearly the courts do not want to be involved in deciding if these are fair.

Regulation 7 provides that written terms must be in 'plain, intelligible language' and that if there is any doubt they must be interpreted in favour of the consumer.

Regulation 8 provides that the effect of a finding that a term is unfair means that that term is not binding. If the remainder of the contract can exist without the unfair term it can still be binding.

5.3 Non-exhaustive list of terms which may be regarded as unfair

Schedule 2 provides examples of terms which have the object of:

(a) excluding liability for death or personal injury;   *29 London Transport*

(b) inappropriately excluding or limiting the consumer's legal rights for non-performance or inadequate performance by the seller or excluding a right of set off;

(c) making the contract binding on the consumer but optional for the seller; *v. unfair*

(d) allowing the seller to keep a deposit if the consumer does not perform but not vice-versa; *— photo Library case*

(e) requiring a consumer to pay compensation out of proportion to a breach;

(f) allowing termination by the seller/supplier but not the consumer, or allowing the seller/supplier to keep sums paid when the seller/supplier terminates;

(g) allowing the seller/supplier to end the contract without reasonable notice except where there are good grounds to do so;

(h) automatic renewal of a fixed-term contract if the deadline for objection is unreasonably early;

(i) irrevocably binding the consumer to terms he had no opportunity of becoming acquainted with;

(j) allowing the seller/supplier to alter the terms of the contract unilaterally without a valid reason specified in the contract;

(k) allowing the seller/supplier unilaterally to alter any characteristics of the product or service without a valid reason;

(l) allowing the price of goods to be determined on delivery, or giving the seller/supplier the power to increase the price without, in both cases, giving the consumer the corresponding right to cancel the contract if the final price is too high;

(m) giving the seller/supplier the right to determine whether goods or services conform with the contract or the exclusive right to interpret the contract;

(n) limiting the seller/supplier's obligations for his agent, or making liability subject to some formality;

(o) making the consumer fulfill all obligations but not the seller/supplier;

(p) allowing the seller/supplier to transfer rights and obligations under the contract thereby reducing guarantees to the consumer without agreement;

(q) excluding or limiting the consumer's legal remedies through exclusive arbitration, restricting evidence or altering the burden of proof.

EXAMPLES

Example (a) is similar to the Unfair Contract Terms Act 1977. s. 2(1), which makes any term which tries to avoid liability for death or injury arising from negligence automatically void.

Example (k) would cover a tour operator altering a holiday destination from Italy to Spain for a reason not stated in the contract: such a term would be unfair.

Many of the terms in the above schedule involve the seller or supplier having rights but no corresponding rights for the consumer.

The Unfair Terms in Consumer Contracts Regulations 1994 were considered in the following case which was brought by the Director General of Fair Trading using his powers under the regulations.

Director General of Fair Trading v *First National Bank* (2001)

The defendant bank lent money on their standard terms. One of these terms provided that if the debtor defaulted the bank could demand payment of the balance and that interest was payable, even if the bank obtained a court judgment against the debtor, until the debt was paid in full. The Director General of Fair Trading argued that this term was 'unfair' under the 1994 Regulations. The Court of Appeal had decided that the term was unfair and a breach of the requirement of good faith because it was not drawn to the consumer's attention. In the House of Lords the bank argued that the payment of interest was the price of lending money. Therefore the term was within reg. 3(2) which provides that the test of fairness does not apply to anything defining the main subject matter or which concerns the adequacy of the price. The House of Lords said that the term did not define the subject matter or the adequacy of the price and was not a 'core' term, so that it was covered by the regulations. The question remained as to whether the term was unfair. The fact was that without such a clause the lender would not be able to charge interest after the court judgment. Many borrowers would not realise that they had to pay interest because the clause was not specifically brought to their attention. However, the term would only be unfair if, 'contrary to the requirement of good faith, it causes a significant imbalance in the parties' rights and obligations to the detriment of the consumer'. Without the term the bank would be losing interest on the money still to be paid and in the circumstances it was not unfair.

5.4 Complaints about unfair terms

Under reg. 10 the Director General of Fair Trading has a duty to consider any complaint that a contract term drawn up for general use is unfair. In addition the Regulations provide that certain 'qualifying bodies' may also take action over unfair terms. These qualifying bodies include the director general for water; the Gas and Electricity Markets Authority; the Financial Services Authority; the rail regulator; weights and measures authorities and the Consumers' Association. With the exception of the Consumers' Association, the qualifying bodies can notify the OFT in writing that they will accept a complaint that a term is unfair and they must then investigate that complaint. They may then accept an undertaking about use of that term or apply for an injunction (under reg. 12) to prevent future use of that term. The injunctions may be used not only for the particular term subject to the complaint but for any similar terms.

The Office of Fair Trading has an 'Unfair Contract Terms Unit' which has been active in enforcing the earlier 1994 Regulations particularly with regard to terms in contracts for the sale of cars and mobile phones.

5.5 Relationship with other rules on exemption clauses

There are now three sets of rules governing exemption clauses, i.e. cor
the Unfair Contract Terms Act 1977 and the 1999 Regulations. All th
consumer contracts, but only the common law and the 1977 Act to cu....
businesses. How all these rules interrelate remains to be seen. The regulations are
wider than the Act in the sense that they apply to all contract terms and not simply to
exemption clauses. However, they are narrower in that they apply only to consumer
contracts. It would have been better if the regulations had been integrated into the
existing statutory rules so that there were no overlaps and potential conflicts.

Vitiating elements

1 Introduction

Even though all the elements of a contract are present, there may be some other factor
which makes the contract invalid. The law will intervene in certain cases on the
ground of public policy, either to protect a public interest which outweighs the interests of the parties, or because the contract is unfair. For example, if the parties make
an illegal contract the courts will not enforce it. If a contract has been made following
a mistake, it may in limited circumstances be treated as void. If one of the parties has
made misrepresentations to the other, or if one party has used physical force or
exerted undue influence on the other the contract is voidable. The law also protects
parties like minors who lack the full capacity to make contracts. A legal adviser will
not often face these problems, but it is nevertheless important to know the rules if
only to eliminate such possibilities.

One important distinction to be aware of is between void and voidable contracts. A
void contract means that no contract has been made and neither party can take legal
action. A *voidable* contract is valid to start with but some factor affects this validity.
The innocent party is then given a choice, either to continue with the contract, which
makes it binding or to avoid the contract, which means neither party is liable for the
future.

2 Illegality

2.1 Introduction

Perhaps the key to understanding illegality is to see that, underlying the categories
into which such contracts are put, is a general principle that, as a matter of public
policy, some agreements should not have the backing of the law. This public policy is
the view taken by the judges which reflects the values of society and consequently it

will change as society's values change. The courts are really attempting to strike a balance between not enforcing contracts which are completely illegal, for example, an agreement to rob banks and divide the takings, *and* enforcing contracts which are slightly illegal, for example which have broken a minor rule. In doing this the courts take a pragmatic approach and have even used the device of the collateral contract to get round illegality and enforce a contract. In 1999 the Law Commission issued Consultation Paper No 154 '*Illegal Transactions: The Effect of Illegality on Contracts and Trusts*' in which it describes the case law in this area as, 'uncertain, at times inconsistent, and . . . by no means readily comprehensible'. The Law Commission aim to review the law on illegal contracts and suggest replacing the complex rules with a discretion given to the courts to decide whether or not to enforce an illegal transaction.

It is proposed to explain illegal contracts using traditional categories. An important distinction is made between illegal contracts and void contracts. *Illegal* contracts are completely prohibited, so it is against the law to make them, whether by statute or at common law. *Void* contracts can be made but cannot be enforced in the courts.

2.2 Contracts illegal by statute

An Act of Parliament or delegated legislation may make certain contracts illegal. This may be done expressly or may be implied from the words of the statute.

Under the Life Assurance Act 1774 it is illegal for someone to take out a life assurance policy on someone else's life, unless they have an *insurable interest* in that life. An insurable interest means a financial interest. The aim of the statute is to stop people gambling on other people's lives by taking out assurance policies on them. If the person taking out the policy has no insurable interest, the policy is illegal and no claim can be made on it.

There are many statutes and regulations governing trade and a minor breach of one of these will not necessarily make a related contract illegal, unless this is expressly made clear.

St John Shipping Corporation v *Joseph Rank Ltd* (1956)

The claimants carried a cargo on their ship for the defendants. The claimants were convicted for overloading the ship in breach of the Merchant Shipping Act 1932. The defendants then refused to pay, arguing the contract was illegal. It was held that this offence did not affect the performance of the contract which was enforceable.

Hughes v *Asset Managers plc* (1995)

In October 1987 the claimant gave the defendants £3m to invest in shares, but one month later after the market crashed the shares were worth only £2m. The Prevention of Fraud (Investments) Act 1958 required all dealers to be licensed. The claimant claimed that although the defendants had a licence, the actual employee who made the contract with the claimant did not have a 'representative's licence' as required by the Act and as a consequence any contract made by such an individual was void. The Court of Appeal said that the Act was passed to protect investors by requiring professional dealers to have a licence. Anyone who dealt without a licence was subject to criminal sanctions, but it did not mean that any contracts they made should be void. The claimant's appeal failed.

2.3 Contracts illegal at common law

A large number of contracts are made illegal at common law, some of the main ones are examined below.

2.3.1 Contracts to commit a crime or tort

A contract to commit a crime, for example to murder someone, is illegal and it is no surprise that the courts would not enforce such an agreement in the unlikely event of such a case coming before them. Similarly an agreement to commit a tort, such as defamation or fraud, cannot be enforced.

Everet v *Williams* (1725)

This was a business agreement between two highwaymen to rob coaches and share the 'profits' equally. The defendant took more than his share and the claimant sued him. It was held that the claimant could not use the courts to enforce this contract. The claimant's barrister was ordered to pay the costs of the case!

Birkett v *Acorn Business Machines Ltd* (1999)

B pretended to hire a fax machine from ABM but actually hired a photocopier. Both parties knew this was done to deceive a finance company. Later B sued to enforce the contract. It was held by the Court of Appeal that public policy required that the courts should not enforce any contract which had an illegal purpose. This contract could not be enforced.

2.3.2 Contracts promoting corruption in public life

Any agreement involving bribery to obtain a public office or honour, or to gain a commercial advantage is illegal.

Parkinson v *College of Ambulance Ltd and Harrison* (1925)

The claimant gave £5,000 to the defendants on the understanding that they would obtain a knighthood for him. They were unable to do so and the claimant claimed the money back. The court held that the agreement to buy an honour was illegal and the money could not be recovered.

2.3.3 Contracts which are sexually immoral

Contracts which are directly immoral, for example an agreement to pay a prostitute, or indirectly immoral, for example to lease a house to a prostitute, are illegal.

Pearce v *Brooks* (1866)

The claimant hired a carriage to the defendant, whom he knew was a prostitute and wanted the carriage for 'business purposes'. The defendant refused to pay for it. The court held that the contract was illegal and the claimant was not entitled to payment.

The above case must now be read in the light of the following recent decision of the Court of Appeal.

Armhouse Lee Ltd v *Chappell* (1996)

The defendants put advertisements for telephone sex lines and dating in the claimant's magazines. The defendants then argued that the contract was illegal as it was for an immoral purpose. The Court asked the question whether the contract could be unenforceable on the ground of public policy as a contract to promote sexual immorality and answered it by saying that there was no generally accepted moral code which condemned such advertisements. Therefore the contract was valid.

2.3.4 Contracts interfering with justice

An agreement not to prosecute someone is an interference with the administration of justice and is illegal.

2.3.5 Contracts damaging to foreign relations

Any agreement which would interfere with the good relations between Britain and other countries is illegal.

Foster v *Driscoll* (1929)

A contract to smuggle whisky into the USA during the prohibition was held to be illegal.

2.3.6 Contracts to trade with an enemy

If Britain is at war with another country, any agreement between individuals in the two countries is illegal.

EXAMPLE

An agreement to supply food to a business in Iraq during the 'Gulf War'.

2.4 Consequences of illegality

A distinction is made between contracts illegal in themselves and contracts which have been illegally carried out.

2.4.1 Contracts illegal in themselves

This is a contract which it is illegal to make. The general rule is that neither party can sue on the contract. Any money paid cannot be recovered. For example, the claimant in *Parkinson* v *College of Ambulance Ltd* could not recover the money he paid for the knighthood. If one party is not equally to blame, he may be able to enforce the contract.

2.4.2 Contracts illegal in performance

Here it is not illegal to make the contract, but it has been performed in an illegal way.

Shaw v *Groom* (1970)

A landlord did not provide a rent book as required by statute and when he sued for arrears of rent the tenant claimed the lease was illegal. It was held that the Rent Acts were to regulate tenancies, not to make them illegal and the landlord was entitled to the arrears.

A party can claim on a contract if the claim does not rely on the illegal act.

Tinsley v *Milligan* (1993)

Miss T and Miss M were lovers who both contributed money to buying a house, which was put in T's name so that M could falsely claim social security. Later they fell out and M claimed a share of the property but T argued that as the arrangement was made for an illegal purpose, M could not claim. The House of Lords said that the test of whether the public conscience would be affronted by allowing the claim was too vague. The proper test was whether M had to rely on the illegality. By contributing to the price M raised the presumption of a resulting trust in her favour. It was T who had brought in the illegality to rebut that presumption. Therefore M's claim succeeded as she did not have to rely on the illegality.

A presumption of advancement was raised in the next case.

Tribe v *Tribe* (1995)

The claimant owned the majority of shares in a family company. The company had the tenancy of premises which needed substantial repairs and the company was responsible for such repairs. The claimant transferred his shares to his son, the defendant, in an attempt to stop the landlord claiming from the claimant. The transfer was stated to be for £78,030, which was neither paid nor ever intended to be. In fact the landlord accepted surrender of the lease, so legally no payment needed to be made by the company. When the claimant asked for the return of the shares his son refused, arguing that there was a presumption of advancement in favour of the son and that the claimant could not rebut this without revealing his illegal purpose. It was held by the Court of Appeal that although the illegal purpose was to defraud the landlord, this had never happened. The claimant could repent before the illegal purpose was carried out and could therefore reclaim the shares from his son.

2.5 Contracts made void by statute

There are many contracts which are made void by statute, two usual examples being wagering contracts and restrictive trading agreements.

2.5.1 Wagering contracts

Under the Gaming Act 1845, s. 18, all wagering contracts are void. This means that although it is not illegal to make a wagering contract in the first instance, such a contract cannot be enforced in a court. A wagering contract is an agreement in which:

(a) there are two parties;

(b) the two parties hold opposite views about something;

(c) the parties stand either to win or lose;

(d) neither party has any other financial interest in the agreement other than the amount of the wager.

EXAMPLE

Alice places a bet of £10 with Basil's Bookmakers, that Party Politics will win the Grand National. The horse wins, but Basil refuses to pay. This is a wager and Alice cannot sue Basil.

A football pools coupon is not a wager as there are more than two parties and the pools company cannot lose as it deducts a sum from the stakes as its profit.

2.5.2 Restrictive trading agreements

Under the Competition Act 1998 agreements which may affect trade within the United Kingdom or have as their object or effect the prevention or restriction of competition are prohibited. This covers, for example, agreements to fix the purchase or selling prices or to control production.

2.6 Contracts made void at common law

Just as the courts have declared some contracts to be illegal, others have been declared void on the grounds of public policy. Three examples are contracts to exclude the courts from disputes, contracts damaging to marriage and contracts in restraint of trade.

2.6.1 Contracts to exclude the courts

Any term in a contract which restricts the right of a party to take a dispute to court is void. This does not make the rest of the contract void.

Baker v *Jones* (1954)

The rules of the British Amateur Weightlifters' Association provided that its central council was the only body which could interpret its rules. It was held that this provision was void, since as a matter of public policy parties to an agreement cannot exclude the courts from interpreting matters of law.

The parties are free to agree that disputes should go to arbitration on matters of fact or law, and this will as a general rule prevent them taking the case to court. However, s. 69 of the Arbitration Act 1996 gives a right of appeal to the High Court on a point of law from the decision of an arbitrator, with the consent of the other party.

2.6.2 Contracts damaging to marriage

Public policy requires marriage to be protected and the courts have recognised a number of agreements in relation to marriage which it treats as void. These include an agreement not to marry anybody or only to marry a particular person; or a marriage brokerage contract by which someone agrees to arrange a marriage for a fee; or an agreement between spouses for future separation, as opposed to immediate separation. It is difficult to see how these can now be justified.

2.6.3 Contracts in restraint of trade

A number of business contracts are treated by the courts as being *prima facie void*, the most important being agreements which restrict employees in their future work; restrictions on the sellers of a business as to their future work; and restrictions on sellers of goods. These are important matters which frequently come before the courts and need to be examined in a separate section below.

2.7 Contracts in restraint of trade

2.7.1 Introduction

Any agreement which restricts a person's freedom to work or run a business how they wish, is treated as being in 'restraint of trade' and is prima facie void. This means that it is initially void and it is up to the party imposing the restraint to show that it is reasonable, and therefore valid. To establish this it must be proved that the restriction is reasonable in:

(a) the interests of the parties—this means that it is not excessive and protects a genuine interest; and

(b) the interests of the public—it is not damaging to the general public. For example, a restriction on someone who is at the forefront in a particular field might be against the public interest.

The restraint must not be excessive in *area, time* and *scope* (i.e. what it forbids).

If a restraint of trade clause is valid, the party relying on it will normally want an injunction rather than damages.

Article 81 (formerly Article 85) of the Treaty of Rome provides that contracts in restraint of trade are void, to the extent that they prevent free trade between member States. As art. 81 has direct effect it could be used in domestic cases.

2.7.2 Restraints imposed on employees

Employers often put a clause in an employee's contract of employment that, on leaving, the employee will not work for a rival employer or set up in competition. Such a restraint is prima facie void unless shown to be reasonable. The employer must have a genuine interest that needs protection, for example special knowledge. The restriction must not be excessive as regards the three factors mentioned above. The courts will take into account changing technology and the nature of the business, and a period of five years in modern times would normally be too long, although it depends on the particular circumstances.

Forster & Sons Ltd v *Suggett* (1918)

The defendant manager of the claimants' glass making factory had knowledge of secret processes. His contract of employment provided that after leaving he would not engage in the business of glass making or any other business connected with glass making, in the United Kingdom for five years. It was held that this restriction was valid because of the special knowledge.

A rather longer period was held valid in the following case.

Fitch v *Dewes* (1921)

A solicitors' managing clerk agreed never to practise within seven miles of Tamworth town hall. The House of Lords held that as long term relationships developed in such a business and it was a small country town, this restriction was valid, even though it was for a very long time!

The restriction on area should not be wider than is necessary to protect the employer's interest.

Mason v Provident Clothing and Supply Co. Ltd (1913)

The claimant was employed to sell clothes and collect money for the defendants, over a small district in London. He agreed not to work for any other clothes firm, within 25 miles of London, for three years after leaving. The House of Lords held that the employers had a legitimate interest to protect in the district he worked, but the area was far too wide and the restriction was invalid.

Employees may also be prevented from soliciting old customers.

Home Counties Dairies Ltd v Skilton (1970)

The defendant was a milkman who agreed not to sell milk or dairy produce for 12 months after leaving the claimant's employment, to anyone who had been a customer in the six months period before he left. He left and obtained a job working for a rival company on the same round. It was held by the Court of Appeal that the term 'dairy produce' was not too wide and could be restricted to things a milkman normally sold. The restriction on selling to former customers was also valid, since without the intervention of the defendant, they might return their custom to the claimant.

2.7.3 Restraints on the seller of a business

Any restrictions on the seller of a business are void unless shown to be reasonable in the interests of the parties and the public. It is easier to enforce these restrictions than the restrictions put on employees. Obviously buyers of businesses need protection from the direct competition of the seller, which would take away something for which they had paid, i.e., the goodwill of the business. It is important that the restriction is not wider than is necessary to protect the buyer's interests.

EXAMPLE

Alice sells a hamburger restaurant to Basil and the contract of sale provides that Alice will not open any restaurant, within one mile, for 12 months.

British Reinforced Concrete Engineering Co. Ltd v Schelff (1921)

The claimant company made road reinforcements and the defendants, a small company, made a different type of 'loop' reinforcements. The defendants sold their 'loop' business to the claimants and agreed not to make or sell any road reinforcements. It was held that this restriction was too wide as the business sold was only for loop reinforcements, therefore the covenant was void.

Apart from the nature of the business, the nature of the industry is also important.

Nordenfelt v Maxim Nordenfelt Guns and Ammunition Co. Ltd (1894)

Nordenfelt owned a worldwide business making guns and ammunition. When he sold the business he agreed that for 25 years he would not make guns or ammunition anywhere in the world or carry on any other business competing with the purchaser in any way. The House of Lords held that the worldwide restriction was valid, taking into account the limited number of manufacturers and customers and the interest which had been sold. An injunction would be granted to stop Nordenfelt working for a competitor. However, the agreement not to carry on any other business was too wide and could be severed.

2.7.4 Restraints on the sellers of goods

A seller of goods may make an agreement to sell only one particular brand of goods. Such contracts are known as 'solus agreements' and they are prima facie void. They are usually imposed on the seller by the manufacturer or producer and may be linked to a mortgage or lease. One example is an agreement by a garage to sell only one brand of petrol.

Esso Petroleum Co. Ltd v _Harper's Garage (Stourport) Ltd_ (1967)

The defendants owned two garages and made agreements for each garage with Esso. The contract provided that the first agreement was to last for four years five months; that the defendants were to buy all fuel from Esso; that the defendants were to get any purchaser to enter a similar agreement. A second agreement was contained in a mortgage of £7,000 for 21 years which could not be redeemed before that period was up. The House of Lords held that Esso's position in the petrol market was an interest worth protecting and solus agreements enabled them to do this by guaranteeing outlets. The contract for four years, five months, was valid but the 21-year contract was unreasonable and void as the period was too long.

2.8 Consequences of a contract being void

If the whole contract is void, then neither party can sue on it. However, money paid may be recovered. If only part of the contract is void, then it may be possible to 'sever' this part leaving the remainder valid. The courts will not re-write the contract and it must be possible to cut out the void part in such a way that the remaining part makes sense (the 'blue pencil test'). How this works in practice can be seen by contrasting the following two cases.

Goldsoll v _Goldman_ (1915)

The claimant bought the defendant's United Kingdom imitation jewellery business. The contract provided that the claimant would not trade in real or imitation jewellery in the United Kingdom, France, the USA, Russia or Spain for two years. The Court of Appeal held that the time period was valid but the scope of the restriction to real jewellery, and the area, were too wide. These parts could be severed and the agreement enforced to cover imitation jewellery in the United Kingdom.

Attwood v _Lamont_ (1920)

The claimant owned a general outfitters at Kidderminster. The head of the tailoring department had agreed that after leaving he would not be concerned in 'the trade or business of a tailor, dress maker, general draper, milliner, hatter, haberdasher, gentlemen's, ladies' or children's outfitter . . . within 10 miles of Kidderminster'. The Court of Appeal held that the business to be protected was one business and not several. It was not possible to sever the other parts from the tailoring and leave that as valid, and therefore the whole agreement was invalid.

3 Mistake

[handwritten: — Voids a contract Caveat emptor — buyer beware]

3.1 Introduction

The meaning of 'mistake' in law is much narrower than its popular meaning. A party to a contract may make a 'mistake' in the popular sense but at common law this will not affect the contract. For example, the buyer of a tennis racket who mistakenly believes it has a graphite frame which in fact is plastic, cannot avoid the contract. For a mistake to affect the contract it must be an 'operative mistake' i.e., a mistake which operates to make the contract void. Establishing a mistake has a drastic effect and means there is no contract. This can equally affect a third party who takes goods from one of the parties to the void contract, because he will have no title to them and will have to return them to the original owner. Such effects are one reason why the courts have confined cases of mistake within narrow limits, as often they are trying to hold the balance between two innocent parties. The courts have recognised a number of types of mistake. In *common mistake* the offer and acceptance correspond and there is agreement but the parties make the same mistake. In *mutual mistake* the parties are at cross purposes and the offer and acceptance do not correspond, so there is no agreement between the parties. In *unilateral mistake* the offer and acceptance do not correspond and only one of the parties makes a mistake, but the other party knows this or must be taken to know. *Non est factum* means 'it is not my deed' and is a special rule which applies to someone who signs a document by mistake. Although at common law a contract will only be void if there is an operative mistake, in equity a party affected may be entitled to relief.

3.2 Common mistake *[handwritten: — both parties made same mistake]*

Here the two parties appear to have made an agreement but it is based on a common mistake. At common law the general rule is that a common mistake will *not* affect the contract. If the subject-matter of the contract does not exist when the contract is made, this will be treated as an operative mistake and the contract will be void.

> EXAMPLE
>
> Alan agrees to sell his tennis racket to Barbara, but at the time of the contract, unknown to both parties, it has been destroyed in a fire. The contract is void.

[handwritten left margin: Common sense!]

Couturier v *Hastie* (1856)

A contract was made to sell a cargo of corn which was on a ship heading for London. Unknown to both parties, at the time of the contract the corn had been sold. It was held by the House of Lords that effectively the corn did not exist and the contract was void, so the buyer did not have to pay.

The above situation is now governed by the Sale of Goods Act 1979 which provides that such a contract is void (s. 6).

A contract will also be void if the purchaser of something already owns it. But the courts have determined that a mistake about the 'quality' of the subject-matter of a contract is not sufficient to amount to an operative mistake.

[handwritten: Mistake as quality. 1st Quality]

EXAMPLE

Alice sells a painting to Basil which both parties mistakenly believe was painted by Lowry. This does not affect the validity of the contract.

Even if a contract is not void at common law, equity may set the contract aside on terms which are just.

Grist v *Bailey* (1966)

The claimant agreed to buy the defendant's house subject to an existing tenancy, which both parties mistakenly believed was protected by the Rent Acts. Because of this mistake the price was fixed at £850 instead of £2,250. It was held that although this mistake did not make the contract void at common law, in equity the claimant's claim for specific performance was refused, on condition that the defendant agreed to sell for £2,250.   *[handwritten: insisting the contract is carried out.]*

3.3 Mutual mistake

Here there is no agreement between the parties. They both make a mistake, but it is not the same mistake.

EXAMPLE

Alan has two cars, a Jaguar and a Mini. He intends to offer to sell the Mini to Barbara, who believes he is offering the Jaguar and she agrees to buy.

The common law applies an *objective test* to these situations and if the reasonable man would say that a contract exists, then in spite of the mistake the contract is binding. If objectively no contract can be said to exist, then the agreement is void.

Wood v *Scarth* (1855)

The defendant offered to let a public house to the claimant for £63 a year, which the claimant accepted. The defendant believed that his clerk had told the claimant that a premium of £500 was also payable. The court held that objectively it was reasonable for the claimant to assume that all he had to pay was £63 and as the defendant had refused to complete the contract, the claimant was entitled to damages.

Even though the contract has not been made void at common law, equity may give relief to a party. Although in the above case equity did not grant specific performance, because on the facts this was regarded as unjust on the defendant, in appropriate circumstances equity could grant specific performance.

3.4 Unilateral mistake

In this case although only one of the parties makes a mistake, the other party knows or must be taken to know of the mistake. There is no correspondence of offer and acceptance. The interpretation adopted by Cheshire, Fifoot and Furmston, *Law of Contract*, 13th ed. (1996), is followed here.

EXAMPLE

Alan sells a painting to Barbara, which Barbara believes is a Lowry. If Alan knows of

Barbara's belief or should know about it, then this is a unilateral mistake—only Barbara is mistaken.

There are two main situations in which such unilateral mistakes occur.

3.4.1 _Mistake of intention_

If one party makes a mistake about their intention and the other party realises this mistake or ought to realise it, the contract will be void.

Hartog v _Colin and Shields_ (1939)

Negotiations for the sale of hare skins were made on the basis of price per skin but the seller offered them at a price per pound. There were three skins to the pound, which meant that they were being offered at one third of the price. The buyer accepted the offer. It was held that the buyer must have known of the mistake, as it was the custom to trade at price per skin, consequently the contract was void.

3.4.2 _Mistake of identity_   _[handwritten: Deliberately misleading the other party]_

Here one party makes a contract with a second party, believing him to be a third party.

> EXAMPLE
>
> Chris pretends to be Bob and makes an offer to Alan, which Alan accepts, believing he is dealing with Bob.

At common law the presumption is that in spite of this mistake, a valid contract has been made. For such a mistake to be an 'operative mistake' and to make the agreement void the mistaken party must show that:

(a) they intended to deal with someone else;

(b) the party they dealt with knew of this intention;

(c) they regarded identity as of crucial importance;

(d) they took reasonable steps to check the identity of the other person.

3.4.2.1 They intended to deal with someone else   To establish this there must be two other legal _persons_ in existence.

King's Norton Metal Co. Ltd v _Edridge, Merrett & Co. Ltd_ (1897)

A rogue had some paper printed with the name 'Hallam & Co', a fictitious company, and used it to order goods on credit from the claimant, which he promptly sold to the defendant. It was held by the Court of Appeal that the claimant must have intended to deal with the writer of the letter, as they could not have intended to give credit to a non-existent company. The contract between the claimant and the rogue could not be void but it was voidable, because of the rogue's fraud in pretending to be someone else. As it had not been avoided at the time of the sale to the defendants, they were entitled to keep the goods.

[handwritten in left margin: The Rogue cases]

3.4.2.2 The party they dealt with knew of this intention   This is normally easy to prove as the other party is often a rogue.

3.4.2.3 They regarded identity as of crucial importance   The identity of the other party must be important to the mistaken person. The law makes a distinction between contracts made 'face to face' and other contracts, for example made by post.

Cundy v Lindsay (1878) *Intended to deal with Blenkiron*

A rogue called Blenkarn ordered goods on credit from the claimant and signed his name to look like Blenkiron, a reputable firm. The rogue immediately resold the goods to the defendant, who bought in good faith. The claimant sued the defendant in the tort of conversion (using the claimant's goods) claiming that the contract with the rogue was void for mistake and therefore the defendant had no title (ownership) to the goods. The House of Lords held that the claimant intended to deal only with Blenkiron, not the writer of the letter and the contract was void, so the goods had to be given back to the claimant.

Cundy v *Lindsay* was distinguished in the following case.

Citibank NA v Brown Shipley & Co. Ltd (1991)

A rogue telephoned a bank posing as a customer and asked them to draw a bank draft on his account to be collected by a messenger. The draft was given to the messenger whom the bank thought was a representative of the customer. The draft was presented to a second bank who telephoned the issuing bank to check that the draft was in order before paying it. The issuing bank now claimed that their contract with the rogue was void on the grounds of mistaken identity. It was held that here the mistake of identity was not between the two parties to the draft, the issuing and receiving banks, but as to the identity of a third party, the rogue. The contract between the banks was not void for mistake and the issuing bank had to bear the loss.

In contracts made face to face, the presumption is that the mistaken party intends to deal with the other party who is physically present.

Phillips v Brooks Ltd (1919) *Leading case on mistake of ID*

A rogue went into the claimant jewellers and selected some jewellery. He then began to write out a cheque, which the claimant hesitated to accept, but the rogue said 'I am Sir George Bullough' and gave an address which the claimant 'checked' in the telephone directory. The rogue was allowed to take away a ring, which he pawned with the defendant. The cheque was not paid and the claimant claimed the ring back, saying that the contract with the rogue was void, so the defendant had no title to it. It was held that the claimant intended to sell to the person in the shop, i.e., the rogue, and not only to Sir George Bullough. When identity was raised, the contract had already been made. The contract with the rogue was not void but voidable because of the fraud, but it had not been avoided before the jewellery was pawned, so the defendant could keep it.

The above case was distinguished in the next one.

Handwritten margin note (top): Not face-to-face but at arm's length situation

Shogun Finance Ltd v Hudson (2001)

A rogue went to a car dealer and used a false name, address and driving licence. He completed a hire purchase form with the claimant finance company and was allowed to take away a car. The rogue sold the car to H, the defendant. The claimant sued in conversion to obtain the car. The Court of Appeal said that this situation could be distinguished from face to face contracts, as the rogue did not deal with the finance company directly but through a form. Neither could it be regarded as being made 'face to face' using the dealer as agent of the finance company, because it was established law that the dealer was not such an agent. As a result the 'contract' made between the finance company and the rogue was void. Therefore the rogue could not pass title to H and as a result H had to give the car to the claimant finance company.

3.4.2.4 They took reasonable steps to check the identity of the other person   In the above case, the jeweller looking in the telephone directory was clearly inadequate.

Equity will generally follow the common law but may set a contract aside or refuse specific performance if the circumstances merit it.

3.5 Non est factum

Handwritten note: This is not my deed – x. special defence

This is a special case in which a party who has signed a document by mistake is claiming 'it is not my act'. The general rule is that if someone signs a document, they are bound by it. The original reason for the rule was to protect illiterate people who were tricked into putting their mark on documents. It was later made available for those who signed documents by mistake but its use in modern times has been very restricted. For a successful plea of *non est factum* the following factors have to be established:

(a) there is a radical difference between the document which was signed and what they thought they were signing;

(b) the signer was not careless in signing.

The following case is the leading case on this topic.

Saunders v Anglia Building Society (1971)

Handwritten note: also Gallie v Lee (same case)

A widow aged 78 years agreed to assign the lease of her house to her nephew. Lee, a family friend, prepared a document and told the claimant that it was a deed of gift to the nephew. The widow did not read the document because she had broken her glasses. In fact it was an assignment for value to Lee. He then mortgaged the house to the defendants but did not pay the mortgage and they claimed the house. The widow claimed she was mistaken about what she signed. The House of Lords held that the document she signed and the document she thought she was signing were not radically different, as they were both assignments of the lease; the widow had been careless in not having the document read to her, so the claim of *non est factum* failed and the building society were entitled to the house.

More recently a claim was successful in the following case.

Handwritten margin notes (left): kept the stock till cheque cleared. the rogue could have cheated the jeweller / strong need to protect (9th) illiterate people / problem: her glasses isn't a good excuse

Lloyds Bank plc v *Waterhouse* (1990)

The defendant, who was illiterate, signed a guarantee in favour of the claimant, which he mistakenly thought covered his son's farm, but which covered all his son's liabilities. The defendant believed that if the guarantee only covered the farm, he could sell it to get his money back on the guarantee. The Court of Appeal held that the mistake about the extent of the guarantee was sufficient for *non est factum*, as there was a fundamental difference between a guarantee for land and an all moneys guarantee. The defendant had not been careless by signing, as he had asked the bank questions about it on several occasions. Therefore he was not liable.

[handwritten margin note: misrep.]

[handwritten note: Bank was at fault b'cos they didn't give him clear explanation of what guarantee implied]

4 Misrepresentation

4.1 Introduction

In making a contract one party may mislead the other by making untrue statements. These statements may become terms of the contract, or may be treated as terms of the contract and the party affected may then claim the remedies available for breach of contract. If neither of these can be established it is still possible to claim misrepresentation. To prove misrepresentation certain requirements must be met, one of the principal ones being that the misrepresentation actually *induced* the person to make the contract. There are three types of misrepresentation: *fraudulent, negligent* and *wholly innocent* and the effect of establishing any one of these is that the contract is voidable. Before the Misrepresentation Act 1967, all cases of non-fraudulent misrepresentation were referred to as *innocent* misrepresentations. The main remedy available is rescission of the contract.

4.2 Definition of misrepresentation

A misrepresentation is an untrue statement of fact, made by one party to a contract, which induces the other party to make the contract.

4.2.1 What makes a statement a misrepresentation?

It must be a statement of fact, so none of the following can amount to a misrepresentation.

4.2.1.1 A mere puff A statement which is clearly sales talk will not be regarded as fact, for example: 'This is the best lager in the world'.

4.2.1.2 A statement of law An untrue statement of law, i.e., what the law is, cannot be a misrepresentation because everyone is presumed to know the law.

> EXAMPLE
>
> Alice buys a television because the salesman tells her that if she buys while Parliament is not sitting she will not need a television licence.

4.2.1.3 A statement of opinion This is not a misrepresentation but if the person making the statement professes to have some special knowledge, the statement is likely to be treated as one of fact.

Bisset v Wilkinson (1927)

The defendant was selling some land and told the claimant it would support 2,000 sheep, although sheep had never been kept there and the claimant knew this. It was held by the Privy Council that this was merely an opinion which the claimant must have realised and it could not be a misrepresentation.

If for example, in the above case, the defendant had been a sheep farmer, then his statement would have been fact rather than opinion.

4.2.1.4 A statement about the future   If a party makes a statement about future conduct but does not do what is promised, the statement does not become a misrepresentation. A statement about the future cannot be a statement of fact by its nature, as no one knows what will happen in the future. But if the person making the statement had no intention of doing the act, this misrepresents his present intention, which can be a statement of fact.

Edgington v Fitzmaurice (1885)

The directors of a company invited loans from the public for the purpose of developing the business. In fact the directors intended to use the money to pay off existing debts. The Court of Appeal held that the statement of intention was a statement of fact and amounted to a fraudulent misrepresentation: ' . . . the state of a man's mind is as much a fact as the state of his digestion' (Bowen LJ).

4.2.1.5 Silence   Simply keeping quiet about something does not amount to a misrepresentation, as there is no general duty to disclose everything in making a contract. However, there are a number of exceptions to this, e.g., statements which become false, half truths and contracts of the utmost good faith.

(A) STATEMENTS WHICH BECOME FALSE

A statement which is true when made may later become false.

With v O'Flanagan (1936)

The defendant doctor was selling his practice and in January told the claimant that it was worth £2,000 a year, but the defendant then became ill and when the contract was signed in May it was only worth £250. It was held that because of the vast change in circumstances, there was a duty to disclose the fall in value, so keeping quiet was a misrepresentation.

(B) HALF TRUTHS

Although what has been said is literally true, it may only be part of the facts and what is unsaid may change the meaning.

Nottingham Patent Brick and Tile Co. v Butler (1885)

The buyer of land asked the seller's solicitor if there were any restrictive covenants on the land and the solicitor said he did not know of any. He did not say that he had not bothered to read the documents. The court held that even though the statement was literally true it was a misrepresentation. There were restrictive covenants and the contract could be rescinded.

(c) UTMOST GOOD FAITH

Some contracts are called *uberrimae fidei* (of the utmost good faith) and in these contracts parties are under a duty to disclose all material facts. A material fact is something which would influence a reasonable person in making the contract. A good example is a contract of life assurance, which requires the person taking out the policy to tell the insurer any material facts about their health. If they fail to do this, the contract may be avoided.

4.2.2 What amounts to an inducement?
It must be shown that the statement met the following conditions.

4.2.2.1 It must be material A statement is only material if it influences a person to make a contract. The courts used to apply an *objective* test of whether the reasonable man would be influenced to make the contract, but a recent case applied a *subjective* test of whether the claimant was induced by the misrepresentation. In *Museprime Properties Ltd* v *Adhill Properties Ltd* (1990) the court said that obviously the more unreasonable the misrepresentation seems to the court, the less likely the claimant will be able to prove that it influenced him.

4.2.2.2 It must have been relied on A party cannot claim misrepresentation if they did not know about it, *or* they relied on their own information *or* they knew the real truth.

Attwood v *Small* (1838)
The seller of a mine made statements about the earnings of a mine but the buyer appointed his own agents, who confirmed the earning capacity. The statement by the seller was not true but the House of Lords held that because the buyer had relied on his own findings he could not claim misrepresentation.

A party who is given the chance to check the truth of a statement but does not, can still rely on misrepresentation.

Redgrave v *Hurd* (1881)
The claimant solicitor was selling his practice and told the defendant that it was worth £400 a year. The claimant produced receipts for £200 and some papers which he claimed showed the rest. The defendant did not examine these papers which only showed £5 more! The Court of Appeal held that the defendant had relied on the statement, it did not matter that he could have discovered the truth.

If one party makes a statement to another party but realises that the information will be given to a third party who is likely to act on it, the maker of the statement will be liable (*Smith* v *Eric S. Bush* (1989), see *Exclusion Clauses,* 4.2.5, above).

4.3 Types of misrepresentation

4.3.1 Introduction
There are three types of misrepresentation, namely fraudulent, negligent and wholly innocent. The importance of the distinction lies in the remedies available for each type.

4.3.2 Fraudulent misrepresentation

A statement is fraudulent if it is made knowing it is false, *or* without belief in its truth, *or* recklessly, which means without caring whether it is true or false. If someone makes a statement which they honestly believe is true, then it cannot be fraudulent. Neither is carelessness in making a statement enough for fraud. A claim for fraudulent mis-representation is a claim in the tort of deceit. The remedies are rescission and damages.

4.3.3 Negligent misrepresentation

This is a false statement made by a person who had no reasonable grounds for believing it to be true. There are two possible ways to claim: either under common law *or* statute.

4.3.3.1 Common law   It was not until *Hedley Byrne & Co. Ltd* v *Heller & Partners Ltd* (1963) that the tort of negligence was extended to cover negligent statements.

Hedley Byrne & Co. Ltd v *Heller & Partners Ltd* (1963)

The claimants intended to make a contract with another company but first asked their bank to find out about that company's financial standing. Their bank was given a reference by the company's bank (defendants) which negligently said that the company was sound. The claimants made the contract and lost £17,000. The House of Lords held that the defendants knew that the information would be given to the claimants and that they would rely on it, therefore there was a 'special relationship' between the parties and a duty of care was owed to the claimants.

Because the advice was given 'without responsibility' the defendants were not liable in the actual case but the principle of the case is important, that if a special relationship can be established a duty will be owed.

4.3.3.2 Statute   The Misrepresentation Act 1967, s. 2(1), provides that if a person makes a contract after a misrepresentation has been made by the other party to the contract, the person making the misrepresentation will be liable in damages unless he proves he had reasonable grounds to believe and did believe that the facts represented were true.

This differs from liability at common law because (a) there is no need to prove a 'special relationship' (b) the person who makes the statement is liable, unless he proves he had reasonable grounds to believe the facts were true; (c) there has to be a contract between the two parties to the misrepresentation. Normally a party will choose to sue under s. 2(1).

F & H Entertainments Ltd v *Leisure Enterprises Ltd* (1976)

The claimants leased a club from the defendants after being told that the rent was £2,400 and no rent review notice had been served, so the rent could not increase. The claimants spent £4,000 on renovations and then got a demand for £6,500 rent as a notice had been served. It was held that as the defendants could not prove they had reasonable grounds to believe their statement was true, it must be negligent. The claimants were entitled to £4,000 damages.

Spice Girls Ltd v *Aprilia World Service BV* (2002)
In March 1998 the claimant group 'currently comprising' five members, made a contract with the defendants. It was agreed that the claimants would promote the defendants' scooters and in return the defendants would sponsor a world tour by the claimants. The defendants produced a commercial and other promotional materials and made some payments to the claimants. In May 1998 one of the group, Geri Halliwell, left. The claimants claimed the remaining payment on the contract. The defendants argued that the group knew, at the time they made the contract, that Geri Halliwell was going to leave and that the defendants had not been told. The fact that all five members took part in the promotional material was a misrepresentation that they would all be together for the period of the promotion. The defendants said that if it had not been for this misrepresentation, they would not have made the contract. The Court of Appeal held that the claimants were liable under s. 2(1) and had to pay damages to the defendants.   *Spice Girls*   *Misrepresentation Act s. 2(1)*

4.3.4 Wholly innocent misrepresentation
This is a false statement which the person makes honestly believing it to be true. Originally the only remedy for such a misrepresentation was rescission of the contract, as damages were not available. This was unsatisfactory because even if the misrepresentation was about something minor the only remedy was to set aside the whole contract. The Misrepresentation Act 1967, s. 2(2), now gives the court a discretion to treat the contract as continuing and award damages in lieu of rescission.

4.4 Remedies for misrepresentation

4.4.1 Introduction
The remedies available include avoiding the contract, rescission, indemnity and damages. A party may claim damages in addition to rescission.

4.4.2 Avoiding the contract
This remedy is available in all cases of misrepresentation. The effect of the misrepresentation is to make the contract voidable and there is a choice of ending the contract or continuing with it. The action to take will depend on the circumstances. The party may simply refuse to carry out his part of the contract. Alternatively he may inform the other party that he wishes to avoid the contract, by sending a formal notice or by conduct.

4.4.3 Rescission — *you have to go to Court*
This remedy is available in all cases of misrepresentation. It is the formal method of ending the contract by applying to the court for an order of rescission. The aim of rescission is to put the parties back in their original position, as though the contract had not been made. If a party does everything in their power to tell the other party they want to end the contract, that will be sufficient.

Car and Universal Finance Co. Ltd v Caldwell (1964)
The owner of a car sold it to a rogue, who gave him a cheque which was not honoured.

The day after the sale the owner told the police and the Automobile Association. Three days later the rogue sold the car to a third party. It was held that the contract was voidable because of the fraudulent misrepresentation and the owner had done everything he could in the circumstances to avoid the contract. As it had been avoided before the sale to the third party, no title was passed to them and the owner could reclaim the car.

Where a right of rescission is available but the court thinks it is not appropriate to grant rescission, it may instead award damages under the Misrepresentation Act 1967, s. 2(2). Guidance on such awards was given *obiter* in the next case.

William Sindall v *Cambridgeshire County Council* (1994)

The claimant bought land from the defendant for over £5m. The claimant then discovered a sewer running under the land, which had not been disclosed. This meant that the land over the sewer could not be built on. During the ensuing delay the value of the land fell by more than half largely due to a general fall in property values. The claimant wished to obtain rescission of the contract on the basis of mistake or misrepresentation. The Court of Appeal held that there had been no misrepresentation by the defendant, and even if there had been a misrepresentation the Court would have exercised its discretion to award damages under s. 2(2). The measure of damages should be the difference in value between what the claimant was misled into believing he was acquiring and the value of what he actually acquired. This assessment was to be made at the time of the contract and should not take into account subsequent losses. The damages would have been the cost of diverting the sewer, approximately £18,000. If losses after the contract had been taken into account, the damages would have been nearly £3m.

Rescission is an equitable remedy and is awarded at the discretion of the court. It will not be granted in the following circumstances.

4.4.3.1 Where restitution is impossible   The normal rule is that to get restitution each party must give back any benefits obtained. If this is not possible then rescission is not available. The rescission does not have to be exact and the court may impose terms to provide a just solution.

4.4.3.2 Affirmation of the contract   If the party affected by the misrepresentation continues with the contract after finding out the truth, then they cannot claim rescission.

4.4.3.3 Lapse of time   If the party affected does not take action to rescind within a reasonable time, the right will be lost. In cases of fraudulent misrepresentation, time only begins to run from the discovery of the fraud.

Leaf v *International Galleries* (1950)

The claimant bought a painting after an innocent misrepresentation was made to him that it was by 'J Constable'. He did not discover this until five years later and claimed rescission immediately. The Court of Appeal held that the claimant had lost his right to rescind after such a period of time.

Mistake of Quality not operative

— Like 4.4.3.1

bona fide

4.4.3.4 Third party acquires rights

If a third party acquires rights in property, in good faith and for value, the party affected by the misrepresentation will lose their right to rescind.

4.4.4 Indemnity

In all cases where the claimants are entitled to rescission, they are also entitled to an *indemnity* where appropriate. An indemnity is not damages but consists only of expenses which had to be incurred in complying with the terms of the contract.

4.4.5 Damages *— if you commit a fraud you pay for it.*

Damages may be claimed as of right only for fraudulent and negligent misrepresentation. Damages may be given for innocent misrepresentation instead of rescission, but this is at the discretion of the court (Misrepresentation Act 1967, s. 2(2)).

For fraudulent misrepresentation, all direct damages may be claimed: they do not have to be foreseeable. Damages may also be claimed for loss of profits (*East* v *Maurer* (1991)).

Smith New Court Securities Ltd v Scrimgeour Vickers Ltd (1996)

fraud

In July 1989 the claimants bought 28 million shares in Ferranti plc from the second defendants (a bank) after a bank employee told them that there were two other bidders, so the claimants bid above the quoted share price. In September Ferranti plc announced it had been the victim of a major fraud and the share price plummeted. The claimants later sold their shares and lost approximately £11m. They claimed damages for fraudulent misrepresentation. The Court of Appeal said that the measure of damages was the difference between the price paid and the price the shares would have fetched on the open market, without the misrepresentation. The Court awarded about £1m damages. The House of Lords said that the victim of a fraudulent misrepresentation was entitled to all direct losses flowing from the transaction induced by the fraud. The normal method of calculating the loss was the price paid less the value of the assets at the date of sale, but the overriding principle was that the claimant should obtain full compensation for the wrong. The normal method did not apply where the claimant was 'locked in' to the property. The claimants were locked in here because they had bought at a high price and could not sensibly sell the shares when the fraud was first announced. They were entitled to damages based on the difference between the contract price and the amount the shares were sold for, which was approximately £11m.

For negligent misrepresentation at common law, only damages which are foreseeable can be claimed.

Tort damages

For misrepresentation under the Misrepresentation Act 1967, s. 2(1), all direct damages can be claimed, on the same basis as fraudulent misrepresentation (*Royscot Trust Ltd* v *Rogerson* (1991)).

Damages in the three instances above are awarded on a tort basis, which means that the aim is to put the claimant in the position they would have been in, if the misrepresentation had not been made. In the case of fraudulent misrepresentation, as loss of profits can now be awarded this puts the claim on a par with a claim for breach of contract.

4.5 Excluding liability for misrepresentation

Under the Misrepresentation Act 1967, s. 3, as amended by the Unfair Contract Terms Act 1977, s. 8, any term of a contract which excludes liability for misrepresentation or restricts the remedies available is subject to the test of *reasonableness* (see *Exclusion Clauses*, 4.2.5, above).

4.6 Criminal liability for misrepresentation

Fraudulent misrepresentation is a crime as well as a tort and the person responsible may be prosecuted. However, the burden of proof, beyond all reasonable doubt, means that prosecution is often unlikely. Under the Property Misdescriptions Act 1991 it is a criminal offence, in the course of an estate agency or property development business, to make a false or misleading statement relating to land about any of the 33 matters set out in an Order made under the Act. For example, to give the wrong size of rooms or wrongly state that a property has been subject to a treatment, such as woodworm treatment. The Act is enforced by trading standards departments.

5 Duress and undue influence

5.1 Introduction

To make a valid contract the parties must act freely. If one of the parties is forced to make the contract by violence or the threat of violence, that is *duress*. If one party uses their influence over another to take unfair advantage of them, that is *undue influence*. In either case the contract is voidable. Undue influence is far more likely to be met in practice than duress.

5.2 Duress

Duress is a common law rule. It means actual violence or the threat of violence, which forces the other party to make a contract. A threat to commit a crime or tort against the person will be duress. Duress includes a threat to one's immediate family. The violence or threat may be made through an agent. – the heavy mob!

Barton v *Armstrong* (1976)

The defendant threatened to kill the claimant unless the claimant bought shares from him at an overvaluation. The claimant made the contract and later claimed duress. It was held by the Privy Council that the contract had been made under duress and could be set aside.

In the past a threat to the goods of another person was not enough to be duress. In recent years the courts have taken a more flexible approach. In *The Sibeon and the Sibotre* (1976) it was said that a threat to slash a valuable painting belonging to the other party would be duress.

The courts have also recognised that 'economic duress', i.e., pressure causing financial loss, is enough to make the contract voidable.

The Atlantic Baron (1978)   *Economic Duress*

The defendants agreed to build a tanker for the claimants, but before they completed it they demanded an extra 10 per cent of the contract price. The claimants initially refused to pay this, but because they wanted the tanker for a charter they agreed. Six months after the tanker was delivered the claimants wished to recover the 10 per cent claiming economic duress by the defendants. It was held that the defendants' threat was economic duress, and the contract was voidable but waiting six months meant that the right was lost.

The difficulty facing the courts is distinguishing between normal commercial pressure and what is sufficient coercion to be duress. In deciding this they will take into account factors like whether the party complained, whether there was an alternative open to them apart from making the contract and whether they acted quickly to avoid the contract when the pressure was removed.

Atlas Express Ltd v Kafco (Importers and Distributors) Ltd (1989)

The claimants made a contract with the defendants, a small company who made basketware, to deliver the defendants' goods to Woolworths. The claimants quoted a price based on large loads and when the defendants produced only small ones, the claimants demanded more money. The defendants agreed as they could not re-arrange deliveries and they depended heavily on the order to Woolworths. Later the defendants refused to pay. It was held that the defendants had acted under economic duress and were therefore not liable to pay the extra money.

Note that there might have been economic duress in *Williams* v *Roffey Bros & Nicholls (Contractors) Ltd* (1990) if the subcontractor had put pressure on the main contractor, to pay more money for finishing the job.

5.3 Undue influence

5.3.1 General principles

The courts of equity developed the doctrine of undue influence because the common law doctrine of duress was so narrow. For undue influence, it has to be shown that one party has exercised improper pressure over another. The House of Lords reviewed the law on undue influence in *Barclays Bank plc* v *O'Brien* (1993) and adopted the following categories of undue influence:

(a) Actual undue influence.

(b) Presumed undue influence:

  (i)   relationships in which undue influence is automatically presumed;

  (ii)   relationships of trust which may raise a presumption of undue influence.

The House of Lords has again reviewed the law in *Royal Bank of Scotland* v *Etridge (No. 2) and other appeals* (2001) and made some important alterations to it.

Burden of Proof on claimant (handwritten margin note)

5.3.2 *Actual undue influence*

The person claiming undue influence must prove that actual undue influence was put on him or her to make the agreement.

Williams v *Bayley* (1866)

A son forged his father's signature on some negotiable instruments. The bank manager told the father: 'This is a serious matter, a case of transportation for life'. The father then agreed to mortgage his coal mine to the bank in return for the forged instruments. It was held that the mortgage could be set aside as the father had proved undue pressure by the bank, which was the implied threat of prosecution of the son.

Previously a claim based on actual undue influence would fail unless it was shown that the agreement was to the 'manifest disadvantage' of the person claiming. This is no longer necessary (*CIBC Mortgages plc* v *Pitt* (1993)).

5.3.3 *Presumed undue influence*

In these cases there is no need to prove actual undue influence.

(a) The law recognises certain relationships in which undue influence is presumed. These relationships include parent and child, doctor and patient, religious adviser and follower, solicitor and client, trustee and beneficiary.

(b) In other relationships, if the person claiming can show that he or she put trust in the wrongdoer in relation to financial matters and that there is a contract which cannot be easily explained by the relationship, this leads to a presumption of undue influence. For example, transactions between husbands and wives could be in this category. In ROYAL BANK OF SCOTLAND *v* ETRIDGE (2001) the House of Lords seems to have abolished the distinction between (a) and (b) above and Lord Nicholls set out the following requirements. The person claiming undue influence must show that they have put trust and confidence in the other party, rather than whether the relationship belongs to a particular type. The person claiming must show (1) that they put trust in the other in financial matters, and (2) that there is a transaction, which given the relationship of the parties, needs some explanation. The bank must then take reasonable steps to see that there was no undue influence. When a wife stands surety for her husband's debts a bank is put on enquiry. These principles could equally apply to other relationships, like cohabitees (whether heterosexual or homosexual) or children and their parents.

Previously, with both the above presumptions, the transaction had to be to the 'manifest disadvantage' of the party claiming undue influence.

National Westminster Bank plc v *Morgan* (1985)

Mr and Mrs Morgan were buying a house in joint names on a building society mortgage. Mr Morgan had financial difficulties in his business and the building society sought possession of the house. The couple asked the claimant bank for a loan to pay the building society mortgage. The bank manager visited Mrs Morgan at home and got her to sign a new mortgage after telling her that it did not cover her husband's business. This statement was made honestly but it was wrong. Shortly after this Mr Morgan died and the bank sought possession of the house. The House of Lords held that there was no presumption of undue influence by the bank and Mrs Morgan could not prove the bank mortgage was a 'manifest disadvantage' to her, rather it was a benefit in allowing her to stay in her home.

The House of Lords, in *Royal Bank of Scotland* v *Etridge (No. 2) and other appeals* (2001) has now said that the requirement of 'manifest disadvantage' can lead to confusion and should not be used. This should be borne in mind when reading the cases decided before the House of Lords decision.

Barclays Bank plc v *Coleman* (2001)

C borrowed money from the bank to buy an investment property and granted the bank a charge over the jointly owned matrimonial home. C and his wife went to a firm of solicitors to execute the charge and were dealt with by S, a legal executive. S confirmed to the bank that the charge had been explained to the wife and that she had signed it of her own free will. Later the bank claimed the property and the wife said that the bank had constructive notice of her husband's undue influence. The Court of Appeal said that with presumed undue influence manifest disadvantage had to be shown. This disadvantage could be small if it was clear and obvious. The charge was an 'all moneys' clause which covered all future borrowings, this had not been pointed out and was a clear disadvantage to the wife. But the bank did not have constructive notice of the wife's rights because it was entitled to rely on the legal executive's certificate which had been given with the authority of the solicitor. The bank could take the house.

The appeal was dealt with by the House of Lords in *Royal Bank of Scotland* v *Etridge (No. 2) and other appeals* (2001) and the court said that the bank could reasonably believe that Mrs C's signature had been obtained properly and her appeal was dismissed.

5.3.4 Undue influence and third parties

Sometimes there are three parties involved in the transaction, for example, if a wife is giving a guarantee to a bank for her husband's debts. Can the husband's undue influence affect the wife's contract of guarantee with the bank?

Two arguments have been used. First, that the husband is the agent of the bank in getting his wife to sign. Secondly, that the wife has a 'special equity' which protects wives who are under the influence of their husbands in financial matters, so creditors are under a duty to check that the wife understood the transaction.

Barclays Bank plc v *O'Brien* (1993)

A husband and wife jointly owned their home and signed a mortgage over it for the husband's business debts without reading the document. The husband had told his wife it was for £60,000 but it was actually for £135,000. The bank staff, contrary to instructions, had not explained the nature of the transaction or that the couple should obtain independent legal advice. Later the bank sought possession of the home. The House of Lords rejected the arguments of agency and special equity. It was accepted that Mrs O'Brien was an intelligent and independent-minded woman, who had not been subject to undue influence. Could the husband's misrepresentation affect the bank's claim to the house? They said that if a wife gave a guarantee for the debts of her husband and the creditor knew they were cohabitees, the guarantee was valid unless there was undue influence or misrepresentation by the husband. In such cases the creditor would have to take reasonable steps to see that the wife had made the agreement freely, otherwise the creditor could be regarded as having 'constructive notice' of the wife's right to set the guarantee aside. The bank would have to tell the wife (without her husband being present) about the risks, the amount of the guarantee, and that she should take independent legal advice. Here the bank knew they were husband and wife and were put on enquiry but had not taken reasonable steps to tell the wife. Therefore the guarantee could be set aside.

This case was distinguished in the next case, decided by the House of Lords on the same day.

CIBC Mortgages plc v Pitt (1993)

The husband wanted to borrow money to speculate on the stock market, using the home as security for the loan. The wife eventually agreed to this under pressure. The claimants lent £150,000 which the husband told them was to pay off the mortgage and to buy a holiday home. The wife did not know the amount of the loan and signed the mortgage without reading it and without obtaining any independent advice. Later the claimants claimed possession. The House of Lords held that the wife had proved actual undue influence by her husband. But the claimants simply knew it was a joint loan to a husband and wife to pay off a mortgage and had no actual or constructive notice of the undue influence. The wife's claim to set the mortgage aside was dismissed.

In *Barclays Bank plc v O'Brien*, the loan was for the husband's business debts, whereas in *CIBC Mortgages plc v Pitt* the loan, as far as the lender knew, was for the joint benefit of the husband and wife. The lender, in the latter case, was therefore not put on enquiry as to whether the wife was subject to undue influence.

Royal Bank of Scotland v Etridge (1997)

A wife signed a mortgage with the claimant bank as security for her husband's business. The bank had appointed a solicitor to act on its behalf and the mortgage was signed in the presence of that solicitor. Later the bank claimed possession and the wife claimed the undue influence of her husband and that the effect of the mortgage had not been explained to her. It was held by the Court of Appeal that where a bank appointed a solicitor to discharge its duty to ensure that the wife obtained independent advice about the effect of a mortgage, the bank remained responsible to see that the duty was carried out. If the duty was not carried out the bank had constructive notice of any undue influence. The bank was in the same position as its agent and had not done enough to ensure that the wife obtained independent advice.

Kenyon-Brown v Desmond Banks & Co. (2000)

Mr KB wished to buy back a controlling interest in his company and Mr and Mrs KB gave the bank a charge over their home for the loan. B, a solicitor, who had acted for Mr and Mrs KB before saw Mrs KB and confirmed this with the bank. When the bank claimed the house Mrs KB said that she had only signed because her husband had told her that otherwise they would be bankrupt. Mrs KB had told B that she understood the transaction and did not wish to go into it further. The Court of Appeal raised the question whether B should have recognised the risk of undue influence and told her to go somewhere else for advice. B was instructed to give Mrs KB independent advice and B had to be satisfied that his client was free from undue influence. B had not ascertained the amount of the loan and did not know her husband had said she would be made bankrupt, which were relevant matters in deciding if she had acted freely. B had not considered whether the mortgage was in the best interests of Mrs KB and he should not have confirmed to the bank that she acted freely. The mortgage could be set aside.

The appeal to the House of Lords was dealt with in *Royal Bank of Scotland* v *Etridge (No. 2) and other appeals* (2001) and the court said that B, the solicitor, had discharged his duty and the appeal was allowed.

Crédit Lyonnaise v Burch (1997)

The defendant was a junior employee of Pelosi, who owned a tour operator. Pelosi asked her to give a mortgage over her flat as security to cover an increase in the company's overdraft. He told her that if she did not do so, the company would go into liquidation and she would lose her job. The bank told the defendant that the mortgage was unlimited. The defendant signed the mortgage at the bank's solicitors in Pelosi's presence. The defendant was not told that the amount of the overdraft was being increased from £250,000 to £270,000. The business went into liquidation and the bank sought possession of the defendant's flat which was worth £100,000. It was held by the Court of Appeal that the relationship of trust and confidence raised a presumption of undue influence. The transaction was a manifest disadvantage to the defendant, as she did not know the extent of her liability and had risked her home to help a company in which she had no direct financial interest. The bank had not taken reasonable steps to avoid constructive notice of the undue influence, as she had not been told the extent of her liability and had not received independent advice. The mortgage could be set aside.

Banco Exterior Internacional v Thomas (1997)

Mrs D's husband died in 1982 and she found herself short of money. In 1983 she met M and developed a close, but not a sexual, friendship with him. M wished to expand his used car business and offered to pay D an income of £500 per month if she would provide a mortgage for his overdraft at the claimant bank. D agreed to this. The bank sent D to a solicitor for advice. D went to the solicitor and signed the mortgage. The deeds for D's house had to be obtained from her former solicitor, who told both D and the bank that he was against the transaction. When M's business got into financial difficulties, the bank claimed D's house. D died before the case came to trial, but her executors argued that D was under the undue influence of M and that the bank had constructive notice of this. The Court of Appeal asked the question whether there was a presumption of undue influence. D had been given advice about the nature of the transaction by an independent solicitor and by her former solicitor but took no steps to set aside the transaction. Any presumption of undue influence was rebutted. The Court also asked whether the bank had constructive notice of the undue influence. It was argued for D that the bank should have made enquiries about the nature of the relationship between D and M. The Court said that a bank has no business enquiring into the personal relationships of those it does business with. The bank's duty was to ensure that D knew what she was doing and wanted to do it, and the bank had fulfilled that duty.

The fact that a solicitor acts for both husband and wife is not in itself sufficient to make a charge void; there has to be evidence of duress or misrepresentation.

The House of Lords has set out guidelines in the following case.

Royal Bank of Scotland v Etridge (No. 2) and other appeals (2001)

The court heard a number of appeals involving wives who had given banks a charge over the matrimonial home as security for their husbands' debts. The court issued the following guidance for use in such circumstances:

(1) A bank is put on enquiry where a wife offers security for her husband's debts, or a husband for his wife's debts. Such a transaction is not to the financial advantage of the wife and the husband may have committed a wrong in persuading the wife to act. The bank does not have to know that the parties are co-habiting or that the wife places trust in the husband.

(2) The bank only needs to take reasonable steps to see that the wife enters the contract with her eyes open and understands the practical implications of the contract. This could be discharged by the bank relying on confirmation by the wife's solicitor that she has been advised accordingly.

(3) The solicitor should advise the wife on the legal and practical implications of the contract. The advice should cover the following as a 'core minimum': the nature of the documents and the practical implications of signing; the seriousness of the risks involved; the purpose of the borrowing; the amount, interest and principal terms; the amount of her liability. The solicitor should also state that the wife has a choice about signing. The solicitor should point out that he would only tell the bank she wished to proceed with her authority. The solicitor should meet the wife without her husband being present.

(4) It was not for the solicitor to veto the transaction by not telling the bank he has explained matters to the wife. Even if the solicitor advises against the wife signing, she can still go ahead.

(5) The solicitor acting for the wife may also act for the husband or the bank provided he is satisfied that this will not lead to a conflict of duty.

(6) As regards future transactions once the bank is put on enquiry it should: (a) communicate directly with the wife and require written confirmation that she has been advised by her solicitor; (b) if the bank does not wish to tell the wife about her husband's finances, it should give the information to the solicitor. This information would include the purpose of the new borrowing, the amount of the debt, the amount of the overdraft, the amount of the new loan. The bank needs the consent of the husband to divulge this information otherwise the loan cannot go ahead; if the bank suspects the wife has been misled by her husband it must tell the wife's solicitor.

The court also said that banks were put on enquiry in all cases where the relationship between the debtor and the person acting as guarantor was non-commercial. So if a wife offers to give security for her husband's debts the bank was put on enquiry. If the bank did not take the required steps, it will be deemed to have notice of any claim by the guarantor that the transaction was made as a result of undue influence or misrepresentation.

If a wife guarantees her husband's debts, this cannot be assumed to be undue influence, although in some cases it will need to be explained. The requirement to prove 'manifest disadvantage' can cause misunderstanding and should no longer be used. Lord Nicholls (who along with Lord Scott gave the two main judgments) said that where a wife guarantees her husband's debts, this is a disadvantage in the narrow sense because she takes on the obligation but receives nothing for it. But in a wider sense such a transaction may be for her benefit, for example, if the husband's business is the source of the family income. Which was the correct approach? 'The answer is neither. The answer lies in discarding a label which gives rise to this sort of ambiguity.' With regard to the second requirement for raising the presumption of undue influence, the amount of the gift and the circumstances had to be considered. For example if the gift was a small one then some proof of the exercise of undue influence was needed.

When a bank is put on enquiry this does not mean that the bank needs to find out if the wife's consent was obtained by undue influence. The most that can be expected is that the bank takes reasonable steps to see that the wife is told the practical implications of signing a guarantee.

Cases decided prior to the above decision must now be read in the light of the above requirements set out by the House of Lords. A bank which takes security from a wife for her husband's debts and wishes to enforce that security must ask three questions. Has the wife produced some evidence of undue influence by her husband? Was the bank put on enquiry? Did the bank take reasonable steps to check that there was no undue influence? The House of Lords was critical of the existing system of independent legal advice where banks took guarantees from wives and described it as 'a charade'.

5.4 Remedies for duress and undue influence

If the other party tries to enforce the contract, the court can prevent this.

The innocent party may wish to claim rescission of the contract, which means that both parties are put back into their original positions. If there is a delay in claiming or if third parties acquire rights in the property, the right to rescission may be lost. Putting the parties in their original position may prove difficult.

Cheese v Thomas (1994)

A house was bought for £83,000, with £43,000 from the claimant and £40,000 on mortgage, from his great nephew, the defendant. The house was put in the defendant's name but the claimant was to have a life interest. When the defendant stopped paying the mortgage, the claimant claimed undue influence and asked for his money back. The house was sold for £55,000 and the claimant claimed £43,000. It was held by the Court of Appeal that the parties should be put into their original positions, as far as possible, but the defendant should not bear the loss. The sale money should be divided in proportion to their contributions to the purchase (i.e., 43:40).

6 Capacity

6.1 Introduction

As a general rule anyone can make a valid contract. However, the law treats certain persons as being under an incapacity, so they do not have the same ability to make contracts as normal adults. These persons include minors, drunks, those suffering mental disorder and corporations. The law recognises that natural persons under an incapacity need protection and rules were made to provide this. Since the age for minors was lowered to 18 years by the Family Law Reform Act 1969, s. 1, this area of contract law has become of less practical importance, as few minors go into business. Similarly with companies, the passing of the Companies Act 1989 means fewer problems with companies acting outside their powers.

6.2 Minors

6.2.1 Introduction

A minor is someone under 18 years of age and if such a person makes a contract it is not generally binding on them. The contracts made by minors fall into three groups, valid, voidable and others.

6.2.2 Valid contracts

A minor may make a valid contract for necessaries or a contract of employment which is for their benefit.

If the minor buys necessaries they have to pay for them. But under the Sale of Goods Act 1979, s. 3(2) the minor only has to pay a reasonable price. They may also sue on the contract. Necessaries have been defined in the Sale of Goods Act 1979, s. 3(3) as 'goods suitable to the condition in life of the minor and to his actual requirements at the time of sale and delivery'. They are not limited to 'necessities' but can cover a wide range of items from food and clothing to education and even a funeral!

In determining whether something is a necessary, the court will take into account both the social status of the minor *and* their existing supply of the item.

Nash v *Inman* (1908)

The defendant, a student at Cambridge University, bought £145 worth of clothes, including eleven fancy waistcoats, from the claimant on credit. The student's father had already given him plenty of clothes. The Court of Appeal held that as regards status the student needed the clothes but as he already had plenty, they could not be necessaries. Therefore he did not have to pay for them.

If the minor enters a contract of employment (sometimes known as 'beneficial contracts of service') that will only be binding if on the whole it is for the benefit of the minor. The fact that some terms are not beneficial will not invalidate the contract.

6.2.3 Voidable contracts

Some contracts which a minor makes are voidable. This means they are binding initially but the minor may reject the contract before reaching 18 years of age *or* within a reasonable time afterwards. The other party to the contract cannot reject it. These contracts involve continuing obligations like agreements to buy or rent land, to buy shares or to enter a partnership.

6.2.4 Other contracts

This covers any contract which is not for necessaries or not voidable. Contracts in this third category are not binding on the minor but are binding on the other party. If a minor ratifies such a contract after reaching full age it is enforceable (Minors' Contracts Act 1987, s. 1). *If child's capital is at risk its void.*

EXAMPLE

Adam, aged 17 years, borrows £500 from the Busy Bank. Adam cannot be sued for this money. *Void against a minor*

6.2.5 Restitution

In cases where a contract is not binding or the minor has repudiated the contract, the court now has power to order the minor to give back any property acquired under the contract. The Minors' Contracts Act 1987, s. 3(1) provides that the court may, if it is just and equitable to do so, require the minor to transfer to the other party any property acquired by the minor or any property representing it.

EXAMPLE

If *Nash* v *Inman* (1908) occurred again, the court could order the minor to give back the waistcoats.

6.3 Corporations

6.3.1 Introduction

A corporation is an artificial person but has legal personality in the same way as a natural person (a human being). A corporation has to be created in some way and this may be done by Royal Charter, Act of Parliament or under the Companies Acts. The latter method is the most important.

6.3.2 Contractual capacity

When a corporation is created its powers are set out in the document creating it. In the case of creation under the Companies Acts the powers are set out in the 'objects clause 'in a document called the memorandum of association. This has to be registered with the Registrar of Companies. In the past a company could only make contracts covered by the objects clause and if it did anything outside the stated objects this was treated as *ultra vires* and void. This caused problems for people making contracts with companies who acted outside their objects, as the contracts would be void. The Companies Act 1989 provides that any contract made by the company, even if outside the objects, is regarded as valid as far as outsiders are concerned (i.e., someone dealing with the company in good faith). However, shareholders may still stop a company making a contract which is outside its objects clause but if the contract has been made, the shareholders cannot claim it is outside the powers of the company.

Discharge of the contract

1 Introduction

To discharge a contract means to bring it to an end. The effect is that the parties do not have to fulfill their primary obligations and carry out the contract. In the case of discharge by breach, the party at fault may still have a secondary obligation to pay damages (see *Contents of a Contract*, 6.1). A contract may be discharged by performance, agreement, frustration and breach. The usual way that a contract is discharged is by each party *performing* their obligations. They may also *agree* to end the contract by making a new contract to this effect. The contract may also end by *frustration*, an outside cause which prevents the contract being carried out. Lastly if one party *breaks* the contract, the other party may treat this as ending it.

2 Discharge by performance

2.1 General rule

Performance is the most obvious way of ending a contract.

> **EXAMPLE**
>
> Alice buys a bar of chocolate from Bertie's shop. When Alice has paid the price and Bertie has handed over the chocolate, the contract has been performed and ends.

The general rule is, that *performance must be precise and exact*. The parties must kee, strictly to what they agreed, if they do something less than or different from what was agreed, this does not discharge the contract. A party who has not performed exactly cannot sue on the contract.

Cutter v Powell (1795)

The claimant's husband signed on as second mate, on a ship sailing from Kingston, Jamaica to Liverpool, for 30 guineas. He died half way through the voyage and his widow sued for part of the contract price. It was held that as Cutter had not carried out his entire duty of sailing to Liverpool, he was not entitled to anything. The payment to Cutter was much more than the normal rate of pay, so this was not as harsh as it seems.

2.2 Exceptions

If the rule that performance must be precise and exact was strictly applied it would cause injustice and the courts have recognised a number of exceptions, e.g., severable obligations, prevention of performance, acceptance of part performance and substantial performance.

2.2.1 *Severable obligations*

A distinction is made between *entire* and *severable* obligations. An *entire* obligation is one which must be completely performed before the party doing it can legally claim payment. A *severable* (or *divisible*) obligation is one which can be broken into independent parts, so payment can be enforced for each part. Whether an obligation is entire or severable depends on the intention of the parties and the terms and nature of the contract.

> EXAMPLES
>
> Alan agrees to take a lorry load of coal from Northampton to Newcastle, for Bob. This is an entire obligation and if Alan only took the coal to Sheffield that would not be sufficient and he would not be entitled to half payment.
>
> Chris agrees to take 10 tonnes of coal from Liverpool to London for Danny. This is a severable obligation and if Chris only takes three tonnes, he can be paid for that, if Danny accepts it.

Most contracts are severable and other examples include delivery of goods in instalments, payment of rent, contracts for work and materials and contracts of employment.

2.2.2 *Preventing performance*

If one party carries out part of the contract, but is stopped from finishing by the other party, then a claim may be made for what has been done. This is a claim for what the work is worth (*quantum meruit*). Alternatively a claim may be made for breach of contract.

Planche v *Colburn* (1831)

The claimant agreed to write a children's book on armour for the defendant for £100. The claimant wrote half of the book and the defendant then cancelled it. It was held that the claimant had not completed the contract so he could not enforce it, but he was entitled to £50 on a *quantum meruit* basis.

2.2.3 Accepting part performance

If one party partly performs the contract and the other party accepts this, it may be possible to say the parties have abandoned the original contract, whether entire or severable, and made a new one. Under the new contract, the party who partly performs is entitled to reasonable remuneration. The party accepting part performance must have a real choice in doing so.

Sumpter v *Hedges* (1898)

The claimant agreed to build two houses on the defendant's land for £565. The claimant did work worth £333 and then stopped. The defendant finished off the buildings, using materials left by the claimant. The claimant then claimed £333. The Court of Appeal held that the defendant could not leave the buildings in a dangerous state and had no choice in finishing them, so the claimant was not entitled to £333, but could claim payment for the materials used by the defendant.

2.2.4 Substantial performance

A party who has substantially carried out the contract may be able to claim payment for what has been done. A claim may not be made if there is a breach of condition or an innominate term which is treated as a condition, for in such cases there cannot be substantial performance. The party who substantially performs may have to pay damages for its own breach to the other party. The courts have shown that there are limits to such a claim and this can be seen by contrasting the following two cases.

Hoenig v *Isaacs* (1952)

The claimant agreed to redecorate the defendant's flat for £750 but the defendant claimed bad workmanship and only paid £400. The cost of putting right the defects was about £55. The claimant sued for the balance of the contract price. The Court of Appeal held that the claimant had substantially performed and the defects could be easily cured, so the claimant was entitled to £750 less £55.

A different conclusion was reached in the following case.

Bolton v *Mahadeva* (1972)

The claimant agreed to install central heating for the defendant for £560. The system was 10 per cent colder than promised and it gave off fumes. The cost of putting these defects right was £174. The defendant refused to pay. The Court of Appeal held that the claimant had *not* substantially performed, as he had not put in a central heating system and was not entitled to any payment. 'It is not merely that so very much of the work was shoddy, but it is the general ineffectiveness of it for its primary purpose that leads me to that conclusion' (Sachs LJ).

The Law Commission has recommended that the law should be changed following *Bolton* v *Mahadeva* and has said that a party who confers a net benefit should receive some payment (Pecuniary Restitution for Breach of Contract (1983) No. 121).

2.3 Tender of performance

A *tender* of performance is an offer to perform the contract. If one party cannot carry out their obligations under the contract without the help of the other party, then the law regards a tender of performance as being the same as performance.

Startup v *Macdonald* (1843)

The claimant agreed to sell ten tons of oil to the defendant and to deliver it during the last 14 days of March. The claimant tried to deliver it on Saturday 31 March at 8.30 p.m. but the defendant refused to take it. It was held that as the claimant had tendered performance, this was the equivalent of performance and he was entitled to damages.

[handwritten margin note: damages for non-acceptance]

Under the Sale of Goods Act 1979, s. 29(5) a tender of goods must be made at a reasonable hour. What is reasonable today will in part depend on the nature of the business, but in most cases delivery at 8.30 p.m. on Saturday would not be reasonable!

2.4 Time of performance

At common law if time was fixed for performance, it was 'of the essence'. This meant it was important and the contract had to be carried out by that date. In equity, time was not of the essence. The Law of Property Act 1925 provided that the equitable principle should prevail. The general rule is that time is not of the essence, even if a date is fixed for performance of the contract. However, it may be of the essence in certain cases:

(a) the contract *provides* that time is of the essence;

(b) it can be implied from the *nature* of the contract or the circumstances;

(c) time can be made of the essence by one party giving *notice* to the other that time is of the essence.

EXAMPLE

Alice is getting married and orders a wedding cake from Basil for 1 June. Time will be of the essence.

In *commercial contracts* time will usually be of the essence.

Where time is of the essence, if performance is late, the innocent party can repudiate the contract. If time is not of the essence, the innocent party cannot end the contract, but may claim damages.

3 Discharge by agreement

3.1 Introduction

A contract is made by agreement and may be ended by agreement. The agreement to discharge a contract may be made orally, by deed, in writing, or by conduct. Discharge may arise from the terms of the *original* contract or from a *new* contract. An example of the former is if a term in a contract of employment provided it would end in 12 months' time. In the case of a new contract, what needs to be done depends on whether the consideration is executory or executed.

3.2 Consideration for discharge

3.2.1 *Executory consideration*
If neither party to the original contract has carried out their part of the contract, then the consideration for the new contract will be a promise not to enforce the original obligations.

EXAMPLE

Alan agrees to sell Basil a video recorder for £300. If neither party has performed their part of the contract and they make a new agreement under which Alan agrees to supply a CD player, each party's consideration for this second contract is giving up their rights under the original contract: Basil gives up the right to a video recorder and Alan gives up the right to £300.

3.2.2 *Executed consideration*
Here the first party has carried out their part of the contract, but the second party is yet to perform. If the first party agrees to discharge the second party, this is not binding because the second party has not provided consideration. For the discharge to be binding it must be by deed or the second party must provide consideration.

EXAMPLE

Alice sells a car to Bob for £1,000. If Alice has delivered the car but Bob has not paid, then if they agree to discharge this contract, Bob must provide consideration.

However, the requirements must now be seen in the light of *Williams* v *Roffey Bros* (1990) in which the claimant carpenters (the second party) did not provide any consideration for the promise of extra money. If the facts meet the requirements set out in this case, no new consideration will be needed.

3.3 Variation and waiver

Variation happens when the parties wish to change the terms of the original contract by making a new contract. What has been said above about consideration applies equally here.

Waiver is changing the terms of a contract without making a new contract. One party allows the other to vary their performance. There is no need for consideration. The party granting the waiver is not allowed to go back on it. It seems to be much the same as the principle of equitable estoppel.

[handwritten annotations in margins and body:]
Cancelling original promise "is as good as" making new contract — mutual release
Sufficient consideration — peppercorn
allowing some liberty but not variation of contract
Consideration should be the £1,000 but she may accept something else instead
usually it's allowing a bit more time.

Perdip buys six apple trees from Olive to be delivered on 1 of May. Perdip agrees to allow delivery two weeks later. Perdip cannot go back on this promise.

4 Discharge by frustration

4.1 Introduction

The old rule was that obligations under a contract were strict and each party was bound to carry out their part of the contract whatever happened. In *Taylor* v *Caldwell* (1863) the courts first set out the principle that if something necessary for the contract ceased to exist, without the fault of the parties, they were excused from the contract. This was later developed into a general *principle of frustration*, that if something happens which makes performance impossible, illegal or radically different from what was undertaken, without the fault of either party, then the contract is frustrated. Both parties are then excused performance. The doctrine of frustration covers a wide variety of situations like illegality, death of a vital party, subject matter destroyed, something becoming unavailable and an event not taking place. Although it is not possible to classify all these situations, it is proposed to use the broad classes of contracts becoming (i) impossible, (ii) illegal or (iii) radically different. These categories must be regarded as flexible.

4.2 Frustration in practice

4.2.1 *Impossible*

A contract may become *impossible* to perform if some physical item needed is destroyed or where a person needed dies or becomes ill. The classic example is provided by the following case.

Taylor v *Caldwell* (1863)

The defendants hired out the Surrey Gardens and Music Hall to the claimants to hold concerts. Before the date of the first concert the hall was burnt down. The claimants had spent money preparing for the concerts and claimed damages. It was held that because the hall no longer existed, without the fault of either party, the contract was frustrated and both parties were excused performance.

Contract has become impossible

If a contract involves a *personal* element and only a particular person is able to carry it out, then the contract will be frustrated. The contract must provide that only that person will perform the contract, or it must be obvious that that is the case.

Ali books Hasan, a famous opera singer, to give a recital in Hyde Park on 1 June. If Hasan is ill on that date, the contract is frustrated.

In cases of a person being unavailable, the court will take into account the likely period of the interruption compared with the period of the contract. Temporary illness is not usually sufficient to amount to frustration.

Morgan v Manser (1947)

An artiste known as 'Cheerful Charlie Chester' signed a ten-year contract with his manager in 1938 but in 1940 was called up for military service and not demobilised until 1946. The court held that this period of absence out of a ten-year contract frustrated it.

Being sent to prison can also frustrate a contract.

Hare v Murphy Bros Ltd (1974)

The claimant was sent to prison for 12 months after being convicted of unlawful wounding in an incident unconnected with his work. He was unable to carry on as a foreman on the defendants' building site. On release from prison, the claimant claimed redundancy when he discovered someone else had taken his job. The Court of Appeal held that, taking into account his position and the length of sentence, the contract was frustrated, which meant the claimant was not entitled to redundancy pay.

In the above case the employer relied on frustration as a defence to the employee's claim, but if the employer had sued the employee, it is less likely the employee would have been able to rely on frustration. A different result was reached in the following later case.

Norris v Southampton City Council (1982)

The claimant was employed as a cleaner by the defendants and was convicted of assault and sent to prison. He was then dismissed and complained to an industrial tribunal that his dismissal was unfair. They held that the contract of employment was frustrated and he was not entitled to compensation. However the Employment Appeal Tribunal held that frustration can only arise if there is no fault by either party. This was the claimant's fault and amounted to a repudiatory breach of contract and the employer had the option of treating it as repudiated.

4.2.2 Illegal

After a contract has been made, but before it has been fully performed, the Government may change the law, so that further performance of the contract becomes *illegal*. This is sometimes known as supervening illegality and its effect is to frustrate the contract.

Denny, Mott & Dickson Ltd v James B. Fraser & Co. Ltd (1944)

A contract was made for the sale of timber, but before it could be performed the Government passed legislation stopping all sales of timber. It was held by the House of Lords that this frustrated the contract.

4.2.3 Radically different

Something may happen after the contract is made which, although it is still physically possible to perform the contract, makes that performance *radically different* from what the parties had in mind. In such a case the contract may be treated as frustrated. A number of cases arose when the coronation of Edward VII was cancelled due to his illness.

Krell v *Henry* (1903)

The claimant owned a room which overlooked the route of the coronation processions of Edward VII. The claimant agreed to let the room to the defendant for two days for £75, with £25 payable in advance. The agreement did not mention the processions. When the processions were cancelled due to the King's illness, the claimant sued for the balance owed. It was held by the Court of Appeal that both parties knew that the purpose of letting the room was to watch the processions, so although it was still physically possible to sit in the room, the foundation of the contract had been taken away and it was frustrated. The defendant did not have to pay the balance. There was a different outcome in the following case.

Herne Bay Steam Boat Co. v *Hutton* (1903)

The defendant hired a boat from the claimant 'for the purpose of watching the Naval Review and a day's cruise round the fleet'. Because of the King's illness, the Review was cancelled. The defendant refused to take the boat, so the claimant used it for ordinary business and claimed the hire charge from the defendant. The defendant argued that the contract was frustrated. The Court of Appeal held that the reason for hiring the boat was no concern of the claimant and anyway it was still possible to cruise round the fleet. The Review was not the foundation of the contract, which was not therefore frustrated. The claimant was entitled to the difference between the cost of hire and the normal day's profit.

should have put in the contract that you wanted to see the King.

The fact that a contract becomes more difficult or more expensive to carry out does not mean it is frustrated.

Davis Contractors Ltd v *Fareham Urban District Council* (1956)

The claimants agreed to build 78 houses for the defendants in eight months for £92,425. Because of shortages of labour and materials the work took 22 months and cost £110,076. The claimants claimed that the contract was frustrated, so they could ignore the contract price and claim the actual cost on a *quantum meruit* basis. The House of Lords held that the contract had not been frustrated: ' . . . it is not hardship or inconvenience or material loss itself which calls the principle of frustration into play' (Lord Radcliffe).

This has been applied in later cases. It was decided that the closing of the Suez Canal did not frustrate a contract to take a cargo from Port Sudan to Hamburg, as it could have gone round the Cape of Good Hope (*Tsakiroglou & Co. Ltd* v *Noblee Thorl GmbH* (1961)). A contract was signed to sell a warehouse for redevelopment for £1,710,000 but the next day the building was listed, so it could not be developed and its value fell to £200,000. Again this was held not to be frustration, it was a risk that both parties knew about and the buyer obtained the property it had agreed to buy (*Amalgamated Investment & Property Co. Ltd* v *John Walker & Sons Ltd* (1976) (CA)).

4.3 Limits on frustration

4.3.1 *Self induced frustration*

The doctrine of frustration only applies if the frustrating event happens *without the fault of either party.* If a party by their own action makes performance of the contract impossible, they cannot claim frustration.

Maritime National Fish Ltd v *Ocean Trawlers Ltd* (1935)

The charterers hired a ship from the owners, which both parties knew needed a licence from the Canadian Government. The charterers had four of their own ships and they applied for five licences. They were only granted three licences and used these for their own ships. They then claimed that the charter was frustrated. It was held by the Privy Council that it was their own choice not to use a licence for the chartered ship and therefore they could not claim frustration.

The courts have not ruled whether a *negligent* act by one of the parties which makes performance impossible can be relied on to frustrate the contract, but it is thought that it cannot.

> EXAMPLE
>
> If the owner of the hall in *Taylor* v *Caldwell* (1863) deliberately burnt it down before the contract was due to start, he could not claim frustration and neither could he claim frustration if he negligently burnt it down.

4.3.2 Provision in contract for frustration

The contract may contain a term dealing with what should happen if a frustrating event occurs. This is known as a *force majeure* clause. In this case the provision in the contract is followed and the doctrine of frustration does *not* apply. The exception is if the contract becomes illegal, when it will be treated as frustrated in all cases. If the term in the contract does not cover the frustrating event or the event is more extreme than was provided for, then the courts may apply the doctrine of frustration.

Jackson v *Union Marine Insurance Co. Ltd* (1874)

This concerned the charter of a ship which was to sail from Liverpool to Newport 'dangers and accidents of navigation excepted' to load its cargo. The ship ran aground in Caernarvon Bay and repairs took eight months. It was held that the clause was not intended to cover such extensive damage and the commercial purpose could not be fulfilled, so the contract was frustrated.

4.3.3 Foreseen events

If one party could foresee or should have foreseen the frustrating event because of their special knowledge, the doctrine of frustration does not apply and that party will be in breach of contract if the event occurs and stops performance. If both parties could or should have foreseen the event it may still be possible to treat the contract as frustrated. It is not a requirement for frustration to apply that the event is unforeseen, as many events are foreseeable but unlikely.

4.4 Effects of frustration

The contract *ends automatically* at the moment of the frustrating event. Neither party has any choice in this and they do not have to carry out any obligations after this event.

4.4.1 Common law

The rule was 'loss lies where it falls', which meant that existing rights and obligations were binding.

EXAMPLE

In *Krell* v *Henry* if the defendant had not paid £25, he would have been liable to pay it. If he had paid it in advance, he could not recover it.

Much depended on the provisions of the contract, if money was payable in advance it remained payable but if it was not payable until performance, it did not have to be paid. The rules were modified by the following case. *[handwritten: law's final attempt at dealing with the money!]*

The Fibrosa Case (1943) *[handwritten: IMP. Common]*

This concerned an English company which agreed to make machinery for a Polish company, to be delivered to Poland. The Polish company paid a deposit of £1,000 but the contract was frustrated by the invasion of Poland and they now reclaimed the £1,000. The House of Lords held that they were entitled to their money back as there had been a total failure of consideration. *[handwritten: the Co. had not delivered anything, Polish Co had all money back.]*

These rules were still unfair and legislation was passed to change them.

4.4.2 Statute

The Law Reform (Frustrated Contracts) Act 1943 was passed to deal with the situation after it has been determined that a contract is frustrated. Its main provisions are as follows. *[handwritten: Tries to be fair between parties]*

(a) Money paid before the frustrating event can be recovered, whether consideration has wholly or only partly failed.

(b) Money payable before the frustrating event, but not paid, does not have to be paid.

(c) A party who has incurred expenses before the frustrating event may claim these up to the limit of the amount paid or payable, if the court considers it just. If nothing is paid or payable, then no expenses may be claimed.

(d) If nothing is to be paid in advance, a party cannot claim expenses, but anyone who has given a valuable benefit to the other party, other than money, may claim a just sum for it.

EXAMPLE

In *Krell* v *Henry* (1903) the defendant hiring the room and paying £25 in advance would be able to claim this back (head (a) above); but the claimant would be entitled to any expenses incurred, like cleaning the room or putting flowers in it, up to £25 (head (c) above).

Gamerco v ICM/Fair Warning Agency Ltd (1995)

G, a pop promoter, made a contract with ICM (who controlled the group Guns 'n' Roses) for the group to play at a stadium in Madrid. A few days before the concert, the authorities discovered that the stadium had structural defects and they banned its use. G had paid money to ICM and both parties had incurred expenses. G reclaimed the money. It was held that the contract was frustrated and G could recover the advance payment. Although the court had a discretion to allow ICM to claim their expenses, because G had also suffered losses it was just in the circumstances not to deduct anything.

The Law Reform (Frustrated Contracts) Act 1943 does not apply in certain cases:

(a) where the parties make express provision for the consequences of frustration;

(b) contracts for the carriage of goods by sea;

(c) contracts of insurance;

(d) contracts for the sale of specific goods which perish.

5 Discharge by breach

5.1 Introduction

A breach of contract happens when one party fails to carry out their part of the contract, or refuses to carry out their part of the contract. One of the effects of breach is sometimes described as a right to discharge the contract, but this is not strictly correct and it is more accurate to say that the innocent party is discharged from their obligations under the contract. For example, it may be at this point that a liquidated damages clause operates, so it is not true to say that the contract has ended. The effect of the breach depends on the type of term which is broken. A breach of condition or innominate term, resulting in serious loss, gives the innocent party a right to treat themselves as discharged from the contract and/or to claim damages. Such breaches are sometimes called *repudiatory breaches*. A breach of warranty or innominate term resulting in minor loss only gives a right to damages. A breach which gives a party the right to treat themselves as discharged from the contract does not end the contract automatically like frustration, but gives the party affected the choice of ending the contract *or* continuing with it. If the innocent party elects to treat themselves as discharged, they are excused further performance and can refuse performance by the other party. If the innocent party elects to continue with the contract, they may claim damages. The breach may be an actual breach or an anticipatory breach.

5.2 Actual breach

This happens if one of the parties fails to carry out their obligations. It may be by not performing what was agreed, for example the seller fails to deliver goods, or by defective performance, for example, the goods delivered are damaged. The innocent party may claim immediately for breach of contract.

5.3 Anticipatory breach

This is a breach which 'occurs' before the date due for performance. One party may inform the other they do not intend to carry out the contract or they may do an act showing this intention, for example, selling goods needed for the contract to a third party. The innocent party can sue immediately for breach of contract *or* wait to see if the contract will be carried out.

Hochster v De La Tour (1853)

Anticipatory breach.

In April the defendant employed the claimant as a courier, to start work on 1 June. In May the defendant wrote saying the contract was cancelled. When the claimant sued, the defendant argued there was no right to sue until the date of performance. It was held that the claimant had an immediate right to sue for breach and was entitled to damages.

The innocent party may elect to treat the contract as continuing. In this case it is 'kept alive for the benefit of both parties', so the innocent party then has to carry out their part of the contract (*White & Carter (Councils) Ltd* v *McGregor* (1961)). In this case Lord Reid stated that the right to perform the contract might not apply if a party 'has no legitimate interest, financial or otherwise, in performing the contract rather than claiming damages' and this qualification was followed in the next case.

Couldn't have easily re-sold the advertising space

The Alaskan Trader (No. 2) (1984)

The charterer of an old ship rejected it before the charter period was up, which was an anticipatory breach. The owners spent £800,000 repairing it and maintaining it with a crew for the remainder of the charter and then sold it for scrap. It was held that the owners had no legitimate interest in continuing to perform the contract and were not entitled to the hire money owing, but only to damages for the charterer's breach.

They went ahead with the Contract

The innocent party may elect to treat the contract as ended.

Vitol v Norelf Ltd (1996)

The claimant buyers agreed to buy a cargo of propane from the defendant sellers. The buyers sent a telex repudiating the contract because delivery was likely to be late. The sellers took no further steps to perform, but shortly after this they sold the cargo at a substantial loss and claimed damages from the buyers. The arbitrator found on the facts, that the claimants had no claim for breach of contract against the defendants and that the claimant's telex amounted to an anticipatory breach. The House of Lords held that a failure to perform may sometimes show an election by the innocent party to treat the contract as ended. The sellers had done nothing to perform the contract and they were entitled to damages.

If the innocent party elects to treat the contract as continuing, there is a danger it may be frustrated.

Avery v Bowden (1855)

The claimant had a ship at Odessa on the Black Sea and made a contract that the defendant would provide a cargo within 45 days. The defendant committed an anticipatory breach by telling the claimant to take the ship away as no cargo could be found, but the claimant kept the ship waiting. Before the 45-day period expired, the Crimean War broke out between England and Russia, making any contracts with Russia illegal.

e claimant sued for breach of contract, it was held that the contract had been ...trated by the outbreak of war and the defendant was not liable for damages.

Remedies for breach of contract

---

1 Introduction

The courts provide a wide range of remedies for the victim of a breach of contract. Although it is common to speak of enforcing a contract, this is an unusual remedy, the main remedy is money compensation, called *damages*. Some remedies were originally developed by the *common law* courts and these may be claimed as of right, which means that once the breach is proved the court will have to grant them. They include damages; repudiation of the contract (available if there is a breach of an important term); and an action for an agreed sum, for example, a debt or the price of goods sold. Other remedies, developed by the courts of *equity*, are discretionary, which means they cannot be claimed automatically but will only be granted in accordance with equitable principles. These remedies include specific performance, to make the other party carry out their obligations; an injunction to prevent a breach of contract; rectification of documents for mistake; and rescission of the contract in cases of mistake, misrepresentation, duress or undue influence. When advising on remedies it is important to remember that it may not be necessary to go to court, for example, in the case of a breach of condition, the innocent party can simply refuse to carry out their part of the contract. This puts the onus on the other party, who may then wish to settle the matter out of court, saving time and money. If court proceedings are inevitable advice must also be given on which court to commence the action in and the possibility of an appeal. Only the main remedies of damages, quantum meruit, specific performance and injunction will be examined in this section, as the others have been covered elsewhere in appropriate sections of the text. It is also important for action to be taken within the time limits laid down by the Limitation Act 1980.

2 Damages

2.1 Types of damages

The claim for damages is for *unliquidated damages*, which means the amount is decided by the court, as opposed to *liquidated damages*, which are a fixed sum. The aim of awarding damages is to compensate the innocent party and there are different types of damages available. *General damages* are awarded for loss which cannot be precisely calculated, for example, inconvenience or pain. *Special damages* can be measured, for example, loss of profit or loss of earnings up to the date of trial.

Nominal damages are a small amount awarded if there has been a breach of contract but no loss suffered.

only loss should be compensated.

Surrey County Council v Bredero Homes Ltd (1992)

The claimant sold land to the defendant, who agreed to build 72 houses on it, in accordance with planning permission. Later the defendant obtained a new planning permission and built 77 houses. The claimant sued for damages for breach of contract, as it would have charged a higher price for more houses. It was held by the Court of Appeal that the aim of damages was to compensate for loss and as the claimant had not suffered any substantial loss, it should get only nominal damages. It was not entitled to the profit made by the defendant on the extra houses.

here was no loss so claimant had not suffered so lost the claim.

In the above case the council might have obtained an injunction or specific performance to enforce the promise in the contract of sale to build 72 houses, if it had acted quickly enough, but it had waited until all the houses had been sold.

In *Surrey County Council* v *Bredero Homes Ltd* (1992) the court followed the general rule for awarding damages for breach of contract and based damages on the loss of the innocent party, not on the gain of the party in breach of contract. But in the next case the court took the latter (and unusual) approach to assessing damages.

Attorney General v Blake (2000)

B worked as an English spy between 1944 and 1961 and he had signed a contract agreeing not to disclose any information obtained in the course of his work. He also became a Russian spy but was convicted for this and imprisoned. He later escaped and went to live in Moscow. In 1989 he wrote a book containing information obtained in his job but the information was no longer regarded as confidential. The book was published by the defendants who agreed to pay B £150,000 and had in fact paid B £60,000. The Attorney General took this action to prevent the balance being paid to B. The House of Lords said that in exceptional circumstances it may be just and equitable to make a defendant account for profits made from a breach of contract. Although no fixed rules could be set down the court had to take into account all the circumstances, including the subject matter of the contract, the purpose of the term broken, the consequences of the breach and all the circumstances. Here, even though the information was no longer confidential, B had broken the term of his contract not to disclose information. The profits made by B were a result of this breach of contract, which was 'closely akin to a fiduciary obligation'. With breach of a fiduciary duty it was common practice to account for the profits made and in the circumstances the Attorney General was entitled to the balance of the profit made by B.

This case shows that the courts have accepted a move away from merely awarding compensatory damages (based on the claimant's loss) for a breach of contract and in exceptional circumstances will award an account of profits.

Damages may be recovered in contract for financial loss or physical suffering or physical inconvenience but not for disappointment or mental distress. This restriction applies to commercial contracts, but was relaxed if the *aim* of the contract was to provide pleasure or comfort or the relief of discomfort. This exception has recently been considered and extended by the House of Lords. The earlier cases are explained below to show how the present position has been reached.

Jarvis v Swans Tours Ltd (1973)

The claimant booked a ski-ing holiday in Switzerland with the defendants and was promised a 'great time'. The hotel owner did not speak English, the bar was open only one evening and the yodeller promised was someone who sang a few songs on their way home from work! The county court assessed damages at 50 per cent of the cost of the holiday and awarded £31.72 but nothing for disappointment. The Court of Appeal held that the claimant was entitled to compensation for loss of enjoyment and awarded total compensation of £125, which included an amount for loss of enjoyment.

The courts applied these rules in the following cases.

Knott v Bolton (1995)

B, an architect, designed a new house for K, who had stressed the importance of having an imposing staircase. Due to design problems the agreed width could not be incorporated in the plan, but K was not told until it was too late. K claimed damages for distress. It was held by the Court of Appeal that there was no general liability in contract for distress, frustration or stress caused by breach of contract unless the object of the contract was the provision of peace of mind, pleasure or relaxation. Here the object of the contract was to design a house and any pleasure was incidental to this.

In *Alexander v Rolls Royce Motor Cars Ltd* (1995), the Court of Appeal said that damages for loss of enjoyment could not be awarded for delay in repairing a Rolls Royce motor car, as this was a normal commercial contract.

Farley v Skinner (2001)

F wanted to buy a house in the country for his retirement. The house was 15 miles from Gatwick Airport and he was worried about the noise. He made a contract with S, a surveyor, to survey the house and specifically asked whether the property would be seriously affected by aircraft noise. S said that it was unlikely the property would suffer greatly from noise and F then bought the house and spent a large sum of money renovating it. He then found that planes flew close and the house was badly affected by noise. F sued S for breach of contract. In the High Court F was awarded £10,000 damages which included compensation for inconvenience, distress and loss of enjoyment. S appealed to the Court of Appeal which allowed S's appeal on the grounds that the object of the contract was not to provide pleasure or relaxation. F then appealed to the House of Lords. The House of Lords said that there was no reason in principle why the scope of a claim for damages should depend on the object of the contract, rather than considering if an important part of the contract was 'to give pleasure, relaxation or peace of mind'. Here the surveyor had been specifically asked to investigate aircraft noise and had a contractual duty of care to do so. Finding out about aircraft noise could also be seen as part of his consideration. S further argued that by staying in the house, rather than selling it, F had failed to mitigate his loss and had forfeited his right to damages but the court said there was no principle to support this argument. The award of £10,000 damages was restored.

The House of Lords overruled *Knott* v *Bolton* (1995) (above). Previous cases must now be read in the light of the above decision.

2.2 The basis of the claim

The general aim of damages is to put the innocent party in the same financial position as if the contract had been carried out. They are compensated for what they expected to get under the contract and this is known as the *expectation loss.*

> EXAMPLE
>
> Alan agrees to sell a car to Bob for £10,000. Alan refuses to deliver. To put Bob in the same position as if the contract was carried out, he needs the same make of car. If the price is £11,000 elsewhere, Bob is entitled to £1,000 damages.

Sometimes a party may not be able to show that they expected to gain from the contract but they may have incurred expenses in carrying out the contract. In this situation they can make a claim for *reliance loss* and the aim is to put them in the position they were in before the contract was made.

Anglia Television Ltd v *Reed* (1971) Olivier   *Reliance loss*

The defendant agreed to play the leading role in a television film for the claimants. The defendant withdrew at the last moment, in breach of contract and the claimants had to abandon the project. The claimants could not prove that the film would have been successful, so they could not claim on the basis of expectation loss. But they had suffered losses in paying a director, script writers, other actors etc. The Court of Appeal held that the claimants were entitled to their claim on the basis that they had relied on the defendant carrying out the contract and had suffered losses because of the breach. 'It seems to me that a plaintiff in such a case as this has an election: he can either claim for his loss of profits; or for his wasted expenditure. But he must elect between them. He cannot claim both' (Lord Denning MR). The court also allowed a claim for the expenses incurred *before* the defendant had been taken on, as both parties must have realised that expenses incurred then would be wasted if the defendant broke the contract.

2.3 Remoteness of damage

If the law gave compensation for *all* the loss caused by a breach of contract, this would put an impossible burden on the party in breach.

> EXAMPLE
>
> Barbara makes a contract to buy a car from Alan's garage. When she goes to collect it, she finds that Alan has sold it to someone else. Barbara has to get the bus to work. She slips getting off the bus and breaks her leg and as a result loses her job as a ballerina, cannot pay her mortgage, and her house is repossessed.

The courts have developed rules to restrict what a party may claim following a breach of contract, but in applying these rules they are really determining policy. The starting point is the following case.

Hadley v Baxendale (1854)

The claimant mill owner arranged for the defendant to take a broken mill shaft to Greenwich, to be used as a pattern for a new shaft. Because of the defendant's delay, the new shaft was a number of days late in arriving. During this time the mill could not be used. The claimant sued for the loss of profits. Alderson B said damages for breach 'should be such as may fairly and reasonably be considered either arising naturally, i.e., according to the usual course of things, from such breach of contract itself, or such as may reasonably be supposed to have been in the contemplation of both parties at the time they made the contract as the probable results of the breach of it'. The court applied this principle to the facts and held that the loss did not arise in the natural course of things, because in most cases a mill should not have to close if the mill shaft was taken away, as the owner should have a spare one. Neither could the loss be regarded as in the minds of the parties, as the defendant did not know the special circumstances that the mill would have to close without the shaft. Therefore the claimant was not entitled to damages for loss of profits.

The principle established in this case is known as the principle of *remoteness of damage*, and under it damages may be claimed if the claimant can establish either:

(a) the loss arises in the natural course of things; or

(b) the loss was in the contemplation of both parties at the time of the contract.

An example of how the principle of remoteness applies is to be found in the following case.

Victoria Laundry (Windsor) Ltd v Newman Industries Ltd (1949)

The defendants agreed to instal a new larger boiler for the claimants' laundry, which the defendants knew was needed urgently for the business. The defendants were five months late in completing the work and the claimants claimed the normal loss of profit they would have made on the boiler plus the loss on some lucrative dyeing contracts for the Ministry of Supply, which they could not do without the boiler. The Court of Appeal held that the claimants could claim the normal loss of profit they would have made on the new boiler, as a loss arising in the natural course of things, but they were not entitled to the loss of profit on the dyeing contracts, which were not in the natural course of things and not in the contemplation of the parties, as the defendants did not know about these contracts.

The court pointed out in the above case that the test applied was not whether the parties actually contemplated the loss at the time of the contract, but whether the *reasonable man* would have done.

The courts have also held that if a particular type of loss is within the contemplation of the parties, damages may be recovered for it, even if the actual loss was greater than the parties could have contemplated (*H. Parsons (Livestock) Ltd* v *Uttley Ingham & Co. Ltd* (1978)).

2.4 The measure of damages

2.4.1 *The market price rule*

When the court has established what loss may be claimed, because it is not too remote, the next question is how much damages should be awarded? In the case of a claim for expectation loss, the aim is to put the innocent party in the same position as if the contract had been carried out.

> EXAMPLES
>
> *Seller fails to deliver goods*
> Where there is a market for the goods, then the loss is the difference between the contract price and the market price, at the time of delivery, if the market price is higher (Sale of Goods Act 1979, s. 51). If there is no market, then the court values the goods.
>
> *Buyer refuses to accept the goods*
> The measure of damages is the difference between the contract price and the market price at the time the goods should have been accepted, if the latter is lower. If the seller finds another buyer at the same or a higher price, then only nominal damages will be awarded.

Charter v *Sullivan* (1957)

The claimants sold a car to the defendant, who refused to accept it but they then sold it to someone else for the same price. The claimants claimed loss of profit on the first sale. The Court of Appeal held that as demand exceeded supply the claimants had not lost any profit because they would have sold every car they had. Nominal damages of £2 were awarded.

However, if supply exceeds demand the seller may claim the loss of profit (*W.L. Thompson Ltd* v *Robinson (Gunmakers) Ltd* (1955)).

2.4.2 *Sub-sales by the buyer*

If the buyer intends to resell the goods and the seller knows this, what damages may the buyer claim?

Bence Graphics v *Fasson UK Ltd* (1997)

The defendants sold vinyl filmto the claimants and the contract provided that the filmwould last five years. The filmwas used to make labels for bulk containers, and the claimants sold the labels to third parties. The defendants knew about this. The film deteriorated before five years and the claimants claimed damages. The High Court awarded damages based on the difference in the value at the time of delivery, which would be nothing, and the value if the labels had complied with the contract, which would be the contract price (approximately £564,000). The Court of Appeal said that where goods were sold on, the measure of damages was the actual loss suffered by the claimants frombreach of those sub-sales. What was in the contemplation of the parties at the time of the contract was the claimants' liability to the ultimate user of the labels. The defendants knew that the film was used to make labels which were sold to third parties, and that a breach of contract by the defendants would mean claims against the claimants by those third parties. Only £22,000 worth of labels had been returned. The defendants' appeal was allowed.

2.4.3 Loss of opportunity

The fact that it may be very difficult to assess damages does not mean that the courts will not award any.

Chaplin v *Hicks* (1911)

The defendant was manager of a theatre and he agreed with the claimant that she could attend an audition with 49 other girls, from which 12 would be selected for a three-year engagement. The claimant was stopped from attending by the defendant's breach. The court held that although the claimant might not have been selected, she had lost the *chance* of selection and she was awarded £100.

2.4.4 Cost of cure

If performance of a contract is defective then the innocent party may claim the cost of curing the defect. But, if the cost of cure is greater than the difference in value between proper and defective performance, damages are the difference in value.

Ruxley Electronics and Construction Ltd v *Forsyth* (1995)

The claimants agreed to build a swimming pool measuring 7′ 6″ at the deep end, for the defendant. When the pool was finished it was only 6′ 9″ at the deep end and 6′ 0″ elsewhere.

The county court found that the pool's being shallower made no difference to its use and value. It would cost £21,560 to cure the defect, because the only way to do this was for the claimants to re-dig the pool. The defendant was awarded £2,500 for 'loss of amenity'. The Court of Appeal, by a majority, reversed this judgment and awarded the defendant the full cost of curing the defect. The House of Lords said that financial loss can be measured in two ways: (i) the difference in value, or (ii) the cost of re-instatement (cure). If the cost of re-instatement is less than the difference in value, the measure of damages will be the cost of re-instatement. But if the cost of re-instatement is out of proportion and unreasonable compared to the benefit obtained, the measure of damages is the difference in value. In applying these rules to the case it was held that although the pool was shallower, this made no difference to its value and it could still be fully used. It would be unreasonable to insist on the cost of re-instatement and the county court judgment was restored.

In most circumstances applying the cost of re-instatement will cause no problems. But in situations like *Ruxley* the consumer seems to lose out, because their particular specifications are not met and they are not put in the position they would have been in if the contract had been correctly performed. The damages awarded on the basis of 'loss of amenity' also seems to conflict with the rule in *Addis* v *Gramophone Co. Ltd* (1909), that as a general rule, no damages can be given for mental distress caused by a breach of contract. *Addis* also said that damages could not include compensation for loss of future employment, but this aspect was distinguished in the following case.

Malik v *BCCI* (1997)

The defendant bank had acted fraudulently and went into liquidation. Although its employees were not involved in the fraud, they had difficulty finding new jobs because of the stigma and they suffered loss. The House of Lords said that the employers were in breach of an implied term not to break the relationship of trust with employees. The employees were entitled to damages for the loss of benefits they would otherwise have had. They were also entitled to damages for loss of future employment prospects if that type of loss was foreseeable.

2.5 Mitigation of damage

The right to compensation for breach of contract is qualified by the duty to *mitigate the loss suffered*. The innocent party must take reasonable steps to reduce the loss caused by the breach. Loss which could have been avoided by taking such steps cannot be claimed as damages. Neither must the innocent party take unreasonable steps which would increase the loss. The important factor is that the innocent party must only take reasonable steps.

> EXAMPLE
>
> Everton Football Club dismiss their manager in breach of contract with two years to run at £1,000,000 a year. The ex-manager has to try to obtain a similar job, not sweeping up after football matches but in some managerial role, to reduce the loss suffered!

An example of someone suggesting unreasonable steps can be found in the following case.

Pilkington v *Wood* (1953)

While acting for the claimant in the purchase of a house, the defendant solicitor accepted a house with a defective title, which was a breach of contract. When sued, the defendant argued that the claimant should have sued the vendor! It was held that it was unreasonable to expect the claimant to take action on a complicated matter which might not have succeeded.

In the case of an anticipatory breach of contract, where the innocent party elects to treat the contract as continuing and see if the other party will perform, there is no duty to mitigate (*White & Carter (Councils) Ltd* v *McGregor* (1961)).

2.6 Contributory negligence

A difficulty arises if the claimant is partly to blame for loss suffered, as to whether damages can be apportioned under the Law Reform (Contributory Negligence) Act 1945 as in the tort of negligence. If the defendant is in breach of contract *and* a corresponding duty of care in tort, then damages may be apportioned, for example

Sayers v *Harlow UDC* (1958). In other cases the Act does not apply and damages cannot be apportioned.

The Law Commission have suggested that where the claimant has suffered damage partly as a result of breach of contract and partly as a result of his own negligence, the damages should be reduced according to the 1945 Act. However, this defence could be excluded or the matter of damages dealt with by a liquidated damages clause (*Contributory Negligence as a Defence in Contract* Law Com. No. 219).

3 Quantum meruit

3.1 Definition

Quantum meruit means 'how much is deserved'. The court will decide how much the claimant deserves for work done for the benefit of the other party. A claim may be made whether or not a contract exists.

3.2 No contract in existence

In some cases a party may have carried out work when no binding contract has been made. A claim may then be made in *quantum meruit* (*British Steel Corporation* v *Cleveland Bridge & Engineering Co. Ltd* (1984)).

Similarly if parties have carried out work under a contract, which unknown to both parties is void, a claim may be made in *quantum meruit*.

Craven-Ellis v Canons Ltd (1936)

The claimant was appointed as managing director of the defendant company but had not bought qualification shares as required, so the contract was void. It was held that the claimant was entitled to claim for work done on a *quantum meruit* basis.

3.3 Existing contract

The normal rule is that where there is a contract, then payment must be made according to the contract. There are some exceptions, when the contract is ignored and a claim may be made in *quantum meruit*. If the contract does not provide for payment, then a reasonable price is payable. This rule is now contained in the Sale of Goods Act 1979, s. 8. If one party is prevented from carrying out the contract by the other party acting in breach, a claim may be made in *quantum meruit* (*Planche* v *Colburn* (1831)). If part performance of an entire contract is accepted, the person partly performing may claim on a *quantum meruit* basis.

4 Specific performance

4.1 Definition

A decree of *specific performance* is an order of the court, telling a party to a contract to carry out their part of the contract. If they do not comply with this order, they are in contempt of court, which is a *criminal offence*. Specific performance is an equitable remedy. A court has power to award damages instead of, or in addition to a decree of specific performance. To be eligible for this remedy certain requirements must be met and it will not be granted for some types of contract.

4.2 Requirements for specific performance

4.2.1 Damages must be inadequate

Specific performance will not be granted if damages are an adequate remedy. Damages will normally be perfectly adequate if a substitute performance is available.

> EXAMPLE
>
> Alice agrees to buy a Sony colour television from Basil Ltd but Basil Ltd refuse to hand it over. Alice will not be entitled to specific performance as it will be easy to obtain the same model elsewhere. Damages will be adequate.

If no substitutes are available, then specific performance may be granted. The classic example is the sale of *land*. Because every 'piece' of land is unique, a contract for the sale of land may be specifically enforced. If the seller refuses to sell, in breach of contract, there is no substitute and the seller can be made to sell. If the buyer refuses to complete, although the seller's interest is simply the price, and this could be obtained from another buyer, under the principle of *mutuality* (see 4.2.3 below), the seller is entitled to specific performance.

> EXAMPLE
>
> Alice agrees to sell her house to Bertie, but changes her mind and refuses to complete the sale. Bertie is entitled to specific performance to make Alice convey the house.

Another example is the sale of *unique goods*, although a court has described a set of Hepplewhite chairs as 'ordinary articles of commerce' and refused to grant specific performance against the seller (*Cohen* v *Roche* (1927)). In the light of this, it is difficult to see when it would be granted apart from items like individual works of art. One example can be found in the following case.

Lamplough v *Lotus Cars Ltd* (1977)

In 1971 the defendants agreed to sell five racing cars to the claimant for £6,750. The cars were to be delivered when they finished racing, but by this time they had won a number of races and were worth £47,000. The defendants refused to deliver them. It was held that damages would not be adequate, therefore specific performance was granted.

4.2.2 At the discretion of the court

Specific performance, like all equitable remedies, is *discretionary*. It cannot be obtained as of right and it is up to the court whether to grant it or not. This decision is not completely arbitrary and the guiding principle is 'Equity will only grant specific performance if, under all the circumstances, it is just and equitable to do so' (*Stickney* v *Keeble* (1915)). In applying this the courts will take the conduct of the claimant into account and if this has been unfair or underhand in any way, they may refuse to grant a decree.

In *Webster* v *Cecil* (1861) the court refused to grant specific performance of the sale of land at £1,250 to the claimant as the defendant had earlier refused an offer of £2,000. The claimant must have realised that when the defendant offered to sell for £1,250, the defendant meant £2,250.

The courts will also take into account hardship to the defendant and if the circumstances have changed drastically since making the contract, specific performance may be refused.

[handwritten margin note: So ct looks at all the circs of each case]

Patel v Ali (1984)

After a contract was made for the sale of a house the seller became disabled and heavily dependent on neighbours for help. It was held that specific performance would be refused, as the claimant could claim damages. *[handwritten: Cl. could claim damages anyway so]*

[handwritten margin note: in other words didn't want to sell + now so broke the contract]

One equitable maxim is 'He who comes to equity must come with clean hands', which means that any person claiming an equitable remedy must have acted fairly towards the other party.

Quadrant Visual Communications Ltd v Hutchison Telephone (UK) Ltd (1993)

The claimants sold their portable phone business to the defendants, who agreed to pay a price based on the number of new subscribers they obtained. Just before the sale the claimants had made a marketing agreement which involved issuing vouchers for free phones, but did not tell the defendants. The claimants now claimed specific performance to obtain the money owed. It was held by the Court of Appeal that the claimants had tricked the defendants by not telling them about the vouchers and specific performance was refused.

4.2.3 Principle of mutuality

This means that specific performance must be available to *both* parties, if it is not, then neither party may claim it. An example is that a minor cannot claim specific performance, as it is not available against them.

4.3 Contracts which cannot be specifically enforced

4.3.1 Contracts of personal service

A contract under which one person is to carry out personal services for another is not specifically enforceable, because this is seen as infringing a person's liberty. It would also be difficult to enforce.

Alice works as a secretary to Basil. Alice is dismissed in breach of contract. Alice cannot obtain a decree of specific performance to make Basil employ her.

4.3.2 Contracts requiring constant supervision

If a contract needs constant supervision to see that it is carried out, the court will not grant specific performance. This rule covers contracts involving obligations of a continuing nature. The following cases may be contrasted.

Ryan v Mutual Tontine Westminster Chambers Association (1893)

The defendants leased a flat to the claimant and the lease provided that a porter would be 'constantly in attendance'. The porter had a part-time job and was frequently missing when needed. The claimant claimed specific performance. The Court of Appeal held that specific performance would not be granted as it would entail day-to-day supervision of the porter.

The above case was distinguished in the following case.

Posner v Scott-Lewis (1986)

The defendants leased a flat to the claimant and the lease provided that a resident porter would be provided to carry out specified duties. There was a non-resident porter, but the claimant claimed specific performance. The court said that in deciding whether to grant a decree the following factors should be taken into account: (a) whether what needed to be done was sufficiently defined; (b) the amount of supervision needed; and (c) the hardships caused to the parties if an order was or was not made. It was held that here the defendants could be ordered to appoint a porter within a given time; this would not need constant supervision as, if it was not complied with, proceedings could be taken; it would not be a hardship to the defendants to make the order. Therefore specific performance was granted.

Co-operative Insurance Society Ltd v Argyll Stores Ltd (1997)

The defendants were the tenants of a loss-making shop in a shopping centre and they wished to close the shop. The claimant landlords asked them to keep the shop open until a new tenant was found, but the defendants closed the shop. The claimants claimed specific performance of a term in the lease that the premises should be kept open for retail trade. The House of Lords said that ordering someone to carry on a business would require constant supervision by the court. If the order was granted the claimants might benefit at the expense of the defendants and the loss suffered by the defendants might be much greater than the loss suffered by the claimants from the breach of contract. Further, it would not be in the public interest to make someone carry on a loss-making business if there was another way of compensating the other party. Specific performance was refused.

Specific performance will not normally be granted for building contracts, as another builder may be taken on to complete the work, so damages are adequate and performance of the contract would need constant supervision. The courts have recognised an exception to this, if the following conditions are met:

(a) the building work required is clearly defined;

(b) the claimant has a substantial interest in the performance of the contract and will not be adequately compensated by damages;

(c) the defendant has possession of the land on which the building is to be done, so another builder cannot be taken on to do the work.

Wolverhampton Corporation v Emmons (1901)

The claimants sold land to the defendants under a contract which provided that the defendants would demolish old council houses and build new ones. The defendants demolished the old houses, but even after plans for the new houses had been approved, the defendants did not build them. It was held that the defendants obligations were clearly defined in detailed plans; damages would be inadequate as the claimants were losing rent on the new houses; and the claimant could not engage another builder as the defendant had possession of the land. Consequently a decree of specific performance was granted.

5 Injunctions

5.1 Introduction

An *injunction* is an equitable remedy and is granted according to the same principles as specific performance, except that there is no need to prove that damages are inadequate. There are different types of injunction available but the relevant ones are *prohibitory* injunctions and *mandatory* injunctions.

5.2 Prohibitory injunctions

A prohibitory injunction is a court order telling a party to a contract *not* to do something. Normally it will only be granted to stop the defendant doing something they have agreed not to do (i.e., to stop them breaking a negative term in the contract).

Lumley v Wagner (1852)

The defendant agreed to sing at the claimant's theatre for three months and during that time not to sing at any other theatre without the claimant's consent. The defendant went to sing somewhere else for more money. The court held that an injunction would be granted to stop the defendant singing elsewhere, as this was a breach of the negative term in the contract.

An injunction will not be granted if its effect is to enforce a contract of personal service. To grant an injunction in these circumstances would be to enforce a contract by the back door, which could not be enforced by a decree of specific performance. Two cases may be contrasted as illustrating how the courts deal with this type of contract.

Warner Bros Pictures Inc v Nelson (1936)

The defendant, the actress Bette Davis, agreed to act for the claimants for 12 months and during that time not to act for anyone else or engage in any other occupation. During this period she acted for another company. It was held that an injunction would be granted to stop her acting for anyone else, but not from engaging in other occupations. The effect was not to force her to act for the claimants, as she could have earned a living some other way.

A different conclusion was reached in the following case.

Page One Records Ltd v Britton (1967)

The claimant was appointed manager of the defendants (the Troggs pop group) for five years, under a contract which provided that the defendants would not appoint anyone else as their manager during this time. The defendants wrongfully dismissed the claimant, who sought an injunction to stop them taking on anyone else as manager. The court took into account that the defendants had no business experience and needed a manager. They could not have earned a living any other way and to stop them employing someone else would be to make them employ the claimant. The court held that an injunction would not be granted.

It seems that if someone has many talents an injunction will be granted but if they only have one way of earning a living it will be refused.

5.3 Mandatory injunctions

A mandatory injunction is a court order telling a party to do some positive act, to put right something they have done in breach of contract. Because of this onerous duty being imposed, they are rarely granted.

EXAMPLE

An order to demolish a wall which has been built in breach of an agreement.

6 Limitation of actions

The Limitation Act 1980 imposes time limits on a person's right to sue for breach of contract. Any claim not brought within the required period is regarded as 'statute barred' and fails. In a simple contract, no action can be taken after six years from the date when the cause of action accrued. If the claim includes damages for personal injuries, it must be made within three years of the date of the breach of contract. If the contract is made by deed, then claims must be made within 12 years. The Limitation Act 1980 does not apply to equitable remedies but the courts apply similar rules by analogy and have a discretion to refuse relief if there has been unconscionable delay.

CONSUMER LAW

Introduction

Everyone is a consumer of goods and services. It has been estimated that an individual will use 50,000 goods and services in his/her lifetime, so it is hardly surprising that everyone has an interest in the control of these goods and services. Although consumer laws existed in early times, for example the Assize of Bread and Ale 1266 which controlled the quantities sold, legal controls are a relatively modern phenomenon. It was not until the development of mass production in the late nineteenth century that the modern consumer emerged. At that time the attitude of the law was reflected in the principle of _caveat emptor_ (let the buyer beware) and protection was minimal. The twentieth century, particularly post World War II, has seen an ever increasing amount of statutory protection for consumers, and local trading standards departments of county councils are now responsible for enforcing approximately 200 statutes from the Explosives Act 1875 to the Licensing (Young Persons) Act 2000.

The role of the law is open to question—how far should it protect the consumer and how far should matters be left to market forces? Although there are opposing schools of thought on this question, consumers often find themselves bewildered in the face of rapid technological change and sophisticated selling techniques. There is also the problem of the inequality of bargaining power as the individual tries to take on the business corporation. The function of the law and the activities of local and central Government in enforcing it and determining future policies must be seen in the context of the work of other interest groups, like the National Consumer Council, sponsored by the Government, and voluntary organisations like the Consumers Association and the Citizens Advice Bureaux, which play an increasingly important role in helping the consumer. The White Paper, _Modern Markets: Confident Consumers_, 1999, puts forward ideas to improve consumer protection including giving companies an OFT 'Seal of Approval'; giving a hallmark for internet traders who guarantee security of payment and privacy of information; new powers to ban companies who repeatedly cheat customers; a new consumer advice network and a review of consumer protection legislation. In October 2001 Consumer Support Networks were set up, under which agencies like the Citizens Advice Bureaux and Trading Standards Departments work together to provide consumer advice. The law must also

be seen in a European setting with the creation of the internal market, the dev
ment of consumer protection policies and the harmonisation of some of the consumer laws of member States of the European Union. The Maastricht Treaty brought
consumer protection to the fore and many of the targets in the Commission's first two
action plans have been achieved, for example, the regulations on timeshares and
distance selling. The institutions of the European Union are in agreement that laws
must be effective and that consumers must have access to justice. One example of the
increasing impact of such laws is that since 1 January 1995 the measure for selling
spirits changed from one sixth of a gill to 25 ml, which is slightly more! The United
Kingdom's record of implementing such directives is not an unblemished one. The
Council has passed a Directive, 99/44, which requires sellers to give a two year minimum guarantee for consumer goods bought within the European Union. If the fault
occurs within the first six months from purchase it is presumed that it was present at
the time of purchase. The Directive applies to both new and second-hand goods. It
should have been implemented by Member States by 1 January 2002. The Sale and
Supply of Goods to Consumers Regulations 2002 will implement the Directive but
have not been brought into force at the time of writing.

Another weapon in the fight for consumer rights has been brought into effect by
the Stop Now Orders (EC Directive) Regulations 2001 which implement Directive 98/
27 on injunctions to protect consumers' interests. These orders apply to any action
which is contrary to certain Directives ('community infringements') which have been
brought into force in the member state. The Orders replace Part III of the Fair Trading
Act 1973 as regards breach of the Directives covered by the Orders. Previously, before
action was taken the Director General had to obtain a written assurance from the
trader that the trader would not break the rules. Under the new system of Stop Now
Orders certain bodies have power to take action, such as the OFT, Ofgem, Ofwat,
Oftel, the Rail Regulator and trading standards authorities. These 'qualified entities'
must first consult the Director General of Fair Trading and the trader and give the
trader the opportunity to stop the breach of the regulations. If the activity is not
stopped within two weeks after the consultation, court proceedings may be taken. The
court may make a Stop Now Order requiring the trader to stop the practice. In
October 2001 the European Commission published a Green Paper, 'European Union
Consumer Protection' (Com (2001) 531 final). The Commission points out that both
consumers and businesses are reluctant to make contracts in other Member States
partly because of differences in the national consumer laws of the Member States. The
main proposal is for common and simple rules setting out principles for fair trading
and consumer protection.

Some of the objectives of the law are to ensure minimum standards for goods and
services; prevent fraudulent practices; control the provision of credit; provide for
adequate information to be given to consumers; and control unsafe goods. It attempts
to achieve these objectives through a mix of criminal sanctions, like the Trade
Descriptions Act 1968, the Weights and Measures Act 1985 and the Food Safety Act
1990, and civil liabilities, for example, the Sale of Goods Act 1979. This section will

examine some of the main provisions set out in the Sale of Goods Act 1979, the Sale and Supply of Goods Act 1994, the Sale of Goods (Amendment) Act 1995, the Supply of Goods and Services Act 1982, the Supply of Goods (Implied Terms) Act 1973, the Consumer Credit Act 1974 and the Consumer Protection Act 1987. There is a growing realisation that the law fails to protect the consumer in many instances and that codes of practice, persuasion and education may be more effective, for example, suppliers of goods and services are now encouraged to reach quality standards such as BSENISO 9000, which is accredited by the British Standards Institute. The impact of government 'deregulation' policy on consumer law will need to be carefully watched to see that it does not erode protection.

Sale of Goods Act 1979

1 Introduction

Every day millions of contracts are made for the sale of goods, for example, buying a teddy bear. The normal rules of contract law apply to such contracts and so does the Sale of Goods Act 1979. This Act sets out wide ranging rules which cover howthe contract is made; the terms implied in the contract; the passing of property in the goods; duties of each party in performing the contract; and the remedies available for breach of contract. This section will examine the implied terms and the rules for passing of property in detail and will briefly look at some of the other rules.

2 Contracts of sale and other contracts

An important distinction is made between contracts for the sale of goods *and* other contracts. The Sale of Goods Act 1979, s. 2(1), defines a contract for the sale of goods:

A contract for the sale of goods is a contract by which the seller transfers or agrees to transfer the property in goods to the buyer for a money consideration, called the price.

The important elements in this are (a) that the buyer must pay money for the goods (this covers cash, cheque and credit) and (b) there must be a transfer of property (or an agreement to transfer property).

The Act also defines goods as including all personal chattels but not choses in action, money, land or fixtures (s. 61(1)).

The distinction between sales of goods and other contracts is less important since the passing of the Supply of Goods and Services Act 1982 (see pp. 143–48).

The following contracts are *not* contracts for the sale of goods and are *not* covered by the Sale of Goods Act 1979:

2.1 Contract of exchange

Here goods are exchanged for other goods. For example, a farmer exchanges potatoes for meat. However, a contract involving part-exchange will normally be a sale of goods.

EXAMPLE

Alice trades in her car at Basil's Garage and is given an allowance against the price of a new car. The Sale of Goods Act will apply to the sale of the new car.

2.2 Contract of hire purchase

Here there is no agreement to sell goods and transfer ownership, although the hirer has an option to buy the goods.

2.3 Contract for goods and services

If the main object is the service, then it is not a sale of goods, for example, having a car serviced involves the provision of some goods like oil and an air filter, but these are secondary to the main purpose, the skill in carrying out the servicing.

2.4 Contract of hire

There is no agreement to sell goods here and the goods have to be returned at the end of the hire period, for example, hiring a television.

2.5 Contract for services

Again, this does not involve the provision of any goods, for example, having windows cleaned.

3 The implied terms

The Sale of Goods Act *implies* certain terms into contracts covered by the Act. The Act distinguishes between *conditions* and *warranties.* Conditions are major terms and if they are broken the innocent party has a choice, *either* to end the contract and claim damages *or* to carry on with the contract and claim damages. Warranties are minor terms of the contract and if they are broken the innocent party must continue with the contract and may only claim damages.

The implied terms are mainly *conditions,* so breach enables the innocent party to end the contract. The implied conditions automatically become part of the contract; there is no need for the buyer to mention them. They provide that the seller has a right to sell the goods; the goods correspond with their description; the goods are of satisfactory quality; the goods are fit for their purpose; and if goods are sold by sample, they will match the sample.

4 Title

4.1 Introduction

A number of different words are used to explain the idea that someone *owns* goods, these are *ownership*, *title* and *property*.

4.2 Right to sell

In every contract for the sale of goods, there is an implied *condition*, that the seller has the right to sell (s. 12(1)).

The effect of this is that the seller must transfer property (i.e. ownership) in the goods to the buyer. Strictly, it does not require the seller to be the owner of the goods, although in most cases this will be so. The seller could have the right to make a third party transfer ownership of goods to the buyer. If the buyer merely gets possession and not ownership, the buyer has a right to end the contract.

Rowland v *Divall* (1923)

The claimant bought a car from the defendant and used it for four months, before discovering it had been stolen. The claimant had to give it back to the true owner and then sued the defendant for the price paid. The defendant claimed that the claimant's use of the car should be taken into account. It was held by the Court of Appeal that the claimant had not been given property in the car and was therefore entitled to return of the price paid. This decision has been criticised, as the claimant obtained free use of the car for four months.

Even though the seller owns the goods, he may not have a right to sell them.

Niblett v *Confectioners' Materials Co.* (1921)

The buyer purchased some tins of condensed milk from abroad, labelled *Nissly*, which infringed the *Nestlé* brand. The milk was detained by Customs until the labels were removed. It was held that, although the seller owned the milk, it was in breach of s. 12(1) because the seller had no right to sell it with the *Nissly* labels on.

4.3 Free from encumbrances and quiet possession

In every contract for the sale of goods, there is an implied warranty: (a) that the goods are free from any charge or encumbrance not disclosed or known to the buyer before the contract is made, and (b) that the buyer will enjoy quiet possession (s. 12(2)).

A charge or encumbrance is a claim over the goods by a third party. Such a claim is rare, but could happen, for example, if a car is in a garage for repair, the owner may sell the car, but the garage may have a lien (i.e. a charge or claim) over the car for work carried out. If the seller tells the buyer of this lien, the seller is not in breach of s. 12(2).

The right to quiet possession means that the buyer will be able to use the goods without interference.

Microbeads AG v *Vinhurst Road Markings Ltd* (1975)

A seller sold some road marking machines to a buyer. After the sale, a third party obtained the patent for such machines and wished to stop the buyer using the machines. The buyer sued the seller for breach of s. 12(1) and (2). It was held that at the time of the sale the seller had the right to pass ownership as no patent had been taken out, so there was no breach of s. 12(1). But there was a breach of s. 12(2) because this relates to the future and here the buyer's quiet possession had been interfered with.

Rubicon Computer Systems Ltd v *United Paints Ltd* (2000)

U bought a computer system from R. After it was installed but before U had paid in full, a dispute arose as to whether R was responsible for transferring information from the old system to the new one. Without U's knowledge, R's representative then installed a time lock on the computer, which made it unusable. R sued for the balance of the price. It was held by the Court of Appeal that the implied term under s. 12(2)(b) applied and installing the time lock was a wrongful interference with goods and a breach of that term. It was also a repudiation of the contract by R. U was entitled to damages.

Note that a breach of s. 12(2) is breach of a warranty and only gives a right to damages.

4.4 Limited title

A seller may transfer a limited title if this is agreed or implied from the circumstances of the contract (s. 12(3)). This could happen, for example, if the seller found goods and sold them, so there was the possibility that someone, i.e. the true owner, had a better title. If this fact is disclosed to the buyer, there is no breach of the condition about title under s. 12(1).

5 Description

Where there is a contract for the sale of goods by description, there is an implied *condition* that the goods will correspond with the description (s. 13(1)).

This condition applies to all sales, both business and private. The sale must be by description, so the goods need to be described in some way. The description may be given by a shop assistant or on a label or in a catalogue. The vast majority of goods are packaged and labelled, so it would be unusual to find a sale which was *not* by description.

EXAMPLE

Alice points to a pile of apples on Bertie's market stall and asks for one kilo of them. If the apples have no notice or label and no description is given by Bertie, this will not be a sale by description.

If the buyer has not seen the goods but relies on a description, it will be a sale by description. Even if the buyer sees the goods, it will still be a sale by description if the goods are described in some way and the buyer relies on that description. In *Grant* v *Australian Knitting Mills Ltd* (1936), Lord Wright said:

It may also be pointed out that there is a sale by description even though the buyer is buying something displayed before him on the counter: a thing is sold by description, though it is specific, so long as it is sold not merely as the specific thing, but as a thing corresponding to a description, e.g. woollen undergarments, a hot water bottle, a secondhand reaping machine, to select a few obvious illustrations.

As regards a sale in a supermarket, the Sale of Goods Act, s. 13(3), provides:

A sale of goods is not prevented from being a sale by description by reason only that, the goods being exposed for sale or hire, are selected by the buyer.

Even though the buyer selects the goods, as long as they are labelled, for example, 'Beans', it will be a sale by description, as the buyer is relying on that description. This aspect of reliance was a significant fact in the following case.

Beale v Taylor (1967)

The defendant advertised his car for sale as a 'Herald Convertible, white, 1961, twin carbs'. The claimant saw the advert, went to see the car and after examining it decided to buy it. Later the claimant discovered that although the back half was a 1961 Herald, the front half was from a 1959 model! At the time of the sale neither party realised this. The Court of Appeal held that, although the claimant had seen the car, he still relied on the description '1961' in the advert. This was clearly a breach of the condition and the claimant was entitled to damages as he wished to keep the car.

One difficulty with s. 13 is whether goods have to comply with *all* parts of the description to satisfy the section? Some cases have suggested that it covers any statements about the goods, so it would include such matters as quantity, weight, ingredients, history, packaging, etc.

Re Moore (1921)

The buyer bought 3,000 tins of fruit, to be packed in cases of 30. Although the correct quantity of fruit was delivered, half was in cases of 24. The Court of Appeal held that being packed in cases of 30 was part of the description and this was clearly a breach. Why should the buyer mention the number in a case if it wasn't important? Also the buyer may have arranged to resell in cases of 30.

A number of rulings followed this decision and sellers were made liable for what often amounted to *technical* breaches of s. 13. The courts later gave it a narrower meaning, so that only words used to identify the kind of goods being sold, could be treated as part of the description and this would not include words used to indicate quality.

The courts re-examined what was needed for a sale by description in the following case.

Harlingdon & Leinster Enterprises Ltd v Christopher Hull Fine Art Ltd (1990)

The defendants were art dealers, who were selling two paintings by Münter, a German painter. The defendants were not experts in such paintings and they told the claimants this. The claimants, who were also art dealers, bought the paintings for £6,000. The invoice contained the word 'Münter'. Later the paintings were found to be fakes and the claimants claimed this was a breach of s. 13. The Court of Appeal held that for a sale by description, there had to be *reliance* on the description by the buyer. The claimants had not relied on the defendants' description of the painting as a 'Münter' but on their own judgment. Slade LJ also said that the use of the name 'Münter' on the invoice was not to be treated as a description, but simply as a way of referring to those specific paintings.

It would seem that as a result of this decision, if sellers of goods said they were not experts, any description applied would not be within s. 13, leaving the buyer without a remedy under that section. Neither did the decision take the amount paid into account, as the plaintiffs paid the original asking price of £6,000 and it would seem reasonable for them to assume that the description 'Münter' should apply. The effect of this decision on sales by description remains to be seen, but it goes against the spirit of the section and it is hoped it will be confined to contracts between businesses.

The new s. 15A inserted by the Sale and Supply of Goods Act 1994, now provides that if a breach is so slight that it would be unreasonable to reject the goods, the breach should not be treated as a breach of condition but as a breach of warranty. In *Re Moore, Re* (1921) above, this would now mean that the buyer could not reject the goods. This provision does not apply to a buyer who 'deals as a consumer'.

A sale will not be a sale by description if it is clear that the buyer buys a specific thing, as it stands, and the seller accepts no responsibility as regards description.

EXAMPLE

Goods sold 'as seen'.

Apart from liability under s. 13, if the sale is in the course of a business, the seller may also commit a *criminal* offence under the Trade Descriptions Act 1968, s. 1(1).

6 Satisfactory quality

The provision in the Sale of Goods Act 1979, s. 14(2) that goods must be of *merchantable quality* had been formulated at the end of the nineteenth century for the purposes of commerce and was of limited use in helping the modern consumer. A Law Commission report in 1987 (Law Commission No. 160 Cm 137) made suggestions for reform which were added to by the DTI, and a private member's bill was passed to implement these proposals which became the Sale and Supply of Goods Act 1994.

Under the Sale of Goods Act, s. 14(2) as amended by the Sale and Supply of Goods Act 1994:

Where the seller sells goods in the course of a business there is an implied term that the goods supplied under the contract are of satisfactory quality.

The 1994 Act, then adds:

(2A) For the purposes of this Act, goods are of satisfactory quality if they meet the standard that a reasonable person would regard as satisfactory, taking account of any description of the goods, the price (if relevant) and all other relevant circumstances.

(2B) For the purposes of this Act, the quality of goods includes their state and condition and the following (among others) are in appropriate cases aspects of the quality of goods—

(a) fitness for all the purposes for which goods of the kind in question are commonly supplied,

(b) appearance and finish,

(c) freedom from minor defects,

(d) safety, and

(e) durability.

The implied term of satisfactory quality is a condition (s. 14(6)).

Whether the old case law on merchantable quality is relevant to the new requirement of satisfactory quality remains to be seen. It can be argued that the old cases are irrelevant in determining *satisfactory quality*, which is a new, improved standard. However, many of the factors set out in s. 14(2B) have been considered by the courts in determining *merchantable quality* and may provide some guidance in determining the new standard.

Liability is strict, which means the seller is liable even though not at fault.

6.1 Goods must be sold in the course of a business

The condition of satisfactory quality will apply only if the seller sells in the course of a business. It does not apply to private sales, for example, by a private individual selling through an advertisement in a newspaper. The buyer's status does not matter, so the buyer may be a private individual or a business. It is of course open to someone who buys from a private seller, to agree an express condition that the goods sold are of satisfactory quality.

The courts have given guidance on what is meant by 'in the course of a business' for the purposes of s. 14(2).

Stevenson v *Rogers* (1998)
The defendant, a fisherman, sold his fishing boat to the claimant. This was only the second boat he had sold in 20 years. Later the claimant sued arguing that the boat was not of merchantable quality. It was held by the High court that the sale was not 'in the course of a business' under s. 14(2) because selling boats was not a regular part of the defendant's business and therefore the implied term of merchantable quality did not apply. The Court of Appeal said that the purpose of s. 14(2) was to widen the protection given to a buyer. The seller did not have to deal regularly in those goods or be a business selling fishing boats but merely had to sell 'in the course of a business'. Those words were simply to distinguish between a sale in the course of a business and a purely private sale. The defendant had sold the boat in the course of the business and therefore the implied condition of merchantable quality applied.

6.2 A reasonable buyer

Goods will be of satisfactory quality if they meet the standard a reasonable buyer would regard as satisfactory. This standard must be applied to the complete range of goods and to varying circumstances, both commercial and consumer. Clearly it is going to vary, so that a reasonable buyer would not expect secondhand goods to be the same as new goods.

6.3 Goods must be of satisfactory quality

In deciding whether goods are of satisfactory quality the factors mentioned in s. 14(2B) are relevant, but other factors may also be taken into account. The courts will need to make an overall judgment and goods will not necessarily be unsatisfactory just because one of these factors is not complied with. The state and condition of goods would cover, for example, a situation where goods are dirty but otherwise satisfactory and these would not be regarded as of satisfactory quality.

6.3.1 Description
The description of goods includes both oral and written statements and statements on the wrapping and labels.

6.3.2 Price
This is taken into account only if it is relevant. The fact that the price is reduced does not mean that goods do not have to be of satisfactory quality. The buyer of an expensive car can expect a higher standard than the buyer of a cheap car, but even in the latter case the buyer can expect the car to work properly.

6.3.3 Fitness for all the purposes
Under s. 14(2B)(a) the goods must be fit for *all* the purposes for which goods of the kind in question are commonly supplied. Under the old requirement of merchantable quality, goods had to be 'fit for the purpose or purposes for which goods of that kind are commonly bought'. This was interpreted in the following case to have been met if the goods were fit for *one* of those purposes.

Aswan Engineering Establishment Company v *Lupdine Ltd* (1987)
The buyer bought some waterproofing compound in plastic pails for export to Kuwait. When the pails arrived in Kuwait, they were stacked six high in intense heat for some days. The pails collapsed and the compound was lost. The buyer claimed that the pails were not of merchantable quality, as they should have been fit for all purposes for which they would commonly be used. The Court of Appeal held that to establish that the pails were not of merchantable quality, it had to be shown they were not fit for any of the purposes they were commonly used for. The pails would have been fit for many of these purposes although not for this particular purpose, so the buyer lost the case.

The new provision demands that goods are fit for *all* the purposes for which they are commonly supplied. They must be suitable for all common purposes. It is up to the court to decide what the common purposes for goods are. If applied to *Aswan* above, and if it was established that such use was one of the common purposes, the seller would be in breach of this term about satisfactory quality, but it seems unlikely to be a common purpose for plastic pails. This change clarifies the law and helps consumers.

6.3.4 Appearance and finish

These concern cosmetic matters and will not usually be serious, although they could be (for example, a scratch on the lens of a pair of binoculars). The importance of these matters was highlighted in the next case.

Rogers v *Parish (Scarborough) Ltd* (1987)

The claimant bought a new Range Rover car for £14,000. The oil seals leaked; the engine and gearbox were noisy; the car misfired; and the bodywork was defective. The garage made several attempts to fix these faults but after six months the claimant rejected the car. It was held by the Court of Appeal that the fact the car could still be driven did not make it of merchantable quality. 'Starting with the purpose for which "goods of that kind" are commonly bought, one would include in respect of any passenger vehicle not merely the buyer's purpose of driving the car from one place to another but of doing so with the appropriate degree of comfort, ease of handling and reliability and, one might add, of pride in the vehicle's outward and interior appearance' (Mustill LJ). The claimant was entitled to his money back.

Clearly, a reasonable person would expect new goods to be generally free from blemishes but not so secondhand goods. If there are some defects in the appearance and finish of goods that does not automatically mean that they are not of satisfactory quality.

6.3.5 Freedom from minor defects

Minor defects have been dealt with separately to avoid argument that a minor defect must concern appearance and finish. Minor defects cover how goods work. If goods are new or expensive, as compared to similar goods, it is more likely they should be free from minor defects or they will fail the test of satisfactory quality. The fact that goods have a minor defect does not mean that they automatically fail the test.

6.3.6 Safety

If goods are unsafe then they are not of satisfactory quality. Under the old law of merchantable quality the courts treated unsafe goods as unmerchantable, but this requirement has now been given statutory force.

6.3.7 Durability

Durability does not require goods to be of satisfactory quality for a particular period of time. It requires that at the time of delivery, the goods should be in such a condition, that they do not become unsatisfactory sooner than a reasonable person would expect.

6.4 Goods supplied

This term from s. 14(2) is wider than simply the *goods* sold under the contract of sale. The condition about satisfactory quality covers any containers or packaging supplied. The old case law will still be useful on this point.

Geddling v *Marsh* (1920)

Mineral water was sold in returnable bottles. One of the bottles exploded due to a defect and injured the buyer. It was argued by the seller that the mineral water was fine and that as the buyer had not bought the bottle there was no liability. It was held that the bottle had been *supplied* and the seller was liable.

The term *goods supplied* also covers foreign matter.

Wilson v *Rickett, Cockerell & Co. Ltd* (1954)

The claimant ordered some coalite from the defendant. When the claimant lit a fire there was an explosion, because unknown to either party the coalite contained a detonator! The Court of Appeal held that the coalite was not of merchantable quality. 'A sack of coal, which contains hidden in it a detonator, is not fit for burning . . .' (per Denning LJ).

6.5 Exceptions to the condition about satisfactory quality

Under s. 14(2C):

The term implied by subsection (2) above does not extend to any matter making the quality of goods unsatisfactory—

    (a) which is specifically drawn to the buyer's attention before the contract is made,

    (b) where the buyer examines the goods before the contract is made, which that examination ought to reveal, or

    (c) in the case of a contract for sale by sample, which would have been apparent on a reasonable examination of the sample.

This may be slightly wider than the old law which referred to 'defects' drawn to the buyer's attention or which ought to have been discovered. The seller is not liable for *any matter* drawn to the attention of the buyer.

Bartlett v *Sidney Marcus Ltd* (1965)

The claimant wished to buy a secondhand car from the defendants' garage. The claimant was told the clutch was defective and the car would cost £950, or the defendants would fix the clutch and charge £975 for the car. The claimant bought the car for £950, but it cost £84 to get the clutch fixed elsewhere and the claimant then claimed the car was not of merchantable quality. The Court of Appeal held that as the buyer had been told about the defective clutch, the car was of merchantable quality. The fact that the defect cost more to put right than the buyer believed, did not make the car unmerchantable.

Under s. 14(2C)(b) if the buyer *examines* the goods and that particular examination should have revealed the defect, the goods will be of satisfactory quality. There is no obligation on the buyer to examine the goods, but if the buyer does examine the goods, obvious defects will be binding, but latent or hidden defects will not be binding.

EXAMPLE

A buyer of a car who does not notice the passenger seat is missing after going for a test drive, cannot complain the car is not satisfactory. But the buyer would not be bound by something he could not discover, for example, a latent defect in the engine.

7 Fitness for purpose

Under s. 14(3):

Where the seller sells goods in the course of a business and the buyer expressly or by implication makes known (a) to the seller . . . any particular purpose for which the goods are being bought, there is an implied condition that the goods supplied under the contract are reasonably fit for that purpose, whether or not that is a purpose for which such goods are commonly supplied, except where the circumstances show that the buyer does not rely, or that it is unreasonable for him to rely, on the skill or judgement of the seller . . . .

7.1 Course of a business

This condition, that goods must be fit for their purpose, applies only to sales in the course of a business. It does not apply to private sales, although someone buying from a private seller could expressly agree the goods must be fit for their purpose.

7.2 Condition

This implied term is a condition and gives the buyer the right to reject the goods if they are not fit for their purpose.

7.3 Goods supplied

The condition of fitness for purpose applies to all the goods supplied under the contract, so it covers the packing, containers and foreign bodies (see 6.4 above).

7.4 Buyer must make known the particular purpose

The condition applies *only* if the buyer makes known the particular purpose for which the goods are wanted. The buyer may expressly say what the purpose is *or* the purpose may be implied.

Baldry v *Marshall* (1925)
The buyer asked the seller for a car which was suitable for a motoring holiday on the Continent. The seller provided a Bugatti. It was held that the buyer had relied on the seller's skill and had been sold a racing car, which was obviously not fit for the purpose made known.

If the goods have only one purpose and the buyer is going to use them for that purpose, then the buyer does not have to say what the purpose is, it will be implied.

Preist v *Last* (1903)
The buyer of a hot-water bottle did not tell the seller why he wanted it. The bottle burst in bed and scalded the buyer's wife. It was held by the Court of Appeal that

hot-water bottles have only one purpose and as it must have been obvious to the seller why the buyer wanted it, the condition of fitness for purpose applied and this was clearly a breach.

If goods can be used for a number of purposes, the buyer must tell the seller the *particular* purpose for which the goods are required.

Griffiths v *Peter Conway Ltd* (1939)

The claimant bought a tweed coat from the defendant but as she had sensitive skin the coat caused dermatitis. The coat would not have affected normal skin. The claimant claimed the coat was not fit for its purpose. The Court of Appeal held that the particular purpose in this case was being worn by someone with sensitive skin. As the buyer had not told the seller of this purpose, the seller was not in breach of the condition of fitness for purpose.

It is important that the seller knows of the particular requirements, as can be seen from the next case.

Slater v *Finning* (1996)

The defendants supplied a new camshaft for the claimant's fishing boat. The camshaft did not work properly, and it was a similar story with replacements. The claimant sold the engine with the new camshaft and it worked in another boat. The claimant claimed breach of s. 14(3). The House of Lords held that the camshaft did not work properly because of a particular peculiarity of the claimant's fishing boat. Neither party knew of the particular circumstances here, but the court said that if the seller did not know of the particular circumstances it made no difference to liability whether or not the buyer knew of those circumstances. There was no breach of s. 14(3).

If the buyer makes known a purpose for the goods which is not a usual or common purpose, the seller will still be liable if the goods are not suitable for that purpose.

7.5 Instructions

If the goods are sold without adequate instructions or warnings, the seller may be in breach of s. 14(3).

Wormell v *RHM Agriculture (East) Ltd* (1987)

The claimant farmer asked the defendant for something suitable to kill wild oats and bought the herbicide recommended for £6,500. The claimant used this late in the season even though the instructions stated 'Damage may occur to crops sprayed after the recommended growth stage'. The herbicide was useless and the claimant sued for breach of s. 14(3). In rejecting the claimant's claim, the Court of Appeal held that the herbicide would have worked if applied at the right time. The court also confirmed that the instructions were part of the goods.

7.6 Duration

Goods must be fit for their purpose at the time of the contract. A defect which appears after the sale will not be a breach of s. 14(3). However, if the defect appears within a reasonable time of the contract, this may be evidence that the goods were not fit for their purpose at the time of the contract (*Crowther* v *Shannon Motor Co.* (1975)).

7.7 Strict liability

Liability under s. 14(3) is strict, which means that the seller is liable if the goods are not fit for their purpose, even though the seller is not at fault.

Frost v *Aylesbury Dairy Company* (1905)

Mr Frost bought milk from the defendants and gave some to his wife. The milk contained typhoid germs and Mrs Frost died of typhoid. The defendants did not know the milk contained these germs and, in the state of scientific knowledge at the time, could not have known. It was held that as the milk was not fit to drink, it did not matter the defendants had taken all possible care, they were strictly liable for breach of s. 14(3).

The duty under s. 14(3) is to supply goods which are *reasonably* fit for their purpose. If the goods are suitable for most purposes but not an unusual purpose, this will not necessarily be a breach of s. 14(3) unless that particular purpose was made known.

7.8 When s. 14(3) does not apply

There are two situations where the condition about fitness for purpose will not apply. These are where the buyer does not rely on the seller's skill *or* it is unreasonable for the buyer to rely on the seller's skill. It is up to the seller to prove either of these cases.

It will not apply where the seller does not know the purpose. It will not apply where the buyer does not give enough information about the purpose to the seller. It will not apply if the buyer has greater knowledge than the seller about the goods. It will apply if the buyer only partly relies on the seller's skill.

Cammell Laird & Co. Ltd v *Manganese Bronze and Brass Co. Ltd* (1934)

The defendants agreed to make two propellers for the claimants. The claimants provided most of the specifications but left the thickness of the propellers up to the defendants. One of the propellers was too thick and was therefore too noisy. It was held by the House of Lords that the claimants had partly relied on the seller's skill and as this propeller was unusable the defendants had supplied goods which were not fit for their purpose.

8 Relationship between section 14(2) and (3)

In deciding if goods are of satisfactory quality, their fitness for purpose is taken into account, so there is overlap between s. 14(2) and (3).

EXAMPLE

Alice buys a tennis racket from Basil's Sports Shop and finds that three of the strings are broken. The racket is not of satisfactory quality and is not fit for its purpose.

But sometimes goods may be fit for their purpose even though they are unsatisfactory.

EXAMPLE

If Alice buys a tennis racket, which has most of the paint scratched off the frame, it is still fit for playing tennis but is not of satisfactory quality.

9 Sale by sample

Under s. 15(1):

A contract of sale is a contract for sale by sample where there is an express or implied term to that effect in the contract.

There must be some evidence that the parties intend the sale to be by sample. The fact that a sample is provided does not automatically mean that it is a sale by sample, as the sample may be used in place of a description.

EXAMPLE

Perfume is not normally sold by sample, even though the buyer may smell the perfume from a sample bottle. This is used in lieu of a description.

If it is a sale by sample, then under s. 15(2):

. . . there is an implied term that

    (a) the bulk shall correspond with the sample in quality;

    (b) [repealed]

    (c) the goods will be free from any defect, making their quality unsatisfactory which would not be apparent on reasonable examination of the sample.

This section applies to both business and private sales.

Under (a) the goods must match the sample shown to the buyer. Under (c) the seller will still be liable for latent defects but not for defects which were obvious to the buyer.

Godley v *Perry* (1960)

The claimant, a six-year-old boy, bought a plastic catapult from the defendant. When he pulled back the elastic, the catapult broke and he was injured in the eye. The defendant had bought the catapults, by sample, from a wholesaler and had tested the sample by pulling back the elastic. It was held that the defendant was liable to the claimant as the catapult was not of merchantable quality or fit for its purpose. But the defendant could recover from the wholesaler, who had been joined as a second defendant, for breach of the condition about sale by sample.

EXAMPLE

Buying a carpet after looking at a sample will be a sale by sample.

10 Excluding the implied terms under sections 12 to 15

10.1 Civil aspects

This has been dealt with above under *Exclusion Clauses*, 4.3.4 'Sale of goods and hire purchase', see p. 65.

The Unfair Contract Terms Act 1977, s. 6, applies to any clause which attempts to exempt the seller from liability under the implied terms of the Sale of Goods Act 1979.

10.1.1 Section 12
Cannot be excluded in *any* sale, whether business or private.

10.1.2 Sections 13 to 15.
(a) Consumer sales: these conditions cannot be excluded.

(b) Non-consumer sales: these conditions may be excluded if this is reasonable.

The Unfair Terms in Consumer Contracts Regulations 1999 apply to consumer contracts and any attempt to exclude liability could be deemed unfair and therefore invalid under the regulations, although reliance on them is superfluous.

10.2 Criminal aspects

The Consumer Transactions (Restrictions on Statements) Order 1976 (as amended 1978) makes it a criminal offence for someone acting in a consumer sale to attempt to take away the rights given by ss. 13 to 15 of the Sale of Goods Act 1979.

It is an offence for someone acting in the course of a business to:

(a) display an exemption notice on business premises;

(b) publish such a notice in an advertisement (also an offence under the Control of Misleading Advertisement Regulations 1988);

(c) put an exemption in a written contract;

(d) supply goods with any statement about the seller's liability in respect of the matters in ss. 13 to 15 without clearly stating that the statement does not affect the consumer's statutory rights.

EXAMPLE

A notice in a shop which states 'No refunds'. This is a criminal offence and is also invalid in civil law.

11 Remedies

Under the Civil Procedure Rules 1998 a claim under £5,000 will be allocated to the 'small claims track' and if the claim is under £15,000 it will be allocated to the 'fast track'. The law provides two remedies for breach of the implied terms, which are damages *or* repudiating the contract and claiming money back. In practice, the consumer may be offered a replacement or repair of the goods, but is not obliged to accept these remedies. However, the buyer loses the right to reject goods once they have been accepted subject to s. 35A below. By s. 11(4):

Subject to section 35A below, where a contract of sale is not severable and the buyer has accepted the goods or part of them, the breach of a condition to be fulfilled by the seller can only be treated as a breach of warranty, and not as a ground for rejecting the goods and treating the contract as repudiated . . . .

The vast majority of sales of goods will not be severable, which means the contract cannot be broken into separate parts and completed separately. If the buyer accepts the goods, then the right to reject them is lost. Acceptance means *legal acceptance* rather than *physical acceptance*.

Under the Sale of Goods Act, s. 35, as amended by the Sale and Supply of Goods Act 1994, s. 2(1), the buyer is deemed to have accepted the goods when:

(a) he tells the seller he accepts them;

(b) after the goods have been delivered he does something inconsistent with the ownership of the seller;

(c) after a reasonable time he keeps the goods without telling the seller he rejects them.

In deciding whether a reasonable time has passed it must be considered whether the buyer has had a reasonable opportunity to examine the goods to see if they conform with the contract (s. 35(5)).

Bernstein v *Pamson Motors (Golders Green) Ltd* (1987)

The claimant bought a new Nissan motor car from the defendants for £8,000. Three weeks later, after about 140 miles, the car broke down on the motorway. This was caused by a small amount of sealant which blocked the oil supply and caused the engine to seize. The claimant wrote immediately rejecting the car because it was not of merchantable quality. It was held that even though the defect was minor it had serious consequences and the car was not of merchantable quality. But the claimant had accepted the car and therefore lost the right to reject it. 'Reasonable time means reasonable time to examine and try out the goods in general terms' (Rougier J). The claimant was entitled to damages to replace the engine but could not reject the car and reclaim the £8,000.

Under the new rules it may be argued that *Bernstein* would be decided differently.

Under s. 35(6) the buyer is not deemed to have accepted the goods by agreeing to repair by the seller, or by re-selling or otherwise disposing of the goods. Previously, agreeing to repair could be seen as acceptance of the goods. Although this is not ruled out under the new provision, generally giving an opportunity to repair would be unlikely to be treated as acceptance. Section 35(6) also solves a previous problem of buyers who resold being treated as accepting the goods by doing an act inconsistent with the seller's ownership.

Under s. 35(7), if the goods are sold in 'commercial units', a buyer who accepts any of the goods in that unit is deemed to have accepted all the goods. A commercial unit is how the goods are sold, so if some of them are taken away this would greatly reduce the value of the remainder. For example, one book taken from a trilogy.

Section 35A, inserted by s. 3 of the Sale and Supply of Goods Act 1994, gives a right of partial rejection of goods. If the buyer has a right to reject goods but accepts some of them, this does not mean the buyer accepts the rest. For example, if some of the goods are not of satisfactory quality, the buyer can reject those goods or reject all the goods. Previously, the law allowed the buyer to reject all or none of the goods.

In non-consumer contracts, s. 15A of the Sale of Goods Act, inserted by s. 5 of the Sale and Supply of Goods Act 1994, provides that where there is a breach of one of the implied terms in ss. 13–15, the right to reject is lost if the breach is so slight that it would be unreasonable to reject the goods. The breach may be treated as a breach of warranty. This restriction on the right to reject applies only where the buyer does not 'deal as consumer', which has the same meaning as under the Unfair Contract Terms Act 1977. This would stop buyers rejecting in circumstances such as *Re Moore, Re* (1921) (see *Description*, 5 above).

12 Transfer of property

12.1 Introduction

The law uses three words, *property, ownership* and *title*, which all mean the same—the right of ownership over goods. The main object of a contract for the sale of goods is to transfer ownership from the seller to the buyer. A distinction is made between this *right of ownership* and *possession* of goods, which means taking physical possession of them. Normally these two rights go together, so someone who has ownership will also have possession. But they may be split up, so that transfer of ownership and possession may take place at different times. Under the Sale of Goods Act these two rights are independent of each other, so that having the right of ownership does not give a right to possession and vice versa.

12.2 Importance of knowing when property passes

It is important to decide if and when property has passed from the seller to the buyer for a number of reasons:

(a) *Risk* passes with property—so the owner bears the risk of accidental damage to the goods.

(b) The buyer cannot *transfer ownership* unless the buyer has ownership—there are some exceptions to this (see 17 below).

(c) If the buyer or seller become *bankrupt*, the trustee in bankruptcy may only claim goods if the bankrupt has ownership of them.

(d) The seller may only sue for the *price* of the goods after property has passed to the buyer.

12.3 Type of goods

It is important to know whether goods are specific or unascertained, in order to decide when property in the goods passes.

12.3.1 Specific goods   These have been defined as 'goods identified and agreed on at the time a contract of sale is made' (s. 61(1)).

EXAMPLE

Alice goes to Bill's Garage, points to a red mini and makes a contract to buy it. That particular red mini is a specific good.

12.3.2 Unascertained goods   These are not defined in the Act but are any goods which are not specific goods. They are goods which have not been identified at the time of the contract. There are three main categories:

(a) *Future goods* These are goods which have to be made or acquired by the seller.

EXAMPLE

If Alice ordered a pink mini from Bill's Garage, and this had to be specially made by the manufacturers, it would be future goods.

(b) *Goods of a particular type* These are goods which match a general description and are also known as generic goods.

EXAMPLE

If Alice asked for 'a red mini'.

(c) *Part of a larger specified quantity* In this case, although the goods are of a particular type, they must come from a given source.

EXAMPLE

Alice goes to the greengrocers, points to a sack of potatoes and asks for 5 kilos from the sack.

When unascertained goods have been set aside for the contract, they become ascertained. As a general rule, it is only then that property in those goods can pass to the buyer, although in some circumstances ownership can pass before the goods are ascertained. Unascertained goods can never become specific goods, because the time for deciding which type of goods are involved is the time the contract is made.

13 Transfer of property in specific goods

The general rule for specific goods is that property 'is transferred to the buyer at such time as the parties intend it to be transferred' (s. 17). This intention can be determined by the terms of the contract, the conduct of the parties, and the circumstances of the case. This rule also applies to ascertained goods.

It is up to the parties to the contract to decide when property will pass. If the contract deals with this the court will follow the contract, otherwise the court has to find what the parties intended from the circumstances. It is unusual for consumer contracts to deal with the transfer of property in the goods. One example is a conditional sale agreement (see *Consumer Credit Act 1974*, 2, below). If the intention of the parties cannot be found, then s. 18 provides rules which apply automatically.

13.1 Section 18, rule 1

Where there is an unconditional contract for the sale of specific goods in a deliverable state, the property in the goods passes to the buyer when the contract is made, and it is immaterial whether the time of payment or the time of delivery or both be postponed.

The contract must not be subject to some condition being fulfilled, for example the goods pass an inspection by a third party. The term 'deliverable state' means that the goods are ready for the buyer and nothing more needs to be done to them.

> EXAMPLE
>
> Alice selects a blue dress from the rack in Basil's store and it is agreed she will pay for it when it is delivered in a week's time. If the dress is destroyed in a fire the next day Alice would have to pay, as property in the dress was transferred to her at the time of the contract.

Tarling v *Baxter* (1827)
A buyer bought a haystack, but it was burned down before it could be taken away. It was held that property had passed at the time of the contract and the buyer had to pay for it.

If after a contract for specific goods has been made there is an agreement about when property is to pass, this agreement will not be effective and rule 1 will apply.

13.2 Section 18, rule 2

Where there is a contract for the sale of specific goods and the seller is bound to do something to the goods, for the purpose of putting them into a deliverable state, the property does not pass until the thing is done and the buyer has notice that it has been done.

Here something needs to be done to the goods and property does not pass until this happens *and* the buyer has been told. The notice required is actual notice, so if the seller sends a letter, it will only be valid notice when the buyer receives it.

> EXAMPLE
>
> Alice selects a blue dress from the rack in Basil's store and arranges to pay for it, in a week's time, when the sleeves have been lengthened. Three days later, before the alterations have been made, the shop is flooded and the dress is ruined. Alice does not have to pay for the dress, as the alterations have not been made and property in the dress remains with Basil.

Underwood Ltd v *Burgh Castle Brick and Cement Syndicate* (1922)
This concerned the sale of machinery weighing 30 tons, which was embedded in

concrete in a factory. It was agreed the seller would put it on the train. The seller accidentally broke it whilst loading it on to the train for transportation to the buyer. It was held by the Court of Appeal that the machinery was not in a deliverable state at the time of the contract, as it had to be freed from the concrete. Rule 2 applied and property was still with the seller, who had to bear the loss.

13.3 Section 18, rule 3

Where there is a contract for the sale of specific goods in a deliverable state but the seller is bound to weigh, measure, test or do some other act or thing with reference to the goods for the purpose of ascertaining the price, the property does not pass until the act or thing is done and the buyer has notice it has been done.

Here the seller has to do something to the goods and it must be in relation to fixing the price of the goods which are sold. This Rule does not apply if the buyer does the weighing etc.

EXAMPLE

Alice selects a roll of blue cloth from the rack in Basil's shop and agrees to buy it. Alice arranges to call back in a week's time when Basil has measured the roll and fixed the price.

Two days after the contract is made the shop is burgled and the cloth stolen. If Basil has measured the roll but not told Alice, then property in the goods has not passed to Alice and she does not have to pay.

13.4 Section 18, rule 4

When goods are delivered to the buyer on approval or on sale or return or other similar terms the property in the goods passes to the buyer:

(a) when he signifies his approval or acceptance to the seller or does any other act adopting the transaction;

(b) if he does not signify his approval or acceptance to the seller but retains the goods without giving notice of rejection, then if a time has been fixed for the return of the goods, on expiration of that time and if no time has been fixed, on the expiration of a reasonable time.

There are three possibilities when property will pass to the buyer:

(a) if the buyer *agrees* to have the goods within the time period;

(b) if the buyer does an act *adopting* the goods within the time period;

(c) if the buyer *keeps* the goods longer than the time period without rejecting them.

EXAMPLE

If Alice buys a blue dress on 14 days' approval from Basil's catalogue, three separate cases may be examined:

(a) If Alice rings Basil after three days and agrees to have the dress, property passes then.

(b) If Alice wears the dress to a party after five days, property passes then.

(c) If Alice keeps the dress after the approval period without telling Basil she does not want it, then property passes after 14 days.

Atari Corp. Ltd v *Electronics Boutique* (1998)

The defendants bought computer games from the claimants on a 'sale or return' basis. They then wrote to the claimants saying that they were not going to stock the games and had told all their shops to return the games to a central warehouse, where the claimants could collect them. The claimants argued (i) that this was not a rejection of the goods because the defendants referred to future action, the goods going to a central point before they could be rejected; (ii) the actual goods being rejected had not been specified; and (iii) the goods were not available for collection when the letter was sent. The Court of Appeal held that the letter was a rejection. Also it was not necessary to identify the precise goods; they could be referred to generically as long as this enabled them to be identified. Further, the goods did not have to be available for collection when the notice of rejection was sent, as long as they were available within a reasonable time. The defendants had rejected the goods.

14 Transfer of property in unascertained goods

14.1 Section 16

Under s. 16:

Subject to section 20A below, where there is a contract for the sale of unascertained goods no property is transferred to the buyer unless and until the goods are ascertained.

Until the goods have been identified, property cannot pass to the buyer. When the goods have been ascertained, then under s. 17 property passes when the parties *intend* it to. Property does not pass immediately the goods become ascertained, but only when the parties intend it to.

If this intention cannot be discovered, then s. 18, rule 5 applies. (See 14.3 below.)

These rules are now subject to the changes made by the Sale of Goods (Amendment) Act 1995 as regards goods forming part of an identified bulk. The 1995 Act adds a new subsection to s. 18, rule 5, the new rule 5(3) now dealing with property passing when a bulk is reduced; it also adds a new s. 20(A) which provides for a buyer from bulk who pays for the goods to have an undivided share in the bulk. These changes were made to deal with the problem that arose under s. 16 that a buyer could pay for unascertained goods, but if the seller then became insolvent the buyer had no claim over the goods. The changes are aimed at commodity traders who wish to claim their share of the bulk, but they may also help individual consumers. It is now important to distinguish between (i) unascertained goods which may be taken from any source, and (ii) unascertained goods taken from an identified bulk.

The two following cases were decided before the Sale of Goods (Amendment) Act

1995, and whether the Act affects them needs to be considered. The seller's existing stock could be an identified bulk if the seller agreed to deliver the goods from that stock.

Re Stapylton Fletcher Ltd and Re Ellis Son & Vidler Ltd, Re (1995)

ESV and SFL were wine merchants. ESV kept the wine purchased by customers in a reserve and kept a card index of customers and the amount of wine allocated to each. SFL did not allocate wine to purchasers and none was put in reserve. A joint receiver was appointed when the two companies could not pay their debts and the receiver claimed the wine. It was held that, as regards ESV, although cases of wine had not been allocated to individual buyers, the wine had been separated from the company's trading assets and had become ascertained. The buyers became tenants in common of the reserve stock. As regards SFL, their buyers had no rights over any wine.

The Privy Council has recently dealt with a claim over unascertained goods.

Re Goldcorp Exchange Ltd (in receivership), Re (1994)

Customers of a company dealing in gold bullion paid for bullion for future delivery. The company explained that this bullion was not set aside for the buyers but was part of the company's stock, although buyers could call for delivery within seven days. The company became insolvent and their bank appointed a receiver. At the time the receiver was appointed, no bullion had been appropriated to individual buyers. The Privy Council, hearing an appeal from the Court of Appeal of New Zealand, held that the bullion purchased was unascertained goods and the company was free to decide from what source it would obtain such goods. No goods had been appropriated to individual contracts, so the buyers did not have title to the bullion. Neither was a trust created over the stock of bullion or the money paid for the bullion, as there was no intention to limit the company's freedom to use these how it wished. The receiver was therefore entitled to the bullion.

14.2 Section 18, rule 5

Where there is a contract for the sale of unascertained or future goods by description, and goods of that description and in a deliverable state are unconditionally appropriated to the contract, either by the seller with the assent of the buyer, or by the buyer with the assent of the seller, the property in the goods then passes to the buyer; and the assent may be express or implied, and may be given either before or after the appropriation is made.

If the seller gives the goods to the buyer or to a carrier to take to the buyer and the seller does not reserve a right of disposal, this is treated as appropriating the goods to the contract.

Two conditions must be met to comply with rule 5:

(a) Goods must be *unconditionally appropriated* to the contract. This means the goods must be set aside for the buyer, but this must be done in such a way that the seller cannot use the goods for someone else.

Carlos Federspiel & Co. SA v Charles Twigg & Co. Ltd (1957)

The seller of bicycles agreed to load them on a ship for transportation to the buyer f.o.b. The bicycles were packed in containers stamped with the buyer's name, but the seller then became insolvent. It was held that property in the bicycles had not passed to the buyer. Only when the bicycles had been put on the ship could they be regarded as irrevocably set aside for the contract.

and

(b) Whichever party does the setting aside, the other party must *agree* to this.

EXAMPLE

Alice chooses a 'Cleanit' brand dishwasher in Bertie's shop and Bertie agrees to deliver one. The dishwasher is unascertained but will become ascertained when Bertie sets one aside for Alice. Alice may be regarded as giving an implied assent to this in advance, as she has seen the model in Bertie's shop.

Property in goods cannot pass if the goods are still unascertained.

Healy v *Howlett & Sons* (1917)

The seller in Ireland put 20 unmarked boxes of mackerel on the train for the buyer, along with another 170 boxes for other buyers. The seller then sent an invoice stating 'At sole risk of purchaser after putting fish on rail here'. When the fish arrived at Holyhead, the railway company put 20 boxes aside for the buyer but by this time the fish had gone bad. It was held that the 20 boxes did not become ascertained until set aside by the railway and property could not pass until then. The seller therefore bore the risk of loss and was not entitled to the price.

The assent may be given after the goods have been appropriated to the contract.

Pignataro v *Gilroy* (1919)

The seller sold 140 bags of rice to the buyer, and at the time of the contract they were unascertained goods. Later the seller gave details of where the rice could be collected, including 15 bags at the seller's premises. The buyer did not go to collect them until nearly one month later and found they had been stolen. It was held that the buyer had assented to the appropriation by doing nothing for so long, therefore property had passed to the buyer under s. 18, rule 5 and the buyer had to bear the loss.

Section 18, rule 5(3) provides (as inserted by the Sale of Goods (Amendment) Act 1995)

Where there is a contract for the sale of a specified quantity of unascertained goods in a deliverable state forming part of a bulk which is identified either in the contract or by subsequent agreement between the parties and the bulk is reduced to (or to less than) that quantity, then, if the buyer under that contract is the only buyer to whom goods are then due out of the bulk.

(a) the remaining goods are . . . appropriated to that contract at the time when the bulk is so reduced; and

(b) the property in those goods then passes to that buyer.

For this rule to apply the parties must agree on a fixed amount of goods from an identified source. This process is known as 'ascertainment by exhaustion'.

EXAMPLE

S sells B 100 tonnes of grain from S's store of 300 tonnes. S then sells and delivers 200 tonnes of grain to X. B will become owner of the remaining 100 tonnes.

15 Reserving a right of disposal

Under s. 19:

Where there is a contract for the sale of specific goods or where goods are subsequently appropriated to the contract, the seller may . . . reserve the right of disposal of the goods until certain conditions are fulfilled; and in such a case, notwithstanding the delivery of the goods to the buyer . . . property in the goods does not pass to the buyer until the conditions . . . are fulfilled.

A 'right of disposal' means the same as property, ownership and title.

This section enables the seller to put a condition in the contract that property in the goods does not pass to the buyer until the buyer has paid for the goods. This protects the seller if the buyer becomes insolvent and cannot pay, because the goods will belong to the seller, who may reclaim them. Otherwise, the seller would simply be an unsecured creditor and unlikely to be repaid in full.

Aluminium Industrie Vaassen BV v *Romalpa Aluminium Ltd* (1976)
The claimants sold foil to the defendants under a contract which provided that the ownership of the foil did not pass to the defendants until they had paid for it and the claimants were entitled to the proceeds of sale of any finished products. The defendants became insolvent before they had paid for the foil and the claimants claimed foil worth £50,000 in the defendants' possession plus £35,000 which was the proceeds of sale of other foil. It was held by the Court of Appeal that the claimants were entitled to both claims because of the clause in the contract of sale.

These clauses became known as *Romalpa* clauses or *reservation of title* clauses. They are clearly effective if the goods sold remain identifiable, but what if the goods are mixed with other goods belonging to the buyer, can the seller claim the new goods?

Re Peachdart Ltd, Re (1983)
The sellers of leather provided in the sale contract that any goods made from the leather belonged to the sellers as did the proceeds of sale of such goods. The buyers made handbags with the leather. It was held that this did not make the sellers owners of the handbags but simply gave them a charge (or claim) over the goods. Such a charge has to be registered with the Registrar of companies and as this had not been done, it was void.

However, in a later case there was a different result.

Hendy Lennox (Industrial Engines) Ltd v *Grahame Puttick Ltd* (1984)

The seller of engines put a reservation of title clause in the sale contract. The buyer put the engines in generators. Later the buyer became insolvent and the seller reclaimed the engines. It was held that engines which had not been put in generators and engines which had been put in generators but could be unbolted, could be reclaimed.

Under the Companies Act 1985, ss. 395 and 396 (as amended by the Companies Act 1989), if a company creates a charge over its assets, that charge must be registered at Companies House, otherwise it is void against a third party who has a claim over those assets. For example, the sellers of the leather in *Re Peachdart Ltd* above. But if a company buys goods from a supplier and the supply contract contains a *Romalpa* clause, the company does not own the goods. Because it does not own them it cannot create a charge over them, so a *Romalpa* clause does not have to be registered to be effective. Depending on the wording of the clause it may be a *Romalpa* clause, which means the seller still owns the goods or it may simply create a *charge* over the goods, which means the buyer owns them, subject to the charge.

The House of Lords has confirmed the position.

Armour v *Thyssen Edelstahlwerke AG* (1991)

T supplied steel to a manufacturer, C, and the contract provided that property remained with T until all debts were paid. C went into receivership without paying and the receiver claimed the steel, which was still in its original form. Had C given T a 'charge' over the steel? It was held that C could not create a charge over the goods until C owned them, which could not happen until C paid for them. Therefore T still owned the steel and could reclaim it.

16 **Transfer of risk**

Under s. 20(1):

Unless otherwise agreed, the goods remain at the seller's risk until the property in them is transferred to the buyer, but when the property in them is transferred to the buyer, the goods are at the buyer's risk whether delivery has been made or not.

The general rule is that risk passes with property.

There are three qualifications on this rule.

(a) s. 20(2);

(b) s. 20(3);

(c) unless otherwise agreed.

(a) 'But where delivery has been delayed through the fault of either buyer or seller the goods are at the risk of the party at fault as regards any loss which might not have occurred but for such fault' (s. 20(2)).

If delivery is delayed because one party is at fault, and that delay causes damage to the goods, the party at fault is responsible.

(b) 'Nothing in this section shall affect the duties or liabilities of seller or buyer as bailee . . . of the goods for the other party' (s. 20(3)).

This means that the person in possession of the goods must take reasonable care of them, even if the other party owns the goods; and if they do not and the goods are damaged, they bear the loss.

(c) 'Unless otherwise agreed'. It is up to the parties to agree when the risk shall pass. It is possible for the risk to pass *before* property in the goods passes.

Sterns Ltd v *Vickers Ltd* (1923)

The sellers sold 120,000 gallons of white spirit to the buyers. This spirit was in a tank of 200,000 gallons on the premises of a third party. The sellers gave the buyers a delivery note, to enable the buyers to collect the spirit. The buyers left the spirit in the tank for their own convenience for a number of months and during this time the spirit deteriorated. Property in the spirit had not passed to the buyers because the 120,000 gallons was still unascertained. The Court of Appeal held that although property had not passed, the parties intended risk to pass because the buyers had accepted a delivery note and therefore the buyers had to bear the loss.

A new s. 20A is added by the Sale of Goods (Amendment) Act 1995. The conditions for s. 20A to apply are:

(a) there is a contract for the sale of a specified quantity of unascertained goods;

(b) the goods are part of a bulk identified in the contract (or by later agreement);

(c) the buyer has paid for the goods (or some of them).

As soon as these conditions are met (or later if the parties agree), property in an undivided share in the bulk is transferred to the buyer who becomes an owner in common. The buyer's share of the bulk will be in proportion to the amount of goods he has paid for. If there is more than one buyer entitled to a share and the bulk is reduced, the buyers' shares are reduced in proportion, so that every buyer obtains a share. This section applies only if there is no contrary intention.

A new s. 20B provides that an owner in common of a bulk is deemed to consent to delivery of goods from the bulk to any other owner in common.

EXAMPLE

B buys and pays for 50 tonnes of grain from S's store of 100 tonnes. Under s. 20A, B immediately becomes an owner in common of the bulk. B and S have equal shares in the bulk.

17 Transfer of property in goods by a non-owner

If someone sells goods they do not own, do the goods belong to the original owner or the new buyer? This creates a problem for the law.

Denning LJ in *Bishopsgate Motor Finance Corporation Ltd* v *Transport Brakes Ltd* (1949) said:

In the development of our law, two principles have striven for mastery. The first is the protection of property. No one can give a better title than he himself possesses. The second is the protection of commercial transactions. The person who takes in good faith and for value without notice should get a good title.

The law has dealt with this problem by having a general rule which protects property rights but allowing a number of exceptions to it for commercial convenience. The general rule is set out in the Sale of Goods Act 1979, s. 21(1):

. . . where goods are sold by a person who is not their owner . . . the buyer acquires no better title to the goods than the seller had.

This rule is known as the *nemo dat* rule, from the maxim *nemo dat quod non habet*, which means no one can give what they have not got.

EXAMPLE

Alice steals Bertie's mountain bike and sells it to Clive for £1,000. Clive will not become owner of the bike and will have to return it to Bertie. Clive can sue Alice for breach of s. 12.

Previously, s. 22 of the Sale of Goods Act provided an exception to the *nemo dat rule*, that if goods were sold in an open market ('market overt'), a buyer who bought in good faith would obtain a good title to the goods. This allowed a buyer to obtain ownership of stolen goods. This rule was abolished by the Sale of Goods (Amendment) Act 1994 which applies to contracts made after 3 January 1995.

The other exceptions to the *nemo dat* rule are explained in the following sections.

18 Estoppel

Under s. 21(1) an exception is made to the *nemo dat* rule if, 'the owner of the goods is by his conduct precluded from denying the sellers authority to sell'. This means that if the true owner allows the buyer to believe that the seller has the right to sell the goods, then ownership will pass to the buyer and the true owner is stopped (or estopped) from saying the seller had no right to sell.

For estoppel to operate, there must be

(a) a representation by the owner, by statement or conduct that the seller can sell the goods;

(b) the buyer must be misled; and

(c) the buyer must act in good faith.

Pickard v *Sears* (1837)

P owned a machine which was being used by A. A owed money to B and B obtained a court order against A's property. B took property from A's premises, including P's machine. P knew this was happening but did nothing about it. B sold the machine to S and P then claimed the machine from S. It was held that because P did not stop B taking the machine, P was stopped from saying the machine did not belong to A. Therefore S could keep it.

Simply giving possession of goods to someone is not a representation they have a right to sell the goods. For example, giving someone a car and the registration document does not enable them to pass ownership to a buyer, because the document is not a document of title.

19 Mercantile agents

Section 21(2) provides that nothing in the Act affects the provisions of the Factors Act 1889. A factor is a professional agent who buys and sells goods for a living.

An agent is someone who acts on behalf of another person (the principal) and is able to make legally binding contracts for that person. If the *nemo dat* rule was strictly enforced, then salespersons would only be able to sell goods if they owned them.

The Factors Act 1889, s. 2(1) provides that if the mercantile agent is:

(a) in possession of the goods (or the documents of title), and

(b) this is with the consent of the owner, and

(c) the agent is acting in the ordinary course of business, and

(d) the buyer acts in good faith

then any sale or pledge by the agent will be 'as valid as if he were expressly authorised by the owner of the goods'.

(a) The agent must have physical possession of the goods and this must be in the capacity of a mercantile agent. For example, if someone leaves a car with a garage to be repaired, the garage cannot sell it and pass a good title, as the garage does not have possession in its capacity as a mercantile agent, but simply as repairers.

(b) The agent must take possession with the consent of the owner. If the agent tricks the owner into parting with possession, this requirement is fulfilled. Also if the agent acts outside their powers, it is still binding on the owner.

(c) The agent must act within the ordinary course of business, so this means during business hours, on business premises and in accordance with normal practice.

(d) The buyer must act in good faith and must not know of any limits on the agent's powers.

Folkes v *King* (1923)

The claimant gave his car to an agent, saying not to sell for less than £575. The agent sold the car to the defendant for £350. It was held that as the agent was in possession, with the consent of the owner, was acting in the ordinary course of business and the buyer bought in good faith, then ownership passed to the defendant, who could keep the car.

20 Common law and statutory powers

The Act provides that it does not affect any common law or statutory powers of sale or court orders which give someone who does not own goods the right to sell them.

Examples of common law powers include pawnbrokers, who may sell goods pledged with them; mortgagees, who may do likewise; and agents of necessity, who may sell goods in an emergency.

Examples of statutory powers include, a bailee, for example, a dry cleaner who sells clothes which have not been collected; a sheriff, who may sell goods seized under a writ of execution; and an innkeeper, who may sell guests' goods to pay the bill.

21 Sale under a voidable title

Under s. 23:

Where the seller of goods has a voidable title to them, but his title has not been avoided at the time of the sale, the buyer acquires a good title to the goods, provided he buys them in good faith and without notice of the seller's defect of title.

A distinction is made between a void contract and a voidable contract. A void contract means that there is no contract and so ownership cannot pass. A voidable contract means that there is a valid contract, but it may be avoided for some reason like misrepresentation, fraud or undue influence. In such a case, it is possible for ownership to pass from one party to another and subsequently to a third person, if the provisions of s. 23 are met. If the buyer resells the goods before the seller avoids the contract, a second buyer will become owner if they buy in good faith and without notice of the defect in the first buyer's title.

The normal way to avoid a voidable contract is to tell the buyer, but this is not practical if the buyer is a rogue who has disappeared. If the seller does everything in his power to avoid such a contract, then it will be treated as avoided.

Car and Universal Finance Co. Ltd v *Caldwell* (1964)

A buyer paid for a car with a worthless cheque, so the contract was voidable for fraud. The buyer then disappeared, but the seller told the police and the AA before the buyer resold. It was held by the Court of Appeal that the contract had been avoided and the original seller was entitled to reclaim the car as ownership had not been passed to the second buyer.

22 Sale by a seller in possession

It is provided in s. 24 that if the seller sells goods but remains in possession of them and resells to a second buyer, who takes the goods in good faith and without notice of the first sale, then the second buyer will obtain a good title to the goods.

This section applies where the seller keeps possession of the goods, although ownership has passed to the buyer.

EXAMPLE

Alice buys an antique mirror from Basil's shop for £100, and agrees to collect it in one week's time. The same day Basil sells the mirror to Clive, who takes it away. Ownership of the mirror passed to Alice when the contract was made, so Basil does not have ownership at the time of the sale to Clive. Under s. 24, if Clive buys in good faith and physically takes possession of the mirror, he becomes owner. Alice can sue Basil for breach of contract or in the tort of conversion.

23 Sale by a buyer in possession

It is provided by s. 25 that if the buyer of goods obtains possession with the consent of the seller and resells to a second buyer, who purchases in good faith and without notice of the first sale, the first buyer is treated as a mercantile agent and can pass ownership to the second buyer.

This only covers cases where someone has 'bought or agreed to buy' and the buyer has possession of the goods but the seller retains ownership. As long as possession has been obtained with consent, it does not matter that the owner has been tricked.

Newtons of Wembley Ltd v *Williams* (1964)

The claimants sold a car to A but A's cheque was dishonoured and three days later the claimants told the police. After this A sold the car to B, who bought in good faith, at an established street market for used cars. B sold to the defendant and the claimant now claimed the car. It was held by the Court of Appeal that A was a buyer in possession with the consent of the owner and he had acted like a mercantile agent by selling in the market. Therefore A passed a good title to B, who in turn passed a good title to the defendant, who could keep the car.

If A had simply sold through an advertisement in a newspaper or to someone he met in the street, this would not be acting as a mercantile agent, but selling in this particular market was treated as a sale by a mercantile agent.

24 Sale of cars on hire-purchase under Part III of the Hire-Purchase Act 1964

A hirer under a hire-purchase agreement has not 'bought or agreed to buy' and is not covered by s. 25, so someone buying from such a hirer would not get ownership.

Part III (s. 27) provides that someone buying from a hirer does get a good title if the following conditions are met:

(a) the seller is hiring under a hire-purchase agreement or a conditional-sale agreement, and

(b) the buyer is a private person (i.e. not a dealer or finance company).

If the car is sold to a private purchaser, who buys in good faith and without knowing of the hire-purchase agreement, the private purchaser will get ownership of the car. Whether a purchaser has acted in good faith is a subjective test—whether *this* purchaser acted honestly.

Dodds v *Yorkshire Bank Finance* (1992)
B had a car under a hire-purchase agreement with YB. B needed money for his business and borrowed money from D and handed over the car. D was suspicious and only agreed to the arrangement after B wrote on the receipt that the car was not subject to a hire-purchase agreement. Later YB took the car from outside D's house. The Court of Appeal held that D's suspicions had been allayed by B and she was a purchaser in good faith, so she obtained a good title to the car under Part III of the Hire-Purchase Act 1964.

Shogun Finance Ltd v *Hudson* (2001)
A rogue went to a car dealer and asked about obtaining a car on hire purchase. The dealer arranged for the claimant to provide finance. The rogue used a false name, address and driving licence, filled in a hire purchase proposal form with the claimant finance company, paid a deposit and was allowed to take the car away. The rogue sold the car to the defendant who bought it in good faith. The claimant finance company sued the defendant in conversion to reclaim the car. It was held by a majority of the Court of Appeal that there was no contract between the finance company and the rogue, who therefore was not a hirer under a hire purchase agreement and Part III of the HPA 1964 did not apply. As a result H did not obtain title to the car and had to give the car to the finance company. In a dissenting judgment Sedley LJ argued that the dealer had made a contract with the rogue not the person he claimed to be.

The court observed that the law was unsatisfactory in such cases and in need of reform.

If the car is sold to a dealer or finance company, they will not become owners, as Part III does not apply. The reason is that dealers and finance companies can subscribe to Hire Purchase Information Limited, which keeps a register of all hire-purchase agreements, so trade purchasers can check the register when someone offers to sell them a car, to see if it is on the register as subject to a hire-purchase agreement. Private purchasers can now search the HPI register for a fee.

If the car is sold to a dealer, who resells to a private purchaser, the private purchaser does obtain ownership under Part III.

25 Reform of rules on passing of property by a non-owner

The DTI published a consultation paper in January 1994, dealing with the general problem of someone buying in good faith from a person who is not the owner. The paper argues that the present *nemo dat* rule and the exceptions are too complex. There are also anomalies, for example, the private buyer of a car which is subject to hire-purchase obtains ownership but the private buyer of a caravan does not. Three proposals were made:

(a) A general principle that if the owner of goods entrusts them to another person, an innocent purchaser should get a good title.

(b) The market overt rule should be abolished. (This was done by the Sale of Goods (Amendment) Act 1994.)

(c) The protection given to purchasers of cars on hire-purchase should apply to all goods on hire-purchase.

26 Duties in performing the contract

26.1 Introduction

The seller's duty is to deliver and the buyer's duty is to accept the goods and pay for them. 'Unless otherwise agreed, delivery of the goods and payment of the price are concurrent conditions' (Sale of Goods Act 1979, s. 28).

26.2 Seller's duty to deliver

Delivery is voluntarily giving possession to another person. This may be done by physical delivery *or* giving someone the means of control, e.g., a key, *or* handing over documents of title *or* giving the goods to an independent carrier.

The place of delivery is the seller's place of business unless agreed otherwise.

If a date is fixed for delivery, this is normally a condition.

The seller must also deliver the correct quantity of goods. If the seller delivers less, the buyer may reject the goods or accept the smaller amount. If the seller delivers more, the buyer may reject or accept all or accept the contract amount. A buyer who does not 'deal as a consumer' may not reject the whole quantity delivered where the difference in quantity is so slight that it would be unreasonable for him to do so.

26.3 Buyer's duty to accept and pay

The Sale of Goods Act 1979 provides for acceptance under s. 35 (see 11, *Remedies*, above).

The buyer need not pay until the goods are delivered. If the buyer pays in advance and no goods are delivered, the buyer can reclaim the price.

27 Remedies under the Sale of Goods Act 1979

27.1 Introduction

Each party to the contract may have rights against the other party (rights *in personam*) and rights against the goods (rights *in rem*).

27.2 Remedies of the Seller

(a) The seller has personal remedies against the buyer: to sue for the contract price if ownership of the goods has passed to the buyer, to sue for damages for non-acceptance if the buyer refuses the goods.

(b) If the seller has not been paid in full, the unpaid seller has the following rights against the goods:

(i) A *right of lien* over the goods. This means a right to keep physical possession of the goods until the seller has been paid. If the seller has lost physical possession then the right of lien is lost.

(ii) A *right of stoppage in transit*. This is a right to stop goods which are on the way to the buyer and keep them until the price has been paid. The right only arises if the buyer has become insolvent and cannot pay his debts, for example, if the seller has given the goods to an independent carrier to take to the buyer and then finds out the buyer is insolvent.

(iii) A *right to resell* the goods. The rights of lien and stoppage in transit do not give the seller a right to resell the goods. The seller may resell in certain circumstances and pass a good title to the goods. These are if the goods are perishable or if the seller tells the buyer he is going to resell and the buyer still does not pay or if the contract gives the seller a right to resell.

27.3 Remedies of the buyer

Damages for non-delivery or for breach of contract.

Reclaim money paid to the seller if the goods are not delivered or the buyer repudiates the contract.

Repudiate for breach of condition. But note that a non-consumer buyer cannot reject for breach of the implied conditions if the breach is slight.

Specific performance, to make the seller deliver (see 'Remedies for breach of contract', 4 'Specific performance', above).

Supply of Goods and Services Act 1982

1 Introduction

The Sale of Goods Act 1979 applies only to contracts under which goods are transferred for money. Before the 1982 Act there were problems as regards other types of contract, for example goods and services provided together, services and hire. What terms should apply to such contracts? The common law would usually imply similar terms to the Sale of Goods Act 1979, for example, as regards the supply of a set of false teeth, it was implied that they should be fit for their purpose (*Samuels* v *Davis*

(1943)). Services may be divided into two main categories: those involving the transfer of ownership or possession of goods and an element of a service; and those which involve a pure service. The 1982 Act, Part I deals with the supply of goods element and Part II deals with services.

The Act may be divided into three parts; those sections dealing with the transfer of ownership of goods; those dealing with the transfer of possession of goods (hire); and those dealing with services.

The 1982 Act does not apply to sale of goods contracts, hire purchase, gifts, mortgages, charges or pledges.

2 Contracts involving the transfer of ownership of goods

If the contract involves both provision of services and goods, then ss. 2 to 5 apply to the 'goods' supplied.

2.1 Title

In a contract for the transfer of goods there is an implied condition that the transferor has a right to transfer the property in the goods (s. 2(1)).

There are also implied warranties that the goods are free from any encumbrances not disclosed and that the buyer will enjoy quiet possession (s. 2(2)).

2.2 Description

If the contract for the transfer of goods is by description, there is an implied condition that the goods will correspond with the description (s. 3).

2.3 Satisfactory quality and fitness for purpose

In the case of a contract for the transfer of goods which is made in the course of a business, there is an implied condition that the goods are of satisfactory quality unless any matter is brought to the buyer's attention or an examination ought to have revealed the defect. There is also an implied condition that the goods must be fit for their purpose, unless the buyer does not rely on the seller.

2.4 Sample

If the contract is made by sample, then there is an implied condition that the goods will match the sample (s. 5).

2.5 Exclusion of liability

The Unfair Contract Terms Act 1977 provides that the condition about title (Supply of Goods and Services Act, s. 2) cannot be excluded; as regards the conditions about description, satisfactory quality and fitness for purpose, in consumer sales these cannot be excluded and in other sales they are subject to the test of reasonableness. The Unfair Terms in Consumer Contracts Regulations 1999 also apply to consumer contracts.

2.6 Minor breaches of condition

In non-consumer sales, if the buyer has the right to treat the contract as repudiated because of a breach of the implied conditions, but the breach is so slight that it would be unreasonable for him to do so, the breach is not to be treated as a breach of condition but as a breach of warranty.

2.7 Distinction between sale of goods and supply of services

The rules on acceptance of *goods* under s. 35 of the Sale of Goods Act have now been made less stringent and closer to the common law rules on affirmation, so there seems to be less need to distinguish between contracts for goods and services.

It may still be worth attempting to establish that a contract is in one category or the other, however. The test used is: What is the substance of the contract?

EXAMPLE

Buying a meal in a restaurant is a sale of goods, but having a picture painted is the provision of a service, the main ingredient being the skill of the artist, although some goods are involved (i.e. paint and canvas).

3 Hire of goods

A hire contract is an agreement under which one person hires out goods to another. This is one type of agreement known as a *bailment*, under which the owner of goods (bailor) gives them to someone else (bailee) for a particular purpose. In the case of hiring goods, the hirer merely obtains possession and at the end of the hire period has to give back the goods. There is no agreement for ownership of the goods to be transferred, so ss. 2 to 5 do not apply. However, the hirer is protected by similar terms in ss. 7 to 10, which apply to consumer and business hire agreements. They do *not* apply to hire-purchase agreements. The implied conditions deal with:

(a) possession

(b) description

(c) satisfactory quality

(d) fitness for purpose

(e) sample.

3.1 Possession

There is an implied condition that the bailor has the right to transfer possession of the goods. There is also an implied warranty that the bailee will enjoy quiet possession and freedom from encumbrances (s. 7).

3.2 Description

If the contract is by description there is an implied condition that the goods will correspond with the description (s. 8).

3.3 Satisfactory quality and fitness for purpose

Where goods are hired in the course of a business, there are implied conditions that the goods will be of satisfactory quality and fit for their purpose (s. 9).

3.4 Sample

If the goods are hired by reference to a sample, there is an implied condition that the goods will match the sample (s. 10).

3.5 Exclusion

The condition about transfer of possession may be excluded if it satisfies the test of reasonableness. The conditions about description, quality, purpose and sample cannot be excluded in consumer sales, and in non-consumer sales such an exclusion must be reasonable. The Unfair Terms in Consumer Contracts Regulations apply in consumer contracts.

3.6 Minor breaches of condition

In non-consumer sales the bailee's right to treat a contract as repudiated for breach of the above conditions is restricted if the breach is slight and it is treated as a breach of warranty.

4 Services

The Act also implies terms into contracts for services. They may apply to a pure service or to the service element in a contract to supply goods and services or to hire contracts which involve some element of service. In the case of provision of goods and services, it is important to determine whether a problem is caused by the goods being faulty, when ss. 2 to 5 apply, or because of the service, when ss. 13 to 15 apply.

EXAMPLE

If Alice has central heating installed and it stops working, the reason may be faulty materials (ss. 2 to 5) or faulty workmanship in installing the system (ss. 13 to 15).

The Act does not apply to employment contracts and the Secretary of State has power to exclude other types of service, for example lawyers acting in court and company directors have been exempted by statutory instrument. Examples of services include hairdressing, accounting, teaching, transport and cleaning.

4.1 Care and skill

Where a service is provided in the course of a business, there is an implied term that it will be carried out with reasonable care and skill (s. 13).

Wilson v *Best Travel Ltd* (1993)

While on holiday in Greece, W fell through a glass patio door in the hotel and was badly injured because the door was fitted with ordinary glass. The brochure from BT stated that even though they did not have day-to-day control, they did 'keep an eye on' accommodation. W claimed breach of the duty of care and skill under the Supply of Goods and Services Act 1982, s. 13, because the hotel was not safe. British standards required safety glass to be used. It was held that BT's duty was to check that local safety regulations had been met, not that they complied with British standards. A hotel should be excluded only if a reasonable man would not take a holiday there because of the particular danger, for example, no fire precautions. As the hotel met Greek standards, BT were not liable.

4.2 Time

Where a service is provided in the course of a business and the time for performance cannot be determined from the contract or the course of dealings, there is an implied term that it will be carried out within a reasonable time. What is a reasonable time is a question of fact (s. 14).

4.3 Charge

Where the consideration is not determined by the contract or in a manner agreed in the contract or in the course of dealings, there is an implied term that the recipient will pay a reasonable charge (s. 15).

4.4 Exclusion

The above terms are subject to the Unfair Contract Terms Act 1977 and in consumer sales or contracts made on written standard terms any attempt to exclude these terms is subject to a test of reasonableness. The Unfair Terms in Consumer Contracts Regulations 1999 also apply in the case of consumer sales.

4.5 Terms

The 1982 Act refers to the above as terms rather than conditions and the effect is to give the courts flexibility to treat a breach as a condition or a warranty, depending on its seriousness.

Supply of Goods (Implied Terms) Act 1973

1 Introduction

A hire-purchase agreement is not covered by the Sale of Goods Act 1979 because there is no sale but simply a hire of goods with an option to purchase. The parties were originally known as the owner and the hirer but since the Consumer Credit Act 1974 they are now the creditor and the debtor. The Supply of Goods (Implied Terms) Act 1973 implies the following terms in all hire-purchase contracts, not simply regulated agreements:

(a) the right to sell;

(b) description;

(c) satisfactory quality;

(d) fitness for purpose;

(e) sample.

2 Right to sell

In every hire-purchase agreement there is an implied term that the creditor will have a right to sell when the property is to pass (s. 8(1)) and an implied warranty that the goods will be free from any encumbrances not disclosed until property is to pass and that the debtor will enjoy quiet possession (s. 8(2)).

The creditor does not need to have the right to sell when the contract is made. The implied warranty that the goods will be free from encumbrances applies to the period of the hire and that of quiet possession also applies to the future.

3 Description

If the contract is made by description, there is an implied term that the goods will correspond with their description (s. 9).

4 Satisfactory quality and fitness for purpose

Where goods are supplied in the course of a business under a hire-purchase agreement, there is an implied term that the goods are of satisfactory quality unless matters are drawn to the debtor's attention or if the debtor examines the goods, as regards matters which that examination ought to reveal. Where the debtor makes known the purpose for which the goods are needed, there is an implied term that the goods are reasonably fit for that purpose, unless the debtor did not rely or it is unreasonable for the debtor to rely on the creditor (s. 10).

5 Sample

Where goods are taken on hire purchase by reference to a sample, there is an implied term that the bulk will correspond with the sample (s. 11).

6 Conditions

The Sale and Supply of Goods Act 1994 provides that the above terms implied under the Supply of Goods (Implied Terms) Act 1973 are to be conditions, except for quiet possession under s. 8(2) which is to be a warranty.

7 Exclusion of implied terms

The terms implied by ss. 8 to 11 are treated in the same way as ss. 12 to 15 of the Sale of Goods Act 1979. Section 8 cannot be excluded. Sections 9 to 11 cannot be excluded in consumer contracts, but in non-consumer agreements they may be if the exclusion is reasonable (s. 6, UCTA 1977). The Unfair Terms in Consumer Contract Regulations also apply to consumer contracts.

8 Minor breaches of condition

A debtor who does not deal as a consumer, who has a right to treat the contract as repudiated for breach of the above conditions (in ss. 9, 10 or 11) is restricted if the breach is slight and may treat it as a breach of warranty.

Consumer Credit Act 1974

1 Introduction

Nearly everyone needs credit at some time. Individuals may wish to buy goods or services on credit or buy a house by taking out a mortgage. Businesses may need credit to start up or to expand. Credit simply means that someone (the creditor) lends a sum of money to another person (the debtor) for a period of time and charges them interest on this loan. Before 1974, in addition to the common law rules, there were numerous statutes dealing with different types of credit from money-lending to pawnbroking but these were piecemeal in their approach. From the debtor's point of view, the history of credit is marked by sharp practices like exhorbitant rates of interest and 'snatchback' of goods on hire purchase. The growth of credit after World War Two, in parallel with increased production of consumer goods, saw an increase in abuses. This was another reflection of the inequalities of bargaining power between creditors and debtors. Demands were made for reform and, following the Report of the Committee on Consumer Credit 1971 (The Crowther Committee), the Consumer Credit Act 1974 was passed. This is a comprehensive statute which deals with all types of credit and, together with the numerous regulations made under it, is a complex measure.

The main provisions of the Act are:

(a) to control who may provide credit through a system of licensing;

(b) to stipulate what information must be given to the debtor;

(c) to regulate the formalities and terms of credit agreements; and

(d) to restrict the remedies available to the creditor.

Although the Act was passed in 1974, most of its provisions did not come into force until May 1985. In June 1994 the Director General of Fair Trading issued a review of the Act (*Consumer Credit Deregulation*) following consulation with interested parties, including the public. The recommendations made include removing business lending from regulation under the Act; simplifying some of the rules, for example, on advertising; and increasing the financial limit for regulated agreements. In 2001 the DTI issued a consultation document 'Tackling Loan Sharks and More' on reforming the Consumer Credit Act 1974 and tackling some of the problems such as the instant availability of credit, penalties for paying loans early, complicated rules on advertising etc. This section will examine the types of credit agreement, advertising, formation, termination and the remedies available in the event of breach.

2 Types of credit

The main types of credit are hire-purchase agreements, credit sale agreements, conditional sale agreements, loans, overdrafts, budget accounts, credit cards, pledges and mortgages of land.

2.1 Hire-purchase

From the consumer's point of view a hire-purchase contract is a way of buying goods on credit. In fact, legally, it is nothing like that. There are two parts to such an agreement, the hire of the goods and an option to purchase, but there is no obligation to buy the goods and they may be given back at the end of the hire period. This type of agreement was commercially popular because the owner of the goods retained ownership unless the hirer exercised his option to purchase. This meant the hirer could not sell the goods during the hire period.

Helby v *Matthews* (1895)
A dealer hired out a piano for 36 months at a rent of 10s 6d per month. The agreement provided that property in the piano would pass to the customer when all the payments had been made, but any time before this the agreement could be ended. A few months after making the agreement, the customer pledged the piano with a pawnbroker. It was held by the House of Lords that the dealer could reclaim the piano from the pawnbroker, as the customer could not pass ownership to the pawnbroker.

2.2 Credit sale

This is an agreement to buy goods and pay later, usually by instalments. Ownership of the goods passes to the buyer as soon as the agreement is made unless the contract provides otherwise, in which case it will be a conditional sale. The buyer under a credit sale agreement may sell the goods and pass on ownership.

2.3 Conditional sale

This is a sale of goods, with payment in instalments, but the agreement provides that ownership does not pass to the buyer until some condition is fulfilled, usually the payment of all the instalments. They are very similar to hire-purchase agreements and the 1974 Act treats them in the same way. But a buyer under a conditional sale agreement is committed to *buying* the goods and may pass title to a third party under s. 25 of the Sale of Goods Act 1979.

2.4 Loan

The creditor gives the debtor a sum of money and it is usually agreed that the debtor will repay in instalments. An example is a bank loan. Because there is no security for this loan, the rate of interest will be higher.

2.5 Overdraft

This is an agreement under which an existing customer is allowed to borrow money through his current account, usually up to a maximum amount. Interest is charged on a daily basis. It is more flexible than a loan and may be repaid at the customer's convenience.

2.6 Budget account

Many large shops operate a system under which the customer agrees to pay a certain amount each month and is then allowed credit up to 12 times the agreed payment. As the outstanding debt is repaid, the customer is allowed more credit, up to the maximum amount and so on. Consequently this is known as *revolving credit* or *running account credit.*

2.7 Credit card

There are different types of credit card schemes.

2.7.1 Bank credit cards
Cards such as Access and Visa allow the holder to obtain goods and services on credit or a cash loan, all subject to a maximum limit. The holder receives a monthly statement and may repay as much as they wish each month.

2.7.2 Charge cards
With cards like American Express there is usually no credit limit but the amount must be repaid in full each month.

2.7.3 Retailers credit cards
Many large businesses issue their own credit cards for use in that business and give a few weeks credit to pay the debt, for example garages.

2.7.4 EFTPOS cards
EFTPOS stands for 'Electronic Funds Transfer at Point of Sale'. This is a system by which certain cards, e.g., Switch, enable a cardholder to pay a shop by electronically transferring money from the cardholder's bank account to the shop's bank account. They are not normally credit cards as the cardholder's account has to have money in it. Even if the cardholder is allowed to overdraw, so it becomes a regulated agreement,

the Consumer Credit Act 1974 provides it is not a D-C-S agreement, and the card-holder's bank is not liable for misrepresentations or breaches of contract by the shop.

2.8 Pledge

A pledge occurs when someone gives *possession* of goods to another as security for a loan. The typical example is a pawnbroker, who will lend money against the security of the goods. If the loan is repaid within say 28 days, the goods are given back to the borrower. Otherwise they may be sold, and ownership is passed to the buyer under common law rules.

2.9 Mortgage of land

A mortgage is a claim over land as security for a loan. Usually the loan will be for the purchase of the land itself but it may be used to buy goods.

3 Terminology of the Act

3.1 Restricted use credit and unrestricted use credit

Restricted use credit (RUC) is credit given to finance a particular transaction in such a way that the creditor can ensure it is only used for that purpose. Examples include hire-purchase, credit sales, conditional sales, budget accounts and credit cards.

> EXAMPLE
>
> Alice obtains a loan from City Bank to buy a car from Bertie's Garage. If the money is paid direct by City Bank to Bertie's Garage, this is a restricted use credit agreement.

With *unrestricted use credit* (UUC) there is no control over how the debtor uses the credit. The standard example is a bank loan.

> EXAMPLE
>
> If City Bank in the above example put the money in Alice's account, this would be an unrestricted use credit agreement, as even though Alice has agreed to use it to buy a car from Bertie's Garage, City Bank cannot ensure that she does this.

3.2 Debtor-creditor-supplier and debtor-creditor agreements

With *debtor-creditor-supplier* (D-C-S) agreements, there is a connection between the creditor and the supplier. It is clearer to think of it as a debtor:creditor-supplier agreement.

If one person supplies the goods and the credit, for example, in a hire-purchase agreement, this is a two party D-C-S.

> EXAMPLE
>
> Alice chooses a car at Bertie's Garage and is introduced to the Crafty Finance Company. Bertie's Garage sell the car to the Crafty Finance Company, who in turn let it on hire purchase to Alice.

If the creditor and the supplier have a 'business arrangement', for example, a finance company has an arrangement with a garage to provide loans to customers, this is a three party D-C-S.

EXAMPLE

Alice chooses a car at Bertie's Garage and Bertie has a business arrangement with the Crafty Finance Company, to provide loans to Bertie's customers. Alice takes out a loan with the Crafty Finance Company and uses that loan to buy the car.

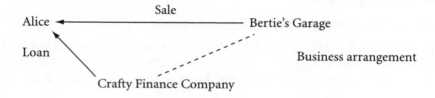

With *debtor-creditor* (D-C) agreements, the supplier has no connection with the person providing the credit.

EXAMPLE

Alice borrows £1,000 from City Bank and then uses the money to book a holiday with Bonny Travel Limited.

The distinction between D-C-S and D-C agreements is important for two main reasons. First, if the debtor cancels a regulated agreement, this automatically cancels any linked transaction, so under a D-C-S agreement any transaction financed by the credit is a linked transaction.

EXAMPLE

Alice wishes to buy a car from Bertie's Garage, who have an arrangement with the Crafty Finance Company to provide credit facilities. Alice obtains a loan from the Crafty Finance Company to buy the car. If Alice later cancels this loan in accordance with the provisions of the Act, the contract with Bertie's Garage for the sale of the car, which is a linked transaction, is automatically cancelled.

If the agreement is a D-C agreement, then cancellation does not have this effect.

EXAMPLE

If Alice had obtained the loan herself from someone unconnected with Bertie's Garage and cancelled it, this would not cancel the contract for the sale of the car.

Secondly, if the debtor under a D-C-S agreement can claim misrepresentation or breach of contract against the supplier, the debtor has a like claim against the creditor. Joint liability does not arise with D-C agreements.

3.3 Fixed sum credit and running account credit

A *fixed sum credit* agreement is an agreement to make a single loan of a fixed amount. For example, a credit sale agreement for £500.

Running account credit (or revolving credit) is a flexible amount of credit subject to a maximum limit. For example, a shop's budget account or an overdraft.

4 Agreements covered by the Act

4.1 Regulated agreements

These may be consumer credit agreements or consumer hire agreements.

A *consumer credit agreement* is an agreement by which one person (creditor) provides credit not exceeding £25,000 to an individual or partnership (debtor). The creditor may be an individual, partnership or a company, but the debtor may only be an individual or a partnership (s. 8).

EXAMPLE

All the agreements in 2 above.

The £25,000 limit only applies to the credit, not the price of the goods or the deposit or interest charges.

EXAMPLE

Alice obtains some new furniture under a hire-purchase agreement with the Crafty Finance Company. The total amount payable is £27,000 of which £2,500 is interest charges and £1,000 is the deposit. This will be a regulated agreement as the amount of credit is £27,000 *less* the interest (£2,500) and the deposit (£1,000) = 23,500.

A *consumer hire agreement* is an agreement for the hiring of goods which meets the following conditions:

(a) it is not a hire-purchase agreement;

(b) it is capable of lasting more than three months;

(c) the hirer does not pay more than £25,000;

(d) the hirer is not a corporation.

EXAMPLE

Hiring a video-recorder for 12 months; hiring a JCB excavator for one month.

Such an agreement does not involve giving credit, because the hirer pays for the use of the goods from the start.

4.2 Partly regulated agreements

There are two types of agreement which must comply with some of the requirements of the Act.

4.2.1 Small agreements

This covers any agreement to provide credit of not more than £50. But some agreements are excluded from this definition—hire purchase, conditional sale or a number of small agreements which together exceed £50; or any regulated consumer hire agreement which does not require payments over £50.

Small D-C-S agreements are exempt from most of the provisions about formalities and cancellation.

4.2.2 Non-commercial agreements

This is a consumer credit or consumer hire agreement not made by the creditor or owner in the course of a business carried on by him. For example, a loan to a friend. These do not have to comply with the formalities and cancellation provisions.

4.3 Exempt agreements

These are *not* regulated by the Act.

(a) Mortgages of land where the creditor is a local authority or other approved body, and the loan is used to buy or improve the land.

(b) D-C-S agreements under which the debtor is to repay in a maximum of four instalments within 12 months, but hire-purchase agreements, conditional sale agreements and pledges are not within this exemption. An example would be a credit sale with less than four payments.

(c) Running account D-C-S agreements under which the debtor must repay in one payment, for example, American Express cards or a milk bill.

(d) Low-cost D-C agreements, where the APR does not exceed 13 per cent or 1 per cent above base rates, for example, low-cost loans to employees.

(e) Credit for overseas trade.

(f) Hire agreements for gas, water, electricity meters and telephone equipment.

4.4 Linked transactions

This is an agreement which is linked in some way to the main agreement. If the debtor withdraws an offer or cancels a regulated agreement, that has the same effect on the linked transaction.

EXAMPLES

(a) An agreement the debtor must make as a condition of the main agreement. For example, if the debtor takes a television on hire purchase and must take out a servicing contract, the servicing contract is a linked transaction.

(b) In a D-C-S agreement any transaction financed by the credit. For example, buying goods with an Access card.

(c)   An agreement the creditor suggests the debtor should make.

5 The licensing system

5.1 Introduction

The Director General of Fair Trading is responsible for administering the licensing system under the Act and for keeping a public register of the licences. There are two types of licence, group and standard. A group licence is used to cover a group of people, if they have other controls over them. For example, the Law Society holds a group licence for practising solicitors. A standard licence is the normal type of licence which is issued to businesses and it lasts for five years.

5.2 Standard licences

Anyone who makes regulated agreements in the course of a business or carries on an ancillary credit business needs a licence. A licence is not needed if the transactions are only occasional. There are six types of standard licence covering the following activities.

5.2.1 Consumer credit
Any business making regulated consumer credit agreements needs this licence.

5.2.2 Consumer hire
Any business hiring out goods.

5.2.3 Credit broker
This covers anyone who introduces customers to providers of credit. It includes introductions for unregulated agreements. For example, a car dealer who introduces customers to a finance company.

5.2.4 Debt adjusting and counselling
This covers advice given, in the course of a business, about debts under consumer credit or hire agreements. Adjusters negotiate with the creditor on the debtor's behalf. Counsellors such as accountants, solicitors, CAB, etc., simply give advice.

5.2.5 Debt collecting
This covers collecting debts and buying debts. For example, debt collection agencies.

5.2.6 Credit reference agency
Any business which collects and sells information about people. Individuals have a right to see the information held on file for a fee of £1 and if it is wrong, the right to correct it.

5.3 Acting without a licence

If someone acts without a licence, they commit a criminal offence. The effect in civil law is that the agreement cannot be enforced unless the Director General makes a validation order. A licence is not needed by local or public authorities, but they still have to comply with the Act.

6 Seeking business

6.1 Advertising

The Act tries to promote 'truth in lending' so that the debtor is not misled by advertisements for credit. The Act creates a number of criminal offences:

(a) giving information which is false or misleading in a material respect (s. 46);

(b) indicating that goods or services will be supplied on credit, if they are not available for cash (s. 45);

(c) breach of regulations made under s. 44.

Dudley MBC v *Colorvision plc* (1997)
C advertised electrical goods on credit stating, 'Your purchase absolutely free if we cannot beat our competitors' prices—ask for details'. The policy operated was that if a customer proved that a competitor had a lower price, the customer would be given some money back but not a full refund. C were prosecuted for publishing a misleading advert under s. 46. On appeal from the magistrates, it was confirmed by the Divisional Court that the test was whether an ordinary person would be misled. An ordinary person would not expect to obtain the goods free in such circumstances, merely a reduction in the price. C were not guilty of an offence.

The advertiser is the main offender but the producer of the advert, the advertising agency and the publisher may all be made liable. A defence is available that the person charged took all reasonable precautions to avoid commission of an offence and the offence was due to a mistake, reliance on information supplied, the act of another, an accident or some other cause beyond his control (s. 168).

The Consumer Credit (Advertisement) Regulations 1989 have been made under s. 44. They permit three types of advert—simple, intermediate and full—and set out what information must be contained in each advert. For example, a 'simple' advertisement may only give the name, address and telephone number of the creditor. It cannot state that credit is available.

The statutory information must be clear and easily legible. The information must be shown together as a whole, except for adverts on the dealers' premises. The annual percentage rate (APR) must be given the same prominence as the period for payment. If the advert concerns a mortgage over the borrower's home, it must contain a warning that the home may be repossessed if payments are not made.

6.2 Canvassing

The law tries to protect consumers from doorstep selling by severely restricting canvassing off trade premises.

Canvassing off trade premises occurs if oral representations are made to the consumer, *and* this is during a visit away from the business premises of the canvasser, creditor, owner, supplier or debtor and the visit is not in response to a request (s 48).

EXAMPLE

Basil, a double glazing salesman, calls at Alice's house and persuades her to sign an agreement for new windows. Basil's licence needs to cover this activity.

It is an offence to canvass D-C agreements off trade premises (s. 49 of the Consumer Credit Act), for example, a cash loan. Other types of agreement may be canvassed off trade premises, provided the licence expressly covers such canvassing. The Director General has determined that an exception to s. 49 is a canvasser who persuades an existing current account holder to take an overdraft. For example, a bank manager who visits a customer to persuade the customer to take an overdraft.

Minors are given special protection as it is an offence to send minors a document inviting them to borrow money or obtain goods or services on credit or to seek further information about it (s. 50).

It is also an offence to issue a credit token to someone who has not asked for it in writing (s. 51).

6.3 Quotations

An individual may ask a creditor for a written quotation in writing, orally on the trader's premises or by telephone.

7 Formation of the credit agreement

7.1 Withdrawal

Normally when the debtor fills in the proposal and gives it to the dealer, that is an offer. This may then be accepted by the finance company. The debtor can withdraw or revoke the offer any time before the finance company accept the offer. The debtor may tell the creditor or the dealer that the offer is withdrawn, as under s. 57 the dealer is agent of the creditor for receiving revocations. The notice of withdrawal may be oral or written, but it must be communicated to the offeree. The effect of withdrawal is as though the agreement had been cancelled, i.e. there is no agreement.

7.2 Formalities

The formalities which must be followed when making a regulated agreement are set out in ss. 60 to 65. The aim is to make sure that the debtor knows the nature of the agreement, what it will cost, the rights and duties the debtor has under it, and the remedies available. All regulated agreements have to comply with these formalities except non-commercial agreements and those which fulfill all the following criteria— they are small, restricted use, D-C-S agreements. For example, a credit sale agreement for £50.

The Consumer Credit (Agreement) Regulations 1983 set out the detail of form, legibility etc. The agreement *must*

(a) Be in writing.

(b) Contain the following information:

    (i)   names and addresses of the parties

    (ii)   cash price

    (iii) amount of any deposit

    (iv) amount of credit

    (v)   APR (annual percentage rate)

    (vi) total amount payable

    (vii) amount of each payment and when payable

    (viii) default charges

    (ix) security provided by the debtor.

(c) Tell the debtor of the following statutory rights:

    (i)   cancellation

    (ii)   terminate early (if hire-purchase or conditional sale)

    (iii) protection for loss of a credit token (e.g. a credit card)

    (iv) to settle early.

(d) Contain all the terms, except for implied terms.

The agreement must be signed by the debtor personally and by or on behalf of the creditor. When the debtor signs, the details of the agreement must have been filled in, so it is not signed in blank.

7.3 Copies

Sections 62 to 63 provide for the debtor to receive a copy or copies of the agreement.

If the debtor signs after the creditor has signed, the agreement is *executed* and the debtor must be given *one* copy at that time. No further copy need be given.

If the debtor signs first, so the agreement is *unexecuted*, then *one* copy must be given to the debtor at that time. A *second* copy must be given or sent to the debtor within seven days of the agreement being executed (i.e. signed by the creditor). In practice this will be the usual situation.

If the agreement is a cancellable one, the above rules are varied as follows:

(a) All copies must contain a notice of the debtor's right to cancel and the name and address of the person to whom it may be given.

(b) Any second copy required must be sent by post.

(c) If the agreement is executed when the debtor signs, then the debtor only gets one copy but must also be sent a notice of the right of cancellation within seven days of the agreement being made. This notice must be sent by post.

EXAMPLE

Alice signs a credit agreement on 1 March, which has not been signed by the finance company. It is an unexecuted agreement and Alice must be given copy one when she signs. On 5 March the credit company sign the agreement and it becomes executed. Alice must be sent or given copy two within seven days of the company signing.

If the agreement could be cancelled, Alice must be sent copy two within seven days of the finance company signing. If this arrived at Alice's home on 14 March, she would have five clear days in which to cancel, i.e. until midnight on 19 March.

7.4 Non-compliance with formalities

If the creditor fails to comply with all the formalities, then the agreement is treated as *improperly executed*. Under s. 65 the creditor cannot enforce the agreement against the debtor without a court order. Under s. 127 the court will enforce the agreement only if it considers it just to do so, taking into account the effect of the contravention on the debtor. The debtor may still treat the agreement as valid and may enforce it against the creditor. For example, if goods taken under a hire-purchase agreement are unfit for their purpose, the debtor may sue under the Supply of Goods (Implied Terms) Act 1973.

PB Leasing v *Patel and Patel* (1995)

P and P made a consumer hire agreement for video cassettes and racks. P and P signed the agreement before the financial details had been filled in, did not read it and they were not given a copy. The dealer who provided the goods went into liquidation and the claimant finance company with whom the agreement had been made sought to enforce it. It was held that as the details had not been filled in and no copy had been given, the agreement was improperly executed and was unenforceable.

Dimond v *Lovell* (1999)

The claimant's car was in an accident caused by the defendant. The claimant hired a car from a company which provided cars for drivers who had not been at fault and claimed the hire charges from the negligent driver. The defendant's insurers argued that the hire agreement was a consumer credit agreement and as it had not been executed in writing it was unenforceable. The claimant did not have to pay for the hire and could not claim from the defendants. It was held by the Court of Appeal that deferring payment was the provision of credit and as the agreement had not been properly executed the claimant did not have to pay. Consequently the claimant could not recover the hire charges from the defendant.

Under s. 127(3) the court must not make an enforcement order for an improperly executed regulated agreement if the provisions for signing were not met unless another document containing all the prescribed terms was signed by the debtor or hirer.

Wilson v *First County Trust* (2001)

W obtained a loan of £5,000 from the defendant pawnbroker and used her car as security. The loan agreement was a regulated agreement under the Consumer Credit

Act 1974 and the amount of credit stated on the form was £5,250, which included a 'document fee' of £250. If an agreement is not properly executed it can only be enforced by a court order under s. 65. But s. 127(3) provided that a court could not make an enforcement order unless a document containing all the prescribed terms had been signed by the debtor. It was held by the Court of Appeal that the amount of credit was £5,000 not the £5,250 stated on the form, which meant that the agreement was not properly executed because it did not state the correct amount of credit. Under s.127(3) the agreement was unenforceable against W and the pawnbroker could not enforce the loan or the security. The question also arose whether s. 127(3) was incompatible with the right to a fair hearing under Article 6 of the European Convention on Human Rights enforceable under the Human Rights Act 1998. The court gave notice to the Crown under s. 5 of the Human Rights Act 1998 that it would consider a declaration of incompatibility. At the later hearing to determine this issue, the court said that although the purpose of s. 127(3) was perfectly lawful, to make sure attention was paid to what was included in such a document, the way this was to be achieved did infringe the Convention. The effect was to prevent the lender having the matter of whether it was enforceable determined by the court. The effect of s. 127(3) was to simply prevent a court making an enforcement order if the document did not include the prescribed terms. Although a court was under a duty to interpret legislation in a way compatible with the Convention, this was not possible here. The court granted a declaration that s. 127(3) was incompatible with the right to a fair trial.

8 Cancellation

8.1 Introduction

The general rule of contract is that once an agreement is made, it is binding. But s. 67 gives the debtor a right to cancel a binding regulated agreement. The aim of the rules is to protect the debtor from doorstep selling, by giving a 'cooling off period', in which the debtor can change his mind.

8.2 Right of cancellation

To have a right of cancellation, two conditions must be fulfilled:

(a) before the agreement, oral statements are made in the debtor's presence by a negotiator; and

(b) the debtor signed the agreement away from the premises of the creditor or anyone acting on behalf of the creditor (s. 67).

EXAMPLE

Alice goes to Bertie's Garage and chooses a car, after Bertie has made certain statements about it. Alice goes for a test drive and decides to have the car on credit. Bertie stops in a lay-by and Alice signs the credit agreement. Alice will have a right to cancel it.

A right of cancellation is also given by the Consumer Protection (Cancellation of Contracts Concluded away from Business Premises) Regulations 1987 for some sales not made on credit. If a contract for goods or services worth more than £35 is made after an unsolicited visit to the consumer's home or workplace, the consumer has a right of cancellation. A written notice must be served within seven days of making the contract and the effect is to treat the contract as if it had never been made. These regulations do not apply to contracts for the sale of land, building contracts, food and drink supplied by regular deliverers or insurance contracts. The regulations do not apply if there is a right of cancellation under s. 67 of the Act. The Consumer Protection (Cancellation of Contracts Concluded away from Business Premises) (Amendment) Regulations 1998 extend the meaning of 'unsolicited visit' to include a visit which follows an earlier unsolicited visit and a visit after an unsolicited telephone call. It also makes it a criminal offence for a trader to make a contract without giving the consumer a written notice of his right to cancel and a cancellation form.

8.3 Agreements which cannot be cancelled

Some agreements cannot be cancelled. They include:

(a) Mortgages of land to buy land or provide a bridging loan.

(b) Non-commercial agreements.

(c) Small D-C-S agreements for restricted use credit.

(d) Agreements for overdrafts.

8.4 Formalities of cancellation

To cancel the agreement, the debtor must serve a written notice of cancellation on the creditor, agent of the creditor, or anyone named in the notice of cancellation. If the notice is sent by post, it takes effect from the date of posting.

The notice of cancellation must be served during the cancellation period. This is up to five days after the debtor receives a second copy of the agreement (if unexecuted on signing) or the notice of cancellation (if executed on signing) (s. 68). If the notice of cancellation is posted, it is effective even if it is delayed or lost.

EXAMPLE

See example in 7.3 above.

8.5 Effect of cancellation

The effect of cancellation is to end the finance agreement and any linked transaction. A distinction is made between D-C-S agreements for restricted use credit and D-C agreements for unrestricted use credit.

8.5.1 D-C-S agreements

Here, the supply of goods is part of the credit agreement, for example hire-purchase, or is a linked transaction. Both the credit agreement and the linked transaction are cancelled. The debtor does not have to make any further payments, he can get back any money paid and goods given in part exchange, or their value, and he has a lien over goods in his possession for the money owed.

The debtor is under a duty to return goods (subject to the right of lien), which means that the goods must be made available for collection. This duty does not apply to goods which are perishable, supplied in an emergency, incorporated in land, or consumed before cancellation. The debtor is also not under a duty to return any services received. Goods supplied in an emergency or incorporated must, however, be paid for. Creditors can protect themselves by not supplying goods or services until the cancellation period runs out.

8.5.2 D-C agreements

Under a D-C agreement the debtor obtains the credit and uses it to buy goods. The contract for the goods is not a linked transaction and is not affected if the credit agreement is cancelled. Although, if the credit agreement is cancelled, the debtor must repay any credit which has been given plus interest. If the credit is repaid within one month of cancellation or before the date of the first instalment, the debtor does not have to pay interest (s. 71).

9 Rights to end the contract

Both the debtor and the creditor have rights to end the contract (i.e. rights of termination).

9.1 Misrepresentation

A misrepresentation is an untrue statement which induces someone to make a contract. If a supplier of goods makes a misrepresentation to a customer and the customer then makes a credit agreement with a creditor, at common law, the customer has no claim against the creditor. But s. 56 of the Act provides that any negotiator in antecedent negotiations is treated as the agent of the creditor. The customer may therefore claim against the creditor. The antecedent negotiations begin when the negotiator and customer first enter into communication, for example, through an advertisement. Any attempt to exclude s. 56 is void.

This is important for D-C-S agreements. In a two-party D-C-S agreement, the debtor may claim against the creditor for misrepresentations made by the supplier. Similarly, in a three-party D-C-S agreement, the debtor may claim against the creditor, although in this case the debtor has a contract with the supplier.

EXAMPLE

Alice chooses a car from Bertie's Garage after Bertie has told her the car will do 60 miles per gallon. Bertie then introduces Alice to Crafty Finance, with whom Bertie has a business arrangement. Alice takes the car under a hire-purchase agreement with Crafty Finance and then discovers that the car will only do 30 miles per gallon. Alice can sue

Crafty Finance under s. 56 and claim rescission of the hire-purchase contract, even though they have not made any misrepresentation to her.

Forthright Finance Ltd v *Ingate* (1997)

I bought a Metro car under a conditional sale agreement with the claimant finance company F Ltd. Before finishing the payments I went to buy a Fiat car from a car dealer. The dealer said that he would take the Metro in part-exchange and pay the balance owing to F Ltd. I then made a second conditional sale agreement with a second finance company, C Ltd. The car dealers did not pay F Ltd and went into liquidation. F Ltd sued I for the money. I claimed that C Ltd should pay, as under s. 56 anything said by the dealer is deemed to be said on behalf of C Ltd. A Divisional Court of the High Court said that s. 56 did not apply because there were two transactions, one about the Metro and the other about the Fiat. The antecedent negotiations did not relate to the goods to be sold, i.e. the Fiat. It was held by the Court of Appeal that the negotiations about the Metro were part of the 'package deal' for the Fiat, which involved both the trade-in and buying the new car. They were therefore part of one transaction relating to the goods to be sold by the car dealer to the finance company, C Ltd, and were therefore within s. 56. C Ltd were liable for the dealer's promise to pay the money to F Ltd.

9.2 Breach of contract

In a three-party D-C-S agreement, s. 75 of the Act provides that a debtor who has a claim against a supplier for misrepresentation or breach of contract, has a 'like claim' against the creditor. The conditions for s. 75 to apply are:

(a) the supplier and creditor are different persons but with some business connection (i.e. it is a three-party D-C-S agreement);

(b) the credit is provided in the course of a business;

(c) the goods or services have a cash price of between £100 and £30,000;

(d) the credit agreement is a regulated agreement, although it may exceed the credit limit.

There is some overlap between ss. 75 and 56, but s. 75 applies only to three-party D-C-S agreements and is subject to lower and upper financial limits. Effectively, s. 75 makes the creditor responsible for the quality of goods or services supplied. It is useful to the consumer if the supplier has gone into liquidation.

EXAMPLE

Alice books a holiday for £1,000 with Basil's Tours, using her Access card. There are numerous breaches of contract. Alice may sue Access or Basil's Tours. If she did sue Access they are entitled to be indemnified by Basil's Tours.

Under s. 75 the creditor is jointly and severally liable to the consumer and this liability covers consequential loss. For example, if a consumer buys a video recorder using a credit card and the video recorder is defective and causes a fire, the creditor is liable for this damage. In May 1995 the Director General of Fair Trading published a report recommending that the liability of lenders should be limited to the amount charged on the card. If this is implemented it will weaken the position of consumers and in the above example the creditor would be liable only up to the cost of the video recorder.

9.3 Early repayment

The debtor has a right at any time to end the agreement by paying early (s. 94). This right cannot be excluded. The debtor may exercise the right by giving written notice to the creditor and paying any amounts due. The debtor is entitled to a rebate on interest.

9.4 Termination of hire-purchase and conditional sale agreements by the debtor

The debtor may terminate a hire-purchase or conditional sale agreement under ss. 99 to 100 any time before exercising the option to purchase or paying the last instalment. There is no right to terminate a credit sale agreement as the debtor has become owner of the goods. The rights under ss. 99 and 100 cannot be excluded or lessened. The debtor must:

(a) give notice of termination to anyone entitled to receive payment;

(b) pay any instalments owing, but not future ones;

(c) pay a sum to bring the amount paid up to one half of the total price payable;

(d) allow the creditor to take back the goods;

(e) pay compensation if there has been a failure to take reasonable care of the goods.

EXAMPLE

Alice 'buys' a motorbike on hire purchase, the total amount payable being £5,000 over 12 months. A few months later, Alice is injured in an accident and decides to terminate the agreement. She will have to let the creditor take the motorbike and pay any outstanding instalments plus a sum to bring the amount paid up to £2,500.

It is not usually a good idea for the debtor to terminate an agreement—it is better to obtain permission to sell the goods and pay off the debt.

9.5 Termination by creditor without debtor's default

Creditors sometimes give themselves the right to terminate the credit agreement, even though the debtor has not broken the agreement. For example, if the debtor is convicted of a crime of dishonesty, or becomes unemployed, or bankrupt. In such cases the creditor is put in a vulnerable position. Under s. 98 the creditor must give the debtor seven days' notice of termination of the agreement. This only applies to agreements with a fixed period of duration, like hire-purchase, credit sale and conditional sale agreements, and does not apply to overdrafts, which may be terminated on demand. The effect of serving this notice is that the agreement is treated as terminated and the debtor must pay any sums due and a sum to bring the amount to half the total price and give back the goods.

9.6 Termination by creditor because of debtor's default

The agreement may provide that if the debtor is in default, the creditor may pursue any of the following options:

(a) terminate the agreement;

(b) demand payment in full;

(c) recover the goods;

(d) treat any rights of the debtor as ended (for example an option to purchase);

(e) enforce any security.

But s. 87 provides that the creditor must serve a default notice on the debtor before taking any of these actions. If the creditor is suing for arrears there is no need to serve a default notice.

The default notice must specify:

(a) the nature of the breach;

(b) if the breach can be remedied, what action must be taken and by what date;

(c) if the breach cannot be remedied, the amount of compensation required and by what date;

(d) the consequences of non-compliance with the notice.

The minimum period for compliance with the notice is seven days. The aim of these provisions is to give the debtor a breathing space to sort out his financial problems. If the debtor takes the steps specified in the notice, the default is treated as never having taken place. Alternatively, the debtor may apply to the court for a time order.

10 Remedies

10.1 Debtor

10.1.1 Damages and repudiation

The rights given by the Sale of Goods Act 1979, the Supply of Goods and Services Act 1982 and the Supply of Goods (Implied Terms) Act 1973 are not affected by the Consumer Credit Act 1974, except in regard to ss. 56 and 75, which have been examined above (see 9.1 and 9.2). In the case of a breach of warranty the debtor may claim damages, and for breach of condition repudiate the contract.

10.1.2 Time order

Although this is not a remedy as such, it does provide relief for the debtor when the creditor wishes to terminate, whether for default by the debtor or otherwise. Under s. 129 the debtor may apply for a time order, which may:

(a) fix a time for payments to be made, taking the debtor's means into account; and/or

(b) fix a time to remedy the breach.

The court will not make a time order where there are no prospects of instalments being paid, for example, the debtor is unemployed (*First National Bank plc* v *Syed* (1991)).

10.1.3 Extortionate credit bargains

Under ss. 137 to 140 the court has power to reopen credit agreements it considers extortionate. This applies to any credit agreement even if it is over the limit or exempt. It covers payments which are grossly exorbitant. In determining this, the court will take all relevant factors into account including: prevailing interest rates; the age, health, business experience and pressure on the debtor; the creditor's relationship to the debtor and the risk taken by the creditor.

A. Ketley Ltd v Scott (1981)

A lender lent £20,500 to a housebuyer at a few hours' notice at 48% interest. The housebuyer had been refused a loan by the bank and was experienced in business. It was held that this was not extortionate.

The debtor may bring an action to have the agreement reopened or may simply raise the matter in any proceedings arising, for example, taken by the creditor to enforce the agreement.

The Office of Fair Trading have recommended that the phrase 'extortionate credit bargain' should be changed to 'unjust credit transaction', which has a wider scope and would make it easier for debtors to get interest rates changed (*Unjust Credit Transactions* (OFT, 1991)).

10.2 Creditor

10.2.1 Action for sums due

This is a claim for any amounts the debtor owes under the agreement.

10.2.2 Termination and repossession

If the debtor commits a repudiatory breach of the agreement, the creditor will have a right to terminate. Even if the breach is not serious, the agreement may give the creditor a right to terminate. If the creditor then chooses to end the agreement, at common law the creditor could reclaim the goods. A problem arises if this involves going on to the debtor's premises, which is trespass. Under s. 92, in the case of regulated agreements, leave of the court is needed to go on to land to retake possession of goods. However, if the debtor consents to entry, the goods may be taken.

In the case of hire-purchase and conditional sale agreements, s. 90 provides that if the debtor:

(a) is in breach of the agreement, and

(b) has not terminated it, and

(c) has paid *one third* of the total price, and

(d) property in the goods remains with the creditor

then the goods are protected goods and the creditor cannot recover the goods from the debtor without a court order. If the creditor does take possession of protected goods without a court order, it is not a crime, but the agreement is automatically terminated and the debtor can reclaim all sums paid (s. 91). If the debtor consents to repossession then s. 91 does not apply and the debtor cannot reclaim payments made.

10.2.3 Damages

Usually a breach of contract will be the debtor not paying instalments, but it may be failing to take care of the goods, as the debtor is a bailee of the goods unless the agreement is a credit sale. Also, if the debtor refuses to give back the goods when the creditor is lawfully entitled to take possession, the debtor is liable in the tort of conversion.

Consumer Protection Act 1987

1 Introduction

One important objective of the law is to try and ensure that goods are safe. It attempts this through a mixture of criminal and civil obligations, which impose standards on the producers of goods. If these standards are not met, those at fault may be prosecuted and fined and the consumer may take civil action for compensation. A range of possibilities are available, all of which have drawbacks. These possibilities include claims in contract, the tort of negligence, the tort of breach of statutory duty, and rights under the Consumer Protection Act 1987, Part I. This section will examine these in turn.

2 Contract

A buyer of goods may sue the seller for breach of the implied terms of the contract under the Sale of Goods Act 1979 or equivalent statutes. These implied terms deal with description, satisfactory quality, fitness for purpose and correspondence with sample. The liability of the seller is strict, which means that irrespective of fault, the seller is liable. The buyer will be able to claim compensation for the following losses arising from the breach of contract, subject to the principle of remoteness of damage:

(a) the price of the goods;

(b) personal injury;

(c) damage to property;

(d) economic loss (i.e. pure financial loss).

There are a number of problems with a claim in contract:

(a) under the rule of privity, only the buyer of the goods may sue (but note that a third party may now have a right to sue under the Contracts (Rights of Third Parties) Act 1999);

(b) the seller may have gone out of business;

(c) taking action through the courts is expensive;

(d) although in a consumer sale the seller cannot exclude liability to the buyer, the supplier may exclude liability to the seller, making the seller solely responsible.

3 Negligence

The buyer has an alternative claim in the tort of negligence against the manufacturer of the product. Anyone else who suffers damage may also sue in negligence. The claimant claiming negligence must prove three things:

(a) the manufacturer owed them a duty of care, to make sure the product was safe;

(b) the manufacturer broke this duty by making a defective product; and

(c) the manufacturer's breach caused damage to the claimant.

The manufacturer is liable to anyone who it is reasonably foreseeable will be affected, if the manufacturer is negligent. The classic example is *Donoghue v Stevenson* (1932), where the manufacturer of a bottle of ginger beer containing a decomposed snail was held liable to the consumer who drank the ginger beer. The manufacturer may be liable to the buyer, the buyer's family, anyone given the goods as a present or complete strangers. The burden of proof is on the claimant and this may be difficult to discharge, particularly in the case of complicated manufactured goods or drugs. The manufacturer will not be liable if the goods should have been checked by an intermediary or they were misused. Also, there is the partial defence of contributory negligence.

If the manufacturer is liable in negligence, the claimant may claim compensation for the following:

(a) personal injury and death;

(b) damage to property.

But not economic loss or the cost of the goods.

4 Breach of statutory duty

Many consumer statutes create criminal offences and anyone who breaks the statute may be prosecuted. Occasionally, such statutes also give the consumer a right to sue in tort for breach of this statutory duty if they suffer damage as a result of the offence.

One example of this is that under the Consumer Protection Act 1987, Part II, it is a criminal offence to break individual safety regulations. If this happens, the consumer may bring a civil action for breach of statutory duty.

5 Consumer Protection Act 1987

5.1 Introduction

The deficiencies of the law were exemplified in the case of the children born with deformities, after their mothers had taken the drug Thalidomide. Because of difficulties in establishing negligence, an out-of-court settlement was made. In the years following, reports by the Law Commission, the Pearson Commission, the Council of Europe, and the European Commission recommended that manufacturers should be strictly liable for damage caused by defective products. In 1985 the Council of Ministers of the European Communities issued a Directive on product liability and gave member states up to 30 July 1988 to implement it. The Consumer Protection Act 1987, Part I implements this Directive and it came into force on 1 March 1988. The rights given by the Consumer Protection Act are in addition to existing rights in contract and tort. The provisions of the Consumer Protection Act 1987, Part I, mean that the consumer does not have to prove negligence in order to claim compensation for a defective product. Part II of the Act imposes criminal liability for breach of the general safety requirement. The Consumer Protection Act repeals earlier legislation, including the Consumer Safety Act 1978, although regulations made under the Consumer Safety Act 1978 are now deemed to be made under the Consumer Protection Act 1987, s. 11, and remain in force. The Act should improve the position of the consumer and will be the first line of attack for someone without a contractual link. However, there are still the problems of establishing the defect caused the damage and the developments risk defence (see below 5.2 and 5.8(e) respectively).

5.2 Basic rule

In theory, one difficulty caused by the Consumer Protection Act is that its wording differs slightly, in places, from the Directive. This should not create a problem because of s. 1(1) which states,

This Part shall have effect for the purpose of making such provision as is necessary in order to comply with the product liability Directive and shall be construed accordingly.

English courts should therefore interpret the Consumer Protection Act in the light of the Directive.

The essence of the Act is that the producer of a defective product is liable for damage caused by that product. By s. 2(1):

. . . where any damage is caused wholly or partly by a defect in a product, every person to whom subsection (2) applies shall be liable for the damage.

Liability is strict and there is no need to establish that the producer was negligent. The Consumer Protection Act does not mention the burden of proof, but the Directive states that the person claiming will have to establish:

(a) that the product was defective;

(b) the damage was suffered; and

(c) that the damage was caused by the defect.

The problem of causation remains and it may prove a stumbling block for claims, particularly against drugs manufacturers or, for example, establishing that smoking a particular brand of cigarettes caused the claimant's lung cancer.

5.3 Product

Section 1(2) provides that 'product' means any goods or electricity and it includes components and raw materials incorporated in other products. Goods is further defined to include 'any substances, growing crops and things comprised in land by virtue of being attached to it and any ship, aircraft or vehicle'. This covers virtually everything.

The exception is buildings. It does not cover buying a house, but if the materials are defective and cause other damage, apart from to the building, the manufacturer is liable. The Act does cover building work on a house, which involves adding material to it.

The Act previously excluded 'game or agricultural produce' which had not undergone an industrial process at the time of supply.

The rule relating to agricultural produce has been changed by Council Directive 99/34 (May 1999) which brings agricultural produce within the rules on product liability. The European Union believed that this was necessary to protect consumers in the light of continuing food scares such as BSE and salmonella. The Consumer Protection Act 1987 (Product Liability) (Modification) Order 2000 implements the Directive and extends Part I of the Consumer Protection Act to primary agricultural products and game.

5.4 Defect

There is a defect 'if the safety of the product is not such as persons generally are entitled to expect' (s. 3(1)). This differs from the Directive which says a product is defective 'When it does not provide the standard of safety which a person is entitled to expect'. The standard applied by the Act is an objective one (persons generally), which is narrower than the subjective standard in the Directive. In determining what persons generally are entitled to expect the courts must take into account 'all the circumstances'. These include matters set out in s. 3(2):

(a) The way in which the goods are sold and the purposes for which they are sold. For example, whether they are sold to children or adults.

(b) Any instructions or warnings given with the goods. For example, with drugs, how and when they should be taken.

(c) What might reasonably be expected to be done with the product. The producer must take into account normal use and foreseeable misuse. For example, using a hover mower to cut a hedge or sniffing glue. A clear warning would avoid liability.

There have been a number of cases which have considered what amounts to a defective product.

Richardson v *LRC Products Ltd* (2000)

R had two children and did not want any more. She used a condom during sexual intercourse but the condom fractured and she became pregnant, She claimed that the condom was defective under s. 3 because of ozone damage in the factory or because it failed. It was held by the High Court that some condoms fractured without being defective. The manufacturer did not claim that the condoms were 100 per cent effective and neither did the public expect them to be so. R could not show there was ozone damage. The condom was not regarded as a defective product.

In any case if the condoms were defective, the defect did not cause the loss because R could have taken the morning after pill.

Foster v *Biosil* (2001)

After a mastectomy F had breast implants which were manufactured by B. Within a short time the implants leaked and had to be replaced. F claimed that the implants were defective under the Consumer Protection Act. It was held in the county court that F had to show both the fact of the defect and the cause. F was unable to show that the leaks were the result of a defect in manufacture and her claim failed.

(d) The time the product was supplied by the producer. This is important in deciding if the goods are safe, not the time the goods were supplied by the retailer.

and nothing in this section shall require a defect to be inferred from the fact alone that the safety of a product which is supplied after that time is greater than the safety of the product in question.

This means that if a manufacturer produces an improved and safer product, this does not prove that the earlier product was defective. If this provision was not included, then manufacturers would not improve products for fear of being sued!

5.5 Damage

The Act provides that the producer is liable for damage caused 'wholly or partly by a defect in a product' (s. 2(1)). It is essential for the person claiming to prove damage. There is liability under s. 5(1) for:

(a) death,

(b) personal injury, and

(c) damage to property (including land).

Liability for damage to property is restricted and no claim may be made for:

(a) damage to the actual product *or* for any product supplied with the defective product in it (s. 5(2)).

EXAMPLE

Alice buys a car with a defective tyre. The car crashes and is wrecked and Alice is injured. Alice may claim for her injuries but not for the tyre (the defective product) or the car.

(b) damage to property not ordinarily intended for private use, occupation or consumption *and* intended by the person suffering the loss mainly for his own private use, occupation or consumption.

EXAMPLE

Basil buys a word processor for his office. Due to a defect it explodes, Basil is injured and his office is damaged. Basil may claim for his injuries but not the damage to the office.

(c) damage not exceeding £275. The object is to cut out small claims.

EXAMPLE

Alice buys a television which is defective. It bursts into flames and destroys her video–recorder which cost £250. Alice cannot claim for the video–recorder, or of course for the television under the Consumer Protection Act 1987.

5.6 Producer

The Act imposes liability on the producer or anyone who has held themselves out as the producer. It covers the following persons:

(a) The manufacturer of the finished product, including the manufacturer of components.

(b) The producer of raw materials, for example coal.

(c) The processor of a product, for example petrol refiner, pea canner.

(d) The seller of own brand goods.

EXAMPLE

Alf's Stores sell beans under Alf's own label which have been made by Bertie's Foods. If the beans are defective and cause damage, Alf is liable. But if the beans have 'Made by Bertie's Foods' on the label, Alf's Stores are not liable.

(e) The importer into the European Union, if this is done in the course of a business. Under the Civil Jurisdiction and Judgments Act 1982 the person suffering damage can take proceedings in the UK courts and have the judgment enforced in the courts of the defendant's state.

(f) The supplier of the product. The supplier is only liable if the person suffering damage asks the supplier to identify the producer, own brander or importer and this request is made within a reasonable time after the damage and the supplier fails to identify any of these within a reasonable time. For example, a retailer who sells a defective product and cannot or will not identify who they obtained it from, will be liable.

The person suing can trace liability along a chain to discover who is responsible. More than one person may be responsible and in such cases liability is joint and several, so each is liable for the full extent of the damage.

5.7 Limits of liability

There are two periods which are relevant, the basic limitation period and the long stop period.

Under the Limitation Act 1980 any claim for personal injury or damage to property must be brought within three years of when the damage was caused by the defective product (patent defect) or three years from when the damage could have been discovered (latent defect).

The Limitation Act 1980 also imposes a 10-year time limit for liability under the Consumer Protection Act. The 10-year period runs from the relevant time the product is supplied. In the case of action against the producer, own brander or importer, it is the time they supplied the product to another. In the case of action against the supplier, it is the time the product was last supplied by a producer, own brander or importer.

It is not possible to exclude liability under the Act (s. 7).

EXAMPLE

Alice buys a hairdryer in March 1993 but it remains unused until March 2002, when Alice suffers severe burns due to a defect in the hairdryer. Alice must sue by March 2003.

5.8 Defences

In a civil action under Part I, the burden of proof is on the defendant to establish any of the following defences s. 4(1)(a) to (f):

(a) *Following the law*   If the person had to follow domestic or European regulations, that is a good defence. There is a similar defence to a prosecution under Part II given by s. 10(3)(a).

Whirlpool (UK) Ltd and Magnet Ltd v *Gloucester County Council* (1993)
A cooker hood, which met regulations, became hot and casing fell off exposing wires. The Divisional Court rejected the suppliers' defence that the hood met the required standards, saying that to comply with s. 10 needed more than this.

This case may have an important bearing on the interpretation of s. 4(1)(a).

(b) *No supply*   The person sued did not supply the product. For example, if the goods were stolen or they were a prototype. Note that in the case of hire-purchase agreements, the Act provides that the dealer supplies the product, not the finance company.

(c) *Non-profit making activity*   The supply was not in the course of a business, or if it was it was not supplied to make a profit.

Goods supplied privately or at a jumble sale.

Veedfald v *Arthus Amtskommune* (2001)

This concerned a kidney which was provided through the state medical system in Belgium. The fluid used for preparing the kidney was contaminated and the kidney could not be used. It was held by the European Court of Justice that the defence under Article 7(c) (s. 4(1)(c)) did not include products supplied by a public health service.

(d) *Subsequent defect*   If it can be shown that the goods were not defective when the defendant supplied them, that is a good defence. In the case of the producer, own brander or importer the time is when they supplied the goods. In the case of the supplier, it is the time of the last supply by the producer, own brander or importer.

EXAMPLE

Alice Ltd supplies minced beef to Bertie's Stores on 1 June. On 2 June an animal liberation group put ground glass in the minced beef, which is sold to Clive who suffers injury. At the time of supply by Alice Ltd, the goods were not defective.

(e) *Scientific and technical knowledge*   That the state of scientific and technical knowledge at the relevant time was not such that a producer of products of the same description might be expected to have discovered the defect. This imposes an objective test, that of the reasonable producer. The Directive refers to knowledge that would enable the producer to discover the defect, which is much wider, and could mean the producer is liable if somewhere there is knowledge which could have led to the defect being discovered.

Because of the differences which were believed to exist between the Directive and the Consumer Protection Act 1987, the European Commission brought an action against the British Government in the European Court of Justice, claiming that the United Kingdom had applied the Directive wrongly. In *EC Commission* v *United Kingdom* (1997) the Court held that s. 4(1)(e) does not conflict with the Directive it was intended to implement, and in reaching this decision the Court took into account s. 1(1) of the Consumer Protection Act 1987 which provides that Part I should be construed to comply with the Directive. This decision means that the consumer will be given greater protection. This defence is sometimes called the 'state of the art' or 'development risks' defence. Member states had the choice of whether to include it or not and some have left it out.

Abouzaid v *Mothercare* (2001)

In 1990 when the claimant was 12 years old he was helping to attach a sleeping bag with an elastic strap to a push chair. He let go of the strap and the metal buckle on the end hit him in the eye, causing loss of vision. The claimant sued the defendant manufacturers under the Consumer Protection Act. The Court of Appeal held that the existence of a defect was to be judged by the expectations of the public. There was a risk of the strap slipping when it would be near the eyes and no warning had been given, so the product was defective. The defendants argued that it could not have realised the risks as there were no accident reports on the product in 1990 and this meant that there was no scientific and technical knowledge available at the time of the accident. But the court said that the fact the defect was not discovered before the accident was not due to the lack of technical knowledge, as the defect could have been discovered by a simple practical test and therefore the defence under s. 4(1)(e) did not apply. The claimant was entitled to damages.

A v *National Blood Authority* (2001)

The claimants were infected with hepatitis C from blood transfusions between 1988 and 1991 and sued under the Consumer Protection Act on the basis that they had been given a 'defective product' because it had the virus. In deciding if the product was defective the court used the wording from Article 6 of the Directive, that it does not provide the safety which 'a person is entitled to expect'. The High Court made a distinction between 'standard' and 'non-standard' products. With a standard product the question was whether it was safe for its foreseeable use. With a non-standard product the question was whether the public accepted that because of its nature some of those products would be defective. Infected blood was a non standard product and the public did not know that blood carried a risk of infection, so they did not accept this risk. The blood was a defective product. The hepatitis C virus had not been identified until May 1989 but no screening test was developed until 1991. The defendants argued that under Article 7 (s. 4(1)(e) of CPA) it was not liable because there was no way to test the blood before 1991. The court said that if there was a known risk with a product, the producer would be liable if they continued to supply the product, even though they could not identify which products were defective. Here there was a known risk of hepatitis C before the test could be developed and the defence under Article 7 (s. 4(1)(e)) failed.

> (f) *Defect in finished product not the component* If the defect is in the finished product in which the component part is incorporated and the defect is due to the design of the finished product or because the producer of the component followed instructions from the producer of the finished product, then the component manufacturer is not liable.

This defence is to provide protection for component suppliers in circumstances where they are not responsible for the defect.

Questions

Law of Contract

1 Michele decided to have a holiday in Cornwall with her boyfriend Danny. She went to the station and booked two tickets to travel from London to Penzance, with Express Trains Ltd, a company which she usually used. Michele put the tickets in her pocket without reading them. On the tickets it stated,

> Express Trains Ltd cannot accept liability for injury to passengers or damage to their belongings in any circumstances. Express Trains Ltd reserve the right to terminate services without notice and no refunds will be given.

About 10 miles from Penzance, due to poor maintenance, a wheel came off the train which Michele and Danny were travelling on, causing the train carriages to be partially derailed. Danny suffered minor cuts from flying glass. Michele's suitcase disappeared in the ensuing commotion. They had to finish their journey by taxi and the taxi fare was paid by Michele.

Advise Michele and Danny.

Outline answer

(a) Explain that the question involves consideration of the rules on exemption clauses, including the common law rules, the Unfair Contract Terms Act 1977 and the Unfair Terms in Consumer Contracts Regulations 1999. The three issues to consider are the loss of the suitcase, the cost of the taxi fare and the injury to Danny.

(b) The first matter to consider is whether the exclusion clause on the ticket has become part of the contract? Could this have been done by notice?; the ticket is a contractual document; she has been given the tickets at the time of making the contract, *Olley* v *Marlborough Court Hotel* (1949); but whether she has been given reasonable notice will depend on whether the exclusion clause was on the front of the ticket or the back, *Thompson* v *LMS Rly* (1930). An alternative possibility is whether the exclusion clause was incorporated by a course of dealing? Michele 'usually' uses Express Trains Ltd but how often is this and can it amount to a course of dealing? Apply *Hollier* v *Rambler Motors Ltd* (1972). Assuming the clause is part of the contract will it be invalid under the other common law rules, the Unfair Contract Terms Act 1977 or the 1999 Regulations?

(c) Michele's suitcase: consider whether the wording of the clause 'damage' covers loss of the suitcase? It may be argued that the *contra proferentem* rule applies, *Houghton* v *Trafalgar Insurance* (1953). Also consider whether the clause passes the test of reasonableness under s. 2(2) Unfair Contract Terms Act 1977; the contract is between an individual and a large company, etc.; distinguish *Watford Electronics Ltd* v *Sanderson Ltd* (2001). Could the clause be unfair under the 1999 Regulations, as it was not individually negotiated and may cause a significant imbalance to Michele's rights?

(d) Taxi fare and refund: is the clause providing no refunds within s.3 Unfair Contract Terms Act 1977? If so, it is subject to a test of reasonableness. Also apply the 1999 Regulations; it can be argued that this term is unfair.

(e) Danny's cuts: explain that the contract was made by Michele and under the rule of privity Danny is not a party and cannot sue in contract; but consider if he is within the Contracts (Rights of Third Parties) Act 1999. An alternative claim would be in the tort of negligence. Under s. 2(1) Unfair Contract Terms Act 1977 any attempt to exclude liability for injury caused by negligence is void; application here; Express Trains Ltd cannot exclude liability.

(f) Give a brief conclusion of the main claims by Michele for her suitcase, the taxi fare and at least a refund of part of her train fare; Danny is entitled to some compensation for his cuts either in contract or failing that in negligence.

2 (a) Kevin owned a restaurant and wanted some leaflets to advertise the Christmas menu, which was available throughout December. He made a contract with Lisa that she would print these leaflets by the end of November, for £1,000. Near the end of November, Kevin was worried that the leaflets would not be ready on time and he offered to pay £200 extra if the leaflets were printed by the end of November. Lisa completed the work on time and has now claimed the £200.

(b) Kevin also owed £3,000 to Mike, a supplier to the restaurant. Mike agreed to accept payment in instalments but after Kevin had paid only a few instalments, Mike demanded the full amount owing.

Advise Kevin in the above situations.

3 (a) How do the courts distinguish between a representation and a term of the contract?

(b) Distinguish between express and implied terms in contracts, using examples to illustrate your answer.

4 (a) Eddie asked Flo, his grandmother, to sign a guarantee for the rent on his flat. Flo was 80 years old and had poor eyesight. In fact, the document she signed was a guarantee for his overdraft at the bank, which was a much larger amount. The bank have now demanded payment.

Advise Flo.

(b) Georgina went into Harry's jewellers shop and told Harry that her name was Lady Isobel and she produced a forged pass for the House of Lords. Georgina then selected an expensive diamond ring and paid with a cheque, which Harry accepted without a guarantee card, as he was certain such an important person would be honest. In fact the cheque was dishonoured and the ring was pawned to James.

Advise Harry.

5 What restrictions does the law impose on a claimant who wishes to claim damages for breach of contract?

Consumer Law

6   (a) Bob owned a used car business. He telephoned Celia, who operated a private hire taxi firm and told her that he had 'a lovely black Rover car' for sale, which would be ideal for her business. Celia went to Bob's showroom and after inspecting the car bought it. Shortly after this she discovered that the car was actually dark blue and she now wishes to reclaim her money.

Advise Celia.

(b) Denise purchased a mountain bike from Bike Shop Ltd, but left it with the shop, so that special tyres could be fitted and agreed to collect it a week later. Later the same day Bike Shop Ltd mistakenly sold the bike to Fred. Denise has now demanded the return of the bike.

Advise all the parties.

7   Your client Ali informs you that in the near future he will be making contracts for expensive treatment to his timber-framed house to protect it from woodworm and for a cruise holiday in the Caribbean. He asks what protection the law provides in these cases.

Advise Ali.

8   (a) Explain the requirements imposed by the Consumer Credit Act 1974, as regards copies of regulated consumer credit agreements.

(b) Explain the circumstances in which a creditor may be made liable for misrepresentation and breach of contract under the Consumer Credit Act 1974.

2

Employment Law

Introduction

The employment law dealt with in this chapter falls into two main categories; namely the law relating to contracts of employment and the law relating to health and safety at work.

Although much of the law described in both of these areas is governed by statute, it is important to recognise that rights and responsibilities of both employer and employee are also derived from common law principles which still apply today.

In some instances this results in more than one set of legal rules applying to the same situation. For example the rules of negligence allow employees who have been injured at work to bring civil actions for damages. Such cases would probably be brought in the county court which can now deal with cases involving claims for compensation of up to £50,000 (or more if both parties agree).

At the same time the Health and Safety at Work etc. Act 1974 sets standards in respect of safe working conditions and practices. If the Health and Safety Executive, which is the enforcing authority for this legislation, considers these standards are not being met, there are a variety of sanctions which it can impose, including initiating criminal proceedings in the magistrates' court.

The Health and Safety Executive can bring a case irrespective of whether someone has been injured in the work environment. The Health and Safety Executive therefore takes proceedings for the purpose of both punishing the offender and setting an example to others who might be tempted to ignore the standards set by the Act.

Any 'person' in law found guilty of an offence under the Act can be fined, and person in this respect includes companies. In extreme cases individuals including company directors and employees may be given prison sentences. The Health and Safety at Work etc. Act 1974 has therefore been passed to act as a deterrent against unsafe practices, whereas the rules of negligence give the injured employee the right to claim compensation.

On other occasions the rules of common law continue to fill gaps left by modern statute in that they apply to civil actions where the statute does not. However the common law right to claim damages for breach of the contract of employment, known as an action for wrongful dismissal, still exists.

Employees who are ineligible to bring a case under statute may bring a civil case in the county court or High Court. Even those who have already been awarded compensation by an industrial tribunal may still bring a separate case for wrongful dismissal, as the case of *O'Laoire v Jackel International Ltd (No. 2)* (CA) (1991) illustrates (this case is dealt with more fully later on).

The rules of common law therefore form a significant part of employment law today and are accordingly described and explained in this chapter.

EXAMPLES OF THE DIVISION BETWEEN COMMON LAW AND STATUTE

Contracts of employment

Common law	Statute
Wrongful dismissal	Unfair dismissal governed by e.g. Employment Rights Act 1996

Health and Safety at Work

Common law	Statute
Rules of negligence	Set of six 1992 regulations E.g. Health and Safety at Work etc. Act 1974

Employment

1 The contract and its formation

This part of the chapter deals with the contract of employment. The underlying rules relating to the formation of a contract of employment are the same as those relating to the general law of contract; namely there must be an offer, acceptance and consideration (normally money-wages/salary in return for work done). Once terms have been accepted they cannot be changed unilaterally by an employer. In *Hayes and Others v Security and Facilities Division* (CA) (2000), an agency of the Cabinet Office, the employers acted unlawfully when reducing a subsistence allowance of £65.50 or £60 (out of London) to a flat £50. The continuance or discontinuance of a contract (of employment) is a matter of contract law and not statute.

Hilton International Hotels (UK) Ltd v Kaissi (EAT) (1994)

While the employee was on maternity leave she wrote to her employers stating that she would not be able to resume work because of a pelvic infection and she would inform her employers when she was fit. This letter was written in February, and had the employee complied with the relevant procedures she had the right to return to work up to mid-May. Five days later (25 February) the hotel's assistant manager wrote to the employee stating that as the hotel had not received any written confirmation of the employee's intention to return to work the employee's employment had been terminated. There was no express or implied agreement between the employee and her employer to bring the contract to an end until the employer's letter on 25 February. That dismissal was unfair because the employer had taken no steps to investigate the position or find out whether she could return to work within a reasonable time. Therefore she was entitled to compensation for unfair dismissal.

All contracts of employment, like other contracts, comprise express and implied terms.

2 Express terms

Examples of express terms include information about weekly wages or monthly salary, holidays, and sick pay. A full example of a contract of employment is given on pp. 214–215.

Although the contract of employment is enforceable as an oral agreement, it is a statutory requirement that the employer provides the employee with written particulars of certain terms within two months of the employee starting work (s. 1, Employment Rights Act 1996).

This does not have to be what the student of law might regard as a 'formal' document. It is, for example, common practice for the employer to write a letter to the successful job applicant setting out the terms that both parties agreed at the interview. However this can and does lead to information being omitted. It is therefore best if the employer draws up a standard set of terms which can be given, suitably modified when necessary, to all employees. The employer should keep a record of when this is issued and a duplicate copy.

Once a written statement has been issued an employment tribunal will only consider the contents of the statement and not what may or may not have been orally agreed between employer and employee.

Eagland v British Telecommunications plc (EAT) (1990)

After the employee complained that she had not been given a written contract, her employer supplied her with written particulars. She then complained to an industrial tribunal that the written particulars were less favourable than the original verbal agreement. On appeal the appeals tribunal held that it was not appropriate for an industrial (now employment) tribunal to remake a contract, and the written information which the employer had provided complied with the legislation. The employee's action therefore failed.

A newly appointed employee should therefore seek to agree, in writing, all contractual details at the earliest possible date.

The Act does not apply to staff employed on a casual basis. In *Carmichael* v

National Power plc (HL) (1999) it was held that staff employed as tour guides, as and when the need arose, were not entitled to a written statement of the terms of their employment. The evidence showed that neither party intended their relationship to be regulated, by contract, when the applicants were not working as guides.

2.1 Remuneration

The consideration given by the employee in return for payment is to undertake all the duties agreed in the contract. In *Cantor Fitzgerald International* v *Callaghan* (CA) (1999) the employers were refusing to honour a package which granted the employees four-year £60,000 forgiveable loans which included arrangements to exclude any prospect of tax liability. Although the amount in issue was not great in relation to the overall package the money at stake was not trivial. The refusal to pay was deliberate and wholly undermined the contract of employment. This constituted repudiatory breach by the employer. Note that under s. 8 of the Employment Rights Act 1996, employees are entitled to an itemised pay statement. An employee who fails to fulfil all these duties will be in breach of contract. When an employee has indicated in advance the intention not to work in accordance with the contract, the employer can treat this as an anticipatory breach. The employer may then advise employees that if they do not undertake all that is required of them they will not be required for work.

Wiluszynski v *Tower Hamlets London Borough Council* (CA) (1989)
The plaintiff was employed by the defendant council as an estate officer. His duties included answering councillors' enquiries. During an industrial dispute the council notified the officers that they would not be required for work, or paid, if they were not prepared to answer enquiries.

During a period in August 1985, although the plaintiff carried out other duties, he did not answer enquiries. It was held that he had broken his contract and accordingly he was not entitled to be paid anything. The fact that he was present at the workplace did not mean that he was employed. An employer is not always expected physically to prevent employees from entering premises.

Where, however, the employee remains employed an employer must obtain the written consent of the employee before making any deductions from wages (s. 13, Employment Rights Act 1996) or before receiving any payments (s. 15).

Pename v *Paterson* (EAT) (1989)
The employee was owed a week's wages when he left without giving notice. It was held that the employers were not entitled to withhold the money they already owed him without his written consent, which they had not obtained.

Normally disputes relating to deductions from wages are heard by industrial tribunals, *but* in *Delaney* v *Staples* (HL) (1992) Miss Delaney's employer had paid her £82 by cheque when he summarily dismissed her. He subsequently stopped the cheque asserting she had taken away confidential information. The House of Lords ruled that for payments to come within the meaning of the Wages Act 1986 they must relate to a period of employment *before* the contract is ended. Therefore, a payment such as this, in lieu of notice was not 'wages' and Miss Delaney's dispute could not be heard by an industrial tribunal.

Other sums not regarded as wages may only be recovered in the county court, as damages.

Industrial action taken by members of a union over a dispute concerning terms and conditions of employment will be classed as a trade dispute under the Trade Union and Labour Relations (Consolidation) Act 1992, s. 244. Consequently in *Wandsworth London Borough Council* v *National Association of Schoolmasters/Union of Women Teachers* (CA) (1993) the union were not liable in tort for inducing a breach of contract in respect of teachers refusing to carry out assessments and tests. By early May 1993 the government announced a change in policy in respect of these tests.

2.1.1 Minimum Wage

The National Minimum Wage Act 1998 sets a national minimum wage of £3.60 per hour for all workers.

Although this Act came into force on 1 April 1999 employers may not be complying with the legislation. For example, at a preliminary hearing in September 1999, brought by a sub post mistress being paid £2.22 per hour the tribunal agreed that she was a worker within the definition of the Act. The Post Office had argued that she was an agent.

In *Edmonds* v *Lawson* (QBD) (1999) a friendly action brought at the instigation of the Bar Council it was held that in accepting an offer of pupillage a barrister was entering into a contract of apprenticeship. This meant that the claimant had become a worker within s. 1(2) of the 1998 Act and was entitled to the National Minimum Wage.

2.2 Notice

In *Skilton* v *T and K Home Improvements Ltd* (CA) (2000) although clause 14:1 of the employee's contract allowed for dismissal without prior notice or pay in nine specific situations, such as for gross misconduct, clause 14:2 stated only that he could be dismissed with immediate effect for failing to meet targets. Therefore in the context of the contract as a whole his right to payment of salary for three months in lieu of notice was not excluded when he was dismissed for missing performance targets.

Notice given in pursuance of a void agreement, nevertheless, determines the relevant date for the end of employment. In *Eastbourne Borough Council* v *Foster* (CA) (2001) the local authority abolished the employee's post as Director of Environment Services before his 50th birthday. Unless he continued to be employed beyond the age of 50 years he would not be entitled to an enhanced pension benefit. He entered into a compromise agreement which was ultra vires and therefore void allowing him to work nine days beyond his 50th birthday. For a period he worked for three days a week and then a dispute arose between him and the Chief Executive. The employee was put on 'garden leave' until 31 August 1999, the date for which the local authority had given notice in the compromise agreement. Consequently he was entitled to his pension.

2.3 Working Time Regulations

The new legal rights available under these regulations are:

(a) entitlement to a break (not defined) when an employee's working day is longer than six hours;

(b) a minimum of 11 consecutive hours' rest on a daily basis;

(c) a minimum of 24 hours' uninterrupted rest every week as well as the 11-hour daily rest period. The weekly rest period may be averaged over a maximum of two weeks or reduced from 35 to 24 hours if there are objective technical or work organisational requirements;

(d) the right not to be required to work more than 48 hours a week. In *Barber* v *RJB Mining UK Ltd* (QBD) (1999) the plaintiffs had been asked to opt out of the 48 hours working time limit. They refused to sign the opt out agreement, although they continued to work under protest, in excess of their contractual hours of 42 hours per week. They sought and were granted both a declaration that they were entitled to refuse to continue working until their average working hours came within the limit imposed under reg. 4(1) and an injunction to enforce this right against the defendants. In *Sindicato de Médicos de Asistencia Pública* v *Conselleria de Sanidad y Consumo de la Generalidad Valenciana* Case-303/98 (Court of Justice of the European Communities) (2000) the court held that medical staff providing primary care at health centres fell within the scope of the Directive which could be transposed in the absence of domestic law. Accordingly time spent at health centres whilst on call was working time. Whilst doctors were merely on call only time spent on the provision of care was working time and doctors on *call* at night could not be regarded as night workers. Work performed while on call constituted shift work;

(e) a minimum of four weeks' paid annual leave. In *Gibson* v *East Riding of Yorkshire District Council* (CA) (2000) the Court of Appeal overruled the EAT deciding that Article 7 of the Working Time Directive had no direct effect on an employee's entitlements. The regulations prescribing rights to annual leave did not come into force until October 1998 whereas her case was presented in July 1997. Consequently she was not entitled at that time to paid annual leave. In *Regina* v *Secretary of State for Trade and Industry, ex parte Broadcasting, Entertainment, Cinematographic and Theatre Union* Case C-173/99 (Court of Justice of the European Communities) (2001) the court stated that the improvement of workers' safety, hygiene and health at work is an objective which should not be subordinated to purely economic considerations. Therefore the right to paid annual leave should apply from the start of employment. The United Kingdom rule that employees are not entitled to paid leave until they have completed 13 weeks of continuous employment is therefore unlawful.

In *Davis and Others* v *M J Wyatt (Decorators) Ltd* (EAT) (2000) an employer acted unlawfully when he reduced the pay of two employees, without their consent, in order to fund his obligation to provide paid annual leave.

(f) night work must not exceed eight hours in a 24-hour period; night workers will be entitled to free and confidential health assessments; and if suffering from health problems related to night work, transferred when possible to suitable day work.

3 Implied terms

There are various examples of contracts where some of the terms automatically (by implication) apply regardless of what the parties may or may not have agreed. The contract of employment is one such example and the following are some implied terms.

3.1 Both parties must cooperate in the performance of their responsibilities

This means that an employee must obey all reasonable instructions given by the employer. These require the employee to undertake work as stated in the contract, or work which has been done in the past, or over a period of time, and has therefore become an accepted part of the employee's duties.

EXAMPLE

If a lorry driver storms off the premises after refusing to take out a lorry at the request of his employer, clearly he will be in breach of contract.

Appropriate disciplinary action is discussed later.

However, in *Macmillan Inc* v *Bishopsgate Investment Trust plc (No. 2)* (1993) the Chancery Division of the High Court held that an employee of a company who gave evidence to the company's liquidator about the affairs of the company was not acting in the course of employment. Consequently he could not be compelled to tell his employers what he said or to hand over a copy of the transcript of evidence.

3.2 Both parties must take reasonable care in performing the contract

For example, an employer must provide safe working conditions. Compensation for injury at work is not limited to physical harm.

Walker v *Northumberland CC* (QBD) (1994)
After suffering two nervous breakdowns brought on by an excessive workload, the plaintiff had to retire from his post as a social services officer responsible for managing four teams of 'field workers', on grounds of permanent ill-health. By the time the plaintiff suffered his second breakdown his superior ought to have foreseen the risk that returning to the same workload would cause another breakdown and termination of the plaintiff's career. In failing to provide the plaintiff with the backup he requested the defendants were in breach of their duty of care to provide a safe workplace and protect the plaintiff against psychiatric damage.

There are an increasing number of reported cases relating to actions against employers where the employee has claimed or is claiming compensation for stress related injury at work. For example two police officers, present after the Dunblane massacre, who helped parents of deceased and injured children are claiming they suffered psychological disorders as a result. It is claimed that there was no stress debriefing and that counselling was inadequate. Both officers are reported to be claiming £400,000. A former teacher at a junior school in Newport Gwent who was already suffering from work related stress was given additional duties which had to be undertaken in what had been her spare time. She accepted £254,362 from Newport County Borough Council in settlement of her claim.

In *Fraser* v *State Hospitals Board for Scotland* (Court of Session) (2000) Lord Carloway held that the relationship between an employer and employee created a relationship of sufficient proximity to create a duty not to cause the employee direct physical or psychiatric injury. However, psychiatric injury did not include unpleasant emotions such as grief, anger and resentment or normal human conditions such as anxiety or stress. This last category seems at odds with specific cases considered by Lord Carloway including the *Walker* decision.

An HSE survey has also shown that half a million United Kingdom workers suffer from work related illness. Those at particular risk include senior executives, managers, clerical and professional staff, teachers, nurses and care workers. The HSE has now prepared a draft code of practice. The code warns that workplace stress may have much greater implications than physical illness. The code expects employers to deal with stress related problems at source.

Employers who do not formulate a policy and procedures to monitor and alleviate stress in the workplace could ultimately face prosecution under the HASAWA as well as civil action by their employees.

However, in three Court of Appeal decisions this year (2002) the court has overruled the previous county court decisions, stating that the signs of stress in an employee must be obvious for an employer to be liable in negligence.

Reporting stress related symptoms once the employee has had a breakdown is too late for the employer to have broken its duty of care (*Somerset CC* v *Barber*). If *other* factors contribute to the depression the employer will not be in breach (*Liverpool CC* v *Hatton*), or if the job itself is not considered over demanding there will be no breach (*Baker Refractories* v *Bishop*). Lady Justice Hale stated, 'If there is no alternative solution, it has to be for the employee to decide whether or not to carry on in the same employment and to take the risk of a breakdown in his health or whether to leave and look for work elsewhere before he becomes unemployable'.

Where, however, an employee warned her employer of excessive workload *before* going off sick the employer was liable (*Sandwell DC* v *Jones*).

An employee must work in a safe manner.

These duties are governed both by statute and by the standards set by the principles of common law and are considered fully in the part of the chapter which deals with health and safety at work.

EXAMPLE

An employee who has been given several warnings for removing a machine guard is failing to comply with more than one statutory requirement. He is also in breach of contract and his employer is entitled to dismiss him.

It is also important to understand that the employee who does not work in a safe manner may not only be dismissed from employment but may also be liable to pay damages for breach of contract.

If the employee has been responsible for an accident and the employer has been made to pay compensation to an injured employee, the employer can in turn claim back an equivalent sum from the negligent employee, such negligence amounting to a breach of contract (*Lister* v *Romford Ice and Cold Storage Co. Ltd* (HL) (1957)).

An employer's duty of care does not extend to answering queries about a former employee's work record. In *Petch* v *Commissioners of Customs and Excise* (CA) (1993) it was held that an employee, who had suffered a mental breakdown as a consequence of his work conditions, was not owed a duty of care when his employers were answering questions about his work record. Consequently his claim for damages based on the contents of the letters they had written, failed. Dillon LJ said that this information equated with information given by an employer in a reference. But in *Spring* v *Guardian Assurance plc* (HL) (1994) the House of Lords has now overruled the earlier decision of the Court of Appeal stating that when an employer gives a reference regarding a former employee the employer *is* under a duty to take reasonable care and will be liable in negligence if it is inaccurate.

An employer must also advise an employee about any wrong doings described in a reference. In *Harris* v *TSB* (CA) (2000) the employee resigned after TSB sent a potential employer details of 17 irregularities in her work. It was held that she had been constructively dismissed.

However, unless a contract of employment is specifically one which provides an employee with particular status, there is no implied term that an employer must conduct his undertaking in a way which will not damage the employee's reputation. In *Malik and Another* v *Bank of Credit and Commerce International SA* (HL) (1997), it was widely thought that the bank had carried on business fraudulently. Employees previously untainted by the fraud were made redundant by the bank's liquidators. It was held that the bank was in breach of an implied term of the contract which required a relationship of trust with their employees. Consequently, the employees were entitled to any forseeable loss of future employment prospects.

3.3 An employee must not make use of confidential information or compete against an employer

There is, however, no overriding obligation for an employee to inform his employer of activities being undertaken outside his work. In *Nottingham University* v *Fishel* (QBD) (2000) the employee, a distinguished clinical embryologist, was employed full-time by the University. In breach of his contract, without formal consent he undertook outside work from private clinics. Even if he had told his employer what he was doing the University could not have undertaken the work without his co-operation. Therefore no loss resulted and no damages could be awarded, although the University was entitled to an account of profits less allowances in respect of work undertaken abroad by other embryologists for which he also received fees.

Contracts of employment often contain what are known as restrictive clauses, that is, clauses which prevent the employee from making use of trade secrets or business connections, or clients (known as the firm's goodwill). All of these are the 'property' of the employer.

EXAMPLE

Y is an employee in a firm of accountants. During the five years he has worked for the firm he has been personally responsible for increasing the client base from 500 to 750. The additional 250 clients 'belong' to the firm.

In order to succeed in enforcing such a clause the employer must show that the clause is reasonable. For example, in *Fitch v Dewes* (HL) (1921) a clause preventing a solicitor's managing clerk from establishing a legal practice within seven miles of the centre of Tamworth, the town where he worked, was enforceable. Although the restriction lasted a lifetime the court accepted that it was reasonable because the clients of the firm were generally lifetime clients, and in *GFI Group Inc.* v *Eaglestone* (QBD) (1994), an options broker whose customer connections had been expensively fostered at the employer's expense would have been held to an obligation under his contract to refrain from engaging in *any* business for 20 weeks after giving his employer notice but for the fact that two other employees were already working for the employee's prospective new employer.

The courts are, however, reluctant to restrict the liberty of individual employees in this way, and in *Provident Financial Group plc* v *Hayward* (CA) (1989) the Court of Appeal would not grant an injunction restraining the defendant employee from working for another company in a similar capacity (financial controller) for the three months his period of notice still had to run.

The Court of Appeal stated that the courts would not normally grant an injunction where to do so would have the effect of compelling the employee to continue working for his previous employer.

3.4 An employer must not break the trust and confidence of an employee

An employer must not break the trust and confidence of an employee, for example, by carrying out an unlawful business such that the employee could not reasonably be expected to tolerate it once it was discovered (*Bank of Credit and Commerce International SA (in liquidation)* v *Ali* (Chancery Division) (1999).

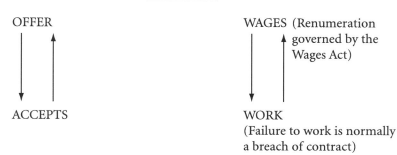

EMPLOYER

OFFER

ACCEPTS

WAGES (Renumeration
governed by the
Wages Act)

WORK
(Failure to work is normally
a breach of contract)

EMPLOYEE

4 Unfair or wrongful dismissal

The preceding section dealt with the formation of the contract of employment, and
the rights and responsibilities which arise once the contract comes into existence.

The following section deals with the rights of an employee not to be either unfairly
or wrongfully dismissed.

4.1 Unfair dismissal

4.1.1 Qualifying period

Subject to the exceptions mentioned later on, under the Employment Rights Act 1996,
a dismissed employee could not bring a claim for unfair dismissal unless continuously
employed for a period of not less than two years (s. 108) ending with the effective date
of termination.

The qualifying start date relates to when employment begins with a new employer.
In *Northern General Hospital National Health Service Trust* v *Gale* (EAT) (1993) the
employee had worked for the Sheffield Health Authority as a student nurse since
November 1987. From July 1990 he worked solely at the Northern General Hospital,
although at this time his contract provided that he agreed to gain experience anywhere in the Sheffield health district. When he was given a full-time post at the
Northern General Hospital on 3 May 1991 it had become a National Health Service
Trust and it was held that this employment was with a different employer so that
when he was unfairly dismissed in 1992 he did not have the necessary two years'
service to make a claim.

An employee who has been continuously employed by the transferor of an undertaking for more than two years (now one year) will be eligible to claim unfair dismissal. The continuity will not be broken by the processes which may take place whilst
the business is being transferred. In *Clark and Tokeley Ltd (t/a Spellbrook Ltd)* v *Oakes*
(CA) (1998) Mr Oakes was dismissed by the liquidators of his former employer's
company on 14 March 1996. Between that date and 21 March, when the business was
acquired by the transferee, the business ticked over. Mr Oakes stayed on together with

a few other employees to provide continuity commencing employment with the transferee on March 21. He was then dismissed by them on 2 April 1996.

The Court of Appeal held that the transfer of an undertaking would be treated as a process and the evidence showed that Mr Oakes was dismissed by the liquidator *during* this process. Consequently he was still employed at the time of transfer. His continuity of employment had not been broken up to the time when he was subsequently dismissed by the transferee on 2 April. He was therefore eligible to claim unfair dismissal and on the full finding of facts by the tribunal the Court of Appeal concluded that the dismissal was unfair.

Work rights are also preserved between subsidiaries which are distinct legal persons. *Allen* v *Amalgamated Construction Co. Ltd* (ECJ Case C234/98) (1999).

The majority of employees affected by the rules are women. In *R* v *Secretary of State for Employment ex parte Equal Opportunities Commission* (HL) (1994), the House of Lords, overruling the Court of Appeal, granted a declaration that the threshold conditions were incompatible with EC law. The declaration was granted against the Secretary of State who had failed to make a case that the rules brought about an increase in the availability of part-time work, i.e a change in UK legislation was therefore needed. However, in *R* v *Secretary of State for Employment ex parte Seymour-Smith and Another* (HL) (1997), the House of Lords was not prepared to uphold a declaration that the two-year qualifying period was discriminatory by the time the Court of Appeal made its judgment in 1995. Evidence, in fact, showed that by 1993 the gap between men and women who qualified for protection for unfair dismissal had narrowed. It was however appropriate for the matter to be referred to the European Court of Justice to ascertain whether as a matter of general principle the two-year rule contravened Article 119 of the European Treaty (if so found then UK law would have to be changed to ensure compatibility with Community law).

In February 1999 the ECJ ruled that a judicial award of compensation constituted pay and the conditions determining whether an employee was entitled where he had been unfairly dismissed fell within Article 119. It was for the national court to take account of all the material legal and factual circumstances to ascertain at what point in time the legality of the two year rule should be assessed. In order to ascertain the legality it must be shown that a significantly smaller percentage of women than men qualified for unfair dismissal. If there was a significantly smaller number the state must show that the rule reflected a legitimate social aim—that the aim was unrelated to any discrimination based on sex—that the member state could reasonably consider that the means chosen were suitable for attaining that aim.

Applying these principles on 17 February 2000 the House of Lords ruled that the prima facie discrimination was justified and although the two year qualifying period had now been reduced to one year this only applied where the effective date of termination was after 1 June 1999.

4.1.2 The Part-time Workers (Prevention of Less Favourable Treatment) Regulations 2000

The Secretary of State has now made regulations under s. 19 of the Employment Relations Act 1999 to ensure that persons in part-time employment are not treated less favourably than those employed full-time. The regulations specify the class of persons taken to be in part-time employment (not identified as full-time) and the circumstances in which they are deemed to be treated less favourably than full-time employees. This is with regard to terms of their contract or other detrimental treatment. However, a part-time employee paid at a lower overtime rate than a full-time employee will not be regarded as being treated less favourably where the hours worked by the part-timer including overtime do not exceed the comparable number of hours the full-time employee is expected to work (reg. 4 (4)). Part-time employees are also entitled to written statements for reasons of less favourable treatment (reg. 6). The Regulations enable tribunals and the EAT to hear complaints relating to infringements (reg. 8) and for unfair dismissal (reg. 7).

Note: The powers that conciliation officers appointed by ACAS have to conciliate tribunal claims also apply to cases brought under reg. 5 (less favourable treatment): the Part-time Workers (Prevention of Less Favourable Treatment) Regulations 2001. The Secretary of State will also issue a code of practice (s. 20, Employment Relations Act 1999).

4.2 Wrongful dismissal

While the qualifying periods in respect of *unfair dismissal* remain, employees who do not qualify may, nevertheless, bring an action for *wrongful dismissal.*

Dietmann v *Brent London Borough Council* (CA) (1988)

A child died as a result of injuries inflicted by the mother's cohabitee. During this time the child was in the council's care. In a subsequent report both the child's social worker and the plaintiff, the social worker's supervisor, were stated to have been grossly negligent. The plaintiff's contract incorporated a disciplinary procedure which stated that employees could be instantly dismissed for gross misconduct.

After the report had been published the council dismissed the plaintiff summarily (instantly) without giving her the chance to appear before a disciplinary panel.

The plaintiff claimed damages for wrongful dismissal and the court found in her favour for two reasons:

(a) Although the plaintiff may have been guilty of gross negligence this did not automatically equate with the term gross misconduct referred to in the plaintiff's contract of employment; gross misconduct meant in this case either dishonest or disruptive conduct. Therefore the council was not entitled to dismiss the plaintiff *without notice*. Disciplinary procedures which are this specific must be very carefully worded.

(b) Even if the plaintiff's gross negligence had amounted to gross misconduct the plaintiff was still entitled to a disciplinary hearing.

Consequently the plaintiff was entitled to damages for breach of contract from the date the council had repudiated (revoked) the contract, to the date when it could have lawfully terminated and held a disciplinary hearing.

Compensation for wrongful dismissal will therefore reflect the loss arising from the employer's breach of contract. Since the object of damages is to place the person in the position (financially) as if the *contract* had not been broken, the court may not take account of any prior *statutory awards* made by an employment tribunal.

In *O'Laoire* v *Jackel International Ltd (No. 2)* (CA) (1991) the plaintiff had been employed as a deputy managing director when he was dismissed. The Court of Appeal was obliged to accept the earlier finding of a tribunal, that the plaintiff had a contractual right eventually to become the company managing director. This meant that his claim in court, for the loss of the managing directorship, did not come under the same head as the compensation of £8,000 already awarded by the tribunal under the statute. Accordingly the plaintiff was entitled to an additional sum representing one month's salary as deputy managing director and five months' salary as managing director. The same principle was applied in *Hopkins* v *Norcros plc* (1994). A wrongfully dismissed employee was entitled to payments from his employer's pension fund and damages for wrongful dismissal could be recovered without deduction of the pension payments, i.e., he had paid pension contributions from his own money and, therefore, they were a separate heading.

Employees who have been dismissed are under a duty to mitigate their loss. In *Cerberus Software Ltd* v *Rowley* (2001) John A Rowley had been shabbily treated when he was summarily dismissed but his contract did not give him an express right to six months salary in lieu of notice. Within a few weeks from the date of the dismissal he found better paid employment. Compensation for wrongful dismissal—breach of contact—could therefore only relate to the time he was unemployed.

Tribunals may now award compensation necessary to put the employee in the same position as if the contract had not been broken, if an order for reinstatement or re-engagement has not been complied with (ss. 117 and 124(3), Employment Rights Act 1996). Tribunals and EATs also have the power to award costs or expenses under clause 22 of the Employment Bill 2001.

In *Le Marechal* v *WSS (Western) Ltd* (CA) (1992) it was stated that the discretion given to the court to grant a new trial where damages for wrongful dismissal had been wrongly and excessively calculated was to be exercised with great caution.

Since 1994 tribunals have had jurisdiction to hear cases for claims for damages for breach of contract—including a situation where a person has contracted to work and the contract is terminated before they start (*Sarker* v *South Tees Acute Hospitals NHS Trust* (EAT) (1997)). However, unlike arbitrators whose jurisdiction is based entirely on the consent of the parties, an employment tribunal derives its jurisdiction from statute and the rules of procedure within the statute. Consequently when a case is remitted by the EAT to a tribunal to determine specific issues a tribunal does not have the jurisdiction to consider other matters.

In *Aparau* v *Iceland Frozen Foods plc* (CA) (1999) the case had been remitted to a tribunal to consider issues relating to wrongful dismissal. The tribunal also allowed the company solicitors to raise the fairness of the dismissal concluding that Mrs Aparau had not been unfairly dismissed. Mrs Aparau appealed against this decision but the decision was upheld by the EAT. The Court of Appeal, however, stated that the tribunal was wrong to re-open the matter itself, even with the tacit consent of the parties.

No doubt, had the tribunal found in favour of Mrs Aparau she would not have lodged these subsequent appeals on a procedural issue.

Ironically, however, it has now been discovered that due to the Tribunals Act 1996 being poorly drafted it is not possible to appeal from a tribunal case involving breach of contract. Whereas s. 136 of the Employment Protection (Consolidation) Act 1978 allowed appeals on a question of law arising from any decision of an employment tribunal, including the 1978 Act itself, similar wording has not been used to allow appeals based on a tribunal's jurisdiction under the 1996 Act.

5 Unfair dismissal—a detailed consideration

When the Employment Protection (Consolidation) Act 1978 applies to an employee who has been dismissed they may claim that they have been unfairly dismissed.

In order to establish that an individual is an employee they must show that there is sufficient control over them by the person they are claiming is their employer. In *Montgomery* v *Johnson Underwood Ltd* (CA) (2001) the Court of Appeal held that an employment agency did not exercise sufficient control to establish the applicant as an employee to make them eligible to bring an action for unfair dismissal.

Once the employee has satisfied one of the qualifying periods discussed earlier there are three further factors to consider:

(a) Has the complaint been lodged in time?

(b) How was the employee's contract terminated?

(c) What was the reason for the dismissal?

A potential claimant should also note that since December 2000 tribunals have power to award costs of up to £10,000 against them, if they are unsuccessful; an increase of £9,500. The deposit for an applicant is also increased from £150 to £500.

5.1 Has the complaint been lodged in time?

Nowadays employees have three months from the effective date of their dismissal in which to lodge their complaint (s. 111(2), Employment Rights Act 1996). The time limit was not always so generous. It used to be as short as four weeks, and, to make matters worse, confusion could arise over the precise date on which the employee had been dismissed.

The legislation was not clear, when an employee was dismissed without notice, whether the day of dismissal was the day on which they were told to leave the premises at which they worked, or the day on which notice would have expired, if it had been given.

The legislation now covers both situations (Employment Rights Act 1996, s. 97).

EXAMPLE

X is dismissed on 31 July with one month's notice. X has three months from 31 August in which to lodge a complaint.

Y is dismissed on 31 July without notice and is told to leave immediately. Y was entitled in the contract to one month's notice. Y, therefore, still has three months from 31 August in which to lodge a complaint.

Before the law was changed employees may well have found that their case, however good, could not be heard by a tribunal because the complaint was lodged 'out of time'.

Dedman v British Building and Engineering Appliances Ltd (CA) (1974)

The plaintiff worked for the defendants as a contracts manager. Without warning he was dismissed on 5 May.

He sought advice from a firm of solicitors who did not lodge his complaint until 23 June. The tribunal considered that he was dismissed on 5 May and therefore the complaint had not been lodged within the four weeks allowed at that time.

The legislation does allow an extension of time if 'it was not reasonably practicable' to lodge the complaint within the time limit. Because Mr Dedman had sought legal advice, the tribunal considered it had been practicable to lodge within the four weeks allowed.

Now that the time limit has been extended to three months, either from the date notice expired, if given, or when it would have expired if given, tribunals are reluctant to give a complainant any further time in which to lodge a complaint.

G W Stephens and Son v Fish (EAT) (1989)

The tribunal in this case, however, took the view that the time limit did not run from the date of the original letter of dismissal.

In 1977 the employee started work as a full time coach driver. His main duty was to drive coal miners to and from their place of work, although he did drive others as well.

In January 1987 his employers lost the contract to transport the miners. On 19 January the plaintiff was given a letter of dismissal, but he did continue working on a part-time basis.

On 27 April 1987 the plaintiff lodged a complaint for unfair dismissal. It was held that, although the letter of 19 January repudiated the full time contract, the plaintiff needed reasonable time to consider if he accepted this repudiation.

When he lodged his complaint this was evidence that he had accepted his employer's repudiation. Therefore the complaint was lodged in time (technically the time limit therefore ran for three months from 27 April).

Draft Regulations laid before Parliament now allow complaints regarding less favourable treatment of fixed-term contract employees. These will also have to be presented within three months of an alleged infringement. For this purpose an infringement will take place on each day of the period during which treatment is less favourable.

5.1.1 Presenting a complaint outside the three-month period

An industrial tribunal may hear a complaint of unfair dismissal more than three months after the contract was terminated if the tribunal considers that it was not practicable for the complaint to be presented before the end of the three-month period (s. 111(2)(b), Employment Rights Act 1996).

The Draft Regulations regarding fixed-term employees also allow tribunals to consider complaints out of time if it is just and equitable to do so.

Marley (UK) Ltd v *Anderson* (EAT) (1994)

The employee was dismissed on 15 November 1991. The reason given was redundancy. His original complaint was not presented until 23 April 1992. On 18 March 1992 the employee discovered that he had probably been dismissed in connection with his work capabilities. He saw specific written evidence to this effect on 24 October 1992. On 9 November 1992 the originating application was amended to add the new complaint. The industrial (now employment) tribunal to which the complaint was lodged ruled it did not have jurisdiction to hear the complaint. On appeal the EAT ruled:

(a) Once sufficient new evidence had come to light (24 October) this was further ground for presenting a complaint outside the three-month period beginning with the effective date of termination. Until this time it had not been reasonably practicable to present a fresh complaint.

(b) All relevant circumstances then needed to be considered to ascertain if the complaint had been presented in reasonable time. In this respect the tribunal had erred in law in saying it did not have jurisdiction because the complaint, based on the second ground, was delayed for over four weeks from when the employee *first* suspected (18 March 1992) that he had been given the wrong reason for dismissal.

Accordingly the case was remitted for consideration by the tribunal.

The offer of another job within the three month period will not make it reasonably impracticable to present a claim within the statutory time limit. In *Noel v London Underground Ltd* (CA) (1999) Ms Noel was employed as a station supervisor from 1990 until 10 April 1997. After an incident involving a passenger she was dismissed. Her internal appeal on 23 April 1997 against the dismissal failed, but a company director reviewed the case and she was offered another job which was at a lower grade and salary. When she underwent a medical examination traces of cannabis were found in her system and the offer of alternative employment was withdrawn on 28 July 1997. She lodged a complaint for unfair dismissal.

The Court of Appeal reversed the decision of the EAT that the tribunal did have the jurisdiction to hear the complaint. It held that the new job was a demotion and the offer could not have rectified the fairness of the dismissal although the employer may have relied on this offer to oppose reinstatement. The tribunal may have decided to make a basic award of compensation. These were, however, separate issues to that of the complaint being lodged in time. It was reasonably practicable for the employee to have lodged her complaint before a tribunal, within the three month period from the effective date of dismissal.

5.2 How was the employee's contract terminated?

Under the current legislation an employee's contract may be terminated in three different ways (s. 95(1), Employment Rights Act 1996):

(a) When the employer terminates the contract either with or without notice, i.e. the employee is dismissed by the employer.

(b) When a fixed term contract is not renewed.

EXAMPLE

X works as a teacher and has been given a series of one year fixed term contracts over a period of five years. In year six, X's contract is not renewed. X has been dismissed and is eligible to bring an action for unfair dismissal. X must then prove that the employer has dismissed him or her unfairly. The plaintiff was able to do this in *Ford* v *Warwickshire County Council* (HL) (1983), where the reason given by the employer was not a satisfactory reason.

Draft Regulations have been laid before Parliament to ensure that fixed-term employees do not receive less favourable rights than those not on fixed terms with regard to:

(a) terms of employment; or

(b) by being subjected to any other detriment by any act or deliberate failure to act.

This does not however apply to either pay or membership of or rights under an occupational pension scheme.

The Draft Regulations also state that as well as circumstances mentioned in s. 95 of the 1996 Act an employee shall be regarded as being:

(a) dismissed if his contract of employment terminates automatically on the completion of a particular task or the occurrence or non-occurrence of an event;

(b) dismissed if his employment is not renewed;

(c) unfairly dismissed if the reason for non-renewal is that the employee has:

(i)   brought proceedings against the employer under these regulations;

(ii)   requested a written statement about less favourable treatment;

(iii) given evidence in connection with proceedings against an employer;

(iv)   done *anything* under the regulations;

(v)   made allegations of infringement;

(vi)   refused to give up a right conferred by the regulations; or that the employer believes or suspects the employee has done or intends to do any of the above.

Note: Employers are prohibited from including unfair dismissal waiver in fixed term employment contracts (s. 18, Employment Relations Act 1999).

(c)   When the *employee* terminates the contract because of the employer's conduct. This is known as a constructive dismissal.

EXAMPLE

The plaintiff was employed as an assistant area manager in London and was then told to work in Liverpool as a retail stock controller. Shortly after the move he suffered a nervous breakdown. When he returned to work he requested an interview with the company's personnel director. When this was refused he resigned. It was held that (i) he had been dismissed and (ii) the dismissal was unfair (*Wetherall (Bond Street W.1) Ltd* v *Lynn* (EAT) (1978)).

When the employers are continuously in breach of a material condition of the terms of employment it is open to the employee to rely on this as a reason for terminating the contract.

Reid v *Camphill Engravers* (EAT) (1990)

The plaintiff worked for the defendants as a shoe repairer. He became aware that he was not being paid the statutory minimum wage and for three years made a number of requests for his pay to be increased. Finally he terminated his employment.

It was held that even if the employee had not reacted to his employer's initial breach, it was always open to him to rely on subsequent breaches which occurred each time his employers paid him less than the wage laid down by statute. Consequently he was constructively dismissed and the dismissal was unfair.

Fear of a *future* substantial change will not be grounds on which to claim unfair dismissal. In *Sita (GB) Ltd* v *Burton and Others* (EAT) (1996) two employees resigned and claimed constructive dismissal because of a fear that an impending transfer of undertaking would substantially change their conditions of employment. The EAT held that the appropriate claim, if one existed, would, however, be under the Transfer of Undertakings (Protection of Employment) Regulations 1981.

5.3 What was the reason given for the dismissal?

An industrial tribunal may not dismiss a complaint at the beginning of a hearing before hearing evidence because it considers that the complaint has no reasonable grounds of success (*Care First Partnership Ltd* v *Roffey and Others* (CA) (2000)).

When dismissing an employee an employer must give, in writing if so requested, one of the reasons listed below, or some other substantial reason (s. 98(1), Employment Rights Act 1996). When considering this a tribunal must look at the reason given, both at the time of dismissal and when the contract of employment terminates if they are not synonymous (*Parkinson* v *March Consulting Ltd* (CA) (1997)).

5.3.1 Capability

Although the statute uses the word 'capability', this really means that an employee can be dismissed for lack of capability. There are a variety of reasons why an employee may not be capable of continuing to do their job to the satisfaction of their employer.

EXAMPLE

A medical condition which has developed since the employee's original date of employment which prevents the employee working fast enough. If an employee is to be dismissed on medical grounds it is, however, important that the employer acts reasonably.

Acting in a reasonable manner means that medical evidence must be considered before the employee is dismissed.

Slaughter v C Brewer and Sons Ltd (EAT) (1990)

The employee suffered pains in her neck and shoulders which prevented her from performing part of her duties, namely unloading delivery lorries. At the end of May 1988 although she agreed to obtain a medical report she refused the employers' offer of a job in their sales office. She was then dismissed.

It was held that the employers had acted unreasonably in dismissing her; they should have obtained a detailed medical report and warned her that she was likely to be dismissed if she refused the offer of alternative employment.

Medical evidence must be unbiased.

East Lindsey District Council v Daubney (EAT) (1977)

The council's personnel director asked the district community physician to indicate whether he felt that Mr Daubney's 'health was such that he should be retired on the grounds of permanent ill health'.

The report which followed was sent direct to the personnel director and, without being given a chance to discuss the matter, Mr Daubney was dismissed.

The dismissal was held to be unfair because neutral language should have been used by the personnel director and no consultation had taken place between the employer and employee after the report had been received.

But in Mitchell v Arkswood Plastics (Engineering) Ltd (EAT) (1993) it was held that an employee was not under an equivalent duty to indicate to his employer what his prospects of recovery were from ill-health.

5.3.2 Qualifications

If an employee gives false information about their qualifications they can be dismissed regardless of how well they might be performing their contractual duties, or for how long they have been working.

EXAMPLE

'Walter Mitty', lecturer, lived an eight-year lie. On 14 October 1991 Paul Carey was given a two-year suspended prison sentence when he admitted before a Crown Court judge that he had obtained pecuniary advantage by deception.

Mid Glamorgan Education Authority had employed Carey over a period of eight years and had paid him £80,000 before they discovered that, as opposed to the eight 'O' levels, two 'A' levels, Bachelor of Education degree and post-graduate diploma which Carey had claimed to have, he had, in fact, five CSE passes. Needless to say, an earlier attempt by Carey to claim unfair dismissal was unsuccessful.

5.3.3 Conduct

Although the statute states that an employee can be dismissed in relation to their 'conduct', in practice this means for misconduct. Misconduct can take many forms and can range from acts of minor misconduct (e.g. occasional lateness) to gross misconduct (e.g. assaulting another employee at the work place).

As already seen in cases like *Dietmann* v *Brent London Borough Council* (CA) (1988), it is also of vital importance for the employer to have a comprehensive disciplinary procedure and, even in cases of alleged gross negligence, to give the employee the opportunity to state their case.

An employer must therefore always act reasonably when dismissing an employee on grounds of misconduct. However the test of reasonableness is not the same in unfair dismissal cases as it is, for example, in a criminal prosecution.

Parr v *Whitbread and Co. plc* (EAT) (1990)

The applicant and three other employees were dismissed when a sum of money was stolen in circumstances where each of the dismissed staff had an equal opportunity of committing the theft. It was held that because the company had carried out a satisfactory investigation to identify those responsible and they reasonably believed that one or more of the four had committed the theft, the applicant had been fairly dismissed.

In an earlier case which went to the Court of Appeal, when two employees had been dismissed on suspicion of theft, Sir David Cairns said the matter had to be looked at in a way 'an ordinary business man would look at it'. Since there were solid and sensible grounds on which the employer could infer or suspect dishonesty both dismissals were fair (*Monie* v *Coral Racing Ltd* (CA) (1981)). Whether or not the particular offence has been committed by the employee is therefore irrelevant, providing that the employer had reasonable grounds at the time of the dismissal for thinking that he had.

In *Ferodo Ltd* v *Barnes* (EAT) (1976) the reason for the dismissal was that after repeated warnings the employers were dissatisfied with the employee's conduct. They considered they were justified in dismissing him after an act of vandalism in their factory toilet which no-one actually saw the employee carry out. The dismissal was held to be fair because the employers had reasonable grounds for thinking it was the employee who had committed the offence.

Where an investigation into the employee's alleged misconduct is necessary it must be full and thorough; if it is insufficient, the test of reasonableness will not be satisfied.

In *Linford Cash and Carry Ltd* v *Thomson and others* (EAT) (1989), dismissing three employees for allegedly forging credit notes, on the uncorroborated statement of one anonymous employee, was held to be unfair.

Evidence may be precluded if it cannot be disclosed on the grounds of national security.

Balfour v Foreign and Commonwealth Office (CA) (1994)

It was held inappropriate for an industrial (now employment) tribunal to go behind a ministerial certificate claiming that national security would be imperilled by disclosure of documents. This is, however, a balancing exercise and since *Conway* v *Rimmer* (1968) it is the court's decision, i.e., there is no absolute immunity from disclosure.

5.4 Effect of further evidence of misconduct

Once an employer has given the reason or reasons for dismissal he is precluded from raising subsequent reasons, after the dismissal has taken place, although further evidence of misconduct may affect the *amount* of compensation a tribunal is prepared to award. This point was established in *W Devis and Sons Ltd* v *Atkins* (HL) (1977), where Lord Diplock stated that if the legislation then in force had allowed an employee who had successfully concealed his fraud until after the date of dismissal, to claim compensation, it would convert the provisions for unfair dismissal 'into a veritable rogue's charter'.

As a consequence of the case the law was changed, and since the Employment Act 1980 an employee is only entitled to any compensation if 'it is just and equitable'.

5.5 The test of reasonableness

To satisfy the test of reasonableness an employer's approach must be the same towards all employees.

Cain v Leeds Western Health Authority (EAT) (1990)

The employee, who worked in a hospital laundry, was dismissed on the ground of gross misconduct for fighting with another employee.

In his submission the employee referred to four cases where employees of the authority had not been dismissed for gross misconduct. Two cases dealt with seven years earlier were rejected as evidence by the tribunal.

The appeals tribunal held that the tribunal should have taken account of all cases cited by the appellant relating to gross misconduct of other employees of the authority.

Acting reasonably means that the employer can take an overview of the employee's conduct. In this respect the final straw which 'breaks the camel's back' and leads to the employee being dismissed can, in itself, be of a minor nature.

Varied but persistent acts of misconduct eventually add up to gross misconduct, as the example disciplinary procedure at the end of this section shows.

In *Auguste Noel Ltd* v *Curtis* (EAT) (1990) the final reason for dismissal was that the employee had damaged two cheeses. Because there had been two previous warnings, within five months, about other acts of misconduct, the dismissal was held to be fair.

5.6 Redundancy

5.6.1 Customary arrangement for selection for redundancy

An employee becomes redundant when the job they were doing ceases to exist.

An employee . . . shall be taken to be dismissed by reason of redundancy if the dismissal is attributable wholly or mainly to . . . the fact that the requirements of [the] business for employees to carry out work of a particular kind . . . have . . . diminished. (Section 11(2) of the Contracts of Employment and Redundancy Payment Act (Northern Ireland) 1965. The current English equivalent is s. 98(2)(c) and s. 139(1)(b)(i) of the Employment Rights Act 1996.)

The House of Lords held in *Murray* v *Foyle Meats Ltd* (HL) (1999) that this means there is no reason in law why the dismissal of an employee should not be attributable to a diminution in the employer's need for employees, irrespective of the terms of their contract or the function which they perform. Therefore, when a decline in Foyle Meats' business occurred, employees who normally worked in the slaughter hall, but who had contracts which also required them to work elsewhere, could be selected for redundancy. Their employer was not required to select employees who had similar contracts but who worked elsewhere.

The House of Lords did, however, state that the dismissal of an employee who could perfectly well have been *re-deployed* or who had been doing work *unaffected* by the fall in demand might require some explanation to establish the necessary casual connection. For example it might be difficult for an employer to justify the dismissal, on the ground of redundancy, of an employee fulfilling a statutory function (e.g. a safety officer appointed to ensure compliance with the Management of Health and Safety at Work Regulations 1999).

Under such circumstances a dismissed employee would be likely succeed in an action for unfair dismissal. Where no customary arrangement exists for employees to be selected for redundancy, an employer may select employees according to the requirements of the business or organisation.

EXAMPLE

X Ltd fails to secure an order. It becomes necessary to make more than 300 employees redundant. It is not unfair, if *no specific arrangement already exists*, for X Ltd to make those redundant from areas of work no longer needed.

Where a customary arrangement exists, an employer must consult with unions prior to dismissal, and/or employees prior to dismissal on matters such as the exact timing of the redundancies and the employees to be selected for redundancy. In *Joshua Wilson and Bros Ltd* v *Union of Shop Distributive and Allied Workers* (EAT) (1978) the owners of a wholesale cash and carry warehouse who had made 21 men redundant were held to be in breach of their obligation to consult representatives of USDAW before issuing redundancy notices. In *Polkey* v *A E Dayton Services Ltd* (HL) (1988) the House of Lords remitted the case to a tribunal for rehearing, stating that at least some aspects of the *manner* of the dismissal should be considered to determine if an employer had acted in a reasonable, and therefore fair, way.

In *Walls Meat Co. Ltd* v *Selby* (CA) (1989) negotiations had taken place prior to notices of dismissal being issued, but between the date notices were given out (15 March) and the date of the employee's dismissal no further negotiations took place. The Court of Appeal upheld the tribunal's decision that the employer had acted unfairly.

Where no customary arrangement exists, an employer is obliged to consult union representatives under the Trade Union and Labour Relations (Consolidation) Act 1992, s. 188, once matters reach the stage where a specific proposal has been formulated (*Hough and others* v *Leyland DAF Ltd* (EAT) (1991). A recognised trade union may complain to a tribunal if this is not complied with.

R v *British Coal Corporation ex parte Vardy* (QBD) (1993)
Decisions had been made to close 10 collieries and review the future of 21 without any consultation with applicable unions. The court decided the appropriate remedy was a declaration that British Coal should not reach a decision on the closures nor should the Secretary of State make available funds to enable British Coal to reach a decision until the correct review procedure had been followed.

If the employee is not represented by a union the employer should negotiate with individual employees. In *Vokes* v *Bear* (NIRC) (1974) a works manager who was dismissed by his employers without warning, and in circumstances described as lacking any humanitarian approach, was held to be entitled to compensation for unfair dismissal.

Despite the examples referred to above there have been decisions, upheld on appeal, where tribunals have not found for the employee. In *British United Shoe Machinery Co. Ltd* v *Clarke* (EAT) (1978) it was accepted that, as there were no alternative jobs and consultation with the employee would have made no difference to him being made redundant, he had not been unfairly dismissed. This was also the view of the Lord Chancellor in the *Polkey* case referred to earlier.

However, it is always sound to advise an employer to consult with individual employees before they are dismissed in order to maintain, as far as possible, good industrial relations and the possibility of a successful case based on lack of reasonable procedure.

5.6.2 Offer of similar work
When an employee is made redundant, if similar work is available the employer should offer this work to the employee. The employer should make a reasonable effort to contact the employee if the latter is no longer at the place of work.

Octavius Atkinson and Sons Ltd v *Morris* (EAT) (1988)
The employee who was a steel erector was made redundant when the job on which he was working was completed. That day, although he left work at 2.00pm, according to a national agreement he was still employed at 4.00pm when another job became avail-

able. By failing to make any effort to contact him at home it was held that the employers had not acted fairly.

The work offered must be of a similar nature.

EXAMPLE

X is employed as a receptionist and is offered a job as a cleaner. He would be entitled to refuse this and would not prejudice his right to redundancy payment. Where the principal reason for the dismissal is redundancy, but it is shown that the employee was selected on grounds relating to union membership this is unfair (Trade Union and Labour Relations (Consolidation) Act 1992, s. 153). There is no qualifying period of employment to bring such a claim (s. 154).

An employee who has been employed continuously for two years or more who is given notice of redundancy is entitled to take reasonable paid time off, during working hours, before the notice expires, to look for new employment or arrange training (Employment Rights Act 1996, ss. 52 and 53).

5.6.3 Transfer of undertakings

Under the Transfer of Undertakings (Protection of Employment) Regulations 1981, employees' rights are protected when an undertaking is transferred from one employer to another. (See for example *Clark Tokeley Ltd (t/a Spellbrook Ltd) v Oakes* (1998) at p. 215). When the transfer involves a substantial and detrimental change in the employee's terms and conditions of employment the employee may terminate his employment, treat themselves as being constructively dismissed (under reg. 4(A) and bring an action against the employer/*transferor* under reg. 5(5). In *Humphreys* v *Oxford University* (CA) (2000) the claimant who was employed to set, mark and moderate GCSE and A level examinations, correctly brought his action against the University of Oxford Delegacy of Local Examinations for wrongful dismissal and not the Associated Examining Board to which the business of the Delegacy had been transferred on 31 March 1995. These regulations will not be applicable when the employer is the same in the new and old undertaking.

In *Governing Body of Clifton Middle School and Others* v *Askew* (CA) (1999) Mr Askew was employed by the local authority, Ealing London Borough Council, at a middle school sharing the same site with a first school. When the local authority decided to amalgamate the two schools Mr Askew was made redundant. At an earlier tribunal hearing it had been decided that Mrs Askew's dismissal by way of redundancy was not unfair. The second issue related to whether he had acquired rights in respect of employment at the new single primary school under the management of a new governing body. The Court of Appeal upheld the EAT ruling that the opening of a new school had not resulted in a change of employer and therefore there was no relevant transfer of undertaking to give rise to a potentially unfair dismissal.

5.6.4 Continuity of employment

Under the Employment Protection (Continuity of Employment) Regulations 1996 an employee's continuity of employment is preserved when he is dismissed and subsequently reinstated or re-employed after, for example making a claim in accordance with a dismissals procedures agreement.

Note that under the Redundancy Payments (Continuity in Local Government etc) (Modification) (Amendment) Order 2001 an individual's service with a succession of local authorities and similar bodies is treated as continuous for the purpose of determining entitlement to a redundancy payment.

5.6.5 Insolvency

An employee of a company which becomes insolvent is entitled to recover redundancy payment from the Secretary of State for Trade and Industry. Currently eligibility for payments is determined by an employment tribunal. However, in *Smith* v *Secretary of State for Trade and Industry* (EAT) (1999) this process was held to be contrary to Article 6 of the European Convention on Human Rights which by October 2000 will be enforced in the Human Rights Act 1998. Article 6 requires, when determining civil rights, everyone to have a fair and public hearing by an independent and impartial tribunal. The EAT held that because employment tribunals have such close links with an executive arm of the Government (a Department of Trade and Industry Agency) they were not independent. Mr Smith's appeal was allowed with further leave to appeal to argue that an employment tribunal could not adjudicate on his complaint. The EAT also held that the tribunal had erred in law in finding that Mr Smith was not an employee who might be entitled to a redundancy payment.

Since this case new appointment procedures have been adopted to ensure there is no reason for any lay member of a tribunal to curry favour by leaning in favour of the Secretary of State in a hearing. Consequently in *Scanfuture UK Ltd* v *Secretary of State for Trade and Industry: Link* v *Same* (EAT) (2000) two cases heard in April 1999, before the rules were changed, were remitted by the EAT to be heard again by a panel composed of members appointed under the new system of open competition.

5.7 Strike action

An employee who goes on unofficial strike may be dismissed. An employee who goes on official strike is protected from dismissal up to the eighth week of the strike (sch. 5, Employment Relations Act 1999).

McKenzie v *Crosville Motor Services Ltd* (EAT) (1990)

In this case it was stated that when an employee is absent during the time of a strike it is their responsibility to inform their employer of the reason for their absence. The plaintiff had been absent from work for five days during which others were on strike. He subsequently claimed that this was for a number of reasons and that he had not been participating in the strike.

It was held by the tribunal that he should have informed his employers, at the time of his absence, that he was not deliberately withdrawing his labour. His dismissal was not, therefore, unfair.

As well as notifying the employer in writing of intended industrial action the union must also describe in writing the employees who have taken or intend to take part in industrial action, and when this is intended, thereby making it easier for the employer to identify the strikers (Trade Union Reform and Employment Rights Act 1993, s. 21). The notice must be at least seven days before the industrial action and after a ballot has been held. If the union does not do this it is not protected from actions in tort by an employer.

It should be noted that under s. 237 of the 1992 Act an employee who goes on *unofficial strike* is precluded from *complaining* to an employment tribunal that he or she has been unfairly dismissed.

A strike is unofficial unless:

(a) the employee is a member of a trade union and the action is authorised or endorsed by the union or a responsible person (e.g. a union official);

(b) there are others who are members taking part if he is not a member.

Under s. 238 of the 1992 Act if an employer waits for three months he may take back, on a selective basis, employees who have been on strike. This enables an employer not to re-employ those he regards, rightly or wrongly, as the 'troublemakers'.

It is possible to dismiss *all* employees who have taken part in strike action and take back some on a selective basis after three months. If only a selected few are taken back within three months, those who are discriminated against are entitled to compensation for unfair dismissal.

In *Crosville Wales Ltd* v *Tracey* (CA) (1995), 73 employees who had taken part in industrial action were unfairly discriminated against when they were dismissed and 22 of their colleagues were re-employed. With regard to their compensation, taking part in such action could not be regarded as grounds for reducing the amount payable to them. The House of Lords has upheld this decision (October 1997). In their Lordships' judgment it was concluded that it is impossible to allocate individual blame in respect of collective industrial action—it has to be shared by all who took part, including those who were taken back on. Therefore any reduction of compensation given to an employee who was not re-engaged should only be what was just and equitable for the individual. This applied whether or not the victimisation was deliberate.

In order for a union to gain protection from liability in tort for acts inducing persons to take part in or continue with industrial action the union must have the support of a ballot. A ballot will not be invalid under the Employment Act 1990 s. 7(3)(a), if some members of the union are already on strike (*Newham London Borough Council* v *National and Local Government Officers Association* (CA) (1993)).

An employee who makes a complaint of unfair treatment arising from an employer's action under s. 238 has six months, beginning with the date of dismissal, in which to lodge the complaint (s. 239).

5.7.2 No compulsion to work
Freedom exists on both sides, however, in that employees cannot be legally compelled,

by the issue of an order of specific performance or an order to implement a contract of employment, to do any work or attend at any place of work.

Employees cannot be restrained by an injunction from threatening to break or breaking their contract (Trade Union and Labour Relations (Consolidation) Act 1992, s. 236).

5.8 Breach of statutory restriction

Under s. 98(2)(d) of the Employment Rights Act 1996, it is unlawful to employ a person if to do so contravenes a statutory provision, e.g. where legislation requires a person to be registered to undertake certain duties. However, in *Sutcliffe and Eaton Ltd v R Pinney* (EAT) (1977), Mr Pinney was dismissed from his job as a hearing aid dispenser after he had failed his examination and his name was removed from the register of hearing aid dispensers making it illegal to act as a dispenser. He had applied for an extension to sit the exam again and to continue to employ him for other duties would not, in itself, have been an offence. The dismissal was unfair.

5.9 Not in a union

Under the Trade Union and Labour Relations (Consolidation) Act 1992, it is now automatically unfair in all circumstances for an employee to be refused employment (s. 137) have action taken against them which is short of dismissal (s. 146) or be dismissed (s. 152) on the grounds of union membership or non-union membership. There is no qualifying period of employment to bring a claim for unfair dismissal if the reason for dismissal was union membership or non-membership (s. 154). Previously it was possible for non-union employees to be dismissed where a ballot-approved closed shop existed.

Employees also have the right not to have action short of dismissal taken against them by their employer for the *purpose* of preventing or deterring their being or seeking to be a member of an independent trade union (Employment Protection (Consolidation) Act 1978, s. 23).

The House of Lords has now ruled (two judges dissenting in part) in *Associated Newspapers* v *Wilson* (1995), that failure to pay increased wages to employees who would not enter into new contracts which terminated collective pay bargaining and union representation, was not action for the purpose of deterring or penalising employees being in a union. The House of Lords accepted that the only witnesses called before the industrial (now employment) tribunal had given evidence that management had no intention of deterring their employees from continuing as members of the NUJ.

Individuals also have the right not to be excluded or expelled from a trade union unless, for example, they do not satisfy the membership rules. An individual who is excluded or expelled can complain to an employment tribunal which can make an award of compensation from *union* funds (Trade Union Reform and Employment Rights Act 1993, s. 14).

5.10 Criminal offences

Under the Trade Union and Labour Relations (Consolidation) Act 1992, s. 240, it is an offence to break a contract of service or hire wilfully and maliciously knowing or having reasonable cause to believe that the probable consequences are:

(a) to endanger human life or cause serious bodily injury; or

(b) to expose valuable property (this includes land, buildings or personal property) to destruction or serious injury.

The maximum penalty is imprisonment for three months and/or a fine at level 2 on the standard scale.

It is also an offence under s. 241 of the 1992 Act to intimidate another person and prevent that person going about his or her lawful pursuits. Intimidation can take various forms:

(a) actual violence to a person, his wife or children, or damage to property,

(b) following the person from place to place,

(c) hiding tools, clothes or other property owned or used by the other or hindering their use,

(d) watching the other's residence or place of business,

(e) following the other with two or more persons in a disorderly manner through a street or road.

A person found guilty of an offence under this section is liable on summary conviction to be imprisoned for up to six months and/or be fined up to level 5 on the standard scale. The police have power to arrest persons they suspect of committing an offence under s. 241.

5.11 Dismissal for health and safety activities (Employment Rights Act 1996, s. 100)

Regardless of length of service it is unfair to dismiss an employee if the reason for the dismissal was that the employee:

(a) having been designated by the employer to carry out activities to prevent or reduce risks to health and safety, carried out or proposed to carry out such activities, e.g., a safety officer or director who proposes to introduce a system of assessment;

(b) being a member of a safety committee or employee safety representative, in accordance with arrangements under an existing Act or as an acknowledged representative, has performed or intends to perform any functions as a committee member or representative;

(c) as an employee makes representations about working conditions to his or her employer;

(d) refuses to work in a place he or she reasonably believes to be dangerous or where he or she believes danger to be serious and imminent;

(e) takes steps to protect him or herself or other persons from what he or she believes to be *serious* and *imminent* danger.

The dismissal will, however, be fair if the employer can show that the employee was negligent.

An employee who has either been designated by the employer to carry out health and safety activities, or who is an employee representative, or who brings circumstances at work to the employer's attention which he believed harmful, has the right not to be subjected to any detriment by any act or deliberate failure to act by his employer (Employment Rights Act 1996, s. 44).

5.12 Proceedings to enforce statutory employment protection

Regardless of length of service, working hours or age, an employee who is dismissed for bringing proceedings against an employer to enforce a statutory employment protection right or alleges an infringement, will have the right to claim for unfair dismissal (Employment Rights Act 1996, s. 104). For example, in *Mennell v Newell and Wright (Transport Contractors) Ltd* (EAT) (1996) the employee, who had been taken on in March 1993, was dismissed in November 1994 after refusing to sign a new contract. The new contract contained a clause which allowed the employer to claim back training costs if the employee left before the expiry of his current contract. The employee's contention, that this was in contravention of the Wages Act 1986, meant that he was entitled to have his case heard before a tribunal to decide the issue.

5.13 Some other substantial reason

In *Ely v YKK Fasteners (UK) Ltd* (CA) (1994), an employee who had originally said he was leaving to work abroad had resigned but he had never given formal notice of termination. Later on he decided not to take up work abroad but by this time his employer had offered his job to someone else and his employment was treated as at an end. The Court of Appeal upheld the employer's contention that its belief that the employee had resigned constituted a substantial reason for dismissal not withstanding it believed he had in effect already dismissed himself.

In determining whether an employer has acted reasonably in dismissing an employee, no account is to be taken of any threat of industrial action (Employment Rights Act 1996, s. 107).

5.14 Dismissal—procedure

As can be seen from a number of the cases referred to earlier, employers must act *reasonably* and *consistently* when dismissing an employee. In order to achieve consistency, and to ensure that employees are treated in like manner, an employer must follow a disciplinary procedure. In *John Lewis plc v Coyne* (EAT) (2000) it was not obvious to an employee that use of the employer's telephone for personal calls was dishonest. Since her employer had not investigated her alleged dishonesty they had not followed a fair disciplinary procedure and her dismissal was unfair.

Although a Chief Constable was rightly interested in the outcome of allegations relating to discrimination it did not prevent him from acting as an adjudicator in disciplinary proceedings brought against the same officer making the allegations (*Regina (Bennion)* v *Chief Constable of Merseyside Police* (CA) (2001).

A contract of employment may define different routes which must be taken when an employee's conduct is being investigated. In *Saeed* v *Royal Wolverhampton Hospitals NHS Trust* (CA) (2001) the Trust's disciplinary procedure, expressly incorporated into the contract of employment, stated that a doctor was entitled to an independent enquiry where professional conduct or competence was being investigated. When personal conduct, relating to performance or behaviour, and not professional skills, was being considered an internal investigation could be carried out. The Trust's internal investigation and subsequent dismissal of the appellant was the correct procedure. The investigation had followed a complaint by a patient who attended accident and emergency for a bruised swollen and disjointed little finger. During the examination the patient complained that the appellant had tapped her breasts and rubbed her stomach.

To ensure the rules of natural justice prevail a member of a disciplinary panel should not allow a quasi prosecutor to remain whilst the panel reaches the decision. In *Regina* v *Secretary of State for Education and Employment and Another ex parte McNally* (CA) (2001) Mr McNally, a teacher, had been accused of inappropriate behaviour towards a pupil. Before considering the evidence the Chairperson asked everyone to leave to enable the panel to deliberate in private. The panel, as representatives of the governing body, had statutory power to require the Chief Education Officer or Head Teacher to withdraw. The acting Chief Education Officer left with everyone else and the panel concluded that no misconduct had taken place. As a consequence the Local Education Authority requested intervention by the Secretary of State who directed the panel to re-hear the allegations.

The Court of Appeal quashed the Secretary of State's decision and restored the panel's original decision stating that it would have been incompatible with the principles of natural justice for a local government officer to be with the disciplinary panel when its members discussed whether misconduct had been proved. An example disciplinary procedure is set out at p. 240 below. It is to be noted that firms with less than 20 employees are exempt from providing particulars of disciplinary procedures.

Under clause 30 of the Employment Bill 2001 employers have to comply with a *statutory* grievance procedure as prescribed in Schedule 2 of the Bill. Clause 34 makes it unfair if the procedure is not completed when an employee is dismissed. Clause 35 requires employers to advise employees of disciplinary rules. If such particulars are not given an employee will be entitled to up to two weeks pay (clause 38). Compromise agreements are made invalid under the Bill under clause 39, i.e. employees will not be required to agree to refrain from bringing actions relating to sex or race discrimination, unfair dismissal, claims relating to minimum wages or the Working Time Regulations.

5.15 Remedies

If a tribunal finds that an employee has been unfairly treated there are a number of remedies which it may award.

5.15.1 Basic award (Employment Rights Act 1996, s. 119)

This is made on the basis of the number of years an employee has worked but it must be just and equitable to make such an award, i.e. it is not granted as of right. Providing an employee is entitled to this award, the tribunal will grant a minimum amount irrespective of the number of years worked. This is not to be less than £3,300, but is subject to contributory fault on the part of the complainant and refusal of an offer of employment which would have reinstated the complainant (s. 122).

5.15.2 Compensatory award (Employment Rights Act 1996, ss. 123 and 124)

In addition to the basic award of compensation a tribunal may award a further sum which it considers to be just and equitable. This award can now be up to £51,700 (Employment Relations Act 1999, s. 34(4)). These awards are now index linked and can be increased or decreased by the Secretary of State (Employment Relations Act 1999, s. 34(1)).

In determining the net loss, such awards will take into account: (i) the amount which had or could have been earned elsewhere during the period in which the contract existed before the unfair dismissal (see, for example, 5.17.4 and *Ministry of Defence* v *Wheeler* (CA) (1997)); (ii) payments which exceed the amount of statutory redundancy pay (*Digital Equipment Co. Ltd* v *Clements* (CA) (1998)).

Currently, under s. 123 compensation can only reflect pure pecuniary loss. Consequently an employee who succeeds in obtaining the statutory maximum for unfair dismissal cannot claim any further sum in common law in respect of damages for psychiatric injury such as injured feelings, mental disorder or damages to reputation arising from the *manner* of the dismissal. The House of Lords so held in *Johnson* v *Unisys Ltd* (HL) (2001), following the decision in *Addis* v *Gramophone Co. Ltd* (1990).

This is in contrast to the decision in *Malik and Another* v *Bank of Credit and Commerce International SA* (1997) where employees could recover for loss of reputation arising from the defendant's *breach* of contract. (See page 213.) The implied term of trust and confidence did not extend to the *manner* of an employee's dismissal and it was not a proper judicial function for the House of Lords to develop the common law to give a parallel remedy, not subject to the statutory limits for unfair dismissal. Under earlier legislation (including the TULRA 1992) tribunals were able to make a just and equitable award which had regard to the infringement which was the subject of complaint. This might include, for example, injury to feelings through (unfairly) not being shortlisted for an internal promotion.

The limit of a compensatory award does not apply if a person is dismissed for Trade Union activities, health and safety activities, or is selected for redundancy because she is pregnant or for reasons connected with her pregnancy (Employment Relations Act 1999, s. 37).

5.15.3 Re-engagement

A tribunal may order that an employee is re-engaged on terms, which so far as reasonably practicable are as favourable as an order for reinstatement. An order for reinstatement requires an employer to treat a complainant in all respects as if he/she had not been dismissed. Accordingly an employee is also entitled to any benefits by way of arrears of pay between his/her dismissal and re-engagement.

5.15.4 Reinstatement

This is an order requiring an employer to employ a complainant on the original terms on which they were employed and to treat the employee as if they had not been dismissed.

Port of London Authority v Payne (CA) (1994)

An industrial tribunal considering the issue of an appropriate remedy for unfair dismissal under the Employment Protection (Consolidation) Act 1978, s. 69, can approach the question whether it would be practicable to order an employer to reinstate or re-engage an employee in two stages.

The first stage would be before any order for reinstatement or re-engagement was made when a provisional decision on practicability based on the evidence before the tribunal could be made.

The second stage would arise if such an order was made but not complied with. The tribunal would then have to make a final conclusion on practicability because it might affect the size of the special award.

Unless it is not reasonably practicable for an employer to comply with an order for reinstatement or re-engagement, a tribunal may make an additional award of compensation if the employee is not re-employed (Employment Relations Act 1999, s. 33). The amount is to be not less than 26 nor more than 52 weeks pay.

5.16 Unfair dismissal—essentials for a claim

To claim unfair dismissal the employee must:

(a) satisfy the qualifying period;

(b) establish that there has been a dismissal;

(c) lodge the complaint in time;

(d) show that the employer has not given a satisfactory reason for dismissal or that the employer has acted unreasonably (there is an equal onus on the employee to prove and the employer to disprove).

5.17 Whistle-blowing

Under the Public Interest Disclosure Act 1998 an employee may make a complaint to an employer and industrial tribunal of harassment.

In *Edgar v Meteorological Office* (EAT) (2001) Mr Edgar, a weatherman, made a formal complaint to his employer of harassment, bullying and management failure. This complaint was upheld after an investigation but after an appeal by Bill Giles in

February 2000, his senior, Mr Edgar was told he could not return to work. When Mr Edgar complained to a tribunal the Meteorological Office submitted that his original complaint on March 11 was prior to the relevant provisions which came into force on 2 July 1999. It was held by the EAT that it was not a requirement in such cases that all the facts should have occurred after the relevant provisions came into force and the alleged detriment was in February 2000 by which time other facts were well known.

EXAMPLE

CONTRACT OF EMPLOYMENT
(as per the Employment Rights Act 1996)

1 This contract is between ....Ltd, herein afterwards referred to as the Company and .... herein afterwards referred to as the employee.

2 The employee's employment commenced on ....

3 The employee's remuneration is ....

4 The employee's remuneration is on a weekly basis. ....

5 (a) The employee's hours of work are 39 hours per week. Start and finish times are in agreement with the Company.

   (b) Overtime is payable at a rate of .....after completion of the above mentioned 39 hours mutually agreed between the Company and the employee.

6 (a) The employee is entitled to 24 working days holiday and 7 days bank holiday—(Christmas Day, Boxing Day, Easter Friday/Monday, Mayday/ Whitsun Monday and August Bank Holiday).

   (b) *Accrued Holiday Pay.*
       If, on leaving, the employee has not taken all of their entitlement, payment in lieu will be as follows.
       Starting with the first full calendar month of employment, the employee will be entitled to $\frac{1}{12}$ of the payment representing the number of holidays to $\frac{1}{12}$ which he/she is entitled. Thereafter for each month's work the fraction will be increased by $\frac{1}{12}$ of the holiday pay entitlement; e.g. maximum of:

       Month 01 - $\frac{1}{12}$ of twenty-four working days
       Month 12 - $\frac{12}{12}$ of twenty-four working days

Less holiday already taken by the employee to the date of leaving.

7 **Incapacity/sickness**
   The Statutory Sick Pay Scheme applies. (For further information see DHSS Booklet NI16/Apl 83.)
   In particular, the employee must provide a self-certificate after three days of illness and a doctor's certificate after seven days to be eligible for Statutory Sick Pay.

8 There are no Pension Schemes in operation within the Company. [Note: if the company offers a pension which 'contracts out' employees from the state scheme, it must refer to its Contracting Out Certificate.]

9 Minimum period of notice required by both the employee and the Company is

one calendar month, after the employee has completed twelve months' service. Prior to this time the period of notice is two weeks.

10   In the event of any gross misconduct dismissal will be instantaneous, after the employee has been given the opportunity to explain his/her actions in the presence of a 'friend' if so requested. [Note: Written details of disciplinary procedures are not necessary if the Company employs fewer than 20 people.]

11   **Job description**
    The duties of the employee consist of. ....
    and they are described ....

12   **Health & safety at work**
    (a) It is recognised that it is the responsibility of the Company to provide a healthy and safe working environment and safe systems of work; and safe plant/ machinery.
    (b) It is also the duty of the employee to take reasonable care of himself/herself and of others and cooperate with the Company in complying with the legislation relating to health and safety at work.

13   **Union membership**
    Employees may or may not belong to a union.

14   A collective agreement reached between the company and the . . . [union] on 1 July 1993 is in force and applies to this contract.

15   The employee is not required to work outside the UK.

16   The period of employment is not a fixed term but employees are subject to the rules set out in clause 10 above and any procedure which may be introduced by the company at a future date.

For and on behalf of   at   place of work

COMPANY DIRECTOR

Employee's Name. ....
Signed ....
Date ....

5.18 Rights in relation to maternity

5.18.1 Pregnancy

Under s. 99(1) of the Employment Rights Act 1996, it is unfair to dismiss an employee because she is pregnant (see *Webb* v *EMO Air Cargo (UK) Ltd* (HL) (1994) at p. **245**).

An employer must undertake risk assessments to determine specific risks to pregnant women and those who are breastfeeding.

Pregnant women have the right, under the Management of Health and Safety at Work (Amendment) Regulations 1999, to be found suitable alternative employment where there is a risk either to their health or the unborn child. If this is not possible their employer must give them time off on full pay. This provision also applies to women once they have given birth if they are breastfeeding and there is a risk, from

EXAMPLE DISCIPLINARY PROCEDURE

ADMINISTRATIVE ACTION TAKEN BY:		ACTION TAKEN FOR:			
		A minor offence	Serious offences	Gross misconduct	APPEALED
The Supervisor	1st	VERBAL WARNING			Departmental Manager in presence of Shop Steward (or next best friend)
or:					
The Supervisor in consultation with employee's Shop Steward	2nd	VERBAL WARNING (recorded) – – – –	– – – – – –	– – – – – –	Works Manager in presence of Shop Steward (or by next best friend)
Departmental Manager in consultation with Shop Steward			FINAL WRITTEN WARNING ———	———		
Departmental Manager Senior Shop Steward Personnel Department				SUSPENSION – – – – – –	Works Manager in presence of Senior Shop Steward (or next best friend)
Works manager Senior Shop Steward Personnel Department				——— DISMISSAL	Works Manager or Managing DFirecxtor and in presence of Senior Shop Steward (or next best friend) or Joint Appeals Committee

At all stages the employee will be given the opportunity to state their case, after, if appropriate, an appropriate 'cooling off' period and in the presence of a union representative or next best friend, if so desired.

work activities, to the baby. The employee must notify her employer in writing of her condition and if requested provide a certificate from a registered medical practitioner (regs 17 and 18). These rights also apply in respect of an employee being suspended from work on maternity grounds, in consequence of any relevant requirement (some thing imposed under a specific provision) or relevant recommendation (recommendation in a code of practice issued under s. 16 of the Health and Safety at Work etc. Act 1974) (Employment Rights Act 1996, s. 66).

EXAMPLE

X works on an assembly line making batteries. When she becomes pregnant it is unsafe for her to continue this work, but a clerical job is available, which she is capable of doing. This work must be offered to her.

Note that other employees, employed for more than one month, or three months in the case of a fixed term contract, suspended from work on medical grounds are entitled to be paid for up to 26 weeks (Employment Rights Act 1996, ss. 64 and 65).

The 1999 Management Regulations also require an employee to introduce general measures to improve safety from hazards specific to pregnant women or young mothers (reg. 16).

5.18.2 Maternity leave (Employment Relations Act 1999, sch. 4)
Maternity leave will not be less than 18 weeks and can be taken when the employee chooses (Employment Relations Act 1999, sch. 4). This may be extended to 26 weeks from 2003. An employee on maternity leave retains the benefits of the terms and conditions of her employment contract and is entitled to return to the same job.

Dismissing a woman in connection with her pregnancy may not be unfair if the employer, through a mistake in law, genuinely believes the employee has not returned to work. In *Halfpenny* v *IGE Medical Systems Ltd* (HL) (2000), due to postnatal depression the employee was unable to return to work at the end of the expiration of 29 weeks from the date of the birth of her baby. Accordingly she submitted a medical certificate and her employers extended her maternity leave to 27 November 1995. She remained unwell and when she failed to return to work on 27 November she was dismissed. The House of Lords held that to gain the right to return to work an employee had to give notice as required by the statute and comply with the contract of employment, by being either physically present, or, if not possible, absent by some other reason permitted by the contract. Once Mrs Halfpenny had given notice of her intention to return and supplied the necessary sick note until 27 November she became entitled to further *contractual* sick leave. She was therefore dismissed when her employers mistakenly thought she had not returned on 27 November, but unlike wrongful dismissal, where any breach was actionable, liability for unfair dismissal depended on the employer's state of mind. The case would therefore be remitted to a tribunal to determine if the employer's mistake of law meant the dismissal was unfair.

Community law does not, however, preclude a clause in an employment contract which makes pay higher than statutory maternity pay, providing the worker returns to work for a least one month after the birth of her child (*Boyle* v *Equal Opportunities Commission* (ECJ) (1998)).

Employees must not be allowed to work during compulsory maternity leave which must not be less than two weeks. Employers who allow an employee to work are guilty of an offence and liable to summary conviction.

5.18.2.1 Additional maternity leave

An employee who has completed one year's service with her employer is entitled to a further 11 weeks' maternity leave. This starts at the end of ordinary maternity leave and finishes 29 weeks after the birth.

An employee must give her employer 21 days notice beforehand of her intention of taking maternity leave and intention of returning to work. Where a woman qualifies for additional maternity leave she must let her employer know when the baby is born so that she and her employer can plan for her return 29 weeks later. An employee who has been continuously employed for one year at the beginning of the eleventh week of confinement has the right to return to work.

The Employment Bill 2001 increases ordinary maternity leave to 26 weeks and an entitlement to an additional maternity leave of 26 weeks giving mothers up to one year's total maternity leave.

Under the Bill there will be two maternity benefits: Statutory Maternity Pay (SMP) – paid by the employer, and Maternity Allowance – paid by the Department for Work and Pensions.

5.18.3 Parental leave

A parent is now entitled to be absent from work for at least three months in order to care for a child or if expecting to have responsibility for a child. Paragraphs 75 and 79 of sch. 4 of the Employment Relations Act 1999 make provision for notices to be given and evidence to be produced in connection with maternity and parental leave, (e.g. the child's birth certificate). Parental leave can be taken at any time up to the child's fifth birthday.

Clauses 1–16 of the Employment Bill 2001 make provision for new rights for paternity and adoption leave and pay. These include:

(a) Two weeks' paternity leave and pay following the birth of a child or the placement of a child for adoption. This must be taken in one single period.

(b) Adoption leave around the placement of a child for adoption for up to one year and up to 26 weeks' paid leave.

An employee who is absent for up to four weeks is entitled to return to the same job. If the absence is for a longer period the employee is entitled to return to the same job unless this is not reasonably practicable. In that case the employee is entitled to a similar job which has the same or better status, terms and conditions as the old job.

5.18.4 Time off for dependants (Employment Relations 1999, sch. 4, part II)

Dependants are entitled to take time off during working hours to provide assistance when a dependant falls ill; gives birth; is injured or assaulted; to make arrangement for care in consequence of the death of a dependant; because of unexpected disruption of care arrangements; or to deal with unexpected incidents involving a child of the employee. The employee must tell the employer the reason for such absence as soon as reasonably practicable and how long they expect to be absent. Complaints for refusal to give time can be made to an industrial tribunal within three months of the date the refusal took place.

5.18.5 Compensation

In *Ministry of Defence* v *Cannock and others* (EAT) (1994) when laying down guidelines for employment tribunals assessing compensation for sex discrimination in cases involving service women dismissed because they were pregnant, the EAT suggested that tribunals needed to keep a sense of proportion and not make excessive awards:

(a) Evaluation of loss should take account of what might have been earned on a balance of probability.

(b) Applicants were entitled to be compensated for such loss as was caused by the wrong provided that it was not too remote.

(c) Applicants were under a duty to mitigate their loss.

The point at which compensation might be reduced to take account of the possibility of a service woman remaining in the service if she had not become pregnant was considered in *Ministry of Defence* v *Wheeler* (CA) (1997), where it was held that compensation for discrimination must take account of actual earnings or those which could have been earned if she had remained in the service, and deduct from this an amount she could have earned elsewhere, if the applicant had taken reasonable steps to mitigate her loss. Only after the net figure had been calculated should a percentage be deducted to reflect that had a service woman not been dismissed (on grounds of pregnancy) she might have left the armed forces anyway.

The argument put forward by the Ministry of Defence that the percentage deduction should take place first was rejected since it would mean that full compensation would not be provided.

5.18.6 Antenatal appointments

Whilst still at work, before the baby is born, a pregnant employee is entitled to paid time off to attend antenatal appointments (Employment Rights Act 1996, ss. 55 and 56).

6 Discrimination: sex discrimination, equal pay and race discrimination

Unequal treatment of men and women is made unlawful in three different areas. These are in relation to:

(a) their sex or marital status;

(b) the amount they are paid;

(c) their race.

(For disability discrimination see 7 below.)

6.1 Sex discrimination

The Sex Discrimination Act 1975 makes discrimination against women or men, or discrimination on the grounds of marital status, unlawful in relation to employment or recruitment arrangements. The law does not however proscribe discrimination on the grounds of sexual orientation. In *Pearce v Governing Body of Mayfield School* (CA) (2001) a lesbian employee of the school was not treated less favourably than a male homosexual teacher when a school did not take steps to prevent pupils calling her a lesbian or dyke. Gender specific abuse was not automatically discrimination.

Once an employee has established that they were unable to comply with a condition to escape dismissal, a tribunal must show that it has objectively weighed the justification for the dismissal. In *Allonby v Accrington and Rossendale College and Others* (CA) (2001) the Court of Appeal remitted the case to a tribunal to determine if the applicant, who had been employed as a part-time lecturer, was justifiably dismissed when her dismissal together with other lecturers fell entirely on the part-time workforce. See also *Whiffen v Milham Ford Girls' School and Another* (CA) (2001) at page 247.

Terms in an agreement which discriminate on grounds of sex can be challenged by individuals in employment tribunals (Trade Union Reform and Employment Rights Act 1993, s. 32).

In *Hall v Woolstone Hall Leisure Ltd* (CA) (2000) the employee was aware her employer was not deducting tax from her wages but her case was based on a breach of the Sex Discrimination Act. Her action for discrimination after being dismissed from her job as a chef when she became pregnant was not therefore banned. No doubt any compensation awarded by a tribunal would nevertheless take into account that her acquiescence meant she had been paid gross to the date of her dismissal.

A person who knowingly aids another to do an act made unlawful by the Race Relations Act is treated as doing an unlawful act of like description. (s. 33(1)). In *Anyanwu and Another v South Bank Student Union and Another* (HL) (2001) the applicants were student members of the South Bank University who became paid officers of the student union. After the University expelled them and excluded them from their premises, the union treated their contracts at an end. Although Lord Bingham doubted whether their allegations were sufficient to support a claim he stated that a majority of the House of Lords did not share this view. Since the University had 'helped or assisted' they had aided in the alleged discrimination and the case would be remitted to a tribunal to apply the plain terms of s. 33.

Section 12 of the Act also makes it unlawful for organisations to discriminate against women by depriving them of membership. It was held by the EAT that this section applied to the National Federation of Self-Employed and Small Businesses Ltd, whose aim is to protect, promote and further the interests of the self-employed

(*National Federation of Self-Employed and Small Businesses Ltd* v *Philpott* (EAT) (1997)).

6.1.1 Direct sex discrimination

Direct sex discrimination occurs when a person is treated less favourably than a person of the opposite sex, but in *Peake* v *Automotive Products Ltd* (CA) (1977) a factory which allowed women employees to leave five minutes earlier than men, in order to avoid the rush at the factory gates, was allowed to continue this practice. The discriminatory conduct was in the interest of safety.

There is nothing in the Sex Discrimination Act 1975 which prevents an employer having a variety of retiring ages for different jobs provided there is no direct or indirect discrimination.

Bullock v *Alice Ottley School* (CA) (1993)

Mrs Bullock was employed as a part-time pantry assistant. She was dismissed at the age of 60 because she had reached the school's retirement age for administrative and domestic staff. Her contention that her job compared to that of maintenance personnel or gardeners who retired at the age of 65 was rejected because there were specific reasons relating to recruitment difficulties which explained why they retired at a later age.

Providing a decision to make staff in a given category redundant applies to all staff there will be no discrimination. In *Taylor* v *Secretary of State for Scotland* (HL) (2000) the applicant was not discriminated against when his employment was terminated at age 58. This was not contrary to his contract which provided an equal opportunities term.

When considering a complaint relating to sex discrimination the House of Lords may refer to the European Court of Justice for a preliminary ruling.

Webb v *Emo Air Cargo (UK) Ltd* (HL) (1994)

Ms Webb had been taken on to cover for another employee who was on maternity leave, when she also became pregnant. She was dismissed and she complained that this was sexual discrimination. The industrial (now employment) tribunal decided that if a man had told his employers he would be absent for a similar period he would have been dismissed. The EAT and Court of Appeal upheld this view but the House of Lords referred the question to the Court of Justice for a preliminary ruling which has now decided that dismissal of a pregnant woman recruited for an indefinite period could not be justified by the fact that she was temporarily prevented from performing her work (case C-32/93). The House of Lords has now ruled that the dismissal of a woman, employed under an 'indefinite' contract, for pregnancy—or maternity—related reasons is directly discriminatory within s. 1(1) of the Sex Discrimination Act 1975. It is not appropriate to compare her position to a hypothetical male because the relevant circumstances of the two can never be the same. The Court of Justice has ruled that this comparison can be made once the period of *maternity leave* has been exhausted (*Haberman-Belterman* (1994)). As yet there is no ruling on the situation where a woman who is employed under a *fixed* term contract becomes unavailable for some or all of the time for pregnancy—or maternity—related reasons. In these circumstances it may be appropriate to compare the woman's position to that of a hypothetical man. However, in *Brown* v *Rentokil* (ECJ) (1998), the Court of Justice has ruled (after reference from the House of Lords) that the community equal treatment directive precludes dismissal of a female worker at any time during her pregnancy when absence is due to illness related to her pregnancy.

The presence of a contractual term providing for dismissal of either sex after a specified number of weeks absence did not affect the issue of discrimination.

In *O'Neill* v *Governors of St Thomas More Roman Catholic Voluntary Aid Upper School* (EAT) (1996) it was held that dismissal which relates purely to an employee becoming pregnant will be discriminatory—irrespective of other surrounding circumstances or the motives of an employer. Employers may therefore feel inclined to look for some other substantial reason when considering the dismissal of an employee who, for example, works in the public domain, if it is considered inappropriate for her to continue to be employed.

When an employer becomes insolvent, as a general principle employees may claim pay to which they were entitled, against the Secretary of State. Whereas it might be assumed that 'pay' would include the payment of a 'debt owed' by the Secretary of State, member states are entitled to make provisions for women absent from work because of pregnancy. Therefore, in *Secretary of State for Employment* v *Clark* (CA) (1996) it was held not discriminatory to prevent the applicant, who was absent on maternity leave at the time of her employer's insolvency, from claiming a shortfall between maternity pay and normal pay, for the 12-week period of notice to which she would otherwise have been entitled.

Promoting women as a national policy in certain employment sectors where women were unrepresented has been held to be discriminatory (*Kalake* v *Freie Hansestadt Bremen* (1995)).

However in *Application by Badeck and Others* (Court of Justice of the European Communities) (2000) (Case C-158/97), national measures which gave priority to women for promotion in sectors of the public service where they were under-represented, were not contrary to Community equal treatment if women were *not* given automatic and unconditional priority when men and women were equally qualified and the personal situations of all candidates were taken into account.

6.1.2 Indirect discrimination
Indirect discrimination occurs when a requirement is applied equally to men and women but a significantly larger proportion of one sex find it harder to fulfil.

EXAMPLE

Setting an age limit of 28 years maximum for entry into the Civil Service at executive officer grade, because at this time women are often raising a family.

Wright v *Rugby Borough Council* (ET) (1984)
Rugby Borough Council was ordered to allow a Town Hall clerk to work at times

enabling her to care for her baby. Before the birth Mrs Wright worked from 8.45am to 5.15pm with a one-hour lunch break. When she returned after the birth the council's chief executive had agreed she could work from 8.30am to 4.30pm with half an hour for lunch. The council's staffing sub-committee disallowed this. The tribunal decided that the council was only serving its own convenience; there was no real need of this requirement. Their decision was, therefore, discriminatory because it affected a far greater proportion of women than men.

More recently, in *Cowley* v *South African Airways* (ET) (1999), Miss Cowley was dismissed by the airline after refusing to work a double shift. The tribunal held:

(a) That whereas her contract implied that overtime would arise from time to time, the requirement to work two shifts back to back did not constitute overtime. She had, therefore, been unfairly dismissed.

(b) Since far fewer women than men would be able to comply with working back to back shifts, because of their domestic commitments, the change in work pattern was also discriminatory.

Employers must now have due regard to female employee's domestic responsibilities, but to date this consideration does not extend to that of the male single parent. If it was to do so it would, of course, raise doubt about the decision in this case.

Indirect discrimination can still take place although a company has made a ruling to promote its business efficiency.

Hussain and others v *J. H. Walker Ltd* (EAT) (1995)

The company had set down a requirement that there should be no holiday for any employees in May, June or July. This meant that the applicants, who were Muslim, could not take time off for the religious festival of Eid. Each was awarded £1,000 damages for upset and distress.

Ratcliffe and others v *North Yorkshire County Council* (HL) (1995)

Paying school dinner ladies less than male comparators was discriminatory. The need to compete with commercial organisations who could provide the same service was not a material factor which could be used as a defence.

Making a female teacher redundant because she was on a series of fixed-term contracts was indirectly discriminatory. It deprived her from participating in the selection process for further employment. In *Whiffen* v *Milham Ford Girls' School and Another* (CA) (2001) the Court of Appeal held the burden was on the employer not simply to justify redundancy because of economic constraints but its *policy* to automatically look to fixed-term contract staff when evidence showed that 100 per cent of male staff were not on fixed-term contracts was discriminatory.

However, in *University of Manchester* v *Jones* (CA) (1993) an advertisement for 'graduates aged 27–35' did not discriminate against women who had been mature students and obtained their degrees at age 25 or over. The advertisement was directed at *all* graduates in this age band and the only permissible pool was graduates in this category. Ms Jones, who graduated at the age of 41, was excluded but she could not claim discrimination by setting her own parameters.

6.1.3 Direct marriage discrimination

This occurs when a married person is treated less favourably, due to their married status, than a single person of the same sex (Sex Discrimination Act 1975, s. 3(1)(a).

EXAMPLE

A married woman is not promoted because she is married.

6.1.4 Indirect marriage discrimination

This occurs when a condition is applied without justification which would apply equally to an unmarried person, but the proportion of married persons who can comply is considerably smaller than the proportion of unmarried persons (Sex Discrimination Act 1975, s. 3(1)(b)).

EXAMPLE

If promotion is offered if employees are prepared to stay away from home for long periods of time (which in reality is not required), this constitutes discrimination on grounds of marital status.

If long periods away from home *were* needed the employer would not be discriminating on grounds of marital status.

If an employer victimises an employee because they are, or intend to be, involved in proceedings under the Sex Discrimination Act 1975 or the Equal Pay Act 1970, this is unlawful (Sex Discrimination Act 1975, s. 4).

6.1.5 Exemptions

There are several situations where the 1975 Act does not apply and there are also certain exemptions granted under the Act.

The 1975 Act is not applicable to work undertaken outside Great Britain (ss. 6(2) and 10). It does not apply to employment in private households (s. 6(3)(a)) or where there are no more than five persons employed (s. 6(3)(b)).

When the Act does apply there are certain occasions when discrimination may be permitted.

6.1.5.1 *Genuine occupational qualifications* Sex discrimination may be allowed where a person's sex is a genuine occupational qualification (Sex Discrimination Act 1975, s. 7).

EXAMPLE

In dramatic performances or some other entertainment where there is a need for a man or vice versa.

Other examples include situations where there is a need to preserve decency or privacy; where the holder of the job can only live in accommodation normally lived in by men, and there are no alternative sleeping arrangements; where the nature of the establishment requires a man to do the particular work, e.g. at a male only prison.

There may be situations where only a woman can do the job and the exemptions would apply equally (Sex Discrimination Act 1975, s. 2).

6.1.5.2 Pregnancy, or childbirth, retirement, death   No account can be taken of any special treatment given to women in connection with pregnancy or childbirth (s. 2(2)) or provisions in the employment field which are more beneficial to one sex or the other in relation to death or retirement (s. 6(4)).

6.1.5.3 Pensions   This last point is now subject to *Barber* v *Guardian Royal Exchange Assurance Co.* (ECJ) (1990). Under the employers' pension scheme, if employees were made redundant women were entitled to their pension at 52 years, whereas men could not claim until they were aged 55. The European Court of Justice ruled that pay includes pensions and therefore this amounted to unlawful treatment of men. Mr Barber was entitled to his pension from the age of 52. This was a 'contracted-out' scheme, paid by an employer, but benefits paid under national social security schemes do not come within the definition of pay and are not subject to European law on equal pay. In *Griffin* v *London Pensions Fund Authority* (EAT) (1993) the applicant's pension was reduced the day before her sixtieth birthday from £1,240 to £1,008, but as it was a statutory pension it was not classed as 'pay' and consequently her claim for equal treatment failed. In *Harvest Town Circle Ltd* v *Rutherford* (EAT) (2001) the Employment Appeals Tribunal stated that given that the State and other pensions were commonly paid from age 65 the existence of possible objective justification seemed obvious. It might be that every employee who remained in work excluded a younger person. A tribunal should take pains to be sufficiently informed. The tribunal should have requested an instruction for the Secretary of State for Employment to consider arguments which justified possible contravention of Article 119 (now 141) of the EC Treaty, if a smaller number of women than men or men than women were able to fulfil the requirement imposed by the Employment Rights Act 1996. Failing to make such a request was an error of law and the case was remitted for re-hearing.

In *Roberts* v *Birds Eye Walls Ltd* (1994), the European Court of Justice stated that it was common ground that a bridging pension fell within the concept of pay within the meaning of Article 119 (now Article 141) of the EC Treaty. However, the amount of the bridging pension paid to a woman who retired early on the grounds of ill health could be reduced after the age of 60 because she was prima facie entitled to a State pension whilst the bridging pension paid to a man was not reduced until five years later.

Some women, like Mrs Roberts, did not draw the full State pension because earlier on as a matter of economic choice they had exercised their right to pay a reduced national insurance contribution. This factor could be taken into account when deciding the amount of the bridging pension.

Consequently paying a reduced amount to women after the age of 60 was not discriminatory.

Similarly in *Neath* v *Hugh Steeper Ltd* (1994) the ECJ ruled that when actuarial factors allowed for different pension entitlements between men and women (e.g., the employer's contribution was higher for females because statistically they live longer) the principle of equality in Article 119 was not broken.

This ruling also stated that Article 119 could be relied on to claim equal pension benefits but only from 17 May 1990.

Equal treatment can be achieved by *lowering* the pension rights of others. In *Coloroll Pension Trustees Ltd* v *Russell and others* (1994), the Court of Justice of the European Communities held that under Article 119 the principle of equal pay for men and women could be relied on against pension scheme trustees as well as employers.

With regard to periods of service completed *after the court's finding* of discrimination but before entry into force of the measures designed to eliminate the discrimination, the principle of equal pay meant that the disadvantaged employee should be granted the same advantages as those previously enjoyed by other employees (i.e., increased benefits). However, with regard to periods of service after entry into force of equal measures, Article 119 did not preclude equal treatment being achieved by reducing the advantages enjoyed by others (i.e., lowering other persons' pensions).

By virtue of the *Barber* judgment, the direct effect of Article 119 could be relied upon for the purpose of claiming equal treatment in relation to occupational pensions, but only with regard to benefits payable for periods of service subsequent to 17 May 1990.

However, in *Vroege* v *NCIV Instituut voor Volkshuisvesting BV and another* (1995), the Court of Justice, in considering when the right to *join* a pension scheme arose, made the following points:

(a) it reaffirmed that pay includes pension;

(b) that the right to *join* a scheme fell within Article 119;

(c) the limits of the effect in time, of the *Barber* judgment, did not, however, apply to the right to join a scheme;

(d) the right to join a scheme runs from 4 August 1976, the date of the judgment in *Defrenne* v *Sabena* (1976), in which the Court of Justice had held for the first time that Article 119 had a direct effect;

(e) nevertheless, a worker who did apply to join a scheme retrospectively would have to pay appropriate contributions relating to the period of membership.

On 9 February 1998 the House of Lords referred to the Court of Justice the following two questions relating to the right of women to join a pension scheme and be awarded arrears of damages:

(a) Whether it is contrary to Article 119 to require a woman to be employed for six months before she can bring a claim relating to equal treatment (Equal Pay Act 1970, s. 2(4), as amended).

(b) Whether lack of entitlement to arrears of damages in respect of a time earlier than two years before the date on which proceedings were begun is also contrary to Article 119 (Equal Pay Act 1970, s.2(5), as amended).

(*Preston and Others* v *Wolverhampton Health Care NHS and Others* (HL) (1998).)

In February 2001 the House of Lords ruled that:

(a) the six month rule did not render the exercise of Community law impossible or excessively difficult;

(b) the two year rule was contrary to Article 119 and future pension benefits had to be calculated by reference to both full and part-time periods of service from the date of the judgment of *Defrenne* v *Sabena* (1976) — see above. (*Preston and Others* v *Wolverhampton Healthcare NHS Trust and Others* (HL) (2001).

Other types of discrimination, for example, relating to disablement allowance, can only be justified on a temporary basis, whilst the system is being changed to ensure equal treatment of men and women (*Thomas* v *Chief Adjudication Officer* (ECJ) (1993)).

However, more recently, in *Graham and others* v *Secretary of State for Social Security and another* (1995), the court ruled that where the discrimination at issue was linked to the setting of different pensionable ages for women and men, legislation (in this instance the Social Security Contributions and Benefits Act 1992) treating men and women differently for invalidity benefits is not unlawful.

In its judgment the Court referred to *Thomas* in respect of what was acceptable discrimination. Therefore, while this form of discrimination is currently acceptable within existing UK legislation, it will be changed to afford equal treatment of women and men in respect of pension entitlements.

Similarly coherence between reduced earnings allowance (REA), designed to compensate for a decrease in earnings as a result of accidents at work or occupational disease, and the old age pension scheme, resulting in discrimination between men and women whose circumstances were similar is currently justified under Article 177 (now 234). (*Heppie and Others* v *Adjudication Officer* Case c-196/98 (Court of Justice of the European Communities) (2000).

6.1.5.4 Contravention of another statute   Section 51 of the 1975 Act allows an employer to discriminate in order to comply with other statutes, e.g. the Health and Safety at Work etc. Act 1974.

Page v Freight Hire Tank Haulage Ltd (EAT) (1981)
A 23-year-old woman heavy goods vehicle driver lost her case claiming compensation for an alleged breach of the Sex Discrimination Act 1975, s. 6(2)(b). She claimed that it was detrimental to her when her employers refused to let her carry loads of chemicals which they said could be dangerous to women of child-bearing age.

The appeals tribunal found that her employers had taken the correct action in order to discharge their responsibility to employees under the Health and Safety at Work etc. Act 1974.

6.2 Equal pay

The Equal Pay Act 1970 was the first legislative provision to require equality at work.

It defined the occasions when both men and women should be given equal treatment by an employer as either:

(a) when employed on like work; or

(b) when employed on work rated as equivalent.

Section 8 of the Sex Discrimination Act 1975 now states that when a woman is employed on either like work or work rated as equivalent to a man's, there is an implied term that none of the terms of her contract will be less favourable than that of a man. This applies to all aspects of the contract, not just pay.

6.2.1 Like work

Sorbie v Trust House Forte Hotels Ltd (EAT) (1977)
Although the employers had changed the job description of a male employee to banqueting supervisor, from waiter, it was still held that he was employed on 'like work' and six waitresses were entitled to the same hourly rate of pay.

Capper Pass Ltd v Lawton (EAT) (1977)
A cook who worked a 40-hour week and provided lunches for between 10 and 20 people in a company directors' dining room was held to be entitled to equal pay with two assistant chefs who worked a 45-hour week and prepared 350 meals a day.

However, in Glasgow City Council and Others v Marshall and Others (HL) (2000) it was held that instructors in special schools who were paid substantially less than qualified teachers doing the same or broadly similar work were not entitled to an equality clause under s. 1 of the Act. The teachers had a teaching qualification; the instructors did not.

6.2.2 Work rated as equivalent
Comparison can be made under this heading when a woman considers she is doing equivalent work but she does not have the same job description or grading as a man.

EXAMPLE

In a factory all male production line workers are graded 10 and are paid a higher wage than all female production workers who are all graded 01.

The employer has made this distinction because he says that the men work overtime. In practice the men work very little overtime, and only on a voluntary basis. The women must be graded as 10, and paid at the higher rate.

Since 1984, where a woman can demonstrate that her work is of *equal value* to that of a man, she is entitled to equal pay, and *vice versa*.

EXAMPLE

A female cook may demonstrate that her work is of equal value to painters and joiners employed by the same employer. In British Coal Corporation v Smith and Others (HL) (1996) it was held there was no material distinction between the work of the applicants and those with whom they sought comparison. The House of Lords decided that in making a comparison with work of equal value, it was necessary to observe common terms and conditions of employment broadly. It was not however necessary to make comparisons between female and male workers. Therefore cleaners and canteen manageresses were able to rely on a comparison of wage structures between themselves and clerical workers employed by British Coal. However, where there is a material distinction between the work done by the persons being compared this will be a defence.

Leverton v *Clwyd County Council* (HL) (1989)

The plaintiff was employed as a nursery nurse. She established that she had the same conditions and terms of work as 11 male clerical officers. Nevertheless the House of Lords upheld the decision of the tribunal that the difference in pay between her and the male employees was genuinely due to material factors.

This defence may also be raised to justify difference in pay when a woman establishes she is doing like work or work rated as equivalent to a man's.

EXAMPLE

X, a man, has worked for Y Ltd for 20 years. He is paid £23,000 a year. Z, a woman, also works for Y Ltd doing like work. She has been employed for 10 years and is paid £15,500 a year. Y Ltd may justify the difference in salary on the length of service of X.

6.2.3 Burden of proof

In *Enderby* v *Frenchay Health Authority* (1994) the ECJ ruled as follows, in respect of questions referred to it by the Court of Appeal:

(a) Where significant statistics disclosed an appreciable difference in pay between two jobs of *equal value* one of which was mainly carried out by women, the other by men, Article 119 (now article 141) of the EC Treaty shifts the burden of proof to the employer to show that there was no discrimination.

(b) This still applies even if the rates of pay were arrived at by a process of collective bargaining.

(c) It was for the national court to determine whether, as a question of fact, different pay rates had to be offered because of a shortage of candidates for one job, resulting in higher salaries for a particular group of employees.

The Court of Appeal has now considered an appeal from the EAT and has concluded that for the purposes of comparison the applicant mirrored the comparator on the incremental pay scale and was not entitled to be placed on the comparator's pay scale at a point commensurate with her *own* years of service. To allow the applicant to receive in 1987 (the date of her claim) not merely the salary of her comparator in that year but his salary plus four annual increments (allowing for her years of service) would be to double count her experience. The tribunal and EAT therefore reached the right conclusions. (*Enderby* v *Frenchay Health Authority and Another (No. 2)* (CA) (2000).

6.2.4 Compensation

The European Court has ruled in *Marshall* v *Southampton and South-West Hampshire*

Area Health Authority (Teaching) (No. 2) (1993) that it is contrary to art. 6 of EC Equal Treatment Directive 76/207 for national provisions (e.g., the Sex Discrimination Act 1975) to set an upper limit on the amount of compensation which a victim may recover. The victim of the discrimination must be 'made whole' by the award and the Court of Justice considered this could not be done by placing a constraint on the amount of compensation the victim might receive.

It is also contrary to Article 119 to restrict, under s. 2(5) of the Equal Pay Act 1970, calculation of loss of equal earnings to two years. The EAT so held in *Levez* v *T M Jennings (Harlow Pools) Ltd*; *Hicking* v *Basford Group Ltd* (EAT) (1999). This followed the earlier decision of the Court of Justice in *Levez* v *T M Jennings (Harlow Pools) Ltd* (ECJ) (1998) in which the Court ruled that community law precluded the application of a rule of national law which limited an employee's entitlement to arrears of remuneration or damages for breach of the principle of equal pay, when the delay in presenting the case was attributable to the employer deliberately misrepresenting the level of remuneration received by persons of the opposite sex performing like work.

6.2.5 Time limits

Complaints can be referred within six months of the date the employee's contract is terminated, whether or not they have been doing the work in respect of which the complaint is made. (*Young* v *National Power plc* (CA) (2000).

6.3 Race discrimination

Any discrimination on grounds of race, nationality or ethnic origin is illegal under the Race Relations Act 1976. In *Crown Suppliers (Property Services Agency)* v *Dawkins* (CA) (1993) a Rastafarian was unsuccessful in his action claiming racial discrimination after not being selected for a van-driving job because of his long hair. Rastafarians are not classed as a separate ethnic group for the purpose of the Race Relations Act 1976.

Discrimination may be *direct*, i.e. where there is specific evidence that a person has been treated less favourably.

EXAMPLE

Use of separate canteens.

Anything done by a person in the course of his employment shall be treated for the purpose of the Act as done by his employer (s. 32(1)). This does not mean within the scope of employment or with the knowledge and approval of the employer. The principal purposes of the Act are educative, persuasive and (where necessary) coercive. Consequently, in *Jones* v *Tower Boot Co. Ltd* (CA) (1996) it was held that the common law principles of vicarious liability were not applicable in making an employer liable for the action of his employees, i.e the act(s) complained of need not be *connected* to employment. The employers were therefore liable in respect of the actions of two employees who had whipped the appellant on the legs with a piece of welt, thrown bolts at him, burnt his arm with a hot screwdriver, tried to put his arm in a lasting machine and called him 'chimp', 'monkey' and 'baboon'.

However in *Sidhu* v *Aerospace Composite Technology Ltd* (CA) (2000) Mr Sidhu had been dismissed following an incident on an outing organised by his employer. He had retaliated after another employee had racially abused and assaulted him. Although his dismissal was unfair the company policy of not taking account of provocation or other mitigating circumstances but simply to consider whether the employee used violent or abusive language was not race specific. It did not amount to direct race discrimination.

Note: See *Health and Safety at Work*, 2.3 in respect of the general principle of vicarious liability.

Refusing to give an employee a short leave of absence to consult an adviser from the Racial Equality Council was, in itself, victimisation within s. 2(1)(a) of the Act (*TNT Express Worldwide (UK) Ltd* v *Brown* (CA) (2000).

Refusing to give an employee a reference because they had made a complaint of racial discrimination victimised the employee since other employees seeking references would not normally have been treated in such a way (*Chief Constable of West Yorkshire Police* v *Khan* (CA) (2000).

Discrimination may be *indirect*.

EXAMPLE

Requiring a manual labourer to sit a mathematics examination.

Indirect discrimination may be justified where a particular standard is set by statute which may, for example, require a knowledge of English.

General Medical Council v Goba (EAT) (1988)

It was held that the required standard of knowledge set down by the Medical Act 1983 did not require persons to sit a written test. Accordingly the applicant, who had failed the test seven times and had been refused registration under the 1983 Act, was entitled to bring a complaint.

However, in *R* v *General Medical Council ex parte Virik* (CA) (1995), the Court of Appeal decided that the distinction made by s. 25 of the Medical Act 1983, whereby a doctor with recognised overseas qualifications enjoyed full registration while those with 'acceptable' overseas qualifications enjoyed only limited registration, was permissible. Those overseas doctors who had not qualified in one of the 22 recognised overseas organisations could not expect their qualifications to be directly comparable to those of doctors who had so qualified.

Discrimination will occur if a person is victimised because they are bringing or are connected with proceedings under the Race Relations Act 1976.

Although the Race Relations Act 1976, s. 54(1), gives the right to make a complaint of discrimination to an industrial tribunal, s. 54(2) excludes a complaint in respect of which an appeal or proceedings in the nature of an appeal may be brought. In *Khan* v *General Medical Council* (EAT) (1993) the right of review of a decision of the GMC to refuse to grant full registration to a doctor qualified in Pakistan was a 'proceeding in the nature of an appeal' and he was therefore excluded from the right to present a claim for unlawful racial discrimination.

In *Post Office* v *Adekeye* (CA) (1996) it was held that under s. 4 of the Act it is unlawful to discriminate against persons only in relation to employment. The Act does not extend to give a remedy to ex-employees who allege that they have been discriminated against when making an *internal* appeal against the decision to dismiss them, i.e from the time of dismissal and during an appeal the applicant was no longer employed.

Discrimination can occur, though, during selection or in relation to internal promotions.

6.3.1 Selection of candidates

Barking and Dagenham London Borough Council v Camara (EAT) (1988)

The applicant, who came from the Gambia, applied for a job as a mobile porter advertised by the council. When he was not selected he complained that he had been unlawfully discriminated against. On appeal it was held that he had not discharged the onus of proving discrimination and accordingly the case was remitted to another tribunal for re-hearing.

However, in *Nagarajan* v *London Regional Transport* (HL) (1999) the applicant had previously worked for both LRT and the London Underground. He had pursued various complaints against both under the Race Relations Act 1976.

In 1993 he applied for a position as a travel information assistant, a post which he had carried out for four months when previously employed by them. After interview he was not employed by them. By a majority the House of Lords upheld the decision of the tribunal which had decided that the applicant had been treated less favourably than others at the interview. Section 2(1) of the 1976 Act relating to selection arrangements, applied whether or not the discrimination was consciously realised. Also, a complaint against an employer would not be affected because different employees were involved in the arrangements.

North West Thames Regional Health Authority v Noone (CA) (1988)

The complainant had been born in Sri Lanka. She had qualified as a doctor and had many years' experience as a pathologist. When she applied to the appellants to work as a consultant microbiologist she was not selected for the job because it was felt that she would not 'fit in'. The Court of Appeal awarded her £3,000 damages for injury to her feelings.

Awards made by tribunals can include injury to health as well as feelings. Consequently in *Sheriff* v *Klyne Tugs (Lowestoft) Ltd* (CA) (1999) a subsequent action was correctly struck out for abuse of process. Mr Sheriff had already been awarded £4,000 at an earlier tribunal hearing on his complaint of racial harassment, abuse, intimidation and bullying. There were no special circumstances allowing new proceedings. The anxiety and depression from which Mr Sheriff claimed he was suffering were known at the time of his complaint and should not be the subject of new proceedings.

The following cases concerned discrimination against contract workers.

Harrods Ltd v *Remick; Harrods Ltd* v *Seeley; Elmi* v *Harrods Ltd* (CA) (1997)

The sale of goods at Harrods, Knightsbridge is organised by licensees providing the workforce. The respondents alleged they had either not been approved or had lost approval to work as a result of racial discrimination. Section 7 of the 1976 Act makes it unlawful to discriminate against contract workers supplied to a principal. The Court of Appeal therefore held that this section did allow the respondents to bring an action against Harrods.

An employer may be able to *justify* conduct which would otherwise be discriminatory. In *Board of Governors of St Matthias Church of England School* v *Crizzle* (EAT) (1993), the EAT accepted that Church of England school governors were entitled to take a decision affecting the way in which that school was managed in spiritual affairs. They were not in breach of the Race Relations Act 1976 when they failed to appoint as head teacher the deputy head teacher who was of Asian origin and not a communicant Christian.

6.3.2 Internal promotion

British Gas plc v *Sharma* (EAT) (1991)

It was held in this case that the appellants had discriminated against the employee, who was Indian, when she was not promoted to the position of clerk with supervisory duties.

It was found that British Gas had departed from its own criteria by appointing someone else who did not have the qualifications laid down in the job specification. Accordingly the applicant, who did possess appropriate qualifications had proved her case.

In *Mecca Leisure Group plc* v *Chatprachong* (EAT) (1993) the operators of a casino had not discriminated in failing to provide opportunities for promotion by not giving English lessons to a Thai croupier to enable him to qualify as a full casino manager.

6.4 Exemptions

Where there is a genuine occupational qualification the discrimination may be exempt, e.g. for the purposes of artistic or photographic modelling.

7 The Disability Discrimination Act 1995

From December 1996 the Disability Discrimination Act 1995 has made it unlawful to discriminate against persons with a disability.

Under the Act discrimination in employment occurs when a disabled person is treated, without justification, less favourably than someone else, as a consequence of their disability (ss. 3 and 4).

The Act applies to any form of direct discrimination in relation to recruitment, promotion, dismissal, transfer of undertaking, training and development (s. 6).

It is unlawful for a principal in relation to contract work to discriminate against a disabled person (s. 12(1)). A principal is defined as a person who makes work available for individuals employed by another person who supplies them.

In *MHC Consulting Services Ltd* v *Tansell* (CA) (2000), T, a computer consultant, was the sole shareholder and employee of Intelligents Ltd. Intelligents Ltd entered into contract with MHC Consulting Services which in turn contracted with Abbey Life Insurance Co. Ltd for the provision of freelance information technology. Several months after T had been working for the insurance company he was diagnosed as suffering from diabetes and shortly afterwards they terminated his services. On a preliminary point the Court of Appeal held that it made no difference to the application of s. 12 that the contract was made by the employment agency and not Intelligents Ltd because (1) they made work available; (2) the applicant was employed by another person; and (3) Intelligents had supplied the applicant.

To ensure that disabled persons are not placed at a substantial disadvantage in relation to able bodied persons, an employer must make reasonable adjustments to the place of work as soon as a disabled person applies for a position. These must fulfil the needs of the disabled person while they continue to be employed.

The Act requires employers to make reasonable changes to physical features of premises and arrangements.

Physical features include: the premises; fixtures; fittings; furniture and stairways. For example, wheelchair access; providing parking spaces; widening entrances and exits; lowering door handles; lowering the height of payphones; changing taps; installing alarms which can be detected by persons with impaired hearing; improved lighting; printing notices and instructions in braille.

Arrangements include: the method and place of recruitment; the terms of the contract; training and benefits. For example, allocation of certain duties originally specified to another employee; alteration of the hours of work to allow the disabled person to travel at times favourable to them; allowing time off work for assessment and treatment; amending the appraisal system; provision of assistance with reading documents; greater supervision; allowing the person to work at other, more suitable premises.

Disability is defined under s. 1 as, a physical or mental *impairment* which has a *substantial long-term adverse* effect on a person's ability to carry out normal day-to-day activities. Physical impairment can affect sense and learning ability. It can be a progressive condition likely to have future effect, e.g. muscular dystrophy. It includes any substantial disability once the effect is noticeable.

In *Goodwin* v *The Patent Office* (EAT) (1999), Mr Goodwin suffered from paranoid schizophrenia. Although he was able to cope at home his behaviour at work was bizarre. The EAT held that his illness fell within the definition of s. 1 stating that evidence must be considered in relation to:

(a) *impairment*, which must be a recognised condition;

(b) *substantial*, which is more than trivial taking into account the effect of medication;

(c) *long term*, which requires assessment of how long the disability will last;

(d) *adverse* which when assessed will still be relevant if the individual is impaired in one respect only.

The effect of any disability must be substantial and not minor. It may be substantial in respect of, say, the time taken to perform an activity or the way in which the activity can be carried out.

Long-term means an impairment which has lasted for at least 12 months, or which may recur at more than 12-month intervals.

Day-to-day activities include physical coordination, mobility, manual dexterity, manual handling, perceiving risk, remembering, speaking, hearing, seeing, and continence.

Employers are not required to make changes for minor disadvantages or if the change would be unreasonable (e.g., the installation of a lift if a stairlift would fulfil the same function). The arrangements which an employer is expected to make are in relation to the job undertaken. In *Kenny v Hampshire Constabulary* (EAT) (1998) a man who suffered from cerebral palsy and who was disabled under the 1995 Act was not unlawfully discriminated against when an offer of employment was withdrawn, because necessary assistance from volunteers to assist him when going to the toilet was not forthcoming. It was going too far to suggest that employers were under a duty to provide carers to attend to a disabled employee's personal needs. The appeal was, however, allowed on the ground that the employers should have waited for the result of a grant application under the Access to Work scheme.

Changes relating to individuals are not required until the employer is aware of the person's disability.

An employer should, however, undertake a risk assessment on being made aware of an employee's disability, to ascertain the likelihood of the employee continuing work. In *Buxton v Equinox Design Ltd* (EAT) (1998) the employee was diagnosed as suffering from multiple sclerosis. A doctor from the Employment Medical Advisory Service made a report recommending retraining and reassessment of risk. Instead, the employee was dismissed.

On complaint to a tribunal his application for unfair dismissal was upheld. He was awarded £7,127 for unfair dismissal and £500 for injury to feelings. The EAT remitted the case for further consideration in respect of the calculation of future loss of earnings.

Employers are now facing an increase in the number of tribunal claims over dismissal because workers can now claim that problems such as long term back ache or mental stress are covered by the new discrimination law. For example, a shift chemist who had poor eyesight was dismissed despite wearing special glasses. He was awarded £103,146 compensation including £3,500 for injury to feelings.

When premises are leased it may be necessary for an employer to obtain the landlord's permission to make alterations (s. 16).

7.1 Recruitment

There should be no indication in advertisements that a person would not be considered for a position because of disability.

Prior to conducting interviews, an employer must make reasonable adjustments which allow disabled persons to take part. What is reasonable may be determined by the extent to which the adjustments improve the situation for the applicant; the ease with which the changes can be made; the cost involved; the employer's resources and the availability of financial assistance.

7.2 Pensions

The Act applies to occupational pension schemes, and discrimination relating to disablement allowances can only be justified on a temporary basis while the system is being changed to ensure equal treatment of men and women (*Thomas* v *Chief Adjudication Officer* (ECJ) (1993). See also *Graham and Others* v *Secretary of State for Social Security and Another* (1995) in relation to equal treatment of men and women in respect of *state* pension entitlements.

7.3 Insurance

An insurance company providing private health care for employees must not treat disabled persons less favourably than other members of the public.

7.4 Trade organisations

Such organisations, e.g. trade unions, must not discriminate on grounds of disability.

7.5 Complaints

Generally complaints are made to employment tribunals, which may declare a practice contrary to the legislation, make recommendations, and award compensation to the applicant. The intention of the 1995 Act must be considered in the context of the employer's duties to employees generally.

In *Post Office* v *Jones* (CA) (2001) the employee who had worked on postal deliveries since 1977 was diagnosed in 1979 with type 2 diabetes. After a heart attack in 1997 he was prescribed insulin and removed from driving duties. The grounds were that drivers taking insulin did not meet the standards for professional drivers required by the Post Office. After review of this decision he was allowed to return to driving for a maximum of two hours every 24 hours. He complained to a tribunal that because of his disability he had been treated less favourably than other employees without justification.

The Court of Appeal held that the tribunal wrongly concluded that the restriction was unjustified and that the risk posed by the employees' insulin requirement was negligible. The tribunal should have confined itself to considering whether the reason given for less favourable treatment was both material and substantial.

In the present case, the employers properly conducted risk assessment provided a reason which was both material and substantial to treat the employee less favourably, even if the tribunal may have come to a different decision regarding risk.

Once a risk assessment has been undertaken clearly employers must be allowed to maintain the appropriate control measures referred to in their assessment. If Mr Jones had been allowed to drive throughout his shift and had been involved in an accident not only would there have been a breach of the Health and Safety at Work (etc) Act but the employee and any others injured as a consequence would have been able to bring civil actions for damages.

See also at 6.1.1 *Peake* v *Automotive Products Ltd* (1977).

Complaints relating to pension schemes are heard by the pensions ombudsman. Advice can be obtained from the National Disability Council.

The Act does not apply to persons with certain types of illness, e.g. kleptomania, exhibitionism, a tendency to commit arson.

From 1 October 1999, service providers are required to take reasonable steps to ensure it is not impossible or unreasonably difficult for disabled people to gain access to the service, to provide reasonable alternatives to making the service available and to provide reasonable auxiliary aids, e.g. Braille price tags in shops.

By January 2001, occupiers of premises to which members of the public have access must also ensure that reasonable adjustments have been made to facilitate disabled access.

Health and safety at work

1 Introduction

The rules of law relating to this topic are both numerous and varied. This section highlights some of the main areas of law but it is by no means a comprehensive text. When giving practical advice to clients it will almost certainly be necessary to go beyond the legal principles and rules referred to here.

The law relating to health and safety dealt with here falls into three categories; namely (i) the common law rules of negligence; (ii) the new regulations implementing European Directives which came into force in January 1993, (iii) the rules laid down by the Health and Safety at Work etc. Act 1974, together with some appropriate regulations.

2 The rules of negligence

An employer owes a common law duty of care to all his employees and other persons who may be using his premises. A common law duty is also owed by a manufacturer of products to persons using them at work.

2.1 Duty to employees

If an employee is injured at work they may be able to claim compensation from their employer, or if an undertaking is transferred under the Transfer of Undertakings (Protection of Employment) Regulations against the transferee in respect of a personal injury which has accrued before the transfer. (*Martin* v *Lancashire County Council* (CA) (2000)). Claims against either a transferee or an employer will depend on whether the injury was caused by an event which the employer could be expected reasonably to foresee.

Doughty v *Turner Manufacturing Co. Ltd* (CA) (1964)

An asbestos and cement cover was knocked into a bath of sulphuric acid which was heated to 800 degrees centigrade. After about 30 to 50 seconds a chemical reaction took place between the acid and the asbestos. The plaintiff was scalded. Since, at this time, the plaintiffs could not have foreseen that such a reaction would take place it was held they were not liable for the resulting injury.

Where, however, an employer can foresee the possibility that *some* injury may occur, and has not taken measures to prevent this, he will be liable for all injury which follows as a consequence.

Robinson v *Post Office* (CA) (1974)

The plaintiff was instructed to climb a ladder provided by his employer. There was oil on one of the rungs and he lost his footing and cut his shin. When he visited his doctor he was given an anti-tetanus injection, which caused severe brain damage. The Post Office admitted breach of duty, in supplying defective equipment, but denied responsibility for the plaintiff's brain damage. The court held that the defendants were liable for everything which arose as a consequence of their negligent act: both the accident and the necessity for an anti-tetanus injection were reasonably foreseeable. Accordingly Mr Robinson was awarded compensation in relation to the brain damage and not merely the cut shin.

The issue of *legal* causation considered in the *Robinson* case must not be confused with the need for judges to weigh up conflicting medical evidence. In *Sewell* v *Electrolux Ltd* (CA) (1997) the Court of Appeal ordered a new trial to determine whether the appellant's back injury was degenerative and therefore *unconnected* with an accident at work, or if the injury had resulted from an accident in respect of which Electrolux admitted liability.

Recently the Court of Appeal has given its response to the Law Commission Report, 'Damages for Personal Injury: Non-Pecuniary Loss' (1999). Determining eight appeal cases the court reviewed the general level of award for pain, suffering and loss of amenity. At the highest level the court saw the need for awards to be increased in the region of one third but there was no need for an increase in awards at present below £10,000. It was therefore, desirable for the Judicial Studies Board to produce a new edition of their guidelines. (*Heil* v *Rankin and Another; and seven other appeals* (CA) (2000).

An employer will also be liable for all financial loss arising from an employee's injury caused predominantly by a failure to provide a safe place of work.

In *Casey* v *Morane Ltd* (CA) (2000) the plaintiff was demoted after he lost a finger in machinery at work. Subsequently, in proceedings he brought in negligence and breach of statutory duty, his employers were held 85 per cent to blame. A 15 per cent fault on the part of the employee would not have been grounds for demotion, therefore he was entitled to the loss of earnings which wrongfully arose from this breach. These were assessed at £119,000.

It is interesting that in *Monie* v *Coral Racing* (see 5.3.3) the Court of Appeal decided it was inappropriate to apply the standards established in criminal law to determine the reasonableness of the employer's action for *unfair* dismissal.

The decision of the House of Lords in *Halfpenny* v *IGE Medical Systems Ltd* (HL) (2001) endorses this, where Lord Brown-Wilkinson stated that liability for *unfair dismissal* depends on the state of mind of the employer unlike wrongful dismissal where any breach of contract, whatever the motivation, was actionable (see 5.17.1).

The contractual duty of care for the safety of employees is no wider than the principles imposed by the law of tort.

Therefore in *Frost* v *Chief Constable of South Yorkshire Police* (HL) (1998), by a majority the House of Lords held that police officers who suffered psychiatric injury after the Hillsborough football stadium disaster could not recover damages. To recover damages for pure psychiatric injury the principles in tort, expounded in *Page* v *Smith* (HL) (1995), required the victim to establish *direct* involvement in the accident, as a *primary* victim. As employees the police officers had no direct involvement. The House of Lords also rejected their claim based on the duty owed towards rescuers since they were not exposed or believed they were exposed to any personal danger.

An employer may still owe a duty of care to employees on occasions outside of their employment, for example when an employer provides transport for an outing. In *Jebson* v *Ministry of Defence* (CA) (2000) the defendants had provided a lorry and driver as transport from camp to Portsmouth for a night out.

The Court of Appeal held that there was a duty to ensure that the transport package was reasonably safe. Since the driver could not see what was happening behind there was also a duty to supervise the men in the back. It was foreseeable that injury could occur, as a result of drunken and rowdy behaviour, on the return trip. The plaintiff, who fell from the back of the lorry when attempting to balance on the tailgate was, however, 75 per cent responsible for his injury.

Liability for personal injury under English law also applies to employees working for subsidiary companies based abroad. In *Lubbe* v *Cape plc* (HL) (2000) the House of Lords allowed an action in the English courts by employees of a South African subsidiary of an English parent company thereby establishing jurisdiction. The employees were alleging failure to protect them against the risk of asbestos. This case endorses the need for employers to properly risk assess the activities of employees who are working abroad. However, the British holidaymaker abroad may not fare as well as his employed counterpart. In *Codd* v *Thomson Tour Operations Ltd* (CA)

(2000) a boy injured in a Spanish hotel lift was unsuccessful in his action for damages. The Court of Appeal stated that the appropriate standards were local safety standards and not the equivalent British standards.

A duty is owed to employees even when an employer is acting as a subcontractor on a site controlled by a main contractor.

Morris v *Breaveglen Ltd* (CA) (1993)

The claimant was wrongly allowed to drive a dumper truck belonging to the main contractor, Sleemans. His own employer, the defendant, was held liable for his injuries caused by the dumper going out of control. An employer cannot avoid liability by delegating the task to another who performs it negligently. See also 5.10 regarding the Construction (Design and Management) Regulations which require a person in control of premises who engages independent contractors, who employ more than five persons, to ensure that the contractors have adequate measures in respect of health and safety.)

Whereas, in *Makepeace* v *Evans Brothers (Reading) (a firm) and Another* (CA) (2000) the main contractor did not owe a duty to an experienced employee of a subcontractor when he borrowed equipment from them – the main contractor. The claimant, an experienced painter, was employed by the first defendants, a sub-contractor of McAlpines. During the course of his work he borrowed a tower scaffold from McAlpines. Either because the tower was erected without stabilisers, or, because Mr Makepeace upset its balance, it toppled over. Mr Makepeace was severely injured. The tower scaffold was an ordinary piece of equipment of a kind frequently used on building sites by painters. It would therefore be extending the nursemaid school of negligence too far to say there was a duty to ask whether he knew how to correctly use the tower. Accordingly the court held that the main contractor owed no duty of care to the subcontractor's employee.

Although *civil* proceedings may *not* be based on a breach of the Health and Safety at Work etc. Act 1974 it does set standards of safety. Section 4 of the Act lays down the duties of persons in control of premises (e.g. a principal contractor) towards persons not in employment but who are using the premises as a place of work (e.g. a sub-contracted painter). One of the duties is to provide plant which is safe and without risks to health. Arguably, a tower scaffold which collapses, for whatever reason, causing the person on it to sustain head injuries leaving them permanently disabled, is not safe or without risk to health. Therefore it is strongly recommended that main contractors develop a CDM plan (see 5.10) which strictly controls the casual use of equipment by subcontractors or their employees.

Nelhams v *Sandells Maintenance Ltd and another* (CA) (1995)

Following the judgment in *Morris* v *Breaveglen Ltd*, an employer was held liable for injuries sustained by one of his employees whilst working for another contractor. However, where no actual blame attached to the claimant's employer, he was entitled to complete indemnity from the contractor under whose instructions the injured employee had been working at the time of the accident.

A subcontractor undertaking work designed by its employer is also under a general

duty to warn the employer of work it knew or ought to have known was dangerous. This duty exists irrespective of the general contractual obligation to obey the
employer's instructions. (*Plant Construction plc* v *Clive Adams Associates and Another*
(CA) (1999)).

2.1.1 Persons using the premises

At any given time it is likely that persons at a place of work will not only include the
employees of the firm but others as well, e.g. the postman delivering the mail, or an
employee of another organisation working at a premises.

For example in *Jameson and Another* v *Central Electricity Generating Board* (HL)
(1998) an employee of Babcock was exposed to asbestos whilst working at the defendant's premises. Shortly before his death he had entered into an agreement with Babcock in full and final settlement of all causes of action in his statement of claim. By a
majority the House of Lords held this extinguished the plaintiff's, and therefore his
widow's, claim under the Fatal Accidents Act 1976 to a further action against the
CEGB. The duty of care in respect of premises applies to persons who either own the
freehold or who have taken on a lease of the premises.

In the latter case the extent of the responsibility will be determined by the terms of
the lease, e.g. a repairing lease will place a greater responsibility on the employer/
leaseholder.

The Occupiers' Liability Act 1984, referred to in Chapter 4 of *Law for Legal
Executives, Part One, Year One*, reiterates the duty established in earlier case law. In
general the duty is to prevent foreseeable accidents to persons either lawfully, or in
some instances, unlawfully, on the premises. (See **Tomlinson** v **Congleton Borough
Council & Another** (CA) (2002) which significantly extends occupiers' liability.)

An occupier must be prepared for children to be less careful than adults. Therefore
in *Jolly* v *Sutton London Borough Council* (HL) (2000) the Council were expected to
foresee not only that children would play on, but also work on, an abandoned boat.
Accordingly the Council were liable when the boat, which was on their land, fell on
the claimant whilst he was attempting to repair and paint the hull.

Occupiers of factories, warehouses and similar premises must therefore, ensure that
risk assessments take into account the possibility of children trespassing on their land
and meddling with equipment creating a potential hazard.

2.2 Duty in respect of products

Manufacturers of goods and products owe a duty of care to the user.

Hill v James Crowe (Cases) Ltd (QBD) (1978)

The manufacturer of a packing case was held to owe a duty of care to a lorry driver
who was injured when he stood on it and it gave way, causing him to fall. The court
accepted that he had fallen because the packing case had been badly made and that the
manufacturers should have foreseen that as a consequence, a person such as the
plaintiff would suffer injury. Applying the rule in *Donoghue* v *Stevenson* (HL) (1932)
the defendants were liable.

Section 2 of the Consumer Protection Act 1987 imposes strict liability on the producer of defective products which cause damage. This Act was passed to implement the Product Liability Directive which states that a product is defective when it does not provide the safety which a person is entitled to expect.

In *A and Others* v *National Blood Authority and Another* (QBD) (2001) Mr Justice Burton held that infected bags of blood were a non-standard product. Members of the public would not expect that a proportion of bags would be infected with hepatitis C. The producers could not rely on the defence that they were unaware of the risk from hepatitis C in blood. The producers were strictly liable to A and the other claimants who became infected with hepatitis C after being given blood transfusions. As a control measure all blood and blood products should have been screened.

2.3 Vicarious liability

An employer will be liable for the negligent acts of an employee committed in the course of employment.

Lister v *Romford Ice and Cold Storage Co. Ltd* (HL) (1957)

A father was negligently run over by his son when the son was reversing a lorry. The accident happened while the son was working in the course of employment. The firm was vicariously liable.

An employer will also be vicariously liable when there is a very close connection between the tort of the employee and his employment.

In *Lister and Others* v *Hesley Hall Ltd* (HL) (2001) the defendants who managed Axeholme House, a boarding annex of Wilsic Hall School, Doncaster, had employed Dennis Grain and his wife to work as warden and housekeeper to take care of the boys in the house. Unbeknown to them, Grain had systematically sexually abused the appellants. Overruling the Court of Appeal's decision in *Trotman* v *North Yorkshire County Council* (1998) the House of Lords held that evidence showed the defendants had entrusted the care of the children to the warden. The warden's torts were so closely connected with his employment it was just and equitable to hold the defendants vicariously liable.

Employers of staff in educational establishments should therefore, include in risk assessments control measures designed to monitor the overall and specific suitability of staff to care, at varying levels, for pupils and students put in their trust.

A local authority will also be vicariously liable when an employee, such as an educational psychologist, called in to advise on the future educational provision for a child, fails to correctly diagnose the child's condition. *Phelps* v *Hillingdon London Borough Council* (HL) (2000).

2.4 The effect of Woolf on accident claims

The implementation of the Woolf Report from 26 April 1999 will undoubtedly increase the numbers of persons claiming compensation for injury sustained in the workplace. Its introduction means that employers and persons in control of premises must have comprehensive records relating to risk management, accident and incident statistics as well as full details of matters relating to any complaints lodged following an accident. This information must be immediately accessible in order to lodge any possible defence to an action within 28 days of service of particulars of claim.

The strict time limit does not, of course, apply until after proceedings have been issued. For those wishing to avoid the additional costs and time now imposed by the need to allocate a case to an appropriate 'track' there is a further incentive to settle before proceedings have been issued.

Consequently, the parties to an action may attempt to negotiate a settlement before litigation is started. The defendant may pay a sum of money into court. If the case goes to trial new evidence produced by the defendant during the case may affect the award of compensation made by the judge. This could be substantially less than the amount originally paid into court. However, in *Ford* v *GKR Construction* (CA) (1999) the Court of Appeal decided that new evidence would not affect the claimant's costs.

2.5 Damages for non-financial loss

The Law Commission has been reviewing the extent of damages for non-financial loss and how they should be determined. Their report, published in April 1999, recommends that the current system of assessment by judges should continue. However, they considered that for serious injuries, damages for non-financial loss were too low. They have recommended an increase of between 50 and 100 per cent. The top of the scale would be at least £225,000 but not more than £300,000.

3 The regulations

3.1 Introduction

In January 1993, to comply with EC Directives, six new UK regulations passed in 1992 came into force. Some of these repealed parts of the Offices, Shops and Railway Premises Act 1963 and the Factories Act 1961 (FA). However, the sections of these Acts which were repealed were generally replaced with equivalent sections under the new regulations. The regulations also establish additional duties for both employers, employees and the selfemployed beyond those previously laid down by the 1963 and 1961 Acts.

The regulations are referred to below and where applicable existing case law is quoted which interpreted similar sections of the earlier legislation.

3.2 Management of Health and Safety at Work Regulations 1999

3.2.1 Risk assessment
These regulations (the 'Management Regulations') require every employer to undertake a risk assessment in respect of risks both to employees (reg. 3(1)(a)) and persons not in employment (reg. 3(1)(b)). The self-employed must also undertake a similar exercise in respect of risks to themselves (reg. 3(2)(a)) and others who may be affected by their undertaking (reg. (3(2)(b)).

The purpose of these assessments is to determine the measures needed to comply with the requirements or prohibitions imposed by 'relevant statutory provisions'. The relevant statutory provisions may include the Health and Safety at Work etc. Act 1974 (HASAWA) (see 4 below) and some or all of the other 1992 regulations and the Fire Precaution (Workplace Regulations) 1997.

Once the initial assessment has been undertaken it has to be reviewed if:

(a) there is reason to suspect that it is no longer valid, or

(b) there has been a significant change in the matters to which it relates (e.g., new machines or a different system of work).

To begin with, undertaking an assessment means identifying foreseeable risks and associated hazards. The difference between risk and hazard and the measures which should have been undertaken can be illustrated by:

Haley v *London Electricity Board* (HL) (1964)

The defendant's employees had dug a hole in the pavement. The plaintiff, who was blind, tripped over a lump hammer (a heavy hammer with a long handle) which had been placed diagonally in front of the hole against some railings. He was deafened as a consequence of falling into the hole.

The court held that since statistically there was a likelihood of blind persons walking along that particular pavement, the risk was foreseeable and consequently the plaintiff's action for damages was successful.

Section 3 of HASAWA 1974 also creates a *statutory* duty towards members of the public in these circumstances. The place of work is the street and the duty is of an employer towards persons *not* in employment. Therefore in order to comply with 'relevant statutory provisions' as required by reg. 3 of the Management Regulations the London Electricity Board would now have to undertake a risk assessment relating to this type of work. In this case the risk was the risk of injury caused by falling into the hole. The hazard was the hole, or to a blind person, the lump hammer which caused him to trip.

Appropriate measures would, therefore, have been either to cover the hole or, if this was not practicable, to fence it with barriers to prevent anyone, including blind persons, falling in. Other measures would include training, instruction and supervision of the employees doing the work (see HASAWA 1974, s. 2(2)(c), discussed in 5.1.3 below).

Once hazard and risk have been identified, an employer who employs five or more people must record the findings and the employees classified as being especially at risk (reg. 3(6)).

The employer must implement preventative and protective measures in accordance with sch. 1 to the 1999 Regulations.

The employer must also make arrangements regarding planning, organisation, control, monitoring and review of the preventative and protective measures (reg. 5(1)) and when more than five persons are employed record these arrangements (reg.

5(2)). Regulation 5 therefore requires an employer to record information about the way in which it is intended to deal with safety matters and the organisational structure of the concern. This information can be included in a safety policy document. This document should refer to all persons affected by the way in which the concern is run—not just employees. Control, monitoring and review measures can be included on the risk assessment sheets which provide information to employees as required by reg. 10.

If the organisation is large, recording and review is best done on a computer, after pro forma hazard sheets have been completed by staff within the organisation. Assessments should involve *all* relevant personnel, making them accountable and engendering a risk culture within the organisation.

Example pro forma hazard sheet

Hazard	Risk	Control	Frequency	Review of Measures
Hole in pavement	Injury by falling	Barriers Training Instruction Superevision	Constant Induction Annual	Annual

Signed: *S. Philips*   Date: 18/04/94
Position: *Supervisor*

The other duties under the Management of Health and Safety at Work Regulations 1992 are as follows.

3.2.2 Health surveillance (reg. 6)
Every employer must undertake appropriate health surveillance of employees which takes account of risks to their health and safety which have been identified by the assessment (e.g., persons exposed to noise, dust or fumes).

3.2.3 Competent persons (reg. 7)
Every employer has to appoint competent persons—defined under reg. 7(5) as persons with sufficient training, experience or knowledge and other qualities to enable them to properly assist in undertaking the measures needed to comply with the statutory provisions. Such persons must be given sufficient time and means to fulfil their function (reg. 7(3)).

The self-employed and persons in partnerships can undertake their own assessments and ensure compliance with the statutes provided they have sufficient training and experience to do so (reg. 7(6) and (7)).

Where there is a competent person in the employer's employment, that person should be appointed in preference to a competent person not in employment (reg. 7(8)).

3.2.4 Procedures for serious and imminent danger and for danger areas (reg. 8)

(a) Employers must have procedures to deal with dangerous occurrences (e.g., fire drills).

(b) Employers must appoint competent persons (e.g., a fire officer) to undertake these procedures.

(c) Access by employees to certain areas of the workplace must be restricted if necessary on health and safety grounds. For example, if dangerous chemicals are stored then employees and others must be told not to enter the storage areas and there must be warning notices.

Employers must arrange contacts with external services (e.g. for emergency medical care and rescue work (reg. 9).

3.2.5 Employers must provide information (reg. 10)

Every employer has to provide employees with comprehensible and relevant information on:

(a) Risks to health and safety identified by the assessments.

(b) Preventative and protective measures. Employees can be provided with printouts of the assessments for their areas.

(c) The emergency procedures referred to in reg. 8 (see 3.2.4 above) and the Fire Precautions (work place) Regulations 1997.

(d) The identity of persons responsible under reg. 8 (see 3.2.4 above) and under the Fire Precaution 1997. These can be identified in the health and safety policy document.

(e) Risks to other employers using the site. This can be done by giving contractors on site a summary of appropriate risks either when they enter the site or in the paperwork sent out before they start work.

3.2.6 Cooperation (reg. 11)

When two or more employers share a workplace they must cooperate with each other to ensure safe and healthy working for everyone using the site (e.g., by sharing applicable information about risk).

3.2.7 Persons working in host employers' or self-employed persons' undertakings (reg. 12)

Employers and the self-employed must provide sufficient information regarding risks to other persons (and their employers) from an outside undertaking working in their undertaking including identification of persons responsible for emergency evacuation.

3.2.8 Capabilities and training (reg. 13)

An employer must take account of employees' capabilities when assigning tasks.

Employees must be provided with adequate training:

(a) when recruited,

(b) on being exposed to new risks (e.g., a change in responsibilities, new
    equipment, new technology, new or different systems).

The training must be repeated or adapted to take account of changes and must be
undertaken in working hours. (See also HASAWA 1974, s. 2(2)(c), discussed in 9.1.3
below regarding the duty to train and instruct).

3.2.9 Employees' duties (reg. 14)

As well as the responsibilities laid down under ss. 7 and 8 of HASAWA 1974 (see 9.2
below), employees must use machinery, equipment, dangerous substances, transport,
means of production and safety devices in accordance with training and instructions
given (reg. 14(1)).

Employees must also *inform* their employer of work situations they consider to be
dangerous or unhealthy (reg. 14(2)(a)) and of any shortcoming in the employer's
arrangements for health and safety (reg. 14(2)(b)), that is, they must advise the
employer about any 'gaps' in the system which they notice. This is as well as taking
reasonable care of themselves and others and cooperating with the employer.

3.2.10 Temporary workers (reg. 15)

There are duties to provide people employed on fixed-term contracts with information about any special occupational skills or qualifications (e.g., electrical qualifications) required to work safely and any health surveillance needed. These duties extend
towards agencies who send out temporary workers and they also place responsibilities
on employers and the self-employed to provide information.

3.2.11 Enforcement

These regulations cannot be used as a basis for any civil action (reg. 22). This is now
under review. A breach can lead to prosecution by the Health and Safety Executive.

3.2.12 Inadmissible defence

It will not be a defence in criminal proceedings for an employer to state the act or
default was that of his employee or competent person appointed under reg. 7 (reg.
21).

EXAMPLE

In order to save on salary A. Principal employs Y, a less than competent lecturer, in the
engineering department. Six months later a student is seriously injured as a consequence
of Y's negligence. A will be personally liable to criminal prosecution and the College
insurers will be liable to compensate the victim.

3.2.13 The health and safety of young persons

The Health and Safety (Young Persons) Regulations 1997 came into force in March
1997. They added to the existing provisions of the Management Regulations and gave
effect to a European Directive (94/33/EC). They have now been incorporated into the
1999 Management Regulations.

Employers must not employ young people to carry out work which is beyond their psychological or physical capacity or which exposes them to harm from radiation, agents which are toxic or carcinogenic or which may cause genetic damage to their health or that of an unborn child (reg. 19 of the 1999 Management Regulations).

An employer must not expose young persons to the risk of an accident which they may not recognise because of their insuffucient attention to safety or lack of experience (reg. 19(2)(d)). Young persons must not be exposed to extreme cold or heat, noise or vibration (reg. 19(2)(e)).

The Regulations make it a requirement to assess risks faced by persons who are under the age of 18 who are employed. The assessments must consider particular risks faced due to inexperience, lack of awareness of risks and the person's immaturity. They take account of the layout of the workplace, equipment and chemicals, the activities which take place and the extent of training for the young person (reg. 3(4) of the Management Regulations 1999).

The employer must also provide information on risks to both the young person when employed and the child's parents *before* employment (reg. 10(2) of the Management Regulations 1999).

Control measures must, therefore, be adopted which are appropriate to the employment of young persons.

3.2.14 Young persons' experience

Employers must recognise, as a general principle, that young employees do not have the same degree of experience as their older counterparts. In *Fraser* v *Winchester Health Authority* (CA) (1999) the claimant, who was a resident support worker, had been sent on a week's camping holiday, with a patient, without supervision or assistance. When she was attempting to change a gas cylinder it was ignited by a candle she had lit. There was an explosion, their tent caught fire and she was burnt.

The Court of Appeal found that she had been given no instruction in changing the cylinder. It was held that although she might appreciate the risk, sending her out with candles and matches could only suggest to her that they might be used as a source of light. She was, however, contributorily negligent and was held one third to blame.

3.2.15 Lone working

There is no general prohibition on lone working but an employer's additional duty to lone workers is to determine what arrangements are needed to prevent an individual being exposed to greater risk than other employees. In assessing risk an employer should consider for example, does the lone worker have access to first aid, is there adequate heating, how can they communicate with others, are females at greater risk, what training should be provided, and whether work equipment poses special risk to the person working alone. Failure to ensure adequate protective measures recorded in risk assessments will be a breach of the management and associated regulations.

3.3 Workplace (Health, Safety and Welfare) Regulations 1992

These regulations (the 'Workplace Regulations') apply to every workplace except ships, certain types of building operation as defined by the Factories Act 1961, s. 176, and mining operations. Also regs 5 to 12 and 14 to 25 are not applicable to aircraft and locomotives and rolling stock when these are a place of work, and regs 5 to 19 and 23 to 25 are not applicable to woods or other land forming part of an agricultural or forestry undertaking (reg. 3).

3.3.1 General duty

Under reg. 4, every employer or person who has control over a workplace, extension, conversion, or modification where any of his employees works must ensure that it conforms with all provisions of the Workplace Regulations that apply to it.

A person who has control of a workplace in connection with carrying on a trade, business or undertaking by him must also ensure that it complies with applicable regulations.

The main duties under the Workplace Regulations are shown below.

The duties under the Factories Act 1961 and Offices, Shops and Railways Premises Act 1963 referred to in the ILEX syllabus in respect of space, temperature, floors, passages, gangways, steps, access, provision of a safe place of work, dust and fumes are now repealed.

3.3.2 Maintenance

The workplace, equipment, devices and systems must be maintained and cleaned in an efficient state, working order and good repair (reg. 5).

3.3.3 Ventilation

There must be effective and suitable ventilation and quantities of purified fresh air for enclosed places of work (reg. 6).

Brookes v J. & P. Coates (UK) Ltd (QBD) (1984)

The claimant contracted byssinosis from working in a cotton mill from 1935 to 1965. The process of spinning cotton gave off very fine dust. His employer knew that cotton dust could cause byssinosis but had failed to take measures to prevent employees from inhaling the dust. It was in breach of duty and accordingly the plaintiff was entitled to compensation.

3.3.4 Temperatures

Temperatures in all workplaces inside buildings must be reasonable. The method of heating or cooling must not result in an escape of fumes, gas or vapour likely to be injurious or offensive to any person. There must be sufficient numbers of thermometers to enable persons at work to check the temperature inside a building (reg. 7).

3.3.5 Lighting

Every workplace must have suitable and sufficient lighting (reg. 8).

3.3.6 Furnishings

Every workplace and the furniture, furnishings and fittings therein shall be kept sufficiently clean. This includes floors, walls and ceilings (reg. 9).

3.3.7 Room dimensions and space

Every room where persons work must have sufficient floor area, height and unoccupied space for the purposes of health, safety and welfare (reg. 10). For workplaces previously covered by the Factories Act 1961, it is sufficient to comply with the requirement that all persons should have a minimum clear working area of 400 cubic feet.

3.3.8 Workstations and seating

A workstation must be suitable both for the persons who may use it and the type of work undertaken there (reg. 11). So far as reasonably practicable it must give protection from adverse weather conditions. Persons must be able to leave it swiftly or be assisted in an emergency and must not be likely to slip or fall at the workstation. A suitable seat must be provided and footrest when necessary.

More specific requirements relate to workstations at which persons operate display screen equipment (see 3.8 below).

3.3.9 Condition of floors and traffic routes

Every floor and surface of a traffic route must be of such construction as to make it suitable for use (reg. 12).

EXAMPLE

Westwood v Post Office (HL) (1973)

Mr Westwood and his companions worked at a Post Office building in Hackney, London. It was a three-storey building with a flat roof. He and others were in the habit of going on to the roof for a 'breather'. When it was not possible to gain access to the roof via the stairway, employees would unlock the door of the lift motor room and climb out on to the roof from a window. There was a notice on the door to the lift motor room which stated 'only authorised attendant is permitted to enter'.

When Mr Westwood was returning on one occasion, a trapdoor in the floor gave way and he fell through to the floor below and was fatally injured. His widow claimed compensation.

The House of Lords held that (a) the requirement in OSRPA, s. 16, to ensure all floors were of sound construction applied to the whole of the premises; (b) the requirement extended to the whole floor areas, including the trapdoor, which was not of sound construction; (c) although there was a notice on the door, and Mr Westwood was not authorised, he was not contributorily negligent. Mr Westwood may have been disobedient, but as the notice said nothing about *danger* he was not negligent. The breach of duty had led to his death. Accordingly his widow was entitled to compensation.

A floor or the surface of a traffic route must be free from holes.

EXAMPLE

Sanders v F. M. Lloyd & Co. Ltd (QBD) (1982)

The floor of the defendant's furnace department had in it three small pits. The plaintiff fell into one of these and sprained his ankle. The defendant's were liable since it did not show that it was impracticable either to cover or rail off the pits.

Where adequate measures have been taken to prevent a person falling into a hole there will be no liability (reg. 12(4)(a)).

A floor or the surface of a traffic route must be free from slopes and not so uneven or slippery as to create a risk to persons or health or safety.

EXAMPLE

Johnston v *Caddies Wainwright Ltd* (CA) (1983)

The plaintiff slipped on a patch of oil. The defendants, who produced no evidence as to what they had done to prevent the oil being there, were held liable for the plaintiff's injuries.

Contrast, however, *Darby* v *GKN Screws and Fasteners Ltd* (QBD) (1986) in which the defendant company was not liable when the plaintiff injured his thumb after slipping on ice. He had arrived at work at 7.45 am. The gang who were spreading rock salt had begun work at 7.30 am, but had not reached the part of the site where the plaintiff slipped. The defendant had discharged its duty to take reasonable care. Similarly in *Dixon* v *London Fire and Civil Defence Authority* (CA) (1993) an employee who slipped on water on a studded tiled floor in a fire station was not able to show that his employer had failed to take reasonable care either to prevent the water, which was endemic in a fire station, being there or to provide a suitable floor surface. Consequently the defendant authority was not liable for his injuries.

Where a handrail has been provided on a slope this will be taken into account in determining the risk created by the slope (reg. 12(4)(b)).

A floor or the surface of a traffic route must have an effective means of drainage when necessary.

So far as reasonably practicable every floor in a workplace and the surface of every traffic route must be kept free from obstruction and from any article or substance which may cause a person to slip, trip or fall (reg. 12(3)).

EXAMPLE

Dorman Long (Steel) Ltd v *Bell* (HL) (1964)

The respondent was making his way around the back of a machine when he tripped or slipped on some backing plates which had been left lying on the floor. The employer argued that his fall was caused by a slippery film on the plates, not on the floor. The argument was rejected. It would have meant that if an employee slipped on a piece of paper lying on the floor the statutory protection would not apply. Mr Bell was, however, 50 per cent to blame for his injury as he should have been looking where he was going.

Cox v *H.C.B. Angus Ltd* (QBD) (1981)

The plaintiff was held to be 50 per cent to blame when his foot slipped on a piece of loose piping inside a fire engine cab. The cab was a place of work, but the plaintiff was negligent in failing to see the pipe.

In *Gunion* v *Roche Products Ltd* (Outer House, Court of Session) (1994), it was held that because something could move in and out of a factory it did not cease to be a place of work. The legislation therefore applied to a fork lift truck—it was a place where a person worked.

Handrails should also be provided on staircases unless they cause an obstruction.

3.3.10 Falls or falling objects

So far as reasonably practicable, measures must be taken to prevent any person falling a distance likely to cause personal injury (reg. 13).

EXAMPLE

Allen v *Avon Rubber Co. Ltd* (CA) (1986)

The duty applied to the edge of a loading bay which should have had a barrier to prevent the plaintiff's fork-lift truck from reversing over the edge.

So far as reasonably practicable, measures must be taken to prevent any person being struck by a falling object likely to cause personal injury. Whether adequate measures have been taken to ensure employees' safety in this respect will be judged purely as a matter of fact.

EXAMPLE

Larner v *British Steel plc* (CA) (1993)

Equipment on which the plaintiff was working fell and severely crushed his right leg. The defendants were liable. It was not necessary for the plaintiff to establish that the accident was foreseeable.

These measures should be preventive measures rather than merely providing personal protective equipment (e.g., a hard hat) or information, instruction, training and supervision (reg. 13(2)). However, where an area creates the risk of falling or injury by being struck, notices should be displayed (reg. 13(4)).

3.3.11 Tanks and pits

Tanks and pits containing dangerous substances (e.g., poisonous or corrosive substances) must be covered over or securely fenced (reg. 13(6)).

3.3.12 Windows

All windows or other transparent surfaces must, where necessary for reasons of health and safety, either be made of safety material or protected against breakage and be marked to make people aware of their presence (reg. 14). Any glass in doors in corridors, for example, should either be toughened or wired glass and clearly marked.

There should be no risk to people either when opening windows, skylights or ventilators or when they are open (reg. 15). This might mean that some windows have to be permanently fixed to prevent them blowing open on windy days and shattering.

It must also be possible to clean windows safely, taking into account the type of equipment available for use (reg. 16).

3.3.13 Traffic routes

The workplace must allow pedestrians and vehicles to circulate safely and there must be suitable and sufficient numbers of traffic routes for persons and vehicles (reg. 17). There must be no danger to the health or safety of persons near to a traffic route. Doors and gates for pedestrians should not lead directly on to a route used by vehicles, and vehicles and pedestrians using the same route must be separated. Signs and notices must be put up to ensure that the routes can be used safely.

3.3.14 Doors and gates

Doors and gates must be suitably constructed with any necessary safety devices (reg. 18). In particular:

(a) Sliding doors must be prevented from coming off their tracks.

(b) Doors which open upwards must have a device which prevents them falling back.

(c) Powered doors should have features which prevent them trapping a person (e.g., a sensor and cut-out device). Where necessary it should also be possible to open them manually.

(d) Persons must have a clear view of what is on the other side of the door if it can be opened by being pushed from either side.

3.3.15 Escalators and moving walkways

Escalators and moving walkways must function safely, be equipped with necessary safety devices and stop controls (reg. 19).

3.3.16 Sanitary conveniences

There must be sufficient numbers of sanitary conveniences (1 per 25 male and female employees) and they must be suitable (reg. 20). They must be adequately ventilated, lit and kept in a clean and orderly condition.

3.3.17 Washing facilities

There must be suitable and sufficient washing facilities which include showers if required for health reasons (reg. 21). Washing facilities must be provided in the vicinity of every sanitary convenience and changing room (reg. 24). They must include a supply of hot and cold or warm water, soap, towels or other means of drying. They must be kept in a clean and orderly condition and be well lit and ventilated.

3.3.18 Drinking water

An adequate supply of drinking water which is easily accessible and conspicuously marked must be provided (reg. 22).

3.3.19 Accommodation for clothing

Provision must be made to store clothing either not taken home but worn during working hours or worn to but not at work (reg. 23). There must be adequate facilities for persons to change their clothing at work where this is necessary (reg. 24).

3.3.20 Facilities for rest and to eat meals

There must be suitable and sufficient rest facilities and, in the case of a new workplace, suitable facilities to eat meals where food would become contaminated if eaten in the workplace (reg. 25).

Rest rooms and rest areas must be arranged so as to protect non-smokers from discomfort caused by tobacco smoke.

Suitable and sufficient facilities must be provided for persons at work to eat meals where they are regularly eaten in the workplace. Since there is a requirement to protect persons in rest rooms from tobacco smoke, it would seem that eating areas should also not be contaminated by tobacco smoke.

Suitable rest facilities must also be provided for women at work who are pregnant.

3.3.21 Enforcement

Civil action based on breach of these regulations is not prevented. Criminal proceedings can lead to a fine of up to £20,000 at first instance.

3.4 Provision and Use of Work Equipment Regulations 1998

The Provision and Use of Work Equipment Regulations 1992 have been entirely repealed. They are replaced by the Provision and Use of Work Equipment Regulations 1998.

These regulations apply to every employer, self-employed person or person who occupies a factory in respect of work equipment used in the premises. They also apply to any person who has control, to any extent, of non-domestic premises made available as a place of work, in respect of work equipment used in these premises.

The main duties under the Provision and Use of Work Equipment Regulations are shown below.

3.4.1 Suitability of work equipment (reg. 4)

Every employer must ensure that work equipment is so constructed or adapted as to be suitable for the purpose for which it is used or provided. When work equipment is selected the employer must take account of work conditions and the risks to health and safety which exist in the premises or undertaking, and any additional risk likely to occur as a result of the use of that equipment. Employers must also ensure that the equipment is used only for operations for which it is suitable.

EXAMPLE

It would not be suitable to use a chisel as a screwdriver.

3.4.2 Maintenance (reg. 5)

Employers must ensure that equipment is properly maintained in an efficient working order and that when applicable maintenance logs are kept up to date.

Regulation 5 (originally reg. 6 in the 1992 Regulations) must be interpreted in the light of previous House of Lords decisions and therefore imposes an absolute duty to maintain equipment. In *Stark* v *The Post Office* (CA) (2000) the defendants supplied the plaintiff with a delivery bicycle. When the front stirrup forming part of the brake broke they were in breach of this duty and accordingly they were liable in damages for the injury he sustained.

3.4.3 Inspection

Equipment must be inspected after installation, prior to service, or, after assembly at a new site location. It must be re-inspected when subject to conditions which might cause deterioration. A record of re-inspection must be kept. Evidence of inspection must be available in respect of equipment either leaving the undertaking or obtained from another undertaking (reg. 6).

3.4.4 Specific risks (reg. 7)

Where the use of equipment is likely to involve a specific risk to health (e.g., a fibreglass sander in a bodyshop) or safety (e.g., a centre lathe) the employer must ensure that use is restricted to persons who use it as part of their work, and that they are adequately trained. Maintenance, servicing or repairs must be undertaken only by authorised persons.

3.4.5 Information and instructions (reg. 8)

Employers must ensure that *all* persons who use work equipment have adequate information and, if applicable, written instructions relating to equipment use. Supervisors and managers must be given adequate information and, if applicable, written instructions. In particular, information and written instructions must include:

(a) the way in which equipment may be used and where it may be used,

(b) any abnormal situation which is foreseeable, and

(c) conclusions to be drawn from experience of the work equipment.

EXAMPLE
Centre drill
Purpose—drilling
Use only in static position.
Use with guard.
Wear protective eye wear.
Use only after instructions for use given, if not already familiar with equipment.
Abnormal occurrence
POWER WILL NOT CUT OFF ON DRILL
RISK OF SHOCK
GO TO MASTER SWITCH IN WORKSHOP AND TURN OFF ALL POWER.

The importance of providing comprehensive instructions has already been illustrated by *Westwood* v *Post Office* (HL) (1973) (see 3.3.9 above).

It may also be noted that these requirements extend beyond those set down by HASAWA, s. 2(2)(c), in that as well as being written, the instructions must refer to abnormal situations.

3.4.6 Training (reg. 9)

Employers must ensure that all persons who work equipment and all managers and supervisors have received adequate training for purposes of health and safety and the methods to be used to operate the equipment. They must also point out any risks and appropriate precautions. This last requirement also extends the duty previously laid down by HASAWA 1974, s. 2(2)(c).

3.4.7 New equipment (provided after 31 December 1992): appropriate standards (reg. 10)

Any such equipment must comply with any Act or instrument which gives effect to one of 17 Community Directives referred to in sch. 1 to these regulations. If it is not subject to any such legislation then it must comply with regs. 11–19 and 22–29 set out below.

3.4.8 Dangerous machinery (reg. 11)

All employers must take measures:

(a) to prevent access to any dangerous part of machinery or rotating stock bar (i.e., guarding),

(b) to stop the movement of any dangerous part of machinery or rotating stock bar (on a lathe) before any person enters a danger zone (e.g., a photoelectric cell which cuts off the power supply when it senses movement) so as to prevent a person being exposed to a hazard in or around a machine.

The guards should enclose every dangerous or rotating part or, where this is not practicable, other types of guard should be fitted.

Kinder v Camberwell Borough Council (KBD) (1944)

The claimant was the operator of a machine which was used for compressing waste paper into bales. This was done by pulling down a handle at the side of the machine which should have been held in place by a cog. Much to Mr Kinder's surprise, on one occasion, when he let go of the handle it flew up and hit him under the chin, knocking out several of his teeth and breaking his jaw. He claimed against his employer. The court decided that the machine was dangerous, that it was not securely guarded and this had caused his injury. Accordingly he was entitled to compensation.

Although the regulation requires that machinery which is dangerous is guarded, the requirement does not extend to material which may become dangerous, but in *Wearing* v *Pirelli Ltd* (HL) (1977) a workman was injured by contact with a thin rubber fabric covering a revolving drum which was a dangerous part of machinery and not securely guarded. Lord Edmund-Davies stated, 'On a practical view of the whole incident the workman was truly injured by the revolving drum itself'. His claim therefore succeeded.

Employees may, however, have their compensation reduced if they are to blame for their injury. In *Rushton* v *Turner Bros Asbestos Co. Ltd* (1959) the claimant had specific-ally asked to operate a machine used for crushing asbestos. The machine was loaded via a trapdoor which slid up and down in two grooves. Occasionally the grooves had to be cleaned out. The claimant's fingers were crushed when he put his hand into the machine while it was still switched on. Although it was held that the machine was dangerous and not adequately guarded, the judge said 'the plaintiff was the sole author of his own misfortune'. Consequently he received nothing.

If it is not practicable to fit guards then jigs, holders or push-sticks must be used. If this is not practicable then adequate training, instruction and supervision must be given (i.e., an employer can only regard this as a last resort in the event that it is not possible to provide guards or other protective devices). Clearly if this is all an employer is able to do to comply with reg. 11 then it is vital to take account of the employee's experience and expertise.

When maintenance work is being undertaken the guards should restrict access to the area where the work is being carried out. If possible, guards should be constructed in such a way that they do not have to be dismantled for maintenance work to be carried out (reg. 11(3)((b)).

3.4.9 Protection against specific hazards (reg. 12)
An employer must prevent or adequately control persons being exposed to the various hazardous situations referred to below. Once a hazard is recognised it is necessary to take *some* type of measures.

> EXAMPLE
>
> As a part of his job X works in a dusty environment but he is only exposed to the dust for 10 minutes each day. There is a risk of lung or other disease but it would not be reasonable to expect his employer to install expensive extraction equipment; instead the employer can provide X with a breathing mask to prevent him inhaling the dust.

The hazards which must be prevented or adequately controlled are those caused by:

(a) substances or articles falling or being ejected,

(b) rupture or disintegration of work equipment,

(c) fire or overheating,

(d) discharge of gas, dust, liquid, vapour or any substance,

(e) explosion.

The preventive measures must, so far as practicable be those *other* than the provision of protective clothing, information, instruction and training.

3.4.10 Temperature (reg. 13)
Preventive measures must be taken to prevent persons being burnt, scalded or seared by extremely hot or cold equipment.

3.4.11 Controls
Equipment must be fitted with suitable controls which can start (reg. 14) and stop (reg. 15) the equipment and also readily accessible emergency stop controls (reg. 16). All such controls must be clearly visible and identifiable by marking where necessary (reg. 17).

Employers must:

(a) ensure, so far as is reasonably practicable, that all control systems of work equipment are safe; and

(b) are chosen making due allowance for the failures and constraints to be expected in the planned circumstances of use.

When in operation a control system must not result in any increased risk to health or safety including any circumstances when a fault occurs or when there is a loss of supply of energy. One control system must not impede the operation of another (reg. 18).

As well as controls for starting and stopping equipment when necessary there must be a means of isolating it completely from its source of energy (reg. 19). For example, in a workshop with a number of electrical appliances each of which can be turned on and off independently both normally and in an emergency, there must also be a master switch which isolates everything.

3.4.12 Stability (reg. 20)
Work equipment must be kept stable by clamping or other means when necessary to prevent risks to health or safety.

3.4.13 Lighting (reg. 21)
Work areas must be suitably illuminated taking into account the operations being carried out.

3.4.14 Maintenance (reg. 22)
When maintenance is being carried out equipment should either be shut down or measures taken to prevent persons being exposed to risks.

3.4.15 Markings and warnings
All work equipment must be clearly marked (reg. 23) and incorporate appropriate warnings (reg. 24).

EXAMPLE

DANGER: ENSURE GUARD IS IN PLACE BEFORE STARTING. READ OTHER INSTRUCTIONS FOR USE BELOW. DANGER: DO NOT USE THIS EQUIPMENT IF NOT TRAINED.

Appropriate warnings include those given by audible devices (e.g., a loud buzzer if a machine is started without a guard, though it should be remembered that when rules laid down by reg. 11 of these regulations are being adhered to, in many instances it will not be possible to start a machine unless the guard is in place).

3.4.16 Mobile work equipment (reg. 25–27)
If any employee is carried on mobile work equipment it must be suitable for this purpose. It must incorporate features for reducing risks to safety including risks from wheels or tracks.

Equipment must be stabilised. It must incorporate a feature which ensures it can do no more than fall on its side and a feature giving sufficient clearance to anyone being carried if it overturns further than on its side.

If there is a risk of a person being crushed it must have a suitable system.

A fork lift truck must be adapted or equipped to reduce to as low as is reasonably practicable the risk to safety if it overturns.

3.4.17 Self-propelled work equipment (reg. 28)

Self-propelled work equipment must have:

(a) a facility to prevent it being started by unauthorised persons;

(b) facility to prevent it from colliding with other rail mounted equipment;

(c) a braking device;

(d) emergency braking and stopping devices;

(e) adequate driver vision or devices for improving visibility;

(f) lighting if used at night;

(g) on-board fire fighting equipment if it carries or tows anything which constitutes a fire hazard.

3.4.18 Remote-controlled self-propelled work equipment (reg. 29)

Employers must ensure that where remote-controlled work equipment involves a risk to safety:

(a) it stops automatically once it leaves the control range;

(b) it incorporates a feature to prevent crushing or impact.

3.14.19 Drive shafts (reg. 30)

Employers are under a duty to ensure that drive shafts used between mobile work equipment and accessories or anything being towed do not seize, or, take all possible measures for the safety of employees if seizure cannot be avoided. There must also be a system for preventing damage to drive shafts.

The Provision and Use of Work Equipment Regulations 1998 also introduces requirements relating to the safe use of Power Presses (Part IV of the Regulations).

3.4.20 Enforcement

Civil action based on a breach of these regulations is not prevented. A criminal prosecution can result in a fine of up to £20,000 at first instance.

3.5 Personal Protective Equipment at Work Regulations 1992

3.5.1 Application

These regulations do not apply to ordinary working clothes or uniforms which do not specifically protect the health or safety of the wearer (reg. 3).

3.5.2 Provision (reg. 4)

Every employer must ensure that suitable and appropriate personal protective equipment is provided to employees who may be exposed to risks to their health and safety whilst at work, unless those risks have been controlled by other means. The clothing must be ergonomically suitable, take account of the state of health of the wearer and fit properly (e.g., a pair of overalls must allow freedom of movement, not cause allergic reaction, and be the correct size for the wearer).

3.5.3 Compatibility (reg. 5)
When employees or the self-employed have to wear more than one type of personal protective equipment each item should be compatible with the other (e.g., protective overalls should fit over safety boots without leaving a gap).

3.5.4 Assessment (reg. 6)
Both employers and the self-employed must make assessments to determine what type of protective equipment is necessary to ensure that it is suitable. The assessment must take account of risk not avoided by other means (e.g., guarding) and define the characteristics which the equipment must have to prevent risk.

This assessment could be undertaken at the same time as that of the general assessment referred to under the Management Regulations and be reflected in the control measures on the hazard identification sheets.

3.5.5 Maintenance (reg. 7)
Employers and the self-employed must ensure that personal protective equipment is properly maintained, is in good repair and works efficiently.

3.5.6 Accommodation (reg. 8)
Appropriate accommodation must be provided for personal protective equipment which is not in use (e.g., lockers or hanging space).

3.5.7 Information, instruction and training (reg. 9)
The requirement for an employer to provide adequate information, instruction and training has already been discussed in relation to the Management Regulations and the Provision and Use of Work Equipment Regulations. Information, training and instruction must also relate to the need to wear personal protective equipment by identifying:

(a) the risks which it will avoid or limit,

(b) its purpose and the way in which it must be used,

(c) what the employee must do to ensure it remains usable (e.g., report defects to supervisor and hand in the equipment).

3.5.8 Use (reg. 10) and reporting loss (reg. 11)
Employers must take all reasonable steps to ensure that personal protective equipment provided is properly used (e.g., supervise employees when necessary), and employees are under a duty to use the equipment (reg. 10(2)).

Employees must also report losses of equipment and defects (reg. 11) (see also reg.

12 of the Management Regulations which requires employees to inform their employer of dangerous or unhealthy situations).

The self-employed must also make full use of personal equipment with which they have been provided and return it after use (reg. 10(3) and (4)).

These regulations revoke, amongst others, the whole of the Protection of Eye Regulations 1974.

3.5.9 Enforcement

Civil action based on a breach of these regulations is not prevented. A criminal prosecution can result in a fine of up to £20,000 at first instance.

3.6 Manual Handling Operations Regulations 1992

3.6.1 Employers and the self-employed

Both employers and the self-employed must either:

(a) so far as is reasonably practicable avoid the need for employees to undertake any manual handling operations at work which involve risk of their being injured, or

(b) where it is not reasonably practical to avoid employees undertaking manual handling operations:

  (i)   make a suitable and sufficient assessment of *all* such manual handling operations. The Court of Appeal has marginalised this requirement. In *Koonjul* v *Thameslink Healthcare Services NHS Trust* (CA) (2000) it held that where an employee carries out innumerable tasks in a small residential home it was unrealistic to assess each task. Consequently the claimant's action for damages based on a breach of the regulations in respect of injury sustained whilst making a low bed failed;

  (ii) take appropriate steps to reduce the risk of injury to the lowest level reasonably practical;

  (iii) provide employees undertaking manual handling with general indicators and precise information on the weight of each load and the heaviest side of any load. In *Swain* v *Denso Martin Ltd* (CA) (2000) the claimant was successful in his action for damages after he suffered crushing to his right hand. The defendants had not undertaken a risk assessment and had therefore failed to provide information about the weight of the load he was moving. It was not a defence to submit that because no assessment had taken place they need not supply the relevant information.

When there has been a significant change in the operations or the assessment is no longer valid it must be reviewed (reg. 4).

An assessment must consider:

(a) The task and what it involves in relation to:

(i)   the distance of the load from the body,

(ii)   the movement required of the body such as twisting or bending,

(iii)   excessive lifting or lowering distances, carrying, pushing or pulling,

(iv)   risk of sudden movement of the load,

(v)   length of time of physical effort,

(vi)   rest periods,

(vii) workrates.

(b) The loads and are they:

(i)   heavy,

(ii)   bulky,

(iii) difficult to grasp,

(iv)   unstable with contents likely to shift,

(v)   sharp.

(c) The environment and does it:

(i)   restrict posture,

(ii)   have uneven or slippery floors,

(iii) different levels,

(iv)   high or low temperatures,

(v)   poor ventilation or lighting.

(d) Individual capacity in relation to the job and does it:

(i)   require excessive strength,

(ii)   create hazards to pregnant women or persons with health problems,

(iii) need special information or training.

(e) Whether other factors hinder movement, e.g., the wearing of personal protective clothing.

The key to complying with these regulations is to undertake an assessment which identifies the different loads each employee will have to lift, ensure they are properly trained in lifting techniques and are aware that they must not attempt to lift loads beyond their capacity.

Mechanical aids (e.g., fork-lift trucks) must also be available where necessary.

3.6.2 Employees (reg. 5)

Employees must ensure that they work to the system provided by the employer and adopt the correct lifting techniques, seeking assistance when necessary.

3.6.3 Enforcement

Civil action based on a breach of these regulations is not prevented. A criminal prosecution can result in a fine of up to £20,000 at first instance.

3.7 The Lifting Operations and Lifting Equipment Regulations 1998

These Regulations require every employer to ensure that:

(a) lifting equipment is of adequate strength and stability for each load, having regard in particular to the stress induced at its mounting or fixing point,

(b) every part of a load and anything attached to it and used in lifting it is of adequate strength.

3.7.1 Lifting equipment for lifting persons

Every employer shall ensure that equipment for lifting persons:

(a) is such as to prevent a person using it being crushed, trapped or struck or falling from the carrier,

(b) so far as reasonably practicable whilst a person is using it whilst carrying out activities from the carrier, being crushed, trapped or struck or falling from the carrier,

(c) has suitable devices to prevent the risk of a carrier falling,

(d) is such that a person trapped in a carrier is not exposed to danger and can be freed.

Employers must ensure that lifting equipment is positioned or installed in such a way as to reduce to as low as reasonably practicable the risk:

(a) of the lifting equipment or a load striking a person or;

(b) from a load:

   (i) drifting;

   (ii) falling freely;

   (iii) being released unintentionally.

Employers must ensure persons cannot fall down shafts or hoistways.

Every employer shall ensure that machinery and accessories for lifting loads are clearly marked to indicate their safe working loads, and equipment for lifting persons is clearly marked to this effect.

Employers must ensure that lifting operations involving lifting equipment are planned by a competent person, appropriately supervised, carried out in a safe manner.

All lifting equipment must be thoroughly examined for any defect before it is put into service unless it has not been used before or the employer has received an EC declaration of conformity made not more than 12 months before the lifting equipment is put into service.

When the safety of lifting equipment depends on the installation conditions it must be thoroughly examined after installation and before being put into service for the first time or after assembly at a new site or location.

When lifting equipment is exposed to conditions which cause it to deteriorate and make it liable to result in dangerous situations it must be thoroughly examined:

(a) every six months when issued for lifting persons;

(b) every 12 months when used for other purposes, or

(c) in accordance with an examination scheme.

If exceptional circumstances are liable to jeopardise the safety of the equipment it must be examined. If appropriate it may also be inspected by a competent person at suitable intervals between thorough examinations.

Lifting equipment must not leave an undertaking or be obtained from elsewhere without physical evidence that the last thorough examination required has been carried out.

Persons making a thorough examination or inspection must notify the employer immediately of any defect in the lifting equipment which is or could become dangerous and as soon as practicable make a written report to the employer and any person from whom the lifting equipment has been hired or leased.

If there is risk of personal injury the person making a thorough inspection must send a copy of the report to the enforcing authority.

When an employer has been notified of such defects he must ensure that the lifting gear is not used until the defect is rectified or from the time the defect becomes a danger to persons.

EC declarations, and reports relating to the inspection or thorough examination of lifting equipment must be kept available for inspection by the enforcing authority.

3.8 Health and Safety (Display Screen Equipment) Regulations 1992

3.8.1 Workstations (reg. 2)
All employers must undertake an analysis of workstations used either by employees or which have been provided for use by the self-employed. The purpose of the analysis is to assess risk to health and safety and reduce it to the lowest possible extent.

A workstation comprises an area where there is:

(a) display screen equipment,

(b) accessories,

(c) disc drive, telephone, modem, printer, document holder, chair, desk, work surface or other item used in conjunction with the display screen equipment.

It also includes the immediate work environment around the display screen (reg. 1(2)(e)).

3.8.2 Requirements for new workstations from 1 January 1993 and existing workstations by 31 December 1996 (reg. 3)

The display screen:

(a) must have well-defined characters,

(b) must have a stable image,

(c) must have a facility for adjusting the brightness,

(d) must swivel and tilt,

(e) should be usable on a separate base,

(f) must be free from reflective glare.

The keyboard must:

(a) be tiltable and separate from the screen to allow the operator to find a comfortable working position, with sufficient space to support the hands,

(b) have a matt surface to avoid reflective glare,

(c) have legible and usable keys.

The work desk must have a sufficiently large, low-reflective surface to allow a flexible arrangement of screen, keyboard, documents and other equipment.

The document holder must be adjustable and minimise the need for uncomfortable head and eye movements.

There must be adequate overall space to allow the operator to work in comfort.

The work chair must be stable and allow easy freedom of movement. The seat must be adjustable in height and the seat back adjustable in height and tilt. A footrest must also be provided for employees or the self-employed if they request one.

The working environment must provide adequate space and light which does not cause glare on the screen. Noise levels must not cause distractions or disturbances.

The heat levels given off by equipment must not cause discomfort and radiation must be reduced to negligible levels.

An adequate level of humidity must be established and maintained.

Software must be suitable for the task, be easy to use and, if appropriate, adaptable to the level of knowledge of the operator.

Users must be made aware of any checking measures in relation to their performance. The display of information must be in a format and at a pace applicable to the user, and provide the user with feedback on its performance.

3.8.3 Daily work (reg. 4)

Employers must plan the work activities of employees to ensure their daily work on display screen equipment is interrupted by breaks or changes of activity to reduce their workload at that equipment.

3.8.4 Eyes and eyesight (reg. 5)

Where a person is already using display screen equipment or will become a user, his or her employer must provide an eyesight test as soon as practicable after this has been requested or before the employee starts using the equipment. This should be repeated at regular intervals and when applicable the employer must provide corrective lenses applicable to the work being done (a suitable pair of glasses).

3.8.5 Training and information (regs. 6 and 7)

Employers must provide employees who use or will use display screen equipment as a significant part of their normal work with health and safety training and adequate information about assessments, requirements for workstations, breaks, eyesight tests and training.

3.8.6 Enforcement

Civil action based on a breach of these regulations is not prevented. A criminal prosecution can result in a fine of up to £20,000 at first instance.

3.8.7 The objectives of prosecutions

In *R* v *F. Howe and Son (Engineers) Ltd* (CA) (1999) Scott Baker J commented that the objective of prosecutions for health and safety offences in the workplace was to achieve a safe working environment for those who worked there and for other members of the public who might be affected. Where the defendant was a company a fine needed to be large enough to bring the message home, not only to those who managed it, but also to its shareholders.

Welcoming the judgment, Health and Safety Commission Chairman, Frank Davies, said:

The Court of Appeal's remarks are very helpful. HSC has long believed that penalties for health and safety prosecutions do not generally match the crime. This has tended to undermine the efforts of health and safety enforcing authorities, and others who have been striving to ensure that prevention of work related death, injury and ill-health care are at the heart of company management practices.

I know that the judgement is also welcomed by Ministers who have shared HSC's concerns over the low level of health and safety penalties.

The judgement sends a clear message to all employers about the need to comply with health and safety law. Employers large or small who ignore health and safety legislation and put their workforce or members of the public at risk may well find themselves at the receiving end of tougher penalties handed down by the courts.

The largest fine ever imposed on a single company—£1.5m—was handed down by the Old Bailey in September 1999 to Great Western Trains Company Ltd following the death of seven rail passengers in the Southall rail accident on 19 September 1997.

Commenting on this and other large fines recently imposed, Jenny Bacon, Director General of the HSE, said: 'These fines are a clear message to all employers—it is lack of safety that costs money, not managing safety properly.'

4 Manslaughter

When employees are killed at work their employer may be successfully prosecuted for manslaughter.

EXAMPLE

In 1997 the Managing Director of a transport firm was imprisoned for 12 months. An employee, who was not wearing personal protective equipment, died after being sprayed in the face with Parachloro-ortho-cresol, a chemical used in the manufacture of pesticides.

Currently a corporation may also be found guilty of manslaughter, for example OLL Ltd were found guilty of manslaughter, after four teenagers drowned on an activity holiday in Lyme Bay, Dorset (*The Times*, 11 November 1997). However, the Law Commission has proposed a new offence of corporate killing. This will be determined by proof of a management failure.

Proof of corporate manslaughter currently requires establishing gross negligence on the part of the company's controlling mind. This may be identified if there is only one person responsible for making management decisions, but under present law it may be impossible to prove when there is a number of directors. Consequently prosecutions are generally brought under health and safety legislation and not for manslaughter.

In *Attorney-General's Reference (No 2 of 1999)* (CA) (2000) Lord Justice Rose stated the three theories of corporate criminal liability: vicarious, identification and personal. It was personal for Great Western Trains to have a safe system of work.

Whereas other companies had incurred personal liability in respect of their breach of statutory obligations (e.g. *R* v *Associated Octel Ltd* (1996) and *R* v *Gateway Foodmarkets Ltd* (1997)) there was no sound basis for suggesting that the courts had started a process of moving from identification (attributing the liability of the company to the mind and will of senior directors and managers) to personal liability as a basis for corporate manslaughter.

This was consistent with the Law Commission Report and the draft Bill to confer liability, based on management failure *not* involving the principle of identification.

Consequently, a non-human defendant cannot currently be convicted of manslaughter by gross negligence in the absence of evidence establishing the guilt of an identified individual.

Although more than 22,000 people have been killed in incidents at work or through commercial enterprise since 1965, only six companies have been prosecuted for manslaughter. See also *Health and Safety at Work etc. Act 1974*, 5.1.

The Turnbull Report is encompassed in a Combined Code of Corporate Governance which applies to all companies listed on the London Stock Exchange. Directors now must declare, in the company's annual report, the risks faced by the company and how these are monitored. Such risks include those relating to health and safety.

A consultative document published by the HSE proposes a draft code, encompassing five action points for directors, including the boards collective recognition of their responsibility for health and safety in their organisation.

In September 2000 the Deputy Prime Minister, John Prescott, announced there would be a shake up in safety. There would be new laws relating to health and safety for the travelling public. The Queen's Speech in December 2000 outlined new powers to make transport operators and employers more responsible for the safety of workers and the travelling public. The Bill also proposed to revitalise health and safety in general.

One of the changes which will have a major impact is the number of safety breaches which can attract a £20,000 fine in the magistrates court, currently limited to £5,000. Magistrates will also be given the power to imprison persons for health and safety offences.

However, despite the overwhelming case for a reform of the law of manslaughter when a company's unsafe system has lead directly to the deaths of employees or members of the public, the Queen's Speech made no reference to proposals to introduce relevant legislation.

5 Health and Safety at Work etc. Act 1974

There were several reasons why this legislation was passed after the report prepared by the Robens Committee. In particular, before the legislation was passed, over five million employees did not have any statutory protection. The Act also sought to involve *all* persons connected with the work environment in safe practices, not just employers. For example, the Act aimed to balance the responsibilities of an employer against those of the employee, and the duties of a manufacturer of products against the industrial user. Finally it facilitated a system of joint consultation between employers and employees by encouraging the formation of safety committees in the work place.

The enforcing authorities may be either the Health and Safety Executive or environmental health officers who are employed by local authorities. In addition to prosecution under s. 38, they have powers to issue improvement notices, prohibition notices, or seize, render harmless or destroy an article or substance if persons are in danger (ss. 18 to 25). Despite the fact that it was unthinkable for Railtrack to re-open until Paddington was re-opened they chose to appeal against a prohibition notice issued under s. 22 of the HASAWA 1974. The notice was issued to stop any activities continuing in the aftermath of the accident at Ladbroke Grove. Mr Justice Sullivan stated in *Railtrack plc* v *Smallwood* (QBD) (2001) that although Railtrack had shut down operations, a belt and braces approach would usually increase public confidence. Whilst Railtrack was entitled to challenge the basis on which the inspector issued the notice, the word 'activities' could not be given a literal meaning, therefore inspectors had power to issue notices both before and in the aftermath of a most serious accident. In 1992–3 the Health and Safety Executive issued 11,857 (provisional figure) improvement and prohibition notices, compared with 12,419 in 1991–2 and 12,738 in 1990–1.

The powers of a health and safety inspector cannot be delegated. Unless proceedings are brought by an inspector justices have no power to hear a case: *R* v *Croydon Justices, Ex parte W. H. Smith Ltd* (QBD) (2000).

Under s. 47 of the 1974 Act civil action is specifically precluded. This is because the Robens Committee considered that using criminal legislation as a platform for civil action would cloud the issue. The aim was to improve working conditions and practices, not to provide a means of obtaining compensation.

All the duties under the Act, referred to below, are to be carried out so far as reasonably practicable. It is practicable to prevent risks which can be foreseen, having regard to the current state of knowledge of those risks.

Under the Act the following persons have duties; an employer (ss. 2, 3); an employee (ss. 7, 8); persons in control of premises (ss. 4, 5); manufacturers, designers, importers, suppliers (s. 6).

5.1 Employer's duties to employees

Companies have a general duty under s. 2(1) to ensure the health, safety and welfare of their employees. For example a prosecution was brought by the HSE in 2001 against Goodyear after an employee who had worked for the company for 36 years, slipped after completing a grinding and polishing operation on the rollers of a calender machine. As he attempted to steady himself his left hand was caught between two unguarded rollers and he lost almost all of the fingers on his hand. The firm was fined £12,000 by the magistrates.

In *R* v *Gateway Foodmarkets Ltd* (CA) (1997) the Duty Manager of a store at Broomshill fell to his death through a trap door in the floor of the lift control room. For approximately a year there had been a problem with the lift. Although this had initially been rectified by a firm of outside contractors, employees at the store had been shown how to rectify the fault themselves. This meant going to the control room. The day before the accident the contractors had undertaken routine maintenance and left open the trap door in the control room. The next day, when the lift jammed, the Manager entered the room, going from bright sunlight into darkness, and fell through the open trap door to his death. It was held that both s. 2 and s. 3 (see 5.3) imposed strict liability subject to what was reasonably practicable, i.e the taking of all reasonable precautions by the company on its *behalf*—including its servants and agents. Since there was a failure at store management level the company was guilty of the offence under s. 2.

Certain activities are not automatically outlawed merely because they are inherently dangerous. Section 1 of the Act is concerned with the requirement that an employer has to ensure, so far as is reasonably practicable, the safety of his employees, i.e this looks at the manner in which the organisation conducts its undertaking. In *Canterbury City Council* v *Howletts and Port Lympne Estates Ltd* (QBD) (1996) it was decided it was not appropriate to impose a prohibition notice on the respondent zoo after an employee was killed by a tiger when cleaning its enclosure.

Health and safety legislation may now also be applied to prosecute directors when employees are involved in road accidents as a consequence of stress or exhaustion. Firms must not set punishing schedules and should pay for hotel rooms if the destination is more than 100 miles away. Companies may face unlimited fines if found guilty of not taking steps to ensure safe driving, including giving training to employees who drive as part of their work.

An employer also has a number of specific duties (s. 2(2)), although, as with *all* aspects of this Act, they are framed in broad terms and are all to be undertaken so far as is reasonably practicable. These duties are only examples of the general duty imposed by s. 2(1).

In *Health and Safety Executive* v *Spindle Select Ltd* (QBD) (1996) it was held that a criminal prosecution need not refer to any paragraphs of s. 2(2) specifically, provided that sufficient particulars were given. Giving further information, at a later date, which referred to more than one aspect of the overall duty was therefore acceptable, e.g that the accused had allegedly both failed to guard a machine and train the injured employee would *not* be duplicitous as alleging two separate offences.

5.1.1 The provision and maintenance of safe plant and systems of work

EXAMPLE

Safe plant would mean a securely fenced machine. Do not forget that many effects of this Act overlap with that of previous legislation. The Health and Safety at Work etc. Act 1974, however, applies in work situations where Acts like the Factories Act 1961 do not.

EXAMPLE

A system of work is safe if there are no obstructions on floors or in gangways. Evidence, however, that there are no other safer ways of doing a job may satisfy the requirements of s. 2(2).

Martin v Boulton and Paul (Steel Construction) Ltd (QBD) (1982)

An employee was knocked off a beam which had been lifted into place by a crane. When the sling on the end of the crane jib was released it knocked the employee off the beam. The magistrates decided that this was a universal practice and other methods were not, in any event, any safer. The defendants had not contravened the section.

Where the degree of risk was considered to be minimal when weighed against the cost, a building society was not required to install anti-bandit screens in all of its branches (*West Bromwich Building Society Ltd* v *Townsend* (QBD) (1983)).

5.1.2 Arrangements for ensuring safety and absence of risks to health in connection with the use, handling, storage and transport of articles and substances

This means, amongst other things, that an employer must ensure that his workforce is properly trained to use and handle articles and substances. Training is also a specific requirement under s. 2(2)(c) of the 1974 Act and regs 8 and 9 of the Provision and Use of Work Equipment Regulations 1992. An employer must ensure that employees understand the need to follow any written instructions on, for example, drums of chemicals relating to the wearing of safety clothing. He must ensure that potentially dangerous chemicals or articles are stored in a safe place and that only an authorised user can gain access.

EXAMPLE

Cleaning chemicals and bleach are always left in an open office area instead of a locked cupboard. This would be a breach of the section. (Note: There are now more specific provisions relating to substances hazardous to health (Control of Substances Hazardous to Health Regulations 1988).)

5.1.3 The provision of information, instruction, training and supervision

The case of *Westwood* v *Post Office* (HL) (1973) referred to at 3.3.9 above illustrates the importance of information and instruction being clear and, in particular, referring to any 'hidden' hazards. When instructing an employee on the use of machinery, it is vital that the employer ensures the employee understands the dangers of the machine. In *Tasci* v *Pekalp of London Ltd* (CA) (2001) the defendants were liable when the plaintiff injured his hand whilst operating a circular sawing machine. The claimant was a refugee with limited English and the employers should not have placed any reliance on what he said about his previous experience. They should have treated him as a novice. Where employees may be expected to undertake different jobs in different parts of the factory, office, or warehouse etc. an employer must provide hazard identification sheets which clearly show what hazards exist, and state why they are hazardous (as required by the Management of Health and Safety at Work Regulations 1999 referred to at 3.2 above). An employee entering the area to work should then read the sheet and, if necessary, be given an explanation of the risks in the area. Some companies would also require the employee to sign a copy of the sheet to signify that they have been told about the hazards and that they understand the danger. If, after this, an employee has an accident employers can demonstrate that they have taken all practicable measures to ensure the employee's safety.

The section (i.e. s. 2) also refers to training. When personnel are being trained they should not only be told *how* to do the particular job but also be made aware of any risks in not following correct procedure, and *why* these risks exist. This is a specific requirement of both regs 8 and 9 of the Provision and Use of Work Equipment Regulations 1992 in relation to information and training about work equipment (see 3.4.4 and 3.4.5 above).

The standard of supervision required is 'so far as is reasonably practicable'. This means that if a supervisor is overseeing, e.g. 20 persons, the supervisor cannot be expected to watch everyone all the time. Therefore, if one employee has an accident this may not necessarily be attributable to lack of supervision.

5.1.4 Maintenance of the place of work and provision of safe entries and exits

The former responsibility requires an employer to keep the place of work in good repair, the latter to ensure that employees can move freely through doorways etc. and, for example, that fire exits are not blocked.

In a situation where fork-lift trucks are driven through entries through which employees may also walk, the areas immediately adjacent should be 'cross-hatched' and warning notices displayed. (See also the Workplace (Health, Safety and Welfare) Regulations 1992, reg. 17, discussed in 3.3.13 above.)

5.1.5 A safe and healthy working environment and adequate facilities

Factors which affect the environment include dust (already referred to in connection with s. 63, Factories Act 1961 at 3.2.8 above) and temperature. While the Health and Safety at Work etc. Act 1974 is not specific about, e.g. a minimum working temperature, the provisions of the old Offices, Shops and Railway Premises Act 1963 may be used as a comparison.

Adequate facilities include provision of such things as toilets, sickbay, first aid and whatever else of that nature may be negotiated between employer and employees.

Under s. 2(3), Health and Safety at Work etc. Act 1974 an employer must also provide information about the way he conducts his business; the document containing this is known as a health and safety policy document. (An employer who employs less than five persons is exempt from this provision.) Information in this document should include a general statement on policy, outlining the legal duties of persons under the Act, procedure in the event of fire and accidents, a list of qualified first aiders, particular areas of risk, storage of chemicals and dangerous materials, persons responsible for different areas of work and information about electrical equipment and noise in the workplace. See the end of this chapter for an example of such a policy document.

5.2 Employee's duties

Section 7 of the Act applies to employees while at work.

Court v Szuba (QBD) (1982)

An employee who worked at a large steel works had a distance of two miles to drive after he had clocked on. Whilst on this 'journey' he had an accident which was his fault. It was held for the purposes of the Act that he was not at work and the prosecution against him failed.

The section requires employees to take reasonable care of both themselves and others who may be affected by their acts or omissions. Employees must also cooperate, to enable their employers to fulfil their own legal duties. It is also an offence for anybody to intentionally or recklessly interfere or misuse anything provided for safety (s. 8), e.g., remove a machine guard.

The case of *Rushton* v *Turner Bros. Asbestos Co. Ltd* (1959) (see p. 249 above) illustrates that the courts are not prepared to award compensation to employees who deliberately place themselves at risk.

Under s. 7 of the Health and Safety at Work etc. Act 1974 employees who either fail to take care, or deliberately place themselves at risk also face prosecution, fine, or even imprisonment. Equally, if they put others at risk or fail to comply with instructions given for reasons of safety, they face criminal prosecution.

It can be seen, therefore, that there is a balance of responsibility between employer and employee. Whilst the greater onus is on the employer, who decides, amongst other things, how much can be spent on the system of work, maintenance and training, an employee is also expected to work safely.

5.3 Employer's duties to persons other than his employees

An employer owes a duty to persons not in his employment, but who may be affected by the way in which he conducts his undertaking (Health and Safety at Work etc. Act 1974, s. 3).

R v Mara (CA) (1987)

A contract cleaning company left its machines at a store which it cleaned. Employees who worked there were also allowed to use the cleaning equipment. One of the employees of the store was killed after receiving an electric shock from one of the machines, which had a damaged cable. The director of the cleaning company was found guilty of failing to conduct his undertaking safely.

In *R v Associated Octel Co. Ltd* (HL) (1996) although the company operated a permit to work it was in a perfunctory manner. If Octel's engineers had followed the correct procedure they would have considered the safety precautions which were necessary when a firm of independent contractors was repairing one of their tanks. As it was, while an employee of the contractors was cleaning a tank with acetone, in preparation for the repair, a light bulb which he was using broke. This ignited the vapour from the acetone and he was badly burned. Following correct procedure, which could have been recorded on the permit to work, would have meant using a special airlamp or a closed container for the acetone. This was not being followed. The defendants had failed to discharge their duty under s. 3.

However, in *R v Nelson Group Services (Maintenance) Ltd* (CA) (1998) the Court of Appeal held that the defendant company was not guilty of an offence under s. 3. A fitter who had been employed and properly trained by the Company had left gas fittings in a condition which exposed the occupier of the house to health and safety risks. The Court of Appeal found that by ensuring the employee had the appropriate skill, instruction and supervision they had done everything which was reasonably practicable, in accordance with s. 3, to prevent risk to the occupier.

It was also held in a prosecution brought by the Health and Safety Executive in 1992 at Lewes Crown Court that directors found guilty of an offence under the Health and Safety at Work etc. Act 1974 may be disqualified from holding office under the Company Directors Disqualification Act 1986, s. 2(1).

R v Board of Trustees of the Science Museum (CA) (1993)

The accused were charged with exposing members of the public to legionella. The prosecution did not have to prove that the public had actually inhaled the bacteria, only that the risk existed.

5.4 Persons in control of premises (s. 4, Health and Safey at Work etc. Act 1974)

Persons in control of premises have a duty to persons who are *not* employees but who are using the premises as a place of work. A person in control may be, e.g. an employer or a landlord or leaseholder. An example of a person who is not an employee using the premises as a place of work would be a maintenance worker who is *not* employed directly by the person in control of the premises.

The duties under this section are twofold. First, to provide *safe premises* and safe means of access and exit from the premises. In essence this is the same as the general responsibility towards employees but, with site contractors in mind, there is the *added* responsibility of safe entrances and exits.

Austin Rover Group Ltd v HM Inspector of Factories (HL) (1989)

A paint spray booth and the sump underneath it needed to be cleaned on a regular basis. The work was contracted out to a firm of specialist industrial cleaners and they had been instructed not to use highly inflammable paint thinners from a pipe in the booth. An employee of the contractor ignored these instructions and allowed the thinners to overflow. Three employees were killed when a fire suddenly started as the thinners were ignited by a non-approved lamp. The court decided that although the contractors were owed a duty under s. 4 that the measures taken were sufficient, the Rover Group were not liable to take measures against the misuse of the premises.

Unlike the decision in *Austin Rover*, an employer's statutory duty to prevent people falling through fragile material is not fulfilled by a system of work based on instructions.

R v Rhone-Poulenc Rover Ltd (1995)

The company was held to be in breach of s. 3 when an employee fell through a roof light, even though his presence on the roof was in disobedience to instructions not to climb on to the roof. Under reg. 36 of the Construction (Working Places) Regulations, roofs more than two metres high must be strong enough to support a person's weight.

Secondly, if any plant (e.g. a ladder) or substance (e.g. cleaning fluid) is provided by the person in control it must be safe and without risk to health. This duty is owed to children attending play centres (*Moualem* v *Carlisle City Council* (QBD) (1994)).

EXAMPLE

X is the landlord of a factory and he provides cleaning contractors with steps, ladders and buckets. All of these must be safe and without risk to health.

Persons in control of premises must also ensure that they use the best practicable means to prevent noxious emissions or offensive substances entering the atmosphere (s. 5).

EXAMPLE

A factory which discharges excessive amounts of cement dust into the air, without taking any measures to prevent this, would be in breach of the section.

5.5 Manufacturers, designers, importers and suppliers have various duties (s. 6, Health and Safety at Work etc. Act 1974).

They must make sure that articles which will be used at work:

(a) are designed and constructed as to be safe. This could be something as simple as a length of wood used for propping up the tailgate of a car while it is going through a spray booth on an assembly line;

(b) are tested. If necessary, where many articles are being produced some should be tested to the point of destruction. If only one article is being made, e.g. a large turbine, it should be 'run-up' to an over-run speed, namely revolutions which exceed its normal running speed;

(c) carry sufficient information about their use to ensure they can be used safely.

EXAMPLE

X Ltd manufacture a chemical of a corrosive nature which is used for cleaning out drains. If they fail to state on the container that it is corrosive, and that appropriate resistant safety gloves should always be worn when the product is being used, they are committing an offence. Where a number of instructions have to be given the label may simply refer the user to an accompanying leaflet.

The duties imposed by this section (i.e. s. 6) have to be balanced against those of the user to use an article in a safe manner. The persons to whom the section applies may obtain a signed undertaking that the *user* will use the product safely. This will have the effect of relieving the first mentioned person (e.g. the supplier) from liability.

5.6 Safety representatives and safety committees

The Act allowed regulations to be passed for the appointment of *employee* safety representatives. The regulations which were subsequently passed in October 1976 and which came into effect one year later, only allowed for the appointment of *trade union* safety representatives.

Such representatives are given various powers, but without any legal duty except that imposed by other sections of the Act. It may therefore be argued that trade union safety representatives have power without responsibility. They may:

(a) investigate potential hazards;

(b) investigate complaints by employees they represent;

(c) make representations on matters arising, including that a process be stopped;

(d) make general representations on matters relating to health, safety and welfare;

(e) carry out inspections of the workplace every three months or when there has been a substantial change in work conditions;

(f) receive information from health and safety inspectors, which includes information about the premises or action which the inspector intends to take;

(g) attend safety committee meetings.

5.6.1 Safety committees

If at least two safety representatives request an employer, in writing, to establish a safety committee he must do so. Once this request is made the employer must consult with recognised trade unions and with the safety representatives who made the request. The committee must be established no later than three months after the request for it. There are no specific guidelines on its composition but an attempt should be made to strike an equal balance between employer and employee representation.

Under the Health and Safety (Consultation with Employees) Regulations 1996 an employer is now obliged to consult with any employees, or their elected representatives, who have not previously been represented, i.e. some employees may already be represented by a trade union safety representative; these regulations allow representation for persons not in a union.

5.7 Employer's Liability (Defective Equipment) Act 1969

Knowles v *Liverpool City Council* (HL) (1993)

Mr Knowles was employed by the appellant council as a labourer flagger. While repairing a pavement, a flagstone he was handling broke causing injury to his finger. The breakage occurred because the manufacturers had not cured the flagstone properly.

The House of Lords held that a flagstone which the respondent was handling in the course of his employment was 'equipment provided by his employer for the purposes of the employer's business' within the meaning of the Employer's Liability (Defective Equipment) Act 1969, s. 1(1)(a), and that consequently the employer was liable under the Act in respect of injuries sustained by the respondent when the flagstone broke due to a defect in its manufacture.

5.8 Construction (Health Safety and Welfare) Regulations 1996

The Construction (Health Safety and Welfare) Regulations 1996 came into force in September 1996. These regulations place similar duties on employers, persons in control of work, the self-employed and employees who are engaged in construction work to those already laid down under the 1974 Act and the 1994 Regulations previously referred to. They do however, introduce standards to certain activities which are specific to work undertaken on construction sites. For example, guard rails to prevent falls when working on platforms (reg. 6); coverings to prevent falls through fragile material (reg. 7); prevention of falling objects and persons being struck (reg. 8); safe procedures in respect of demolition (reg. 10); use of explosives (reg. 11); excavations (reg. 12); protection from adverse weather conditions (reg. 24).

5.9 Confined Spaces Regulations 1997

Under these regulations, which come into force in January 1998:

(a) persons shall not enter a confined space unless it is not reasonably practicable to undertake the work without such entry (reg. 4(a));

(b) persons shall not enter, work in, or leave a confined space unless the system of work is safe (reg. 4(b));

(c) emergency arrangements shall exist to rescue persons who may become trapped (reg. 5).

A confined space means any place such as a chamber, tent, vat, silo, pit, trench, pip, sewer, flue, well or other similar place.

5.10 Construction (Design and Management) Regulations

These regulations, which came into force at the beginning of 1995, require a principal contractor (when more than five persons are employed) who undertakes work which will last longer than 30 days or involve more than 500 person days of construction work (e.g., 50 people x 10 days) to produce *a health and safety plan*. This must be supplied to the client's planning supervisor for the Health and Safety file.

The health and safety plan must:

(a) be drawn up prior to and supplied with the tender;

(b) set out arrangements to control risk, i.e. production of relevant risk assessment sheets and control measures;

(c) show how the construction work will be managed, e.g., line of sub-contractors through all stages of construction;

(d) show how persons will be monitored, i.e. *who* and *how* their competence will be checked.

The contractor must also:

(a) ensure that no unauthorised persons can enter areas where construction work is taking place;

(b) put up warning notices;

(c) direct other contractors on site;

(d) provide contractors with relevant health and safety information, e.g., particular risks from work in progress;

(e) ensure that *other employers* provide their employees with health and safety information;

(f) review and update the plan as necessary.

Remember that as a general principle your own employees are still your responsibility even if they are using other contractors' equipment (*Morris* v *Breaveglen Ltd* (CA) (1993), an employee should have been warned not to use another employer's dumper truck).

5.11 Control of Substances Hazardous to Health Regulations 1994 and Amendment Regulations 1996

Under these regulations employers must ensure that assessments are undertaken to identify all hazardous substances to which employees or others may be exposed in the workplace, e.g., softwood dust, cotton dust, foundry fumes, chemicals and micro-biological agents. The risk must be either prevented or controlled. For example in 2001 the University of Birmingham Medical School, which handles tuberculosis, was fined £10,000 for failing to test ventilation systems over a three-year period and ensure filters were effective. The assessments must include the maximum exposure limits to these substances and identify relevant control measures. Control measures can include:

(a) eliminating the task and therefore the need to use the chemical;

(b) substituting the product for a less hazardous substance;

(c) using the substance in a less harmful form, e.g. liquid rather than spray.

In the light of the findings by medical researchers in the USA, such assessments should not only focus separately on substances, but also on combinations to which persons may be exposed.

Users of hazardous substances have the right to obtain information about the hazards from the supplier under the Chemicals (Hazard Information and Packaging for Supply) Regulations 1994.

The Chemicals (Hazard Information and Packaging for Supply) (Amendment) Regulations 1999, in force from April 1999, revises the list of dangerous chemicals which suppliers must label. It adds around 60 new substances to the list.

5.12 Asbestos

Regulations have been proposed to prevent exposure to asbestos, adding to existing requirements under the Health and Safety at Work etc. Act 1974, the Management of Health and Safety at Work Regulations 1999 and the Workplace Regulations 1992, as well as specific regulations controlling asbestos. The proposed new regulations will require a written statement saying exactly how work involving asbestos will be undertaken.

5.13 The Fire Precaution (Workplace) Regulations 1997 (consolidated in the 1999 Management Regulations) and amended by the Fire Precautions (Workplace) (Amendment) Regulations 1999

A workplace was covered by the Fire Precaution (Workplace) Regulations 1997 unless it was covered by an alternative provision which was generally a fire certificate issued by the local authority under the Fire Precautions Act 1971.

The 1999 Fire Precautions (Workplace) (Amendment) Regulations remove this distinction. The requirements of the 1997 Regulations therefore apply to both premises with or without a fire certificate.

The 1997 Regulations extended employers' duties to undertaking assessments relating to risks created by fire. Where assessments are undertaken on premises without a fire certificate an employer must be guided by a competent person.

Minimum standards of precaution are laid down in the 1997 Regulations. As well as competent assistance these are:

(a) adequate security to help prevent arson;

(b) prohibiting smoking;

(c) keeping heat sources away from combustible material;

(d) ensuring the non-accumulation of excess paper or waste;

(e) control of contractors using welding equipment or blow lamps on site;

(f) minimising purchase and use of substances which are a fire hazard;

(g) regular checks on electrical appliances and wiring;

(h) avoiding use of portable heaters and where these are in use ensuring lack of obstruction;

(i) regular cleaning and control of cooking;

(j) measures to prevent fires taking hold.

Other measures which need to be in place relate to the outbreak of fire. For example:

(a) detection;

(b) alarms to warn of fire;

(c) fire doors;

(d) evacuation procedures;

(e) maintenance and signing of clear emergency escape routes and exits;

(f) fire signs, which must be rectangular or square showing a white pictogram which may include an arrow on a green background. The background must be at least 50% of the sign's area and be adequately illuminated;

(g) fire fighting equipment which may include, hoses, blankets, wall mounted extinguishers.

Occupiers of premises which are rented have similar duties. Occupiers should therefore ensure, within the terms of the lease, precisely who is responsible for the various aspects of fire safety.

5.13.1 Certificates
A fire certificate must be applied for in the case of:

(a) offices;

(b) shops;

(c) factories;

(d) railway premises,

when more than ten persons are employed other than on the ground floor at any of the above premises, and in:

(a) buildings with two or more individual offices, shops, factories or railway premises where the aggregate of people exceeds ten;

(b) factories where explosive or highly flammable materials are stored or used unless the fire authority has confirmed no serious risk to employees;

(c) hotels or boarding houses which sleep more than six guests.

A fire certificate sets out the minimum standards required by the fire authority. These may need to be exceeded to comply with other health and safety legislation, e.g. the specific safety of traffic routes under the Workplace Regulations.

The fire certificate specifies:

(a) the use of the premises;

(b) the means of escape in the event of fire;

(c) how to ensure the means of escape can be safely and effectively used (e.g. use of signs and fire doors);

(d) availability of fire fighting equipment;

(e) the way in which people are warned of a fire (e.g. bells, klaxon);

(f) particulars of explosive material.

Other details may include:

(g) how means of escape are to be maintained.

(h) how employees are to be trained.

5.13.2 Risk Assessments

All employers responsible for buildings (including sports grounds and sub surface Railway Stations), *whether or not requiring* a fire certificate must manage fire risks by:

(a) appointing a competent person;

(b) assessing potential risk created by fire and determining appropriate control measures to prevent fire and protect persons in the event of an outbreak of fire;

(c) ensuring the implementation of appropriate control measures;

(d) implementing emergency procedures in the event of fire (e.g. fire notices advising persons what to do, fire induction sessions, appointment of fire marshals).

Fire risk assessments can be separate or integrated with general risk assessments. These should be monitored and reviewed. When five or more staff are employed they must be recorded.

The employer must provide sufficient information and training to ensure that everyone in a workplace knows how, and is able to, react in the following situations:

(a) discovering a fire hazard (e.g. faulty electrical wiring);

(b) hearing the fire alarm.

5.14 Procedures for accident reporting

The Reporting of Injuries, Diseases and Dangerous Occurrences Regulations 1995 (in force April 1996) require accidents at work to be reported when:

(a) any person dies as a result of an accident arising out of work;

(b) any person suffers a major injury arising out of work;

(c) any person not at work suffers an injury as a result of an accident arising out of or in connection with work and that person is taken from the site to hospital for treatment;

(d) any person not at work suffers a major injury as a result of an accident arising out of or in connection with work at a hospital;

(e) there is a dangerous occurrence.

The report must either be made within 10 working days of the accident on form F2508 or by fax, telephone or through the Internet, to a national contact centre based in Wales.

A consultative document published by the Health and Safety Commission proposes that there will be a new duty to investigate all accidents which occur in the workplace. Compulsory accident investigation is therefore likely by the end of 2002.

6 Sample health and safety policy document

This sample document is an example of a general statement of safety policy. A full policy document would also include a number of appendices referring to e.g. fire precautions, evacuation in the event of fire, fire regulations notice, first aid, procedures in the event of accidents, details of areas requiring particular attention to safety and health, list of qualified first aiders, storage of chemicals and dangerous materials, staff possessing expertise in various areas, safety procedures and instructions, safety literature, use of scaffolding ladders, COSHH (Control of Substances Hazardous to Health) inspection of electrical equipment, sample risk assessment sheets.

Sample Document

---

1   **Main Objectives**

1.1 The Company management will take all practicable steps to ensure and to promote the health and safety at work of all staff and to safeguard appropriately members of the general public legitimately on the premises.

1.2 *Management of Safety at Work Regulations 1999*
In accordance with Management of Safety at Work Regulations 1999 the Com-

pany operates a system of risk assessment. Initial information has and, since work situations change, will be recorded by appropriate staff completing forms which identify any hazards relating to the system of work, together with associated risks and control measures. The frequency of the control is also identified.

The information is stored on computer and staff are asked at regular intervals to verify that these arrangements still exist.

The intention of the regulations and the system is, therefore, to develop and maintain a safety culture throughout the Company by involving all employees in the implementation and monitoring of this programme. Example forms and a completed printout are shown in the appendices to this document.

Any employee who wishes to obtain more information about risk assessment or specific risks within his or her area of work should ask his or her line manager.

1.3 Persons on the premises must follow codes of good practice and work in a safe and healthy manner.

1.4 Employees are under a duty whilst at work to take reasonable care of the safety of themselves and of other persons, e.g., other members of staff, visitors and contractors.

1.5 Under regulation 14 of the Management of Safety at Work Regulations 1999 employees have a duty to inform management of any work situations considered dangerous or unhealthy and also any shortcomings in the arrangements for health and safety.

1.6 All training programmes for staff and others will include specific reference to health and safety.

1.7 Health and safety training is regarded as an ongoing requirement but, in particular, training will be undertaken to ensure staff are familiar with, and adhere to, changes in the legal requirements.

2   Health and Safety Organisation and Practices Applicable to the Company

2.1 There are three main aspects to the organisational structure of health and safety at the Company. These are:

(a) various production teams, headed by a supervisor who is responsible for imparting, receiving information and acting on advice or instructions from the safety officer,

(b) the risk assessment programmes outlined in 1.2 above,

(c) the Health and Safety Committee, which comprises representatives from all areas of the workplace.

2.2 Employee safety representatives are given time within working hours to carry out their responsibilities and to attend training courses on safety.

2.3 Managers and supervisors are responsible for ensuring staff are adequately trained, and for good safety practices within their designated areas of responsibility.

2.4 Managers and supervisors have a duty to ensure that all staff are made aware of any specific health and safety practices and draw attention to special tasks within their designated areas of responsibility. A similar duty exists towards visitors and others using the premises, including independent contractors.

2.5 Managers and supervisors will ensure that copies of any special regulations or practices within their areas of responsibility are displayed.

3 Reporting and Recording of Accidents

3.1 All accidents and injuries must be reported without delay in the appropriate accident book.

3.2 If an accident is notifiable then obtain HSE F2508 from the safety officer. Complete and return this immediately.

3.3 Dangerous occurrences where serious injury might have resulted must also be reported. If in doubt, ask.

4 Medication

Although certain staff are trained in first aid under *no* circumstances should *any* staff dispense any form of medication to others during the course of their employment. Remember, persons may also suffer from allergies including reaction to sticking plasters.

5 Training and Supervision

5.1 Arrangements will be made for all members of staff to receive the appropriate training in the use of new processes, machines and dangerous materials with which they may become involved in carrying out their duties. This training will be carried out by trained and experienced members of staff or arranged through the external supplier of equipment and other courses.

5.2 Persons working with chemicals or electricity, or in an environment affected by noise levels above 85 decibels, should be familiar with appropriate regulations. Currently assessments have been undertaken in accordance with COSHH Regulations. Copies of these are available from the safety officer.

5.3 *Use of VDUs; Lifting and Carrying*

Any employee who thinks his or her health is affected by working with VDUs at the Company, and any employee involved in lifting and carrying who wants advice on lifting techniques and/or the weight of items they are lifting should discuss this with their line manager.

5.4 *Health Screening*

Health screening is available for any employee who either:

(a) considers he or she is exposed to specific health risks (e.g., from dust, chemicals, acid, suds, certain materials used in welding);

or

(b) who may suffer from specific allergic reactions.

6 Outside Contractors

6.1 Persons working on site who have been employed by the Company are owed similar duties of care as those owed towards employees. It is, therefore, the responsibility of whoever has engaged them to advise them of any hazards and risks which they would not be expected to know.

6.2 If any equipment is provided, the provider must ensure it is safe and without risk to health.

6.3 It is also the responsibility of independent contractors to work in a safe and healthy manner. Therefore, before commencing work they *must* be issued with and return a signed copy of the Health and Safety Declaration.

7 Distribution

This document is issued to all full and part-time staff.

Questions

Employment Law

---

1 (a) Outline and explain some of the main reasons why the Health and Safety at Work etc. Act 1974 was passed.

   (b) X, who is employed by Y Ltd, claims that she is suffering from stress after witnessing the fatal injury of a colleague at work. Since the incident X has been given no counselling, Y Ltd have no procedures in place relating to stress counselling and the action which managers should take when they are aware of an employee suffering from stress. They have not undertaken any management training in stress recognition.

What action may be taken by:

   (i)   X?

   (ii) the Health and Safety Executive?

Advise X Ltd and the chemical manufacturers with regard to their civil and criminal liability.

Outline answer

(a) Reference to reasons for HASAWA 1974, e.g., many employees previously not given statutory protection; all persons at work given responsibilities; the Act established a mechanism of joint consultation—explain these.

(b)

   (i)   Action in damages (these may be substantial).

         Lack of help/failure to provide safe system e.g *Walker* v *Northumberland C.C* (QBD) (1994): victim directly involved *Page* v *Smith* (HL) (1995). Employers knew of the likelihood of stress (*Sandwell D.C.* v *Jones*) (2002).

Contrast *Frost* v *Chief Constable of South Yorkshire* (HL) (1998).

Y Ltd will be unable to produce any records relating to risk assessments, and management control measures; policy and procedures relating to stress counselling.

   (ii) The Health and Safety Executive may issue an improvement notice giving Y Ltd a fixed time in which to introduce procedure and training relating to stress management. If Y Ltd fail to comply they face prosecution under HASAWA 1974; Management Regulations.

2 Give some examples of express terms in a contract of employment.

3   Give some examples of implied terms in a contract of employment.

4   What action can an employer take if an employee is in breach of contract?

5   What can an employer do to protect confidential information?

6   Distinguish wrongful and unfair dismissal.

7   What are the ways in which a contract of employment may be terminated?

8   What remedies are available to an employee who proves unfair dismissal?

9   Summarise an employee's rights and responsibilities in relation to maternity.

10 Distinguish direct and indirect race discrimination.

11 Explain the term vicarious liability.

12 Illustrate how contributory negligence affects any claims for compensation in respect of injury in the work place.

13 Give one example of the effects of the imposition of EC standards on UK employment law.

14 Briefly explain the impact of the Management of Health and Safety at Work Regulations 1999 and associated regulations on employers, including those aspects relating to young persons, fire and pregnant women.

15 Outline and explain the duties in respect of machinery, floors and traffic routes laid down by the Provision and Use of Work Equipment Regulations 1998 and the Workplace (Health, Safety and Welfare) Regulations 1992, respectively.

16 Do you consider the Health and Safety (Display Screen Equipment) Regulations 1992 give sufficient protection to users of this type of equipment?

17 Outline the effects of the Disability Discrimination Act 1995.

18 What must the Crown Prosecution Service currently establish to succeed in a prosecution for manslaughter against a corporation?

3

Family Law

Introduction

The practitioner in family law faces some particularly difficult problems. Not only is a detailed knowledge of the law necessary, but also an understanding of the way in which the law operates in practice. The Matrimonial Practice syllabus covers basic divorce procedure, and applications to the magistrates for financial provision and protection from violence in the home. This indicates how difficult issues may arise not only when a husband and wife are separating for good, but also when their marriage is still continuing. A different approach is necessary when the affairs of a married couple need to be finalised, as opposed to the situation where an application to the magistrates' family proceedings court may only represent temporary discord in a relationship. The law, however, is remarkably similar in many respects, both in the grounds that must be proved, and the matters that the court has to consider before making a financial order. The financial orders that the court can make are very different however, and this is a factor that must be considered by the practitioner when advising a client. For example, a client who needs a share of the property that has been accumulated during the marriage may find that the magistrates' powers are too limited to be of any help. It may therefore be necessary to discuss proceedings in the divorce court, even though the client has no thoughts of a divorce at this stage.

A familiarity with the procedure for divorce will make it clear that the practitioner is rarely going to be involved in issues of law. It is vital to be aware of the law underlying the procedure however, to ensure that the proceedings progress smoothly. For example, a divorce is usually granted after the petitioner has filed a simple affidavit expanding the basic facts alleged in the petition. A misunderstanding of the law may easily lead to the affidavit being rejected however, and the client being subjected to the worry and expense of a court hearing. An even worse outcome could occur. For example, a suggestion that a two-year separation was not originally caused by a desire to live apart could lead to the petition being dismissed altogether. A good knowledge of the law is therefore a vital preventative measure!

In financial matters, every case that the practitioner comes across is different, and complex in its own way. The majority of these cases should not get to court however, if both parties have sound legal advice. The costs of court proceedings in such matters are prohibitive, and usually destined to be paid from the limited resources available to be divided between the two parties. This is because of the legal aid rules which will often enable the Legal Services Commission to recover claims under a legal aid certificate by imposing a statutory charge on any property involved in the dispute. There is therefore, a duty on the practitioner to devise a fair settlement as quickly as possible and to embody this in an agreed court order. This can only be done with a sure knowledge of the law, and a sound understanding of the principles which the courts follow when such matters are before them. These principles are set out primarily in statutory guidelines, but it is also necessary to know how the courts have interpreted them.

There are special difficulties facing the practitioner when children are involved. Financial questions will almost always involve children, and particular consideration has to be given to them especially in the light of the powers of the Child Support Agency. In addition however, there may be other separate issues, such as which of the parties is going to look after the children, and the extent to which the other is going to have contact with them. It may be that the dispute is not between the parents themselves, but between the parents and the local authority, as when a child is taken into care. The Children Act 1989 completely revised the law affecting children, procedures have been introduced to give effect to the basic principles of the Act and the law is now being developed by the courts from those principles. A thorough knowledge of the provisions of the Act is therefore essential to an understanding of those developments as they occur.

Finally, in October 2000 the Human Rights Act 1998 came into force so that the European Convention on Human Rights is now directly enforceable against public authorities. Furthermore, the English courts must now interpret legislation so that it complies with the Convention as far as possible. Although there have only been a few significant cases to date, Convention rights such as Article 8 (the right to respect for private and family life) and Article 12 (the right to marry and found a family) are likely to affect family law in many ways. It is beyond the scope of this chapter to try to anticipate every area where this might occur, but notes on existing case-law of the European Court of Human Rights have been included where it seems most likely to have an important effect. These should be noted as examples of how the Convention and the jurisprudence of the European Court could affect the development of English family law over the next few years.

Requirements for a valid marriage

1 The nature of marriage

1.1 Marriage as a status

A marriage can be brought into effect in English law only if there is an agreement between a man and a woman to get married. To that extent therefore it is similar to any other contract, and before such actions were abolished by the Law Reform (Miscellaneous Provisions) Act 1970, it was even possible to sue the other person for breach of promise to marry. As soon as a marriage has taken place however, the husband and wife are bound by certain rights and obligations regardless of their own wishes. This is because marriage creates a *status*, and that status cannot be changed by the agreement of the parties, but only by operation of law. Thus any agreement between the parties will be void insofar as it attempts to restrict the rights and obligations which are attached to marriage by law.

Brodie v Brodie (1917)

Before their marriage the man persuaded the woman to enter into an agreement that they would not live together after the marriage. The woman subsequently applied for an order for 'the restitution of conjugal rights' (an action which has since been abolished). The court granted her application, holding that all married couples are entitled to have their spouses live with them, and that therefore the agreement was void and of no legal effect.

This aspect of English marriage law has been criticised on the grounds that marriage is now much more a matter of personal choice than it was at the beginning of the century, and that therefore there is no longer a 'typical' marriage. Nowadays over one third of modern marriages involve at least one person who has been married before, and more women in particular are postponing marriage until later in life, in order to concentrate on building a career. It is argued that the refusal by the courts to allow pre-marriage contracts fails to allow a couple to agree in advance exactly what the nature of their marriage will be, and what it will mean to them.

1.2 Rights and duties on marriage

At common law a marriage entitled each party to the other's *consortium*. This expression is impossible to define satisfactorily, but certainly means that each is entitled to live with the other, and thereby to share all the comforts and responsibilities necessarily arising out of that relationship.

> EXAMPLE
>
> Spouses should communicate, respond physically and sexually to each other, care for each other and respect each other's confidences.

The concept is not important nowadays in itself. It is no longer possible for a husband to bring an action in tort for the loss of his wife's consortium for example (Administration of Justice Act 1982, s. 2), and the 'right' to consortium cannot be enforced.

R v Jackson (1891)

The wife refused to live with her husband after he returned from a trip abroad. He obtained an order for the 'restitution of conjugal rights' (now abolished; see 1.1 above), but she still refused to live with him. He therefore took her to his house by force, and prevented her from leaving. She applied for a writ of habeas corpus and the Court of Appeal unanimously ordered her release.

Similarly the House of Lords has now stated that a husband cannot force his wife to have sexual intercourse against her will (*R* v *R* (1991), where a husband's conviction for attempted rape was upheld). However the concept underlies such ideas as 'unreasonable behaviour' in divorce law (see *Invalidity and Failure of Marriage*, 3.3). It is also possible that certain special aspects are capable of being enforced.

Argyll v *Argyll* (1965)

The husband had divorced his wife on the grounds of her adultery, and two years later started to publish a series of articles about her in a newspaper. The High Court granted the wife an injunction to prevent publication of any secrets that she had communicated to her husband in confidence during the marriage.

Perhaps the most important right which married couples have nowadays is the right to be supported financially by their spouses. This right certainly derives from the concept of consortium, and will be looked at later in detail (see *Financial Provision in the Family Proceedings Court*).

1.3 Restrictions on marriage

Since 1753 there have been prescribed formalities that a couple must go through before they are validly married. These consist firstly of preliminary matters such as the calling of banns or obtaining a licence, and secondly of a subsequent ceremony in church or a register office (or premises approved by the local authority under the Marriage Act 1994). Most of these regulations are set out in the Marriage Act 1949. More important however are the restrictions which prevent certain people from getting married. These were developed by the common law based largely on teachings of the Christian church, and were stated authoritatively in the following case.

Hyde v *Hyde and Woodmansee* (1866)

An Englishman had gone to the USA to marry a Mormon woman. At that time the Mormon marriage ceremony allowed the man to take additional wives. Eventually the man renounced the Mormon religion and returned to England. He learned that his wife was living with another man and so sought to divorce her in England. The court however decided on a preliminary point that the couple were not legally married in the first place! The judge stated that in English law a marriage must be 'the voluntary union for life of one man and one woman to the exclusion of all others', and the Mormon ceremony clearly did not exclude 'all others'.

The common law also followed Church teaching in laying down restrictions based on the relationship between the parties (both by blood and marriage). The parties also had to be over the legal age of puberty, namely 14 years for a boy and 12 years for a girl. Surprisingly this remained the law until 1929, when the minimum age of 16 years was fixed for both males and females. Collectively these various restrictions are known as the *capacity* to marry, and must be distinguished carefully from the *formalities* which are necessary to create a valid marriage. The rules relating to the capacity to marry are set out in the Matrimonial Causes Act 1973, s. 11. There are five in total: the prohibited degrees of relationship; age; gender; single status; and polygamous marriages abroad. These will be looked at individually in detail in sections 2 to 6 below.

2 The prohibited degrees of Relationship

2.1 Consanguinity and affinity

Under the Marriage Act 1949, s. 1, and the Matrimonial Causes Act 1973, s. 11(a)(i), no valid marriage can take place where the parties are within the prohibited degrees of relationship. The law distinguishes between relationships of *consanguinity* and relationships by *affinity*. *Consanguinity* refers to the relationship between persons who are related genetically (or 'by blood'). *Affinity* is a relationship created solely by marriage.

> EXAMPLE
>
> Parents and their children, brothers and sisters, uncles/aunts and nephews/nieces are all relationships of consanguinity. Parents-in-law, brothers/sisters-in-law are relationships by affinity. Half-brothers/sisters (where they have the same mother but different fathers, or *vice versa*) are relationships of consanguinity; step-brothers/sisters (where their genetic parents are completely different, but the mother of one has married the father of the other) are relationships by affinity.

The reason for preventing marriages between blood relations was undoubtedly based on genetic considerations. Thus it is accepted that there is a higher chance of mutant genes being 'reinforced' where blood relations have children, the result possibly being that those children would be deformed. Church teaching was that a man and a woman became 'one flesh' on marriage. It thus followed that your spouse's blood relations became your blood relations in the eyes of the Church, and as it was the Church that laid down the rules relating to capacity to marry, this principle prevented many people from marrying. This was clearly a fiction, however, and the tendency throughout the twentieth century has been to reduce restrictions based on affinity. For reasons of social policy, however, certain restrictions have remained.

2.2 The development of the modern law

At the beginning of the twentieth century it was impossible to marry a person who was related to you by affinity, even after the death of your spouse. Thus a man could not marry his deceased wife's sister, nor a woman her deceased husband's brother. These restrictions were gradually abolished, and eventually the Marriage (Enabling) Act 1960 allowed such people to marry even where the original marriage had only been terminated by divorce. A man could still not marry his mother-in-law (or a woman her father-in-law) however, even when their original spouses were dead. Nor could a person marry a step-child, even where they had only ever known each other as adults. As the number of divorces increased every year, so did the number of situations where such people had a legitimate desire to marry. Some people were able to obtain a private Act of Parliament to allow them to marry, and the social policy behind the restrictions was eventually rethought. It became accepted that the real danger was the risk of sexual abuse of the young by those in authority over them. As a result the Marriage (Prohibited Degrees of Relationship) Act 1986 allowed marriages between in-laws and step-relations where there was no possibility of abuse of authority.

2.3 The modern law

The prohibited degrees are set out in schedules to the Marriage Act 1949, as amended, and in the Marriage (Prohibited Degrees of Relationship) Act 1986. There are now three categories.

2.3.1 *Degrees of consanguinity*

A man may not marry his grand-mother, mother, daughter, grand-daughter; nor his sister, aunt or niece. The corresponding restrictions apply to women. Note therefore that you may marry your great-grand-parent! These restrictions also cover adoptive parents and children.

2.3.2 *Step-relations*

A man may marry his step-daughter if both of them are over 21, and she has never lived with him as if she were his daughter. The same rules apply to other types of step-relationship, and equally to women.

> EXAMPLE
>
> John and Linda are married. Linda's daughter from her previous marriage is living with her ex-husband, but John's son from his previous relationship lives with them and is looked after by Linda. John and Linda get divorced, and John meets Linda's daughter. He may marry her as soon as she is 21 years old. Linda may not marry John's son.

2.3.3 *Daughters-in-law*

A man may marry his son's ex-wife if they are both over 21 and both his wife and his son are dead. Again, the same rules apply to women. Presumably these more stringent conditions apply to in-laws in order to discourage parents from becoming sexual competitors to their children. There is no guarantee that this will be completely effective however, as sexual competition does not depend on the prospect of marriage!

> EXAMPLE
>
> John's son Harold marries Susan. John begins an affair with Susan, and eventually he leaves his wife Linda, and Susan leaves Harold. John and Susan may live together, but may only marry when both Linda and Harold are dead.

2.4 Effects of the law

2.4.1 *The criminal law*

The prohibited degrees must not be confused with the crime of incest (Sexual Offences Act 1956). First, the crime of incest is much more limited in scope—it is not a crime to have sexual intercourse with your uncle/aunt, for example. Secondly, a marriage to a person within the prohibited degrees will be automatically void (see 7 below), but will only be a crime if sexual intercourse took place in the *knowledge* that it was incestuous.

2.4.2 Adoption

Although adoption is supposed to create a clean break between the genetic parents and their child, they (and their descendants, namely grand-children) still remain within the prohibited degrees. Unless adopted children take specific steps to trace their genetic parents, however, they cannot possibly know whether their proposed spouse is related by blood or not. Such a marriage would nevertheless be void. On the other hand, although adopted children are supposed to be completely integrated into their 'new' family, they are not prohibited from marrying their adoptive brother/sister.

2.4.3 Anomalies

Marriages where there is a relationship of consanguinity are prohibited because of the genetic risks. These are only risks however, not certainties; and other people who are carriers of a genetic disease are allowed to marry and have children when the risks of deformed off-spring are much higher. The social policy of restricting some marriages where there is a relationship of affinity could also be applied to other situations. The children of unmarried cohabitants are not protected in this way, nor are some adopted children, as noted in 2.4.2 above.

3 Age

Under the Marriage Act 1949, s. 2, and the Matrimonial Causes Act 1973, s. 11(a)(ii), no valid marriage can take place where either party is under the age of 16. This restriction seems uncontroversial, although it has only been the law since 1929. It should be noted that a marriage where one party is under 16 cannot be 'affirmed' when that party has come of age. No valid marriage will have taken place, and therefore the proper formalities must be gone through all over again. The position must be distinguished carefully from that relating to marriages where one party is over 16 but under 18 years of age. Under the Marriage Act 1949, s. 3, parental consent is necessary, but only as part of the formalities. A failure to comply with that requirement does not affect the validity of the marriage.

4 Single status

Under the Matrimonial Causes Act 1973, s. 11(b), a valid marriage cannot take place where at the time of the ceremony either party is already married to another person. This must be distinguished from the crime of bigamy (Offences against the Person Act 1861). The crime is not committed when the accused can show that he believed that his first marriage no longer subsisted. The second marriage will still be invalid however.

EXAMPLE

Harold is married to Susan, but has not heard from her since she went on safari ten years ago. Believing her to be dead, he goes through a ceremony of marriage with Jennifer. Susan then reappears. Harold's 'marriage' to Jennifer is invalid, and he will therefore still be married to Susan. He will not be guilty of bigamy, as he honestly and reasonably believed Susan to be dead.

5 Gender

5.1 Introduction

Under the Matrimonial Causes Act 1973, s. 11(c), a marriage will only be valid if both parties are respectively male and female. This clearly prohibits single-sex, or homosexual, marriages having any legal effect, although informal ceremonies may be available. The prohibition is well established throughout the world, although several European countries allow homosexual couples to 'register' their relationship. The only area of doubt therefore concerns the exact meaning of 'male and female', especially at a time when 'sex-change' operations are sophisticated and even available through the National Health Service. Such operations are accepted for certain state purposes, such as passport details, National Insurance registration etc. The registrar of births will not, however, allow a birth certificate to be changed in these circumstances.

5.2 Transsexuals

A person who feels psychologically a member of the other sex can undergo surgery and hormone therapy, the result of which will be that he (or she) will physically resemble that other sex. It would seem however that this 'sex-change' will have no legal effect as far as the law of marriage is concerned.

Corbett v Corbett (1970)

George Jamieson was a merchant seaman who underwent a sex-change operation, so that he physically resembled a woman. He changed his name to April Ashley, and had some success as a female model. He was wooed by Arthur Corbett, who was aware of his previous identity, and they went through a ceremony of marriage. The relationship broke down, and the High Court had to decide if the marriage was valid or not in accordance with the common law restriction to 'one man and one woman'(see Hyde v Hyde and Woodmansee (1866) at 1.3 above). The court ruled that a person's gender is fixed at birth, in accordance with biological criteria. As an operation only changes physical appearance, and a person's psychology is not relevant, every person must therefore remain the gender noted on his or her birth certificate. The 'marriage' between April Ashley and Arthur Corbett was therefore of no legal effect.

This decision has been followed by the criminal courts in respect of the charge of being a 'man living on the earnings of prostitution' (*R* v *Tan* (1983)) and confirmed by the Court of Appeal in the following case.

Bellinger v Bellinger (2001)

Mrs Bellinger had been classified as a man when she was born but underwent gender reassignment surgery after many years of dressing and living as a woman. She went through a ceremony of marriage with Mr Bellinger in 1981, and he was fully aware of her past history. After 20 years of happy marriage she applied to the court, with Mr Bellinger's support, for a declaration that their marriage was valid. The Court of Appeal ruled that the marriage was void, but did so reluctantly and only by a majority of 2 to 1.

5.3 The European Convention on Human Rights

Applications to the European Court of Human Rights have been made, basically on the grounds that the law as reflected by the decision in *Corbett* is contrary to Article 12 of the Convention. This Article guarantees the 'right to marry', and both Mark Rees (*Rees* v *UK* (1987)) and Caroline Cossey (*Cossey* v *UK* (1991)) were post-operative transsexuals who wished to marry a person of their own 'biological' gender. Both applications were dismissed, but in *Cossey* v *UK* the court was divided, and stated that the issue would have to be reviewed in the future. The decisions were upheld in general terms in *B* v *France* (1992), but again the court noted that attitudes towards transsexuals were changing. It was also ruled that, in any event, a person's 'new' gender should be recorded in certain official documents such as identity cards, in order to protect their right to privacy under Article 8 of the Convention. This is in fact allowed in the UK already. These decisions have been followed most recently in *Sheffield and Horsham* v *UK* (1998), but it seems that there is some support for the complaints. There have been many dissenting judgments to the majority decision of the court, especially under Article 8 (the majority in *Sheffield and Horsham* v *UK* was only 2—11 in favour, 9 against). It is the right to respect for family life in particular under this Article which may give rise to further applications in the English courts, now the Human Rights Act 1998 has come into force.

5.4 The future

Opinion in England seems to be moving towards recognition of the needs of single-sex couples. An informal registration system was introduced in London by the Mayor, Ken Livingstone, in September 2001 and the Civil Partnerships Bill 2002 provides for a detailed scheme of formal registration of partnerships regardless of the sex of the parties. A registered partnership would allow the parties to agree that they would have similar legal rights and obligations as a married couple, and the courts would therefore have wide powers to make orders for financial provision on the breakdown of the relationship. The Bill is unlikely to become law because it is only a private member's bill, but it has gained much support for its aims. Transsexuals would be able to take advantage of such a system as their legal sex would be irrelevant, but they may be able to marry in their 'new' gender anyway. First, even if European Convention on Human Rights jurisprudence does not force the English courts to overrule the decision in *Corbett*, it could yet be overturned if scientific proof becomes available to the effect that psychological identity is caused by biological factors. The narrowness of the decision in *Bellinger* certainly suggests that English judges would be receptive to such arguments. Secondly, the Home Office *Report of the Interdepartmental Working Group on Transsexual People* (2000) noted that England was one of the few European countries which still did not allow gender-reassignment surgery to have legal effects and suggested that there should be consultation on the possibility of suitable legislation.

6 Polygamous marriages

A ceremony which anticipated the possibility of either party taking another spouse in the future could not be contracted validly in England, as it would not comply with the formalities laid down in the Marriage Act 1949. It is possible, however, that such a ceremony could be a permissible form of marriage in another country, and under the Private International Law (Miscellaneous Provisions) Act 1995 it would now create a valid marriage in English law, even if either party is domiciled in England and Wales at the time. The prohibition against further marriages remains however (see 4 above), so that a party domiciled in England and Wales could not marry a second person, no matter what the original ceremony purported to allow.

7 Void and voidable marriages

A marriage ceremony has no legal effect if either party has not the capacity to marry, under any of the headings above. In addition, certain formalities laid down in the Marriage Act 1949 must also be complied with. In such circumstances the marriage is said to be *void*. The effect is that no marriage has ever taken place, and it is not necessary for a court order to be obtained to terminate it.

EXAMPLE

Harold is married to Susan, but he believes her to be dead. He therefore goes through a ceremony of marriage to Jennifer. Unknown to Harold Susan is still alive, but she dies soon after the date of his 'wedding' to Jennifer. Harold then leaves Jennifer and marries Perdip. He is now legally married to Perdip. His 'marriage' to Jennifer was void, because he was still married to Susan. As Susan has now died, and no marriage to Jennifer ever existed, he is free to marry Perdip!

The number of situations where a marriage is void is now strictly limited to the five set out above, as long as the proper formalities have been complied with. There are, however, certain other defects which are seen as affecting a marriage from the outset, and which therefore render it *voidable*. These will be looked at in *Invalidity and Failure of Marriage*, as they require a court order, or 'decree', to terminate the marriage. The process is therefore more properly viewed as similar to divorce, rather than having anything to do with the validity of the marriage. These defects (inability to consummate the marriage is one example) would once have rendered the marriage void under canon (Church) law as well, but it was necessary to restrict the process as too many marriages could fall foul of the rules, and be found to be void even after the death of one of the parties! As this could have far-reaching effects on issues of inheritance, it was vital to introduce an element of certainty into the law by ensuring that most of the defects could only form the basis of a petition to invalidate the marriage by one of the parties. It is this distinction between *void* and *voidable* marriages which has been carried over into modern marriage law, although the original reason for the distinction is no longer valid (see *Invalidity and Failure of Marriage*, 2.1).

Invalidity and failure of marriage

1 Methods of terminating a marriage

1.1 The necessity for a final decree

Because marriage is a status (see *Requirements for a Valid Marriage*, 1.1) it cannot be brought to an end purely by agreement between the parties, and it is therefore always necessary to obtain a court order which formally terminates the marriage. Such an order is known as a *decree*, and can only be obtained after set procedures have been complied with by the applicant (known as the *petitioner*). Note however that this assumes that a valid marriage has been entered into in the first place. If the marriage was void (see *Requirements for a Valid Marriage*, 7) then there is nothing to be terminated. There are three types of final decree that can be obtained, namely decrees of *nullity, divorce* and *judicial separation*. It is useful at this stage to look briefly at the reasons for having these three different methods of terminating a marriage.

1.2 The three decrees in outline

It has already been noted that there are historical reasons for the distinction between void and voidable marriages (see *Requirements for a Valid Marriage*, 7). A marriage which is voidable can be annulled by obtaining a decree of nullity on one of six grounds under the Matrimonial Causes Act 1973, s. 12 (see 2 below). In theory, by granting a decree of nullity the court acknowledges that there was a serious defect in the marriage from its inception, although that defect was not so serious as to render the marriage void. A decree of divorce on the other hand can only be granted after the petitioner has proved one or more of five facts under the Matrimonial Causes Act 1973, s. 1(2) (see 3 below). The difference in theory is that a decree of divorce recognises that the marriage has broken down because of something that has gone wrong *after* the date of the marriage. In law both decrees have exactly the same effect, in that the marriage is terminated and both parties may re-marry. There are, however, some practical differences which will be considered at the end of this section (see 5 below). The third type of decree is that of judicial separation. This decree will be granted where the petitioner proves one or more of the same facts as for a decree of divorce. Under the Matrimonial Causes Act 1973, s. 17, however, there are certain technical differences (see 4 below). The most important difference is that, although the parties will be regarded as formally separated, neither of them will be able to re-marry. This type of decree does not actually dissolve the marriage therefore, and is available for those persons who object to the idea of divorce (perhaps for religious reasons), but who wish to terminate their relationship permanently.

1.3 The importance of a final decree

A decree of nullity or divorce will enable either party to the original marriage to re-marry. Perhaps more important, however, is the fact that all three decrees allow the court to award financial provision under the Matrimonial Causes Act 1973, s. 23 (see *Financial Provision after a Final Decree*). In particular the courts have the power to re-distribute all property owned by the parties to the marriage, including the power to transfer ownership of property from one person to another. This is a very wide power which is not available to the courts where the parties are merely separating on a temporary basis (see *Financial Provision in the Family Proceedings Court*).

2 Nullity

2.1 Introduction

Under the Matrimonial Causes Act 1973, s. 12, there are six grounds under which a marriage is voidable. These can only affect marriages celebrated after 31 July 1971, that being the date on which the original legislation (the Nullity of Marriage Act 1971) came into force. The court will declare a *decree nisi* of nullity when the relevant ground or grounds have been proved by the petitioner. This may then be made *absolute* after a period of six weeks has expired, whereupon the marriage becomes annulled. Under the Matrimonial Causes Act 1973, s. 16, the marriage will neverthe-less be treated as having existed up until the date of the decree absolute. This appears to contradict the theory behind the principle of nullity, namely that the marriage has been defective from the very beginning and is therefore invalid. It is questionable therefore whether there is any point in retaining this method of terminating a mar-riage, when a decree of divorce has exactly the same effect. Although some people might, for religious or moral reasons, feel less constrained in terminating their mar-riage by a decree of nullity rather than divorce, the actual grounds which have to be proved are usually of a more personal and embarrassing nature. Each of these grounds will now be looked at in detail, but it should be noted which of them can be used by either party, and which can only be used when the respondent is at fault. After the six grounds have been considered, it will be necessary to look at the situations where a petition cannot be brought at all, i.e. the *bars* (see 2.8 below).

2.2 Incapacity to consummate the marriage

[handwritten: Nullity Nullifies the marriage]

Under the Matrimonial Causes Act 1973, s. 12(a), a marriage is voidable if it has not been consummated because of the incapacity of either party. It is thus possible for a person to petition for a decree of nullity on the grounds of his own incapacity. Although this provision is clearly based on old canon law theory, it is nevertheless a complete statement of the law. It is therefore a purely technical provision that depends upon the parties having one act of ordinary sexual intercourse *after* the date of the marriage (see, for example, *Ford* v *Ford* (1987), 2.3 below).

[handwritten margin note: If you've had this one act of S.I. after you marriage you can't petition for nullity on these grounds]

> EXAMPLE
>
> A couple have lived together for several years and have two children. They marry, but on the way from the reception to their hotel they are involved in a car accident which renders the man impotent. The marriage is therefore voidable by either party. If the accident had occurred the following day, after one act of sexual intercourse, the marriage would not have been voidable. *[handwritten: — Because it would have been consummated.]*

It does not matter why the party is incapable, nor even whether the party would be capable with another partner! Psychological impotence is therefore as valid a ground as physical impotence, but it must be a recognisable medical condition.

Singh v *Singh* (1971)

A young Sikh girl was persuaded by her parents to enter into a marriage with a man she had never met before. After the marriage she refused to have anything to do with him, and eventually petitioned for a decree of nullity on the grounds that she was incapable of having sexual intercouse with him. The court held that she had merely taken a positive decision not to consummate the marriage, and that did not amount to an 'invincible repugnance' to have sexual intercourse. The petition was therefore refused.

[handwritten margin note: Not that she had no capacity]

The court might also be faced with difficulties if there is a physical problem which could be remedied by medical treatment. Evidence would need to be given as to the nature of the treatment that would be necessary, and whether it would be reasonable to expect the party to go through with it. It seems wrong to expect any person to have to submit to such a distressing examination of their personal medical problems, and unlikely that anybody would want to when the divorce process is so much more private (see 3.9 below).

2.3 Wilful refusal to consummate a marriage

[handwritten: Nullity nullifies the marriage.]

Under the Matrimonial Causes Act 1973, s. 12(b), a marriage is voidable if it has not been consummated because of the wilful refusal of the respondent. It is therefore not possible for the petitioner to rely upon his own refusal, only his own incapacity. The line between a refusal based on unwillingness, and a refusal based on 'invincible repugnance', is therefore an important one.

[handwritten margin note: She should have pleaded her case on grounds of incapacity or her own part]

In the case of *Singh* v *Singh* (1971) above, the girl's petition did not succeed because her refusal to consummate the marriage was a rational decision, rather than a psychological repugnance towards the man. It was therefore a case of *wilful refusal* rather than *incapacity*, and she could not bring a petition on the grounds of her own refusal.

The refusal must be final, and not merely a momentary lack of interest or nervousness. The court will therefore have to look at the behaviour of the parties throughout the marriage.

Ford v *Ford* (1987)   *[handwritten: FORD PRISON!]*

The parties had had sexual intercourse on a few occasions, and were married after the man had been sent to prison. There were several occasions during unsupervised visits when it would have been possible to have had sexual intercourse, although it would have been in breach of prison rules, but the man refused. When he was allowed a home visit on the condition that he stay with his wife, he again refused to have sexual intercourse with her, and insisted that she take him to the house of a former girl-friend. In the light of all these circumstances the court ruled that there was a settled refusal to have sexual intercourse, and granted the wife's petition.

The refusal must be *wilful* however, and therefore the court must consider whether the respondent was justified in refusing. If it is the behaviour of the other person which justifies a refusal, then it is that behaviour which amounts to wilful refusal.

Kaur v *Singh* (1972)

Two Sikhs went through a civil ceremony of marriage, but both knew that it was Sikh custom that the husband arrange an additional religious ceremony before the marriage would be regarded as complete. The husband refused to do so, and so the wife refused to consummate the marriage. Her petition for nullity was granted on the grounds of his wilful refusal.

This principle could cause particular difficulties where both parties put conditions upon sexual intercourse. The court would then have to assess which condition was more reasonable, although the burden of proof is of course on the petitioner.

The husband refuses to use a condom, but the wife refuses to have sexual intercourse unless he does. On the one hand the husband is ready to have normal intercourse, but on the other hand the wife might be justifiably afraid of pregnancy.

It should be noted finally that this ground is completely inconsistent with the theoretical basis for annulment. It is clearly a problem that has arisen during the course of the marriage, rather than a defect that existed at the time of the ceremony. It is also a proper basis for a divorce on the grounds of the respondent's behaviour (see 3.3 below), even where one or more acts of sexual intercourse have taken place. There seems little justification for retaining it as a special method of terminating the marriage therefore, although it may become more important when the law of divorce has been reformed (see 3.10.2 below).

2.4 Lack of consent

Under the Matrimonial Causes Act 1973, s. 12(c), a marriage is voidable if either party did not validly consent to it. The section goes on to give three specific categories, namely *duress*, *mistake* and *unsoundness of mind*. These are only examples however, as lack of consent induced in any other way will also make the marriage voidable.

2.4.1 Duress

If a person is forced to go through a marriage ceremony by threats, it is possible that the marriage will be voidable. The difficulty, however, is in finding the right balance between total acceptance of the state of mind of the parties (a purely subjective test), and a need for certainty based on more visible criteria (an objective test). On the one hand, if a person has entered a marriage for any reason other than a true desire to marry, there has been no true consent and the marriage should be annulled. On the other hand, this would enable anybody to allege a state of mind at the time of the ceremony, which would be impossible to disprove and thus effectively allow nullity on demand. The following two cases illustrate the balance that the courts have reached.

Hirani v Hirani (1982)

A young Hindu girl had formed an attachment to a Muslim boy. Her parents arranged a marriage to a Hindu man whom she had never seen, and told her that if she did not go through with the ceremony she would have to leave. She married the man, but left him after six weeks and went to live with her Muslim boyfriend. Her petition for nullity was granted, as the court found that she was so dependent upon her parents before the marriage that her will was overcome by their threats.

No valid consent on her part

In the case of *Singh* v *Singh* (1971) however (see 2.2 above), the Sikh girl went through with the marriage out of 'proper respect' for her parents and Sikh traditions. The court ruled that this was not sufficient to amount to duress. It seems clear therefore that the petitioner must be able to prove fear of some consequence, rather than just a desire to avoid a disagreeable situation. The fear may be induced by a person or circumstances, and the petitioner will be judged according to his or her strength of will. This could have strange results however, and so it is uncertain whether the courts would follow these principles completely.

> EXAMPLE
>
> A man living in England is so terrified by what he sees as the rising tide of violence in the streets, that he marries a French woman so that he can go and live in France. He subsequently regrets his actions and seeks to annul the marriage. It does not matter that a reasonable person would not suffer the same fear, nor that the threats were not specific. It is difficult to see the courts allowing his petition however.

It should be noted, though, that decisions by the Scottish courts have gone even further than *Hirani*.

Mahmud v *Mahmud* (1994)

The applicant was a man who had been living with his partner for several years, and they had one child with another on its way. For all of this time the applicant's family had been pressurising him to marry a woman from their community, and eventually he gave in when his father died and his family insisted that it had been his dying wish that his son would be 'properly' married. Despite the fact that the applicant was clearly capable of looking after himself, the court granted his petition and annulled the marriage.

duress

2.4.2 Mistake

A mistake as to the personality, wealth, or other characteristics of a person is not sufficient to annul a marriage, even if the mistake was induced by fraud. Even a mistake as to the effects of the marriage is not sufficient.

Kassim v *Kassim* (1962)

The man thought that the marriage ceremony was polygamous, and that he would therefore be entitled to take other wives. His petition was refused.

There are two categories of mistake which will render a marriage voidable however. Firstly, mistake as to the identity of the other person, and secondly mistake as to the nature of the ceremony. The first category is perhaps unlikely, unless the bride is wearing a very thick veil! There are some circumstances where a petition may be successful, however.

Militante v *Ogunwomoju* (1994)

The wife found out that her husband had married her under an assumed name when he was arrested and deported as an illegal immigrant. The Family Division judge granted the decree of nullity on the grounds that the husband's fraud as to his identity had vitiated the wife's consent.

This decision must be doubted, however, as it seems to be more a case of 'the wrong name' rather than 'the wrong man'.

The second category is quite possible, especially where the ceremony is being conducted in an unfamiliar language.

Mehta v *Mehta* (1945)

An English woman met an Indian man in England and went to India with him. She went through a ceremony with him, but did not understand it because it was in Hindustani, which she could not speak. She later found that it was a wedding ceremony, and her petition to annul the marriage was granted.

2.4.3 Unsoundness of mind

The party to the marriage must have been unable to understand the nature of marriage at the time of the ceremony, owing to mental disorder. It is unlikely that this ground will be used now that there is a special provision for mental disorder under the Matrimonial Causes Act 1973, s. 12(d) (see 2.5 below).

2.4.4 Other circumstances

Lack of true consent may have been caused by intoxication by drink or drugs. One or both of the parties may also have been performing the ceremony as a joke, with no intention that it should result in a true marriage. The courts have refused to annul 'sham' marriages however.

Messina v *Smith* (1971)
The woman went through the ceremony purely so that she would be able to obtain a British passport. Her petition was refused.

2.5 Mental illness

Under the Matrimonial Causes Act 1973, s. 12(d), a marriage will be voidable where, at the time of the ceremony, either of the parties was suffering from a mental disorder which made them unfitted for marriage. The disorder must be within the meaning of the Mental Health Act 1983. This provision is meant to cover the situation where a valid consent was given, but subsequently it has become clear that the mental disorder is so serious that a normal married life between the parties is not feasible.

2.6 Venereal disease

Under the Matrimonial Causes Act 1973, s. 12(e), the marriage can be annulled if the respondent was suffering from a venereal disease in a communicable form, and the petitioner was unaware of it.

2.7 Pregnancy

Under the Matrimonial Causes Act 1973, s. 12(f), the marriage can be annulled if the respondent was pregnant by another man at the time of the ceremony, and the petitioner was unaware of the fact.

2.8 Bars

There are two specific bars to the granting of a decree of nullity, set out in the Matrimonial Causes Act 1973, s. 13.

2.8.1 Time
The petition for nullity must be issued within three years of the date of the marriage, unless the grounds are inability or wilful refusal to consummate. Leave to present a petition outside this period may be given where the petitioner was suffering from a mental disorder which makes it fair that the period of time should be extended.

2.8.2 Knowledge
The respondent may oppose the petition on the grounds that the petitioner 'with knowledge that it was open to him to have the marriage avoided, so conducted himself in relation to the respondent as to lead the respondent reasonably to believe that he would not seek to do so'. This is meant to cover the situation where two people marry in the full knowledge that one of them is suffering from a disability, or where it

is agreed that they will not have a sexual relationship. It clearly seems unfair that either party should then be able to use the other's disability, or refusal to consummate, as grounds for annulling the marriage. However, there is a further condition that 'it would be unjust to the respondent to grant the decree'. As the court can grant full financial relief, and as the marriage could be terminated by divorce after five years anyway (see 3.6 below), it is difficult to think of any situation where the courts would see any point in refusing a decree! There has been no reported case to date in which a respondent has successfully pleaded this bar.

3 Divorce

3.1 The ground for divorce

3.1.1 Proving the ground

The basis for divorce used to be the *matrimonial offence*. The law was changed substantially by the Divorce Reform Act 1969, and was later consolidated with the law on nullity and other matters in the Matrimonial Causes Act 1973. Under the Matrimonial Causes Act 1973, s. 1(1), either party to a marriage may present a petition for divorce on the ground that the marriage has broken down irretrievably. *Irretrievable breakdown* is therefore the sole ground for divorce. In effect however this is a fiction, because s. 1(2) goes on to state that the court shall not hold the marriage to have broken down irretrievably unless one of five facts is proved. Each of these facts will be considered in detail, but it is worth noting them in outline at this stage:

* Adultery
* Behaviour
* Desertion for two years
* Separation for two years
* Separation for five years.

In particular it should be noted that the first three facts are all related to the *fault* of the respondent. Thus the concept of the matrimonial offence has been retained to some extent. The last two, however, contain no allegations of fault at all, and relate purely to the objective fact of separation for a period of time. It was the introduction of these which was the innovation of the Divorce Law Reform Act 1969, and which also caused much controversy at the time. As will be seen later in more detail (see 3.5 and 3.6 below), the different periods are to allow divorce by consent after two years' separation, and divorce despite the objections of the respondent after five years' separation.

3.1.2 The importance of the facts

The necessity to prove one of these facts serves to emphasise that divorce is not regarded as a matter which can be left to the two parties. In every case the court must be satisfied that one of the facts has been proved, even if both parties are agreed that the marriage has broken down irretrievably. Under the Matrimonial Causes Act 1973,

s. 1(3), it is the duty of the court to enquire into the facts alleged by the petitioner. In practice, however, the courts are reluctant to follow this procedure more than is absolutely necessary.

Grenfell v *Grenfell* (1978) — no enquiry into the allegations - divorce granted on basis of 5 yrs separation

The wife had petitioned for divorce, citing lengthy allegations of misbehaviour on the part of the husband. He denied these allegations (which ran to several pages of the petition), but petitioned for divorce himself on the basis that they had been separated for five years. The Court of Appeal refused to enquire into the wife's allegations, as one fact (five years' separation) had been proved and the marriage could therefore be terminated on that basis.

The court will have to allow an enquiry into the facts in certain circumstances however.

Bonnesen v *Bonnesen* (1989)

The husband had obtained a decree nisi based on his wife's behaviour. His wife was suffering from mental illness, and by mistake the Official Solicitor had failed to defend the petition on her behalf. On the application of the Official Solicitor, the court set aside the decree nisi and insisted that the husband prove his allegations, although the wife could not give any evidence to the contrary, and it was clear that the marriage had broken down irretrievably.

3.1.3 The relevance of irretrievable breakdown

Under s. 1(4), Matrimonial Causes Act 1973 the court must also be satisfied that the marriage has broken down irretrievably, even when a fact has been proved. There is, however, no reported case of a divorce being refused by the court purely on the basis that the marriage has not broken down irretrievably, once a fact has been proved. The Matrimonial Causes Act 1973, s. 6, stipulates that divorce procedure must include consideration of the possibility of a reconciliation between the parties, and allows the court to adjourn proceedings for attempts at reconciliation to take place. It should be noted, however, that the typical divorce procedure effectively prevents any real investigation by the court of either the state of the marriage, or even the facts that have been alleged (see 3.9 below).

3.1.4 The decree of divorce

Under the Matrimonial Causes Act 1973, s. 1(5), a decree nisi of divorce will be granted once a relevant fact (and irretrievable breakdown) has been proved. After a period of six weeks, the divorce can then be made absolute, by a simple application by the petitioner. The marriage will not be terminated until the decree has been made absolute, but the court can reduce the six-week period in the exceptional circumstances of a particular case.

3.2 Adultery

Under the Matrimonial Causes Act 1973, s. 1(2)(a), the court may find that a marriage has broken down irretrievably if the petitioner proves that the respondent has committed adultery, and that he finds it intolerable to live with the respondent. 'Adultery' means normal heterosexual intercourse between the respondent and another person of the opposite sex. The respondent must have consented, and therefore the victim of a rape will obviously not have committed adultery. The petitioner must also find it 'intolerable' to live with the respondent. This need not be because of the adultery.

Cleary v Cleary (1974)

After the husband found out about his wife's adultery, they lived together for six weeks. She then left, and petitioned for divorce herself some months later. The husband crosspetitioned on the grounds of her earlier adultery, but said that the reason he did not want to live with her was that there was 'no future for the marriage'. The judge refused his petition, but it was allowed on appeal by the Court of Appeal.

It is therefore possible for one act of adultery to justify a petition for divorce in seemingly unjust circumstances.

EXAMPLE

Unknown to his wife, a man is carrying on an affair with another woman. He persuades his wife to go to a party where everybody swaps partners for the evening, and they both have sexual intercourse with other people. The next day he starts divorce proceedings on the basis of her one act of adultery, stating that he finds it intolerable to live with her because he wants to live with the other woman.

Although this seems unfair, the basis of the divorce legislation is that 'irretrievable breakdown' is now the ground for divorce, not fault. But if that is the case, and if the reason for granting the divorce is because one party finds it intolerable to live with the other, why is it necessary to insist upon an act of adultery as a pre-condition?

3.3 Behaviour

Under the Matrimonial Causes Act 1973, s. 1(2)(b), the court may find that a marriage has broken down irretrievably if the petitioner proves that the respondent has behaved in such a way that the petitioner can no longer reasonably be expected to live with the respondent. The expression 'unreasonable behaviour' is therefore not strictly accurate, although it is a useful shorthand expression. Instead it should be noted that there are two separate requirements, namely the existence of some form of misbehaviour by the respondent, and a judgment as to whether the petitioner can be expected to continue living with the respondent as a result.

3.3.1 The respondent's misbehaviour

Any sort of behaviour can be relevant under this heading, except mere desertion. This is dealt with separately under s. 1(2)(c), Matrimonial Causes Act 1973 (see 3.4 below). There are many cases where quite minor problems have been held to justify a divorce. The following case is an example of an extremely flimsy petition.

Richards v Richards (1984)

The wife's divorce petition was granted on allegations that her husband had forgotten her birthday and their wedding anniversary and failed to give her presents at Christ-mas or when their child was born. He compounded this dreadful behaviour by refus-ing to take her out and by failing to get rid of their dog (which was causing damage around the house).

The court will be prepared to look at the totality of the respondent's behaviour when it is really his character that is the problem, rather than specific instances of behaviour.

Livingstone-Stallard v Livingstone-Stallard (1974)

The husband was a very domineering man, and attempted to impose his old-fashioned ideas on his wife. One of many apparently trivial examples was his treat-ment of his wife when he found that she had invited the wedding-photographer in, and given him a glass of sherry while they went through the photographs. He scolded his wife because she had allowed a tradesman in, and given him alcohol. She should have known that such men are likely to be inflamed by alcohol into trying to take advantage of a woman on her own. Her petition was granted because of his *character rather than terrible things he had done* domineering attitudes, as evidenced by such incidents.

The respondent need not be to blame for the behaviour. Thus it may be possible to base a petition on behaviour caused by the respondent's illness.

Thurlow v Thurlow (1975) *in sickness + in health?*

The wife was often bed-ridden and suffered from epilepsy. As a result she would throw household objects around, and wander into the street at night. The husband was granted a divorce on that basis.

It is more difficult to see how a divorce could be granted if the respondent is merely ill, and therefore the petitioner's complaint is that the respondent needs constant care and cannot reciprocate in any way. The court was reluctant to grant a divorce in the following case, where the circumstances were similar in principle.

Carter-Fea v Carter-Fea (1987) *Why For Richer for Poorer?*

The husband got into financial difficulties, with the result that the wife suffered the strain of coping with visits from the court bailiffs, avoiding creditors, and worrying about the repossession of her home by the bank. Her petition was granted, but the court made it clear that mere financial difficulties would not always justify a divorce.

It is therefore not clear whether illness or other difficulties can justify a divorce based on the respondent's behaviour if they do not result in positive behaviour by the respondent.

3.3.2 Whether the petitioner should live with the respondent

In the first place the court will look at the character and personality of the petitioner. Thus it will take into account whether the petitioner has particular likes or dislikes which make the respondent's behaviour more difficult to bear. It will also take into account the petitioner's behaviour, as this could affect the issue.

EXAMPLE

Swearing and aggressive behaviour would normally be unacceptable. If both parties behave in the same way however, it would be difficult for either of them to rely on such behaviour by the other as the basis for a divorce petition.

The respondent's behaviour will then be assessed on the basis of what is reasonable, and not all of the petitioner's views will be accepted.

Pheasant v Pheasant (1972)

The sole basis of the husband's allegations was that his wife had not given him the spontaneous demonstrations of affection which his nature demanded. Although he clearly regarded the marriage as at an end because of that, his petition was refused.

3.4 Desertion

Under the Matrimonial Causes Act 1973, s. 1(2)(c), the court may find that a marriage has broken down irretrievably if the petitioner proves that the respondent has deserted the petitioner for two years immediately preceding the presentation of the petition. The two-year period must therefore have elapsed by the time that the petition is filed at the court, and it is not sufficient that it has elapsed by the time of the court hearing. The respondent must still be in desertion at the time that the petition is filed. Desertion requires two separate elements, namely a period of *separation* and an *intention* to separate.

3.4.1 Separation

This is also an important element in the facts that require separation for a fixed period (see 3.5 and 3.6 below). There must be a physical living apart, but this can occur in the same house. The court must therefore assess the extent to which the parties lived separately.

Le Brocq v Le Brocq (1964)

The husband and wife slept in different rooms, and avoided each other. The wife continued to cook for both of them however, and the husband gave her house-keeping. The petition was refused.

The court must also sometimes look at the nature of the relationship between the parties, as this may put their behaviour into a different light.

Fuller v Fuller (1973)

The husband and wife had lived apart for four years, and the wife was now living with another man. The husband suffered a heart-attack and the wife allowed him to move in with them as a paying lodger. Although she now cooked for him and did his laundry, it was clear that it was purely as a business arrangement, and the petition was granted.

3.4.2 Intention

The respondent must have intended the marital relationship to be brought to an end by their separation. It will not be desertion therefore if the parties have separated by agreement. If one party leaves the other for a good reason, that will also not amount to desertion.

If a husband is sent to prison, he will not be in desertion. If he leaves while he is mentally ill, and not responsible for his actions, he cannot be said to have the necessary intention. If he leaves because his wife's behaviour is so bad that he cannot put up with it, again he will not be deserting her.

In fact, if it is the other party's conduct that causes the separation, it is that party who would be regarded as being in desertion. This situation is known as *constructive desertion*. Constructive desertion is rarely applicable nowadays, because the petitioner can use s. 1(2)(b), Matrimonial Causes Act 1973 instead. Indeed the fact of desertion forms the basis of less than two per cent of all divorce petitions. ⟍ Behaviour

3.5 Two years' separation

Under the Matrimonial Causes Act 1973, s. 1(2)(d), the court may find that a marriage has broken down irretrievably if the parties have lived apart for two years immediately preceding the presentation of the petition, and the respondent agrees to the divorce being granted. As with desertion, the two-year period must have expired when the petition is filed, rather than when the case comes before the court. There are thus two crucial elements, namely *separation* and *consent*.

3.5.1 Separation

Under s. 2(6), Matrimonial Causes Act 1973 this can occur in the same house, as long as the parties are living in different *households*. The same principles apply therefore as in the case of desertion (see 3.4.1 above). There is no provision that there needs to be anything other than a mere living apart, but the courts have implied into the Act a mental element similar to that needed for desertion.

Santos v *Santos* (1972)

A wife left her husband in Spain and came to England. She returned to Spain three times (amounting in total to less than six months; see 3.7.1 below). On each occasion she used the same room as her husband, and occasionally the same bed. On her petition for divorce after a total period of separation of two years, the Court of Appeal ruled that the period of living apart for the purposes of the 1973 Act could not start to run until one party decided that the marriage was at an end. Time would start to run however, even though that decision might not have been communicated to the other party.

A secret intention to live apart will therefore suffice. As the parties are divorcing by consent, they need only be careful as to how they give their evidence as to the period of separation.

A wife is given a job abroad, and takes it with her husband's agreement. After two years they decide that the marriage is at an end. If the wife petitions for divorce, all she need say is that, when she took the job, she had secretly decided that the marriage was at an end. It is clearly impossible for the court to say whether she is lying or not.

The possibility of this situation arising is increased by the method of giving evidence under the typical procedure for divorce. This will be considered briefly (see 3.9 below), but reference should also be made to the Matrimonial Practice syllabus, and the form of affidavit used when a *special procedure* divorce is being applied for.

3.5.2 Consent

This must be given by the respondent on a form issued by the court (see the Matrimonial Practice syllabus and the standard form of Acknowledgement of Service). Consent can be withdrawn at any time up to the granting of the decree nisi. Thereafter under the Matrimonial Causes Act 1973, s. 10(1), the court can rescind the decree nisi if the respondent proves that he was misled by the petitioner about any matter which he took into account when deciding whether to give his consent or not.

3.6 Separation for five years

Under the Matrimonial Causes Act 1973, s. 1(2)(e), the court may find that a marriage has broken down irretrievably if the parties have lived apart for five years, whether the respondent agrees to the divorce or not. The same considerations apply to the meaning of 'living apart' as apply to the previous fact, and in particular s. 2(6). On the face of it, this allows a petitioner to obtain a divorce against even the most unwilling of spouses (see *Grenfell* v *Grenfell* (1978) at 3.1.2 above). There is, however, a possible defence even to this fact, which will be considered in the context of bars to divorce generally (see 3.8.2 below).

3.7 Separation and reconciliation

There are various provisions in the Matrimonial Causes Act 1973 to encourage reconciliation between the parties. Some of these are procedural, and will be encountered in the Matrimonial Practice syllabus. Generally, the court has the power to adjourn the proceedings at any time if it feels that there is a reasonable possibility of a reconciliation being effected. This is a theme throughout the Act, and there are two particular provisions which merit consideration. First, the method of calculating the periods of separation needed for a divorce on the facts of desertion or separation for two or five years. Secondly, the provisions which apply when adultery or behaviour are the relevant facts, and the parties have carried on living together.

3.7.1 Continuous separation

Under the Matrimonial Causes Act 1973, s. 2(5), a period or periods of living together totalling no more than six months, will not interrupt the 'continuous period'. Those times spent together will not count towards the relevant period however. This is to ensure that two spouses who are living apart will not be dissuaded from attempting a reconciliation by the thought that they will have to start counting all over again should the attempt fail.

6 mths apart   4 tog.
12 mths apart   2 tog.
                 6 mths   FAMILY LAW   335
18

EXAMPLE

A husband leaves his wife for six months. They then live together for four months to see if they can resolve their problems. They split up again and live apart for a further 12 months.

Once again they attempt a reconciliation, and live together for two months. Should they now separate again, they will only have to wait a further six months before being able to start divorce proceedings on the basis of two years' separation or desertion (or three years and six months for a divorce on the basis of five years' separation). See also the facts of *Santos* v *Santos* (1972) (see 3.5.1 above).

Take the 6 mths out of the period of 18 that they've been apart + they only need 6 mths apart to qualify.

3.7.2 Living together after adultery or behaviour

The difficulty here is that this could be evidence that the marriage has not broken down irretrievably. Once again, however, the innocent party should not be under pressure to separate immediately and thus destroy any possibility of a reconciliation. Accordingly under the Matrimonial Causes Act 1973, s. 2(2) and (3), the court cannot take into account any periods of living together totalling no more than six months when considering whether the marriage has irretrievably broken down or not.

up to 6 mths tog. can be ignored.

EXAMPLE

A husband finds out that his wife has committed adultery. He leaves immediately, but comes back after four months to attempt a reconciliation. After two months he leaves again and starts divorce proceedings alleging her adultery. The period when they lived together cannot affect the divorce. The same principle would apply if he had left after the last incident of behaviour on her part which formed the basis of a subsequent petition.

If the periods together do total more than six months, then under s. 2(2) the act of adultery cannot be relied on. Under s. 2(3) however, any incidents of behaviour can still be relied upon in a petition under s. 1(2)(b), but the court can now look upon the periods of living together as evidence that the marriage has not broken down irretrievably.

EXAMPLE

A wife alleges several acts of violence against her husband in a divorce petition based on his behaviour. She has lived with him for more than six months since the last act of violence, but can convince the court that she had no choice as she could not find anywhere else to go, and was too frightened of him to try and live apart under the same roof.

3.8 Bars to divorce

3.8.1 Short marriages

Under the Matrimonial Causes Act 1973, s. 3, no petition for divorce may be presented unless the parties have been married for one year. This was introduced by an amendment in the Matrimonial and Family Proceedings Act 1984, as previously the restriction was three years unless the petitioner could prove exceptional hardship or that the respondent had been guilty of exceptional depravity. The bar is now absolute, but it does not prevent the petitioner from relying upon events that occurred during that time. *So it can be less than 1 yr.*

EXAMPLE

A husband and wife separate the day after their marriage, after the wife discovers that her husband committed adultery at the reception. She can bring proceedings for divorce based on his adultery, as soon as the one year has elapsed. Alternatively they can divorce after two years' separation, calculated from the day after the marriage.

3.8.2 Grave hardship

Under the Matrimonial Causes Act 1973, s. 5, a petition alleging five years' separation can be opposed on the grounds that a divorce would cause the respondent 'grave financial or other hardship' and that 'it would in all the circumstances be wrong to dissolve the marriage'. The effect is therefore to provide a defence to such a petition after all, even if the marriage has irretrievably broken down. Financial hardship can normally be resolved in ancillary proceedings (see *Financial Provision after a Final Decree*), and is normally caused by the separation of the spouses and the breakdown of their relationship, rather than the divorce itself. The typical problems encountered by a petitioner under this section must therefore relate to financial benefits which depend upon the status of being married.

EXAMPLE

During a marriage a husband has made contributions to his employers' pension scheme. His wife is entitled under the scheme to considerable benefits should he die while they are still married. A divorce would therefore lose her this protection, and it is now too late in her life for her to build up her own pension rights. The court cannot under present law transfer the benefits of the husband's pension to her.

Normally this problem will be overcome by the petitioner making suitable other arrangements. The respondent may still be worse off, but the hardship must be 'grave' before it can prevent the divorce going through. There has been no known case where 'other hardship' has been successfully pleaded by a respondent. The courts have occasionally considered social difficulties that the respondent may suffer, and the following case is the nearest that a court has come to allowing such difficulties as a defence.

Banik v *Banik* (1973)

A Hindu woman resisted her husband's petition based on five years' separation, on the grounds that the attitudes and conventions of her community would render her a social outcast if she were divorced. The Court of Appeal considered that this gave rise to a valid defence on the face of it, and the case was sent back to the divorce court for her arguments to be considered on their merits.

Only five per cent of all divorces are on the basis of five years' separation, and therefore this provision is of little practical relevance except in the specific financial circumstances detailed above. Even those situations are perhaps best dealt with by a suitable application for financial relief after the decree, especially now that the courts have the power to split a pension fund (see *Financial Provision after a Final Decree*, 2.9.3).

3.8.3 *General financial protection*

A respondent to a petition based on either of the separation facts may oppose the granting of the decree absolute under the Matrimonial Causes Act 1973, s. 10(2). The court must then consider the financial position of the respondent after the divorce, in the light of all the circumstances including health, age, earning capacity and financial resources and obligations of both parties. The court must not make the decree absolute unless it is satisfied that the petitioner has made reasonable financial provision for the respondent, or is prepared to accept an undertaking to that effect. The court has all the necessary powers to achieve these ends after the divorce (see *Financial Provision after a Final Decree*), but this provision can be useful in that the petitioner may have a more powerful incentive to comply if the divorce depends upon it! There may even be situations where the court's powers would not be adequate, as where the petitioner benefits under a discretionary trust and has no other assets that the court could redistribute to take such possibilities into account. Nevertheless, the last time that statistics were kept (1975), there were only 701 applications under this section, and it is rarely used. There has been a recent example of the procedure being used successfully, however.

Garcia v Garcia (1992)
The wife's application for the decree absolute to be postponed was granted, because of the husband's substantial maintenance arrears under a separation agreement registered in Spain.

3.8.4 *Children*

Under the Matrimonial Causes Act 1973, s. 41, as amended by the Children Act 1989, the court will consider whether to exercise any of its wide powers under the Children Act 1989 (see *Children*, 2) in respect of any relevant children. This provision applies to any child under 16 who has been treated by the husband and wife as a member of their family but excludes children who have been officially fostered by them. Step-children of one of the parties are therefore covered, as are children who have been looked after by them under a private arrangement. The court may also extend the provision to cover children over 16, which it would probably do if they are still receiving education or training. In the Matrimonial Practice syllabus you will see how the parties must complete a special document which provides full details of the proposed arrangements for any relevant children. This will include information about their residence, education, financial support and contact with the parent with whom the child will not be living. After considering these matters, if the court thinks that it should, or is likely to have to, exercise any of its powers under the Children Act 1989, and that there are exceptional circumstances concerning the interests of the child, then it may direct that the decree is not to be made absolute until it orders otherwise. The effect of this provision is to encourage the husband and wife to consider how the divorce will affect their children in the knowledge that any obvious problems will delay the divorce while the court investigates.

3.9 Divorce law and procedure

A divorce may now be granted under a *special procedure*, which does not require the petitioner to attend court. Reference should be made to the Matrimonial Practice syllabus for the exact procedure, but the principal element is the affidavit in support of the petition which must be completed and sworn by the petitioner. This is then scrutinised by the district judge, who will grant a certificate that the relevant fact is proved. The decree nisi is then granted by a judge in open court in the normal way but without any consideration of the facts. This procedure was brought in by new regulations rather than primary legislation, between 1973 and 1977. The vast majority of all divorces are now dealt with on this basis, and this has undoubtedly had an effect upon the substantive law. As over 99 per cent of divorces are undefended, the facts alleged in the petition are not countered by the respondent, but neither are they now subject to cross-examination by the court. As long as the special procedure affidavit is completed carefully by the petitioner, there is little possibility that the district judge will be able to detect any falsehoods. As a result, very few couples are now bothered to wait until two years' separation has expired, as a divorce can be obtained much more quickly by one of them alleging adultery or behaviour. Over 75 per cent of all divorces are now granted on one of those facts. These procedural changes have thus rendered most of the substantive law of divorce meaningless, as in practice a divorce can be obtained by consent if the parties are willing to bend the truth, or exaggerate slightly. On the other hand, the unnecessary use of the 'fault' provisions can encourage feelings of bitterness, and induce antagonism between the parties. As a result, the need for reform has been recognised.

3.10 Divorce reform

3.10.1 Reports and proposals

The perceived deficiencies in the existing divorce law, noted in 3.9 above, prompted the Law Commission and (eventually) the Government to consider reforming the law and procedure once again. First there were two reports by the Law Commission (*Facing the Future*, 1988; and *The Ground for Divorce*, 1990) which considered alternatives and recommended a new procedure. The idea at the heart of these documents was that 'fault' is inappropriate as a ground for divorce, and the best of the other options would be to reform the procedure so that the only way to obtain a divorce would be for one party to file a formal request for divorce with the court. After a fixed period of time the divorce would be granted automatically unless the court thought that important ancillary matters (such as financial matters, or arrangements for the children) still needed to be resolved. The parties would thus be encouraged to consider the implications of the breakdown of their marriage, and would be assisted (by 'mediation') to agree ancillary matters in a constructive atmosphere. The Government responded after some delay and issued a Consultation Paper in December 1993 entitled *Looking to the Future: Mediation and the Ground for Divorce*, essentially proposing that the Law Commission's scheme be enacted. Again there was further delay before a White Paper with the same title was published in April 1995, but the proposals outlined in this document were quickly embodied in the Family Law Bill introduced into Parliament at the beginning of 1996. This Bill suffered many amendments in both the House of Lords and the House of Commons, mainly at the hands of those who saw it as an attack on the institution of marriage. In particular the abolition of fault as an element of the divorce process caused almost as much controversy as it had in 1969 (see 3.1.1 above), and most amendments were aimed at making the new process longer or more difficult. The Family Law Act received the Royal Assent in July 1996, but the divorce provisions were to be brought into force at a later date.

3.10.2 *The Family Law Act 1996 divorce provisions*
The new law was to allow divorce after a period of 12 months' notice (18 months if there were minor children or one party requested the extra time). The process was to be started by a compulsory *information meeting*, followed by a three month wait before the notice of the intended divorce could be registered. After this notice another period of nine months (or 15 months) would commence, called the period for reflection and consideration. At the end of this second period a divorce order could be requested, as long as all financial matters and arrangements for the children had been settled. During the period of reflection and consideration the parties would be encouraged to use mediation to settle any disputes (see 3.10.3 below) instead of having recourse to lawyers and court proceedings, and the Government clearly hoped that the combined system of information meetings and mediation would encourage reconciliation as well as persuading people not to use solicitors. In June 1999, however, the Lord Chancellor announced that the divorce provisions would not be brought into force in 2000 as originally planned. This was because pilot projects to assess the impact of the system of information meetings were not going well in that they did not appear to be achieving what the Government hoped. The final reports were presented in September 2000 and showed that, far from saving marriages or encouraging mediation, information meetings seemed to convince people that they should continue with the divorce and see a solicitor for legal advice. After a further delay, the Lord Chancellor announced in January 2001 that the relevant part of the Act would actually be repealed. There has been little evidence since of the Government's intentions, but it is notable that in October 1999 the new president of the Family Division, Dame Elizabeth Butler-Sloss LJ, described the present divorce system as a 'hypocritical charade', so that reform is clearly needed. The provisions in respect of mediation have been implemented independently of the divorce law, however, and are part of the Legal Services Commission's scheme for legal aid.

3.10.3 *Mediation*
Mediation is a method of enabling parties to reach agreement on disputed matters without having recourse to court proceedings. There will usually be a series of meet-

ings run by qualified mediators, with legal advisers being excluded (although the mediators themselves may be legally qualified). The parties will be encouraged to talk informally about their dispute so that differences are minimised and areas of common agreement emphasised. Under the Act, for the purposes of legal aid, mediation is presumed to be more appropriate than court proceedings. This means that a person needing legal aid to pursue or defend a claim (whether for financial provision or in respect of a dispute concerning children) will have to try mediation first. There is some concern that mediation allows aggressive spouses to dominate their partners and, although there are provisions to allow the presumption to be rebutted, it is inevitable that some people will be forced into mediation against their wills. This seems contrary to the whole philosophy behind such schemes, and research conducted on the effectiveness of publicly-funded mediation suggests that many people return to using a solicitor after trying mediation, with the result that the Legal Services Commission may end up financing solicitors' fees as well as (not instead of) the costs of mediation. This has undoubtedly caused the Government some embarrassment and the scheme is being reviewed, but publicly-funded mediation now seems so embedded in the practice of family law that it is difficult to see how it could be abandoned.

4 Judicial separation

4.1 Grounds for a decree

Under the Matrimonial Causes Act 1973, s. 17, a decree will be granted to a petitioner who establishes any of the facts on which a petition for divorce can be based. The court is not required to consider irretrievable breakdown however. A simple decree is then granted, without the necessity for a decree nisi and decree absolute (see 3.1.4 above).

4.2 Procedures

A decree may be refused under Matrimonial Causes Act 1973, s. 41, as for divorce (see 3.8.4 above). However, none of the other bars set out in 3.8 above applies.

4.3 Effects of a decree

The most important legal consequence is that the court will have the same wide powers to grant financial provision, as on a decree of nullity or divorce (see *Financial Provision after a Final Decree*). Otherwise, the idea that the parties are no longer obliged to live together has little practical effect. The right to consortium cannot be enforced in any event (see *Requirements for a Valid Marriage*, 1.2), and a decree of judicial separation does not automatically mean that one spouse must leave the matrimonial home. Neither party may re-marry of course, and the full divorce procedure must still be gone through to terminate the marriage fully (although an established fact under a previous judicial separation petition can be used again). Automatic rights on intestacy (see Intestacy in chapter 4, *Wills, Probate and Succession*) are revoked however, under the Matrimonial Causes Act 1973, s. 18(2).

5 Methods of terminating a marriage compared

It is useful to conclude this section by reviewing the use made in practice of the three methods. Approximately 150,000 divorces are granted every year, compared with 400 decrees of nullity and 1,500 decrees of judicial separation. Thus 99 per cent of people who are separating permanently choose to dissolve their marriage by divorce. Undoubtedly the main reason why nullity or judicial separation procedures are used at all is that many people have religious or moral objections to divorce. Judicial separation used to be popular when divorces were restricted by the rule that a petition could not usually be granted until the parties had been married for three years. It was thus a useful way of finalising financial matters when the parties were determined to go their separate ways immediately, even though they would have to wait another year or two for the formality of a divorce. Since 1985 however (see 3.8. above), the reduction in that period to one year has meant that most couples have either been married long enough to qualify, or are prepared to wait the few months until their first wedding anniversary. Parties to a marriage who have strong religious or moral beliefs, or who have only been married a short time, must always be advised of the alternatives of nullity or judicial separation. They should also be warned however of the unsuitability of nullity procedure (see 2.1 above), the simplicity of divorce law and procedure, and the availability of divorce after five years' separation.

Financial provision after a final decree

1 Introduction

1.1 The statutory background

Under the Matrimonial Causes Act 1973, s. 23, the court has wide powers to grant financial provision on or after a decree of divorce, nullity or judicial separation. When compared with the orders that the court can make during the marriage (see *Financial Provision in the Family Proceedings Court*), it is noticeable how extensive its powers are. The different orders that the court can make will be considered in more detail (see 2 below), but it is worth noting at this stage that the court can not only award maintenance and lump sums to both the spouses and the children of the family (subject to the Child Support Act 1991; see *Children*, 4.3), but can also transfer the ownership or possession of property, including the matrimonial home, and split up a pension fund. The court's powers are unlimited, and so millions of pounds might be at stake. On the other hand (and more frequently), the court might have to juggle the finances of a couple who have no capital other than their home. This can cause particular difficulties if one spouse has no income other than state benefits, and the other has only a small income. The primary concern of the court will be to ensure that both spouses have somewhere to live, and in particular that the children will have a settled home. Clearly, however, only one spouse can continue to live in the former matrimonial home, and somehow the mortgage or rent must be paid from the income available. The sale of the home will not resolve the problem, as the proceeds of sale will not usually be sufficient to buy even one house, let alone two. In order to guide the way in which the courts deal with these difficult problems, there are several factors set out in the Matrimonial Causes Act 1973, s. 25, which a court must take into account before making an order. These guidelines are an important part of the legislation, and must be looked at carefully (see 3 below). The majority of cases are resolved by negotiation and agreement between the parties' legal advisors, the final agreement being embodied in a *consent order*. The practitioner must therefore be familiar with the different ways which the courts have evolved to minimise the financial hardship caused by the termination of a marriage (see 2.7 and 4 below), so that similar methods can be employed in such agreements.

1.2 Who can apply? *either*

Either husband or wife can apply, and it makes no difference whether the applicant is the petitioner or the respondent. There is no difference in law between a wife's or a husband's application, although in practice it is usually the husband who has the higher income. The courts must also recognise that the wife's earning capacity is diminished considerably if she has spent several years out of paid employment while bringing up the children. These practical considerations are covered by a proper application of the guidelines under s. 25 of the Matrimonial Causes Act 1973.

1.3 Commencement of proceedings

1.3.1 Procedure for making an application

The petitioner's applications for financial relief must be included in the petition. The standard format is covered in the Matrimonial Practice syllabus, and it is usual to include every order that the petitioner might need. When the petitioner wishes the court to consider any of the applications, a notice of intention to proceed must be issued and served on the respondent. The respondent will usually commence proceedings by notice only, although if the petition is defended, the respondent's applications must be included in the answer.

1.3.2 When the orders will be made

The court can usually make orders for the children at any time during the proceedings (see 2.8 below) although basic maintenance orders are now the responsibility of the Child Support Agency (see *Children*, 4.3). All other orders can only be made on or after decree nisi, and under the Matrimonial Causes Act 1973, s. 23(5), they cannot come into effect until after decree absolute. This restriction does not apply to proceedings for judicial separation, which are concluded as soon as the decree is granted. Until decree absolute, either party is entitled to *maintenance pending suit* (see 2.1 below). Maintenance orders can be backdated to the date when the application was first made. This may be the date of the presentation of the petition for applications included in it.

2 Orders available to the court

2.1 Maintenance pending suit   s.22

Under the Matrimonial Causes Act 1973, s. 22, the court may require either party to make such periodical payments to the other as the court thinks is reasonable, up to and including decree absolute. This is known as *maintenance pending suit,* the 'suit' being the divorce, nullity or judicial separation proceedings. Maintenance pending suit is meant to cover the immediate needs of a spouse, and will not be necessary if the other spouse is making voluntary payments, or if a magistrates' order is in force.

2.2 Periodical payments   s. 23(1)

2.2.1 The basic order _ a

Under the Matrimonial Causes Act 1973, s. 23(1)(a), the court may make an order that either party to the marriage make periodical payments for such term as the court may specify. The order will thus direct one spouse to make regular payments to the other of a specified sum. The period will typically be weekly, monthly or annually, but any period is possible. The court is not restricted in any way as to the value of the order. The amount of the order will remain the same unless it is varied after a subsequent application to the court. It can then be increased or decreased, depending on how circumstances have changed.

> EXAMPLE
>
> A husband is ordered to pay £50 per week to his ex-wife. If he loses his job, or learns that his ex-wife has increased her income substantially, he can apply to have the order reduced. Similarly, the woman can apply for an increase in the amount of the order if her circumstances change for the worse, or if her ex-husband's income increases.

If the court considers that maintenance should be paid by one party (for example, the husband), but that he has insufficient income at the moment, it is possible to make a *nominal order.* This could be, for example, £1 per annum. That order could then be increased if the husband's income increases sufficiently to enable him to pay maintenance.

2.2.2 Secured periodical payment orders _ b   s.23(1)(b)

If an order is not paid, the court can enforce payment in various ways. They can order that the maintenance be deducted from the payer's wages before he receives them, for example, and as a last resort a sentence of imprisonment can be imposed. If the court has reason to believe that the payer might default, and that these normal methods of enforcement would be ineffective, it is possible under s. 23(1)(b), Matrimonial Causes Act 1973 to order the payer to provide security for the order. A specified capital fund (for example, shares or property) must then be set aside, and can be used to pay the order should the payer default.

EXAMPLE

A man is ordered to pay maintenance to his ex-wife, but has shown himself to be unwilling to meet such orders in the past. She learns that he has accepted a job abroad, in a country where an English court order cannot be enforced. She asks the court to secure the maintenance order by placing a charge on the ex-husband's house, which he intends to rent out while he is abroad. *goes on to Land Registry*

2.2.3 Duration of periodical payments orders s. 28(1)a

Under the Matrimonial Causes Act 1973, s. 28(1)(a), the death of either party will bring the order to an end, except that a secured order will continue after the death of the payer. The remarriage of the person to whom the payments are made will also terminate the order automatically. Unmarried cohabitation will not bring an order to an end however, although it might entitle the payer to apply for a reduction in the amount of the order, perhaps to a nominal figure (see 3.3.2 below). Apart from these situations, the order will continue indefinitely, or until any date fixed by the court (as in a *clean break* situation; see 3.4 below).

Death & re-marriage rehabilitation co-habitation maybe

2.3 Lump sum orders

2.3.1 The basic order

Under the Matrimonial Causes Act 1973, s. 23(1)(c), the court may make an order that either party to the marriage shall pay to the other party a specified lump sum or sums. In every case this will be one or more payments of a fixed sum of money, and therefore the order cannot be subsequently varied, even if the parties' circumstances change. The court can, however, allow payment of a lump sum in instalments, in which case the time allowed for payment can be varied.

2.3.2 Additional orders

If payment is to be made by instalments, under s. 23(3)(c) the court can order that payment of the instalments be protected by security. Furthermore, under s. 23(6), the court may order that interest be payable on the full amount until it is paid.

2.3.3 The purpose of a lump sum order

Under the Matrimonial Causes Act 1973, s. 23(3)(a), a lump sum order may be made for the purpose of enabling a spouse to meet any debts incurred when maintaining herself or the children before making her application for financial relief. This is only really an example however, and there is no restriction on the purposes of a lump sum order, or the amount that may be awarded. The order may seek to redistribute the matrimonial assets, if one party has the major share of savings accumulated during the marriage. Alternatively, it may be part of a package whereby one party receives the former matrimonial home, and the other is compensated by a lump sum order. In particular, such orders are made when the court is seeking to produce a clean break (see 3.4.4 below).

2.4 Transfer of property orders

Under the Matrimonial Causes Act 1973, s. 24(1)(a), the court may make an order that a party to the marriage shall transfer specified property to the other party (or to a child of the family, or to any other person for the benefit of a child). This can be any property, such as shares, household goods, a car, even the family pets. The most important item that will be dealt with under this heading however, is the former matrimonial home.

2.5 Settlement of property

Under the Matrimonial Causes Act 1973, s. 24(1)(b),(c) and (d), the court can order one party to the marriage to settle property for the benefit of the other party or a child of the family. This means typically that the property will be placed in trust for the benefit of one party, perhaps for life, or until remarriage, or until the children have grown up. The court can also vary existing settlements, although this power is not so important nowadays, as there are few formal settlements, and the power to transfer property is sufficient for most purposes. Again, these powers can be used for any type of property, so that one party could be given a life interest in a sum of money, or a fund of shares for example. More typically, however, it is used to deal with the former matrimonial home, to ensure that the children have a settled home with one parent. Some examples of the different ways in which this power is used will be considered (see 2.7 below).

2.6 Sale of property

Under the Matrimonial Causes Act 1973, s. 24A, the court has wide powers to order a sale of property, and to direct payments out of the proceeds of sale. This power will be used to give effect to the orders already mentioned.

> EXAMPLE
>
> A husband owns substantial share-holdings. In the divorce proceedings his ex-wife is awarded a lump sum. The court can order that the shares be sold, and that part of the proceeds be paid to the ex-wife in satisfaction of the lump sum order.

2.7 Typical property orders

In most cases the only asset of any value owned by the parties is their former matrimonial home. This house may be in joint names, or the court could transfer full ownership or a share of it to one party. If the house is in joint names, this is technically a settlement (a trust of land, under the Trusts of Land and Appointment of Trustees Act 1996) which can be varied by the court (see 2.5 above). The dilemma usually faced by the court is that, on the one hand, the house must be preserved as a home for one party, typically the wife. This will be principally for the benefit of the children who will be looked after by her, and therefore be living with her. On the other hand, the house also represents the life-savings of the husband, who is now expected to set up home elsewhere and start a new life. The dilemma is basically insurmountable, but there are two typical orders that the courts can make which alleviate the situation. The first type of order was made in the following case, and bears its name: the '*Mesher* order'.

Mesher v *Mesher* (1980)

The matrimonial home was in the joint names of the husband and wife, and the wife still lived there with the two children of the marriage. Although the house was subject to a mortgage, there would be a considerable amount of money left over if the house were sold and the mortgage paid off. The husband had already purchased another house for himself, and was about to remarry. The Court of Appeal ordered that the trust for sale continue, but that it was not to be enforced (i.e. the house sold) until the child of the marriage reached the age of 17.

This type of order has been largely superseded by an order which gives more protection for the wife, as a *Mesher* order can leave her with insufficient money to house herself in the future.

Martin v *Martin* (1978)

The husband had left his wife to live with another woman in her council flat. The wife was still living in the matrimonial home, and there were no children of the marriage. The Court of Appeal ordered that the house would be settled on trust for the wife for her life, or until she remarried or ceased to live there.

The vital issue therefore is the necessity to ensure that both parties have secure housing. If one party (typically the husband) has, or can obtain, alternative accommodation, and it is not reasonable to expect his wife to do the same, the order should ensure that the matrimonial home is a secure home for her as long as she wishes to live there.

2.8 Child orders

The court can make any of the orders set out above, either for a child of the family or for a specified person for the benefit of a child, except that periodical payments for a natural child of both parties can only be dealt with by the Child Support Agency (see *Children*, 4.3). Lump sums and security can be ordered at any time during the proceedings, and even if the petition is dismissed. Transfer of property orders or variation of settlements can only be made after decree nisi. Under the Children Act 1989, s. 105(1), the phrase *child of the family* covers children of both parties or any child who has been treated by both parties as their own child (not being a child officially placed with them as foster parents). This will include, for example, step-children. There are special guidelines to which the court must have regard when considering an order for financial relief in respect of a child, and additional guidelines if the payer is not the biological parent of the child (see 3.5 below). Periodical payment orders for children will in the first place last only until the child leaves school. They may be extended beyond that date however if there are special circumstances. They may even extend beyond the age of 18 if the child is to attend an educational establishment, or there are special circumstances such as disability or ill-health.

2.9 Pensions

2.9.1 Pensions as capital

In some marriages one person (typically the man) will be in permanent full-time employment, while the other (typically the woman) will have a much less structured employment record because of the need to look after the children of the marriage. In this situation the man will build up a large fund with a pension company by making regular monthly payments throughout his working life. The woman will probably rely upon her husband doing this, rather than trying to build up her own pension fund. She will feel secure in the knowledge that, in her old age, she will either be supported by her husband's pension income, or receive it directly herself as his widow. The pension fund therefore represents the couple's joint savings just as much as a joint bank account or the matrimonial home, and as it will amount in value to many thousands of pounds, it is an extremely important asset which should be shared by both of them.

2.9.2 The basic position

When making financial orders on termination of a marriage, the court must take the value of the pension fund into account (3.3.8, below). This may prove impossible, however, if the person holding the pension rights has no other capital. In such a situation the only thing that can be done is to delay the divorce itself (*Invalidity and Failure of Marriage*, 3.8.2). This is an unsatisfactory solution, and will be done by the court only if there is a real possibility that the owner of the pension rights can be 'persuaded' in that way to find some extra capital.

2.9.3 Special orders

The Pensions Act 1995 allows the court to order that the pension company must earmark part of the pension fund for retirement benefits for the other spouse. This means that, when the pension becomes payable, both parties to the marriage will benefit. The problem here, however, is that this will prevent a 'clean-break' between the parties (3.4.1 below) and will leave the woman dependent upon the man's decision as to when to retire. In order to give the woman more independence therefore, an amendment was made to the Family Law Act 1996 to allow the courts to order an immediate splitting of the pension fund, in effect producing two separate funds, one for each party to the marriage. The Government was unhappy about this, and issued a White Paper ('Pension Rights on Divorce') in February 1997 outlining the necessary technical details which would have to be implemented. The provisions are now embodied in the Welfare Reform and Pensions Act 1999, and regulations brought the provisions into force in December 2000. The courts therefore now have two additional orders which they can make: a *pension earmarking* order or a *pension splitting* (also known as a *pension sharing*) order. These are alternatives, however, and so only one can be made in respect of any one pension fund.

3 Statutory guidelines

3.1 Introduction

[handwritten: Section 25 is important — 8 factors to consider]

Under the Matrimonial Causes Act 1973, s. 25, there are certain factors to which the court must have regard when it considers whether to grant financial relief in the first place, and also what order or orders to make. These guidelines were first introduced in the Matrimonial Proceedings and Property Act 1970, but were subsequently amended by the Matrimonial and Family Proceedings Act 1984. It is worth noting that the 1970 Act removed the principle that financial relief should be based on the doctrine of the 'matrimonial offence', i.e. awarded on the basis of which party was 'innocent' and which was 'guilty' of causing the breakdown of the marriage. The court was still supposed to strive to ensure that the parties did not suffer financially from the divorce, although this was patently an impossible task. The 1984 Act removed that principle, and now the court merely has to consider certain specific factors. The first consideration must be the *welfare of any child*, after which *all the circumstances* must be taken into account. Certain particular factors are listed. Finally, under s. 25A of the Matrimonial Causes Act 1973 (introduced by the Matrimonial and Family Proceedings Act 1984), the court must try to encourage *self-sufficiency*, by terminating the right of each spouse to be maintained by the other indefinitely. Special guidelines for *child orders* are also included in s. 25 of the 1973 Act. There are thus four separate sets of guidelines, and each will now be looked at in turn.

3.2 The welfare of any child

Under s. 25(1) of the Matrimonial Causes Act 1973, it is the duty of the court to give first consideration to the welfare, while a minor, of any child of the family who has not attained the age of 18. This is so even though the court is considering orders for the spouses themselves. The effect of this provision is that the court will normally refuse to order a sale of the former matrimonial home, to ensure that the children can continue living there with the parent who is going to look after them on a day to day basis. The provision does not override all other considerations however.

Suter v *Suter* (1987)

After the divorce, the wife remained in the former matrimonial home with the two children of the marriage. The husband was ordered to transfer the house to her, and to pay her enough maintenance to ensure that she could keep up the house as a home for the children. This was despite the fact that her new boy-friend was now staying every night at the house. The Court of Appeal stated that the need of the children for a secure home was important, but did not override other relevant factors, such as the wife's conduct, and the possibility that her boy-friend could contribute to the household expenses. The maintenance order was therefore reduced to a nominal sum.

3.3 All the circumstances of the case

Under s. 25(1) of the Matrimonial Causes Act 1973, the court has a duty to consider all the circumstances of the case, but under s. 25(2) it must have particular regard to eight specific factors. Each of these will now be considered briefly.

3.3.1 Financial resources

Both parties must provide evidence of their income and capital, including any possible increase in the foreseeable future. The court must also consider their earning capacity, and the possibility that they could increase their income.

> EXAMPLE
>
> A husband proves that he is now earning £150 per week. During the marriage, however, he used to earn over £200, and it is clear that he has merely stopped working over-time. His ex-wife earns £80 per week as a cleaner. She used to work as a secretary before their child was born, and could do so again after a short period of retraining. Both would be assessed on what they could be earning, rather than on what they are actually earning.

It should be noted that means-tested state benefits are not relevant. Periodical payment orders may make no difference to the persons in whose favour they are made, if the amount of the order will merely be deducted from their state benefits. The court must ignore this however, and calculate the order as if they had no income at all. All other resources are relevant however, including capital assets and even assets acquired after the breakdown of the marriage.

Schuller v *Schuller* (1990)

The wife left the matrimonial home, but the husband stayed and petitioned for divorce. A decree absolute was eventually granted, but the wife then inherited a large sum of money before the matter of financial provision came before the court. The Court of Appeal ruled that her inheritance should be taken into account, and accordingly she should only receive a small share of the value of the former matrimonial home.

What cannot be taken into account is the possibility of a future inheritance. Not only might the will be changed, but there is also no telling how long it will be before the testator dies (*H* v *H* (*Financial Provision: Capital Assets*) (1993)).

3.3.2 Financial needs and obligations

This will usually mean housing costs (rent or mortgage payments), travelling expenses to work, food and regular bills for gas, electricity etc. Excessive expenditure will obviously not be taken into account. The financial burden of a new family may be relevant. On the other hand, if one party to the marriage is now living with somebody else, the court can take that person's income into account to the extent that it reduces the financial burden (see *Suter* v *Suter* at 3.2 above). It is important to note, however, that an order will still be justified even if the applicant has no financial needs at all, as long as there are other relevant factors (see *Smith* v *Smith* (1991) at 3.3.6 below).

3.3.3 Standard of living

The court need not limit the award to basic needs and thus can make an award to allow a luxurious life-style, if that is what the parties were used to during the marriage.

3.3.4 Age and length of marriage

The age of the parties will normally be more relevant to the issue of whether they can be expected to get employment or not. The length of the marriage is perhaps more relevant in itself, as the court will be less inclined to award substantial financial relief if the parties have been married only for a short time. It may be that the courts will now give some weight to pre-marital cohabitation. In *B* v *B (Consent Order: Variation)* (1995), the marriage had broken down after only two years, but the Family Division judge took into account the fact that the wife had committed herself to the relationship before the marriage by living with the man for 14 years and bearing him a child. It should be noted, however, that this factor may be much less relevant if there are children of the marriage.

C v C (Financial Relief: Short Marriage) (1997)

The wife applied for ancillary relief for herself and the one child of the marriage. Despite the fact that the marriage had lasted less than 10 months, the Court of Appeal upheld an order whereby the husband had to pay a substantial lump sum and periodical payments for the wife and child.

3.3.5 Physical or mental disability

This is hardly a separate matter, as it will be covered under the heading of financial resources and needs. It is not important as a heading in its own right.

3.3.6 Contributions to the welfare of the family

Under this heading the court must give recognition to the extent to which one party (usually the wife) looked after the home and brought up the children, while the other accumulated wealth by working. The court should also look to contributions in the foreseeable future which will be made in the same way. There is certainly a greater awareness of the value of such non-financial contributions (see *White* v *White* (2000) at 3.3.9 below). This in itself will justify the court making a transfer of property order in favour of a wife when the former matrimonial home is in the sole name of the husband, even though he has made all the mortgage payments. This principle will also justify a large order which is unrelated to the issue of 'needs'.

Gojkovic v Gojkovic (1992)

The husband was a multi-millionaire in the hotel business. His wife had made exceptional contributions to the business in the early, difficult years, and even when it was well established. The Court of Appeal approved a lump sum award to the wife of one million pounds.

This principle may even justify an order where the applicant has no financial needs at all, as in the following unusual case.

***Smith* v *Smith* (1991)** ⟵ *MR.* *Change of circumstance.*

After their divorce, the husband was ordered to pay his wife a large lump sum. Six months later she committed suicide. The husband appealed against the lump sum order, as the basis of the order had been the need to enable the wife to maintain secure housing for herself. His needs were now more important, as he was elderly and in ill-health. The Court of Appeal ruled that the wife's contributions to the marriage still merited a large order regardless of her needs, but that the order would be reduced to take account of the change in the balance of their respective needs.

3.3.7 *Conduct*   25(2)g   *extreme conduct*   *physical injury   alcoholism*

The court must take into account the conduct of each of the parties 'if that conduct is such that it would be inequitable to disregard it'. In the case of *Wachtel* v *Wachtel* (1973), the Court of Appeal ruled that the conduct of the parties would not be relevant to the issue of financial relief unless the behaviour of one of them had been 'both obvious and gross'. The position appears to have remained the same, and therefore the conduct of the parties will rarely be relevant. Any gross misbehaviour can be taken into account however, whether it is related to the breakdown of the marriage or not, and even when it has occurred after the parties have separated. In exceptional circumstances the court will have to consider the behaviour of both parties, to ascertain if the imbalance in their respective behaviour is such that it would be inequitable to disregard it.

Kyte v *Kyte* (1988)

Cross-decrees were awarded, to the wife on the grounds of her husband's behaviour, and to the husband on the grounds of his wife's adultery. The husband had suffered from severe depression, and his behaviour had undoubtedly caused the wife much distress (see *Thurlow* v *Thurlow* (1976), *Invalidity and Failure of Marriage*, 3.3.1). However the wife had formed an adulterous relationship, withdrawn her support and understanding, and then encouraged her husband to commit suicide so that her lover could move in with her. On that basis the balance was clearly against the wife, and the lump sum order in her favour was reduced considerably by the Court of Appeal.

3.3.8 *Financial benefits lost by termination of the marriage*

This will apply only to decrees of nullity or divorce. It is meant to allow the court to take into account the fact that one party will lose pension rights because of the termination of the marriage. A lump sum or transfer of property order may compensate for the possible loss of a widow's pension, for example, or a *pension earmarking* or *pension sharing* order could be made (see 2.9 above).

3.3.9 Applying the guidelines

The House of Lords has emphasised that the ranking and relative weight of the different guidelines are largely a matter of discretion for the trial judge.

Piglowska v Piglowska (1999)

On the first hearing the district judge awarded the matrimonial home to the wife but ordered that she should pay £10,000 to the husband, who would also have their flat in Spain. After two more appeals, the Court of Appeal overturned that order and ruled that the home should be sold and the proceeds divided, so that each party would be able to buy another home in England. The House of Lords restored the original order and made several specific and general criticisms. Specifically, there is no principle that both parties have a right to be able to purchase accommodation. The decision of the district judge to put more weight on the wife's need for the home and her overall contribution to the marriage was justifiable and within the proper exercise of his discretion. Generally, many cases involve judgments on matters where there is no commonly held view and appeal courts must allow for a variety of attitudes to family values ('a degree of pluralism').

In an even more significant case, the House of Lords has considered the basic principles which should be applied when a court is exercising its discretion under the s. 25 guidelines.

White v White (2000)

The husband and wife were divorcing after more than 30 years of marriage, during which time they had built up a farming business worth over £4 million. The trial judge awarded the wife one-fifth of the joint assets on the basis that it was impractical for her to run a farming business herself and that the sums awarded would satisfy her reasonable needs. The case eventually reached the House of Lords, who allowed an increase in the wife's share to approximately two-fifths and rejected the idea that she should not carry on farming herself. They stated that all financial provision should be judged against the 'yardstick of equality'. This is not a guideline in itself, but merely an exercise to ensure that there is no unfair discrimination against the spouse who has acted as home-maker while the other spouse has accumulated the family's wealth. There is therefore no limit of 'reasonable needs' on the amount to which a spouse may be entitled.

The full impact of this decision has yet to be ascertained, especially in cases which do not involve such large amounts of money. It is clear, however, that the courts will now be obliged to justify a departure from the 'yardstick of equality'. This may be done where one spouse has been personally responsible for the creation of their wealth.

Cowan v Cowan (2001)

Mr and Mrs Cowan were divorcing after nearly 40 years of marriage. The husband had run a small business supplying polythene for the building industry but had an inspired idea to produce bin-liners for local authorities. This resulted in a multi-million pound enterprise which produced considerable wealth for the family, the total assets being valued at about £8 million. The Court of Appeal recognised that the wife had contributed both by working in the business in the early years and also by supporting the family, but held that the husband's genius and special business skills merited a departure from equality in the division of assets. Accordingly, the wife was awarded £3 million, approximately 38 per cent of the assets.

3.4 Self-sufficiency

3.4.1 The clean-break concept

Since the Divorce Reform Act 1969, divorce law has concentrated on recognising the reality of the termination of the relationship (see *Invalidity and Failure of Marriage*, 3.1.1). The courts have followed this principle by encouraging the parties to start new lives with the minimum of bitterness and recrimination. As has already been noted, the courts have adhered to the spirit of the 1969 legislation by minimising the opportunities for the parties to bring the issue of fault into the proceedings (see for example *Grenfell* v *Grenfell* (1978), *Invalidity and Failure of Marriage*, 3.1.2. Also 3.3.7 above). After decree absolute however, the parties must still have contact with each other if there are children, as one party will look after themfrom day to day, and the other will have to visit them and pay maintenance for their up-keep. This continuing aspect of their relationship is unavoidable, but in addition one party (typically the husband) may be ordered to pay maintenance to his former spouse as well as to the children. The amount of this order will always depend on the exact financial circumstances of each party, and may also be affected by a new relationship or marriage (see 2.2.1, 2.2.3 and 3.3.2 above). This will obviously encourage the parties to worry constantly about each other, rather than to get on with their new lives. The most effective way to achieve a clean break therefore, is to terminate the life-time right to maintenance once the marriage has been terminated. This approach is now encouraged by the Matrimonial Causes Act 1973, s. 25A. Before this section was introduced by the Matrimonial and Family Proceedings Act 1984, the court could not cancel spouses' rights to maintenance without their consent, although agreements to that effect were often reached between the parties. Under s. 25A, the court now has both the power and the duty to impose a clean break, if possible.

3.4.2 The statutory duty

Under s. 25A(1) of the Matrimonial Causes Act 1973, when making an order for financial provision, the court must consider 'whether it would be appropriate so to exercise [its] powers that the financial obligations of each party towards the other will be terminated as soon after the grant of the decree as the court considers just and reasonable'. Under s. 25A(3), it may then dismiss either party's claim for maintenance and direct that no application may be made in the future. Furthermore, under s. 25A(2), even when the court makes a periodical payments order, it must again consider the possibility of limiting the period of time for which the payments must be made, so that the maintenance order will only last as long as is 'sufficient to enable the party in whose favour the order is made to adjust without undue hardship to the termination of his or her financial dependence on the other party'. There are thus two distinct stages. First, should a maintenance order be made at all? Secondly, if an order is necessary, can it be for only a limited period of time?

3.4.3 Variation of orders

If the court orders that the periodical payments order will cease after a specified period of time, the party affected can nevertheless apply in the future for the period to be extended, if circumstances have changed. Under s. 28(1A) of the Matrimonial Causes Act 1973 (also introduced by the 1984 Act), at the time of specifying the time when periodical payments are to come to an end, the court may also direct that the party shall not be entitled to apply for an extension of the period and this should be included in a consent order if it is the parties' intention (*Richardson* v *Richardson* (1993)). On the other hand, the court can terminate an unrestricted periodical payments order on an application by either party to vary the original order, and (if appropriate) award a lump sum and/or transfer of property order instead, thus imposing a clean-break at this later stage. Once made, a clean-break order cannot be varied except in exceptional circumstances. Technically this can be done only by allowing an appeal against the original order. In *Barder* v *Barder* (1987) the House of Lords allowed such an appeal where the wife killed both the children and committed suicide some weeks after the order was made, leaving all the property awarded to her to her relatives (see also *Smith* v *Smith* (1991), 3.3.6 above).

3.4.4 The court's discretion

Although the court must consider a clean-break order, it nevertheless has a discretion as to whether to make one or not, and also what type of order to make. The court is unlikely to order a clean break where one party has to care for children of the family (see for example *Suter* v *Suter* (1987), 3.2 above). The court may even decide that a nominal order is appropriate as a safety-net where there is little chance of the payer ever earning enough to justify increasing it. This extreme point of view would mean that a clean break would almost never be justified, but it was reached in the following case.

Whiting v Whiting (1988)

A nominal order had been made against the husband on the divorce. He subsequently applied for the order to be dismissed as he had been made redundant, and was unlikely to be able to get another job, other than part-time work. On the other hand his ex-wife was working full-time as a teacher. The judge refused the application, and the Court of Appeal would not reverse his decision.

If the court does decide to terminate one party's right to maintenance, it will usually compensate that party by ordering a lump sum or transfer of property.

EXAMPLE

After separation the wife has remained in the matrimonial home, and is living off a small income. The husband is now living with another woman in her house, and intends to marry her. The court could order a transfer of full ownership of the matrimonial home to the wife but dismiss her right to claim maintenance.

Where one party is wealthy, this arrangement is fairly straightforward. Where there is no money or property available, the decision is more difficult, but a clean break may still be feasible.

Seaton v *Seaton* (1986)

The husband was severely disabled after a stroke and heart attack, and would probably have to go into a home for continual nursing. The wife had a small income as a teacher, and would not be able to make a significant contribution to improve his standard of living. The Court of Appeal refused to overturn an order dismissing the husband's entitlement to maintenance.

3.5 Child orders

Under the Matrimonial Causes Act 1973, s. 25(3), in addition to the guidelines already mentioned (see 3.3 above), the court must have regard to certain particular matters when considering financial provision for a child of the family. These include the financial resources and needs of the child, any physical or mental disbility, and 'the manner in which he was being and in which the parties to the marriage expected him to be educated or trained'. Furthermore, if the child in question is not the biological child of the payer, under s. 25(4) the court must consider three additional matters. First, the extent to which the person assumed responsibility for the child's mainten- ance. It may be that it was only on the basis that the child would otherwise have felt 'left out', and it would thus be unfair to penalise such altruistic actions. Secondly, whether the person knew that the child was not his own. Thirdly, the liability of any other person to maintain the child, i.e. the natural parent.

4 The interrelationship of orders

In conclusion it should be noted that the court must consider the total effect of the proposed orders. In a typical situation, there will be a transfer of property order in respect of the matrimonial home in favour of the wife. The husband's financial interest in the house may be recognised by a lump sum order in his favour, secured on the house but not to be enforced until certain events occur (such as in *Martin* v *Martin*, see 2.7 above). The husband will have to pay maintenance for the children of the family who are living with the wife. His obligation to maintain the wife may be dismissed, or at least reduced to take account of the amount that he is having to pay for the children, and his responsibilities towards his 'new' family. If there are other assets accumulated during the marriage which are in the sole name of either of them, for example savings in a building society account, a lump sum order may be necessary to distribute them fairly. There may even need to be a transfer of property order in respect of the contents of the former matrimonial home, although the parties can usually agree on that matter. Finally, if one spouse has been paying into a pension fund, the court will also have to consider how to deal with that asset. There is no such thing as a 'typical' case however, and these examples are very basic. The way in which all these different factors interrelate is a matter for an experienced lawyer, and is perhaps the most testing aspect of the work of a family practitioner.

Financial provision in the family proceedings court

1 The domestic jurisdiction of the magistrates

[handwritten: Can't effect a divorce but can give financial relief]

1.1 Introduction

Magistrates have powers to award financial relief to married couples, and when hearing such cases, as a result of the Children Act 1989 they are now called the family proceedings court (see *Children*, 1.2.2). They cannot terminate a marriage, or order a judicial separation, and their powers are therefore limited to what is commonly called a 'legal separation'. This is a misleading expression, as the magistrates merely award financial relief, and have no say over whether a couple should or should not live together (although cohabitation may affect the validity of the order; see 1.4.2 below). The expression does at least suggest the basis of the magistrates' jurisdiction in domestic matters however, namely that they are dealing with a temporary situation, and are not involved in a final distribution of the income and assets of the parties. This jurisdiction in domestic matters is perhaps taken for granted, but it is really an anomaly. After all, the major jurisdiction of the magistrates is in criminal matters. It is certainly questionable whether it is appropriate for delicate matrimonial disputes to be dealt with in the atmosphere and surroundings of a court which normally deals with criminal offences. Most magistrates' courts minimise these problems by setting aside special days or separate courtrooms for domestic matters, and the magistrates themselves must receive special training before being qualified to sit in the family proceedings court.

[handwritten margin note: Domestic Proceedings + Mags Cts Act 1978]

1.2 The origins and scope of the jurisdiction

The jurisdiction of the magistrates in these matters arose during the nineteenth century, when they were given the power to award maintenance to a wife if they had convicted her husband of a serious assault upon her. The scope of their powers was then extended over the years, as the magistrates' court came to be regarded as the most suitable forum for the matrimonial disputes of the poor. It was certainly a more accessible and cheaper forum than the High Court, or even the county courts, when they were formed. The law remained rather archaic however, and the reforms in the law of divorce introduced in 1969 (see *Invalidity and Failure of Marriage*, 3.1) made it vital to modernise it. Accordingly the Domestic Proceedings and Magistrates' Courts Act 1978 repealed the old law, and introduced a new basis for domestic proceedings before the magistrates. In particular, the concept of the matrimonial offence was abolished, and husbands and wives were put on exactly the same footing. There are now four grounds on which a party to a marriage can apply for financial relief, and these will be considered in detail (see 2 below). The method of application is fully covered in the Matrimonial Practice syllabus, but it should be noted here that it is by way of complaint and summons. The terminology is therefore different from that used in the divorce court (i.e. *petitioner* and *respondent*), and the expressions *applicant* and *respondent* are used instead. One important point is that the general time limit applicable to proceedings in the magistrates' court also applies to matrimonial proceedings. The complaint must therefore be laid within six months of the date of the events which form the basis of the application. This section will look at all of the relevant law relating to proceedings in the magistrates' court, but a brief mention will also be made of the power of the county court to award maintenance in certain circumstances (see 5 below).

1.3 Orders available to the court

These are set out in the Domestic Proceedings and Magistrates' Courts Act 1978, s. 2. They are available to the court if one of the grounds has been proved, except that orders to or for the benefit of a child of the family may be made in any event.

1.3.1 Periodical payments

The court may award any amount, payable over any period, to either spouse and any child of the family. Maintenance for children, however, will normally be dealt with by the Child Support Agency (see *Children*, 4.3). The magistrates' powers are therefore identical to those of the divorce court, except that there is no power to order security (see *Financial Provision after a Final Decree*, 2.2.2). This power is, however, available to the county court in some circumstances (see 5 below). Application can be made to vary a periodical payments order should circumstances change.

1.3.2 Lump sum

The court may order that a specified lump sum be paid to either spouse, or to any child of the family. The maximum that may be awarded is at present £1,000 under each order. Thus a wife looking after three children of the family may be awarded £4,000 in total. Under s. 2(2) of the Domestic Proceedings and Magistrates' Courts Act 1978, a lump sum order may be made for the purpose of enabling the applicant to meet any liabilities or expenses incurred before the date of the application.

> EXAMPLE
>
> An unemployed wife is deserted by her husband, and he leaves her no money. As a result the rent falls into arrears, and gas and electricity bills remain unpaid. The rent arrears and outstanding bills are suitable grounds for a lump sum order to be made in her favour.

This provision is similar to that for lump sum orders on a final decree (see *Financial Provision after a Final Decree*, 2.3.3). In effect it is only an example of the proper purpose of a lump sum order, and there are no restrictions on the court's powers apart from the £1,000 limit. It is clear however that the court should not use the power merely to redistribute matrimonial assets, but only to meet a specific need. The court can allow payment by instalments, and so although the amount of the order cannot be varied once made, the time allowed for payment can. The following case is an example of how the court should exercise its powers.

Burridge v Burridge (1983)

The husband and wife were separated, and the wife had accumulated debts of £800. The husband was unemployed, but was expected to obtain a job within six weeks of the hearing. On that basis the magistrates ordered him to pay to the wife a lump sum of £500 for her, and £150 for each of the two children. They allowed him to pay the total at the rate of £10 per week. On the husband's appeal, the High Court agreed that the terms of the order were satisfactory, but sent the case back for the magistrates to reconsider whether the husband's job prospects were too optimistic.

Unlike the divorce court, under s. 20 of the Domestic Proceedings and Magistrates' Courts Act 1978 the magistrates also have the power to award further lump sums on an application to vary.

1.4 Duration of orders

1.4.1 Divorce and remarriage

Periodical payments orders will continue during subsequent divorce, nullity or judicial separation proceedings, and may even remain in force after the final decree. The divorce court has the power under the Domestic Proceedings and Magistrates' Courts Act 1978, s. 28, to cancel a magistrates' order, but often merely allows the order to continue. Should the spouse receiving the payments remarry however, the order will cease automatically.

1.4.2 Cohabitation

An order can be made while the parties are still living together, but under s. 25(1) it will cease to be enforceable after they have cohabited for a continuous period of six months. The same provision will apply if they resume cohabitation after having lived apart for a while.

1.5 Statutory guidelines

Under the Domestic Proceedings and Magistrates' Courts Act 1978, s. 3(1), before making an order for financial relief, the court must consider certain matters. These are identical to those set out in the Matrimonial Causes Act 1973, s. 25 (see *Financial Provision after a Final Decree*, 3). Thus, first consideration must be given to the welfare of any child of the family. Thereafter, the same particular matters are listed, omitting only reference to benefits which the applicant may lose on termination of the marriage (as, of course, the marriage is not being terminated!). In particular, the magistrates are in a position to rely on local knowledge.

Munt v Munt (1983)

The husband was unemployed, but the magistrates decided that he was capable of

weekly periodical payments

getting seasonal unskilled work, of which there was plenty available in that locality. On that basis they ordered him to make weekly periodical payments, to commence in two months time. The husband appealed, but the High Court ruled that this was a proper decision for the magistrates to make.

2 Grounds for an order

2.1 Failure to maintain

Under the Domestic Proceedings and Magistrates' Courts Act 1978, s. 1(a) and (b), either party may apply for an order on the grounds that the other party has failed to provide reasonable maintenance for the applicant, or failed to provide or make a proper contribution towards maintenance for any child of the family. There is no guidance in the Act as to how 'reasonable maintenance' should be assessed, but it seems logical that the magistrates should use the criteria set out in s. 3. The mere fact that the applicant has (for example) committed adultery will not therefore automatically justify the respondent's failure, but it may be relevant under the heading of *conduct* (see *Financial Provision after a Final Decree*, 3.3.7). Furthermore, the section is so worded that a failure to maintain a spouse will be grounds for making orders in favour of a child, and vice versa.

> EXAMPLE
>
> A husband leaves his wife and refuses to give her any money, except sufficient to enable her to look after their child. She could apply to the magistrates' court for financial relief for herself and the child.

2.2 Behaviour

Under the Domestic Proceedings and Magistrates' Courts Act 1978, s. 1(c), either party to a marriage can apply for an order on the grounds that the other has behaved in such a way that the applicant cannot reasonably be expected to live with the respondent. This is identical to the appropriate fact under the Matrimonial Causes Act 1973, s. 1(2)(b) which can be used as evidence that a marriage has broken down irretrievably (see *Invalidity and Failure of Marriage*, 3.3). In the following case the High Court ruled that the magistrates must apply the same approach as the divorce court.

Bergin v *Bergin* (1983)

There had been assaults by the husband on his wife, and finally one evening he came home drunk and started throwing furniture around. The wife left to stay with a friend and started proceedings in the magistrates' court for financial provision on the grounds of his behaviour. The magistrates refused her application because she had lived with him for some time after the assaults, and therefore could not be said to be in fear of him. On her appeal, the High Court stated that the magistrates had followed the wrong approach, and it was clear that any right-thinking person would conclude that this woman could not reasonably be expected to live with her husband.

As adultery is not a separate ground for an order in the magistrates' court, it would need to be cited as 'behaviour' under this heading. Finally, it should also be noted that the six months time limit (see 1.2 above) only applies to the last incident of behaviour.

Buxton v *Buxton* (1967)

The wife's application was based on the old law of *persistent cruelty*. She had suffered from her husband's excessive drinking, indifference towards her, and his domineering treatment of her. After a dispute he threatened to claim custody of their child, and issued a summons to that effect, purely to intimidate her further. After five months she finally started proceedings against him in the magistrates' court, based on his behaviour. The High Court ruled that the husband's final act of cruelty in claiming custody could be viewed in the light of all his previous behaviour, even that which had occurred more than six months previously.

2.3 Desertion

Under the Domestic Proceedings and Magistrates' Courts Act 1978, s. 1(d), either party can apply for an order on the grounds that the other party has deserted the applicant. The basic law will be the same as that which applies to divorce proceedings (see *Invalidity and Failure of Marriage*, 3.4), except that the desertion need not have existed for any specific period of time.

2.4 Voluntary separation

Under the Domestic Proceedings and Magistrates' Courts Act 1978, s. 7, the court may make an order if the parties have been living apart by agreement for three months, and the applicant has been receiving voluntary maintenance from the other party. The court can make an order for the average payments made by the respondent for the last three months. The court must not, however, make an order that is either more or less than the order they would normally make. If they feel that the payments made by the respondent are inadequate, they can deal with the case on the basis of 'failure to maintain'.

> EXAMPLE
>
> A couple separate by agreement, and the husband makes occasional payments to his wife. The first month he gives her £100, the second month £200, and the third month £130. On the wife's application, the magistrates could make an order for £110 per month, unless they considered that amount too much or too little. If they considered it too little, they could order periodical payments on the basis of failure to maintain.

In theory this procedure would be useful to a spouse who wanted to ensure regular payments in the future. In practice it is little used.

2.5 The grounds in practice

There is little point in a spouse applying for a magistrates' court order unless financial relief is required. Financial relief will not be required if the other party is providing reasonable maintenance. Therefore in practice the only ground that needs to be used is 'failure to provide reasonable maintenance'. To use allegations of behaviour or desertion will probably only exacerbate ill-feeling between the parties. The inclusion of these two 'fault' grounds in the 1978 Act was probably for the same reasons as the retention of 'fault' grounds in the divorce reform legislation nine years earlier, namely a reluctance to break completely with the concept of the matrimonial offence as the basis for family law. There is an argument that sometimes a spouse may wish to obtain an order as security for future payments. The procedure under s. 7 could be used, but in practice any application to the court is only likely to make the other party uncooperative. The Family Law Act 1996 included a provision to abolish the grounds of behaviour and desertion as soon as the new divorce law came into force. Now that the Act is to be repealed, the law relating to magistrates court provision is in just as urgent need of reform (see *Invalidity and Failure of Marriage*, 3.10.2).

3 Consent orders

Under the Domestic Proceedings and Magistrates' Courts Act 1978, s. 6, either party to a marriage may apply to the court for an order to be made on terms agreed between them. This procedure may be followed even where there is a subsisting application under s. 1, whereupon that application will be treated as withdrawn.

EXAMPLE

A wife applies for maintenance from her husband on the grounds of his failure to provide reasonable maintenance for her and their child. At first he opposes her application, and a date is fixed for a full hearing before the magistrates. During this time however, they reach agreement on the amount that he should pay. That agreement could form the basis for an application under s. 6, whereupon her application on the grounds of his failure to maintain would be withdrawn.

The court can make any order which could be made under s. 2, but only if there is proof of an agreement, and there is no reason to think that the order would be contrary to the interests of justice. In addition, any agreement for financial provision for a child of the family must make a proper contribution towards the needs of that child and will also remain susceptible to an assessment under the Child Support Act 1991. The court will therefore need some information as to the financial resources and needs of both parties and the children. They will not be too concerned as to the effect of the agreement between the parties insofar as it relates to their own situation (as long as it is not clearly unfair), but will scrutinise a proposed order for a child much more carefully. If the court considers that the agreement is unsatisfactory in any respect, it can make an order on other terms, if the parties agree.

4 Child orders

4.1 In matrimonial proceedings

The court can award either or both periodical payments or a lump sum order (limited to £1,000 for each child), to or for the benefit of any child of the family but subject to the powers of the Child Support Agency for assessing and collecting periodical payments for maintenance for natural children of the parties. The expression *child of the family* has the same meaning as in the divorce court (see *Financial Provision after a Final Decree*, 2.8), under the Children Act 1989, s. 105(1). Thus a child of the family is either a child of both of the parties, or any other child who has been treated by both of them as their child (not being a child who has been placed officially with them as foster parents). There are also special guidelines under s. 3, Domestic Proceedings and Magistrates' Courts Act 1978, which are identical to those to which the divorce court must have consideration. Thus, under s. 3(3), the court must have regard to the financial resources and needs of the child, and the manner in which the child was being, and in which the parties expected him to be educated or trained. If the child is not the child of the respondent (e.g. a step-child of the respondent), under s. 3(4) the court must also consider the extent to, and the basis on which, the respondent accepted responsibility for the child's maintenance, whether he did so in the knowledge that it was not his child, and the liability of any other person to support the child (e.g. the other natural parent).

4.2 In independent proceedings

The magistrates can make the same orders in proceedings brought under the Children Act 1989. A wide range of persons can apply for such orders, including unmarried parents of children. The same principles apply (see *Children*, 4.1 and 4.2).

5 Orders in the High Court or county court

Under the Matrimonial Causes Act 1973, s. 27, the High Court or county court can make an order for financial relief if a party to a marriage can prove that the other party has failed to provide reasonable maintenance for the applicant, or to provide or make a proper contribution towards reasonable maintenance for any child of the family. The grounds are therefore identical to those under the Domestic Proceedings and Magistrates' Courts Act 1978 (see 2.1 above), and the court's jurisdiction is the same (i.e. married couples who are not seeking to terminate their marriage or relationship). The procedure is little used, as the magistrates' court procedure is much quicker and cheaper. The only advantage in making an application under this provision is that the court's powers are much wider. There is no limit on the lump sum that can be awarded, and security can be ordered for periodical payments or instalments of a lump sum. There is also no bar on the order continuing should the parties cohabit for more than six months (see 1.4.2 above). The court can still not make transfer of property or settlement orders however (except in favour or for the benefit of a child of the family; see *Children*, 4.1), and therefore if one party to a marriage needs the greater powers of the High Court or county court, it would be better to seek a judicial separation (see *Invalidity and Failure of Marriage*, 1.1 and 1.3).

Children

1 Introduction

1.1 The law relating to children

Financial provision for children has already been considered to some extent (see *Financial Provision after a Final Decree*, 2.8 and 3.5, and *Financial Provision in the Family Proceedings Court*, 4). During the early 1990s, there were fundamental changes to this and many other aspects of the law relating to children. It is therefore important to look again at the question of financial provision in the context of this new structure. The Children Act 1989, which came into force on 14 October 1991, laid down basic principles for dealing with disputes concerning or involving children in both the private and public domains. The Child Support Act 1991, which came into force on 5 April 1993, created the Child Support Agency, and under its aegis a totally new system for the assessment and collection of child maintenance. Individually, these two Acts represented radical reforms. Collectively, they have comprehensively overhauled the whole system of child law and effectively created a new structure within which all proceedings affecting children must operate. This structure will be covered under three headings. First, private disputes between parents who have separated, concerning which of them is going to look after the children, and the extent to which the other can be involved in their upbringing (see 2 below). Secondly, the public domain, concerning the role of local authorities in protecting children and promoting their welfare, often in opposition to the child's parents (see 3 below). Thirdly and finally, the issue of maintenance of children, looking in particular at the role of the Child Support Agency and the residual powers of the courts (see 4 below). It is first necessary to look at the Children Act 1989, however, as this was the starting-point for all of the reforms, and established several basic principles which underpin all aspects of child law.

1.2 The Children Act 1989

1.2.1 Social problems

During the 1980s there was a succession of incidents and scandals concerning the treatment of children, which brought into the open the deficiencies in the law as it then stood. There were detailed enquiries into the deaths of Jasmine Beckford and Kimberley Carlile, which had occurred despite the attentions of the authorities. A number of surveys and investigations made it clear that physical and sexual abuse of children was only too common. The House of Lords was asked to rule on the balance between the parents' right to be informed if contraceptive advice is being given to their child, and the child's right to confidential medical advice and assistance (*Gillick* v *West Norfolk and Wisbech AHA* (1986)). The enquiry into the handling of child abuse allegations in Cleveland was concerned with the balance between the powers of local authorities to intervene to protect children, and the interests of the parents and the children themselves. It thus became accepted that children were not being properly protected, either in the area of private disputes between their parents or guardians, or in the area of public powers as wielded by local authorities. The Act itself sets out a framework within which all these problem areas are covered, with some detail as to specific principles, duties and responsibilities. There is also a substantial body of even more detailed rules and guidance, set out in regulations made under the Act and covering every aspect of the proper approach towards child care. Some of these regulations will be referred to by way of example, but you should be aware that there are many more which are not mentioned, purely for reasons of space. The Department of Health's *The Children Act 1989 Guidance and Regulations*, is published in nine volumes, with a separate index, and is recommended to the specialist or enthusiast. It should also be noted that the Children Act 1989 has not proved to be a magic wand, eradicating all the problems which beset the care and protection of children. The Beckford and Carlile cases of the 1980s have been more than matched for tragedy by the suffering of Adjo 'Anna' Climbie throughout 1999–2000. The inquiry headed by Lord Laming has highlighted the failure to protect Anna by a variety of agencies, including Haringey social services department, two hospitals and two police child protection units. The second phase of the inquiry, starting work in March 2002, will concentrate on ways to try to prevent similar tragedies occurring again and this may result in further amendments to the law such as the provision of a national database of vulnerable children. The law regulating disputes between parents has also been questioned, with a growing recognition of the need to protect children from the psychological effects of observing violence, even when they themselves are in no danger of being assaulted (see 1.3.3 below).

1.2.2 Procedural problems

Before the Children Act 1989, a proper scheme for the care of children was hampered by the number of different procedures which were available, each of which had its own legislative background. There was a choice of proceedings in the magistrates court, High Court or county court, each of which had different powers. The orders that the court could make might also depend on the exact nature of the proceedings before it. The selection of the court and statute under which the case should be brought could be a difficult strategic decision for the practitioner, when the real issue should always be what is best for the welfare of the child concerned. At the centre of the new procedure, therefore, is the idea of *concurrent jurisdiction*. This means that the same orders are available to the court, whichever court is hearing the case, and whatever the circumstances.

Thus it does not matter whether it is the magistrates' court, the county court or the High Court which is hearing the case. Nor does it matter whether the issue arose in other family proceedings (e.g. divorce), or is the subject of a specific application. A particularly important aspect of this system is that the same range of orders is now available in private and public proceedings.

EXAMPLE

If two parents are in dispute over who should look after their children, the court can consider involving the local authority, and thus making a care or supervision order (see 2.7 below). On the other hand, in care proceedings the court could make a residence order in favour of one parent, perhaps with conditions attached (see 2.2 below), instead of a full care order.

The court system itself has also been re-organised in order to reflect this principle. Magistrates now sit as the family proceedings court, although in effect this is only a change of name for the previous domestic panels of the magistrates' courts. County courts may be designated a *family hearing centre* and/or a *care centre*, and judges are specially trained to deal with child matters. The Family Division of the High Court continues to deal with child matters as before. There are two sets of rules governing procedure, namely the Family Proceedings Courts (Children Act 1989) Rules 1991 for magistrates' proceedings, and the Family Proceedings Rules 1991 for High Court and county court cases. Both sets of rules are similar in content however, and even follow the same numbering system. There is thus now a unified, three-tier court system, and although most cases should now commence in the family proceedings court (proceedings in a divorce county court which involve a child of the family are an obvious exception), the Rules allow an easy transfer of cases between courts. Thus a case can be transferred from a family proceedings court to a county court or the High Court if it is particularly complex, or vice versa if it can be dealt with more quickly and efficiently in that way. Similarly, if proceedings involving the same child are commenced in different courts, all proceedings can be transferred to the one court which is most suitable. The main exception to this principle is that care proceedings and applications for emergency protection orders (see 3.1 below) must be commenced in a family proceedings court, under the Children (Allocation of Proceedings) Order 1991. The magistrates also have limited powers in financial matters (see 4.1 below).

It was eventually recognised that the unified court system also required an integrated system of personnel to provide the necessary welfare functions. The Criminal Justice and Court Services Act 2000 therefore set up a new service, the *Children and Family Court Advisory and Support Service* (CAFCASS), which began operating in April 2001. Unfortunately this new service has experienced several problems with staffing and resources, and its close relationship with the Lord Chancellor's department has been criticised as compromising the independence of its officers. The Magistrates' Courts Services Inspectorate has the responsibility of ensuring that CAFCASS meets certain standards and it is expected that the first inspections will take place late in 2002.

1.3 Basic principles of the Children Act 1989

There are certain key principles set out in the Act which encapsulate its philosophy towards the care of children.

1.3.1 *A new model of parenthood*

If married, both parents are to <u>retain *parental responsibility*</u>, even if they separate. Under s. 3(1), this means 'all the rights, duties, powers, responsibilities and authority which by law a parent of a child has in relation to the child and his property'. An unmarried father can either enter into a formal *parental responsibility agreement* with the mother, or obtain an order giving him parental responsibility. The concept of 'custody' is thus abolished, and the emphasis placed on the need for both parents to have a share in decisions affecting their children. The courts appear prepared to grant such orders so as to enhance the possibility of a relationship between the father and the child, even where this is unlikely in the short term.

Re H (A Minor) (Parental Responsibility) (1993)

The woman had left the man with whom she had been living, taking their two-year-old child with her. She subsequently married another man and <u>moved to Scotland</u>, and the contact order originally granted to the father was revoked by the court. Nevertheless the Court of Appeal granted a <u>parental relationship order.</u> Not only was the father qualified for such an order, but it would also give him appropriate status should the mother and her husband seek to adopt the child (thus needing his consent), or should their marriage break down.

    The matters to be considered by the courts when dealing with an application for parental responsibility were confirmed in *Re H (Parental Responsibility: Contact)* (1998). They are, first, the <u>degree of commitment</u> shown by the father towards the child. Secondly, the <u>degree of attachment</u> between the father and the child. Thirdly, the father's <u>reasons for applying</u> for the order. The unmarried father, therefore, has no rights concerning his child until or unless a court order is made in his favour or a formal agreement entered into. In *B* v *UK* (2000), the European Court of Human Rights ruled that this difference in treatment of married and unmarried fathers is not in breach of the Convention as it is justifiable on many grounds. The Government, however, intends to go some way to meeting the concerns of such men by legislating to provide that any father named on a child's birth certificate will have automatic parental responsibility and a provision to this effect has been included in the Adoption and Children Bill 2002. Medical advances such as in vitro fertilisation (IVF) have given rise to other practical and ethical problems, however, which are testing the general principles outlined in *Re H* (1993).

Re D (A Child) (2001)

A woman had unsuccessful IVF treatment with donated sperm while in a settled relationship with a man, the applicant in this case. Their relationship broke down but she deceived the provider of the treatment into allowing her to try again, and this time she conceived and gave birth. It was accepted (possibly wrongly) that under the Human Fertilisation and Embryology Act 1990, the applicant would be treated as the father. The Court of Appeal refused to grant an order for parental responsibility, however, as the applicant had 'no forum in which to exercise' the right. This appears to conflict with the principle enunciated in *Re H* (1993) and

[handwritten marginalia: father's status in relation to the child was maintained]

other cases, that an order is appropriate even if the father is not in a position to exercise it.

This model of parenthood is reflected in the new orders that the court can make, and although these will be looked at in detail (see 2 below), it is worth noting the two most important at this stage. The first is the *residence order*, which replaces the idea of custody, and merely establishes where children are to live. The second is the *contact order*, which replaces the idea of access, and determines the nature and frequency of contact between children and the parent with whom they are not living. The child is also recognised as an independent person who should be fully involved in decision-making, and the need to obtain the child's views is emphasised (see 1.3.3 below). On occasions, this may necessitate children having separate legal representation, especially as they get older. Finally, children should always be cared for within the family, unless their interests require them to live away from home (e.g. in local authority care). Even then, the parents should continue to be closely involved in decisions about their children's upbringing.

1.3.2 The welfare principle

The welfare principle has been retained under s. 1(1), Children Act 1989, which states that 'the child's welfare shall be the court's paramount consideration' when dealing with any question concerning a child's upbringing or property. This derives ultimately from the Guardianship of Infants Act 1925, although most recently the principle was stated in the Guardianship of Minors Act 1971. It is not a new principle, therefore, and in *J* v *C* (1969) the House of Lords explained that it meant that the welfare of the child 'determines the course to be followed' by the court. This would therefore exclude other considerations, such as which parent 'deserves' to look after the child. It should be noted, however, that this seems to be in conflict with the European Convention of Human Rights. In *W* v *UK* (1987) the European Court of Human Rights ruled that Article 8 of the Convention (the right to respect for private and family life) protects the parents' right to the company of their child. Any action which involves curtailment of this right is therefore in breach of the Convention unless specifically justified. The effect of this is that the court's decision should be much more of a balancing exercise between the rights of the parents and the interests of the child and although the House of Lords has stated that Article 8 has no effect on the welfare principle in the context of adoption proceedings (*Re B (Adoption: Natural Parent)* (2001)), the rights of a parent have been been considered by the courts in this way.

Re T (Paternity: Ordering Blood Tests) (2001)

By agreement with her husband, in order to conceive a child, the mother of T had sexual intercourse with several different men, but most frequently with the applicant in this case. He applied for blood tests to be ordered to establish his paternity and, if he was the father, for parental rights and contact orders. The High Court judge ordered the necessary blood tests, even though it was unlikely that a finding of paternity would result in parental rights and contact orders. His ruling involved a recognition of the rights of the applicant to have his right to family life respected under Article 8 by at least having the possibility of a relationship with his biological son considered.

1.3.3 *The checklist*   ⌐ 7 items

Over the years the courts had acknowledged various factors which were considered particularly important when reaching a decision in a case involving the welfare of a child. In order to encourage consistency in decision-making and private arrangements between parents without recourse to the courts, these factors are now rationalised and set out in a checklist in s. 1(3). Of the seven items, perhaps the most important is the first, namely that the court must have regard to the 'ascertainable wishes and feelings of the child concerned, considered in the light of his age and understanding'. This may mean that the child will be provided with separate legal representation, known as a '*guardian ad litem*'. Usually a report from the court welfare officer will be a sufficient indication of the child's own wishes, but the *guardian ad litem* will also focus on the child's interests, and may on occasions disagree with arrangements which have been agreed by all other parties (see, for example, *Re D (A Minor) (Care or Supervision)* (1993), 3.2.3 below). It will then be up to the court to decide the weight to be given to the child's 'wishes and feelings', being particularly aware of the danger that the child might have been unduly influenced by an adult. The courts have shown themselves quite ready to respect the child's views, however, especially where other factors are equally balanced.

Re P (A Minor) (Education) (1992)

After their divorce the wife lived with the younger child in the former matrimonial home while the husband lived with the 14-year-old son. The husband paid the school fees for both children to attend private schools, but the time came when there was the possibility of the elder boy moving to a prestigious boarding-school with a special music scholarship. The mother was keen for him to do so, and the boy's present school recommended the move. The boy was also enthusiastic, but eventually decided that he wanted to stay at his day-school, so that he could see more of his father. The father felt that he could not afford the increased fees. The Court of Appeal felt that they had a duty to respect the boy's wishes, as he was mature, sensible, and had reasoned his decision soundly.

The other factors in the checklist also merit close consideration, however. The second is the child's 'physical, emotional and educational needs', which will clearly operate in conjunction with 'how capable each of his parents, and any other person in relation to whom the court considers the question to be relevant, is of meeting his needs'. Furthermore, another factor is the 'age, sex, background and any character-istics of his which the court considers relevant'. The needs of a particular child will therefore depend upon those characteristics, and include considerations such as the child's religion, race or ethnicity, and perhaps even socio-economic group. There must then be an assessment by the court of the respective capabilities of the compet-ing adults to provide appropriate accommodation, food and clothing, day-to-day care, sound moral guidance and emotional attachment, and educational opportunities both in school and at home. It is difficult for the courts to avoid sometimes controversial value judgments, such as objecting to one parent's strong religious beliefs (where they belong to a sect seen as harmful), 'alternative' lifestyle, or even sexual orientation (as in the case of a lesbian mother or homosexual father). The courts have avoided laying down precise rules, except that they are usually in favour of the mother having care of a young child.

Re W (A Minor) (Residence Order) (1992)

The parents of a newly born baby were unmarried, but the mother agreed that the father should bring the child up, allowed him to collect the baby from the hospital, and then entered into a formal parental responsibility agreement (see 1.3.1 above) with him. Two weeks later she changed her mind, and the Court of Appeal granted her a residence order on the basis that there was a presumption that the mother was the best person to look after a baby. This presumption is rebuttable, however (see *Re B (A Minor) (Residence Order: Ex Parte)* (1992) below).

There is also a strong presumption that a child should be brought up by a natural parent.

Re D (Care: Natural Parent Presumption) (1999)

Three children were in care and the local authority had to determine where they were going to live. It was agreed that the two eldest should live with their grandparents, but their father wished to look after the youngest. The Court of Appeal ruled in favour of the father, stating that the proper approach was to begin by asking if there were compelling reasons against placing the child with its natural parent.

The court must also consider 'the likely effect upon him of any change in his circumstances'. It seems to be accepted now that a child needs stability, and that it can be harmful to move a child away from familiar surroundings and established friends. There is, however, a distinct preference for the *status quo* in the short term at least, especially in the light of the priority now given to expeditious determination of such cases (see 1.3.5 below).

Re B (A Minor) (Residence Order: Ex Parte) (1992)

The wife left her husband and four children to live with another man, but returned and abducted the youngest child, a four-year-old boy. The Court of Appeal ruled that the court could make an *ex parte* order (i.e., without giving the mother notice of the hearing) granting a residence order to the father. The court emphasised that this was an unusual situation (see 2.6.3 below), but not only were they concerned about the character of the mother's new partner, they also felt strongly that children had a right to remain where they were until a proper, considered decision had been made about their future. A full hearing of the case, with all parties involved, had to take place as soon as possible.

It is perhaps to be expected that the court must also consider 'any harm which he has suffered or is at risk of suffering'. This refers to more than physical ill-treatment, however, and will cover impairment of the child's intellectual, emotional and social development. It is under this heading in particular that the court will decide on the relevance of such difficult issues as the parent's sexual orientation, with the assistance of expert evidence. Thus in *C* v *C* *(A Minor) (Custody: Appeal)* (1991), the Court of Appeal ruled that the mother's lesbian relationship was an important factor, and sent the case back to the High Court for a full rehearing of the issues. The matter was finally resolved after expert evidence.

C v *C* *(Custody of Child) (No. 2)* (1992)

After the marriage had broken down the wife lived on her own with the child. She had then got a job as a prison warder in a women's prison, fallen in love with one of the prisoners, and after her release set up home with her and the child. An expert on homosexual relationships gave evidence to the effect that the child would not suffer harm because of the mother's relationship with the other woman. The court weighed the pros and cons and finally made a residence order in favour of the mother on the basis that 'the importance to the child of the mother's relationship with her dominated all other factors'.

A particular problem has been the extent to which violence by one parent against the other should affect contact with the child by the violent parent. A proposed amendment to the Adoption and Children Bill 2002 seeks to extend the definition of 'harm' to include 'suffering as a result of witnessing the ill-treatment of another person'.

Finally, the only factor not directly related to the child's welfare is 'the range of powers available to the court under this Act in the proceedings in question'. On the positive side, this means that the court must always consider the best way to meet the child's needs. On the negative side, the court must accept the practical limitations imposed upon it. It is not always appropriate to try to force on someone a responsibility which he or she is unwilling to take, and sometimes it is not even possible to do so (see *Nottingham County Council* v *P* (1993), 3.1 below). In *Re B (A Minor) (Residence Order: Ex Parte)* (1992) (above) the Court of Appeal made an *ex parte* residence order despite the fact that the Family Proceedings Rules do not appear to allow this. This suggests that there are gaps in the Act, and that the courts may have to be inventive in some situations.

1.3.4 *The 'no order' principle*

Under s. 1(5), a general policy of non-intervention is stated. Thus the court should not make an order unless it considers that it would be better for the child than making no order at all. It is therefore important to consider the precise benefit that the child will derive from any proposed order.

EXAMPLE

It used to be standard practice during divorce proceedings to make a custody order in respect of one parent and an access order in favour of the other. Now, as both parents retain parental responsibility (see 1.3.1 above), a residence or contact order will only be needed (for example) to provide security where there is a real dispute between the parents, or where the child will be taken abroad on occasions.

The courts do appear to regard a maintenance order as being necessary in most circumstances.

K v H *(Child Maintenance)* (1993)

The unmarried and separated parents of a two-year-old child agreed that the father would pay £20 per week to the mother. This voluntary arrangement stood for a year, and accordingly, when they applied for a formal court order, the magistrates refused because of the 'no order' principle. The Family Division judge made the order, however, as this would give the benefit of security and the ability to enforce arrears should they ever accrue in the future.

1.3.5 *Avoidance of delay*

Under s. 1(2), the court must have regard to the principle that delay in hearing a case is likely to prejudice the child's welfare. This principle was adopted by the courts even before the Act came into force.

Re G *(Child Case: Avoiding Delay)* (1991)

The case concerned a dispute between the local authority and the child's mother as to when and how the child should be returned to the mother's care. The High Court hearing the case refused to accept an agreement between the parties for the matter to be adjourned for further medical reports, taking note of the principles in the Children Act 1989 which would come into force later that year. Instead the court made an order in favour of the local authority's proposals.

The court is also encouraged to hold preliminary hearings and to set a time-table for future hearings, to ensure that there is no unnecessary delay. At the same time the courts have recognised that 'planned and purposeful delay may well be beneficial' (see *Hounslow London Borough Council* v *A* (1993), 3.2.2 below).

> EXAMPLE
>
> Rather than place a child into the care of the local authority, other possibilities should be fully assessed first. There may have been unexpected developments which mean that there is a real possibility that the parents are now capable of looking after the child (see *Re B (Minors) (Care: Contact: Local Authority's Plans)* (1993), 3.4.2 below), or that another suitable home is available (see *Hounslow London Borough Council* v *A* (1993), 3.2.2 below). This will usually mean that a welfare report will have to be prepared, and an adjournment for that purpose is quite satisfactory.

1.4 Jurisdiction under the Children Act 1989

1.4.1 *Proceedings covered by the Children Act 1989*

The orders under the Act are available either by way of a new application under the Act itself, or in the course of *family proceedings*. Under s. 8(4), this phrase is defined to cover many different proceedings, including proceedings under the Matrimonial Causes Act 1973 (e.g. petitions for divorce, nullity or judicial separation and financial provision after a decree); the Adoption Act 1976; the Domestic Proceedings and Magistrates' Courts Act 1978; and proceedings for injunctions for domestic violence.

Thus, even where the basic proceedings are unsuccessful, the court can still make orders in respect of children.

EXAMPLE

If a petition for divorce is presented, the court has the power to make orders in respect of the children even if the petition is dismissed, or if a decree is granted but no order for financial provision is made. The court can make child orders on application by either party to the marriage, or of its own volition.

1.4.2 Children covered by the Act

Under s. 10(1), the court can make orders in respect of _any child_, if an issue as to that child's welfare arises in the proceedings. The definition is therefore even wider than the concept of a 'child of the family' (see _Financial Provision after a Final Decree_, 2.8 and _Financial Provision in the Magistrates' Court_, 4). There are however restrictions under s. 9(7) concerning children over the age of 16, and applications in respect of children who are not 'children of the family' may require leave of the court (see 1.4.3 below).

1.4.3 Who may apply under the Act?

Under s. 10(4), three categories of person have the automatic right to apply for any s. 8 order (see 2.1 below). They are firstly, the parents of the child (including the unmarried father); secondly, the guardians of the child; and thirdly, persons who have had a residence order made in their favour. Under s. 10(5), a further three categories may apply for the basic _residence_ or _contact_ orders. They are firstly, either party to a marriage, in respect of a child of the family; secondly, persons with whom the child has lived for at least three years within the previous five years; and thirdly, persons who have obtained the consent of the parents (or of everybody who has the benefit of a residence order in respect of the child, or of the local authority if the child is in care). Further categories may be added by rules of court, especially grand-parents, who appear to have lost the rights that they previously had. Otherwise, all other persons can only apply with prior leave of the court, including the children themselves. In that situation, under s. 10(8), the court is required to ascertain that the child has sufficient understanding to make the proposed application. This require-ment should ensure that no child is unduly influenced by an adult as a way round the regulations.

EXAMPLE

A local authority places John, a 14-year-old boy, with foster parents. After some time the authority decides to move John, but both he and the foster parents wish the arrangement to continue. As John has not lived with them for three years, the foster parents would need the authority's permission before they could apply for a residence order. If that permission is not forthcoming, John could apply for leave to bring an application himself. The court would be careful to ensure that he was not being unduly influenced by the foster parents.

In other situations, under s. 10(9) the court must consider the applicant's connection with the child, the risk of the case disrupting his life, and the local authority's plans and parents' wishes if he is in care. There are additional restrictions affecting foster parents in particular. These are to reassure the parents of a child who is to be fostered, so that there will be no sense of competition between them and the foster parents which might upset the arrangements and disturb the child. Thus, short-term foster parents who are not relatives of the child must also obtain the permission of the local authority before they can even apply for leave to apply for an order. They will therefore have three hurdles to clear before being able to obtain a residence order (permission/leave/grounds for an order). It has been decided by the Court of Appeal that, once the matter is before the court (i.e., as a result of someone else's application), the court has the power to grant a residence order in favour of such foster parents (*Gloucestershire County Council* v *P* (1999)). It remains clear, however, that only after three years of fostering the child will they be able to apply to the court as of right.

2 The orders available under the Children Act 1989

2.1 Introduction

The key principle of *parental responsibility* (see 1.3.1 above) is meant to ensure that both parties retain their status as parents, even if one has to lose some day to day influence over the child's upbringing. The concept of custody has therefore been abolished, as this was seen as an attempt to allocate rights over the child to one parent, at the expense of the other.

It is always going to be necessary, however, to arrange for the child to live predominantly with one party, and it is inevitably this party who will need to exercise parental responsibility on a day to day basis. *Residence* and *contact* orders will therefore allocate the child's time between the parents, and it is hoped that this will encourage both parents to cooperate and share important decision making, and thereby reduce the potential for disputes. In practice however, the effects of a *residence order* are similar to those of an old-fashioned custody order. There are two other orders available, which are a means of restricting the responsibility of the parents, namely the *prohibited steps* and *specific issue orders.* The four orders are defined under s. 8(1), and not surprisingly are known collectively as *s. 8 orders*. There are useful examples of how these orders can be used in one of the Matrimonial Practice case studies.

[handwritten margin note: A bit like Specific performance — injunction]

2.2 Residence orders

This is an order 'settling the arrangements to be made as to the person with whom a child is to live'. Such an order will have several effects apart from simply determining where the child is going to live. First, under s. 12(2) it will give parental responsibility, if the person concerned is a non-parent, but without giving full parental powers. Such a person will not be able to consent to adoption, for example, or appoint a guardian for the child. Secondly, under s. 13, no one may change the child's name, or remove the child from the United Kingdom for more than one month, without the written consent of every person with parental responsibility, or the permission of the court. Under s. 11(7), the court may also attach detailed provisions to the order, affecting the person with the order, a parent or person with parental responsibility, or a person with whom the child is living.

EXAMPLE

The court may wish to prevent the parent with the order from taking the child abroad at all, or from moving to another part of the United Kingdom too far from the other parent.

The court should not impose a condition of residence at a specific address, even where this is intended to ensure that the other parent can maintain contact (*Re E (Residence: Imposition of Conditions), Re* (1997). This question whether the child should be moved away from the non-resident parent has caused the courts some difficulties.

M v M (Minors) (Removal from Jurisdiction) (1992)

The husband and wife had divorced after 12 years of marriage, and the wife looked after the two children. The husband had continual problems in keeping up contact with the children, because of the wife's attitude, and eventually she applied for permission to take the children to live in France (where she was born). The court welfare officer recommended that the children would be better off staying in England. The Court of Appeal ruled that the basic principle is that a reasonable proposal should be granted, unless it is clearly adverse to the interests of the children. Here, a move to France would inevitably result in a complete loss of contact with their father, because of the mother's attitude. Accordingly the case was sent back for a rehearing of all the issues.

This approach has been confirmed by the Court of Appeal in subsequent decisions, and in particular it has been ruled that it does not breach the European Convention on Human Rights (*Re A (Permission to Remove Child from Jurisdiction: Human Rights)* (2000)).

Under s. 11(4), the court may even make a residence order in favour of two people who are living apart, and specify the periods during which the child is to live with each of them.

In *Re H (A Minor) (Shared Residence)* (1994) the Court of Appeal emphasised that such an order should only be made in exceptional circumstances, however, as the child should have one settled home. Travelling to and fro will almost certainly confuse and worry children in such circumstances, and may also subject them to the stresses of competing interests if the parents are not in complete agreement. Normally this situation would be best dealt with by a residence order and contact order.

2.3 Contact orders

This is an order which requires 'the person with whom the child lives or is to live to allow the child to visit or stay with the person named in the order, or for that person and the child otherwise to have contact with each other'. The wording emphasises that the order is for the benefit of the child, rather than the other person and there is an assumption that a child will benefit from contact with both parents.

Re H (Minors) (Access) (1992)

The parents of two children separated and the children lived with their mother. The father had contact with them for five months, but the mother then refused to allow him to see them any more. Eventually she moved away from the area and married another man. Despite intermittent efforts to resume contact, over three years had passed when the father's application came before the Court of Appeal. The court ruled that it was wrong to deprive children of the long-term benefits of contact with their father except in exceptional circumstances, and accordingly granted a contact order for a gradual resumption of contact with the position to be reviewed in the near future.

There is a growing body of cases where this presumption has been rebutted, however. A particular difficulty arises when the parent with care of the child (most typically, the mother) has previously suffered violence at the hands of the parent seeking contact. The court will then have to consider the deeply entrenched fear of the mother for her own safety, but in the context of the interests of the child and the rights of the father.

Re K (Contact: Mother's Anxiety) (1999)

When they had lived together the child's father had been violent towards the mother and after they separated he had once kidnapped the child and been sent to prison as a result. The mother now suffered uncontrollable and severe stress when the father had contact with the child, although otherwise the sessions had gone well. The Family Division judge was satsified that the mother's anxiety was genuine and therefore cancelled direct contact and substituted indirect contact by letters, presents and photos. There was a two-fold danger that, not only would her distress be conveyed to the child, but also that the child would then suffer emotional harm from divided loyalties.

The principles to be applied in such cases were outlined by the Court of Appeal in the following case, the issue being considered so important as to justify hearing four cases together.

Re L (A Child) (Contact: Domestic Violence) (2000)

The mere fact that there has been domestic violence does not automatically prohibit contact, and the court must in any event decide whether allegations are true. The court must then weigh the advantages (e.g. seeing the father can be beneficial to the child's sense of identity and contact may enable the violent parent to reform) against the disadvantages. These can include the risk of violence to the child, or perpetuation of a bullying relationship. There is also the possibility that contact may awaken frightening memories of witnessing past violence.

There is also a provision in the Adoption and Children Bill 2002 for funding to be provided for special 'contact centres', where parents posing a risk to their child can be carefully supervised. Even where there has been no previous violence, however, it is not unusual for the parent with care to be hostile to the whole idea of contact. The court can try to encourage and persuade such a parent to be cooperative, but, at the end of the day, can only threaten punishment (e.g. imprisonment) for contempt of court. The only possible alternative is to grant a residence order to the other parent instead, but it is unlikely that either step would be in the interests of the child. There are no easy solutions to this problem, and the Advisory Board on Family Law has now issued a report *Making Contact Work* (February 2002) recommending a clear two-stage process of advice and persuasion followed by punitive sanctions as a last resort.

The order will usually be worded broadly, to allow reasonable contact, although the presumption against making orders at all (see 1.3.3 above) should perhaps reduce the number of orders in such terms. The court may define the nature and frequency of contact.

EXAMPLE

If contact is to be by visiting, then it might be necessary to state the regularity of visits, where they are to take place, and how long each visit is to last. Visits could also be supervised by a relative, friend or court welfare officer. If face to face contact is undesirable, it would be possible to specify letters or telephone calls instead.

Under s. 11(7), conditions can be attached in the same way as for residence orders.

2.4 Prohibited steps orders

This is an order preventing any person taking 'a step which could be taken by a parent in meeting his parental responsibility for a child'. The court can therefore specify issues relating to the upbringing of the child which must be referred to the court before any action is taken. This is likely to be rare in practice, as the court already has powers to attach conditions to residence and contact orders. The courts are also constrained from making a prohibited steps order which has the same effect as a residence or contact order. Such an order may be an appropriate way to prevent any contact with a child at all, as a contact order with conditions preventing contact seems paradoxical! The order must relate to matters which are aspects of parental responsibility, however.

Croydon London Borough Council v *A* (1992)

The local authority had applied for an interim care order because the elder of two young boys had been assaulted by his father. The magistrates made a prohibited steps order to prevent contact between not only the father and the children, but also between the mother and the father. The Family Division judge ruled that the issue of contact between the mother and father was not relevant to the issue of parental responsibility and therefore a prohibited steps order could not be used for that purpose.

2.5 Specific issue orders

This is an order 'giving directions for the purpose of determining a specific question which has arisen, or may arise, in connection with any aspect of parental responsibility for a child'. This will enable the court to resolve any disputes between the parents with the minimum of interference, in that it will not always be necessary or desirable to make a full residence or contact order. Again, the courts cannot make a specific issue order which has the same effect as a residence or contact order and it is limited to issues of parental responsibility.

Pearson v *Franklin* (1994)
The unmarried parents of the children lived in a rented house. The mother applied for a specific issue order to remove the father. The Court of Appeal ruled that the order should not be used for this purpose, as rights of occupation should be dealt with by an application for a transfer of property order (see *K* v *K (Minors: Property Transfer)* (1992), 4.1 below).

It is, however, particularly useful for the classic emergency when a child needs to have urgent medical treatment contrary to one parent's wishes.

Re R (A Minor) (Blood Transfusion) (1993)
A 10-month-old child with leukaemia needed a blood transfusion, but the parents could not consent because of their religious beliefs as Jehovah's Witnesses. A specific issue order was made by the Family Division judge to allow appropriate medical treatment to take place, as long as the parents' wishes were respected as far as possible.

2.6 Restrictions on s. 8 orders

2.6.1 *Key principles*
An order should not be made unless it is better than making no order at all, nor should conditions be attached unless that would be better than making just the basic order. The welfare principle also applies both to the making of orders and the attaching of conditions (see 1.3 above).

2.6.2 *Local authorities*
Under the Children Act 1989, s. 9, the orders cannot be made in favour of a local authority, nor have conditions attached which would have the same effect. This is to ensure that the role of local authorities is restricted to the protection of children, without allowing unwarranted interference in the private lives of families (see 1.2 above).

2.6.3 *Procedure*
It has already been noted that prohibited steps orders and specific issue orders cannot be made with a view to achieving the same result as a residence or contact order. This is mainly because those orders can be made without giving notice of the application to the parties who are going to be affected by them, unlike residence and contact orders (but see *Re B (A Minor) (Residence Order: Ex Parte)* (1992), 1.3.3 above). This concern that the full procedure should be followed except in unusual circumstances also explains the remarks made in *Re R (A Minor) (Blood Transfusion)*

(1993) (2.5 above) that, even where an *ex parte* application is permissible, 'strenuous efforts' should be made to have a full *inter partes* hearing whenever possible.

2.6.4 Duration

Apart from exceptional circumstances and where they are specifically extended, s. 8 orders cannot be made after a child's 16th birthday, and will cease automatically on that date. Residence and contact orders will also cease to have effect if the two parents concerned live together for more than six months, with the one exception of a residence order in favour of both of them.

2.7 Other orders

Apart from the orders available under s. 8, the courts can also grant parental rights under s. 4 to an unmarried father, and make a *family assistance order* under s. 16. This order will require a social worker to be available 'to advise, assist and befriend' the persons named in the order, and may also require the named persons to allow visits. The court must be satisfied that it could make a s. 8 order, that the circumstances are exceptional, and that everyone consents to the order. This procedure is intended to provide short-term assistance where the family is going through a particularly difficult time. The order will only last for a maximum period of six months, therefore, and may even be for a shorter specified period. If the court feels that there are long-term problems, under the Children Act 1989, s. 37, it can direct the local authority to investigate the child's circumstances with a view to instituting proceedings for a full care or supervision order. One of the aims of the Children Act 1989 was to establish a clear distinction between the private and public domains of child law, and this procedure in particular operates to blur that distinction. Furthermore, there is evidence of a wide range of interpretations as to what are 'exceptional circumstances', and large discrepancies in the number of such orders being made in different parts of the country. Such orders should certainly be regarded as a clear exception to the general rule, and their use should be strictly limited to appropriate situations where there is a real concern about the child's welfare.

EXAMPLE

The court should not be tempted to use the procedure to obtain a quick welfare report on the child, or to enable the appointment of a guardian *ad litem* (a solicitor to represent the child—see 1.3.3 above) at public expense.

This distinction between private and public proceedings should be borne in mind in the next section, which will look specifically at the area of public child law by focusing on the duties and responsibilities of local authorities under the Children Act 1989.

3 Local authorities

3.1 The role of local authorities

The key duties of a local authority in respect of children are, first, to promote the proper upbringing of children by their own families, and to check that other institutions which look after children away from home are complying with their responsibility for the children's welfare. Secondly, to protect children who are in need. Primarily, the local authority should try to meet these two duties by agreement with the parents and, under s. 17, it has a positive duty to attempt to do so within the child's own family. If, however, this is not possible, there is a range of powers available under the Act which can be utilised. Thus the local authority can bring care proceedings under s. 31, whereupon the court can make a care order, a supervision order, or any of the s. 8 orders. If a child is in urgent need of protection, the authority can seek an emergency protection order under s. 44, or a child assessment order under s. 43. These powers are carefully circumscribed however, to ensure that a proper balance is maintained between the need to protect children, and the right of families to freedom from unnecessary intrusion and disturbance. This balance can sometimes be difficult to maintain, and the result may be that the Children Act 1989 does not protect children as fully as it should.

Human rights Act

Nottingham County Council v *P* (1993)

There were serious allegations against a father that he had sexually abused his three daughters. After proceedings for an emergency protection order (see 3.3.2 below), the local authority applied for a prohibited steps order to remove the father from the home. It did not want a full care order, as it was felt that the authority could not control the children outside their own home. The Court of Appeal ruled that a prohibited steps order could not be made as it was the equivalent of a residence or contact order (2.6 above). Neither could it make a residence order in favour of the local authority, as this was not an appropriate alternative to a care order, and it was tantamount to imposing a duty on the authority which it was not willing to accept. Thus, if a local authority refuses to take care proceedings, there is no order which can be made to protect the child.

This deficiency should be overcome by a provision in the Family Law Act 1996, which allows the court to attach an *exclusion requirement* to an emergency protection order or interim care order, to force the abuser to leave the home. There may be other circumstances where the court is left powerless because of the refusal of a local authority to take action, and this could be in breach of the European Convention on Human Rights.

Z and others v UK (2001)

The applicants were brothers and sisters who had spent their early childhood in dreadful conditions despite the local authority's knowledge that their parents were incapable of looking after them properly. The House of Lords had ruled that they could not sue the local authority for damages. The European Court of Human Rights held that there had been a breach of Article 3 (the right not to be subjected to inhuman and degrading treatment) because of the State's failure to remedy the parental neglect; and Article 13 (the right to an effective remedy) because of the children's inability to obtain compensation.

3.2 Care proceedings

3.2.1 Investigation and prosecution

Under the Children Act 1989, s. 47, local authorities must investigate all cases where they have a reasonable belief that a child is suffering or likely to suffer harm. They are empowered to call on other authorities (e.g. housing, education and health authorities and the NSPCC), which must assist unless it would be unreasonable in all the circumstances of the case. A special government publication, *Working Together under the Children Act 1989*, gives guidance to these and other agencies who might become involved. It identifies the various stages which a case should go through, and recommends good practice for each agency at every stage. In this way it is intended to encourage cooperation between agencies, and to prevent mistakes such as those identified in the Cleveland Report although the report into the Climbie case shows that problems still occur (see 1.2.1 above). Further guidance has also been provided by *The Framework for the Assessment of Children in Need and their Families* (April 2000), published jointly by the Department of Health, Education and Employment and the Home Office. The onus, however, is always clearly on the local authority itself to consider whether it is necessary to exercise any of their powers under the Act, either by providing assistance, or by taking care proceedings. In fact, under s. 47(6), if an authority has been unable to gain access to a child, it must take proceedings unless it is satisfied that his welfare can be safeguarded without so doing. As it is unlikely that this would be the case, it is almost always going to be incumbent upon the authority to take action. The imposition of this duty is a clear response to the situation which the authorities encountered in the Jasmine Beckford and Kimberley Carlile cases, where they were continually obstructed in their attempts to see the children, and relied instead on the word of the adults concerned.

3.2.2 *The standard for intervention*

In order to protect families from unwarranted intervention and disturbance, the Children Act 1989, s. 31(2), sets tests which must be met before the court can consider making a care or supervision order. These are known as the *threshold criteria*. Even if these are met, however, the court must still go on to apply the welfare principle (using the checklist), and must not make an order unless it is better than making no order at all (see 1.3.3 above). The court must be satisfied that, first, the child is suffering or likely to suffer significant harm. The interpretation of this provision has led to conflicting decisions in the Court of Appeal and the House of Lords.

Re M (A Minor) (Care Order: Threshold Conditions) (1994)
The local authority applied for a care order in respect of a two-year-old boy whose father had murdered his mother 18 months previously. In the meantime the child had

been placed with foster parents, but the dead mother's other three children from another relationship had been living with her cousin. The cousin had also had regular contact with the little boy, and now applied for a residence order so that she could take him to live with his half-brothers and sisters. As the father was now serving a life sentence of imprisonment for murder he was no longer a threat. The Court of Appeal ruled that, although the threshold criteria were clearly met at the time that the whole process started, the relevant time was the date of the court hearing. The child was no longer suffering harm, nor was he likely to, as there was a good home awaiting him. A residence order was accordingly made in favour of the cousin. The House of Lords reversed this decision and made a care order. They ruled that the relevant date was the date at which the local authority started proceedings to protect the child, and that therefore they had jurisdiction to make a care order. It did not follow that such an order should be made, but they felt that a care order would enable the local authority to monitor the progress of the child as there was a real possibility of problems in the future. The child would continue living with the cousin, however, as he had been thriving in her care while waiting for the appeal to the House of Lords to be dealt with.

The House of Lords' decision on the point of law enables local authorities to pursue care proceedings even when a child is being cared for by relatives, and in particular this means that a *guardian ad litem* (see 1.3.3, above) can make an independent investigation of the issues. The decision to make a care order on the facts can be criticised, however, as an order under s. 8 would have met their major concerns without prejudicing the cousin's responsibility for making day-to-day decisions about the child's care.

The word 'likely' implies that the risk of significant harm is more than merely 'possible', but not necessarily as much as 'probable'. This issue is also tied up with the question of the standard of proof required where the court is concerned with serious allegations against third parties.

Re H (Minors) (Sexual Abuse: Standard of Proof) (1996)

The local authority applied for a care order in respect of three girls following allegations by their older sister that she had been sexually abused by the man who was living with their mother. Her allegations had earlier formed the basis of unsuccessful criminal proceedings against the man, but the local authority argued that the standard of proof in care proceedings ('the balance of probabilities') was lower than that in criminal cases ('beyond reasonable doubt'). The House of Lords confirmed the decision of the original judge and the Court of Appeal that no care order should be made. They ruled that 'likely' meant 'a real possibility', and that the more serious the allegations, the stronger the evidence needed to prove them.

This decision clearly attempts to balance the need to protect children against the need to be fair to the people against whom serious allegations are being made. As such it is possibly a reaction to the outcry against the events in Orkney, where several children were removed from their parents in distressing circumstances after far-fetched (and subsequently unproved) allegations of organised ritual sexual abuse. The decision has been criticised, however, as meaning that the worse the danger that children are in, the less likely it will be that the courts will protect them from it.

The court must be satisfied secondly that the harm is attributable either to the care given to the child (or likely to be given to him if the order were not made), or the child being beyond parental control. The standard of care which should be given to a child by his parent is 'what it would be reasonable to expect a parent to give'. Under s. 31(9), 'harm' is defined as 'ill-treatment or the impairment of health or development'. This is a wide definition, and would cover not only physical violence, neglect or sexual abuse, but also unconventional life-styles which adversely affect the child's educational or social abilities. The harm must be 'significant' under s. 31(10) by comparison 'with that which could reasonably be expected of a similar child'.

EXAMPLE

A child with physical or mental handicaps will be assessed according to the average child with a similar handicap, but in the light of what it would be reasonable to expect the parents to do.

Allowances cannot be made for the parents' own disadvantages or disabilities. This is because the test refers to 'a parent', and not 'this parent'.

EXAMPLE

If a parent is unable to care properly for her child because she is mentally handicapped herself, it does not matter that she cannnot be said to be to blame in any way for the harm that is being caused to the child. A more difficult situation arises if the lack of care is due to the parents' poverty. Is it fair to judge them by middle-class standards?

Notable exceptions from the grounds for an order are failure to attend school, and the commission of criminal offences by the child. Truancy must now be dealt with in other ways, by the local education authority either prosecuting the parents, or obtaining an *education supervision order*. Either situation can now only be grounds for an order if the *threshold criteria* are satisfied.

EXAMPLE

If a child is not attending school and her parents are at fault, the harm to the child's educational standards may be so serious as to merit an order. Usually, however, the local education authority can achieve the same results by other proceedings, and these would be preferred. If a child is involved in criminal activities which are physically dangerous (e.g. drug dealing), or which are affecting her social development because of the extent of her involvement (e.g. a regular shop-lifting gang), then care proceedings may be necessary.

It is not always necessary to find that a parent had personal responsibility for the harm.

Lancashire County Council v *A* (2000)
A baby suffered non-accidental injuries but there was no proof as to whether they

were caused by the mother, father or child-minder. The Court of Appeal ruled that the injured child should be placed in care, as the term 'attributable' only required an objective lack of care by the parents and did not necessitate a precise finding of responsibility. The important issue was that the child was in need of protection. The child-minder's baby should not be placed in care, however, as it had not suffered harm to date and there was no evidence of future risk. The House of Lords rejected the appeal by the parents of the injured baby.

Whether or not the *threshold criteria* are met, the court can instead make any of the s. 8 orders, as the proceedings are classified as *family proceedings* (see 1.4.1 above). This possibility must be considered carefully by the court.

Hounslow London Borough Council v A (1993)

The local authority was applying for a care order in respect of a baby. The mother had a long history of alcohol abuse, and had been separated from the father for some time. The baby had been taken from her for its own protection, and placed with foster parents. The father, who was now living with another woman, applied for a residence order in respect of the baby. Although there was some evidence that the father could not offer a safe home for the child, the Family Division judge ruled that an interim care order should be made (see 3.2.5 below) so that the situation could be properly assessed and the father's application given full consideration.

It should be recalled, however, that s. 8 orders should not be used for a purpose for which they were not designed (see 2.4 and 2.5 above).

3.2.3 Care orders

Under s. 33, a care order gives parental responsibility to the local authority, which must receive the child into its care and keep him as long as the order remains in force. It also terminates existing s. 8 orders. The parents also retain their parental responsibility, but the local authority may determine the extent to which it can be exercised by them. The key principle remains that the parents should still be involved in decision-making as far as is possible (see 1.3.1 above), and under s. 34 the authority must allow the child reasonable contact with them (see 3.4.2 below). In exceptional cases, where only a care order will give sufficient protection, the child may continue to live with the parents.

Re D (A Minor) (Care or Supervision) (1993)

The father of the child had been imprisoned following the mistreatment of children, and the death of one child, during a previous relationship. His new partner had just given birth to his child, and the local authority applied for a supervision order (see 3.2.4 below). The child's *guardian ad litem* (see 1.3.3 above) argued that only a full care order would protect the child, and the Family Division judge agreed. The safety of the child overrode the local authority's argument that a care order might undermine the spirit of cooperation at present in existence.

The care order will also involve a *care plan*, which includes an assessment of the child's needs, details of placement and contact, a timetable of arrangements, and information on the support to be provided by the local authority. There has been a growing emphasis on care plans, and the Adoption and Children Bill 2002 contains a provision to the effect that a care order cannot be made until such a plan has been considered by the court. The House of Lords has also confirmed that the courts cannot use the elements of a plan in order to interfere with the day-to-day detail of the manner in which a local authority exercises its responsibilities. A decision of the Court of Appeal had proposed an innovative new scheme.

Re W and B (Children) (Care Plan) (2001)

The mother was ready to agree to care orders in respect of her three children, but only on the basis that the care plan would be adhered to. The plan revolved around rehabilitation of the children to her care and included a package of support and treatment measures to that end. The orders were made without any guarantees, however, and after only four months it was clear that the local authority would not be able to adhere to the plan because of budgetary constraints. The mother appealed against the care orders on the grounds that they breached Article 8 of the European Convention on Human Rights (her and the children's right to respect for their family life). The court agreed to the extent that they would read certain additional provisions into the Children Act 1989 so that it would comply with the Convention. First, the court had the power to make an interim care order (see 3.2.5 below) if a care plan was not watertight. Secondly, the plan should contain *starred milestones* to denote its essential elements. Thirdly, the local authority must inform the children's *guardian ad litem* if it could not achieve one of the milestones within a reasonable time, and the guardian could then apply to the court for directions.

In March 2002 the House of Lords overruled this decision on the grounds that it amounted to judicial innovation rather than legitimate interpretation of the Children Act. Their lordships also stated that the lack of supervision by the courts of local authorities is not in conflict with the Convention. The Children Act requires local authorities to review the care order every six months, and a failure to do so and take action if the plan was failing would amount to a breach of the child's human rights. Proceedings could then be taken against the authority under the Human Rights Act 1998 itself. They did comment, however, that the Court of Appeal had identified several practical and legal problems and that these should be considered properly by the government. This suggests that the provisions in the Adoption and Children Bill may have to be reviewed.

The authority's responsibility is also limited, in that it cannot consent to adoption, appoint a guardian or change the child's religion. The child's surname cannot be changed, nor can the child be removed from the United Kingdom for more than one month, unless the parents consent in writing or a court order is obtained. A care order will last until the child is 18, unless discharged by the court either specifically or by making a residence order under s. 8 (see 3.2.6 below).

3.2.4 Supervision orders

Under s. 35, a supervision order places the child under the supervision of a social worker, who must advise, assist and befriend him. The order will last for one year unless extended. The supervisor has no right of entry into the child's home, and cannot remove the child. Under s. 35(1)(b), the supervisor must take reasonable steps to ensure that the order is effective, and under sch. 3 can impose conditions upon the child and the parents. These can include a condition of residence in a particular place, and taking part in specified activities. Changes of address must be notified in any event, and the child can be required to submit to medical or psychiatric examination (unless he is mature and does not consent). If the order is breached or ignored by the child or parents, the supervisor can seek to vary it, but otherwise there are no real sanctions which can be applied for a breach of a supervision order. It may be that disobedience to a specific order of the court would amount to contempt of court, and be punishable as such, but this would not be a satisfactory way to respond and there is no evidence that the courts are taking such a course. Furthermore, if a care order is sought in place of a supervision order, the *threshold criteria* must be applied again. The order therefore relies in the main on the cooperation of the child's parents. If this cooperation can be relied upon in the first place, there may be little point in the local authority running the risk of creating ill-feeling by making an application to the court, as this will inevitably involve making allegations against the parents. On the other hand, if the parents' cooperation cannot be relied upon, a supervision order is unlikely to give the child sufficient protection. In the past, social workers have been sceptical about the effectiveness of similar types of order. Although the new order under the Children Act 1989 enables the court to impose specific requirements upon parents, it is still doubtful whether local authorities will prefer it to, for example, a care order with a high degree of parental contact (see *Re D (A Minor) (Care or Supervision)* (1993), 3.2.3 above). In 1998 there were approximately 1,000 supervision orders made, as opposed to 6,000 care orders.

3.2.5 Interim orders

Under s. 38, the court may make an interim care or supervision order for up to eight weeks, with further extensions of four weeks. An interim order will have the same legal effect as a full order, and can only be made if the court is satisfied that there are reasonable grounds for believing that the case meets the *threshold criteria*, but needs to adjourn the hearing or investigate the child's circumstances. These investigations may involve medical or psychiatric examinations, or other types of assessment (*Re C (Interim Care Order: Residential Assessment)* (1997)). The court can order the local authority to conduct an assessment even if it disagrees (see *Re B (Minors) (Care: Contact: Local Authority's Plans)* (1993), 3.4.2 below). At the adjourned hearing, a full order will be considered or the application dismissed (subject to the power to extend the interim order).

3.2.6 Discharge of orders

Under s. 39, application to discharge an order may be made by the local authority, any person with parental responsibility, or the child. Any other interested person can instead apply for a residence order (see 2.5 above), and if granted this will have the effect of discharging the care or supervision order. This can only be done with leave (see 1.4.3 above), with the important exception of an unmarried father. The better alternative may be for him to apply for a parental responsibility order first, as the courts are responsive to such applications (see *Re H (A Minor) (Parental Responsibility)* (1993), 1.3.1 above).

EXAMPLE

The parental responsibility order will give the father a free choice to apply either for a residence order in his favour, or for the care order (or supervision order) to be discharged. He may not be ready to give the child a home immediately, in which case a residence order would clearly be inappropriate.

The local authority is required to review a care order every six months, with a view to considering its discharge. Any application for discharge will be judged on the welfare principle, with reference to the checklist.

3.2.7 The Human Rights Act 1998

After October 2000 (see *Introduction*) a key issue throughout all these processes and procedures may be that the parents' rights under Article 8 of the Convention (the right to respect for private and family life) will have to be considered more carefully. In *McMichael* v *UK* (1995), the European Court of Human Rights ruled that parents must be involved in any decision-making process to such an extent that their rights under Article 8 are protected. The English High Court has taken the same view in respect of a local authority child protection conference, even though no decision as such was being made (*R* v *Cornwall County Council ex parte LH* (2000)). Furthermore, this is a continuing obligation, as the European Court has emphasised that any care order should be discontinued whenever, and as soon as, possible, in order to re-unite the parent and child and thus comply with their mutual right to family life, although ultimately the best interests of the child would override the rights of the parent (*Johansen* v *Norway* (1997)).

3.3 Emergency protection

3.3.1 Introduction

On occasions it is necessary to remove children immediately, pending a hearing before the court when an interim care order can be sought. To a certain extent the police have been able to exercise this role, but the Children Act 1989, s. 46, limits this to situations where the child is likely to suffer significant harm, and only allows detention for a maximum of 72 hours. The police are also obliged to contact the parents and the local authority. The usual procedure would be for the police themselves, or the local authority, to then apply to the court for an *emergency protection order*, or a*child assessment order* if investigation of the child's circumstances is necessary.

3.3.2 Emergency protection orders

There are two situations where this order may be necessary. First, under the Children Act 1989, s. 44, any person may apply to the court for an order empowering them to remove a child (or prevent its removal if already in a safe place), where it is felt that the child is in immediate danger. The court must be satisfied that there is reasonable cause to believe that the child is likely to suffer significant harm if he is not removed. Secondly, where the local authority (or NSPCC) needs access to the child because of worries about his welfare, and access is being denied. In this second situation the test is not so severe, as the court need only be satisfied that the applicant has reasonable grounds for believing that (in the case of a local authority application), access is required 'as a matter of urgency', or (in the case of an application by the NSPCC), that the applicant has reasonable cause to suspect that the child is suffering, or is likely to suffer significant harm. The effect of an emergency protection order is that the child must be produced to the applicant, who may then remove him. The applicant also obtains parental responsibility. Under s. 45, the order will last for a maximum of eight days, and may be extended once for a further seven days upon an application by a local authority or the NSPCC. Even this limited period was felt to be too long however, particularly as the order can be obtained without giving notice to the parents. On the other hand, the authority needs a minimum secure period in which a proper assessment of the child can take place. Accordingly, if the parents, persons with parental responsibility, or anyone with whom the child was living were not present at the first hearing, they can apply to discharge the order after 72 hours, as can the child himself. This emergency protection is deliberately limited in its extent, and the onus is on the local authority to start care proceedings as soon as possible if it feels that the child is in need of more lasting protection.

3.3.3 Child assessment orders

Under s. 43, a local authority (or the NSPCC) may apply for this order, which will enable it to remove the child for up to seven days, but purely for the purpose of assessment. Notice of the application must be given, and the court must be satisfied that the applicant has reasonable cause to suspect that the child is suffering, or is likely to suffer significant harm. Furthermore, the court must also be satisfied that an assessment is necessary and is unlikely to be possible without a court order. As the court cannot make this order if it feels that it ought to make an emergency protection order instead, and as the local authority can use the emergency protection procedure to remove the child if access has been denied, very few child assessment orders are made. This is particularly so as an emergency protection order can be made without notice, imposes a less severe test for a local authority application, and can last for up to 15 days (thus giving a more realistic chance of assessing the child).

3.3.4 Other orders

When an emergency protection order is granted, the court may also authorise entry and search of specific premises. If the whereabouts of a child cannot be ascertained, the court may order that a named person disclose this information. Finally, if there is reason to believe that access to the child will be denied, the court may authorise a police constable to assist and to use reasonable force.

3.4 Children in care

3.4.1 Local authorities' powers and duties

Because of the power that the local authority has over children in its care, the Act sets out the extent of the authority's duties and detailed guidance is given in further regulations. Thus, under s. 22, the local authority must 'safeguard and promote' the child's welfare, and specifically take into account when doing so the child's 'religious persuasion, racial origin and cultural and linguistic background'. A key element in caring for children will be the choice of their home during the time that they are in care. Under s. 23, accommodation must be near to their former home, and with any brothers and sisters who are also in care. The same section allows (in order of preference) placement with the child's own family (as in *Re D (A Minor) (Care or Supervision)* (1993), 3.2.3 above), with relatives or friends, or in a children's home. Guidance on the proper procedures is set out in the Arrangements for Placement of Children (General) Regulations 1991, with further detailed guidance in regulations specific to each situation. The Jasmine Beckford enquiry, for example (see 1.2 above), revealed a lack of supervision after Jasmine had been returned to live with her parents, despite the fact that she was still in care. The Placement of Children with Parents etc. Regulations 1991 therefore stipulate a variety of safeguards, such as preliminary enquiries and interviews, notification to all other relevant official bodies, and a timetable of visits and private interviews with the child. But s. 22 is intended to encourage positive steps to promote children's welfare, and therefore the Review of Children's Cases Regulations 1991 provides for regular reconsideration of plans for the child's future, with the views of the child's parents and the child itself being a particularly important part of the process. Finally, under s. 24, the local authority must not only prepare children for independence or for a return to their homes, but also provide after-care. This may consist of moral support and advice, or even financial assistance towards living expenses, education or training. The growing importance of this aspect of the duties of a local authority led to additional requirements being imposed upon them under the Children (Leaving Care) Act 2000 and the associated provisions of the Children (Leaving Care) Regulations 2001. The local authority must assess the needs of all relevant children, appoint a personal adviser and support them up to the age of 21 under a *pathway plan* designed for their individual needs. The children will not be eligible for State benefits but will continue to receive support and accomodation from the local authority instead.

3.4.2 Disputes with parents

As parents retain parental responsibility even though their children are in care, they have a right to be kept informed of their children's welfare, and to participate as much as possible in decision-making. The authority has a positive duty to promote contact between children and their family and friends, and under s. 34 the court may hear applications concerning contact, and make orders with or without conditions. Anyone (including the child) can apply for an order granting contact. The court can also prohibit contact, but only the child or the local

authority can make such an application. The courts are thus in control of this important aspect of the child's welfare, and have shown themselves ready to disagree with the
local authority's plans.

Re B (Minors) (Care: Contact: Local Authority's Plans) (1993)

Two children had been in the care of the local authority for nearly two years as the
mother had proved incapable of looking after them. The authority was now applying
to stop all contact between the mother and the children, with a view to placing the
children for adoption. In the meantime, however, the mother had had another baby,
and had been assessed as providing 'excellent' care for it. The Court of Appeal stated
that the courts should not normally interfere with local authority's plans, but only
where the circumstances were exceptional. In this case there was a real possibility that
the mother could now cope with all three children, and therefore the case should be
adjourned so that she could be properly assessed.

The issue is most likely to occur when continued contact would put the safety of
the child at risk. In those situations the court will have to weigh that risk against
the presumption that contact with their parents is in the best interests of children,
especially where continued contact would disrupt the search for a new family for
a child.

Birmingham City Council v H (1994)

The child's mother was herself a child, and her behaviour was seen as presenting a
serious risk to the safety of her baby. The House of Lords ruled that the interests of the
baby were paramount, and that they saw no reason to overturn the finding of the trial
judge that the mother's condition was unlikely to improve. That being the case, the
facts were exceptional enough to justify the decision that contact should be
terminated so that the baby could be found a long-term home by adoption.

Under s. 34, and the Contact with Children Regulations 1991, the local authority
can refuse contact for up to seven days in an emergency, as long as written notice is
given to all concerned.

Other matters may be the subject of a complaint through a formal complaints
procedure, which the authority must set up under s. 26. This procedure can be used by
the children themselves, their parents or those with parental responsibility, foster
parents and any other person who has a reasonable interest in a child's welfare. The
procedure is governed by the Representations Procedure (Children) Regulations 1991
and must involve a person who is completely independent of the authority. There is
provision for an appeals procedure, and strict time-limits of 28 days for the complaint
or appeal to be dealt with, and for the complainant to be notified of the local authority's final proposals. Thereafter, under s. 84, an application can be made to the Secretary of State to consider whether the local authority has failed to comply with its
duties under the Act. It is perhaps more likely that an individual case (as opposed to
an issue of general policy) would be the subject of an application for judicial review of
the authority's decision. Furthermore, as a result of the decision of the House of Lords
in Re W and B (Children) (Care Plan) (2001) (see 3.2.3 above), the local authority

itself must keep the important elements ('starred milestones') of the care plan under review, and take action if it seems likely that they cannot keep to them.

4 Financial provision

4.1 Applications and orders

Under the Children Act 1989, s. 15 and sch. 1, application can be made for financial provision for children. The applicant may be the parent or guardian of the child, or a person in whose favour a residence order is in force. Even the child himself can apply, if he is over 18, in full-time education or training, and his parents are separated. The order will be made against a parent of the child, and for all purposes of the Act it does not matter whether the parents are (or have been) married or not. The court may order periodical payments, a lump sum, or transfer or settle property. In this instance, however, the principle of concurrent jurisdiction (see 1.3.2 above) does not apply. Thus the family proceedings court is limited to its basic powers of periodical payments, and lump sums of £1,000 for each child. The effect of this is that an unmarried parent who wishes to claim a share of property must apply to the county court or High Court, where such an order can at least be made in favour of the child. Two important cases show how these principles can operate in practice.

K v K (Minors: Property Transfer) (1992)

An unmarried couple had four children, and lived in a council house. The woman applied for the joint tenancy to be transferred into her sole name on the grounds that this would be 'for the benefit of the children' as provided for in the Children Act 1989, sch. 1. The Court of Appeal ruled that 'benefit' included non-financial benefit, such as the need to provide a secure home for the children, and that therefore the order could be made despite the fact that the children would not receive any direct interest in the property. The court emphasised, however, that all the matters set out in sch. 1, para. 4, must be considered (see 4.2 below), and that the father's interest in the property should be protected wherever possible.

Re J (A Minor: Property Transfer) (1993)

This again involved an unmarried couple, and the mother applying for the joint tenancy in a council house to be transferred to her sole name 'for the benefit of the children' under sch. 1. In this case, however, the man was not the father of any of the children. The Family Division judge ruled that, although a stepfather can be regarded as a 'parent' (under sch. 1, para. 16), this cannot be extended to cover an unmarried cohabitee. Accordingly the order could not be made.

This procedure can therefore be used by one of an unmarried couple to obtain a property transfer order, as long as it can be regarded as being 'for the benefit of' any children. The person against whom the order is sought must be a 'parent' within the meaning of sch. 1, para. 16. A married parent has the option of commencing divorce proceedings, and seeking a transfer of property order there (see *Financial Provision after a Final Decree*, 2.4 and 2.5). The crucial difference is that transfer of property orders involving unmarried parents will be more limited in scope, especially where they concern ownership of property rather than a tenancy.

T v S *(Financial Provision for Children)* (1994)

The father of five children was ordered to buy a house where they could live with their mother. In the High Court, the judge ruled that the house should be placed in trust so that it would revert to the unrestricted ownership of the father as soon as the youngest child finished full-time education. The judge specifically ruled out any provision which would have the effect of providing a windfall to the mother, but commented that it was unfortunate that the law did not allow him to make provision for her purely because she was not married to the father of her children.

4.2 Guidelines

Under sch. 1 para. 4, the court must have regard to all the circumstances of the case, and certain matters in particular. These are identical to those set out in the Matrimonial Causes Act 1973 (see *Financial Provision after a Final Decree*, 3.5) and the Domestic Proceedings and Magistrates' Courts Act 1978 (see *Financial Provision in the Family Proceedings Court*, 4.1).

4.3 Child Support Act 1991

4.3.1 *Introduction*

The principal aim of the Child Support Act 1991 is to take the assessment of maintenance for children away from the courts, ostensibly in order to make the amounts of awards more realistic and collection more effective. It does this first by making the amount of maintenance largely a matter of arithmetical calculation, and secondly by transferring responsibility for assessment and collection of child maintenance to a new body, the Child Support Agency. It applies to all children regardless of whether their parents are married or not, and irrespective of the proceedings in which the issue of maintenance arises. The Act received the royal assent in July 1991, but the first provisions did not come into force until April 1993. The first three years of the Act's operation saw much controversy. The concentration on cases where state benefits were involved produced allegations that the Act was primarily a device to save money for the Government. Certainly the recipients of child maintenance derived no benefit in these cases, because any amount received by the parent looking after the children was merely deducted from the state benefits that she already received. The amounts which fathers were ordered to pay under the new method of calculation also caused some controversy, because they increased existing orders by up to four times the amounts previously fixed by the courts. The work of the Child Support Agency was even blamed for several suicides. In February 1994, the Government made some changes to the regulations and in January 1995 published a White Paper *Improving Child Support* setting out its proposals for more fundamental changes to the Act. Some of these changes were brought into force in April 1995 by changing existing regulations, but primary legislation was also needed. Accordingly the Child Support Act 1995 was passed, setting up a departures system to allow the normal formula for assessment to be modified when the paying parent has unusual expenses. Continuing criticisms of the system led the Government to consider further, more radical reforms, starting with yet another Consultation Paper (*Children First* (1998)) and White Paper (*Children's Rights and Parents' Responsibilities* (1999)). These proposals are now embodied in the Child Support Pensions and Social Security Act 2000. They were due to come into force in April 2002 but implementation has been postponed for further testing of the Agency's computer system.

4.3.2 Basic principles

Under s. 1(1) of the Act, every parent of a 'qualifying child' is responsible for that child's maintenance. A 'qualifying child' is one who is living with only one (or neither) parent, and who is under 16 or under 19 but still in full-time education up to A-level standard. Where a child is being looked after on a day-to-day basis by one person (typically one of the parents), any parent not living with the child (the non-resident parent) is liable to pay maintenance for the child in accordance with an assessment under the Act. This assessment is made on an arithmetical basis (i.e., with no discretionary elements at all) by applying the 'statutory formula' (see 4.3.3 below). The assessment and collection of maintenance under the Act is undertaken by a new section of the Department of Social Security called the Child Support Agency, staffed by child support officers. The Agency has powers to trace absent parents and to enforce collection of maintenance by applying to the magistrates' court to seize their goods, attach their earnings, or even commit them to prison. The Agency will take on this role upon an application by either the parent having care of the child, or by the non-resident parent. Where the parent with care is in receipt of state benefits, she is presumed to have authorised the Agency to collect maintenance, and must provide the necessary information to enable it to do so. This provision is necessary because many women and children will be no better off if maintenance is collected from the father, as every pound collected will be offset by a reduction in their benefits. On the other hand, they are likely to lose the cooperation and support of the father as a result, or suffer renewed harassment from a man they would rather forget all about. Not surprisingly, therefore, many women consider the collection of maintenance to be more trouble that it is worth, and that it actually operates to the detriment of them and the child. The only exception to the rule is when the Agency considers that there are reasonable grounds for believing that the parent with care, or any child living with her, would be at risk of suffering harm or undue distress. If the parent with care cannot prove this but still refuses to cooperate, her benefits can be reduced according to a maximum amount and period set out in detailed regulations. The provision was carefully worded so that it depends upon whether the Agency considers that a refusal to cooperate is justified or not, not whether it is, in fact, justified. Some additional support is available for parents with care (see 4.3.6 below). The new scheme will apply to new cases as from the date of implementation, and to existing liabilities after a transition period. Parents will still be able to have agreed orders made by the court, but after an agreement has been in force for 12 months an application can be made for a Child Support Agency assessment after giving two months notice to the other parent.

4.3.3 The statutory formula

The Child Support Pensions and Social Security Act 2000 replaces the original formula with a simpler system for calculating maintenance liability. The net income of the non-resident parent (NRP) is calculated by deducting tax, insurance and pension contributions. The NRP must then pay 15 per cent of net income for one child, 20 per cent for two and 25 per cent for three or more children. The maximum figure for assessment purposes is fixed at £2,000 per week at present, but this figure can be changed by regulation. This means that, in effect, the maximum amount payable per week at present is £300 for one child, £400 for two children and £500 for three or more. If the NRP earns under £200 per week net, a lesser percentage is payable. Under £100 per week only a fixed sum is paid. The minimum sum payable is £5 per week, although there are some circumstances where a 'nil rate' is payable (e.g. where net income is under £5 per week or the NRP is a prisoner).

4.3.4 Deductions

Reductions will be allowed if the NRP has a second family and for any time that the NRP looks after the children over 52 days per year (i.e. during staying contact). Where there is a second family, the NRP's net income is reduced by the same percentage as for the basic assessment. Thus, a NRP with two children but living in another relationship with three children would have his net income reduced by 25 per cent and would then have to pay 20 per cent of that figure for his own two children.

> EXAMPLE
>
> A man has left his wife and three children and is now living with another woman and her two children. His net income is £350 per week. This is reduced by 20 per cent because of his new responsibilities for two children, leaving £280 per week net. He must pay 25 per cent of this for his own three children, i.e. £70 per week.

If the NRP's children stay with him for 52 nights of the year, the amount payable is reduced by one-seventh; 104 to 155 nights, by two-sevenths; 156 to 174 nights, by three-sevenths; and 175 or more nights, by one-half. If the NRP's net income is less than £100 per week and his children stay with him for 52 nights or more, nothing is payable.

> EXAMPLE
>
> The man in the first example has his own children to stay with him every other week-end, totalling 52 nights over the course of the year. He would only have to pay six-sevenths of £70, i.e. £60 per week.

4.3.5 Applications for variation

This replaces the departures system (4.3.1 above) and will allow special expenses relating to other forms of support of the child, contact arrangements or other special circumstances.

EXAMPLE

These could be expenses for the care of a chronically sick or disabled child; debts incurred for the child before maintenance was payable; boarding school fees.

On the other hand, the residential parent can ask for an increase where there are suspicious circumstances concerning the NRP's purported income (e.g., there is evidence that income has been diverted or has not been declared). Applications for variation must be made to a special tribunal.

4.3.6 Additional support
Parents receiving working families tax credit will have child support payments disregarded, so that there will be no corresponding deduction from their benefits. Enforcement of assessments has also been toughened up considerably, with new powers of investigation and penalties (including criminal offences) for non-compliance.

4.3.7 Disputes
Appeals against assessments can be made to a Child Support Appeal Tribunal, and thereafter to a Child Support Commissioner, but only to deal with mistakes of fact or law, such as incorrect calculations. Disputes about parentage must be dealt with through the courts. Every parent is liable for an assessment under the Act, whether the parents are divorced, separated or have never lived together at all; and whether they are married or unmarried. 'Parent' is not defined precisely under the Act, but under s. 26(2), parenthood can be assumed if there is an existing court order establishing that fact, or if the person has adopted the child. There are also special provisions covering Scotland and procedures under the Human Fertilisation and Embryology Act 1990. If a person denies that he is the child's father then a child support officer must apply to the court under s. 27 for the appropriate declaration, whereupon the court will consider all the evidence as to parenthood.

4.3.8 Criticisms
The new system has all the virtues of simplicity and clarity, but has to pay the price of seeming rather crude at times. The danger is that this could give rise to discord between the parents which would inevitably affect their relationship with the children. For example, the income of the parent with care is completely disregarded, no matter how much higher it may be than that of the NRP. Although it is arguable that the costs of maintaining a child remain the same and the NRP should always pay a proportion of that cost, in practice this could lead to ill-feeling where there is a clear discrepancy in income. Similarly, the direct link between the amounts payable and the extent of overnight contact goes against previous practice. The parent with care may be aggrieved because her basic overheads are not reduced merely because the children are away for a night or two, but her income will be. The NRP may be tempted to demand staying contact merely to reduce his payments, not considering the best interests of the children or his new family. Finally, the reductions for children in the NRP's new household will inevitably seem unfair to the parent with care, especially if

they are children from the NRP's new partner's previous relationship(s). It may be thought that these problems are insuperable, however, and certainly the practitioner should be aware of the gap that exists between how people should think and behave where children are concerned, and how they think and behave in reality. Parents paying maintenance for their children often relate it to the amount of contact they have with them, and are more likely to keep up payments if they feel they are 'getting something out of it'. They also form new relationships and have to balance their new lives with their responsibilities to their former families. The reality is that income may be limited and the present household is the one they live in all day, every day; their own children live on the other side of town and they now only see them once or twice a week. In those circumstances it is not easy to keep their different responsibilities clear and distinct. The scheme certainly recognises some of these realities, but whether it is merely creating new problems may require the benefits of hindsight.

4.4 Child maintenance, the courts and the Child Support Act 1991

4.4.1 Introduction
To conclude this section it is useful to review the division of responsibility for child maintenance between the courts and the Child Support Agency. The basic rule is that, under the Child Support Act 1991, s. 8, no court shall exercise its normal powers to make, vary or revive a child maintenance order. It may, however, revoke such an order. There are various exceptions, however, which will now be outlined.

4.4.2 Children of the family
As the Child Support Act 1991 applies only to natural parents, the courts will still need to consider maintenance for step-children, or any other children who come under the wider definition of 'child of the family'. A wide discretion is needed to assess maintenance in these cases, because of the many factors that need to be considered under the relevant guidelines (see *Financial Provision after a Final Decree*, 2.8, and *Financial Provision in the Family Proceedings Court*, 4.1).

4.4.3 Children over 19
Some children in full-time higher education may still need maintenance, but are outside the scope of the Act (see 4.3.2 above).

4.4.4 Non-maintenance orders
The Child Support Act 1991 applies only to periodical payments orders. It will still be necessary to apply to the courts for other financial relief for a child, such as a lump-sum order, security or transfer of property order.

4.4.5 Additional calculations
As noted in 4.3.3 above, there is a ceiling for assessment where the non-resident parent has a large income. In such cases it is possible for the courts to 'top up' the Child Support Agency assessment by making an additional order.

4.4.6 Special needs

If there are special expenses associated with the maintenance of the child because of school or other education fees, or a particular disability, the court can be asked to make an order in addition to the Child Support Agency assessment to cover those expenses. The new system of applications for variation (see 4.3.5 above) should remove much of the need for such cases, however.

Questions

1   Alan and Susan were married last year. Alan did not want to get married, but Susan threatened to report his father to the police for fraud unless he agreed. Four weeks ago Susan suffered a stroke, and has been been in a coma ever since. Alan has now learned that her condition is irreversible, and he seeks your advice as to whether he can end the marriage.

Outline answer

(a) The marriage appears valid on the face of it, and therefore the only methods of terminating it will be by nullity or divorce proceedings.

(b) Outline the law of nullity by reference to the Matrimonial Causes Act 1973, s. 12. Distinguish an annulled marriage from a void marriage.

(c) A possible ground for annulling the marriage is Alan's lack of consent. Explain the law relating to duress, referring to *Hirani* v *Hirani* (1982) and *Singh* v *Singh* (1971). Was Alan's will overcome by Susan's threat? How realistic was her threat? Does it matter how real her threat was, if Alan was completely affected by it?

(d) Divorce may be another possibility if they have been married for 12 months. Outline the law of divorce by reference to the Matrimonial Causes Act 1973, s. 1.

(e) The 'fact' which could be used here is that relating to Susan's behaviour, under s. 1(2)(b). Explain the subjective and objective approach as in *Pheasant* v *Pheasant* (1972). What is the effect of Susan's illness on Alan? Explain the problem of purely negative behaviour and refer to *Thurlow* v *Thurlow* (1976) and *Carter-Fea* v *Carter-Fea* (1987). Is Susan's condition 'behaviour' for the purposes of the 1973 Act?

(f) Conclude by summarising your advice to Alan.

2   John and Linda have been married for six months and have one child aged two months. Linda was pregnant by another man when she married John, but he was aware that the baby was not his. John is employed as an accountant, but is now refusing to give Linda any more housekeeping for the baby, saying that he does not see why he should support someone else's child. He has also started shouting and swearing at Linda for no reason, and refusing to talk to her apart from that. Advise Linda as to how she may obtain financial provision from John without having to start divorce proceedings.

3   Floyd and Gina have been married for ten years and have two children aged six and four. Floyd is employed as a carpenter on a low wage. Gina is unemployed, but used to work as a secretary before she had the children. The house is in Floyd's sole name, and is worth £10,000 after deducting the outstanding mortgage. Floyd and Gina are getting divorced and Gina is to look after the children.

(a) Explain what financial provision could be awarded to Gina, and the matters that would be taken into account by the court.

(b) Outline briefly how maintenance for the children would be dealt with.

4   Explain, with reference to decided cases, the orders available under the Children Act 1989, s. 8, for regulating the residence of children or contact with them.

5   Discuss whether the law relating to capacity to marry unreasonably restricts the freedom of every person to marry the partner of their choice.

4

Wills, Probate and Succession

Introduction

The distribution of a person's 'estate' (i.e., possessions including land) depends on whether the person died testate (i.e., having made a valid will which is still in existence at the date of death), or intestate (i.e., without leaving a valid will in existence at the date of death). Recent figures show that as few as one third of persons capable of making a will have in fact done so. There may be many reasons for not making a will but there are very important reasons why a person should make a will, not the least of which is that by making a will a person ensures that his or her estate will pass to the persons whom he or she chooses (the beneficiaries). If a person does not leave a valid will then statute (the Administration of Estates Act 1925, as amended) specifies who is entitled to inherit that person's estate on his or her death.

This chapter will cover, individually, the following eight topics:

(1) Introductory principles covering the formalities and validity of wills and codicils.

(2) Main clauses in a will.

(3) *Gifts contained in wills*. The different types of gift which may be made by will, and both the effect of a beneficiary dying before (predeceasing) a testator and the effect of the testator disposing, prior to his death, of items which he has specifically mentioned in his will.

(4) Revocation of wills.

(5) *Intestacy*. Dealing with the distribution of an estate where there is no valid will or the will does not dispose of the whole of the estate. This section also covers the types of gift which are often referred to as 'death bed gifts', more properly termed 'donationes mortis causa'. This type of gift falls between 'inter vivos' gifts, i.e., lifetime gifts and gifts contained in a will. There are certain specific requirements which must be met for such a 'death bed gift' to be effective.

(6) *Personal representatives*. In outline, the types of formal papers or 'grant' which must be applied for by the personal representatives, who are the people who have the job of sorting out a deceased person's estate. Personal representatives

will be either executors named in a valid will or administrators where there is an intestacy (i.e., where a person dies intestate), or where there is a valid will of which, for some reason, there are no executors (e.g., the persons named as executors have predeceased the testator).

There are three basic types of grant. These are:

(a) grant of probate—where executors prove a will;

(b) grant of letters of administration—where a person dies intestate and administrators obtain the grant;

(c) grant of letters of administration with will annexed—where there is a valid will of which there are no proving executors and administrators obtain the grant.

This section will also cover the powers and responsibilities of personal representatives.

(7) *Inheritance (Provision for Family and Dependants) Act 1975.* When, and by whom, a claim may be made against the estate of a deceased person by a person who has not been specifically provided for either under the terms of a will or the rules of intestacy.

(8) *Inheritance tax.* An introduction to inheritance tax, being the relevant tax in respect of the estate of a deceased person. It will be seen later, however, that not all estates actually end up being liable to pay inheritance tax as there are important statutory exemptions and reliefs.

Introductory principles—formalities and validity

1 Wills and codicils

1.1 Wills

A will is a testamentary document, that is a document (not a deed) by which a person (the testator) sets out his requirements and wishes regarding the administration (the collection of the assets and payment of the debts and liabilities) and the ultimate disposal of his estate. The will must comply with the statutory requirements of the Wills Act 1837 (as amended) to be valid. Briefly, it must be in writing, signed by the testator and witnessed by two people (these requirements will be explained in detail later in this chapter). In the absence of such compliance it will not be enforceable. See the specimen will set out on pp. 407–409 for an example of a simple will.

1.2 Codicils

A codicil is a testamentary document made subsequent to a valid will, which amends or adds to the will. The codicil must state that it is made subsequent to the will and any previous codicils and it must comply with the same formal requirements as a will. A codicil may deal either with the dispositions contained in the will (e.g., by adding or deleting legacies) or with formalities covered by the will (e.g., the appointment of executors or amendments to the trustee powers).

EXAMPLE

Arthur makes a will leaving legacies of £100 each to his nephew John and his niece Jill. Two years after making his will another nephew, Richard, is born and Arthur wishes to leave a similar legacy to him. This can be done by a codicil rather than a new will.

The reasons for making a will and the reasons for the dispositions in it are irrelevant to its validity. If, for example, the testator wishes to make it clear that he does not wish a person to benefit, this will not invalidate the will.

EXAMPLE

'I wish to record in my will, for the avoidance of doubt, that I have intentionally made no provision for my son William in my will because I do not believe he deserves anything from me.'

Any personal comments or explanations are not prohibited but are more usually contained in a letter placed with the will.

2 Capacity

In order for a will to be valid the testator must have the necessary testamentary capacity; that is, he must be:

(a) over the age of 18; and

(b) of sound mind, i.e., he must not be mentally incapable.

Subsequent failing of mental capacity will not affect a valid will, but if there is any doubt as to mental capacity it should be settled by taking medical advice. It may be helpful to have the testator's doctor as one of the witnesses to the will because, if the validity of a will is in doubt, an affidavit of due execution (that is a statement sworn on oath concerning the circumstances surrounding the signing of the will) will be required by the court before a grant of probate will be issued, and the appropriate persons to make such an affidavit are the witnesses to the will.

Affidavits of due execution, types of grant and method of application are discussed more fully later.

3 *Animus testandi* (intention of making a will)

Although a will may be valid on the face of it, it will be invalid if the testator did not have the necessary intention to make a will, or if any undue influence or fraud was used to cause him to make his will. If it is claimed that either undue influence or fraud was used to persuade the testator to make his will, it is up to the person making the claim to substantiate it. There is no automatic presumption of undue influence.

EXAMPLE

A is a wealthy but frail old man. He is persuaded by his nurse B to make a will leaving everything to B. A takes no independent advice and B provides the witnesses to the will.

A's children contest the will but would have to prove undue influence to rebut the presumption that the will was validly executed. Suspicion alone is not enough.

However, where a will is prepared by a person who is to receive a substantial gift under the terms of the will, the court will require evidence that the testator knew what he was doing and understood the effect of the will and the gift.

A testator should know, and understand the effect of, the contents of his will. Although a testator may have thought out what he requires in his will, discussion and explanation will be needed if his requirements are affected by statutory provisions.

EXAMPLE

Richard wishes to leave everything to his son but does not wish to make any provision for what should happen to his estate in the event of his son predeceasing him.

Any gifts to issue (i.e., direct lineal descendants, which means only children and their children and their children and so on) are governed by s. 33, Wills Act 1837. Section 33 provides that, in the absence of a contrary provision in the will, any gift by a person to his issue (i.e. direct lineal descendants) which fails, will pass to any issue of the proposed beneficiary alive at the death of the testator. This may not represent the testator's requirements and it should be explained that, in order to avoid this, a 'substitutionary' gift, that is a provision as to what should happen if the beneficiary predeceases, should be made. Such a substitutionary gift is a sufficient indication of contrary intention to prevent s. 33 taking effect.

EXAMPLE

If in the previous example Richard had provided that in the event of his son predeceasing him everything was to go to a named charity, this would have been a contrary intention and would prevent s. 33 applying.

4 Preparing the will

Instructions for a will should always be taken from the testator or confirmed with him. If someone purports to be giving instruction for a third party it may be that the third party does not know or approve of the instructions and would be surprised to receive a draft of his supposed will!

Usually a draft will, that is the first copy of the will prepared in accordance with the testator's instructions and containing any necessary formalities, is prepared for approval by the testator. This is then either submitted to him for approval, or he is invited to make an appointment to call at the solicitor's office to discuss the contents of the draft before a final print of the will is prepared for signature. This final print is known as the engrossment and it must be signed by the testator in accordance with the formalities required by the Wills Act 1837 as amended by the Administration of Justice Act 1982.

Any unusual or complicated requirements or technical clauses must be carefully explained as clearly as possible to ensure that the testator is fully aware of the implications of the terms and requirements set out in his will.

EXAMPLE

The additional trustee powers often set out in a will are by their very nature technical, but they are included so as to give the trustees more freedom in the exercise of their duties under the terms of the will than they are given by statute. To understand the additional or extended powers the statutory powers and their effect must also be explained. (See specimen draft will on pp. 407–409 for extended trustee powers and *Main Clauses in a Will.*)

5   Statutory requirements for a valid will

To be valid a will must comply with the statutory formalities required by s. 9, Wills Act 1837, as amended, which states:

No will shall be valid unless—

(a) it is in writing, and signed by the testator, or by some other person in his presence and by his direction; and

(b) it appears that the testator intended by his signature to give effect to the will; and

(c) the signature is made or acknowledged by the testator in the presence of two or more witnesses present at the same time; and

(d) each witness either—

  (i)   attests and signs the will; or

  (ii) acknowledges his signature, in the presence of the testator (but not necessarily in the presence of any other witnesses),

but no form of attestation shall be necessary.

Note that the original s. 9 was replaced by s. 17, Administration of Justice Act 1982 as regards deaths after 1 January 1983. (It does not affect wills of testators who died before that date.)

5.1   'In writing and signed by the testator'

This means that the will must be in writing. The will can take any form whether it is handwritten or printed and may be produced on anything from a stationer's will form, to a piece of paper, to a form produced by a solicitor. A handwritten will is known as a 'holograph' will. There is no particular form or order of wording which is required to make a valid will, although normally the first clauses deal with the revocation of earlier wills and the appointment of executors and trustees; subsequent clauses deal with the disposition of the estate and later clauses deal with trustee powers.

5.1.1 Who may sign a will?

Section 9(a) of the Wills Act 1837 provides that the will may be signed by the testator or 'by some other person in his presence and by his direction'. This means that if a will purports to be signed by someone other than the testator it must be clear that it was with the knowledge of the testator and at his request. In such a case the attestation clause should specify the circumstances under which the will was signed and witnessed. All wills should contain an attestation clause but s. 9 specifically provides that one is not required for the validity of the will.

> EXAMPLE
>
> An attestation clause to be used where a testator is blind and someone signs on his behalf might read as follows:
>
> Signed by A with the name of the testator (after the will had been read over to him and he had indicated his full understanding and approval of it) by his direction and in his presence and ours and then by us in his presence.

5.1.2 Position of the testator's signature

Prior to 1983 a will had to be signed 'at the foot or end thereof or in such a way at or under or beside or opposite to the end that it was apparent that the testator intended to give effect to his will' (s. 9, Wills Act 1837, as amended by the Wills Act 1852). Section 9, as now amended, sets out the present requirements concerning the position of the testator's signature on a will, and s. 9(b) provides that as long as the testator intended his signature to give effect to the will, then it will be valid no matter where it is signed. This means that the signature no longer has to be 'at the foot or end thereof', although in practice it usually is.

However, a 1991 case has raised the question of whether the testamentary dispositions must be set out before the testator signs the will. In _Wood v Smith_ (1991), the testator made a handwritten will two days before he died which commenced 'my will by Percy Winterbone'. It was witnessed but the testator did not add his signature again at the end. At the first hearing it was held by the deputy Chancery Division judge that the writing of the name was a signature, but that the will was invalid as no dispositions existed at the time the signature was made, the signature being at the head of an otherwise blank piece of paper.

On appeal (1992), the Court of Appeal held that, provided the signing and writing of the subsequent dispositions all formed part of one operation, as in this case, then it would be a valid will. (Students should note that the appeal failed on other grounds.)

5.1.3 Meaning of 'signature'

The signature does not have to be a signed name. A signature can be made by a mark commonly, but not always, a cross, and thumb prints or initials have been accepted as signatures. However, great care is required where a signature comprises only a set of initials. Where alterations are made in the body of a will (e.g. manuscript alterations of typing errors) then the alterations are initialled by the testator and the witnesses to signify that those alterations were made before the will was signed. If the signature to the will comprises only the testator's initials, then it must be made absolutely clear that those initials are intended to be a signature in respect of the whole will.

The will may be signed on the testator's behalf by some other person, even by one of the witnesses, so long as it is at the testator's 'direction and in his presence'. Therefore a testator can ask someone else to sign for him and on his behalf, but the testator himself must be present when such signature is made and the attestation clause must state the circumstances (see the previous example of the attestation clause for a blind testator who does not sign for himself). This means that no-one can sign a will for a person without that person being present.

5.2 'The signature is made or acknowledged by the testator in the presence of two or more witnesses present at the same time'

5.2.1 Acknowledgment of testator's signature

Nothing alters the basic necessity that, in order for a will to be valid, it must be signed by the testator in the presence of two witnesses. However, s. 9 of the Wills Act 1837 extends the meaning of signature to include 'acknowledgement' of a signature which was made prior to the execution. If a testator signs his will he may then acknowledge that signature to the two witnesses who must both be present at the time of acknowledgement and they must see the signature.

> EXAMPLE
>
> A writes out his will during the morning and signs it but has no witnesses present. In the afternoon B and C call on A. A shows his will to them and points to the signature, saying, 'that is my signature' or words to that effect. In A's presence B and C then sign the will as witnesses. A's will has been validly executed.

Contrast this with the position where A writes his will in the morning and signs it but has no witnesses present. B calls on A in the afternoon and A acknowledges his signature to B who signs as a witness and leaves. In the evening C calls on A, who again acknowledges his signature and C signs as the second witness. The will has not been validly executed because B and C were not both present at the same time when the signature was acknowledged.

5.2.2 Acknowledgment of witness's signature

If a witness has signed before the testator, the witness may also subsequently acknowledge his signature in the presence of the testator. Section 9(d), Wills Act 1837 provides that the witnesses must sign or acknowledge their signatures in the presence of the testator, but not necessarily in the presence of each other.

5.2.3 Attestation clause

Although an attestation clause is not required by law, it is normal practice to use one and the usual attestation clauses all provide for the will to be signed by the testator in the presence of the witnesses who then sign in the presence of the testator and of each other.

EXAMPLE

'Signed by the above named Arthur Jones in our presence and attested by us in the presence of him and of each other.'

5.3 Competence of witnesses

A witness must not be blind and must not be of unsound mind. Both witnesses must be present when the testator signs the will, or acknowledges his signature and both witnesses must either see the testator signing the will or see the testator's signature if he acknowledges it. It is not necessary for the witnesses to read or know the contents of the will but, since the witnesses must either see the testator signing or see his signature, a blind person cannot be a competent witness.

5.3.1 May a beneficiary be a witness?

Under s. 15 of the Wills Act 1837 a beneficiary who witnesses a will, or whose spouse witnesses a will, loses his beneficial interest. However, under s. 1 of the Wills Act 1968 if the will is validly executed without that witness, then the beneficial interest is saved (e.g. if there were more than two witnesses).

EXAMPLE

A makes a will which includes a gift to B. Unusually there are three witnesses to the will, B, C and D. Section 15 of the Wills Act 1837 would mean that B cannot inherit his gift on A's death, but s. 1 of the Wills Act 1968 saves B's gift because there were two other witnesses.

It is worth noting in this respect that s. 9 of the Wills Act 1837 specifically provides that the testator's signature must be made in the presence of 'two or more witnesses . . .'. It is, however, unusual for there to be more than two witnesses.

6 Privileged wills (wills of soldiers on actual military service and sailors at sea)

Although under normal circumstance s. 9 of the Wills Act 1837 must be complied with for a will to be valid, s. 11 of the Wills Act 1837 and s. 3 of the Wills (Soldiers and Sailors) Act 1918 enables soldiers on actual military service and seamen at sea to make a valid will, even though they are unable to comply with s. 9; for example, there may be no witnesses available, or it may not be possible to make a written will. Such privileged testators may be under the age of 18 and the will remains valid even after the end of service. Any such will is revoked by the testator's subsequent marriage in the same way as a will made in normal circumstances is so revoked.

Any form of words is acceptable for a privileged will so long as it is clear from the words used that the testator intended them to have testamentary effect, that is, that he intended to make a will.

By s. 5(2) of the Wills (Soldiers and Sailors) Act 1918 the word 'soldier' is deemed to include a member of the Royal Air Force.

The courts have interpreted the phrases 'actual military service' and 'sailors at sea' in various cases and have found seamen to have been at sea even though they were on leave and on shore during or prior to a voyage, but not where they were ashore on leave and not under instructions to join a ship.

Re Rapley (1983)

The court held that a 15-year-old seaman who made an unwitnessed will when not under instructions to join a ship was not 'at sea' and the will was held to be invalid.

In another case the courts considered that a soldier was on actual military service even though no war had actually been declared.

Re Jones (Deceased) (1981)

A soldier stationed in Northern Ireland, who was fatally injured, made a verbal will in the presence of two officers in favour of his fiancée. This was held to be a valid will even though he had made a previous formal will and even though no state of war had been declared at the time the privileged will was made.

SPECIMEN WILL

THIS IS THE LAST WILL of me Joseph Porter of Ship House Sea Lane Littleisland

[handwritten margin note: Revocation]

    1 I HEREBY REVOKE all former testamentary dispositions previously made by me

[handwritten margin note: Executor]

    2 I APPOINT my Wife Josephine Porter the sole Executrix of this Will but if she shall predecease me or shall be unwilling or unable to prove it or shall die without having proved it then I APPOINT Ralph Rackstraw and Jane Rackstraw both of The Cabin Sea Lane Littleisland to be the Executors and Trustees hereof

[handwritten margin note: Trustees but allowing for other people to take over]

    3 IN THIS Will the expression 'my Trustees' shall where the context permits mean its trustees for the time being whether they are original additional or substituted or (where the context requires) my Personal Representatives for the time being

[handwritten margin note: guardians]

    4 IF my wife the said Josephine Porter does not survive me I APPOINT the said Ralph Rackstraw and the said Jane Rackstraw to be the guardians of any child of mine who is a minor at my death

[handwritten margin note: estate but allowing for debts to be settled]

    5 I GIVE all my estate (out of which shall be paid my funeral and testamentary expenses my debts (and legacies) and all Inheritance Tax payable on or by reason of my death in respect of my estate):

    (a) To my said Wife if she shall survive me for the period of twenty one days

    (b) If my said Wife shall not survive me for that period or the gift should otherwise fail then to my Trustees:

(i)   Upon trust as to such estate (which together with the property representing it for the time being is referred to in this Will as 'the Trust Fund') to
sell it or (if they see fit and without being liable for loss) to retain it or any
part of it in the state in which it is at the time of my death and

(ii) To hold the Trust Fund upon trust absolutely for such of my children
living at my death as shall reach the age of eighteen years and if more than
one in equal shares But if any child of mine shall die (whether in my
lifetime or after my death) before attaining a vested interest but leaving a
child or children alive at or born after my own death who shall reach the
age of eighteen years then such child or children shall take absolutely and
if more than one in equal shares so much of the Trust Fund as that child
of mine would have taken had such child lived to attain a vested interest

(iii) If the Trust Fund shall not vest absolutely in some person or persons
under the preceding trusts then the Trust Fund (subject to the trust
powers and provisions hereby or by statute vested in my Trustees in
respect thereof and to every exercise of the same by my Trustees) shall be
held by my Trustees in trust for The Royal National Lifeboat Institution

6 MY TRUSTEES shall have the following powers in addition to their powers
under the general law:

(a)   To raise at any time and from time to time the whole or any part of the vested
or contingent share or shares in the Trust Fund of any beneficiary hereunder
and pay the same to or apply the same for the advancement maintenance
education or otherwise for the benefit of him or her

(b)   To invest trust money and transpose investments with the same unrestricted
freedom in their choice of investment as if they were absolute owners beneficially entitled and to purchase retain or improve a house or other dwelling for
the occupation of anyone who is or could become a beneficiary under the trust

(c)   To insure against loss or damage by fire or from any other risk any property for
the time being comprised in the Trust Fund to any amount and to pay the
insurance premiums out of the income or capital of the Trust Fund or the
property itself and any money received by my Trustees under such a policy
shall be treated as if it were the proceeds of sale of the property insured

(d)   To exercise all the powers of appropriation and other incidental powers conferred on personal representatives by Section 41 of the Administration of
Estates Act 1925 without any of the consents required by that section and even
though one or more of them may be beneficially entitled

(e)   To permit any trustee who is a professional or business man to charge and be
paid all usual professional and other fees for work done by him or his firm
including work which a trustee not being a professional or business man could
have done personally

(f)   To treat as income all the income from any part of my estate whatever the

[handwritten margin notes: "absolutely meaning with No conditions attached"; "So if one dies before age 18 the share will not pass to its estate but pass to the remaining survivors in equal part"]

period in respect of which it shall accrue and to disregard the Apportionment Act 1870 and any Act replacing it and the rules of Equity relating to apportionments

AS WITNESS my hand this   day of   Two thousand and .....
SIGNED by the above named Joseph Porter ⎤
in our presence and attested by us in   ⎬
the presence of him and of each other   ⎦

Main clauses in a will

---

1 Introduction

A formal will consists of clauses dealing with the formalities and clauses dealing with the disposition of the testator's estate.

The formalities include the appointment of executors, the expression of any wishes concerning funeral arrangements, the extension of trustee powers and the revocation of any former wills.

2 The revocation of former wills

A will normally contains an express revocation of any former wills and codicils made by the testator. If the current will disposes of the whole of the testator's estate, that is, it includes a residuary gift of the whole of his estate not otherwise disposed of by the will or by any codicil, then this would serve as an automatic revocation of any earlier will, but it is normal to include an express revocation. This is often incorporated as either the first or the last clause in the will.

EXAMPLE

'I hereby revoke all former testamentary dispositions previously made by me.'

3 Appointment of executors

Amongst the earlier provisions in the will is normally the appointment of the executors. This may be an appointment of only executors or, as is more common, an appointment of executors and trustees. Many wills appoint the same person as both executor and trustee and a combined clause is normally used.

EXAMPLE

'I appoint A of . . . and B of . . . to be the executors and trustees of this my will.'

However, if a testator wishes to appoint separate trustees, there will be a separate clause.

EXAMPLE

'I appoint A of . . . and B of . . . to be the executors of this my will and I appoint C of . . . and D of . . . to be the trustees hereof.'

In some circumstances a testator may wish to appoint 'special executors' to deal with specific parts of his estate, e.g., he may wish to appoint a literary executor to deal only with his literary works, or a business executor to deal only with his business interests.

EXAMPLE

'I appoint A of . . . to be the executor of this my will to administer only my literary estate . . .'

Such a clause will usually define 'literary estate' and indicate which part of the estate should bear the cost of obtaining the grant to the literary estate.

Anyone may be appointed as an executor but a grant will not be made to anyone who lacks capacity, i.e., a minor or a person of unsound mind (see *Personal Representatives*).

4 Funeral arrangements and special wishes concerning a body

If the testator has some specific requirements concerning the disposal of his body, or specific wishes as to funeral or cremation requirements, these may be included towards the beginning of the will so that they are quickly obvious to anyone reading the will. Such requirements however, can only be expressed as 'wishes' of the testator and are not binding on his executors.

If a testator includes these wishes only in his will it is possible that funeral arrangements may be made before anyone becomes aware of them. It is preferable, therefore, for such wishes to be made known to the executors, or to the testator's family, in addition to or instead of including them in the will. This will at least ensure that someone is aware of the wishes and can take them into consideration before making the funeral arrangements.

5 Appointment of guardians

If the testator wishes to appoint guardians in respect of his minor children this appointment is normally found towards the beginning of the will.

Since the Children Act 1989 the word 'guardian' only describes someone who is not a parent of the child. Under the Act a parent has the right to appoint a guardian to act on his death only if the parent has parental responsibility for the child.

Where a child's parents were married to one another at the time of the child's birth each parent has parental responsibility. In other cases the mother has parental responsibility, but the father does not have it unless he acquires it under the Act, which he may do either by court order or by agreement between the parents.

If a surviving parent has parental responsibility the responsibility continues and the appointment of the guardian by the will of the deceased parent does not normally take effect until there is no such surviving parent. Only when there is no parent with parental responsibility will the appointment of the guardian take effect. At that stage the guardian himself acquires parental responsibility.

6 Dispositions in the will

The above clauses deal with the non-beneficial matters in the will. Having dealt with those matters it is then usual to set out the dispositions required by the testator. These dispositions can range from a simple gift of the whole estate to a single beneficiary, to a whole series of different gifts to a wide variety of beneficiaries.

The gifts may include 'pecuniary legacies' (gifts of sums of money; see example 1 below) and 'specific legacies' (gifts of particular described items; see example 2 below). See also the specimen will on pp. 407–409.

EXAMPLE

1 'I give free of tax to A the sum of £250.'

EXAMPLE

2 'I give free of tax to B my grandfather clock.'

7 Extension of trustee powers

(*References in the examples in 7 are to the clauses in the specimen will on pp. 407–409.*) Trusts may sometimes arise under the terms of a will, e.g., because there are minority interests (i.e., gifts to children who may be under the age of 18 at the time the will comes into effect and who will not be able to receive their gift until they attain the age of 18); or life interests (i.e., a gift made to someone only for the period of his life). Where a trust arises the trustees are the people who will look after the estate until someone finally becomes entitled to it in his own right.

The trustees' powers are set out in the Trustee Act 1925 as amended or extended by the Trusts of Land and Appointment of Trustees Act 1996 and the Trustee Act 2000 and as to investment in the Trustee Investment Act 1961 and Part II of the Trustee Act 2000.

The Trustee Act 2000 was the first major reform of trustee legislation since the Trustee Act 1925. Most provisions of the Act came into force on 1 February 2001. The Act operates by default in that its provisions are not meant to replace the use of specific provisions in a will or trust deed but to supplement them with powers which might not be specifically included and in the case of trusts arising on intestacy to provide powers not otherwise given to the trustee.

The Act specifically contains in s. 1 a statutory duty of care which applies whether trustees are using powers given by the Act or other powers. Schedule 1 of the Act contains provisions about when the duty of care is applicable, e.g. when exercising powers of investment, to acquire land, to delegate, or to insure, however conferred. The duty itself is defined by s. 1 which states that whenever the duty applies a trustee must:

exercise such care and skill as is reasonable in the circumstances having regard in particular:

(a) to any special knowledge or experience that he has or holds himself out as having and

(b) if he acts as Trustee in the course of a business or profession to any special knowledge or experience that it is reasonable to expect of a person acting in the course of that kind of business or profession

Although the Trustee Act 2000 includes or extends powers set out in the earlier Acts it does not preclude the need for powers to be included in a will or trust deed. Some common extensions of trustee powers are considered below.

7.1 Powers of maintenance and advancement

EXAMPLE

Clause 6(a) of the specimen will.

Section 31 of the Trustee Act 1925 permits trustees to use income from trust property for 'the maintenance education and benefit . . . ' of a minor, whether he has a vested interest (i.e., he is absolutely entitled to the trust property but cannot give a valid receipt for it until he is 18), or a contingent interest (i.e., the gift is made subject to the beneficiary meeting a specified contingency, frequently the attaining of a certain age). If the interest is contingent then the income cannot be used if someone else is entitled to it in the meantime.

Under s. 31 any unused income must be accumulated, i.e. added to the capital. It is in fact s. 31 which permits accumulation.

The powers under s. 31 are often extended by the will to enable the trustees to use income which has been accumulated as if it were income from the current year for the specified purposes.

EXAMPLE

A testator may have left his whole estate to his two children subject to their attaining 18, and at the date of his death both are under 18 and both are at public school. Under s. 31 the trustees would be able to use the income from their share in the estate to provide any school fees (assuming that the income was sufficient).

Section 32 of the Trustee Act 1925 concerns capital and under this section trustees are able to advance (i.e., pay to or on behalf of a beneficiary for the purpose of his advancement or benefit) up to one half of the share of capital to which he will become entitled. This power is often extended by the will to enable the trustees to advance the whole of any such sum.

Any sum so advanced has to be brought into account by the beneficiary when he becomes absolutely entitled, i.e., any sums received by way of advancement are deducted from the share of the estate due to him.

EXAMPLE

If in the example for s. 31 above there was not enough income to pay the school fees, then the trustees could use their discretion to advance part of the capital due to make up the shortfall.

7.2 Powers of investment

Although the statutory powers given to trustees have been extended by Part II (ss. 3–7) of the Trustee Act 2000 so as to give trustees power to invest as if they were absolutely entitled to the trust assets, it will still be common practice for the power to invest to be included in the will so as to give the trustees power to invest in such manner as they think fit. Such a clause is often worded so as to enable the trustees to invest as if they were beneficial owners, and means that they can take financial advice and invest accordingly. However, the new statutory duty of care imposed on trustees by the Trustee Act 2000 will apply even if the power to invest is in the will.

EXAMPLE

Clause 6(b) of the specimen will.

7.3 Powers to purchase or retain a residence

Sometimes a testator will require a residence to be retained or purchased so as to provide a home for a beneficiary. Clause 6(b) of the specimen will includes the authority to retain or purchase a property for this purpose as an investment, but if the testator specifically wishes to provide a residence a more detailed clause should be considered. A more detailed clause can be used to set out any additional powers which may be necessary, for example relating to responsibility for the general upkeep and maintenance of the property and the payment of outgoings.

Although the Trusts of Land and Appointment of Trustees Act 1996 gives trustees power to purchase a legal estate in land and by s. 12 gives any beneficiary entitled to an interest in possession in land subject to a trust of land a right to occupy it (if the purposes of the trust include making it available for occupation), and Part III of the Trustee Act 2000 (ss. 8–10) gives trustees power to invest in land in the United Kingdom for specified purposes, it is still wise to include a specific power for trustees to retain or purchase land for this purpose as there may not be any land forming part of the residue.

Section 6 of the 1996 Act sets out the general powers of trustees under the 1996 Act and s. 6(1) provides 'for the purpose of exercising their functions as trustees, the trustees of land have in relation to the land subject to the trust all the powers of an absolute owner'. A testator may therefore wish to exclude or modify the provisions of

s. 6. He may also wish to modify the provisions of s. 12 which give the beneficiary rights of occupation.

7.4 Powers of insurance

Trustees did have power to insure trust property under the original s. 19 of the Trustee Act 1925. However, this only gave a power to insure rather than imposing a duty to do so, and only in respect of loss or damage by fire, and only up to three quarters of the value of the property. By s. 34 of the Trustee Act 2000 a new s. 19 was substituted which gives trustees power to insure trust property against whatever risks they consider appropriate and to pay premiums out of the trust fund *but* as bare trustees are subject to contrary directions by the beneficiaries it will still be better to include a specific provision.

The clause will usually also specify the source from which the premiums may be paid, for example the trust fund or the income from the property insured.

Although s. 6 of the Trusts of Land and Appointment of Trustees Act 1996 gives the trustees powers of an absolute owner and they can therefore insure land, it is still necessary to extend or refer to the powers given under s. 19, Trustee Act 1925 as that still applies to personal property, i.e. everything other than land.

EXAMPLE

Clause 6(c) of the specimen will.

7.5 Powers of appropriation

It is not uncommon for a will to provide that the trustees are entitled to appropriate (i.e. to use) any assets to meet a legacy, without the consent of the beneficiaries of the will. This is an extension of the general power to appropriate given under s. 41, Administration of Estates Act 1925 to personal representatives which requires the consent of the beneficiaries in whose favour the appropriation is made.

EXAMPLE

Clause 6(d) of the specimen will.

7.6 Charging clause

Usually executors are not paid for their work and are only entitled to out of pocket expenses from the estate. Prior to the Trustee Act 2000 if professional executors were appointed (e.g. accountants or solicitors) the will had to contain a charging clause to enable the executors to make a charge for their time and services in connection with the administration of the estate. Without that they would be unable to make their usual professional charges.

However by s. 29 of the Trustee Act 2000 (which does not override express provisions in the will) personal representatives who act in a professional capacity are entitled to receive reasonable remuneration for services provided even if the services are capable of being provided by a lay person. However s. 29 specifically provides that 'each other trustee must agree in writing' to the remuneration which means that a sole personal representative would *not* be covered by the Act and it is still necessary to include a specific provision in the will to enable a sole personal representative to charge for his professional services.

Note also ss. 28 and 30 which provide that charges made by a professional personal representative will be treated as remuneration for services *not* as a gift for the purposes of s. 15, Wills Act 1837 and s. 34, Administration of Estates Act 1925 which means that the benefit of a charging clause will not be lost if a solicitor (or his spouse) witnesses a will which contains a charging clause (s. 28, Trustee Act 2000). These provisions are only effective for deaths after 1 February 2001 in respect of personal representatives.

EXAMPLE

Clause 6(e) of the specimen will.

7.7 Powers to carry on a business

If the testator has a business he may wish to appoint special executors (see *Personal Representatives*) to carry on or to deal with his business, or he may give his trustees extended powers to do this, i.e., by specifying that they are entitled to employ one of their number or any other person to run the business, or to employ any staff required and in some circumstances to use other assets of the estate to enable the business to continue running.

Such powers may be required either to keep the business going in order to sell it as a going concern at some future time, or to preserve the business for a beneficiary who at the time of death is under age.

Without the extended powers, trustees could only do whatever is necessary to enable the business to be sold as part of the general administration of the estate.

In addition to the extended powers to carry on the business, there is usually an indemnity in favour of the trustees, i.e., a provision that they will not be personally liable for any debts incurred in carrying on the business.

8 Attestation clause

If an attestation clause in appropriate form is not included in the will, the Probate Registry will require an affidavit from one or both of the witnesses confirming that the requirements of the Wills Act 1837, as amended, have been complied with.

Gifts contained in Wills

1 Introduction

A testator may use his will to leave gifts to any beneficiary he chooses.

A testator may use his will to make provision for his family and dependants (i.e., persons supported by and dependent on the testator) as well as making gifts to family, friends and others, e.g. charities.

If a testator does not adequately provide in his will for family and dependants then these persons may make a claim under the Inheritance (Provision for Family and Dependants) Act 1975 (see further the section on *Inheritance (Provision for Family and Dependants) Act 1975*).

2 Inheritance tax considerations

Before considering the various types of gift, it is necessary to consider the effects of inheritance tax on testamentary gifts (i.e. gifts set out in wills).

Inheritance tax is considered later in the section on *Inheritance Tax,* but briefly it is the tax which is payable in respect of the estate of a deceased person on the net value of the estate for tax purposes. If the net value of the estate for tax purposes currently exceeds £250,000, then tax is payable at the rate of 40 per cent on the excess over £250,000.

The general rule relating to both real property, i.e. freehold land (also referred to as 'realty') and personal property, i.e. everything other than freehold land (also referred to as 'personalty') under the Inheritance Tax Act 1984 is that all tax for which the personal representatives are responsible falls to be paid out of residue (as it is treated as a general testamentary and administration expense), so long as the property on which it is payable:

(a) is in the UK;

(b) vests in the personal representatives;

(c) was not comprised in a settlement immediately before the testator's death.

This means that if the testator says *nothing* about the tax in his gifts then they will be free of tax so long as they fall within the above description.

However, present day thinking is that it is better to stipulate in respect of each individual gift whether or not it is to be free of tax. This would also make the position clear if in the future the rules are changed.

EXAMPLE

'I GIVE free of tax the sum of ONE HUNDRED POUNDS to my niece ELIZABETH JONES.'

EXAMPLE

'I GIVE subject to tax the sum of ONE HUNDRED POUNDS to my niece ELIZABETH JONES.'

Since jointly owned property does not vest in the personal representatives, a clause in the will which states that all inheritance tax is to be paid out of the residue of the estate will cover the tax due on the value of the deceased's share of such property.

EXAMPLE

'I GIVE all the rest of my estate (out of which shall be paid my funeral and testamentary expenses my debts and legacies and all inheritance tax payable on or in respect of my estate) . . . '

3 Categories of gift

There are two basic categories of testamentary gift although it is common nowadays for wills merely to refer to 'giving'.

EXAMPLE

'I GIVE the sum of ONE HUNDRED POUNDS free of tax . . . '

The two categories of gift are devises, dealing with real property and bequests (or legacies), dealing with personalty. Legacies or bequests may be further divided into:

(a) specific;

(b) general;

(c) demonstrative.

Each of these will be considered separately at 5 below.

4 Gifts of land

4.1 Real property

Real property is land, which includes everything fixed to it and situated above and below it.

A devise of land will not include a gift of leasehold property since strictly speaking leases are personalty.

EXAMPLE

'I DEVISE my freehold property situate and known as Greentrees Lower Hill Glenglade to my son ARTHUR JONES absolutely.'

4.2 Leasehold land

Leasehold land is personalty. Personalty is further subdivided into chattels (i.e. things) real and chattels personal.

A lease is the only thing which can exist as a chattel real but, as it falls within the definition of personalty, a gift which is intended to include a lease must be by bequest.

EXAMPLE

'I BEQUEATH my leasehold property known as Flat 6 Green Road Blackheath free of tax to . . . '

4.3 Distinction between freehold and leasehold

It is important to distinguish between freeholds and leaseholds if the correct terms of gift, i.e. devise and bequest, are to be used. If a gift purports to be a general devise it will not pass leasehold land.

EXAMPLE

'I DEVISE all my land which I may own at the date of my death free of tax to . . . '

In the above example if the testator owns both freehold and leasehold land at the date of his death, the gift as worded will only pass the freehold land even if he intended to give both the freehold and the leasehold land.

In order to pass both the freehold and the leasehold in the above example the gift should either use the word 'give' or both the terms 'devise and bequeath'.

EXAMPLE

'I GIVE all my freehold and leasehold property which I may own at the date of my death free of tax to . . . '

or

'I DEVISE AND BEQUEATH all my freehold and leasehold property which I may own at the date of my death free of tax to . . . '

To be absolutely clear what it is intended to give, it is better to refer to the type of title it is intended to pass, i.e. freehold or leasehold or both. Remember that a testator will not know what type of title to land he may hold at the time of his death and so reference to both is preferable (unless this would not be his intention).

It may be that a testator only wishes certain categories of property owned by him to pass under the terms of a particular gift.

EXAMPLE

Testator only wishes any property he lives in as his principal residence to pass to a particular beneficiary.

The gift can be limited accordingly but can still leave leeway for either freehold or leasehold land to pass, depending on the type of title to the testator's principal private residence held at the date of death.

EXAMPLE

'I GIVE any freehold or leasehold property which I may own and in which I reside as my principal residence at the date of my death free of tax to . . . '

4.4 Other considerations

Two other points should also be considered when drafting a gift of freehold or lease-hold property. These are:

(a) whether the gift is to be free of tax (see 2 above); and

(b) whether the gift is to be free of any mortgage or charge secured on the property at the date of death.

4.4.1 Free of tax or not

To be absolutely clear it is better to state in the gift whatever is required.

EXAMPLE

(a) 'I GIVE any freehold or leasehold property which I may own at the date of my death free of tax to . . . '

or

(b) 'I GIVE any freehold or leasehold property which I may own at the date of my death subject to tax to . . . '

In example (a) above the gift would be free of tax and in example (b) it would be subject to tax. This would mean that when the tax bill in respect of the whole estate has been calculated, a further calculation is required to work out the proportion of the total tax on the estate which is attributable to the gift.

4.4.2 Free of mortgage or charge

Although it is common to provide when dealing with the residue of an estate (i.e., everything which is not specifically disposed of in the will by gifts contained in it) that all 'funeral and testamentary expenses and all inheritance tax' should be paid from the residue, s. 35, Administration of Estates Act 1925 specifically provides that this does *not* include mortgages and charges secured on the deceased's property. Therefore the gift must specify if it is to be free of these.

EXAMPLE

The following words should be added to the clause making the gift of property 'the gift made by this clause is free of any money charged or otherwise secured on the property given . . . ' The clause should then go on to stipulate from where any such charges should be paid e.g. out of residue.

If it is not specifically freed from these charges then the gift passes to the beneficiary subject to these charges and this may not be what the testator intended.

Specific instructions should be taken from the testator as to his requirements on this point. Even if the testator does not have a mortgage or charge at the time of making the will, it should be pointed out to him that circumstances may change and he should bear that in mind when making his will. It should also be pointed out that it may be necessary to consider amending his will in the future if he has not made provision at this stage merely because he does not have a mortgage at the time of making his will, but would wish the property to pass free of mortgages and charges.

Similarly if the testator makes a gift free of charge but subsequently changes his mind, he will need to amend his original gift. This can be done by way of a codicil if appropriate, i.e., if there are no other, or only a few, amendments to the will which, on the whole, remains satisfactory.

4.5 Failure of gifts of property—*ademption*

If a testator makes a gift of a specific property, whether leasehold or freehold, by reference to its address, and he no longer owns that particular property at the date of his death, then the gift will adeem, i.e. fail and the beneficiary will not receive anything.

> EXAMPLE
>
> 'I GIVE my freehold property situate and known as 10 Green Lane Basingstoke free of tax to . . . ' If the testator no longer owns 10 Green Lane at the date of his death the gift will adeem.

The gift will not fail, however, if the testator shows a contrary intention, i.e., he makes a provision to ensure that, even if he does not own a particular property at his death, then the gift is to be of any other property which he may own at the date of his death.

> EXAMPLE
>
> 'I GIVE all that my freehold property situate at and known as 10 Green Lane Basingstoke or any other freehold or leasehold property which I may own at the date of my death to . . . '

The testator may also provide, if he wishes, that if at the time of death he has contracted to sell one property and to buy another, then the one he is buying is to be the property referred to in the gift.

4.6 General considerations

Great care must be taken both in the taking of instructions from the testator and drafting the clauses in the will to deal with the gifts of land. The main points to consider are:

(a) does the testator only want to give his existing property?

(b) does the testator wish to ensure that any property he owns at the date of his death will pass under the gift?

(c) does the testator wish to limit the property, e.g., to include only that in which he resides at the date of his death as his principal or only residence?

(d) what provisions does the testator wish to make if he has contracted to sell a property and to buy another as at the date of his death?

(e) is the gift to be free of or subject to tax?

(f) how are any mortgages or charges on the property to be dealt with?

(g) is the property freehold or leasehold?

5 Legacies or bequests—gifts of personalty

5.1 Specific legacies and ademption

A specific legacy is a gift set out in a will of a specific, clearly identifiable item which must be clearly ascertainable.

EXAMPLE

'I GIVE my three stone diamond engagement ring free of tax to . . . '

So long as the testator has only one ring which meets the description it will be clear what is intended to pass under the gift. It is therefore vitally important that the subject matter of a specific gift is clearly described.

If the gift is of an unspecified item, it will not be a specific gift but a general gift.

EXAMPLE

'I GIVE a three stone diamond ring free of tax to . . . '

5.1.1 Ademption

If a testator gives an item of personalty by will which at the date of death he no longer possesses then the gift is said to *adeem*. This means that the gift fails and nothing will pass to the beneficiary. There is no liability on the estate to provide the item.

Only specific gifts can adeem since general gifts are payable out of the undisposed estate, i.e., out of the residue which consists of all property real and personal not given by specific gift.

5.2 General legacies

A general legacy is a gift of an unspecified item which the testator may or may not possess at the date of his death but which could be purchased to fulfil the gift.

EXAMPLE

'I GIVE a set of four dining chairs free of tax to . . . ' If at the date of death the testator does not possess a set of four dining chairs his personal representatives will have to purchase a set to fulfil the gift. This is in direct contrast to the doctrine of ademption in respect of specific gifts.

5.2.1 Pecuniary legacies

These are a category of general legacy since they are gifts of sums of money out of the general estate (unless they are demonstrative legacies; as to which, see 5.3 below.)

EXAMPLE

'I GIVE the sum of one hundred pounds free of tax to . . . '

5.2.2 Failure of general legacies

General legacies will only fail or be reduced if there is insufficient in the estate to pay all the liabilities and gifts. Such a failure or reduction is known as 'abatement'; see 5.4 below.

5.3 Demonstrative legacies

These are gifts of a general nature which are to be provided from a specific fund.

'I GIVE free of tax a grandfather clock to be purchased out of the monies in my Greenback Building Society account to . . . '

If there is insufficient money in the Greenback Building Society account to buy a grandfather clock then any balance required will have to be found from the residue.

Demonstrative legacies, although payable from a specific fund do not adeem as the gift itself is of a general nature.

5.4 Abatement

If the estate is insolvent, i.e. there is not enough money to meet all the liabilities and gifts set out in the will, then the value of the gifts is reduced or 'abated' to provide enough to meet the liabilities.

The order of abatement, i.e. the order in which the assets in the estate are taken to pay off liabilities, is set out in Schedule 1 to the Administration of Estates Act 1925:

1   Property of the deceased undisposed of by will, subject to the retention thereout of a fund sufficient to meet any pecuniary legacies.

2   Property of the deceased not specifically devised or bequeathed but included (either by a specific or general description) in a residuary gift, subject to the retention out of such property of a fund sufficient to meet any pecuniary legacies, so far as not provided for as aforesaid.

3   Property of the deceased specifically appropriated or devised or bequeathed (either by a specific or general description) for the payment of debts.

4   Property of the deceased charged with, or devised or bequeathed (either by a specific or general description) subject to a charge for the payment of debts.

5   The fund, if any, retained to meet pecuniary legacies.

6   Property specifically devised or bequeathed, rateably according to value.

7   Property appointed by will under a general power, including the statutory power to dispose of entailed interests, rateably according to value.

The Act also provides that the order of abatement may be varied by the terms of the will.

The testator may provide that the specific gifts should be abated first before any pecuniary legacies which would normally abate first.

It will be seen from the list in Schedule 1 above that the last items to be reduced are the actual gifts or legacies in the will, since the liabilities are first met from residue, or any part of the estate of which there is an intestacy, followed by any gifts subject to the payment of liabilities.

So far as the order of discharge of liabilities is concerned, funeral, testamentary and administration expenses have priority followed by secured debts and then other debts, 'preferential debts', e.g., income tax and national insurance taking priority over 'ordinary debts' e.g., telephone bill.

5.5 Lapse

Normally any gift will lapse (i.e. fail) if the beneficiary predeceases the testator, unless the testator has included a contrary intention in the gift.

EXAMPLE

'I GIVE free of tax my gold wristwatch to Arthur Smith.' If Arthur Smith predeceases the testator then the gift fails and falls into residue.

EXAMPLE

'I GIVE free of tax my gold wristwatch to Arthur Smith but if he predeceases me then to John Smith.' If Arthur Smith predeceases the testator but John Smith is alive at the testator's death then John will inherit and the gift will not fail.

It should be noted, however, that s. 33, Wills Act 1837, as amended, provides an exception to the general rule of lapse. This section provides that any gift to issue will not lapse if there is issue of that issue alive at the testator's death (see *Introductory Principles—Formalities and Validity*).

Section 33 only applies to gifts to issue and only applies in the absence of a contrary intention shown in the will.

EXAMPLE

'I GIVE free of tax the sum of one hundred pounds to my son.'

If the son predeceases the testator but leaves a child of his own, alive at the death of the testator, then that child, i.e. the testator's grandchild, will be entitled to the gift. *But* note that a contrary intention would avoid this.

EXAMPLE

'I GIVE free of tax the sum of one hundred pounds to my son but if he shall predecease me then to the Royal National Lifeboat Institution.'

If the son predeceases the testator the gift will not go to the issue but to the substituted beneficiary.

6 Residuary gifts

Although a will may contain gifts of certain items in an estate, not every single item will normally be dealt with individually and a 'residuary gift' is included to deal with everything not specifically mentioned either as a specific or general legacy.

EXAMPLE

'I GIVE all the rest of my estate both real and personal to . . .'

This gift will cover everything not otherwise disposed of in the will and avoids an intestacy as to part of the estate. The residuary gift is a sort of 'sweeping up' clause.

In some wills there are no specific, general or demonstrative gifts, merely a gift of the whole estate which will act in the same way as the residuary gift in that it will pass everything without itemising all the testator's property.

Clause 5 of the specimen will on pp. 407–408 contains the residuary gift. In the first instance the whole residue passes to the testator's spouse absolutely under clause 5(a). Clause 5(b) then provides a substitutionary gift in the event of the gift to the spouse failing. This substitutionary gift passes the residue to the trustees on trust for sale. Although the Trusts of Land and Appointment of Trustees Act 1996 introduced the trust of land, it is still appropriate in residuary gifts to make the gift to trustees 'on trust for sale' because there is no certainty that land will be included in the residue and the 1996 Act does not cover trusts of personal property.

The doctrine of lapse applies to residuary legacies as to other legacies and, if there is no substitutionary beneficiary, then the residue will be distributed according to the rules of intestacy. Again the effect of s. 33, Wills Act 1837 should be borne in mind if the residuary gift is to a child or other issue.

It is not unusual for a will to contain a 'long stop' substitution in respect of the residue; see clause 5(b)(iii) in the specimen will on pp. 407–408. In the absence of any relatives or friends whom the testator may wish to benefit, he may specify, e.g., a charity as the substitutionary beneficiary.

7 The survivorship period

Any gift contained in a will can be made subject to a survivorship period, i.e. the gift will pass to the beneficiary only provided he or she survives for a specified period, usually 21 or 28 days or one calendar month. The survivorship period cannot be unduly long. It is not unusual for, say, residuary gifts to surviving spouses to be made subject to a survivorship period (see clause 5(b) in the specimen will at pp. 407–408).

8 Circumstances in which a beneficiary may lose a beneficial interest

8.1 Forfeiture

Under the common law rules a person convicted of causing the death of another cannot benefit from his victim's death, either under the terms of the victim's will or under the rules on intestacy. The rule affects not only the person convicted but also anyone claiming through or under him, therefore his issue will also be unable to take unless they are entitled in their own right.

If the person is convicted of murder there can be no relaxation or modification of the rule. However, if he is convicted of manslaughter the application of the rule will depend on whether he was guilty of deliberate and intentional violent acts.

The rule does not apply if the killer was insane.

8.1.1 Forfeiture Act 1982

(not applicable where there is a conviction of murder) In the case of manslaughter or unlawful killing this Act modifies the general rule so that if, taking into account the conduct of the parties and any other matters the court considers material, the court considers it just to modify the rules it will do so either in whole or part.

> EXAMPLE
>
> If the killer brings a claim under the Inheritance (Provision for Family and Dependants) Act 1975 the court may consider the claim, but not if the killer was convicted of murder.

Re K (Deceased) (1985)

The widow of the deceased was convicted of manslaughter following her killing of her husband, the deceased, during an argument. Throughout the marriage she had been subjected to violent physical attacks. The court held that the forfeiture rule could be modified to enable her to benefit under the deceased's will.

Re Jones, Jones v Midland Bank Trust Co. Ltd (1998)

The deceased's son was convicted of her manslaughter. By her will she had left everything to her son but if he predeceased her then to her two nephews. The son applied for relief under the Forfeiture Act and at first instance the will was construed as if he had predeceased her. However, on appeal by the deceased's next of kin who would benefit on her intestacy it was held that the residuary estate should pass as on the deceased's intestacy.

Application for modification of the rule must be brought within three months of the conviction; s. 2(3), Forfeiture Act 1982.

8.2 Beneficiary as attesting witness

As to the general rule that a beneficiary who witnesses a will loses the beneficial interest, although the validity of the will is not affected, see *Introductory Principles— Formalities and Validity*. Section 1, Wills Act 1968 provides that if a will is validly witnessed without the beneficiary, then the beneficiary will retain his beneficial interest.

It is also to be noted that not only does a witness lose any benefit under the will, but any spouse of the witness will also lose any benefit under the will, unless saved by s. 1, Wills Act 1968.

In this respect it should also be noted that prior to the Trustee Act 2000 if a solicitor or the partners in a firm of solicitors were appointed as executors, then since a charging clause was treated for the purposes of s. 15, Wills Act 1837 as a beneficial interest, the solicitor or a partner in the firm (or their respective spouses) should not have witnessed the will, otherwise the right to charge for the firm's services in the administration would have been lost. However, s. 28, Trustee Act 2000 specifically provides that such charges are to be treated as remuneration for services and *not* as a gift under s. 15, Wills Act 1837 (see p. 414).

Revocation of wills

Once a will has been validly executed it becomes a valid testamentary document. However, the terms of the will do not come into effect until the testator's death. At any time between the execution of the will and the date of his death the testator may revoke (i.e. cancel) or amend the will.

The Wills Act 1837 (as amended) also provides that a will is revoked by intentional destruction by the testator, marriage or remarriage of the testator and divorce of the testator. It should be noted that it is only a limited revocation in respect of divorce.

1 Voluntary revocation—s. 20 of the Wills Act 1837

1.1 Revocation by a later will or codicil

A later will containing an express revocation clause will revoke an earlier will.

If the later will contains no revocation clause and makes no gift of the residue, then the later will only revokes those parts of an earlier will which are inconsistent with the later will. In these circumstances those parts of the earlier will which are not inconsistent with the later will remain valid to deal with property not disposed of by the later will.

A codicil may amend or add to the terms of a will and may serve to revoke parts of an earlier will.

1.2 Destruction

A will is revoked if the testator destroys it intentionally.

By s. 20 of the Wills Act 1837 the testator must intend to revoke his will by the destruction. This is defined by the section as 'burning tearing or otherwise destroying the same'.

The destruction must be by the testator personally or done on his behalf and in his presence.

EXAMPLE

If A tears his will into small pieces and then throws it into the fire with the intention of revoking it, his actions will amount to a successful revocation within the terms of the section. Similarly, if A asks B to tear up A's will and then to burn it, and B does this in A's presence this will amount to revocation by A.

Any unintentional destruction of a will does not amount to revocation and the executors would have to rely on other evidence of the contents when applying for the grant, e.g., a draft or made up copy of the will or even oral evidence of the contents. If a will has been destroyed, or there is some other reason for not submitting the original will, the District judge or Registrar will require affidavit evidence as to the reason for the submission of some other evidence of the contents of the will (e.g. a copy will) instead of the submission of the original will.

EXAMPLE

A has made a valid will of which he also has a copy. While disposing of some papers on the fire he accidentally throws away his will which is completely destroyed before he realizes his mistake. This would not amount to intended destruction and would not be a revocation of the will. If A died without making a replacement will, the copy will would have to be submitted to probate as evidence of the contents of the will.

If a testator destroys a will with the intention that a new will shall be effective and then for any reason the new will is ineffective *and* there is clear evidence that the testator's only reason for revoking the old will was to make the new one effective then the old will remains effective. This is known as the doctrine of dependent relative revocation.

In the Estate of Davies (1951)
The testatrix executed a new will and an earlier will was destroyed in her presence. The second will was ineffective and it was held that the doctrine of dependent relative revocation applied to revive the earlier will.

Similarly if a testator destroys a later will mistakenly believing that it will revive an earlier will and it can be established that the testator carried out the destruction in that mistaken belief, then the later will remains effective.

In the Estate of Bridgewater (1965)
The testator had made three wills. He destroyed the latest will in the mistaken belief that the second will would be revived. The third will was admitted to probate.

A will cannot be destroyed by someone other than the testator except on the testator's instructions and in his presence. Even then, if the testator did not intend the will to be destroyed, the destruction will not revoke the will.

If a will has marks on it which could indicate attempted destruction then, when it is submitted for probate, the District judge or Registrar will require evidence, in the form of an affidavit of plight and condition, explaining the state of the will (see *Personal Representatives*).

EXAMPLE

If there are some scorch marks on the will which are there as a result of the testator accidentally putting his will on the ironing board next to a hot iron with no intention of destroying the will, then the marks will have to be explained to the satisfaction of the district judge in an affidavit of plight and condition.

If a will which is known to have been in the testator's possession is not found at his death, there is a rebuttable presumption that it has been destroyed by the testator with the intent to revoke.

1.3 'Some writing declaring an intention to revoke'

Section 20 of the Wills Act 1837 also provides that a will may be revoked by 'some writing' so long as it declares 'an intention to revoke' the will and the writing is executed in accordance with the same formalities as required to make a valid will.

> **EXAMPLE**
>
> A testator suddenly decides to revoke his will but does not have the original in his possession and so cannot destroy it. He does not wish to make another will or a codicil. In these circumstances this part of s. 20 would enable him to revoke his will by writing a revocation and signing it in the presence of witnesses in accordance with s. 9, Wills Act 1837.

2 Revocation by marriage or remarriage

Section 18 of the Wills Act 1837, as amended, provides that a will is revoked by the testator's marriage unless the will was made in contemplation of the specific marriage which subsequently occurred. This is referred to as a will 'made in contemplation of marriage'. Such wills must include the name of the intended spouse and the marriage must take place. A will cannot be made in contemplation of some unspecified marriage!

In all other cases marriage or remarriage will revoke a will. Testators should therefore always be advised that, in the event of marriage or remarriage in the future, they should reconsider their wills.

3 Revocation by dissolution or annulment of marriage

Section 18A of the Wills Act 1837 (as amended by the Law Reform (Succession) Act 1995) provides that where a testator's marriage is dissolved or annulled after the testator has made a will then, by s. 18A(1)(a), any provisions appointing the former spouse as an executor or trustee, or conferring a power of appointment on the former spouse take effect as if the former spouse had died on the date the marriage was dissolved or annulled and, by s. 18A(1)(b), any property or interest in any property devised or bequeathed to the former spouse passes as if the former spouse had died on the date the marriage was dissolved or annulled.

Section 18(A)(1) has effect on wills made by a person dying on or after 1 January 1996 regardless of the date of the will, or the dissolution or annulment of the marriage. The section will take effect unless there is any contrary intention in the will.

Section 18A specifically provides that revocation under this section is without prejudice to any right of a former spouse to make an application under the Inheritance (Provision for Family and Dependants) Act 1975 (and see the section later in this chapter *Inheritance (Provision for Family and Dependants) Act 1975*). This means that although a former spouse will lose any testamentary benefit, he or she may still claim for provision from the estate if there is a valid claim under the 1975 Act.

Intestacy

1 Total or partial intestacy?

When a person dies without having made a valid will he is said to be wholly intestate, and the distribution of his estate is dealt with according to the rules laid down in Part IV, Administration of Estates Act 1925, as amended (see 3.1 below). The most recent amendment is contained in the Law Reform (Succession) Act 1995 which introduced a 'survivorship period' of 28 days in respect of spouses (see p. 430).

The law also stipulates the order in which persons are entitled to apply for a grant of letters of administration. This is covered by rule 22 of the Non-Contentious Probate Rules 1987 (see *Personal Representatives*).

A person who makes a valid will which does not dispose of his whole estate is said to die partially intestate.

EXAMPLE

residue of estate not disposed of

Testator makes a will which does not contain a residuary gift. This would create a partial intestacy as the residue of his estate would not be disposed of by his will.

The executors of the will (or administrators with will annexed) would be the persons responsible for dealing with the distribution of the residue in accordance with the intestacy rules as set out in the Administration of Estates Act 1925.

This section will deal with total intestacy.

2 The statutory trust for sale

On a total intestacy, that is where a person does not make a valid will, under the terms of s. 33 of the Administration of Estates Act 1925 (as amended by the Trusts of Land and Appointment of Trustees Act 1996) the deceased's estate vests in (i.e. passes to) his personal representatives (i.e. his administrators) on trust for sale with power to sell it. This is 'the statutory trust for sale' which enables the Administrators to deal with the estate both prior to and after any sale. Section 33(1) of the Administration of Estates Act 1925 (as amended) states:

TOLATA '96

On the death of a person intestate as to any real or personal estate that estate shall be held in trust by his personal representatives with the power to sell it.

If there is sufficient cash in the estate to meet all the liabilities, the administrators may vest any assets in those entitled to the estate.

Handwritten margin notes (left, top to bottom): Doesn't have to sell the estate / Power to / Pay off the debts

A surviving spouse, where there is no issue or close relatives, may have all the real and tangible assets vested in him or her rather than these being sold and the cash paid to him or her.

Section 33, Administration of Estates Act 1925 also contains powers for the administrators to pay sums due from the estate in respect of funeral and testamentary expenses and liabilities, and powers of investment pending distribution; see 4 below.

3 Who is entitled to the estate?

It must be noted that following the Law Reform (Succession) Act 1995, in respect of deaths occurring on or after 1 January 1996, all benefits in favour of a surviving spouse are subject to the spouse surviving the intestate for a period of 28 days beginning with the day on which the intestate died. If a spouse survives the intestate but dies before the end of the 28-day period, by s. 1(1) of the Act the spouse is treated as if he or she had not survived the intestate. *ie that the estates are then treated as separate for tax purposes*.

Details of the persons entitled to the estate on an intestacy are set out in s. 46, Administration of Estates Act 1925. The table which follows summarises the position.

3.1 Distribution of assets on intestacy

Handwritten margin note (left): S.46 A of Estates Act 25

Surviving Relative	Entitlement
1 Surviving spouse with no children (or issue) or other close relative. (Close relatives in order of priority: (a) parents (b) brothers/sisters of the whole blood or their issue.)	Surviving spouse receives everything.
2 Surviving spouse and children (or issue) who attain 18 or marry under that age.	1 Spouse receives: (a) personal chattels including cars, books, jewellery and household items butnot business chattels or money; (b) statutory legacy—£125,000; (c) life interest in half of the rest of the estate (reversion to issue at 18 or on earlier marriage).
Note that the balance of the residuary estate is held on the statutory trusts for the following:	2 Children receive other half of residue at 18 or on earlier marriage plus balance on death of spouse.

Surviving Relative	Entitlement
(a) half for surviving spouse for life; (b) half for issue who become entitled to their share at 18 or on earlier marriage.	NB If any child dies under 18 without marrying (and without children alive at the death of the intestate) his share will go to the others, or, if none, to the spouse or other close relatives subject to a larger statutory legacy to the spouse (see below).
3 No spouse but children or other issue. (Note that 'issue' includes illegitimate children if death after 1 January 1970. The estate is held on the statutory trusts until beneficiaries attain 18; each becomes entitled to his share at that time or on earlier marriage.	Children receive whole estate in equal shares at 18 or on earlier marriage. If any child dies under 18 leaving issue, alive at the death of the intestate the issue will take in equal shares (if more than one) the share of the deceased parent, at 18 or on earlier marriage.
4 Surviving spouse with no issue but close relatives (i.e. parent(s) or brothers/sisters of the whole blood).	1 Spouse receives: (a) personal chattels; (b) statutory legacy—£2000,000; (c) half of the remainder absulutely. 2 Close relatives receive the other half of the remainder absolutely. Parents take in priority to brothers and sisters.
5 No surviving spouse or issue but surviving close relatives.	Whole estate to: (a) parent or parents equally; (b) if no parent, to brothers/sisters of whole blood (or issue of any brother/sister who predeceased the intestate) equally. NB Issue will only be entitled to the share to which their parent would have been entitled.
6 No spouse, issue or close relatives.	Whole estate passes to other relatives in (a) brothers/sisters of half blood; (b) grandparents; (c) uncles/aunts being brothers/sisters of whole blood of a parent of the deceased;

Surviving Relative	Entitlement
	(d) uncles/aunts being brothers/ sisters of half blood of a parent of deceased. Note in all cases if more than one person is entitled they share equally, and if any person who would have been entitled predeceases the deceased leaving issue alive at the death of the intestate then the issue will take the share which his/her parent would have taken and, if more than one, in equal shares at 18 or on earlier marriage.

In the absence of any of these relatives, the estate passes to the Crown, the Duchy of Lancaster or the Duchy of Cornwall as *bona vacantia*.

The Administration of Estates Act 1925 appears to distribute on the basis that the intestate would have wished his estate to pass to his relatives, those closest taking in priority to those most distant.

If a person dies intestate while there is a decree of judicial separation in force and the separation is continuing at the date of death then under s. 18(2), Matrimonial Causes Act 1973, any property as to which he or she dies intestate passes as if the other party to the marriage was already dead.

3.2 'The statutory legacy'

The values of the statutory legacies, that is the sums due to a surviving spouse under an intestacy in accordance with the table set out above, are periodically increased by statutory instrument to take into account up to date values and inflation.

Set out below are some examples of the statutory legacies for a surviving spouse with issue where death has occurred in the periods specified:

(a) Where death occurred between 1 January 1953 and 1 January 1967 the statutory legacy was £5,000.

(b) Where death occurred between 1 March 1981 and 1 June 1987 the statutory legacy was £40,000

(c) Where death occurred between 1 June 1987 and 1 December 1993 the statutory legacy was £75,000.

In all the above cases in addition to the statutory legacy the surviving spouse receives the personal chattels (as defined by s. 55(1)(x), Administration of Estates Act 1925), and a life interest in half the residue (plus interest thereon up to the date of payment) with reversion to the issue.

A dies intestate on 5 March 1994 leaving an estate valued at £250,000 net including personal chattels valued at £5,000. He leaves a widow and two adult children. The widow receives all personal chattels plus the statutory legacy of £125,000. The remainder of the estate is divided into two equal shares of £60,000 each. One share goes to the children and the other share is invested and the widow receives the income for her lifetime. On her death the second share passes to the children.

It should be noted that where there is a spouse and no issue, but close relatives, then the statutory legacy is increased to £200,000 and the spouse receives half the rest absolutely. No life interest arises.

3.3 Life interest

Where a life interest arises this means that the capital sum in which the life interest exists is invested and only the income is paid to the beneficiary. Such a beneficiary is called a 'life tenant'. If the estate in which the life interest exists comprises real property then the life tenant would be entitled to live in the property.

3.4 Reversion to issue

Where the Administration of Estates Act 1925 speaks of a 'reversion to issue' it means that on the death of the life tenant (the spouse in this case), the capital which was invested becomes due to the issue of the intestate. If at the date of the life tenant's death the issue are below the age of 18, then the invested capital is held on the statutory trusts by the intestate's administrators until the issue reach 18 or marry below that age. If issue are already aged 18 at the date of death of the tenant for life then they receive the capital absolutely.

3.5 Beneficiary predeceasing the intestate leaving issue alive at the intestate's death

If a relative who is a beneficiary predeceases the intestate but leaves issue, i.e., children, grandchildren or great grandchildren or other direct lineal descendants alive at the death of the intestate, then that issue will take the share which his, her or their parent would have taken if their parent had not predeceased the intestate. If there is more than one person entitled then they will take in equal shares by families.

A, a widow, dies intestate leaving a son and daughter, and two grandchildren who are the children of a daughter who predeceased the intestate. In this case the intestate's estate will be split three ways with one third going to the son, one third to the daughter and one third being split equally between the grandchildren who take the share which their mother would have taken had she not predeceased the intestate.

3.6 Repeal of provisions on bringing into account sums received

Prior to the Law Reform (Succession) Act 1995, under s. 47(1)(iii) of the Administration of Estates Act 1925 any sums paid by an intestate to his or her child or other issue by way of advancement or on the marriage of such person had to be brought into account and set against his or her share of the estate. This section and part of s. 49, Administration of Estates Act 1925 (dealing with partial intestacy and the bringing into account of sums received under the will by a spouse or issue of the deceased) were repealed by s. 1(2) of the Law Reform (Succession) Act 1995 in respect of persons dying on or after 1 January 1996.

4 Other powers and duties under s. 33, Administration of Estates Act 1925   *Intestacy*

4.1 Payment of debts and liabilities

The administrators' first duty is to pay the funeral testamentary and administration expenses and all debts and liabilities in the estate. These will be paid either from the cash in the estate or out of the proceeds of sale of assets if insufficient cash is available. Unless there is insufficient cash without the sale of personal chattels, these should not be sold.

Anything left after the payment of these sums is the 'residuary estate' which is distributed in accordance with the 1925 Act.

4.2 Powers of investment

Also included in s. 33, Administration of Estates Act 1925 is the power of investment for administrators where a life or minority interest arises and pending distribution of the estate (s. 33(3)).

EXAMPLE

A dies intestate, leaving a spouse and two children under 18 who, because of the value of the estate, are all entitled to share in the estate (in accordance with the table set out at 3.1 above). By s. 33(3) the administrators have power to invest the sums to be held during the spouse's life interest, and the sums held until the children become entitled at 18 (or on earlier marriage).

5 The matrimonial home

If the net value of an intestate's estate is below the value of the statutory legacy due to a surviving spouse then any property (or the intestates share in any property) in which the surviving spouse was residing at the time of the intestate's death passes to the spouse. If the value of the net estate exceeds the statutory legacy then the surviving spouse will not automatically receive the property (or share in it) in which he or she resides. There are, however, several ways in which the surviving spouse can take the property.

5.1 Appropriation

Under s. 41, Administration of Estates Act 1925, personal representatives have a general power to appropriate property in or towards satisfaction of any interest in an estate and if they so choose could appropriate the property in which a surviving spouse resides. However s. 41 gives the personal representatives only a power not a duty to appropriate. Under the Intestates' Estates Act 1952 (hereafter referred to as the 1952 Act) a surviving spouse may (by giving written notice to the personal representatives within 12 months of the date of the grant of representation) require the personal representatives to exercise their power of appropriation in respect of any property in which the surviving spouse was living at the time of the intestate's death in or towards satisfaction of any absolute interest the surviving spouse has in the intestate's estate. If the value of the property exceeds the entitlement of the surviving spouse he or she can pay the difference. The 1952 Act provides a statutory right for the surviving spouse to acquire the property in which he or she is residing at the date of the intestate's death (but there are exclusions of the right). Normally personal representatives could not be compelled to exercise their powers under s. 41.

The 12-month period for exercise of the statutory rights may be extended and during that period the personal representatives must not dispose of the property without the written consent of the surviving spouse.

5.2 Leasehold property

If the property is leasehold and is held on a lease under which the intestate had a right to acquire the freehold or an extended lease under the Leasehold Reform Act 1967 then the surviving spouse will have the same right. By s. 7 of the Leasehold Reform Act 1967 a member of the deceased tenant's family, which includes a surviving spouse, can claim to be treated as having been the tenant and occupied the house as his or her residence during any period when resident in it as his or her only or main residence and the deceased was occupying it as his or her residence.

5.3 Purchase from the personal representatives

A surviving spouse may always seek to purchase any asset from the estate including the house in which he or she resided at the date of the intestate's death but if the surviving spouse is the only personal representative the consent of the court or the other beneficiaries will be required. If the surviving spouse is one of two or more personal representatives then the 1952 Act provides that the general rule should not prevent the purchase by the surviving spouse.

6 Possible hardship caused by present intestacy rules

A Law Commission report in 1989 on the rules on intestacy came to the conclusion that the present rules should be amended, so that where there is a surviving spouse the whole estate will pass to the surviving spouse. At the present time, however, the rules on intestacy remain unchanged. As the rules stand they can cause hardship where there is a surviving spouse and issue and the value of the estate is above the amount of the statutory legacy. This can mean that the surviving spouse does not automatically inherit the *whole* estate.

However, there is a procedure whereby, on an intestacy where there is a surviving spouse and issue and where all the beneficiaries agree, the intestacy rules can be rearranged to enable the whole estate to pass to the surviving spouse, or to be split in such other manner as the spouse and issue agree between themselves. This is achieved by a deed of arrangement or variation, but such an arrangement is only applicable where all the beneficiaries are of full age and able to agree about the redistribution of the estate.

7 Commorientes and intestacy

[handwritten: If they've made wills then youngest survives eldest. If they are intestate estates are separate]

When two people die in circumstances where it is impossible to tell who died first (commorientes), then the general rule under s. 184, Law of Property Act 1925 is that the youngest is deemed to have survived the eldest. However, the general rule is not applicable when dealing with the rights to a spouse's estate on intestacy.

[handwritten left margin: if you die intestate your estates are treated separately]

Section 46(3) of the Administration of Estates Act 1925, as amended, specifically provides that where a husband or wife would have been deemed to survive under s. 184 of the Law of Property Act 1925, then by virtue of s. 46(3) of the Administration of Estates Act 1925 they shall not be treated as having survived for the purpose of inheriting the estate of the elder spouse. This means that the younger spouse will not receive anything under the rules of intestacy as each spouse will be treated as not leaving a surviving spouse. Note also that for deaths since 1 January 1996 a spouse must survive for 28 days before becoming entitled in any event.

EXAMPLE

A and his younger wife B are both killed in a plane crash. It is impossible to establish the order of death. Both died intestate. Under s. 46(3) of the Administration of Estates Act 1925, B will not be treated as surviving A and therefore will not take any of A's estate. Similarly, A will not take B's estate under the general rule as B will be deemed to survive.

8 Donationes mortis causa—'death bed gifts'

[handwritten: ie not mentioned in a will]

This type of gift is included in this section since it is not a testamentary gift. However, neither is it strictly anything to do with intestacy!

Such a gift is, as the name suggests, a gift which is made by a person who is dying. It is made in anticipation of the death of the person making the gift. The donor, i.e. the person making the gift, must be aware of what he is doing and intend to make the gift.

For any lifetime gift to be valid and effective the subject matter of the gift must actually be handed to the recipient, together with anything else necessary to complete the passing of title. *[handwritten: eg. Key to box etc. deeds, etc.]*

[handwritten left margin: 2 provisos knowledge intention]

EXAMPLES

1   A hands a necklace to B and tells B he can keep it. This is a valid gift.

2   A hands a share certificate to B and tells him he can have the shares. This is not a

valid gift of the shares. A must also hand to B a completed stock transfer form to make a valid gift of the shares.

In the case of a donatio mortis causa, however, the handing over of something representing the subject matter of the gift is sufficient evidence of intention to make a gift, even if such handing over does not formally transfer legal title.

EXAMPLE

As in example 2 above, A hands a share certificate to B and tells B to keep the shares, but this time A is on his deathbed and dies a few hours later. The gift of the shares to B is effective, even in the absence of a stock transfer form, because it is a valid gift in contemplation of death.

In the case of a donatio mortis causa the gift will only take effect if the donor subsequently dies and the gift was made in contemplation of death. If the beneficiary predeceases the donor, or the donor does not die, the gift does not become effective.

It was always assumed that real property could not be the subject matter of a donatio mortis causa but following a recent case, *Sen* v *Headley* (1991), this is no longer the case. In this case the court found that real property could pass if what was handed to the beneficiary was sufficient evidence of intention to give the real property.

Sen v *Headley* (1991)

The deceased and the plaintiff had been cohabitees for 10 years from 1954. After that date they saw less of each other but remained close and the deceased continued to be treated as part of the plaintiff's family. When the deceased was in hospital the plaintiff visited daily and they discussed what should happen to the deceased's house. The deceased told the plaintiff that the house and contents were hers and that the deeds were kept in a steel box and that she had the keys to the box. The plaintiff found the box and using a key, which she thought the deceased had put into her handbag on one of her visits to the hospital, she opened the box and took possession of the deeds. The Court of Appeal held that this constituted a valid donatio mortis causa.

As such gifts are similar to legacies they are subject to the debts of the estate if there are not enough other assets to meet the debts.

Personal representatives

1 Appointment of personal representatives

'Personal representative' is the generic term used to describe both executors and administrators. These are the persons who deal with the administration and winding up of a deceased person's estate. Executors are appointed by will; administrators are appointed by the court either:

(a) where there is an intestacy; or

(b) where there are no proving executors, either because the executors appointed by the will are unwilling or unable to act or no executors were appointed by the will.

2 Appointment of executors

2.1 Introduction

Any valid will may (and normally does) contain an appointment of executors who will be the persons chosen by the testator to deal with his estate after the coming into effect of the will. The will is valid once it has been signed in accordance with s. 9, Wills Act 1837, but does not come into effect until the death of the testator. A testator does not have to obtain the executor's consent to the appointment, but it is always advisable to discuss the appointment direct with the person chosen because he may not wish to act and the testator can then appoint someone else.

Any number of persons can be appointed as executors although the number who will be permitted to apply for the grant of probate (i.e. the grant from the court confirming the authority of the executors to deal with the estate) will be limited to four.

As well as individuals, a firm (e.g. of solicitors) or a trust corporation (e.g. a bank trust company) or the public trustee may be appointed as executor.

The will normally contains a clause towards the beginning dealing with the specific appointment of the executor. If there is any likelihood of a trust arising, then trustees are appointed either in the same clause, or by a separate clause if different persons are to be appointed to act as trustees from those appointed to act as executors.

If a trust is likely to arise, e.g. because there is a life or minority interest (i.e. someone will only be entitled to something under the will for the period of his life, or there is a gift to someone under the age of 18), then it is usually advisable to appoint more than one executor and trustee so that if anything happens to one there is still someone chosen by the testator to deal with the trust.

This is in contrast to the rules concerning administration where there must be a grant to at least two administrators or a trust corporation if a life or minority interest arises.

Normally a testator appoints the same person to act as both executor and trustee.

2.2 Special executors

If the testator wishes to appoint executors to deal with only a specified part of his estate then he may do so. Such executors are referred to as 'special executors' and they only have power to deal with the part of the estate in respect of which they have been appointed, e.g. they may be business executors who will deal with the testator's business interests, or literary executors who will deal with his literary interests. Such executors or trustees will be appointed by a separate clause.

2.3 Appointment of individuals as executors

The chosen individual or individuals are referred to by name and it is usual to include each individual's address particularly if they are not close relatives of the testator. Anyone of sound mind may be appointed as an executor although a grant will not be made to anyone under a disability, e.g. a minor. (A minor is a person under the age of 18.)

However, the appointment of a minor does not invalidate either the appointment or the will but means that, if there are no other executors named or no other executors who are of full age, then a grant of letters of administration with will annexed for the use and benefit of the minor will be necessary. This will be granted to the parents or surviving parent with parental responsibility or guardian of the minor until he attains the age of 18, when he can then apply for a grant of probate to deal with any part of the estate still unadministered at that date. This means that when the minor reaches 18 he will be able to make his own application for a grant of probate and he will deal with the rest of the administration of the estate. If the administration has already been completed, there will of course be nothing in respect of which he could apply for a grant and therefore no application will be made.

If the minor is only one of several executors who are appointed by the will and there are other executors who are willing and able to prove, then a simple grant of probate will be applied for by the other executor or executors with 'power reserved' to the minor executor who will then be entitled to apply for a grant of double probate when he reaches 18. Such a grant of double probate will run concurrently with the original grant and will be in respect of such part of the estate remaining unadministered at the time the grant of double probate is applied for. See 2.6 below for grants 'with power reserved'.

2.4 Appointment of firms or trust corporations as executors

As well as individuals, firms or trust corporations may be appointed as executors of a will. If a firm of solicitors is appointed to act, the normal appointment is of 'the partners in the firm of ABC or the firm which succeeds to that firm and carries on its practice ... ' Such appointment often also includes a wish that only a specified number of the partners should prove the will. The will can appoint only the partners as executors or can appoint the partners as executors jointly with an individual or individuals (e.g. members of the testator's family). Before the Trustee Act 2000 the will had to include a 'charging clause' to enable such executors to be able to charge for their services. However, by s. 29, Trustee Act 2000 such executors are entitled to receive reasonable remuneration *but* the section will *not* apply to a sole executor, in which case a charging clause *must* still be included. Thus it may still be preferable to include a charging clause in case events occur which mean that there is only one partner.

If a trust corporation is appointed, or the Public Trustee, then it or he may also be appointed either alone or jointly with other individuals. The wording for the appointment should be checked with the trust corporation concerned as it will often provide specimen clauses of appointment and charging clauses although it should be noted that s. 29, Trustee Act 2000 also applies to trust corporations.

2.5 Appointment by implication or 'according to the tenor' of the will

Although the executor will normally be expressly appointed and therefore clearly identifiable as the executor of the will, there are occasions when the testator does not specifically name a person 'as executor' but words the will in such a way that it implies an intention on the testator's part that some person should act as executor, e.g. *Re Cook's Goods* (1902) where a person was specified to deal with the payment of debts. Only an executor would be expected to deal with debts.

However such an appointment will only arise where it is clear from the wording in the will that the testator has given to the person named the duties of an executor.

2.6 Executors who are unwilling or unable to prove

The fact that the testator has chosen someone as his executor does not mean that that person is bound to act. Any executor of a will who does not wish to act can either 'renounce probate' or have 'power reserved' to him if there are other executors willing and able to act. The fact that an executor does not have to take up the appointment is good reason for the testator always to check with the person he proposes to appoint that such person will be willing to act in the administration of the estate.

2.6.1 Renunciation

If an executor does not wish to act and has not done anything in respect of the administration of the estate, then he can renounce his right to the issue of the grant, including his right to a grant in some other capacity, e.g. as the appropriate person entitled to a grant of letters of administration with will annexed. If there is a will with no proving executor, then rule 20 of the Non-Contentious Probate Rules 1987 sets out the list of persons entitled to such a grant and the executor may fall within that list (see 3.3 below). Therefore if he intends to renounce all rights to any grant to the estate this must be clear. The renunciation must be in writing which is then submitted to the Probate Registry when the application for the grant is eventually made.

2.6.2 Power reserved

If an executor does not wish formally to renounce probate and he is one of several executors who are capable of applying for the grant, then the other executor or executors can make the application for the grant with 'power reserved' to the executor who does not wish to prove. This means that if at any time in the future the executor to whom power was reserved wishes to prove, he can apply for a grant of double probate in respect of any part of the estate remaining unadministered at that time.

This procedure is particularly useful where a minor is one of several executors named in the will and the other executors are capable of applying for the grant. In such circumstances the application can be made with power reserved to the minor and then, if the minor wishes to prove when he attains the age of 18, he can apply for a grant of double probate in respect of the unadministered estate. He does not, however, have to apply for the grant if he does not wish to do so.

It will be seen from the above that an application 'with power reserved' is only applicable where there is another executor or executors who are willing and able to apply for a grant of probate in addition to the executor to whom power is to be reserved.

If power is reserved to an executor rule 27 of the Non-Contentious Probate Rules 1987 provides that notice must be given to the executor to whom power is to be reserved that the other executors intend to apply for the grant. No copy of such notice needs to be sent to the Probate Registry, but the oath which will be sworn by the executors in connection with the application for the grant will state that the notice has been given and will name the executor to whom power is reserved.

In certain circumstances, if it is not possible to give such notice, then a written application should be made to the Registry to dispense with the notice prior to the application for the grant. If such application is not made before the grant, the letter of application will need to be submitted at the same time as the application for the grant but may delay the issue of the grant if the District judge or Registrar is unable to grant the dispensation.

2.7 Lack of proving executors

The lack of appointment of executors in a will, or the lack of executors willing and able to prove, does not affect the validity of a will and the appropriate grant will not be a grant of probate but a grant of letters of administration with will annexed. In any case where the grant is of letters of administration the persons appointed will be administrators not executors.

3 Appointment of administrators

3.1 When appointed

Administrators will be appointed either:

(a) on complete intestacy, i.e. where there is no valid will; or

(b) Where there is a valid will of which there are no proving executors.

[handwritten note: People who wrote their own wills may not know to appoint executors]

3.2 Intestacy

3.2.1 *Rule 22 of the Non-Contentious Probate Rules 1987*

This rule sets out the order of persons entitled in priority to apply for a grant of letters of administration which follows closely the order of persons entitled to an estate on intestacy. Only one person need apply, unless under the intestacy rules there is a minor beneficiary, or a life interest to the spouse arises, when there must be at least two administrators.

The order of persons entitled in priority to apply for a grant of letters of administration under rule 22 is as follows:

(i) spouse (the spouse must survive the deceased for 28 days in order to have a beneficial interest and should not therefore swear the oath until the period of 28 days has elapsed);

(ii) children of the deceased and the issue of any child who predeceased the deceased;

(iii) parents of the deceased;

(iv) brothers and sisters of the whole blood and the issue of any who predeceased the deceased;

(v) brothers and sisters of the half blood and the issue of any who predeceased the deceased;

(vi) grandparents;

(vii) uncles and aunts of the whole blood and the issue of any who predeceased the deceased;

(viii) uncles and aunts of the half blood and the issue of any who predeceased the deceased;

(ix) the treasury solicitor, if he is claiming the estate bona vacantia for the Crown;

(x) a creditor of the deceased.

3.2.2 *Persons of equal degree*

Persons of equal degree in the same class of administrators can apply for a grant without notifying others of the same degree of their intention. Application must be made by persons in the order specified by this rule. The oath, i.e the sworn statement made by the appropriate person to apply for the grant, will 'clear off' anyone with a better right to apply. This means that the oath will show that the person making the application is in fact the person, or one of the persons entitled to the estate of the deceased, or will include details as to why someone with a better entitlement to the grant is not making the application, e.g., because an administrator has renounced the right to a grant or does not wish to apply for the grant personally and has appointed an attorney to apply for the grant of administration for 'his use and benefit'.

3.2.3 *Person entitled to a grant dying before the grant is made*

If a person entitled to the grant survives the intestate but dies before applying for the grant, then that person's personal representatives may apply for a grant to the estate of the intestate. However, if there are other persons entitled to the grant in the same class of priority then they will be preferred to the personal representatives of a deceased administrator.

The personal representatives of a surviving spouse of an intestate will only be entitled to apply for a grant to the estate of the intestate if the spouse was entitled to the whole of the intestate's estate. In all other cases the other persons entitled to the estate will have priority.

3.3 Appointment of administrators where there is a valid will

3.3.1 *Rule 20 of the Non-Contentious Probate Rules 1987*

This rule sets out the order of persons entitled in priority to apply for a grant where there is a valid will. In the absence of proving executors the grant will be a grant of letters of administration with will annexed and such a grant will be made to the administrators selected according to the priority set out in rule 20 after the executor i.e.:

(i)   Any residuary legatee or devisee holding in trust for any person.

(ii) Any other residuary legatee or devisee (including one for life) or where the residue is not wholly disposed of by the will, any person entitled to share in the undisposed of residue. There is a proviso that, unless the District judge or Registrar otherwise directs, residuary beneficiaries with vested interests are preferred to those with contingent interests and also, where the residue is not wholly disposed of, the District judge or Registrar may allow a grant to be made to any beneficiary entitled to share in the estate which is disposed of without regard to persons entitled to the undisposed of residue.

(iii) The personal representatives of any residuary beneficiary (but not one for life or holding in trust for any other person) or of any person entitled to share in any residue not disposed of by the will.

(iv) Any other legatee or devisee or any creditor. There is a provision that the beneficiary whose legacy is vested will be preferred to one whose interest is contingent.

(v)   The personal representatives of any other legatees or devisees (but not for life or one holding in trust for any other person) or of any creditor of the deceased.

3.3.2 Persons of equal degree

As with an application for a grant of simple administration, persons of equal degree can apply without giving notice to others of the same degree, but any applicants with prior title must be cleared off and if necessary evidence of renunciation produced.

4 Grant of letters of administration *de bonis non administratis*

4.1 Death before administration completed

Once a grant of probate or administration has been obtained then the persons appointed deal with the administration of the estate. However, if a sole or last surviving executor or administrator dies without completing the administration, then application must be made for a grant of letters of administration de bonis non administratis in order to deal with any part of the estate which remains to be administered. The persons entitled to the grant are selected in accordance with priority under rule 20 of the Non-Contentious Probate Rules 1987 if there is a will, or rule 22 if there is no will.

4.2 Chain of executorship

However, a grant de bonis non administratis will not be necessary in the following circumstances:

(a) if the sole executor or person entitled to a grant of administration dies before applying for the grant; or

(b) if the sole or last surviving executor, having proved the testator's will, himself dies leaving a will appointing an executor who takes out probate of that will. This is known as a chain of executorship and in such cases the executor of the executor's will is the appropriate person to deal not only with his testator's will but also to complete the administration of the estate of the will of which his testator was an executor.

EXAMPLE

A appoints B executor of his will. A dies and B obtains a grant of probate to A's estate. B has made a will appointing X as executor. B dies before completing the administration of A's estate. If X proves B's will he will also have to complete the administration of A's estate.

It must be noted that a chain of executorship cannot arise if there was originally an intestacy.

EXAMPLE

A dies intestate and B obtains a grant of letters of administration to his estate. B appoints X as executor of his will. B dies without completing the administration of A's estate. There is no chain of executorship as B was not an executor of A, he was an administrator appointed in accordance with the rules of intestacy. A grant de bonis non administratis will be required to complete the administration of A's estate.

5 Powers and duties of personal representatives

5.1 Personal representatives' authority

The executor's authority to act in an estate is derived from the will but the administrator's power to act in the estate derives from the grant of letters of administration.

5.2 Obtaining the appropriate grant

This will entail establishing full and true details of all the assets and liabilities in the estate in order to ascertain the papers which will be required to obtain the grant in respect of the estate. If the gross value of the estate exceeds £210,000 (or £200,000 if the date of death is before 6 April 2000 but after 6 April 1998—there are other limits prior to that date) then a detailed account of the assets and liabilities in the estate must be completed and, if the net estate exceeds £250,000 (or £242,000 if the date of death was before 6 April 2002) after deduction of any exemptions and reliefs, inheritance tax will be payable and it is the personal representative's duty to deal with the payment of the tax. (See *Inheritance Tax* for a more detailed discussion of inheritance tax and the exemptions and reliefs from tax.)

When applying for a grant the personal representatives must submit to the Probate Registry such of the following as are relevant:

(a) oath—required for all types of grant;

(b) the original will or a copy if the original is not available (relevant where the application is for a grant of probate or letters of administration with will annexed);

(c) any other affidavit evidence which may be required, e.g. as to the condition of the will;

(d) if any inheritance tax account is required for any reason then a Probate summary (D18—see 6.2.3 below) is required;

(e) the appropriate fees, i.e. set fees according to the net value of the estate for probate purposes: if this value is less than £5,000 the court fee is nil; above £5,000 the fee is £50 (Non-Contentious Probate Fees Order 1999). A fee of £1 for each office copy of the grant, which may be required should be added to the fee. An office copy of the grant is a sealed copy of the grant prepared by the court. The original grant is sealed by the court and incorporates a copy of the will which is also sealed by the court;

(f) it should also be noted that the Probate Registry now like to see a copy of the death certificate.

5.3 Collection of assets

Having obtained the relevant grant, the personal representatives must proceed to collect in the assets of the estate by producing to the asset holders the grant, or an office copy of the grant, for registration in their records as evidence of the personal representatives' right to deal with the assets. The asset holders will require the personal representatives to sign any relevant claim, withdrawal or transfer forms in order to deal with the payment of the assets to the estate.

5.4 Payment of liabilities

Having collected the assets, the personal representatives should then proceed to deal with the payment of any liabilities out of the sums collected. Normally liabilities will fall to be paid from the residue, but if there is a will which provides that some other funds should be used to pay either all or some specific liabilities, then the personal representatives should act in accordance with the terms of the will.

5.5 Advertisements for creditors

The personal representatives should consider whether advertisements for creditors under s. 27, Trustee Act 1925 are required in respect of the estate. Section 27 provides that if personal representatives make an advertisement for creditors of the estate in accordance with the section (i.e. advertisements are placed both in the London Gazette and a local newspaper or newspapers, inviting anyone who has a claim against the estate to make such claim within two months of the date of such advertisement appearing), and then proceed to distribute the estate after the two months has elapsed, there can be no claim against the personal representatives personally for distributing the estate. Any valid claim would have to be pursued against the beneficiaries of the estate. Compliance with the section therefore provides a protection for personal representatives against claims of which they did not have knowledge at the time of distribution.

In this connection it should be noted that as administrators derive their authority from the grant the advertisement should not be made until after the grant has been issued. If it is made before that time the personal representatives must ensure that at least two months will remain after the date of the grant for claims to be made. Contrast the position of executors who derive their authority from the will and who can therefore place the advertisement before the grant is issued.

It is up to the personal representatives to decide if advertisements for creditors are necessary but if a person who has no knowledge of the deceased's affairs is appointed, then the advertisements should always be made unless that person is also the sole beneficiary, in which case any claim could still be made against him as beneficiary rather than as personal representative. If professional persons are appointed they should *always* make the advertisements.

5.6 Distribution

When all assets have been collected, liabilities have been paid (including inheritance tax) and any advertisements for creditors have expired, it is the personal representatives' duty to distribute the estate either in accordance with the terms of the will or under the rules of intestacy. Providing six months have elapsed since the grant they are protected from claims under the Inheritance (Provisions for Family and Dependants) Act 1975 (for which see below). Before finally distributing the estate, however, it may be necessary to deal with other outstanding matters in the administration; e.g.:

(a) To check the position with regard to income and capital gains tax in respect of the estate and up to the date of death by submitting any claims for repayment of tax or agreeing and making any payments of tax due from the estate. In this respect any income and capital gains arising during the administration of the estate are liable to tax.

(b) To obtain a certificate of discharge of inheritance tax. This is done by submitting a form of application to the Capital Taxes Office which will issue a certificate to the effect that the inheritance tax position as regards assets declared is clear. (This will not avoid tax if some additional assets turn up at a later date which either make the estate taxable or increase the amount of tax due).

(c) Interim distributions may be made, e.g., if large sums have been collected but some matters remain to be resolved.

Once all outstanding matters have been dealt with, the final estate accounts are then prepared by the solicitors acting for the personal representatives and sent to the personal representatives for approval. When the accounts have been approved, the estate is then distributed, i.e., paid out to the persons entitled. If there are any legacies given by a will these may be paid out before the final distribution if the circumstances permit, but it will be up to the personal representatives to authorise such payment.

When payment is made from the estate it is usual to obtain receipts from the beneficiaries, or any person specified in any will as appropriate to give a receipt (e.g. a charity's treasurer).

It is usual to send a copy of the approved accounts to the residuary beneficiaries as well as to the personal representatives when finally distributing the estate.

6 Applying for the grant

6.1 The oath

Whatever type of grant is applied for it will be necessary to submit an *oath* which will either be an oath for executors in the case of an application for a grant of probate, or an oath for administrators in all other cases.

The oath is a sworn statement showing the name, address, postcode (if known) and entitlement of the applicant(s) and also details of the name, address, postcode (if known), dates of birth and death and domicile of the deceased. It also contains statements as to whether any minority or life interest arises (in the case of intestacy), whether there is any interest in settled land and that the applicant will 'collect get in and administer the estate according to the law'.

If an inheritance tax account is required the oath will show the actual figures shown in the account as the net and gross figures for probate purposes. (Such figures do not include anything passing by survivorship as the grant is not required for that, although the values are included for tax purposes.) If no inheritance tax account is required the gross value will be sworn as not exceeding the relevant excepted estates figure (i.e., currently £210,000 for deaths since 6 April 2000). The net value should be rounded up to the next whole thousand and sworn as 'not exceeding . . .' that figure (from 13 April 2002).

There are different forms of wording in the oath depending on the type of grant but the basic content and purpose of the oath is the same for both an oath for executors and an oath for administrators.

The oath for administrators will clear off persons with any better right to the grant and the oath for executors will describe the persons applying by reference to their appointment.

If power is reserved to an executor or excutors the oath will contain a statement that notice of the application has been given to them.

EXAMPLE

'I am the executor named in the will' or 'We are the executors named in the will' or 'I am one of/we are two of the executors named in the will'.

'I am the lawful husband and the only person entitled to the estate of the said deceased' (oath for administrator where the deceased left no issue, parents, brother or sisters of the whole blood or their issue).

'I am the son of the deceased and one of the persons entitled to share in the estate of the said deceased' (oath for administrators where the deceased left adult children but no spouse).

The oath is normally sworn to on the testament by the applicant but if this is not acceptable to the applicant, e.g., because of particular religious beliefs or because the applicant has no religious belief, then the jurat (the part of the oath which shows how it is sworn to) is amended to show that the applicant has chosen to *affirm*. This is equally binding on the applicant as an oath sworn on a testament and whether there is an oath or an affirmation, it is administered by a solicitor (or other person entitled to administer oaths) who has not been involved in the preparation of the oath and does not work for, and is not a partner in the firm which prepared the oath.

6.2 Inheritance tax account

(Students should read this section in conjunction with the section *Inheritance Tax* at the end of this chapter.)

6.2.1 Delivery of accounts

By s. 216, Inheritance Tax Act 1984 personal representatives are required to deliver an inheritance tax account within 12 months of the end of the month of death, unless the estate is an excepted estate (defined below). Before applying for the grant the personal representatives must decide whether an account is required. This depends initially on the gross value of the estate. With effect from 5 May 2000, if the gross value is less than £210,000 in respect of persons dying on or after 6 April 2000 the estate may be an excepted estate if it complies with the other requirements of s. 256, Inheritance Tax Act 1984; i.e.:

(a) the gross value is below £210,000 (or £200,000 if the date of death was between 6 April 1998 and 5 April 2000);

(b) not more than £50,000 worth of the estate is situate outside the UK (if death was prior to that date other limits apply);

(c) the estate consists only of property passing under the will or intestacy of the deceased or by nomination or survivorship;

(d) the value of lifetime transfers of cash, quoted shares or quoted securities made by the deceased (including potentially exempt transfers (see p. 464)) chargeable to tax does not exceed £75,000 (in respect of deaths prior to 6 April 1996 an estate would only be excepted provided there were no lifetime gifts which were not exempt and between 6 April 1996 and 5 April 1998 provided the value of lifetime transfers of items as above did not exceed £50,000);

(e) the deceased died after 1 April 1981 and was domiciled in the UK.

If the estate complies with the above then no account is required, although the tax office has the right to call for an account within 35 days of the grant being made.

If the estate does not comply with the requirements of s. 256 then an account will be required.

It should also be noted that if assets subsequently appear which mean that an estate which previously complied with s. 256 no longer complies, then the personal representatives must submit an account within six months of becoming aware of the assets.

6.2.2 Type of Inland Revenue account

As from February 2000 there is only one form of Inland Revenue account, the IHT 200. Prior to the introduction of this Form the most commonly used accounts were:

(a) IHT 200 (Old Form)—a 12-page account for use where the deceased died domiciled in the United Kingdom and the estate was neither an excepted estate nor one where any other form of account was applicable.

(b) IHT 202—a four-page account for use where the deceased died domiciled in the United Kingdom and an account was required but no tax was payable because after deduction of exemptions and reliefs the net estate did not exceed the threshold below which no tax was payable and the gross value of the estate before deduction of exemptions and reliefs did not exceed twice the inheritance tax threshold at the date of death and the deceased had not made any chargeable lifetime gifts and did not have any interest in settled property.

(c) IHT 201—for use where the deceased died domiciled other than in the United Kingdom.

Following the introduction of the new IHT 200 there is now only one form of account which replaces the three mentioned above. This new Form IHT 200 is now the prescribed form of account under s. 257, IHTA 1984 for all estates other than excepted estates, for deaths after 18 March 1986.

The Form is free and is obtained from the Capital Taxes Office. In addition to the Form the Capital Taxes Office provide a 'Practitioners' Guide' (Form 215) which contains one section entitled 'How to fill in Form 200', which deals separately with each part of the Form 200, and separate notes on how to complete and what to include in each of the 18 supplementary pages.

6.2.3 Purpose and contents of inheritance tax account

The purpose of the account is to give to the Inland Revenue Capital Taxes Office full details of all assets and liabilities of an estate. If the estate is taxable or the deceased was not domiciled in the United Kingdom the account together with all supplementary pages including the probate summary, D18, and any other documents required (see below) must be submitted to the Revenue, together with any tax due, before the application is made for the grant. The D18 is completed by the Capital Taxes Office and is returned to the applicant and is then sent with the application for the grant to the Probate Registry.

In other cases the D18 is sent with the application for the grant to the Probate Registry and at the same time the IHT 200 together with the supplementary pages (excluding D18) and any other documents are sent to the Capital Taxes Office.

It must be noted that if the estate is not an excepted estate then the full form of account must be used. Therefore, even if no tax is payable, the account must be used if the deceased held any life interest or any other interest in the estate of someone else, or had made any potentially exempt transfers, (PETs) which exceed the permitted amount or gifts with reservation (see further—Inheritance Tax).

6.2.4 Form of the new IHT 200

The IHT 200 is an eight-page Form and in addition to the Form there are 18 supplementary pages i.e.:

D1	The wll
D2	Domicile outside the United Kingdom
D3	Gifts and other transfers of value
D4	Joint and Nominated assets
D5	Assets held in trust (settled property)
D6	Pensions
D7	Stocks and Shares
D8	Debts due to the estate
D9	Life Insurance and annuities
D10	Household and personal goods
D11	Interest in another estate
D12	Land, buildings and interests in land
D13	Agricultural relief
D14	Business relief, business or partnership interests
D15	Foreign assets
D16	Debts owed by the estate
D17	Continuation sheet for additional information
D18	Probate summary

As will be seen below, not all the supplementary pages will be required in each case. As the Form IHT 200 is completed the relevant supplementary pages should be selected and completed and only those completed pages are sent to the Capital Taxes Office. There is also a check list to ensure nothing is forgotten when sending papers to the Capital Taxes Office. The check list is not submitted.

6.2.5 IHT 200

Page 1 contains at A details of the Probate Registry to which the application is being made for the grant; at B details of the name, address, dates of birth and death, marital status, surviving relatives, domicile, occupation, National Insurance Number, tax district and reference of the deceased; at C names, addresses, telephone and FAX numbers and contact reference of the firm or person dealing with the estate.

Page 2 contains section D—supplementary pages. There is a series of questions to be answered 'yes' or 'no' and if the answer is yes the appropriate supplementary page has to be completed e.g.:

Did the deceased leave a will?—if yes complete D1.

Did the deceased hold any joint assets?—if yes complete D4.

Did the deceased own any stocks or shares?—if yes complete D7.

Did the deceased own any land or buildings?—if yes complete D12.

When this page has been completed it should be clear which supplementary pages will be required. Each supplementary page number is given in a coloured box in section D and each supplementary page has the same colour coding on the corner so as to be clearly identifiable.

Page 3 contains at E a question only relevant to domicile in Scotland and at F details of the estate in the United Kingdom where tax may not be paid by instalments. The importance of establishing whether something is instalment option property is that the persons liable to pay the tax on it can elect to pay the tax by 10 annual instalments. If the instalment option property is sold within the 10 years then the balance of the tax falls due on the sale.

Items included at F include anything which the deceased could have disposed of personally and liabilities under this section include the funeral account and expenses. Assets held as a joint tenant with any other person or situated abroad are not included in this section but the value of nominated assets and the deceased's share as tenant in common are. The types of assets listed in F include investments, Premium Bonds, National Savings investments e.g. Savings Certificates (listed on D17), Bank and Building Society Accounts (listed on form D17), cash, debts and rents due to the deceased, income due, life insurance policies, income or capital gains tax repayments due, personal chattels e.g. clothes, jewellery and furniture, the deceased's interest in the unadministered estate of someone else, in fact anything which is of value and which was in the deceased's name in the United Kingdom and which is not instalment option property.

Tax on non-instalment option property must be paid before the application for the grant can be submitted and interest is due on outstanding tax six months from the end of the month of death.

Page 4 continues with F and lists the liabilities which are deducted from the assets including separately the funeral expenses (which can include the reasonable cost of a headstone). Any exemptions and reliefs claimed against section F property are also deducted at the end of F. This then produces a net figure for chargeable assets where tax may not be paid by instalments.

Page 5 contains G—details of the estate in the United Kingdom where tax may be paid by instalments. This includes land and buildings owned by the deceased (both freehold and leasehold) including the deceased's residence, certain shares and securities and business interests. Business interests include a business owned solely by the deceased, partnership interests and shares in a company which gave the deceased a controlling interest. Shares may also be instalment option property if they are unquoted shares which are valued at £20,000 or more and either the nominal value of the shares is not less than 10% of all the shares in the company or they are ordinary shares and their nominal value is not less than 10% of the nominal value of the ordinary shares in the company. Also if the shares held are not quoted and the tax on the shares plus other instalment option property is not less than 20% of the tax for which the person liable for the tax is liable, then they will be instalment option property.

At the beginning of G is the election whether the tax on the property is to be paid by instalments.

EXAMPLE

If a father leaves his house to his two sons, they may wish to continue living there. There may be insufficient cash in the estate to pay the tax and keep the house. By taking the instalment option the tax payment can be spread over 10 years.

Page 5 also contains details of the liabilities which are attributable to the instalment option property.

EXAMPLE

A owns a freehold property which is subject to a mortgage to XYZ Building Society. The mortgage will be deducted from the value of the property, which will be instalment option property.

The liabilities and any exemptions and reliefs claimed against section G property are deducted at the end of G thus leaving a net figure for chargeable assets in the United Kingdom where tax may be paid by instalments.

Page 6 contains H which is a summary of the chargeable estate. The notes at the start of this section refer to completion of a further form—IHT (WS). This is the Inheritance Tax worksheet which is used to work out the value of the estate and the tax. The IHT (WS) is not submitted to the Capital Taxes Office but the various totals taken from the IHT to complete the IHT (WS) are then transferred back to section H—Page 6—IHT 200 which is split into three parts i.e.:

Assets where tax may not be paid by instalments including:

The total from F (box 30)
Joint property passing by survivorship D4
Foreign property D15
Settled property on which the Trustee wishes to pay tax now D5

Assets where tax may be paid by instalments including:

The total from G
Joint property passing by survivorship D4
Foreign property D15
Settled property on which the Trustee wishes to pay tax now D5

Other property taken into account to calculate the total tax:

Settled property D5
Gifts with reservation D3

The totals of each of the above sections are then added together to produce the total value of the chargeable estate on death and then the cumulative total of lifetime transfers (i.e. PETs) is added to calculate the aggregate chargeable transfer i.e. the figure on which tax is calculated.

Page 7 contains J—Calculating the Tax Liability—again details are transferred from the IHT (WS). This section is split into two parts:

calculating the total tax payable and
calculating the tax payable on delivery of the Account.

The tax payable on delivery of the account will be the tax which may not be paid by instalments, less any double taxation relief (i.e. this relief applies because the deceased inherited assets on the death of someone else and the two deaths occurred within five years of each other. If tax was paid on the first death the tax on the second death is reduced on a sliding scale depending on the year in which the second death occurred e.g. if the second death is within one year of the first then there is a 100 per cent reduction decreasing to a 20 per cent reduction if the second death is between four and five years of the first).

If interest is due that will be added as will the instalments due in respect of instalment option property (plus interest if applicable).

Finally on Page 7 K includes the 'authority for repayment of Inheritance Tax' i.e. details of the party to whom a repayment should be made if there is an overpayment of tax. Without this authority, any repayment cheque will be in favour of all persons who signed the Form. The authority can be in favour of e.g. only one of the personal representatives or the firm of solicitors or other agent acting for the personal representatives.

Page 8 contains L, the declaration which is signed by the personal representatives stating the type of grant applied for (e.g. Probate or Letters of Administration), confirming that to the best of their knowledge, information and belief the information in the account and the supplementary pages is correct, that they have made the fullest enquiries reasonably practicable to establish the values and that if any values are provisional they will inform the Capital Taxes Office as soon as exact values are known.

There is a statement by the personal representatives that they understand that they may be liable to prosecution if they conceal information which affects the inheritance tax liability or if they deliberately include false information and also that they may be liable to financial penalties in the event of fraud or negligence or failure by them to remedy anything which is incorrect in the account within a reasonable time of it coming to their notice.

Finally there is a statement that the personal representatives understand that the account is only inspected in detail after the grant issues, that the Capital Taxes Office may ask questions, that further tax and interest calculations may be necessary and that interest may be payable on unpaid instalments.

6.2.6 Supplementary pages to IHT 200

If any of the supplementary pages are required all relevant questions on each page must be completed and the information carried to the IHT 200 as necessary.

6.2.7 Form D18

The D18 must be completed in all cases and either sent to the Capital Taxes Office or with the application for the grant of probate as appropriate (see 6.2.3 above).

The D18 contains at A the name and address of the Solicitor or other person to contact (from C Page 1 IHT 200) and the name of the Probate Registry, at B the name, address, date of death and domicile of the deceased and at C a summary for probate purposes from the IHT 200 i.e. the gross and the net estate for probate purposes and details of the tax paid (or if no tax is due it will show NIL). It should be noted that the only figures taken into account for probate purposes are those relating to assets for which the grant is required. Property passing by survivorship is *not* included.

6.2.8 Delivery of reduced account

Subsequent to the introduction of Form IHT200 in May 2000 the Capital Taxes Office then introduced in October 2000 provisions whereby a reduced Inland Revenue Account can now be delivered if the following conditions are met:

(a) the deceased died domiciled in the United Kingdom;

(b) most of the assets passing by will or intestacy pass directly:

  (i) to the surviving spouse or into a trust under which the surviving spouse has the right to benefit and the spouse was domiciled in the United Kingdom at the date of death; OR

  (ii) to a charity registered in the United Kingdom or a body listed in sch. 3 to the Inheritance Tax Act 1984 or to be held on trusts established in the United Kingdom for charitable purposes; AND

(c) the gross value of assets passing to beneficiaries other than as at (b) above plus any other assets chargeable on death (e.g. joint assets held with someone other than the surviving spouse or trust property) plus the chargeable value of gifts made within seven years of death is less than the inheritance tax threshold current at the date of death.

If the above conditions are fulfilled the form of the reduced Inland Revenue Account is still the IHT200 but with the following amendments:

Page 1	Still completed in full
Page 2	All questions must be answered and if Questions 1–6 or 15 are answered 'yes' then the relevant supplementary pages must be completed. However if the reply to Questions 7–14 or 16 is 'yes' there is no need to fill in the relevant supplementary pages if *all* the items pass to an exempt beneficiary. Also if the guide to IHT200 requires Form D17 to be competed as to e.g. bank accounts there is *no* need to complete D17 if all items pass to exempt beneficiaries
Pages 3–5	All boxes must be completed but where the assets pass to exempt beneficiaries an estimated value may be given
Pages 6 and 7	These should be completed even though there should not be any tax to pay

Page 8   Should be completed in full *but* Box L3 should *not* include items with an estimated value which pass to an exempt beneficiary

It should also be noted that if a deed of variation is signed and an election made so that assets previously exempt from inheritance tax become chargeable then the relevant supplementary pages must be completed and if previously estimated values were given for any such assets then a corrective account with market values must be delivered. Also if having delivered a reduced account it becomes obvious that a full account should have been delivered then again the relevant supplementary pages must be completed and delivered with a corrective account.

7 Other affidavit evidence

7.1 Non-Contentious Probate Rules 1987

The Non-Contentious Probate Rules 1987, rules 12 to 15 set out various circumstances in which the District judge or Registrar will require evidence in addition to the usual oath by personal representatives.

Rule 12—Evidence as to due execution of the will.
Rule 13—Evidence as to execution of a will by a blind or illiterate testator.
Rule 14—Evidence as to terms, condition and date of execution of a will.
Rule 15—Evidence where there appears to be an attempted revocation of a will.

7.2 Affidavit of due execution of a will

Under rule 12, where a will contains no attestation clause, or the clause is insufficient, or there is any doubt about the execution, the District judge or Registrar will require an affidavit of due execution. This will normally be required from the witnesses to the will. If the witnesses are unavailable, the District judge or Registrar may accept an affidavit from someone else present when the will was signed. Failing such persons he may accept affidavit evidence from someone else to show that the signature is the testator's own handwriting, or as to any other fact which would lead to a presumption of due execution.

However, if the District judge or Registrar is satisfied that the distribution of the estate is not affected by the will he may accept it for probate without any such evidence.

If the will is that of a blind or illiterate testator, or there is any doubt that the testator knew and approved the contents of the will, the District judge or Registrar will have to be satisfied that the testator knew the contents of the will (rule 13, Non-Contentious Probate Rules 1987). If the attestation clause sets out the circumstances of the signing and witnessing, i.e. that a will was read over to a blind testator before the signature and witnessing, then no further evidence will normally be required.

7.3 Affidavit of plight and condition

7.3.1 Alterations in a will

By rule 14, Non-Contentious Probate Rules 1987, where there is any 'obliteration, interlineation or other alteration' which has not been validated by the testator and the witnesses, either by signing or placing their initials at the side of the amendment (or by the re-execution of the will), then the District judge or Registrar will require evidence to show that the amendments were present at the time the will was executed. If no evidence can be given then the will will be admitted to probate as if the amendments had not been made. If the amendment is an obliteration which makes it impossible to read what has been obliterated, probate will be granted with a space where words have been obliterated.

However, rule 12(2) provides that no additional evidence will be required if the amendment 'appears to the District judge or Registrar to be of no practical importance'.

It is therefore vital that, if any amendments are made to a will, before it is executed, they are all signed or initialled by the testator and both the witnesses before the will is executed in order to validate them.

7.3.2 Marks on the will

If there are any marks on the will, or it appears from the state of it that the testator may have attempted to revoke it, then the state of the will must be explained to the satisfaction of the District judge or Registrar, usually by the person finding it.

EXAMPLE

Following a fire at his home A is taken to hospital where he subsequently dies. B helps to clear up in A's house and finds A's will which has been damaged in the fire. B takes the will to A's solicitor. The District judge or Registrar will require an affidavit of plight and condition from B explaining the state of the will and the circumstance of his finding of the will.

If a will has any marks on it to show that something may have been attached to it, e.g. marks left by a staple, pin or paperclip, then the District judge or Registrar will require an affidavit as to what was attached so as to ensure that it was not some other testamentary document, e.g. a codicil. Sometimes a District judge or Registrar will accept a letter from a solicitor if he can explain the marks.

EXAMPLE

Following A's death, when his solicitor takes A's will from its envelope, a rusty paperclip attaching a note to A's will containing details of a beneficiary's address, falls to pieces leaving a rusty mark on A's will. A letter from the solicitor will usually be acceptable to the District judge or Registrar.

Affidavits of plight and condition will usually be required from the person finding the will or having knowledge of the reason for the state of the will.

Inheritance (Provision for Family and Dependants) Act 1975

1 Introduction

As we have already seen, if a person dies testate he has made a valid will which disposes of his estate according to his wishes. If a person dies intestate the law stipulates who is to inherit his estate.

In both cases the distribution of the estate is clear-cut so long as there is no one who believes that he should have been provided for, either under the will or intestacy rules, but who has not been so provided for.

There are occasions, however, when neither the will nor statute takes into account the persons who ought to receive something and who are, or who believe they are, entitled to receive something from the deceased's estate. Generally, other than a spouse, only someone who is a '*dependant*' of the deceased will have a valid claim against the estate.

Any claim by spouse, cohabitee or a dependant will, in respect of a death after 31 March 1976, arise under the Inheritance (Provision for Family and Dependants) Act 1975 and will have to be pursued under the provisions of the Act, which sets out the classes of persons entitled to claim; when the claim must be made; what provision the courts can order and the considerations the court must take into account when deciding an application.

It is of course open to the parties to settle a claim without court proceedings. One method of doing this would be for all the beneficiaries and the claimant to enter into a deed of arrangement. This is a process whereby a deceased's estate under a will or intestacy may be redistributed by those concerned, and this redistribution will be accepted by the Revenue for tax purposes as a distribution by the deceased, provided that notice of the deed is given to the Revenue within six months of the date of the deed and the deed is made not more than two years after death. The redistribution is therefore effectively treated as a disposition made by the deceased.

2 Against whom may a claim be made?

By s. 1(1), Inheritance (Provision for Family and Dependants) Act 1975 a claim can only be made against the estate of a deceased who died domiciled in England and Wales.

3 When must the claim be made?

By s. 4 of the 1973 Act an application must be made to the court within six months of the date of grant of representation being issued to the personal representatives. The court may in certain circumstances grant permission for a later application.

This is at the court's discretion, and although the Act does not specify the matters which the court should consider it will look at all the circumstances and consider whether an extension is required 'in the interests of justice'.

The burden is on the applicant to show exceptional circumstances and that he has an arguable case. The court will consider, e.g., the reason for the delay, whether negotiations have taken place in the time limit, whether the estate has been distributed and whether refusal would cause hardship or be unfair to the applicant and leave him with no other remedy.

Bouette v *Rose* (2000)

Louise Bouette, who was disabled at birth as a result of medical negligence (for which she was awarded £250,000) died aged 14 having been looked after by her mother since birth, her father having left when she was eight months old. Her mother received maintenance from the Court of Protection from Louise's fund which after her death was to be divided equally between her Parents. The Court of Appeal on Appeal, granted Mrs Bouette leave to apply out of time to pursue a claim under s. 1(1)(e) as a dependant on the basis that Louise needed her mother's constant care and therefore Mrs Bouette's needs were Louise's needs and there was a dependency and moral obligation on Louise to provide for her mother.

4 Who may claim under the Inheritance (Provision for Family and Dependants) Act 1975?

Section 1 of the 1975 Act lists the persons who may make a claim under the Act.

> 1.—(1) Where after the commencement of this Act a person dies domiciled in England and Wales and is survived by any of the following persons—
> (a) the wife or husband of the deceased;
> (b) a former wife or former husband of the deceased who has not remarried;
> (ba) any person (not being a person included in paragraphs (a) or (b) above) to whom subsection (1A) below applies;
> (c) a child of the deceased;
> (d) any person (not being a child of the deceased) who, in the case of any marriage to which the deceased was at any time a party, was treated by the deceased as a child of the family in relation to that marriage;
> (e) any person (not being a person included in the foregoing parapraphs of this subsection) who immediately before the death of the deceased was being maintained, either wholly or partly, by the deceased;

that person may apply to the court for an order under section 2 of this Act on the ground that the disposition of the deceased's estate effected by his will or the law relating to intestacy, or the combination of his will and that law, is not such as to make reasonable financial provision for the applicant . . .

> 1.—(1)(A) This subsection applies to a person if the deceased died on or after 1st January 1996 and, during the whole of the period of two years ending immediately before the date when the deceased died, the person was living—

(a) in the same household as the deceased, and

(b) as the husband or wife of the deceased. $Co-habitees$

Sections 1(1)(ba) and 1(1A) were added to s. 1, Inheritance (Provision for Family and Dependants) Act 1975 by the Law Reform (Succession) Act 1995.

The wife or husband of the deceased includes a judicially separated spouse, and a child includes an illegitimate child or child 'en ventre sa mere', but does not include a child adopted after his deceased parent's death but before he makes an application under the Act.

4.1 Who may be a dependant?

It will be seen from the list of persons who may claim that as well as 'family', a cohabitee falls within the definition of a dependant. This is desirable since the trend to cohabit has increased over recent years. Situations arose before the Inheritance (Provision for Family and Dependants) Act 1975 where couples had not married but had lived together as man and wife for many years. If one of them died intestate the survivor was not entitled to anything under the rules of intestacy. Clearly this was not a desirable situation. Since the passing of the Act, although the survivor still has to take court action for provision (in the absence of a claim being agreed with the beneficiaries), at least the Act recognises the survivor's rights and it is open to the court to award the survivor a sum similar to that which a surviving spouse could have expected.

In any cases which fall within s. 1(1)(e), the applicant must have been maintained by the deceased 'immediately before the death of the deceased'.

Jelley v *Iliffe* (1981)

Mr Jelley, the applicant, applied under s. 1(1)(e) for an order that he was entitled to reasonable financial provision from the estate of the deceased with whom he went to live, in her house, eight years before she died.

The 1975 Act is not designed to allow spurious claims by all and sundry who think they are entitled to something. It will only give rights to persons who are within the definition of family and dependants in s. 1.

5 What must the applicant prove?

An applicant must prove that he or she was dependent on the deceased, was maintained in some way by the deceased and that the distribution of the estate does not make 'reasonable financial provision' for the applicant. It is insufficient merely to show that the applicant is a relative if he or she has never relied on the deceased for maintenance.

The courts do, however, have other matters to take into account (see 6 below) and, especially where there is an intestacy, the courts have been prepared to allow claims where there was a moral obligation on the deceased, e.g. because the claimant had provided considerable services, even though there was no financial dependency. This is unlikely, however, to be allowed where there is a will, particularly if it is a fairly recent one.

The court may also consider who would in fact inherit under the rules of intestacy and may take a more generous view if it is, e.g. a distant relative and the claimant is someone who has been treated by the deceased as 'a child of the family'.

By s. 1(2), Inheritance (Provision for Family and Dependants) Act 1975 'reasonable financial provision' in the case of a spouse is 'such financial provision as it would be reasonable in all the circumstances of the case for a husband or wife to receive whether or not that provision is required for his or her maintenance'. Provision for a spouse is not limited to 'maintenance' and could include the transfer of property and or lump sum payments.

In all other cases 'reasonable financial provision' is defined as 'such financial provision as it would be reasonable in all the circumstances of the case for the applicant to receive for his maintenance'. Provision in these cases is limited to maintenance only.

Harlow v *National Westminster Bank* (1994)
The applicant, a successful businessman, applied for provision from his father's estate. His parents had separated when he was three and no financial provision was made for him. It was held on appeal that the court should consider only the obligations at the time of death and the applicant was unsuccessful.

By s. 1(3) of the 1975 Act a person claiming under s. (1)(e) is treated as being maintained if the deceased 'was making a substantial contribution in money or money's worth towards the reasonable needs of that person'. In such cases the person making the claim must not have been doing anything for which the contribution was intended as a payment.

Maintenance is not defined by the 1975 Act but where the claim is other than by a spouse it seems that the courts take into account all the circumstances, and will need to be satisfied that the contribution by the deceased was a substantial contribution towards the needs of the applicant.

Re Coventry, Coventry v *Coventry* (1979)
The judge stated that 'it does not mean just enough to enable a person to get by; on the other hand, it does not mean anything which may be regarded as reasonably desirable for his general benefit or welfare'.

6 Matters which the court must consider when making orders for provision (s. 3, Inheritance (Provision for Family and Dependants) Act 1975)

Section 3 of the 1975 Act sets out the general matters which the court must consider when making an order under the Act, i.e. the financial resources and needs of the applicant and any beneficiary of the estate (and also of any other applicant under the Act), at the time of the application or in the foreseeable future; any obligations and responsibilities which the deceased had towards the applicant or any beneficiary of the estate; the size and nature of the estate; any physical or mental disability of the applicant or a beneficiary of the estate and finally, by s. 3(1)(g), 'any other matter, including the conduct of the applicant or any other person which in the circum-stances of the case the court may consider relevant'.

In addition to these general considerations in each case, subsections (2), (2A), (3) and (4) of s. 3 set out other specific considerations depending on within which class the applicant falls.

6.1 Application by a spouse (s. 3(2))

This subsection deals with the different matters which must also be considered if the applicant is a spouse or former spouse who has not remarried, i.e. the age of the applicant, the duration of the marriage and any contributions by the applicant to the welfare of the deceased's family including 'contributions made by looking after the home or caring for the family'.

A court must also consider what the applicant could have expected to be awarded on a divorce, unless there was a decree of judicial separation in force and continuing at the date of death.

Re Moody (deceased), Moody v Stevenson (1992)
The applicant lived in a house owned by his wife who made no provision for him in her will on the basis that he had 'adequate resources of his own'. The court ordered that he be allowed to live in the property as long as he was willing and able to do so subject to compensating for any deterioration in the property during that time.

Re Adams (2001)
The deceased and his wife had been married for 54 years and had 12 children. The deceased left his wife the household goods and personal effects and a legacy of £10,000. The widow claimed that was not reasonable provision and claimed the family home. Three of her children opposed the claim but agreed the provision made was not reasonable. It was held that the will did not contain reasonable provision taking into account amongst other things—that the widow would have received on divorce (and following *White* v *White* (2001)—a divorce case in which one of the consider-ations was equality between the spouses if they contributed equally with no bias in favour of the money earner and against the homemaker). The widow was awarded the family home but the legacy was reduced to £5,000.

6.1.1 Applications by persons under s. 1(1)(ba)
This subsection deals with the different matters which must also be considered if the applicant was, immediately before the date when the deceased died, living with the deceased (and had been for the whole of two years ending immediately before the date the deceased died) as the husband or wife of the deceased, i.e., the age of the applicant and the length of the period during which the applicant lived as the husband or wife of the deceased and in the same household as the deceased, and any contribu-tions made by the applicant to the welfare of the family of the deceased, including contributions made by looking after the home or caring for the family.

6.2 Application by child or person treated as child of the family (s. 3(3))

This subsection deals with the different matters which must also be considered if the applicant is a child, or person treated as a child of the deceased. In both cases the court must consider 'the manner in which the applicant was being or in which he might expect to be educated or trained.' Additionally, in the case of a person 'treated as a child of the family,' the Court must consider the basis on which responsibility had been assumed, the period over which that responsibility had been assumed, whether the deceased assumed that responsibility knowing the applicant was not the deceased's own child and whether it is anyone else's responsibility to maintain the child. Child can include a grown-up child.

Leach v *Lindeman* (1985)

The court held that a grown up stepdaughter could claim on her stepmother's intestacy on the basis that the rules of intestacy did not make reasonable provision for her as a child of the family in relation to the marriage of her father with her stepmother.

Snapes v *Aram* (CA) (1998)

On an appeal against an award of maintenance granted to a daughter from her father's estate after an increase in the value of the estate it was held that 'there was no requirement to prove moral obligation or special circumstances and that the Court could take into account the fact that the father's will contained an expression of wishes that if his wife survived him she should make provision for, inter alia, the daughter, and also the fact that at the date of the hearing the value of the property had increased. (See s. 3(1)(g) and 3(5).)

6.3 Application by persons under s. 1(1)(e) (s. 3(4))

Under s. 3(4) the court must consider 'the extent to which and the basis on which the deceased assumed responsibility for the maintenance of the applicant and the length of time for which the deceased discharged that responsibility'.

6.4 Other considerations under s. 3

On any application the court considers the facts as known at the time of the application (s. 3(5)). Under s. 3(6) the earning capacity of the applicant is taken into account when considering financial resources, and financial obligations are taken into account when looking at financial needs.

7 Orders which may be made

If reasonable financial provision is not made by the will or intestacy rules, the court may make various orders taking into consideration the matters referred to in 6 above.

Section 2, Inheritance (Provision for Family and Dependants) Act 1975 sets out the orders which a court may make, i.e.:

(a) periodic payments;

(b) lump sum payments, which may be by instalments (s. 2(1)(b) and s. 7(1));

(c) transfer of property orders;

(d) settlement for the benefit of the applicant of property in the estate;

(e) the purchase of such property as the court may specify out of the estate and the transfer of such property to or on settlement for the applicant;

(f) orders varying any ante or post nuptial settlements for the benefit of the surviving spouse or child or person treated as a child of that marriage.

Any orders made may contain whatever provisions the court consider necessary for making the orders effective, e.g. periodic payments may be in such sum and for whatever period the court stipulates.

The court also has power under s. 5 to make interim orders and when doing so should, so far as possible, take into consideration the same matters as those referred to in an application under s. 2.

8 Conclusion

Although it is not perhaps satisfactory that a valid claimant should have to take court proceedings in order to obtain his or her share of the deceased's estate, at least it has been recognised by the 1975 Act that situations can arise where a testator does not make adequate provision for someone he should provide for, and that the intestacy rules may not recognise all the persons entitled to share in an estate on intestacy.

Inheritance tax

1 What is inheritance tax?

During an individual's lifetime he will be subject to various taxes, both in respect of income (i.e., income tax which is charged on income from all sources) and capital gains (i.e., capital gains tax which is charged on gains made by the disposal of a capital asset, e.g. shares and real property). In both cases there are allowances and exemptions which mean that the whole of a person's income or capital gains may not be subject to tax.

On death an individual does not escape a tax liability. The tax chargeable on death is inheritance tax. As with lifetime taxes there are exemptions and reliefs which mean that the whole value of a person's estate may not be taxable on death.

If the net value of an individual's taxable estate is below the threshold above which tax is chargeable, currently £250,000, then no inheritance tax will be chargeable on the estate on death. If, however, the net taxable estate is above that threshold, then inheritance tax will be chargeable at the rate of 40 per cent on the sum above that figure.

EXAMPLE

A dies leaving a net taxable estate of £260,000. Tax will be charged at 40 per cent on the sum of £10,000, being the excess over the tax threshold.

The principal Act dealing with inheritance tax is the Inheritance Tax Act 1984 (formerly the Capital Transfer Tax Act 1984). The Inheritance Tax Act 1984 will be referred to in the rest of this chapter as IHTA 1984.

2 Introduction of inheritance tax

The name 'inheritance tax' was introduced by the Finance Act 1986 and it is now the relevant tax in respect of deaths on or after 1 March 1986. Prior to that date the relevant tax was known as capital transfer tax, which itself replaced estate duty in respect of deaths on or after 13 March 1975.

3 When is inheritance tax chargeable?

Inheritance tax is chargeable in respect of ' . . . a transfer of value which is made by an individual but is not . . . an exempt transfer' (s. 2(1), IHTA 1984). This means that the tax is potentially chargeable in respect of lifetime gifts as well as on death.

By s. 4 of the IHTA 1984, in respect of a death, there is a deemed transfer of value of the assets in the deceased's estate at the moment of death. Tax is therefore chargeable on the net value of the estate. This value will include all assets in the deceased's sole name, the value of the deceased's share of any jointly owned property and any interests in possession in settled property (i.e. anything which the deceased was receiving by way of an interest in someone else's estate or an interest in a trust).

The net value will also include the value of any outright gifts made by the deceased within seven years prior to his death. Such a gift is known as a potentially exempt transfer (PET) and the value as at the date of the gift is included in the value of the deceased's estate at the date of death.

The net value will also include the value, as at the date of death, of any gifts which the deceased made which were not outright gifts but were gifts in which the deceased retained some continuing interest. These are known as 'gifts with reservation'.

3.1 Potentially exempt transfers

If an individual makes an outright gift during his lifetime to another individual (or into an accumulation and maintenance trust or a trust for a disabled person) and then survives for seven years, the value of that gift does *not* form part of his estate for inheritance tax purposes on death. Gifts other than as referred to above will be included in the estate for tax purposes on death.

If, however, the individual does not survive for the period of seven years, then the value of the gift as at the date of the gift is added to the value of the estate at death. For tax purposes this increases the value of the estate on death by the value of the gift as at the date of the gift.

However, by s. 7, IHTA 1984 the amount of tax attributable to the gift is reduced on a sliding scale if the person making the gift survives for more than three years after making the gift, i.e.:

death in the fourth year—80 per cent of the tax is payable;
death in the fifth year—60 per cent of the tax is payable;
death in the sixth year—40 per cent of the tax is payable;
death in the seventh year—20 per cent of the tax is payable.

3.2 Exempt transfers

Details of exempt transfer are set out in ss. 18–28, IHTA 1984. These include:

(i)   Transfers between spouses in life or on death without limit unless the deceased is domiciled outside the UK when there is a limit of £55,000 (s. 18, IHTA 1984).

(ii)   Gifts of up to £3,000 in any one year. Any unused part of the £3,000 can be carried forward to the next year but it can only be carried forward for one year, i.e. the total exemption for any two year period cannot exceed £6,000 (s. 19, IHTA 1984).

(iii)   Small gifts not exceeding £250 annually (s. 20, IHTA 1984).

(iv)   Gifts which are part of normal expenditure out of income and which do not reduce the transferor's standard of living (s. 21, IHTA 1984).

(v)   Gifts in consideration of marriage of up to £5,000 where the gift is made by a parent to a child; up to £2,500 where the gift is made by either party to the marriage or by a grandparent or remoter ancestor of either party; up to £1,000 in any other case (s. 22, IHTA 1984).

(vi)   Gifts to charities either in life or on death (s. 23, IHTA 1984).

Other exemptions include gifts to political parties and registered housing associations, gifts for national purposes to specified bodies and gifts for 'public benefit'.

4 Transfer of value

A transfer of value is defined by s. 3(1) of the IHTA 1984 as '. . . a disposition made by a person (the transferor) as a result of which the value of his estate immediately after the disposition is less than it would be but for the disposition; and the amount by which it is less is the value transferred by the transfer'.

The important point to note is that the value transferred is the *reduction* in value to the transferor not necessarily the value of the item to the transferee, which may be more or less than the value to the transferor.

EXAMPLE

A owns a valuable collection of toy lead figures valued at £20,000 as a collection. A has been told that if he gives one item from the collection (valued individually at £2,000) this will reduce the value of the collection to £l5,000. If A gives the item to B it will be treated as a transfer of value of £5,000 being the reduction in value to A, rather than the £2,000 value of the item on its own.

The word 'disposition' is not defined by the Act but it is clear from the Act that it is taken to mean the reduction in value of the transferor's estate, which may occur either through an act (e.g. giving something away or selling it at a reduced value) or through an omission. By virtue of s. 3(3) of the IHTA 1984 it is necessary, however, that the value of another person's estate is increased by the transferor's omission. It is not normally necessary to look at the effect of a transfer on the transferee's estate; see the example above.

5 Rate of tax

On death, tax is charged at the rate current at the date of death. The rate of tax may be altered in any government Budget and the current rate is 40 per cent where the net taxable value is in excess of the current threshold i.e. £250,000.

Prior to 1988 there were different rates of tax in respect of different bands of the estate, e.g., in respect of death between 17 March 1987 and 14 March 1988 (during which time the tax threshold was £90,000) the lowest rate of tax was 30 per cent between £90,000 and £140,000; the highest rate of tax was 60 per cent over £330,000. Each band of the estate was taxed at the appropriate rate.

6 Reliefs from tax

Part V of the IHTA 1984 sets out the various reliefs from inheritance tax which may be claimed in respect of certain types of property. These reliefs take the form of a reduction in the value of the asset to be taxed. The basic reliefs available are in respect of business and agricultural property and woodlands.

As from 10 March 1992, following the government's Budget, the reliefs are as follows:

ASSET	RELIEF
1 Business interests in a partnership or as a sole proprietor of a business.	100 per cent
2(a) Controlling holdings in unquoted trading companies and unquoted shares in a company.	100 per cent
(b) A minority holding in unquoted trading companies not giving control.	100 per cent

ASSET	RELIEF
3 Controlling holdings in fully quoted trading companies.	50 per cent
4 Agricultural property	
(a) owner occupied farms;	100 per cent
(b) farms subject to a tenancy which could be terminated within 12 months;	100 per cent
(c) farms subject to other tenancies (for land let after 31 August 1995—100 per cent).	50 per cent
5 Assets owned by a partner or controlling shareholder personally and used in the business or company.	50 per cent

Questions

1   C has died leaving a will appointing X, Y and Z as executors. X and Y come to see you and explain that as Z is out of the country on business he would prefer not to be involved with the administration of the estate.

When you look at the will you see:

(a)   The amount of a legacy has been altered from £200 to £2,000. This alteration has been initialled by C and both of the witnesses.

(b)   A legacy of £50 to Q has been crossed out in red ink but is still legible.

(c)   C has left a legacy to P who has also witnessed the will.

(d)   The will has been signed by C and witnessed by P and R but it does not contain an attestation clause.

Advise X and Y:

(a)   Whether they alone can prove the will and what will be required in respect of Z.

(b)   As to the effect of the alterations in the will.

(c)   The effect of P witnessing the will.

(d)   Whether the lack of an attestation clause is relevant.

Outline answer

Consider the following points:

(a)   Discuss the permitted number of proving executors and the alternative methods of dealing with non-proving executors.

(b)   The general effect of attested and non-attested alterations in a will.

(c)   The requirements of s. 9, Wills Act 1837, as amended, and the effect of s. 15 of the Wills Act 1837 and s. 1 of the Wills Act 1968.

(d)   The requirements of s. 9 of the Wills Act 1837 as to attestation clauses generally and the requirements of the District judge or Registrar if no such clause is used.

(e)   Conclusion—summarise the position.

2   C is going on holiday and wishes to make a home-made will. Advise him whether he can do this and of the statutory requirements with which he must comply in order to make a valid will. Explain the effect of non-compliance with these requirements. C also asks if he can leave a legacy to his executor.

3   C has asked you to draft a will for him and wishes to know the difference between a specific legacy and a general legacy. He also wishes to know what will happen to the subject matter of a gift if the beneficiary predeceases him, or if he, C, has disposed of the

subject matter of the gift prior to his death. Also, can he ensure that he does not leave any of his estate out of his will?

4   C, who is B's brother and the executor named in B's will, tells you that B has died and hands to you B's will. In the will, B has left everything to C. You see that the will has not been signed or witnessed.

C tells you that apart from a nephew aged 19 and a niece aged 16, being the children of a sister of C and B and who predeceased B, he, C, is the only other relative of B.

   Advise C who is entitled to B's estate and why. Who will deal with the administration of the estate?

5   C, a widow, has died leaving a will appointing her two adult children, X and Y, as executors. C's estate is worth £260,000 gross (£257,000 net). X and Y tell you that the estate comprises of a freehold property worth £175,000 and the balance of the estate comprises personal chattels and cash.

Advise X and Y:

(a)   Who is entitled to apply for what type of grant to the estate.

(b)   Who is entitled to the estate.

(c)   As to the inheritance tax position.

6   C is the brother of B and the appropriate person to be the administrator of B's estate. B was a bachelor and C tells you that B was cohabiting with Y at the time of his death.

Explain to C:

(a)   How the grant of letters of administration will be obtained and in particular what documents C will have to sign.

(b)   How the value of the estate affects whether or not any inheritance tax account will be required.

(c)   How C can protect himself against claims from creditors after he has completed the administration of the estate.

(d)   How Y might be entitled to make a claim against the estate.

Index

Abatement 422–3
Acceptance
  certainty 13
  communication *see*
      Communication of
      acceptance
  conditional 12–13
  counter offers 12
  fact of 10–14
  methods 18–19
  must fit offer 12
  tenders 13
  termination of offer by 20–2
  without knowing 19–20
Ademption 420, 421
Administration
  chain of executorship 443–4
  death before administration
      completed 443
  grant of letters of 400, 443–4
  persons entitled to grant
      dying 442
Administrators
  appointment
    intestacy 441–2
    timing 441
    where valid will 442–3
  intestacy 441–2
  persons of equal degree 442
Adoption, capacity to marry 317
Adultery 329–30
  living together after 335
Advancement presumption 81
Advertisements
  auctions 7
  credit supply 182
  for creditors in probate 445–6
  offer of contract 8–9
Affinity 315
Agency
  apparent authority 41
  mercantile agents 163–4
  undisclosed principle 41
Agreements
  business 24–6
  collective 26–7
  composition agreements 33–4
  contract 5–45
  credit *see* Credit
  discharge by 111–13

social 22–4
solus agreements 85
Agricultural produce 196
Appropriation powers
  personal representatives
      434–5
  trustees 414
Asbestos 302
Auctions 7
  'without reserve' 65

Bailment 170
Bank credit cards 175, 176
Bargaining powers 68
Battle of the forms 65
Beckford, Jasmine 363, 364
Behaviour
  dismissal for misconduct
      225–6
  divorce and 330–2
  financial provisions and
      after final decree 351
      for married couples 359–60
  living together after 335
Bids, referential 10
Breach of contract
  damages
    account for profits 121
    basis of claim 123
    contributory negligence
        127–8
    cost of cure 126–7
    failure to deliver 125
    general 120
    liquidated 120
    loss of amenity 126
    loss of opportunity 126
    market price rule 125
    measure of 125–7
    mitigation of loss 127
    nominal 121
    refusal to accept delivery
        125
    remoteness 123–5
    special 120
    sub-sales by buyer 125–6
    unliquidated 120
  discharge by
    actual breach 118
    anticipatory breach 118–20

failure to deliver 125
refusal to accept delivery 125
remedies 120–33
  damages *see* damages
  injunctions
    mandatory 132, 133
    prohibitory 132–3
  limitation of action 133
  quantum meruit 109, 128
specific performance
  constant supervision 131
  definition 128–9
  discretion of court 129–30
  inadequate damages 129
  mutuality principle 130
  personal service 130
  requirements for 129–30
  unenforceable contracts
      130–2
  termination of credit
      agreement 189–90
Budget accounts 175
Buildings, consumer protection
      for materials 196
Business efficacy test 51

Capacity
  contract and
    corporations 107–8
    minors 106–7
    non-consummation and 323
    wills and 401
Capital gains tax 463
Care orders 383–4
Care proceedings
  intervention standard 380–3
  investigation and prosecution
      380
Carlile, Kimberley 363, 364
Caveat emptor 134
Charge cards 175, 176
Child assessment orders 387
Child of the family 362, 395
Child orders
  after final decree 346–7,
      348–9, 355
  married couples 361–2
Child Support Act 1991 363,
      391–5
  basic principles 392–3

departure system 393–4
maintenance 395–6
parentage disputes 394
statutory formula 393
Child Support Agency 392–3, 395
Child Support Appeal Tribunal
    394
Child Support Pensions and
        Social Security Act
        2000
    additional support 394
    applications for variation
        393–4
    deductions 393
    disputes 394
    maintenance calculation 393
Children 363–96
    care orders 383–4
    child assessment orders 387
    child of the family 362, 395
    Children Act
        applicants 372–3
        basic principles 365–71
        checklist 368–70
        concurrent jurisdiction 364
        duration of orders 378
        jurisdiction under 371–3
        'no order' principle 370–1
        parental responsibility
            366–7, 369, 373
        procedural problems 364–5
        restrictions on s.8 orders
            377–8
        s.8 orders 373
        social problems 363–4
        welfare principle 367–8,
            377
    see also individual orders
    concurrent jurisdiction 364
    contact orders 367, 373,
        374–6, 377
    delay 371
    duration of orders 378
    emergency protection orders
        386–7
    family assistance order 378
    financial provision 346–7,
        348–9, 355, 361–2
    applications and orders
        390–1
    Child Support Act 1991
        391–5
    Child Support Pensions and
        Social Security Act
        2000 393–5

guardian ad litem 368, 378
Human Rights Act 386
in vitro fertilisation 366
lesbian mother 369, 370
local authorities see Local
    authorities and
    children
medical treatment against
    parent's wishes 377
non-intervention policy 370–1
parental responsibility 366–7,
    369, 370, 373
prohibited steps orders 373,
    376, 377
provision on divorce 339
residence orders 367, 369,
    373–4, 377
specific issue order 373, 376–7
supervision orders 384–5
welfare principle 367–8, 377
Children Act 1989 see Children
Choses in action 37
Citizens Advice Bureaux 134
Clauses of contract see Contracts,
    clauses and exclusion
    clauses
Clean-break principle 353
Climbie, Adjo 'Anna' 364
Codicils 400–1
Comfort letter 25–6
Commorientes 436
Communication of acceptance
    authorised person, by 15–16
    dispensing with 17
    exceptions 17–18
    general rule 14–15
    postal rule 18
    silence 16
    unilateral contracts 17
Composition agreements 33–4
Conditions 53–4
    Sale of Goods Act 1979 137
Conduct
    financial provisions and
        after final decree 351
    for married couples 359–60
    see also Behaviour; Misconduct
Confined Spaces Regulations
    1997 300–1
Consanguinity 315
Consent orders 361
Consideration 27–35
    composition agreements 33–4
    definition 28
    for discharge 112

exceptions to rule
    bills of exchange 29
    business situations 29
    previous request 29
executed 28, 112
executory 28, 112
existing duties
    imposed by contract with
        third party 32
    imposed by existing
        contract 31–2
    imposed by law 31
failure test 27
forbearance to sue 30–1
moves from promisee 30
must be sufficient 30
need not be adequate 29
part payment 32–4
past 28–9
Pinnel's case 32–3
promissory estoppel 34–5
rules 29–32
total failure test 27
trivial items 30
Consortium 314
Construction (Design and
    Management)
    Regulations 301
Construction (Health, Safety and
    Welfare) Regulations
    1996 300
Constructive dismissal 223
Consumer Credit Act 1974 174–93
    see also Credit
Consumer credit agreements 37
Consumer hire agreement 137,
    179
Consumer law
    caveat emptor 134
    Consumer Protection Act
        1987 193–201
    see also Consumer
        protection
contracts
    of exchange 137
    for goods and services 137
    hire 137, 179
    of hire purchase 137
    implied terms 137
    involving transfer of
        ownership of goods
        169–70
    sale contracts compared
        with other 136–7
    for services 137

credit *see* Credit
description 139–41, 169, 170
duties in performing contract
  buyer's 167
  seller's 167
estoppel 162–3
European law 135
exclusion clauses
  civil law 150
  criminal law 150
fitness for all purposes
  duration 147–8
  instructions 147
  Sale and Supply of Goods
    Act 1994 142, 143
  strict liability 148
fitness for purpose
  condition 146
  in course of business 146
  goods supplied 146
  hire of goods 170, 171
  particular purpose 146–7
  Supply of Goods (Implied
    Terms) Act 1973 173
  Supply of Goods and
    Services Act 1982 169,
    170, 171
hire of goods 137, 170–1, 179
hire purchase
  contracts 137
  sale of cars on 165–6
instructions 147
internet trading 134
mercantile agents 163–4
merchantable quality
  in course of business 141
  Sale of Goods Act 1979
    141
objectives 135
protection of consumer *see*
    Consumer protection
questions 203–4
remedies 150–2, 167–8
  of buyer 168
  of seller 168
repudiation 168
resale right 168
reservation of right of
    disposal 159–60
right of lien 168
risk transfer 152, 160–1
Romalpa clauses 159–60
Sale of Goods Act 1979
    136–68
  see also main heading

sales
  by buyer in possession 165
  by seller in possession 164–5
  of cars on hire purchase
    165–6
  common law powers 164
  contracts compared with
    other contracts 136–7
  statutory powers 164
  under voidable title 164
samples 149, 169, 173
  hire of goods and 170, 171
satisfactory quality 141–6
  appearance 144
  in course of business 142
  description 143
  durability 144
  exceptions to condition
    145–6
  finish 144
  fitness *see* fitness for all
    purposes
  freedom from minor
    defects 144
  goods supplied 144–5
  price 143
  reasonable buyer 142–3
  safety 144
  Supply of Goods (Implied
    Terms) Act 1973 173
  Supply of Goods and
    Services Act 1982 169,
    170, 171
'seal of approval' (OFT) 134
services 171–2
specific performance 168
stoppage in transit 168
Supply of Goods (Implied
    Terms) Act 1973
    172–4
Supply of Goods and Services
    Act 1982 169–72
  see also main heading
title 169
  encumbrances 138
  limited 139
  quiet possession 138
  right to sell 138
transfer of property 152
  in future goods 153
  in goods by non-owner
    162, 166–7
  in specific goods 153–6
  in unascertained goods
    153, 156–9

transfer of risk 152, 160–1
Consumer protection
  basic rule 195–6
  breach of statutory duty
    194–5
  buildings 196
  Consumer Protection Act
    1987 195–201
  contract actions 193–4
  damage 197–8
  'defect' meaning 196–7
  defences 199–201
  development risk defence
    200
  game or agricultural produce
    196
  internet trading 134
  latent defects 199
  limits of liability 199
  negligence actions 194
  producer liability 198–9
  product 196
  'seal of approval' (OFT)
    134
  state of art defence 200
  subsequent defect 200
  see also Unfair Contract Terms
    Act; Unfair Terms in
    Consumer Contracts
    Regulations
Consumers Association 76
Contact order 367, 373, 374–6,
    377
Continuity of employment
  redundancy 229–30
  unfair dismissal 215–16
Contra proferentem rule 62
Contracts 1–133
  acceptance *see* Acceptance
  advertisements 8–9
  agency
    apparent authority 41
    undisclosed principle 41
  agreement *see* Agreements
  auctions 7
  battle of the forms 65
  breach *see* Breach of contract
  business bias 3–4
  business efficacy 51
  capacity
    corporations 107–8
    minors 106–7
  clauses
    honour clauses 24–5
    indemnity 38–9, 59, 73

limitation 58–9, 70
liquidated damages clauses 56
penalty clauses 56
collateral contracts
  exclusion clauses 64–5
  privity exception 42
  representations or terms 45–6
communication of acceptance
  see Communication of acceptance
conditions 53–4, 137
consideration *see* Consideration
consumer law *see* Consumer law, contracts
contents *see* conditions; express terms; implied terms; parole evidence rule; representations; warranties
counter offer 12
  termination of offer by 21
deeds 5, 36
discharge *see* Discharge of contract
duress 98–9, 105–6
employment *see* Employment contract
exclusion clauses
  collateral contracts 64–5
  common law rules 59–65
  construction 62–3
  contra proferentem rule 62
  disclaimer 59
  fundamental breach doctrine 63
  incorporation 59–60
  indemnity *see* clauses
  inducements 68
  knowledge 68
  limitation *see* clauses
  main purposes rule 63
  misrepresentation 64
  notice 60–1
  overriding oral promise 64
  reasonableness test 68
  statutory rules 65–6
  third parties 64
  unfair contract terms *see* Unfair Contract Terms Act
  use of 58
express terms 40, 50

employment contract 206–7
formation 5–45
  see also Acceptance; Agreements; Consideration; Intention to contract; Offer; Privity of contract
freedom of contract 5
frustration *see* Frustration of guarantee 38–9
honour clauses 24–5
Human Rights Act 1
illegality *see* Illegality of contract
implied terms 49
  by courts 51
  by custom 50
  by statute 50–1
  description 51
  employment contract 211–15
  Sale of Goods Act 1979 137
  incorporation 59–60
  course of dealing 61–2
  notice 60–1
  signature 60
indemnity *see* clauses
information requests 9
innominate terms 53, 54–5
intention *see* Intention to contract
invitation to treat 6–7
legally binding 1, 2, 5, 10–14
letter of comfort 25–6
misrepresentation *see* Misrepresentation
mistake *see* Mistake
nature of 2–5
necessaries 106, 107
offer *see* Offer
'officious bystander test' 51, 52
parole evidence rule 48–9
  exceptions 49
performance *see* Discharge of contract, performance
personal service 130
privity *see* Privity of contract
questions 202–3
referential bids 10
representations
  collateral contracts 47–8

terms compared 45–6
repudiation 168, 191
requirements as to form 35–9
  deed, made by 36
  writing 36–8
restitution 107
restraint of trade
  imposed on employee 83–4
  on seller of business 84–5
  on seller of goods 85
sale contracts *see* Consumer law, contracts
for sale of land 36–7
secondary obligations 56–7
sexually immoral 79–80
simple 5
specialty 5
specific performance *see* Specific performance
statement of price 9
tenders 9–10
  acceptance 13
termination of offer *see* Termination of offer
terms *see* Terms of contract
tort compared 4–5
undue influence 98, 99–105
Unfair Contract Terms Act *see* Unfair Contract Terms Act
unilateral contracts 17
vitiating elements 77–108
void *see* Void contracts
voidable contracts 77, 107
warranties 53, 137
Contributory negligence, breach of contract damages 127–8
Control of Substances Hazardous to Health Regulations 1996 301–2
Corporations, contract capacity 107–8
Corruption of public life contract 79
Counter offer 12
  termination of offer by 21
Covenants on land, privity 41
Credit
  advertising 182
  agreement formation
    copies 184–5
    formalities 183–4
    non-compliance with formalities 185–6

withdrawal 183
budget accounts 175, 176
cancellation
    formalities 187
    right of 186–7
    unable to cancel 187
canvassing 182–3
charge cards 175, 176
conditional sales 175–6
    termination rights 190
Consumer Credit Act 1974
    174–93
consumer credit agreements
    37
    in writing 37
consumer hire agreement 179
credit cards 175, 176
debt collection 181
debtor-creditor agreements
    177–9, 188
debtor-creditor-supplier
    agreements 177–9,
    187–8
EFTPOS cards 176–7
exempt agreements 180
extortionate credit bargains
    192
fixed sum 179
hire purchase see Hire
    purchase
licensing system
    acting without licence
    181–2
    standard licences 181
linked transactions 180–1
loans 176
mortgage of land 175, 177
non-commercial agreements
    180
overdraft 176
partly regulated agreements
    180
pledge 175, 177
quotations 183
regulated agreements 179
remedies
    creditor 192–3
    damages and repudiation
    191, 193
    debtors 191–2
    extortionate credit bargains
    192
    time order 191–2
restricted use credit 177
running account credit 179

sale by 175
seeking business 182
small agreements 180
termination rights 188–91
    breach of contract 189–90
    by creditor with debtor
    default 191
    by creditor without debtor
    default 190–1
    conditional sales 190
    early repayment 190
    hire-purchase agreements
    190
    misrepresentation 188–9
unrestricted use credit 177
Credit broker 181
Credit reference agency 181
Custody of children 369

Damages
    Consumer Credit Act remedy
    191, 193
    misrepresentation remedy
    97–8
    see also Breach of contract,
    damages
Death
    donatio mortis causa 436–7
    exclusion of liability 74
    termination of offer by 22
Debt collection 181
Debtor-creditor agreements
    177–9
    cancellation 188
Debtor-creditor-supplier
    agreements 177–9
    cancellation 187–8
Deeds 5, 36
Defects
    in finished product not
    components 201
    latent 199
    meaning 196–7
    patent 199
    subsequent 200
Dependants
    inheritance provision see
    Probate
    time off work 242–3
Description 139–41, 169, 170
Desertion
    divorce
    constructive 333
    intention 332–3
    separation 332

married couples 360
Development risk defence 200
Director General of Fair Trading,
    role 76
Disability discrimination
    1995 Act 257–9
    arrangements 258
    changes to physical features of
    premises 258
    complaints 260–1
    disability definition 258
    insurance 260
    pensions 260
    recruitment 260
    trade organisations 260
Discharge of contract
    agreement
    consideration for 112
    variation and waiver 112–13
    breach
    actual 118
    anticipatory 118–20
    frustration see Frustration
    performance
    exceptions 109–10
    general rule 108–9
    part performance 110
    prevention of 109–10
    severable obligations 109
    substantial 110
    tender of 111
    time of 111
Disclaimer 59
Dismissal
    constructive 223
    procedure 234–5
    redundancy 227–30
    strike action 230–2
    unfair see Unfair dismissal
    wrongful 215, 217–19
Distance selling contracts 37–8
Divorce
    adultery 329–30
    living together after 335
    bars to
    children 337–8
    general financial protection
    337
    grave hardship 336
    length of marriage 335–6
    behaviour 330–2
    living together after 335
    children, provision for 339
    compulsory information
    meeting 339

'cooling off' period 339
decree 329
desertion
    constructive 333
    intention 332–3
    separation 332
ground 338
    importance of facts 328–9
    irretrievable breakdown
        329
    proving 328
information meeting 339
irretrievable breakdown 329
living together after adultery
        or behaviour 335
mediation 338, 339–40
no fault 338, 339
pensions 347–8
procedure 338
reconciliation 334–5
reflection and consideration
        339
reform proposals 338–40
separation
    2 years and consent 333–4
    5 years 334
    continuous 334–5
    desertion and 332
    reconciliation and 334–5
Donatio mortis causa 436–7
Duress
    contracts 98–9
    economic 99
    marriage 325–6
    remedies 105–6

Electronic Funds Transfer at
        Point of Sale
        (EFTPOS) 176
Emergency protection 386–7
    child assessment orders 387
    emergency protection orders
        386–7
Employer's Liability (Defective
        Equipment) Act 1969
        300
Employment contract 206–7
    breach of trust or confidence
        214
    confidential information use
        213–14
    cooperation in performance
        211
    example of 238–9
    express terms 207–11

implied terms 211–15
    minors 106
    national minimum wage 209
    notice 209
    reasonable care 211–13
    remuneration 208–9
    termination
        dismissal procedure 234–5
        fixed term employees 222–3
        methods 222–3
        notice 209
        see also individual reasons eg
            Redundancy; Unfair
            dismissal
Working Time Regulations
        210–11
Employment law 206–310
    continuity of employment
        215–16
    redundancy 229–30
    unfair dismissal 215–16
contract of employment *see*
        Employment contract
dependants 242–3
disability discrimination
    1995 Act 257–9
    arrangements 258
    changes to physical features
        of premises 258
    complaints 260–1
    disability definition 258
    insurance 260
    pensions 260
    recruitment 260
    trade organisations 260
disciplinary procedure
    example 240
discrimination *see* disability,
        marital status, racial
        and sex
        discrimination
dismissal
    constructive 223
    redundancy 227–30
    strike action 230–2
    unfair *see* Unfair dismissal
    wrongful 215, 217–19
health *see* Health and safety at
        work
manslaughter 291–2
marital status discrimination
    248
maternity
    ante-natal appointments
        243

compensation for service
        women 243
    leave 241–2
    pregnancy 239, 241
    right to return to work
        242
parental leave 242
part time employment 217
qualifying periods 219
    unfair dismissal 215–16
questions 309–10
race discrimination 254–7
    candidate selection 256
    contract workers 256–7
    exemptions 257
    internal promotion 257
    separate canteens 254–5
re-engagement 237
reinstatement 237
restraint of trade contracts
    imposed on employee 83–4
    on seller of business 84–5
    on seller of goods 85
restrictive trading agreements
    82
safety *see* Health and safety at
        work
sex discrimination 244–5
    contravention of other
        statute 251
    direct 245–6
    equal pay 251–2
        burden of proof 253
        compensation 253–4
        time limits 254
    exemptions 248–51
    genuine occupational
        qualifications 248–9
    indirect 246–8
    like work 252
    marital status 248
    pensions 249–51
    work rated as equivalent
        252–3
solus agreements 85
special knowledge 83
Equal pay 251–2
    time limits 254
Estoppel
    consumer law 162–3
    promissory *see* Promissory
        estoppel
European Convention on Human
        Rights
    children 386

family law 312
Exclusion clauses
  collateral contracts 64–5
  common law rules 59–65
  construction 62–3
  consumer law
    civil law 150
    criminal law 150
  contra proferentem rule 62
  disclaimer 59
  fundamental breach doctrine
    63
  incorporation 59–60
  indemnity 38–9, 59, 73
  inducements 68
  knowledge 68
  limitation 58–9, 70
  main purposes rule 63
  misrepresentation 64
  notice 60–1
  overriding oral promise 64
  reasonableness test 68
  statutory rules 65–6
  third parties 64
  unfair contract terms *see*
    Unfair Contract
    Terms Act
  use of 58
Executors
  appointment of 409–10,
    438–41
    'according to tenor' of will
      440
    by implication 440
  chain of executorship 443–4
  firms or trust corporations
    439
  individuals as 439
  lack of proving executors 441
  power reserved 440–1
  renunciation 440
  special 438
  unwilling or unable to prove
    440
Express terms *see* Contracts,
  express terms
Extortionate credit bargains 192

Family assistance order 378
Family law 311–98
  children *see* Children
  clean-break principle 353
  divorce *see* Divorce
  financial provisions *see*
    Financial provisions

human rights and 312
legal separation 356
marriage *see* Marriage
questions 397–8
Family Proceedings Court 356–7,
  365
Financial provisions
  after final decree
    age and length of marriage
      350
    applicants 342
    benefits loss 351
    child orders 346–7, 355
    clean-break 353
    commencement of
      proceedings 342–3
    conduct 351
    contribution to family
      welfare 350
    disabilities 350
    discretion of court 354–5
    financial needs and
      obligations 349–50
    financial resources 349
    interrelationship of orders
      355–6
    lump sum orders 344–5
    maintenance pending suit
      343
    Martin order 346
    Mesher order 346
    pensions 347–8
    periodical payments 343–4
    property orders 345–6
    sale of property 345
    settlement of property 345
    standard of living 350–1
    statutory background
      341–2
    statutory guidelines
      348–55
    transfer of property orders
      345
    variation of orders 354
    welfare of child 348–9
  for children 348–9, 355, 361–2
    applications and orders
      390–1
    Child Support Act 1991
      391–5
    Child Support Pensions and
      Social Security Act
      2000 393–5
  magistrates' courts *see* married
    couples

married couples 356–62
  child orders 361–2
  cohabitation 358
  consent orders 361
  grounds for order
    behaviour 359–60
    desertion 360
    failure to maintain 359
    voluntary separation
      360
  High Court or county court
    orders 362
  jurisdiction of court 356–7
  lump sums 357–8
  periodical payments 357
Fire Precautions (Workplace)
  Regulations 1997
    302–4
  fire certificate 303–4
  risk assessment 304
Fire Precautions (Workplace)
  Regulations 1999 302
Fixed sum credit 179
Foreign relations, illegal contracts
  damaging to 80
Frustration
  effects of 116–18
  foreseen events 116
  illegality 114
  impossibility 113–14
  limits on 115–16
  provision for 116
  radical difference 114–15
  self-induced 115–16
Funeral arrangements in will 410

Game 196
Gifts *see* Wills, gifts
Goods and services contracts 137
Guarantees
  contracts of guarantee 38–9
  manufacturers' 73
Guardian *ad litem* 368, 378
Guardians, appointment in will
  410–11

Hazardous substances 301–2
Health and safety at work
  1974 Act 292–305
  accident reporting and
    recording 305, 307
  accommodation
    clothing 277
    protective equipment 284
  asbestos 302

assessment 284
capabilities 270–1
compatibility of equipment
        284
competent persons 269
Confined Spaces Regulations
        1997 300–1
Construction (Design and
        Management)
        Regulations 301
Construction (Health, Safety
        and Welfare)
        Regulations 1996
        300
Control of Substances
        Hazardous to Health
        Regulations 1996
        301–2
controls for machinery 281–2
danger area provisions 270
dangerous machinery 280–1
defective equipment 300
doors 277
drinking water 277
drive shafts 283
dust 296
duties
    of employees 286, 296–7
        cooperation 270
        to inform 270, 271, 272
    of employers 262–5, 293–6
        information provision
            270, 271, 272
        general 271, 273
        regarding products 265–6
    to persons other than
        employees 297
    to persons using premises
        265
eating places 278
Employer's Liability (Defective
        Equipment) Act 1969
        300
equipment risks 278
escalators 277
eyes and eyesight 289–90
falls and falling objects 276
fire certificates 303–4
Fire Precautions (Workplace)
        Regulations 1997
        302–4
Fire Precautions (Workplace)
        Regulations 1999 302
floors 274–6
fumes 296

furnishings 273
gates 277
hazard sheet 269
hazardous substances 301–2
Health and Safety at Work
        (etc) Act 1974 261
health and safety document 296
    sample 305–8
health screening or
        surveillance 269, 308
information provision 284,
        290, 295
inspection 279
instructions 279, 284, 295
legionella 297
lifting operations and
        equipment 287–8
lighting 273, 282
lone working 272
maintenance 273, 278–9, 282,
        284
Management Regulations
        1992 267–72
manslaughter 291–2
Manual Handling Operations
        Regulations 1992
        285–7
manufactures, designers,
        importers and
        suppliers 299
markings 282
mechanical aids 286
medication 307
mobile work equipment 282–3
moving walkways 277
negligence rules 261–7
new equipment 280
objectives of prosecution 290
Offices, Shops and Railway
        Premises Act 1963
        267
outside contractors 308
Personal Protective Equipment
        at Work Regulations
        1992 283–5
persons in control of premises
        298
pits 276
Provision and Use of Work
        Equipment
        Regulations 1992
        278–83
Provision and Use of Work
        Equipment
        Regulations 1998 283

rest facilities 278
risk assessment 267–9
    fire 304
room dimensions 274
safe access 295–6
safe exits 295–6
safe plant 294
safe premises 298
safe systems of work 294
safety committees 300
safety policy document 269,
        296, 305–8
safety representatives 299
sample documents 305–8
sanitary conveniences 277
seating 274
self-employed undertakings
        270, 271
self-propelled work
        equipment 283
serious and imminent danger
        provisions 270
space 274
specific hazards 281
stability of machinery 282
suitability of equipment 278
supervision 307–8
tanks 276
temperature 273, 281, 296
temporary workers 271
traffic routes 274–6, 277
training 270–1, 279–80, 284,
        290, 295, 307–8
VDUs 288–9, 307
ventilation 273
vicarious liability 266
warnings 282
washing facilities 277
windows 276
Workplace Regulations 1992
        272–8
    enforcement 278
workstations 274, 288–90
    daily work 289
    eyesight 289–90
    training and information
        290
    VDUs 288–9, 307
young persons regulations
        271–2
Hire contracts 137
Hire of goods 170
Hire purchase
    Consumer Credit Act 1974
        175

contracts 137
  sale of cars on 165–6
  termination rights 190
Homosexuals, marriage and 318
Honour clauses 24–5
Human Rights Act 1998
  children 386
  contracts 1
  family law 312

Identity mistake
  contracts 88–90
  marriage 326
Illegality of contract 77–8
  at common law 79–80
  by statute 78–9
  committing crime or tort 79
  consequences of 80–1
  damaging to foreign relations
      80
  illegal in performance 80–1
  illegal in themselves 80
  interfering with justice 80
  promoting corruption in
      public life 79
  sexually immoral 79–80
  trading with enemy 80
  see also Void and Voidable
      contracts
Implied terms 49
  by courts 51
  by custom 50
  by statute 50–1
  description 51
  employment contract 211–15
  Sale of Goods Act 1979 137
Indemnity
  clause 38–9, 59, 73
  misrepresentation remedy 97
  Unfair Contract Terms Act 73
Inducement 68, 93
Information meeting 339
Inheritance tax 463–7
  account
    D18 454
    delivery of account 448–9
    IHT 200 449, 450–3
    IHT 201 449
    IHT 202 449
    purpose and content
        449–50
    reduced account delivery
        454–5
    types of account 449
  exempt transfers 465

gifts 416–17
  introduction 464
  potentially exempt transfers
      464–5
  rate 466
  reliefs 466–7
  transfer of value 465–6
  when chargeable 464
Injunctions
  mandatory 132, 133
  prohibitory 132–3
Insurance
  disability discrimination 260
  trustees powers 414
Intention
  mistake of 88
  to create legal agreement 22–7
Intention to contract
  business agreements 24–6
  collective agreements 26–7
  honour clauses 24–5
  social agreements 22–4
Interfering with justice 80
Internet trading 134
Intestacy
  account sums received 433–4
  appointment of
      administrators 441–2
  beneficiary predeceases
      intestate 433
  commorientes and 436
  death bed gifts 436–7
  distribution of estate 430–2
  donatio mortis causa 436–7
  hardship caused by 435–6
  investment powers 434
  life interests 433
  matrimonial home 434–5
  partial 429
  payments of debts and
      liabilities 434
  persons entitled to estate
      430–4
  reversion to issue 433
  statutory legacy 432–3
  statutory trust for sale
      429–30
  total 429
  see also Personal
      representatives;
      Probate; Wills
Invitations to treat 6–7

Judicial separation
  effects of decree 340–1

grounds 340
procedures 340

Land gifts
  free of mortgage or charge
      419–20
  free of tax or not 419
  freehold property 418
  leasehold property 417, 418
  real property 417
Land sale contracts 36–7
Latent defects 199
Letter of comfort 25–6
Letter of intent 14
Letters of administration see
      Administration
Lien right 168
Lifting operations and
      equipment 287–8
Like work 252
Limitation clauses 58–9, 70
Liquidated damages clauses 56
Loans 176
Local authorities and children
      377
  care orders 383–4
  care proceedings
    intervention standard
        380–3
    investigation and
        prosecution 380
  children in care
    disputes with parents
        388–90
    powers and duties 388
  discharge of orders 385–6
  interim orders 385
  role of 379–80
  supervision orders 384–5
Lump sum payments
  additional orders 344
  after final decree 344–5
  married couples 357–8
  purpose 344–5
  to dependants in probate 462
  variation of orders 354

Maintenance pending suit 343
Manslaughter at work 291–2
Marriage
  affinity 315
  age of parties 314, 317
  capacity to marry
    adoption 317
    affinity 315

age of parties 314, 317
consanguinity 315, 316, 317
daughters-in-law 316
gender of parties 318–20
prohibited degrees 315–17
single status 317–18
step relations 316
transsexuals 318–19
consanguinity 315, 316, 317
consortium 314
contracts damaging to 82
criminal law 316–17
formalities 314–15
polygamous 320
prohibited degrees 315–17
rape within 314
restrictions on 314–15
revocation of will and 428
rights and duties 313–14
status 312–13
termination of
    comparison of methods 341
    importance of final decree 322
    methods 321–2
    necessity of final degree 321
    see also Divorce; Judicial separation; Nullity
void 320–1
voidable 320–1
    lack of consent 325–7
    mental illness 327
    pregnancy by another 327
    venereal disease 327
Martin order 346
Maternity
    employment provisions 239, 241–3
    nullity of marriage and 327
    unfair dismissal
        ante-natal appointments 243
        leave 241–2
        pregnancy 239, 241
        right to return to work 242
Matrimonial home, on intestacy 434–5
Mediation, divorce and 338, 339–40
Mercantile agents 163–4
Merchantable quality see Consumer law, merchantable quality

Mesher order 346
Minors
    beneficial contract of service 106, 107
    capacity to make will 401
    contract capacity 106–7
    contract of employment 106, 107
    contract for necessaries 106, 107
Mirror image rule 12
Misconduct
    dismissal for 225–6
    divorce and 330–2
    living together after 335
    see also Behaviour; Conduct
Misrepresentation
    criminal liability 98
    definition 91
    excluding liability 98
    exclusion clauses 64
    fraudulent 93, 94
    half truths 92
    inducement 93
    'mere puff' 91
    negligent 93, 94
    reliance upon 93
    remedies
        affirmation of contract 96
        avoiding contract 95
        damages 97–8
        indemnity 97
        lapse of time 96
        recission 95–6
        restitution impossible 96
        third party acquires rights 97
    sales talk 91
    silence 92
    statement about future 92
    statement of law 91
    statement of opinion 91–2
    statements which become false 92
    statute 94–5
    termination of credit agreement 188–9
    Unfair Contract Terms Act 73–4
    utmost good faith 93
    wholly innocent 93, 95
Mistake
    contracts
        common 86–7
        of identity 88–90

of intention 88
    mutual 86, 87
    non est factum 86, 90–1
    operative 86
    unilateral 87–90
    nullity of marriage and 326
Mitigation of loss, breach of contract 127
Mortgage of land 175, 177
Mutuality principle 130

National Consumer Council 134
National minimum wage 209
Necessaries, contracts for 106, 107
Negligence
    contributory 127–8
    protection of consumer 194
Negotiable instruments 37
Non est factum 86, 90–1
Non-consummation
    incapacity 323
    wilful refusal 323–5
Notice, termination of employment 209
Nullity 322–8
    lack of consent
        duress 325–6
        mistake 326
        unsound mind 326
    mental illness 327
    non-consummation
        incapacity 323
        wilful refusal 323–5
    pregnancy by another 327
    venereal disease 327

Offer
    advertisements 8–9
    auctions 7
    conditional, failure of condition 21
    counter offers 12, 21
    display of goods 7–8
    information requests 9
    invitations to treat compared 6–7
    statement of price 9
    tenders 9–10
    termination see Termination of offer
Office of Fair Trading
    'seal of approval' 134
    Unfair Contract Terms Unit 76

'Officious bystander test' 51, 52
Overdraft 176

Parental leave 242
Parental responsibility 366–7,
    369, 370, 373
Parole evidence rule 48–9
    exceptions 50
Part time employment 217
Past consideration 28–9
Patent defects 199
Penalty clauses 56
Pensions
    disability discrimination 260
    divorce and 347–8
    earmarking 348
    sex discrimination 249–51
    sharing 348
Performance
    discharge of contract by
        exceptions 109–10
        general rule 108–9
        part performance 110
        prevention of 109–10
        severable obligations 109
        substantial 110
        tender of 111
        time of 111
    specific see Specific
        performance
Periodical payments
    after final decree 343–4
    duration 344
    married couples 357
    secured 343–4
    to dependants in probate 462
    variation of orders 354
Personal injury liability 74
Personal representatives 399,
    400
    administrators
        appointment
            intestacy 441–2
            timing 441
            where valid will 442–3
        intestacy 441–2
        persons of equal degree
            442, 443
    affidavit evidence
        alterations to will 455–6
        due execution of will 455
        marks on will 456
        plight and condition 455–6
    appointments 437–8
        administrators 441–2

executors 409–10, 438–41
appropriation powers 434–5
chain of executorship 443–4
executors
    appointment 409–10,
        438–41
    'according to tenor' of
        will 440
    by implication 440
    chain of executorship
        443–4
    firms or trust corporations
        439
    individuals as 439
    lack of proving executors
        441
    power reserved 440–1
    renunciation 440
    special 438
    unwilling or unable to
        prove 440
grant
    applications 447–55
    obtaining appropriate
        grant 444–5
inheritance tax account
    D18 454
    delivery of account 448–9
    IHT 200 449, 450–3
    IHT 201 449
    IHT 202 449
    purpose and content of
        449–50
    reduced account delivery
        454–5
    types of account 449
oath 447–8
powers and duties
    advertisements for
        creditors 445–6
    authority 444
    collection of assets 445
    distribution 446–7
    obtaining appropriate
        grant 444–5
    payments of liabilities 445
    see also Intestacy; Probate;
        Wills
Personal service contract 130
Personalty 421–3
Pinnel's case rule 32–3
Pledge 175, 177
Postal rule 18
Potentially exempt transfers
    464–5

Pre-contract performance 11
Pregnancy
    employment provisions 239,
        241
    nullity of marriage and 327
Presumption of advancement 81
Privity of contract 6, 39–45
    agency 41
    avoidance 42–4
    changes to contract 44
    collateral contracts 42
    conferring benefit on third
        party 44–5
    covenants on land 41
    defences 44
    statutory exceptions 40–1
    trusts 41–2
Probate
    dependants, provisions for
        457–63
        claimants 458–9
        factors to consider 460–2
        orders 462–3
        proofs required 459–60
        when made 457–8
    gifts in wills see Wills, gifts
    grant 400
    legacies see Wills, gifts
    trustees see Wills, trustees
        powers
    see also Intestacy: Personal
        representatives; Wills
Prohibited steps orders 373, 376,
    377
Promissory estoppel
    defence to claim 35
    estoppel principle 34
    existing legal relationship 34
    inequitable to go back on
        promise 35
    promise 34–5
    reliance on promise 35
    suspension of rights 35

Quantum meruit 109, 128

Race discrimination 254–7
    candidate selection 256
    contract workers 256–7
    exemptions 257
    internal promotion 257
    separate canteens 254–5
Re-engagement 237
Reasonableness test, unfair
    dismissal 226

Redundancy
  continuity of employment
    229–30
  customary arrangements for
    selection 227–8
  similar work offer 228–9
  transfer of undertakings 229
Referential bids 10
Regulated credit agreements 179
  partly regulated 180
Reinstatement 237
Reliance, misrepresentation and
    93
Remedies
  breach of contract see Breach
    of contract
  consumer law 150–2, 167–8
  credit see Credit, remedies
  duress 105–6
  misrepresentation 95–8
  Sale of Goods Act 1979 167–8
  undue influence 105–6
Remoteness of damage 123–5
Remuneration
  employment contract 208–9
  national minimum wage 209
Representations
  importance of statement 46
  manner of making statement
    46
  special knowledge or skill
    46–7
  time of statement 47
Repudiation 168, 191
Resale right 168
Rescission 95–6
Residence orders 367, 369, 373–4,
    377
Restraint of trade contract
  imposed on employee 83–4
  on seller of business 84–5
  on seller of goods 85
Restricted use credit 177
Restrictive trading agreements 82
Retailers credit cards 176
Right of lien 168
Romalpa clauses 159–60
Running account credit 179

Safety see Health and safety at
    work
Sale of Goods Act 1979
  conditions 137
  contracts
    of exchange 137

for goods and services 137
  of hire 137
  of hire purchase 137
  implied terms 137
  for services 137
description 139–41
merchantable quality 141
  in course of business 141
remedies
  of buyer 168
  of seller 168
title
  encumbrances 138
  limited 139
  quiet possession 138
  right to sell 138
warranties 137
see also Consumer law
Sale and Supply of Goods Act
    1994 see Consumer
    law
Samples 149, 169, 173
Scientific and technical
    knowledge defence
    200
Separation
  divorce and see Divorce
  legal 356
  voluntary 360
Services, contracts for 137
Sex discrimination 244–5
  contravention of other statute
    251
  direct 245–6
  equal pay 251–2
    burden of proof 253
    compensation 253–4
    time limits 254
  exemptions 248–51
  genuine occupational
    qualifications 248–9
  indirect 246–8
  like work 252
  marital status 248
  pensions 249–51
  work rated as equivalent
    252–3
Sexually immoral contract 79–80
Silence
  acceptance and 16
  misrepresentation and 92
Social agreements 22–4
Solus agreements 85
Special knowledge 83
Specific issue order 373, 376–7

Specific performance
  consumer contracts 168
  definition 128–9
  discretion of court 129–30
  inadequate damages 129
  mutuality principle 130
  personal service contracts 130
  requirements for 129–30
  supervision 131
  unenforceable contracts
    130–2
State of the art defence 200
Stoppage in transit right 168
Strike action 230–2
Supervision, specific performance
    and requirement for
    131
Supervision orders 384–5
Supply of Goods (Implied Terms)
    Act 1973 172–3
  conditions 173
  description 173
  exclusion of implied terms
    174
  fitness for purpose 173
  minor breaches of condition
    174
  right to sell 173
  samples 173
  satisfactory quality 173
Supply of Goods and Services
    Act 1982 168–72
  breaches of condition 170
  exclusion of liability 169
  fitness for purpose 169
    hire of goods 170, 171
  sale of goods and supply of
    services 170
  samples 169
  satisfactory quality 169
    hire of goods 170, 171
  services
    care and skill 171–2
    charge 172
    exclusion 172
    terms 172
    time 172
  transfer of ownership of goods
    contracts 170
  see also Consumer law
Survivorship period 424

Tenders
  acceptance 13
  offers 9–10

Termination of employment
  dismissal procedure 234–5
  methods 222–3
  notice 209
  see also individual reasons eg
      Redundancy; Unfair
      dismissal
Termination of offer
  acceptance 20
  counter offer 21
  death 22
  failure of condition 21
  lapse of time 21
  rejection 20
  revocation 20–1
Terms of contract
  express 50, 207–11
  implied see Implied terms
  importance of statement 46
  innominate 53, 54–5
  intention of parties and 55
  intermediate see innominate
  made on last set of terms sent
      65
  manner of making statement
      46
  representations and 45–6
  secondary obligations 56–7
  special knowledge or skill
      46–7
  time of statement 47
  see also Unfair Terms in
      Consumer Contracts
      Regulations
Title
  consumer law 138–9, 169
  encumbrances 138
  limited 139
  quiet possession 138
  right to sell 138
Torts 4–5
Trade organisations, disability
      discrimination 260
Trade union membership
  closed shops 232
  strike action 230–2
Trading with enemy 80
Transfer of property orders
  after final decree 345
  Martin order 346
  Mesher order 346
  sale of property 345
  settlement of property 345
  to dependants in probate
      463

Transfer of undertakings,
      redundancy 229
Transsexual marriage 318–19
Troublemakers 231
Trustees see Wills, trustees
      powers
Trusts, privity of contract 41–2

Uberrimae fidei 93
Undue influence 98, 99–105
  actual 99, 100
  independent advice 102–3,
      104–5
  manifest disadvantage 100–1,
      105
  presumed 99, 100–1
  remedies 105–6
  third parties 101–5
Unfair Contract Terms Act
  applications 66
  breach of contract 71–2
  business liability definition 67
  complaints 76
  consumer sales 73
  damage to property 71
  'dealing as consumer'
      meaning 67
  death or injury 70
  exclusion clauses see Exclusion
      clauses
  hire purchase 72–3
  indemnity clause 73
  inducements 68
  knowledge of exclusion 68
  limitation clauses 58–9
  manufacturers' guarantees 73
  misrepresentation 73–4
  negligence 68
  non-consumer sales 73
  reasonableness test 68, 71–2
  relative bargaining strength 68
  sale of goods 72–3
  terms regarded as unfair 74–6
  see also Unfair Terms in
      Consumer Contracts
      Regulations
Unfair Contract Terms Unit 77
Unfair dismissal 215–17,
      219–43
  breach of statutory restriction
      232
  capability 224
  closed shops 232
  continuous employment
      215–16

criminal offences 233
essentials for claim 237
health and safety activities
      233–4
maternity
  ante-natal appointments
      243
  leave 241–2
  pregnancy 239, 241
  right to return to work 242
means of terminating
      employment 222–3
misconduct 225–6
  further evidence of 226
part time employment 217
qualifications 224–5
qualifying periods 215–16,
      219
reason given for dismissal
      223–6
reasonableness test 226
remedies
  basic awards 236
  compensatory award 236
  re-engagement 237
  reinstatement 237
strike action 230–2
taking action to enforce
      statutory protection
      234
time for lodging complaint
      219–22
  presentation outside limit
      221–2
whistle-blowing 237–8
Unfair Terms in Consumer
      Contracts
      Regulations 57, 74–7
  'consumer use' 73
  death or injury liability 74
  Director General of Fair
      Trading 76
Unofficial strike action 231
Unrestricted use credit 177
Unsound mind 326
Utmost good faith 93

VDUs 288–9, 307
Venereal disease 327
Void contracts 77
  at common law 82
  by statute 81–2
  consequences of 85
  damaging to marriage 82
  excluding the court 82

restraint of trade *see* Restraint
    of trade
restrictive trading agreements
    82
wagering contracts 81–2
Void marriage 320–1
Voidable contracts 77, 107
Voidable marriage 320–1

Wagering agreements 81–2
Warranties 53
    Sale of Goods Act 1979 137
Welfare principle 367–8, 377
Whistle-blowers 237–8
Wills 400
    affidavits
        alterations to will 455–6
        due execution 455
        marks on will 456
        plight and condition 455–6
    alterations 455–6
    appointment of executors
        409–10
    appointment of guardians
        410–11
    attestation clause 404, 405–6,
        415
    capacity 401
    codicils 400–1
    dependants, provisions for
        457–63
        claimants 458–9
        factors to consider 460–2
        orders 462–3
        proofs required 459–60
        when made 457–8
    dispositions 411
    forfeiture 424–5
    funeral arrangements 410

gifts 415–26
    abatement 422–3
    ademption 420, 421
    categories of 417
    demonstrative legacies 422
    failure 420
    general considerations
        420
    general legacies 421
    inheritance tax
        considerations
        416–17
    land 417–20
    lapse 423
    pecuniary legacies 421
    personalty 421–3
    real property 417
    residuary legacies 423–4
    specific legacies and
        ademption 421
    survivorship period 424
holograph 403
inheritance tax considerations
    see Inheritance tax
intention to make 401–2
loss of beneficial interest 406,
    424–5
persons who may make 404
preparation 402–3
privileged 406–7
questions 468–9
revocation
    by dissolution or
        annulment of
        marriage 428–9
    by later will or codicil 426
    by marriage 428
    destruction 426–7
    of former wills 409

written declaration of
    intention 428
signature
    acknowledgment 405
    meaning 404–5
    position 404
    of witness 405
specimen 407–9
statutory requirements 403–6
trustees powers 411–15
    appropriation power 414
    charging clauses 414–15
    insurance powers 414
    investment power 413
    maintenance and
        advancement 412–13
    purchase or retention of
        residence 413–14
    to carry on business 415
undue influence 401–2
witnesses
    acknowledgment of
        signature 405
    beneficiary, as 406, 424–5
    competence 406
    'in writing and signed' 403
    see also Intestacy; Personal
        representatives;
        Probate
Witnesses *see* Wills
Working Time Regulations
    210–11
Workstations
    daily work 289
    eyes and eyesight 289–90
    health and safety 288–90
    training and information 290
    VDUs 288–9, 307
Wrongful dismissal 215, 217–19